KILLING SHORE

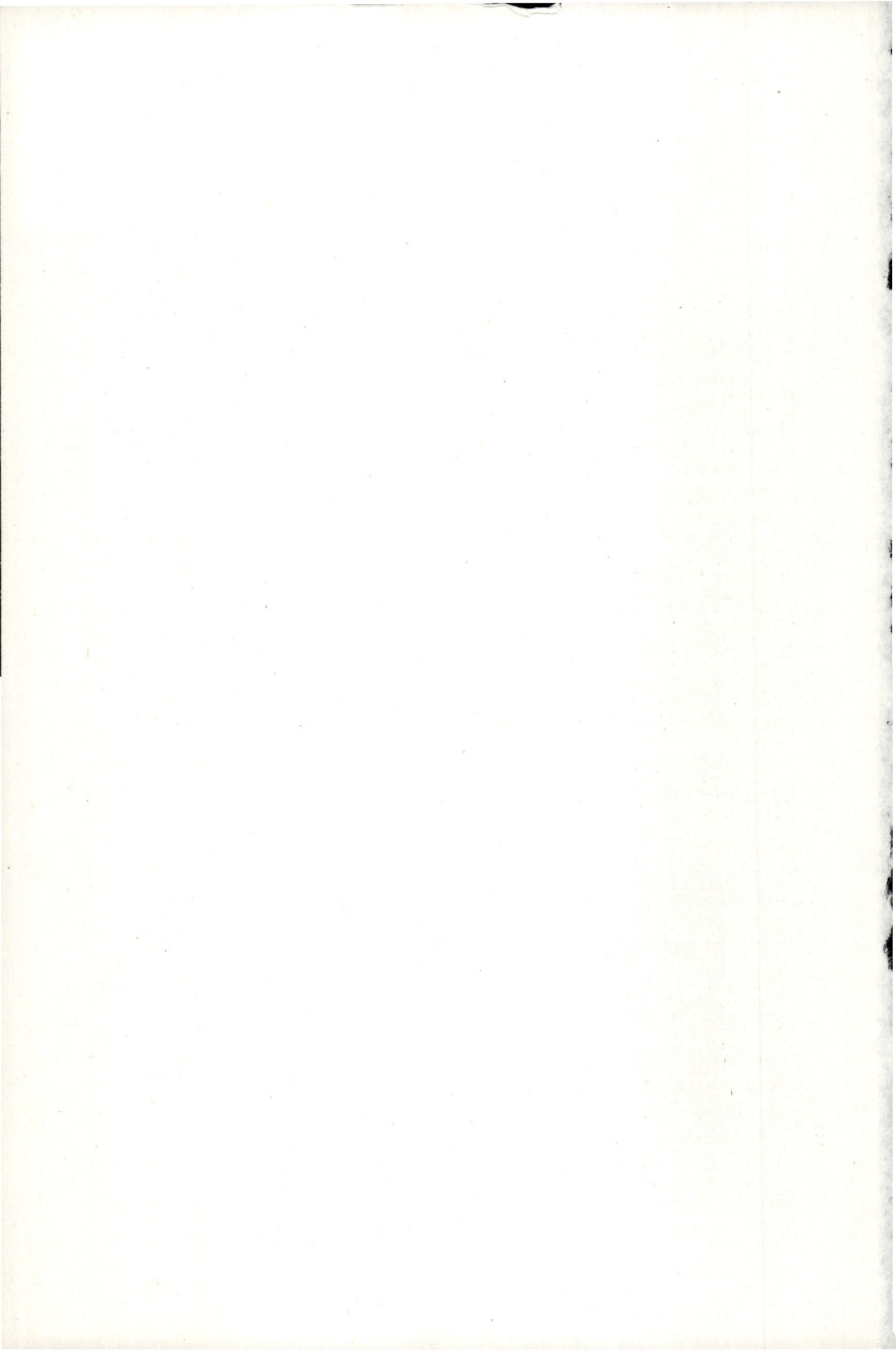

KILLING SHORE

The True Story of Hitler's U-boats Off the New Jersey Coast

K. A. NELSON

BROOKLINE
books
Havertown, Pennsylvania

Brookline Books is an imprint of Casemate Publishers

First published in the United States of America and Great Britain in 2024.
Reprinted as a paperback in 2025 by
BROOKLINE BOOKS
1950 Lawrence Road, Havertown, PA 19083, USA
and
47 Church Street, Barnsley, S70 2AS, UK

Paperback Edition: ISBN 978-1-955041-55-3
Digital Edition: ISBN 978-1-955041-30-0

A CIP record for this book is available from the British Library

Printed and bound in the United Kingdom by CPI Group (UK) Ltd, Croydon, CR0 4YY
Typeset in India by DiTech Publishing Services

For a complete list of Brookline Books titles, please contact:

CASEMATE PUBLISHERS (US)
Telephone (610) 853-9131
Fax (610) 853-9146
Email: casemate@casematepublishers.com
www.casematepublishers.com

CASEMATE PUBLISHERS (UK)
Telephone (0)1226 734350
Email: casemate@casemateuk.com
www.casemateuk.com

Cover images:
Front: a Type VIIC U-boat and a freighter being shelled, both during WWII (locations unknown).
Back: The *R.P. Resor* burns after being torpedoed off New Jersey in February 1942.

The Publisher's authorised representative in the EU for product safety is Authorised Rep Compliance Ltd., Ground Floor, 71 Lower Baggot Street, Dublin D02 P593, Ireland.
http://www.arccompliance.com

For

Eileen C. Gaynor
15 May 1963–24 June 2021

and

Captain Samuel A. Schultz, USMC
10 February 1990–3 April 2018

Contents

Preface

History has a way of feeling far away in both time and space. This is particularly true in the American experience, the United States being effectively a continent-island geographically removed from most of the world. Long considered a blessing, this oceanic moat kept foreign threats at arm's length while facilitating access to global markets for ships carrying American exports. The sea therefore represented the United States' guarantor of prosperity and security well into the 20th century.

This perspective even survived World War I, during which the waters off the Jersey Shore briefly became a peripheral battlefield in 1918. Even so, few Americans recognized that summer for the omen it was. Just one generation after the "war to end all wars," the same ocean that had long impeded would-be aggressors instead carried them again to America's doorstep. Although the arrival of Hitler's U-boats in 1942 was not a surprise, what followed proved bloodier and more brutal than even the Germans had foreseen.

The Nazi assault began just six weeks after Pearl Harbor, and the ensuing months constituted what historian Michael Gannon described as "one of the greatest maritime disasters in history and the American nation's worst-ever defeat at sea." The storm would claim hundreds of ships and thousands of lives before it abated. Curious explorers can even lay hands on the physical remnants of these events, at the modest price of only the proper experience and equipment.

The seeds of what would eventually become this story were sown over the course of several dives on New Jersey's wartime wrecks. It was, more than anything else, their silence that struck me. These ships' last moments afloat were wrought with chaos, explosions, terror, and flames—yet they lie today in absolute, noiseless stillness. Finning over the derelict remains of smashed hulls and corroded boilers set me wondering: *What happened here? What were the final moments like? Who were the men on either end of this violence?*

Ideas for how to answer these questions were germinating in my imagination by 2019. One afternoon that summer found me at a grocery store, where I spotted an elderly customer bedecked in a jacket and baseball cap identifying him as a US Merchant Marine veteran of World War II. I approached and expressed my gratitude for his service before introducing myself as a Marine Corps veteran with an interest in the role of merchant shipping in the world wars.

The man's politeness did not conceal his lack of interest in conversing, so I kept my intrusion short. Before parting ways, however, I mentioned my dives on the wrecks of ships torpedoed by U-boats off New Jersey. A change passed over his face at the word "U-boats," and the tone of his reply was solemn: "Oh, they were out there, alright." Something substantive seemed to loom behind his words, and the observation hardly begged a question.

The elderly mariner had once labored under the threat of the deck being ripped out from under his feet in a sudden cataclysm of steel and fire. If he did not drown or burn to death then he would have found himself adrift on a seemingly endless sea, probably at night and possibly in the dead of winter. Lacking a raft or lifeboat in the Atlantic meant a quick death by hypothermia, regardless of the season. Even escaping this fate could entail interminable days of waves, thirst, sunburn, and hunger—enough for the living to envy the dead. "To perish or be cast adrift in such dreadful waters," wrote historian Lisle Rose, "was an ordeal past comprehension."

Whether or not this man endured any such trial, he was a witness to an era that had by then nearly passed from living memory. Despite continuing public interest in World War II, however, *Killing Shore*'s subject receded from America's collective memory even before my lifetime. That Nazi Germany once launched a prolonged and devastating assault along US shores is largely unknown by modern Americans, although this is less than surprising if one considers the Battle of the Atlantic's historiography.

Samuel Eliot Morison described World War II's longest campaign and history's most destructive naval conflict as "exceedingly difficult to relate in an acceptable literary form." This is partly because, as Jonathan Dimbleby explained, the Atlantic war "played out far from the correspondent's notebook or the photographer's lens." Its scale and complexity have largely relegated it to broad-brush treatments, and relatively few historians have endeavored to portray what its veterans and casualties experienced. For this reason, among others, *Killing Shore* was crafted with three primary purposes in mind.

The first purpose is to recount the war that raged offshore from Maine to Texas (and throughout the Western Hemisphere) and reached its grisly apex during the first half of 1942. By portraying the U-boat campaign in American waters through the prism of one US state, it presents a broad and complex subject by focusing on a narrow slice of the same. Likewise, although each chapter in Part II tells the story of a different ship, this is not an anthology of disparate events. These accounts and their broader historical context are instead presented as a single narrative.

This story's second purpose is to capture what a US Navy report from June 1942 identified as "an element in warfare that is frequently overlooked," that is, "the individual man." He is "forgotten amid the campaigns, the statistics, the correspondence, and the impressive movements of large forces," the unnamed staff officer wrote. "A convoy makes safe passage, a tanker moves through a swept channel, a merchant vessel slips unseen through the black night—and where is the single man in all this?"

To state that a ship was sunk is one thing, but to portray the actual experiences of victims, attackers, and rescuers is a very different undertaking. The characters in the following pages were ordinary people every bit as real as the elderly mariner at the supermarket. Many perished within sight of New Jersey's boardwalks, and the effort that produced this book was girded by the conviction that their stories deserve to be told as they were experienced. Dan Lieb, president of the New Jersey Historical Divers Association, put it best during an interview with *South Jersey Magazine* in 2016:

"Shipwrecks are very much human stories, and I like being able to tell them."

Killing Shore also serves a third purpose. Thousands of ships and lives lost during mankind's bloodiest war were "minor in themselves when weighed in the scales of global war," Johnathan Dimbleby wrote. "Such losses were easily overlooked and rapidly forgotten except by those who grieved for the loved ones they had lost." Indeed, only one of the eleven vessels featured in Part II has previously been the subject of a long-form narrative backed by serious scholarship. This book consequently represents the definitive account of what the men aboard these ships experienced in New Jersey waters.

This is not a work of historical fiction, nor is it "based on a true story." These are instead real events reconstructed with as much factual accuracy as available sources allow. Accessibility was also a primary consideration: *Killing Shore* was always intended as a work of popular history that any interested reader can understand and appreciate. For this reason, relevant scientific, nautical, and military topics are explained throughout.

New Jersey serves as *Killing Shore*'s primary setting, but there was nothing particularly unique about the Garden State's wartime experience. An alternate version of this book could easily use North Carolina or Florida as its geographic frame. New Jersey was chosen partly for its proximity to my own native soil (the Philadelphia area) and partly for the inspiration drawn from diving the state's war wrecks.

Another motivation, however, lay in the opportunity to tell a story that has never really been told. Little has been written about the ships most prominently portrayed in Part II, and myths and misconceptions persist even among the wreck divers most familiar with them. Finally, although other nonfiction books portray U-boat operations along New England, the Gulf coast, and North Carolina, no comparable long-form account exists for New Jersey. *Killing Shore* is therefore as much a work of local history as a chronicle of combat and survival at sea.

Sometimes history hits closer to home than you'd think.

K. A. Nelson
February 2023

Sources and Methodology

Killing Shore's main story was largely drawn from three categories of primary sources. One was American and British military files such as after-action reports and POW interrogation records. Another was wartime newspapers, which proved an important source of minor details often absent from official documentation. Finally, the German perspective was sourced primarily from the logbooks (*Kriegstagebücher*, or KTBs) of individual U-boats and the headquarters staff. These three categories of documentation were supplemented by books, journal articles, genealogical records, websites, and other sources.

Firsthand accounts were leveraged to the greatest extent possible, although this required scrutiny to weed out the errors and ambiguities inherent to all eyewitness recollections. Numerous characters were brought to life in part by memories and photographs provided to the author by their children, grandchildren, and nephews. Biased or inaccurate sources like Karl Dönitz's memoirs were cited only in specific contexts, and pseudohistory from the likes of Sharkhunters International or Franz Kurowski was excluded entirely.

No facts have been changed or altered for dramatic effect. Small gaps in the historical record, however, were bridged using intuition and deduction. Sparingly performed to advance the narrative, this included reconstructing some dialogue. Other dialogue was drawn verbatim from primary sources, as were all radio messages. All persons portrayed are real people, and no details about them have been altered insofar as they are known.

All sources are cited using endnotes. To find the source(s) for any content in this book, simply find the next endnote in the text and then reference the "Endnotes" section. Source citations were consolidated to no more than one endnote per paragraph for readability's sake. Full details about many sources are listed in the bibliography. Some endnotes also include remarks about historical accuracy and attribution.

Distances, ocean depths, and seafloor topography were verified using Google Earth and other cartographic tools. Units of measurement were converted from metric to imperial for a primarily American readership, and distances are in statute miles, or "ground miles," unless nautical miles are specified. All times are in Eastern War Time (today, Eastern Daylight Time). All statistics about tonnage, sinkings, and fatalities related to U-boat attacks were calculated by the author using raw data sourced from Uboat.net.

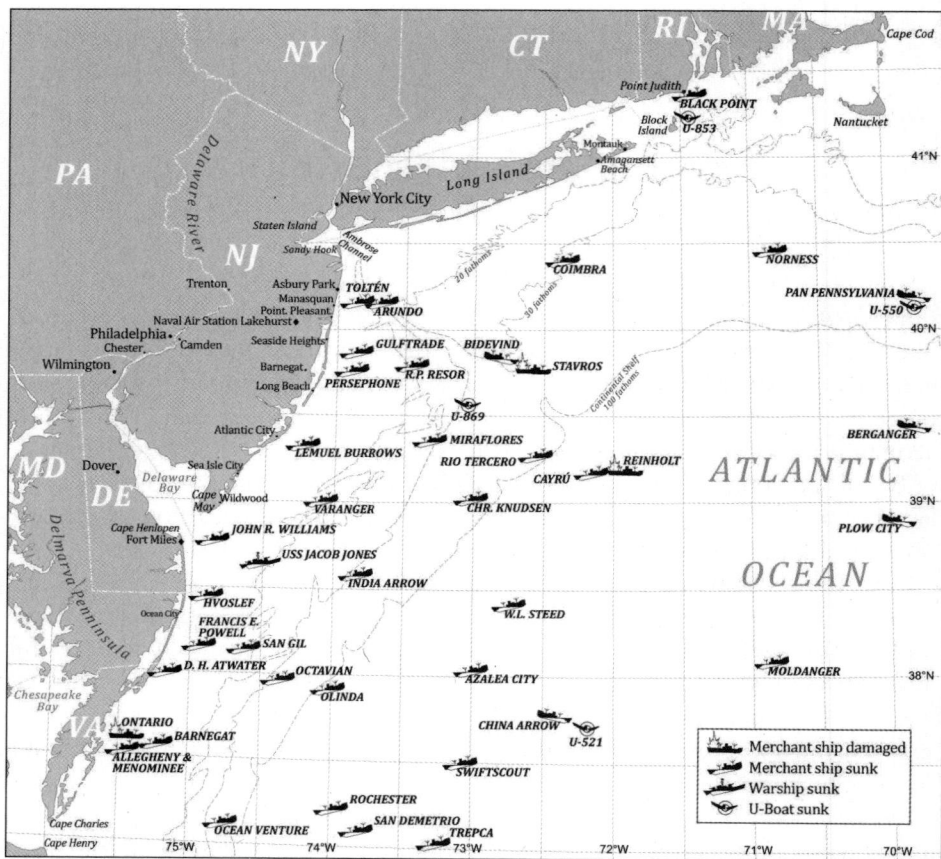

All vessels sunk or damaged by combat operations in the area shown, 1942–45. (Custom art by Bob Pratt)

Part I

CHAPTER ONE

Eins Zwei Drei

"The nation still stirs uneasily, like a man half-awake on a morning of disaster, still half-hoping that the evil thing is in the dream and not a reality."
—*New York Times* (8 March 1942)

14 January 1942
Grid quadrant CA 2896
21:56

Thirty-seven days after the Japanese attack on Pearl Harbor, *Kapitänleutnant* Reinhard Hardegen ordered the *U-123* to a stop. The roar of the U-boat's diesel engines faded to a whir before ceasing entirely. An uncanny silence prevailing within the vessel's musky confines was mirrored by the chilly winter night around it. The U-boat was on the surface, where submarines of that era usually traveled. It was impossible to dive here, anyway, as the depth was less than 40 feet.

Kapitänleutnant Hardegen was standing on the *U-123*'s bridge, or open-air command station atop the conning tower. Huddled around him were a half-dozen other unshaven young men sporting a mishmash of dark-colored attire. A double-breasted leather coat insulated the U-boat commander's lanky frame while atop his unkempt hair sat a military-style hat with a dark blue brim and white, rumpled-looking crown. Its brim's edge was embroidered with gilt thread and its center band displayed oak leaves flanking a tricolor roundel. Above this, centered on the white crown, gleamed a gold insignia of an eagle clutching a swastika.

The Germans clustered on the conning tower murmured as they marveled at the distant spectacle off the *U-123*'s starboard bow. By their feet, another young man's face peered out from the open hatchway. Clouds of hot breath rose in the cold air. One of the four lookouts was staring agape in the same direction as his crewmates. His inattentiveness went unnoticed by Hardegen, who was similarly transfixed by the sight before them.

A few dozen miles northwest lay the blazing incandescence of New York City. It was unlike anything the U-boat crewmen had ever seen. Even before the war, when Europe's cities were still illuminated at night, there was no sight so stunning anywhere on the continent. Manhattan's electric luster cast a sail of light far into the sky that shimmered and shifted in front of the waning moon. "I cannot describe the feeling with words, but it was unbelievably beautiful and great," Hardegen later wrote. "I would have given away a kingdom for this moment, if I had one."

Hardegen oriented himself geographically. To the north, the lights of Rockaway Beach shined off the U-boat's starboard beam. West of here, off the starboard bow, the dark ocean terminated on a stretch of beach featuring a lighted circular shape which Hardegen recognized as Coney Island's Ferris wheel. Faint points of light marked cars driving along Atlantic Avenue, and a neon blur indicated where Nathan's Famous Hot Dog Stand stood open for business even at this cold and late hour. Beyond Coney Island glimmered Brooklyn.

The U-boat commander identified Staten Island farther west and forward of his bow. On the opposite side of Ambrose Channel from Staten Island was the low, dark shape of the Sandy Hook barrier spit that extends from northern New Jersey and marks the southern boundary of the entrance to New York Harbor. The *U-123* was too far south and east of the Narrows—the tidal strait separating Staten Island from Brooklyn—to discern individual buildings in Manhattan, but the electric radiance insinuated the skyline's grandeur.

The *U-123* commander contemplated the symbolic weight of the dazzling view. "For the first time in this war, a German soldier looked upon the coast of the USA," he later reflected. A smirk blossomed under three weeks' growth of beard. Without taking his eyes off New York, Hardegen remarked to *Oberleutnant* Rudolf Hoffmann: "I have a feeling the Americans are going to be very surprised when they find out we're here."[1]

***

The handbook for their trade depicted the ideal U-boat commander as possessing "an aggressive spirit, a capacity for making quick decisions, initiative, tenacious endurance, and unfailing skill." Hardegen possessed all these in spades, just as surely as he lacked humility and discretion. His radioman felt that "sometimes he took too many risks," his peers thought him a braggart, and his superiors knew him to disobey direct orders when it suited him. These same superiors nonetheless also recognized an aggressive commander with a stellar combat record and a penchant for independent action. "A commander who missed his targets, that would demoralize an entire crew," explained *U-123* boatswain Walter Kaeding. "But you can't say that about Hardegen."

Reinhard Hardegen, age 28, was tall and thin with a gaunt face garnished by a short and scraggly beard that was red, unlike the hair on his scalp. A naval pilot before transferring to the U-boat fleet, a 1936 plane crash had left him with a shortened leg and chronic stomach bleeding that medically disqualified him from U-boat service. He had evaded his medical records until they reached the attention of the U-boat fleet commander, but the admiral recognized Hardegen's "dash and tenacity" and only issued a good-humored scolding.

Hardegen's inclination to irritate superiors would be on full display six months after his New York voyage. Invited to dine with Adolf Hitler after being awarded the coveted Knight's Cross with Oak Leaves medal, Hardegen left the dictator red with anger by castigating him for allowing Germany's naval aviation capability to be absorbed by the air force. A mortified General Alfred Jodl sternly admonished him after the meal, but the *U-123* commander was unfazed: "*Herr General*, the Führer has the right to hear the truth, and I have the duty to speak it."

"I've always loved the sea since an early age," Hardegen explained. "So you could say it was in my blood." He was just 4 years old when his father, a teacher and accomplished history author, was killed in action during World War I. Young Reinhard was subsequently raised under the tutelage of renowned naval commander and family friend Paul König.

School records indicate that his nonconformist tendencies predated his military career. "Hardegen constantly ill-mannered," "Hardegen interrupts the class," and "Hardegen eats breakfast during the lesson" were among a litany of offenses against good order and discipline. He preferred sailing to studying, and only his dream of becoming a naval officer forced an improvement in his behavioral and academic performance. A recommendation from König helped secure Hardegen's admission to Germany's naval academy at Mürwik.[2]

***

The *U-123*, known to its crewmen as the "*Eins Zwei Drei*" (One, Two, Three), was a Type IXB U-boat measuring 251 feet long and 22 feet wide at the beam. Two diesel engines manufactured by Maschinenfabrik Augsburg-Nürnberg AG provided a top speed of 18.2 knots (20.9 miles per hour, or mph) on the surface. The boat had an operational range of 12,000 nautical miles at 10 knots. Electric motors provided a maximum underwater speed of 7.3 knots (8.4 mph) with the battery fully charged, though this was only sustainable for about an hour. The *U-123*'s armament consisted of twenty-two torpedoes complemented by a 105mm gun, a 37mm gun, and a 20mm gun.

Three weeks earlier, the *U-123* and its crew of four officers and forty-eight enlisted men had departed from the port of Lorient in German-occupied France. Hardegen knew that putting to sea on Christmas Eve risked having drunk and homesick men aboard, so he opted to sail on 23 December instead. The U-boat slipped its mooring lines while a pierside band played "*Wir fahren gegen Engeland*":

> Farewell, my darling, farewell, my darling,
> For we sail, for we sail,
> For we sail against England, England.

It seemed as appropriate a tune as any, considering that not even Hardegen knew where they were going. His instructions were to proceed west and open the sealed orders after reaching 20° West longitude. The U-boat's official logbook reflected his curiosity by noting that their assigned route took them past "all six contemplated patrol areas." And so they ventured *Westwärts*—westward—a word that encapsulated the sense of glory and adventure that still held U-boat men in its thrall in December 1941.

The *U-123* submerged the following day to celebrate Christmas 66 feet under the Bay of Biscay. Gifts secreted aboard by Hardegen were distributed by *Leutnant* Horst von Schroeter, formally designated as "*Knecht Ruprecht*," one of Saint Nicholas' helpers in German folklore. Pancakes and wine punch were served, and the crew gathered around a Christmas tree in the control room where Hardegen read the story of Christ's birth from the Gospel of Luke. "The war was forgotten for a few hours," he wrote in the log.[3]

Upon reaching 20° West two days after Christmas, Kapitänleutnant Hardegen retreated to the alcove just forward of the control room which constituted the captain's quarters. He drew its green curtain closed, then doffed and placed aside his reefer jacket cut from dark blue doeskin-type fabric and featuring a gold eagle and swastika embroidered on the right breast. Hardegen then removed a large blue envelope from the boat's safe, gently slid out its contents, and laid them out on his schoolhouse-sized desk. His face tensed quizzically.

In addition to the operations order, the envelope contained a 1939 World's Fair handbook and a tourist guide to New York City. There were no nautical charts or pilot books, nothing that showed depths, navigational buoys, or lighthouses, not to mention shoals and other hazards. A bemused Hardegen realized that war with America had arrived so suddenly that the naval high command had not even possessed charts of the US coast. Inside the tourist book's back cover he found a folded map portraying ports and bays in somewhat more detail.

His eye was drawn to the entrance to Lower New York Bay, which was labeled "Ambrose Channel." The map also indicated the location of Ambrose Channel's lightship, a type of navigational aid. In addition to tourist information, the envelope contained a standard large-scale 1870G *Nord-Atlantischer Ozean* map. This copy of the map featured several areas along the East Coast which some staff officer had labeled with Roman numerals.

The operations order directed the *U-123* to grid square "CA," which spanned the US East Coast from Boston, Massachusetts to Cape Hatteras, North Carolina. Specifically, the Eins Zwei Drei was assigned a quadrant within CA formed by squares CA 28, CA 29, CA 52, and CA 53. Hardegen consulted the 1870G map and saw that this encompassed all of Long Island in addition to most of New Jersey's coast out to roughly 150 miles offshore.

The orders read: "Off the American littoral you will attack unescorted, independently sailing coastwise merchant traffic … Following initial attacks at destination New York, *U-123* will pursue targets as far south as Cape Hatteras." The orders further specified the date on which the U-boats could begin engaging targets at will, and they reiterated the imperative not to transmit any messages whatsoever. "You will maintain strict radio silence until after your attacks commence."

Only broadly familiar with the geography, Hardegen found New York City on the map and traced his eyes south along the coast. His gaze passed New Jersey, the Delaware Bay, then the Chesapeake Bay. He found Cape Hatteras among North Carolina's barrier islands nearly 400 miles south of New York. A smile spread across his face.

Hardegen had long hungered for a bite of the Americans. On earlier combat patrols, he had watched "neutral" American merchant ships bringing cargo unmolested to Britain while US Navy destroyers and Coast Guard cutters patrolled the north-central Atlantic. But now the leash was off, and Hardegen relished the opportunity to teach them some humility.[4]

***

The 3,600-mile voyage to New York took the *U-123* through all the fury of a North Atlantic winter. The U-boat pitched and rolled hideously as 30-foot waves crashed down and exploded into foaming torrents against the foredeck, the noise of which was thunderous even inside the boat. Winds of 35 mph lashed the faces of the four lookouts posted on the bridge atop the conning tower. Each wave attempted twice to claim them from their swaying perch, first when its weight broke over their heads and then again when it washed back out over the bridge and gun platform to rejoin the boiling sea.

The U-boat climbed each dark mountain, its sharp bow rearing high on the crest before the entire vessel tipped forward and skidded down into the deep trough to bury its nose in the bedrock of the next wave. Bronze propellers revolved in the air for a moment, then the sea crashed down again and enveloped the boat. It emerged again each time to continue its odyssey through a frigid seascape of white-crested hills chasing one another eastward. "The North Atlantic is where the seaman takes his graduate course in weather," wrote US Coast Guard veteran John Waters, "and the curriculum is tough."

The *U-123* was approximately 250 miles southeast of the Canadian port of Halifax, Nova Scotia on 9 January 1942 when Hardegen received his final coordinating instructions via an encoded wireless transmission: "OCCUPY FOLLOWING ATTACK AREAS: ZAPP ATTACK AREA ROMAN NUMERAL I. HARDEGEN II. FOLKERS III. BLEICHRODT IV AND V. KALS VI." He consulted the 1870G map again and saw that the coastline in his assigned zone ran from Long Island, New York to Atlantic City, New Jersey. The message continued. "BDU COUNTS ON YOUR ARRIVING IN ATTACK AREA ON 13 JANUARY." Its final sentence designated the U-boats as "GROUP PAUKENSCHLAG."[5]

In addition to radio silence, the five U-boats of *Gruppe Paukenschlag* were instructed not to conduct any attacks before reaching their attack zones off North

America. The only exception was if a ship of 10,000 or more gross registered tons presented itself, and the *U-123* encountered just such a target on the night of 11 January when a lookout spotted a large two-masted ship 316 miles east of Cape Cod, Massachusetts. "These steamers and all other English and American ships with double masts are about 10,000 gross registered tons or more," Hardegen explained in the log, "so I am allowed to attack."

The British freighter *Cyclops* survived two U-boat attacks during World War I and had narrowly escaped Japan's capture of Hong Kong the previous month, but her good fortune was now depleted. Hardegen chased down the *Cyclops* and put a torpedo into her hull, prompting the passengers and crewmen to abandon ship. While a trio of sailors fired the U-boat's 20mm gun at the *Cyclops'* midship house to silence her distress call, Hardegen saw the merchant crew attempting to re-board. A second torpedo then broke the 485-foot ship in half. Torpedoes killed only 2 of 181 passengers and crew, but 86 more would die from hypothermia before a Canadian destroyer rescued the survivors and landed them at Halifax, Nova Scotia.

Hardegen's copy of Erich Gröner's *Merchant Fleets of the World* revealed that the *Cyclops* was only 9,076 gross registered tons, but he knew that nobody whose opinion mattered would care. He was instead concerned with the detour's impact on his timetable. As the *U-123* resumed her course with both propellers turning at 300 revolutions per minute (rpm), Hardegen remarked in the U-boat's logbook that "I have lost a lot of time and have to hurry to be in the patrol area on 13 January."[6]

***

At 21:28 on 13 January, four days after sinking the *Cyclops*, Hardegen finally laid eyes on the American coast. Mercifully calm weather and clear visibility enabled him to spot a distant light pulsing in a dot-dot-dash pattern. "Light to starboard. Probably the Montauk lighthouse," he noted, referring to the easternmost tip of Long Island. More artificial illumination soon appeared on the dark horizon. "Glow from the direction of New York and the cities on the Narragansett Bay."

Three hours later and 68 miles southeast of Montauk Point, Hardegen's lookouts spotted a much nearer light off the port bow. The *U-123* approached to find the tanker *Norness*, which was sailing under Panamanian registry with a mostly Norwegian crew. The ship was laden with fuel oil and sailing a straight course with navigation and running lights on, as if in peacetime. Hardegen closed to within 900 yards on the surface before loosing a pair of torpedoes.

One torpedo missed, but the *Norness* lurched when the other struck under her aft mast to satisfying effect. "Heavy detonation. 50 meter high column of fire, 200 meter high black mushroom cloud … impressive view against the bright starlit sky," Hardegen observed. The tanker was listing to starboard with its stern slouching low in the water when a third torpedo crashed into the hull amidships. "Again a very strong detonation, high column of fire," yet this was still not a mortal blow. "Tanker now lies on even keel again," an annoyed Hardegen observed. "Does not sink."

The *U-123* launched another, but a depth-keeping malfunction caused the torpedo to pass harmlessly beneath the *Norness'* keel. "Now I have to sacrifice a fifth torpedo," the incensed U-boat commander explained, "because he has to go, or else he can be towed in." The merchant crew was rowing a single crowded lifeboat away from the abandoned *Norness* when the fifth torpedo exploded against her engine room with a thunderous roar. The aft compartments now flooded rapidly as the *Norness* listed further, her masts toppling against the deck. "The stern hits the bottom at seventy meters, the bow protrudes about thirty meters vertically from the sea," Hardegen noted. "An interesting menace to navigation."

All but two of the *Norness'* forty-one crewmen survived the attack. Not until the following morning would the US Navy blimp *K-3* sight the shipwreck's bow and men huddled on a raft nearby. A Navy destroyer and a Coast Guard cutter then rescued thirty survivors and a fishing boat picked up the remaining nine. The *Norness* later fully sank.

The sun was rising astern by 06:38. Even the daredevil *U-123* commander recognized the danger of traveling on the surface so close to shore during daylight, so he elected to submerge and wait on the seafloor until nightfall. The chief engineering officer directed the sailors in the control room to flood the boat's ballast tanks and steer it downward to the seafloor. The crew passed the daylight hours sleeping and conducting torpedo maintenance 180 feet beneath the sea while Hardegen pored over his maps.[7]

After sunset on 14 January, the *U-123* surfaced and resumed its westward course as the German radioman on duty tuned in to American radio frequencies. "Heard announcement by the Navy Department, Washington in American broadcast that a tanker was probably torpedoed by a U-boat 60 NM south of Block Island," Hardegen wrote in the log. The same message was repeated on the 600-meter frequency, then by German naval headquarters. Hardegen relished the recognition by friend and foe alike that he was boldly sauntering through the Americans' front gate. *Knock, knock.*

Lacking proper charts, the *U-123* followed the Long Island coast toward the Lower Bay. "I could see on Coney Island, the houses and lights and motorcars and so on," Hardegen would later recount, "therefore navigation was very easy." A stationary light ahead became visible at 20:09. Presuming it to be the Fire Island lightship, he ordered the helmsman to steer toward it. "Twenty meters under the keel!" shouted boatswain Walter Kaeding from the control room. "Fifteen meters! … Ten meters!" The irritated captain interjected: "Which idiot is depth-sounding? They can hear us on shore!"

Five minutes later, Hardegen's heart leapt into his throat when he suddenly sighted the white flash of surf breaking over sand dead ahead—the "lightship" was, in fact, a beachside building. "Both back emergency full!!" he bellowed. The *U-123* halted jarringly, pushing a comber of its own toward the beach. Diesels snarled as the propellers were thrown into reverse. Beyond the surf, Hardegen could see dunes, a lit hotel, and the darkened silhouettes of trees. Chastened, he resumed following Long Island's shoreline at a safer distance.

Hardegen ordered the helmsman to steer well clear of the fishing boats swarming innocuously around them, each a point of light moving on its own course. "No mines, then …" observed Oberleutnant Hoffman, his second-in-command. "Yeah, nothing to chew on either," the commander replied. "I advance further," his log noted. The Ambrose Channel and Fire Island lightships both seemed to be either off or relocated elsewhere, but Manhattan's radiant glow swelled off the starboard bow as the Germans approached the Narrows.

Hardegen soon halted the *U-123* and invited the rest of the crew up to the bridge for their first view of New York. They took turns ascending the conning tower ladder to marvel at the incandescent tableau. The city carried a symbolic resonance beyond that of simply a large metropolis. Here was the land of cowboys, gangsters, swing music, and Hollywood. Washington, D.C. may have governed the United States, but New York embodied it. "You just imagine to yourself: America," an enraptured Walter Kaeding reflected, "and there it is."

Alwin Tölle was snapping photos. Tölle was not a U-boat sailor, but rather a photographer assigned to document the historic mission. Later claims that the Germans had watched people dancing on the roof of the Waldorf Astoria hotel were mere sensationalism, however. Tölle was too far away for such images, so Ufa Film Studios would instead fabricate close-up photos of Manhattan for Joseph Goebbels' propaganda reels.

To the *U-123* commander, the lustrous panorama also embodied that particularly American arrogance which had come to annoy him. German cities had been blacked out for over two years, and yet here were the Yankees with their damn lights on. Yet even in his most triumphant moment, Hardegen felt a twinge of guilt and nostalgia. This was, after all, not his first visit to New York.[8]

His naval academy education had included a round-the-globe training cruise aboard the light cruiser *Karlsruhe* in 1933. Among the ports of call was Pearl Harbor in Hawaii, where he met an American commander's daughter who arranged for him to tour a US Navy submarine. Later, in New York City, he rode the elevator to the top of the Empire State Building. He would recall of America that he was "amazed at the people and how kind they were to us."

Yet Hardegen had developed considerable scorn for the Americans during the more than two years since the war began. His vanity and nationalism also made him an enthusiastic mouthpiece for Hitler's propaganda; Hardegen would be credited with authoring the 1943 propaganda book *To Action Stations! U-boats Against England and America*, which extolled the U-boat sailors' rugged warrior spirit while deriding the "soft" and "degenerate" Americans.

These ridiculous claims were, however, wrapped around a kernel of truth. Hardegen had been stunned by the relative spaciousness and luxury of the US Navy submarine he toured in Hawaii, which contrasted starkly with Germany's cramped and austere U-boats. "As far as the German soldier is concerned, private wishes and conveniences quite naturally take a back seat," he boasted in 1943. "The American, however, places great value on his so-called comfort … Recent history has shown us just how well they stand up in combat."[9]

Hardegen lingered near Sandy Hook, New Jersey in the hope of catching a merchantman departing or entering New York Harbor, but none presented itself. He reasoned that by backtracking eastward, toward the open ocean, he might cross a ship's path. "Come to one-zero-zero," he ordered the helmsman seated below the open hatch in the conning tower compartment. At around 01:00, Hardegen retired below deck to catch some sleep. His respite would be brief.

"*Kommandant auf Brücke!*"

The *U-123* was 86 miles east of Sandy Hook at 01:40 when Hardegen was awakened by the second watch officer's voice. Donning his leather coat and white cap, he rushed into the control room and up the ladder. He emerged into the winter chill where the bridge watch indicated a ship roughly 2 miles astern.

Lifting his binoculars, Hardegen sighted a large tanker on an eastward heading, indicating that it had just departed Ambrose Channel. The ship was not hard to see, as it was conspicuously backlit by New York's lights in addition to having all its own lights on. "Don't these crass *Schweine* know there's a war on?" Hardegen quipped derisively. He ordered his helmsman to slowly turn the *U-123* for a head-on approach.

The U-boat crept forward while its commander assessed the target. The tanker's beam and masts suggested its large size, and the hull riding low in the water indicated a full cargo. "He seems bigger than *Norness*, especially the superstructure on the stern," the log stated. "Amazingly long." A sailor emerged from the hatch carrying an optical targeting device that resembled a large set of binoculars. Oberleutnant Rudolf Hoffman installed it on a post extending to chest height from the bridge's deck and pressed his face against the eyepiece.

As the first watch officer, Hoffman now took over execution of the attack. In what Hardegen described as a "textbook approach," Hoffman ordered the helmsman to steer to port and orient the U-boat's bow perpendicular to the tanker's track. He then centered the targeting reticle on its midship house as the *U-123* maneuvered into attack position. "Flood tube one for surfaced firing and open tube door," the first watch officer ordered. "Running depth … two-point-five meters."

The unwitting victim's shadowy form grew nearer. "Target angle starboard zero-nine-five, target speed ten-point-five," Hoffman announced. "Range nine-zero-zero." A voice from below the hatch echoed his words in confirmation. His gaze tracked the ship through the optic while ready reports were shouted from below, then issued the order to fire. "*Rohr eins, LOS!*" Hoffman shouted as he punched the firing lever.

Fifty-eight seconds later, the torpedo slammed into the ship's starboard side just aft of the bridge. The blast reverberated across the sea as flames mushroomed skyward in a grisly palette of red, orange, and black that illuminated Hardegen's toothy grin. Burning oil showered the tanker's deck as the fire quickly spread. "The effect was stunning," he wrote in the U-boat's log. "A fierce detonation, a column of fire rose over 200 meters high, and the whole sky was as bright as day."

The stricken vessel lost headway and began listing to starboard as Reinhard Hardegen and Rudolf Hoffman surveyed their handiwork. Flames engulfing the tanker's bridge indicated that there would be no distress message. However, they spotted flashlight beams near the stern, where the fire's glow illuminated a naval cannon mounted on the aft deck. Seeking to finish off the ship before its crew could shoot back, Hoffman fired another torpedo from one of the U-123's two stern tubes.

It struck home 45 seconds later: "Heavy detonation, high columns of fire, black mushroom cloud." The tanker finally succumbed, sinking aft until its stern was scraping the seafloor 177 feet below and its bow protruded forlornly from the surface amid a burning oil slick. "These are some pretty buoys we're leaving for the Yankees as replacement for the lightships," Hardegen quipped, amusing himself so much that he recorded his wisecrack in the log.[10]

The flaming wreck they left behind was the British-flagged tanker *Coimbra*, which had been carrying a cargo of lubricating oil to Britain. Ten of her forty-six crewmen survived and were rescued that afternoon by the US Navy destroyers USS *Rowan* (DD-405) and USS *Mayrant* (DD-402). An eleventh survivor had a mental breakdown in the liferaft and died shortly after rescue. Like the *Norness*, the partially exposed wreck of the *Coimbra* later fully sank.

Lights ashore, lights at sea, and the apparent absence of the US Navy left Hardegen dumbfounded at the United States' apparent disregard for the realities of war. A dozen U-boats could easily turn the entire East Coast into a maritime graveyard, he reasoned, later remarking that "it's a pity there weren't a couple of minelaying boats with me on the night I was off New York to plaster the place with mines." To have sent only five U-boats seemed like a squandered opportunity. After returning to port, Hardegen would urge the U-boat fleet's commanding admiral to dispatch every available boat to the American coast. The admiral would need little convincing.

The U-123 turned south after sinking the *Coimbra*. Remaining surfaced, it hugged New Jersey's shoreline while the lookouts scanned the horizon for merchant ships. Lighthouses winked as automobiles cruising blithely along coastal roadways formed a ribbon of light off the boat's starboard beam. The Germans were 8 miles off Wildwood, New Jersey when Leutnant Horst von Schroeter directed Kapitänleutnant Hardegen's attention to the southwest where searchlight beams were visible at the Delaware Bay entrance. "It was a special experience for us to be that close to the American shore, to be able to see the cars driving on land, to see the lights on the streets, to smell the forests," von Schroeter later recalled. "We were that close."

At dawn, the *U-123* dived to cruise underwater. This more than halved its speed, but also concealed it from visual detection. The batteries were running low by that afternoon, and the U-boat surfaced 15 miles off the Jersey Shore at 16:23. The Germans maintained a southward heading as whirling propellers turned the drive shaft that recharged the batteries. Exactly thirty-eight minutes later, an American patrol aircraft appeared in the overcast sky.

"*ALAAAARRMM!!!*"

The emergency bell rang as men on the bridge tumbled unceremoniously down into the control room and the chief engineer initiated the crash-dive procedure. Hardegen slammed the hatch shut behind him, muffling the angry rasp of aircraft engines swelling louder as the American plane swooped low over the ruffled water. Clattering diesel pistons gave way to humming electric motors, the winter sea closed over the deck, and the Eins Zwei Drei slid beneath the waves.

Seconds later, the boat trembled as four explosions reverberated through the water; the aircraft's depth charges had fallen well starboard of the *U-123*. The American air crew was presumably jittery, inexperienced, or both. Reinhard Hardegen noted in his log: "They were badly aimed. The Yankees have much to learn."[11]

Indeed, they did.

CHAPTER TWO

The Third Dimension of Warfare

"Briefly stated, I consider that at the present moment we are losing the war."
—Rear Admiral William Sims, US Navy (April 1917)

1 July 1916
Beach Haven, New Jersey
18:06

Twenty-five years before Reinhard Hardegen's *U-123* reached New York City, a July sun was retreating above Long Beach Island on the coast of New Jersey. At the barrier island's southern end, lingering daylight held the tranquil resort town of Beach Haven in a pleasant 78° Fahrenheit embrace. Nothing about the sun's impassive glow suggested that it had also shined upon thirty-one thousand young men slaughtered earlier that day near the Somme River in France. Beach Haven's cool coastal breeze was a welcome relief for the Vansant family, who had just escaped the sweltering humidity of Philadelphia, Pennsylvania to spend the 4th of July weekend at the beach.

World War I was raging on the far side of the Atlantic, where night had just fallen on the deadliest day in British military history. Some Americans vaguely understood that 1916 may be the nation's last summer of peace, nevertheless, the war's horrors soured few moods along the New Jersey coast. One exception was President Woodrow Wilson, the state's former governor, who was managing his administration from Asbury Park that summer. Wilson's highest priority was preserving American neutrality, and he was running for reelection under the slogan "He Kept Us Out of the War!"

Wedged against the Atlantic Ocean by New York to its north and Pennsylvania to its west, New Jersey was one of the thirteen colonies that rebelled against the British crown in 1776. The fourth-smallest and tenth-most populous state in 1916, it was purportedly described as "a barrel tapped at both ends" by Benjamin Franklin; New Jersey's northern and southern regions have long been closely linked with neighboring New York City and Philadelphia, respectively. The state's coastline, the "Jersey Shore," had recently become a popular summer destination due in part to railroads that made it accessible to the middle class. The Pennsylvania Railroad brought legions of families from Philadelphia, Pennsylvania across the Delaware River to Jersey Shore destinations like Atlantic City, dubbed the "Queen of Resorts."

Not coincidentally, recreational swimming had also grown increasingly popular since the turn of the century. According to author Michael Capuzzo: "Along the beaches of the Jersey Shore that summer [of 1916] was perhaps the largest number in the world, perhaps in any era to date, of human beings in the water." Life here altogether seemed to embody the optimism and vitality of the United States in the early 20th century. The nation's tranquility, however, was about to end violently. Neither President Wilson nor the millions flocking seaward for the holiday weekend had any inkling that death lurked just offshore.

As the sun waned, a handsome 23-year-old Ivy League graduate named Charles Vansant helped his family check in to the Engleside Hotel before rushing to the beach. Trudging across the dunes, he befriended a wandering Chesapeake Bay retriever and greeted an acquaintance, lifeguard and Olympic swimmer Alexander Ott. Vansant's father and sister soon arrived and saw him playing with the dog in the outgoing tide.

Nothing about the unusually clear sea swirling around Vansant's legs conjured the Jersey Shore's history as one of the nation's deadliest coastlines. Together with New York's Long Island, New Jersey formed half of a funnel that concentrated traffic in and out of New York City, the nation's busiest port. This increased a ship's odds of collision, but those straying too far inshore risked falling victim to New Jersey's notorious rocks, sandbars, and shoals. So many ships have been wrecked here over the centuries that poet Walt Whitman described the state's waters as "unshovelled, ever-ready graves."

The ocean was refreshing despite its chill, and Vansant waded chest deep as the dog paddled in lively pursuit. He dived to stay ahead of his canine companion and transitioned into an athletic crawl stroke as he swam past the breakers. A few beachgoers, however, saw the dog abruptly change course and begin swimming back to shore. The young man turned and called out, but his four-legged friend soon trotted out of the water and shook himself off.

The young man began wading back toward shore. Vansant was 20 yards from the waterline when he noticed a handful of people shouting out to sea—shouting toward him. "Watch out!" they called. Vansant could not discern their words, nor did he see the sleek and dark shape cruising nearer from behind. "WATCH OUT!" Even if he had sighted the gray object slicing through the water toward him, it was already too late.

Vansant's body suddenly jerked forward as he cried out in shock and pain. Disbelief swashed over the onlookers. He began thrashing wildly, bloodcurdling screams carrying over the beach. Lifeguard Alexander Ott sat rigidly upright. He saw Vansant, in barely 4 feet of water, flailing against a shark that had seized him in its viselike maw of serrated teeth. Ott had scarcely processed what he was seeing before he set off sprinting across the sand. He splashed through the surf toward Vansant as several Good Samaritans followed.

The shark had ceased its assault and vanished by the time Ott arrived. He immediately locked his arms around Vansant's chest and began dragging his grievously wounded acquaintance to shore. Other men waded into the waist-deep surf behind him as the lifeguard trudged backward. Suddenly, Ott shouted in alarm as Vansant's weakening body was yanked powerfully in the opposite direction.

The shark had returned and buried its teeth again into Vansant's flesh, its black and expressionless eyes seeming to stare straight through Alexander Ott. A tug-of-war ensued as the shark's prey shrieked, his primal terror mirrored by long-skirted mothers wailing on the beach. The beast was dark, angular, and unfathomably strong, perhaps 10 feet in length and weighing 500 pounds. Alone against the shark, Ott hollered for assistance as the surf boiled a gruesome pinkish hue.

His arms stayed clamped around Vansant's torso as a human chain muscled them—Vansant, Ott, and the shark—toward the beach. The thrashing monster refused to yield, its underside scraping the sand while its teeth remained embedded down to Vansant's femur. The shark nearly beached itself before finally releasing its victim. It then writhed powerfully as it slithered seaward, disappearing in a vortex of foam.

Vansant's sister and father had watched the nightmare unfold, and they now stared numbly as the rescuers laid Charles' maimed body on the sand. Motionless and pale, his left leg was almost entirely severed. A bright river of crimson from his femoral artery flowed down the beach, connecting his motionless form to the vast Atlantic into which his attacker had vanished.[1]

***

Charles Vansant's grisly death marked the United States' first fatal shark attack, yet the shocking spectacle barely made headlines beyond southern New Jersey and Philadelphia. Even the *New York Times* only published the story on page eighteen. The incident likely would have garnered more publicity three years earlier, but other events were occupying global attention in July 1916.

The world that Vansant left behind was engulfed in World War I, a conflict unlike any yet seen. Although Europe had experienced nearly a hundred years of relative peace and stability following Napoleon's defeat in 1815, geopolitical maneuvering in the late 19th and early 20th centuries gradually entangled the continent in a spider's web of alliances and treaties. "It is militarism run stark mad. There is too much hatred, too many jealousies," stated an American diplomat a few months before war broke out. "All that is needed is a spark to set the whole thing off."

That spark was lit two years before Vansant's death when the heir to the Austro-Hungarian Empire's throne was assassinated in June 1914. This triggered a chain reaction of accusations and ultimatums that quickly arrayed the world's most powerful nations against one another. The "Great War," as it was then known, pitted the "Triple Entente" of Britain, France, and Russia against the "Central Powers" of

Germany, Austria-Hungary, and the Ottoman Empire. The United States remained neutral, having little interest in being dragged into what most Americans viewed as an Old World blood feud.

The pre-war tension's greatest catalyst was the new continental power that emerged in 1871 when the kingdom of Prussia unified most of Europe's German states into the German Empire. Prussian monarch Wilhelm I thereby became the *Kaiser*, or emperor, of the new German *Reich* (realm or domain). A latecomer to the imperial arena of great power politics, the nation's geopolitical ambitions were expressed in an 1897 speech by statesman Bernhard von Bülow. "We do not want to put anyone into the shade," von Bülow declared, "but we demand a place for ourselves in the sun."

German leaders realized that attaining world power status demanded a first-rate navy, and this effort's most important patron entered the scene when Wilhelm I's impulsive and emotionally unbalanced son took the throne in 1888. A cousin of both the British king and the Russian czar, Kaiser Wilhelm II envied the prestige of his British relatives and their Royal Navy, the most powerful armada on earth. German ascendance engendered British mistrust, and the two nations were locked in a naval arms race by 1902 as each built warships of increasing size, speed, and firepower.

Naval doctrine of that era was centered on the "battlefleet," or force of large ships armed with heavy guns. Future wars at sea, it was believed, would be decided by decisive clashes of battlefleets exchanging salvos of naval artillery. This was seemingly validated in 1905 when Japan annihilated the Russian fleet at the Battle of Tsushima, effectively deciding the Russo-Japanese War with a single blow.

The Russo-Japanese War also saw the employment of a revolutionary new weapon first fielded in the 1870s: the torpedo. A self-propelled underwater projectile with an explosive charge in its nose, the torpedo could be launched from warships, shore installations, and (eventually) submarines. Its deadliness lay in its ability to strike below the waterline, which increased the odds of sinking a ship. Navies responded by redesigning their warships with double hulls, armor belts, and watertight compartments to survive flooding.

Torpedoes soon featured combustion engines that increased their speed and range, and gyroscopes further raised the ante by making them the first guided missiles. The world's navies also developed small and fast "torpedo boats" to deploy this new weapon at close range under cover of darkness. Their value was proved at the Battle of Tsushima when Japanese torpedo boats wreaked havoc on the Russian fleet, yet doctrinal orthodoxy and national pride remained centered on battleships and cruisers, collectively known as capital ships.

The strength of the Royal Navy and the *Kaiserliche Marine*, or Imperial German Navy, was therefore focused in their battlefleets: Britain's Grand Fleet and Germany's High Seas Fleet. The Kaiserliche Marine had just emerged as the world's second-most powerful navy when the naval arms race further intensified in 1906. That year saw

Britain launch HMS *Dreadnought*, a battleship of unprecedented speed and firepower armed with guns capable of engaging targets from beyond torpedo range.

For the Germans, the mighty *Dreadnought* was the armor-clad embodiment of British dominance at sea. Even at the Great War's outbreak eight years later, the Kaiser's admirals knew that the High Seas Fleet could not go toe-to-toe against the Grand Fleet. They lacked an alternative strategy, but one would soon present itself.[2]

***

The first use of a submarine in combat was actually a feat of American ingenuity. By the summer of 1776, the Royal Navy had blockaded the rebellious American colonies and was landing troops ashore to trap General George Washington's Continental Army in New York City. It was during this direst hour that Yale graduate and fervent patriot David Bushnell completed a new weapon as audacious as it was novel.

Bushnell's invention was the *Turtle*, an egg-shaped wooden craft that floated vertically like a barrel. A tank in the bottom could be flooded to submerge the vessel, and its one-man crew powered it via two hand-cranked propellers. The *Turtle* was surprisingly stable and even featured a compass, depth gauge, and ventilation system that automatically closed upon submerging. Praised by George Washington as "an effort of genius," the craft was intended to stealthily approach an enemy ship and attach a keg of gunpowder by screwing an augur into the ship's hull before escaping undetected.

The fanciful concept very nearly worked. In September 1776, a Continental Army sergeant piloted the *Turtle* under cover of darkness toward the frigate HMS *Eagle* in New York Harbor. The sergeant was attempting to drill into the *Eagle*'s hull when British sentries spotted him. He quickly lit the explosive keg's fuse and released it to float away, where it detonated as the *Turtle* escaped. Though little noticed by the wider world, the unsuccessful attack marked the crossing of a major threshold in naval warfare.

Although submarines remained little more than novelties as the 20th century dawned, a few prescient naval officers recognized their potential. When the American submarine *Holland VI* was completed in 1899, the US Navy's chief engineer extolled its ability to conduct "an attack upon the enemy unseen and undetectable … she is an engine of warfare of terrible potency." Britain's Admiral Lord John "Jackie" Fisher subsequently concluded that submarines must have some value if "a common-sense, level-headed nation like that of the United States has tried and adopted them." Fisher wrote five years later: "I don't think it is even faintly realized the immense, impending revolution which the submarines will effect as offensive weapons of war."

The adoption of submarines nonetheless faced multiple challenges. Small vessels that skulked under the waves and struck by surprise challenged naval officers' gentlemanly self-image, one British admiral describing them in 1902 as "underhanded, unfair, and damned un-English." Everything about the submarine seemed an affront to the battlefleet's grandeur and the perceived chivalry of war at sea. Not long after his son was killed on the Western Front in 1915, British poet Rudyard Kipling wrote:

> They bear, in place of classic names,
> Letters and numbers on their skin.
> They play their grisly blindfold games
> In little boxes made of tin.

The world's naval powers all possessed submarines by 1914, yet their actual tactical and strategic potential remained unclear. Germany arrived last to the game, with the Kaiserliche Marine possessing no submarines until 1906 and only twenty-eight when the Great War began in 1914. This was a third as many as Britain, half as many as France, and fewer than even Russia. The German boats (submarines are traditionally considered "boats" rather than ships) were of comparable quality to British ones, albeit generally more conservative and practical in design.

Germany's submarine fleet would grow, however, both in quantity and as a looming menace in the minds of millions. Even into the 21st century, they would not be spoken of merely as submarines. Rather, their German-language name would become an international byword for lurking terror and sudden death on the high seas. The *Unterseeboot*, or "U-boat," was about to make its debut.[3]

***

The Germans have long been victims of geography. Their lands in Central Europe have historically been bordered by multiple rival powers, and more so in 1914 than ever before. Kaiser Wilhelm II described his nation as "menaced on every side" with "the bayonets of Europe pointed at her." This was true enough, as was the Kaiser's culpability in exacerbating these circumstances through his own geopolitical blundering.

His nation also suffered from an additional geographic liability in the form of sea access. Germany's comparatively small coastlines on the Baltic Sea and North Sea meant that any German ship—military or civilian—had to pass through British-controlled waters to reach the open Atlantic. A Royal Navy attaché in Berlin expressed British concerns in 1908. "At the bottom of every German's heart," the officer wrote, lay the desire for "a brave breaking-through of the lines which he feels are encircling him."

It was this strategic anxiety that underscored the German Empire's plans for a major war, a scenario the Kaiser's officers spoke of as "*der Tag*" (The Day). The plan was for German armies to quickly knock France out of the war before pivoting east to defeat Russia. Its success hinged on speed, as Britain's economic and naval strength made prolonged conflict a risky proposition. A short war, won by a decisive one-two punch, would leave the Central Powers commanding the continent and Germany with direct access to the Atlantic via the French coast. Britain and whatever remained of its alliance, it was believed, would then be forced to sue for peace.

Events unfolded differently. German troops swept through Belgium and into France during the war's first weeks, but the offensive was halted by British and French forces in September 1914 at the Marne River north of Paris. The full horror of industrial warfare revealed itself as machine guns and artillery shredded both sides' attempts to overwhelm the other. The war quickly reached a grim stalemate, and the opposing armies began digging in for a long and uncertain bloodletting.

Concurrently, the Kaiserliche Marine's inferiority to the Royal Navy proved to have ramifications beyond national pride when Britain established a blockade to prevent essential military and industrial cargo from reaching German ports. The Kaiser's admirals had assumed that an enemy blockade would be established close to shore, where it could be defeated by torpedoes and mines, but the British also recognized this danger. The Royal Navy therefore kept far from a potential trap by using the English Channel and the North Sea between Scotland and Norway as distant chokepoints.

The High Seas Fleet made no direct attempt to break the blockade because German admirals were unwilling to risk its destruction in a large battle. The Royal Navy was a "foe whose trenches could not be taken by storm," one German naval intelligence officer lamented. "It was a specter, an intangible phantom against which strategy, tactics, and all the courage of the German soldier were helpless." The war's stalemate, it seemed, had extended even to the sea.[4]

While trenches were being gouged from French and Belgian fields on 5 September 1914, the British scout cruiser HMS *Pathfinder* became the first vessel ever sunk by a submarine-launched torpedo. The *U-21*'s sinking of the *Pathfinder* claimed 259 lives, but an even more calamitous event seventeen days later shook the Royal Navy to its institutional oak. The *U-9* was on patrol off the Dutch coast when it sank three cruisers in ninety minutes with the loss of 1,459 British lives. Even a *U-9* officer described the scene as "tragic horror." An additional 525 were killed when the same U-boat sank another cruiser the following month.

Any doubts about the submarine's tactical potential were now dispelled. They could also be produced faster and with fewer resources than capital ships, making them particularly appealing to the blockaded and resource-strapped Germans. No nation, however, had seriously considered using submarines for large-scale "commerce raiding," or attacking civilian cargo ships. This was typically carried out by auxiliary cruisers (heavily armed ocean liners). Germany had deployed several auxiliary cruisers as commerce raiders, though the Royal Navy was efficiently making their careers short-lived. But although the British ruled the ocean waves, the Germans would soon find their solution beneath them.

The first sinking of a merchant ship by a submarine occurred off southern Norway on 20 October 1914. The *U-17* halted the British freighter *Glitra* by signaling that the ship would be torpedoed if she did not consent to a search, then a German boarding party armed with pistols came aboard. They declared that her cargo of coal, oil, and iron constituted contraband, and the U-boat sailors allowed the crew to abandon ship before scuttling the *Glitra* by opening its seacocks. The sinking was a bloodless and relatively gentlemanly affair, but the loss of a single freighter effected no measurable impact on Britain's sprawling war economy. Losing thousands of such ships, however, would be a different matter entirely.

German leaders increasingly recognized this as their enemies' Achilles' heel. Britain imported all its oil, cotton, and rubber, two-thirds of its food, and most of its wool and iron ore. Most of the Allies' munitions were produced in the neutral United States. All these goods arrived by ship: freighters carried solid cargo while tankers hauled crude oil and refined fuels. Ocean liners like the *Olympic*, one of the *Titanic*'s two sister ships, served as troopships (the other sister, *Britannic*, was sunk by a mine while serving as a hospital ship). Most merchant vessels were slow, all of them lacked armor, and they were weakly constructed compared to warships.

Sending enough of these civilian-manned ships to the bottom could defeat the "Allied Powers"—as the Triple Entente and its broader coalition became known—by denying them the equipment, food, and raw materials necessary to wage war. This was hardly a secret. Britain's prime minister declared in December 1916 that merchant shipping was "the jugular vein, which, if severed, will destroy the life of the nation." International law, however, mandated adherence to "prize rules" which required a submarine to halt a merchant vessel, search its cargo, then allow the crew to evacuate before sinking it. Prize rules therefore negated a U-boat's stealth advantage and left it vulnerable to the defensive guns installed on some merchant ships.[5]

German hopes for a decisive victory withered as 1915 approached. Voices in Berlin began clamoring for "unrestricted submarine warfare," or commerce raiding by U-boats that disregarded prize rules by attacking merchant ships without warning. This proposal was not initially approved due to both ethical concerns and uncertainty regarding how neutral nations would respond. Such a policy could provoke so much wrath, warned the foreign minister, that Germany "would be beaten to death like a mad dog." The British considered it improbable for the same reason. "I do not believe this would ever be done by a civilized power," wrote First Lord of the Admiralty Winston Churchill, who doubted there existed "a nation vile enough to systematically adopt such methods."

Yet it was not Britain that made Germany reluctant to initiate unrestricted submarine warfare—it was the United States. Berlin was determined not to provoke the Americans, but how would Washington respond when its ships and citizens became collateral damage? "There is no question that ruthless U-boat warfare will lead to a breach with America," warned Germany's chancellor. "If she declares war, America, with all her reserves, will be at the disposal of the Allies," another civilian politician cautioned. "I can see in the employment of the [U-boat] nothing but catastrophe."

Many in Berlin felt that circumstances were not dire enough to warrant such a drastic measure. The blockade as established in August 1914 was not a mortal blow to their war economy because neutral nations' vessels could still deliver goods to German ports and the Royal Navy could not legally seize neutral ships in international waters. The tipping point, however, came in November 1914 when Britain declared the entire North Sea a war zone: all ships seeking to pass the blockade would now be searched. In one stroke, Britain effectively severed German access to the global market.

Unrestricted submarine warfare suddenly became more palatable. "England wants to starve us: we can play the same game," boasted Grand Admiral Alfred von Tirpitz, who insisted that U-boats "surround England, [and] torpedo every English ship or those of its allies." Admiral Hugo von Pohl asserted that "we can wound England most seriously by injuring her trade," though he acknowledged that attacking merchant ships without warning would "send [civilian crewmen] to the bottom with their ships."

And so the Kaiser's government announced in February 1915 that "the waters around Great Britain and Ireland, including the whole of the English Channel, are hereby declared to be a war zone … every enemy merchant vessel encountered in this zone will be destroyed." Neutral nations' ships would not be deliberately targeted, though Germany warned that "it may not always be possible to prevent attacks on enemy ships from harming neutral ships." In fact, instilling fear in neutral merchant fleets was the campaign's secondary goal; the Kaiserliche Marine estimated that one-quarter of the cargo reaching British ports was carried by neutral ships.

The unrestricted submarine offensive of 1915 proved underwhelming. Only a few dozen ships were sunk and no significant impact on Britain's war economy was achieved. It also elicited protests from across the Atlantic when an American tanker was torpedoed in error, though this brought the United States no closer to fighting. Some Americans held pro-German sympathies, and many believed that Britain's blockade was no less morally repugnant than Germany's unrestricted submarine warfare. Public opinion strongly supported neutrality, but an incident south of Ireland in May 1915 would strain this nearly to the breaking point.[6]

The British ocean liner *Lusitania* was bound from New York City to Liverpool on 7 May 1915 when a torpedo slammed into her hull and sank her within minutes. Among the 1,198 fatalities were 124 Americans and 94 children, sparking global condemnation. One US newspaper decried it as "nothing short of savagery," while another declared that "bloodlust has toppled reason from its throne." A rumor that the German-owned radio station in Tuckerton, New Jersey transmitted the attack order underscored American perceptions of murderous treachery. "It seems inconceivable that we can refrain from taking action in this matter," declared former president Theodore "Teddy" Roosevelt, "for we owe it not only to humanity, but to our own national self-respect."

Sentiments like Roosevelt's did not go unnoticed in Berlin. In fact, the prospect of the United States joining the Allies so unnerved German leaders that American opinion effectively came to govern U-boat policy. Continued protests from Washington caused the unrestricted campaign to be suspended in September 1915. Renewed in the spring of 1916, it was halted again less than two months later when further American casualties occurred.

It was becoming clear that no gentlemanly half-measures would succeed in starving Britain into submission. Fully realizing the U-boat's strategic potential would instead require a naval offensive more ruthless than any yet seen in the history of war at sea. As *U-53* commander Hans Rose remarked in 1916, "It was war, which demanded victims, even if it was occasionally fought in patent leather shoes."[7]

***

6 July 1916
Spring Lake, New Jersey
14:22

More than a year after the *Lusitania* sinking, the shark swam north along the Jersey Shore after killing Charles Vansant in Beach Haven. It followed the offshore sand ridges past the state's barrier islands for five days until reaching Spring Lake, a seaside haven for the moneyed upper classes of Philadelphia and New York City. Many vacationers stayed at the posh Essex and Sussex Hotel where the staff worked under bell captain Charles Bruder, a 28-year-old Swiss Army veteran.

Bruder used his lunch break on 6 July to cool off with a swim. Hurrying across a beach crowded with men in striped tank top-style swimsuits and women in long summer dresses and wide-brimmed hats, Bruder threw himself into the surf and swam athletically out to sea. Minutes later, a few beachgoers sighted a commotion a few hundred yards offshore as bloodcurdling shrieking sounded.

Two lifeguards hurriedly rowed toward Bruder as they watched the bell captain claw himself to the surface only to be yanked down once more. The shark attacked and turned away before attacking again "like an airplane attacking a zeppelin," according to the *Philadelphia Inquirer*. Bruder's assailant, unseen except for its telltale dorsal fin, grated and shredded him with a bite force exceeding 2,000 pounds per square inch.

By the time the lifeguards hauled Bruder into the boat, his left leg had been ripped off above the knee and his right leg now ended where the exposed tibia and fibula bones protruded halfway between his knee and missing right foot. He died before reaching the beach, where some women fainted at the sight of his mangled body. A wealthy benefactor offered to ship Bruder's body home to his family, but the Swiss government declined because U-boats had made transatlantic voyages too dangerous.

Panic exploded across the Jersey Shore in the aftermath of the second fatal shark attack in six days. The authorities emplaced steel nets to protect swimmers, many of whom quit the water and were replaced by a flotilla of motorboats carrying volunteers wielding harpoons and rifles. It was in this flurry of fear and confusion that a different underwater threat appeared along US shores for the first time.[8]

***

While the shark seized US public attention during the summer of 1916, Britain's blockade had left Germany critically short of raw materials necessary for military production. At the same time, incidents like the *Lusitania* sinking fueled highly effective British propaganda that condemned German sailors as "pirates" with a "sheer love of cruelty." The U-boats' malevolent reputation was not merely a public relations issue but rather a strategic liability that threatened to turn American public opinion in favor of joining the Allies. It was eventually decided to tackle both challenges via an unprecedented mission. A U-boat would sail to the United States on a pre-arranged visit to humanize U-boat crewmen to the American public and bring back vital resources.

The purpose-built cargo U-boat *Deutschland* departed for the United States commanded by Kapitänleutnant Paul König (later mentor to a young Reinhard Hardegen). König passed unseen through the Royal Navy blockade, rounded the Scottish coast, then cruised on the surface for the remainder of the 3,800-mile voyage. On 9 July 1916, three days after Charles Bruder became the second New Jersey shark victim, the first-ever transatlantic submarine voyage concluded with fanfare when the *Deutschland* arrived in Baltimore, Maryland.

The U-boat's arrival enthralled the American populace and sparked a media sensation. Historian Michael Hadley wrote: "Had the Germans designed the voyage ... to dispel the myth of the 'marauding and merciless Hun,' they could scarcely have offered the American press a better package." König was feted at a dinner presided over by Baltimore's mayor, and the U-boat officers were even hosted at the White House by the Assistant Secretary of the Navy, a spry New Yorker named Franklin Delano Roosevelt. König also furtively met with a German espionage ring in Baltimore, and its operatives stood guard over the *Deutschland* while it was docked.

Even this historic event could not escape the shadow of the Jersey Shore's burgeoning shark hysteria. Lurid rumors abounded that the *Deutschland* was equipped with some secret technology that provoked shark attacks, or that sharks had followed the U-boat to the East Coast because they associated submarines with feasts of human flesh. When US officials encountered difficulty arranging an inspection of the *Deutschland* in Baltimore, one cartoonist drew König's U-boat with a shark's teeth and fin tossing Uncle Sam into the air.

Sharks have been feared by seafarers for centuries. Their name derives from the German word *schurke*, meaning scoundrel or villain, and *Moby Dick* author Herman Melville wrote of the great white shark's "transcendent horrors." Advancements in scientific knowledge had washed away these anxieties by the early 20th century, though much about sharks remained unknown to science. No fatal shark attack had ever been documented in American waters before the 1916 New Jersey incidents, and it was widely believed that no shark species posed any threat to humans.

The U-boat docked in Baltimore therefore represented July's second disconcerting revelation about the sea's dangers. The *Deutschland* carried no torpedoes, yet its dark and hulking shape served as a reminder that sharks were neither the ocean's only underwater predators nor the only ones capable of stalking the East Coast. Paul König's visit was intended solely as a commercial enterprise and publicity event, nevertheless, a few Americans saw the ostensibly friendly port call as a veiled threat: *You are not beyond our U-boats' reach.*[9]

The shark conveyed a similar message three days later. It continued swimming north after killing Charles Bruder, hugging the New Jersey coast and rounding the Sandy Hook barrier spit before passing through Raritan Bay. The shark then entered Matawan Creek; fresh water is an environment that bull sharks occasionally visit and in which great whites can survive for limited periods. It swam inland, following the winding creek through the marshes to the New Jersey town of Matawan. There, on the hot and humid afternoon of 12 July 1916, it struck again.

Several boys were swimming in the creek when one witnessed "the biggest, blackest fish [he] had ever seen" seize 11-year-old Lester Stilwell by the arm and shake him "like a cat shakes a mouse." Stilwell was dragged under, and the boys ran screaming into town. When their ghastly story elicited skepticism, they hurried to 24-year-old Stanley Fisher, described by newspapers as "a friend of all the boys in town." Matawan's most eligible bachelor and the son of a merchant ship captain, Fisher's tall and brawny physique belied his vocation as the town's tailor.

Rushing to the creek with other local men, Fisher leapt into the water to search for Stilwell's body. More than two hundred townspeople had converged on the banks when Fisher suddenly cried out in alarm as the beast, lurking unseen, ambushed him. Onlookers glimpsed a thrashing tail and flashes of white underbelly as Fisher fought back, striking the shark repeatedly with his fists. A witness recalled that he "seemed to be holding his own" against the shark, which retreated long enough for Fisher to reach shore—minus 10 pounds of flesh. Another boy became the fifth victim an hour later. He survived, but Stanley Fisher died that evening at Monmouth Memorial Hospital.

"WHOLE OF NEW JERSEY COAST INFESTED WITH MAN-EATING MONSTERS!" exclaimed the *New York Herald*'s front page as shark panic gripped the nation. Underlying the widespread fear was a chilling sense of powerlessness against a threat that moved unseen in the depths and attacked at will, chasing Americans from their own waters. Terrified citizens claimed to witness shark fins swarming off beaches up and down the Jersey Shore, and the Maryland State Police even reported a shark in Annapolis Harbor not far from where the U-boat *Deutschland* sat docked. Man was not powerless against the threat, however, and retaliation was thorough and brutal.

Fishing boats trailed glinting hooks baited with meat as fishermen slaughtered one shark after another. Matawan locals dropped dynamite in the creek while firing rifles and shotguns at any sign of movement. Grinning sailors aboard the battleship USS *Texas* (BB-35) were photographed beside a 15-foot hammerhead they had killed. President Wilson even mobilized the newly established US Coast Guard, and the cutter USCGC *Mohawk* was dispatched to the Jersey Shore with the task of "clearing the coast of the dangerous fish." As the *New York Times* stated, "The one purpose in which everybody shares is to get the shark, to kill it, and to see its body drawn up on the shore, where all may look and be assured it will destroy no more."

Two days after the Matawan Creek attacks, a pair of fishermen 4 miles off the creek mouth in Raritan Bay snagged something very large in their net. They hauled up a great white shark nearly the length of their boat, its jaws snapping as a powerful tail thrashed wildly. As one fisherman struggled to keep their boat from capsizing, the other bludgeoned the shark to death with an oar. Human remains found in its stomach led most experts to conclude that the "New Jersey man-eater" had been slain.

The *Deutschland* departed Baltimore twenty-three days later carrying nearly 900 tons of nickel, tin, and rubber. Paul König and his cargo U-boat would return to the United States later that year, but this second port call would be overshadowed by an even more ominous visitor. It was not the shark, as the attacks ceased after the Raritan Bay great white was slain. October's visitor instead also traveled from the far side of the Atlantic. Unlike Paul König, however, he did not arrive unarmed.[10]

***

The US Navy submarine *D-2* was patrolling 3 miles east of Point Judith, Rhode Island, on 7 October 1916 when its crew spotted the *U-53*. The *D-2* assumed a parallel course and the German commander, Kapitänleutnant Hans Rose, requested permission via megaphone to enter the harbor at Newport, Rhode Island. Rose received clearance and replied: "I salute our American comrades and follow in your wake." The *U-53* crewmen stood on deck in dress uniforms under the German Empire's fluttering white-and-black war flag as the U-boat entered Newport and anchored near a US Navy scout cruiser.

Hans Rose, age 31, would later reflect on the incongruity of his circumstances. Yesterday he had been "full of murderous thoughts on the filthy tower," and this morning he stood "at the dripping periscope, dressed in oily fatigues." Now, with his goatee and mustache neatly trimmed, he was on American soil, bedecked in a "spotless uniform with a chest full of medals," while chatting with two US Navy admirals. "Strange existence," he reflected.

The *U-53* commander informed the surprised American officers that he only intended to remain in port for a few hours. Rose invited his US Navy counterparts aboard for drinks while onlookers gawked at his crew lounging on the deck as records played on the boat's phonograph. American visitors noted that the German sailors seemed relaxed, disciplined, and healthy.

The *U-53* departed at 17:30 and promptly submerged to avoid detection. Rose steered toward the Nantucket lightship, explaining in his log that "the trade routes from New York, Philadelphia, Baltimore, and Providence all run together just a few nautical miles south of here." The *U-53* continued to just beyond the 3-mile limit marking international waters. As a clear day dawned on 8 October 1916, Hans Rose commenced a display of the same destructive efficiency that would make him the war's fifth-most successful U-boat ace.

He proceeded to sink five ships by stopping each with warning shots from his deck gun before allowing its crew to evacuate. Maydays filled the airwaves as US Navy destroyers arrived on the scene. Being neutral warships in international waters, however, they could only watch the destruction unfold from a few hundred yards away. One destroyer strayed between the *U-53* and its target, prompting Rose to signal: "GET OUT OF MY WAY, I AM GOING TO TORPEDO THAT SHIP." After expending their last torpedo, the Germans turned for home.

One newspaper deemed the episode an "indiscriminate massacre," although there were no fatalities. The only casualty was a mother who broke her hand when she reached overboard for her daughter's doll just as a wave smashed their lifeboat against the ship's hull. Hans Rose's famous chivalry was also on display as the *U-53* towed each lifeboat to the nearby lightship. President Wilson's administration took no action beyond summoning Germany's ambassador for a rebuke, but the incident's implications were clear to former president Teddy Roosevelt. "War has been creeping nearer and nearer," the twenty-sixth president observed, "until it stares at us from just beyond our three-mile limit."[11]

***

Newport residents noted the strong physiques and health of Hans Rose's crew, yet the average German citizen cut an increasingly different image. In addition to cutting off metals and oil, Britain's blockade blocked most of Germany's food imports. The winter of 1915–16 became known as the "Turnip Winter" for the prevalence of that dreary vegetable in the citizenry's diet. One *U-53* sailor decried "a system of war that had thrust into the hands of innocent German children a slice of raw onion for their supper." In Berlin, an American journalist saw women and children whose "skin was drawn hard to the bones and bloodless. Eyes had fallen deeper into the sockets. From the lips all color was gone."

Although German armies were trouncing czarist Russia in Eastern Europe, the Western Front stalemate persisted. France and Belgium's trenches were a muddy hell that millions of men on both sides shared with swarms of lice, rats, and flies. The stench of decomposing corpses was omnipresent, and artillery shells fell in a ceaseless hail that ravaged body and mind alike. Underlying the horror was its apparent futility. The Battle of the Somme in 1916 killed or wounded a million men—unleashing "all the horrors of all the ages," wrote Winston Churchill—yet even this failed to shift the battle lines appreciably in either direction.

That same year saw the Great War's only major clash of battlefleets. Submarines played little role in the large but anticlimactic Battle of Jutland, but nor did the decisive slugging match of heavy guns ever transpire. The two fleets instead fought a series of skirmishes and repeatedly broke contact while their destroyer screens threw salvos of torpedoes. Nearly nine thousand men were killed at Jutland without either side achieving a clear victory.

German victory could now "only be obtained by destroying the economic resources of Great Britain," the High Seas Fleet commander informed Kaiser Wilhelm. "Namely, by the employment of U-boats against British commerce." The Kaiserliche Marine estimated that Britain was being sustained by 11 million gross registered tons of shipping, 3 million of which sailed under neutral flags. They calculated that sinking 600,000 gross registered tons per month, and scaring off 10 percent of neutral tonnage, would seal the nation's fate. "An unrestricted submarine campaign … is the right means to bring the war to a victorious end," the naval chief of staff asserted. "Indeed, it is the only means to that end."

Confidence was boosted by an enlarged U-boat fleet. The Kaiserliche Marine had only been able to maintain fifteen or sixteen boats on patrol at any given time in 1915, but this had risen to roughly forty by early 1917. "England would be defeated in six months, at most," the High Seas Fleet commander declared on 1 February 1917. The tantalizing prospect of victory also spurred an imprudent reassessment of the threat posed by the United States, the intervention of which Germany now accepted as a foregone conclusion.

The Germans believed that the U-boat stranglehold would crush Britain "before a single American had set foot on the continent." Even if it did not, the crown prince assured his father's advisors that "America is not a serious military opponent. Its million-man army exists only on paper." At the same time, Admiral Eduard von Capelle declared that "[American] entrance means nothing. I repeat … nothing." He snidely added, "And when [US troops] have been trained, how are they to cross the ocean?" General Erich von Ludendorff was even more blunt: "I do not give a damn about America."

And so unrestricted U-boat warfare resumed on 1 February 1917. Relations between Berlin and Washington, already deteriorating, broke altogether two days later when President Woodrow Wilson's administration severed diplomatic relations with the German Empire. American public opinion still opposed direct involvement in the war, but another disastrous German policy decision was about to change that.

In January 1917, British intelligence intercepted a secret German telegram to the Mexican government. It was decoded and passed to the United States, and

President Wilson was stunned when handed a copy on 25 February. The message from German foreign secretary Arthur Zimmerman proposed an alliance: if the U-boat campaign were to drive the Americans to join the Allies, then Berlin would financially and politically support a Mexican attack against the southwestern United States. When newspapers published the "Zimmerman Telegram" on 1 March, many Americans suspected a British forgery until Zimmerman himself publicly confirmed its authenticity two days later.

"It was as if a gigantic bolt had struck from the blue across the American continent," wrote historian Arthur Link. "No other event of the war to this point, not even the sinking of the *Lusitania*, so stunned the American people." But the republic would not enter hostilities by fiat. Monarchs and cabinet ministers had taken the other combatant nations into war, but only in the United States did elected representatives vote on it. Congress voted in favor of hostilities by 82–6 in the Senate and 373–50 in the House of Representatives, and President Wilson signed the declaration of war on 6 April 1917. In Germany, Admiral Franz von Hipper responded wryly: "The U-boats will now have the last word."[12]

Entry into the Great War sparked a litany of urgent manufacturing initiatives in the United States. Among the highest priorities was merchant ship construction (Britain's prime minister begged for "ships, ships, and more ships"). The resulting shipbuilding program was centered at the Hog Island shipyard at the confluence of the Schuylkill and Delaware Rivers in Philadelphia, Pennsylvania. The construction effort's belated start, however, meant that none of the "Hog Islanders" would see service in World War I.

Just as merchant ships could not be built overnight, neither could an army. A few thousand American troops arrived in France during the summer of 1917, but training, equipping, and deploying the newly established American Expeditionary Force required months. The US Navy's modernization and expansion effort included building hundreds of "subchasers" in the form of 110-foot wooden-hulled vessels and 200-foot steel-hulled "Eagle boats." The new Caldwell, Clemson, and Wickes-class destroyers would soon join the fleet as well, though none were yet in service.

The Navy did, however, have other destroyers ready to fight. The newly commissioned USS *Jacob Jones* (DD-61) and five other Atlantic Fleet destroyers reached Ireland only a month after the United States declared war. They commenced combat operations immediately, their crews becoming the first American servicemen to fight in World War I.[13]

***

By the time USS *Jacob Jones* and her squadron mates arrived in May 1917, the unrestricted submarine campaign had cost the Allies over one thousand merchant ships. One of every four vessels leaving the British Isles on a round-trip voyage was sunk before it returned. Rising insurance rates immobilized Norway's merchant fleet and threatened to cripple Britain's, and many neutral ships now refused to leave port. Winston Churchill wrote that the Western Approaches, or waters immediately west of the British Isles, were "becoming a veritable cemetery of British shipping." April 1917 was the most catastrophic month yet, with an average of thirteen ships sunk per day.

Britain had only six weeks of food stores remaining by May. One German politician hardly embellished the situation when he boasted that the island nation faced "a situation unparalleled in her history," and Winston Churchill would recall that "the danger of [the Allies'] collapse in 1918 began to loom black and imminent." The U-boats also threatened to render moot America's entry into the war. Even if US troops could be safely transported to Europe, the dire shipping situation meant they could not be properly supplied.

As President Wilson prepared to declare war, US Navy Rear Admiral William Sims departed for Britain on a secret mission. Sims traveled via passenger ship in civilian clothes under a false identity, and by 10 April he was seated across from Admiral Sir John Jellicoe, Britain's First Sea Lord, in London. Sims was shocked at the figures his Royal Navy counterpart showed him. "It looks like the Germans are winning the war," the American officer observed. "They will win," Jellicoe replied bluntly, "unless we can stop these losses—and stop them soon."[14]

The U-boat itself, however, constituted a seemingly insurmountable tactical challenge. "The submarine presents a problem such as the world at large has never dreamed of before," wrote Ensign George S. Dole, who served aboard US Navy subchasers in 1917–18. As naval historian Jan Breemer would explain, "Never before had a weapon been created that so defied man's scientific ability to produce quickly a counter-weapon." Previous threats entailed only the variables of distance and horizontal movement, Breemer wrote, but the U-boat's ability to operate underwater made it "the first man-made weapon to go about its war-making business in the third dimension." ENS Dole concluded: "The Kaiser's deep-sea monsters represent the most perfect engines of evil genius man has ever been able to devise."

Merchant ships were not always defenseless, however. Many were outfitted with naval guns for self-defense. The ocean liner *Olympic* was carrying American troops across the English Channel in May 1918 when she spotted a U-boat and promptly rammed it; the boat sank and the German survivors were rescued by a nearby US Navy destroyer. A few U-boats were also lured to their destruction by Royal Navy "Q-ships," or seemingly defenseless merchant vessels actually crewed by naval sailors and heavily armed with hidden weaponry.

Nevertheless, although Allied warships could shoot or ram a surfaced U-boat or lay nets and mines in waters U-boats were expected to traverse, they still lacked reliable means of locating and destroying a submerged enemy. Even the 1915 introduction of an underwater explosive device called the "depth charge" was of limited effectiveness unless a submerged U-boat's location could be accurately pinpointed. By the time

Admiral Sims reached London in April 1917, statistics reflected just one U-boat sunk for every 167 Allied merchant ships lost.

Desperate naval policymakers finally resorted to a practice not employed since the Napoleonic era: convoys. Opponents cited the difficulty of organizing thousands of ships of differing speeds, routes, and nationalities. Other concerns included claims that convoying would only offer the U-boats more targets, and that merchant crews were not skilled enough to maintain formation. Historian Paul Halpern also noted that convoying was seen as "a tedious business and not one proper to an aggressive fighting navy." The losses of April 1917 demanded drastic measures, however, and that same month saw a trial convoy implementation achieve a 75 percent drop in sinkings. Finally, on 26 April, the British Admiralty decided to "introduce a comprehensive scheme of convoy."

"The oceans at once became bare and empty," one German officer wrote. Indeed, the primary benefit of convoying was that it made ships harder for U-boats to find. Convoys lured U-boats like moths to a flame when they were spotted, but the presence of escorting destroyers forced them to attack convoys while submerged, denying them both speed and visual awareness. Rear Admiral Sims explained that convoying "compelled the submarine to encounter its most formidable antagonist, the destroyer, and risk destruction every time it attacked merchant vessels." Coordinated attacks by multiple U-boats seemingly offered promise, although the Germans were unable to advance this concept beyond experimentation.

Though the Allies never defeated the U-boat tactically during World War I, they thwarted it strategically through the convoy system. The one-in-four sinking rate of April 1917 fell to fewer than one-in-twenty by year's end, even as Germany's own losses mounted. The Allies sank only twenty-three U-boats (excluding mine-related sinkings) prior to the introduction of convoys, but they destroyed more than twice that number thereafter.

Convoying staunched the massacre of Allied shipping during the latter half of 1917, yet the situation on Europe's battlefields swung precipitously against the Allies in December when Germany signed a peace treaty with Russia's new communist government. The Bolsheviks' capitulation presented a window of opportunity: Germany could now focus the majority of its combat power on the Western Front while most of the American Expeditionary Force had not yet arrived. German generals began preparing an all-out attack to defeat the Allies before US troops reached Europe in force.

The Spring Offensive, which the Germans termed the "*Kaiserschlacht*" (Kaiser's battle), was unleashed in March 1918. Casualties were horrific on both sides, but novel "stormtrooper" tactics breached Allied lines at multiple points amid a hurricane of bullets and shrapnel. German armies were soon advancing on Paris, but Berlin's final bid for victory would not be limited to the mud and barbed wire of the Western Front.[15]

***

The first indication that the East Coast of the United States was under attack came on 19 May 1918 when a radio station in Atlantic City, New Jersey received a distress call from a steamship being fired upon 300 miles off the Delmarva Peninsula. Less than twenty-four hours later, another ship reported being attacked 150 miles off Delmarva. A third vessel was shelled the next day, this time only 80 miles offshore.

The Kaiser was initially reluctant to extend the war to North America, yet it was clear by early 1918 that the U-boats had scarcely dented the deluge of American strength flowing into British and French ports. The U-boats dispatched to the United States in 1918 were therefore intended to attack troop transports and merchant ships, though their principal objective was more modest. Enemy forces marauding within sight of American beaches, the Germans reasoned, would draw US naval forces away from the primary U-boat operational areas in the Western Approaches.

The U-boats dispatched to the East Coast in 1918 were *U-Kreuzers,* or "U-cruisers." Most had been designed as cargo-carrying blockade runners like Paul König's *Deutschland.* Wide and ponderous in appearance and carrying enough fuel to operate along the eastern seaboard for up to a month, the U-Kreuzers were among the largest and most heavily armed U-boats of either world war. Their weaponry consisted of eighteen torpedoes and two 150mm guns, and some boasted an additional pair of 88mm guns.

The first U-boat arrived on 21 May when the *U-151* reached North Carolina. While cruising north along the coast, the *U-151* sank three small vessels by halting each with warning shots, ordering the crew to evacuate, then boarding it and placing explosives below decks. Their occupants were taken prisoner aboard the U-Kreuzer.

The *U-151* laid six mines in the shipping channel at the mouth of the Chesapeake Bay on the night of 24 May, then eight more off the Delaware Bay. The Germans submerged to lay the Delaware Bay mines and, upon surfacing, found themselves amid several merchant ships in heavy fog. The U-boat escaped on the surface by sounding its horn like another fishing boat or tug, then cut telegraph cables on the seafloor southeast of Sandy Hook before turning south again. But the interloper's most brazen gambit was still to come. On the morning of Sunday, 2 June 1918, none of the New Jersey residents preparing for church knew that a storm was about to break offshore.

It began 70 miles east-southeast of Atlantic City when the *U-151* halted and sank the schooner *Isabel B. Wiley.* After similarly dispatching the freighter *Winneconne,* the U-boat cut a 40-by-20-mile rectangular pattern while sinking two more schooners, the freighter *Texel,* and the passenger ship *Carolina.* Most were sunk by boarding them and planting explosives below decks. This left more than four hundred people (and the *Texel*'s cat) adrift in lifeboats, and the Germans used the opportunity to offload the prisoners they had held for several days.

Carolina passenger Mrs C.H. Westbrook would recount that "thoughts of Hun atrocities filled my mind," and *U-151* officer Frederick Körner wrote that "a great wailing of women's voices rose. There was praying and pleading." Many passengers "thought we were going to use them for target practice," but the only fatalities occurred when thirteen drowned after a lifeboat capsized. The *Haskell*'s captain later described Frederick Körner as "so polite it almost got on our nerves," and another *Carolina* passenger recalled that "[Körner] said in perfectly good English that he was sorry about this. But war is war." The *U-151* sank six vessels off the Jersey Shore on 2 June 1918, known thereafter as "Black Sunday."

The *Texel* survivors rowed 50 miles to Atlantic City Inlet, and the freighter *San Saba* later rescued others adrift off Barnegat Light. A crowded lifeboat from the *Carolina* reached an Atlantic City beach while Philadelphia's LuLu Temple Shriners band was playing on the boardwalk. Bystanders rushed toward the waterline to assist as the Shriners began an impromptu rendition of the National Anthem. The *Atlantic City Gazette* told of survivors who "stood with tears streaming down their cheeks … others were swearing, spilling their wrath at the Kaiser."

On 3 June, the day after Black Sunday, the tanker *Herbert L. Pratt* was steaming to Philadelphia when one of the *U-151*'s mines exploded and ripped open her hull near the bow. The ship's radio operator broadcast a mayday while her captain made a dash for the Delaware Bay. The flooding was more than the pumps could counteract, and the *Herbert L. Pratt* partially sank 3 miles south of the breakwater. There were no casualties, but the partly submerged tanker stood as a warning to passing ships.

"U-BOATS OFF SHORE!" declared the *New York Times* as a paroxysm of fear gripped the East Coast. Where Jersey Shore residents and vacationers had claimed to witness shark fins swarming the glinting coastal waters two summers earlier, they now seemed to spot German periscopes behind every wave. The destroyer USS *Preble* (DD-12) reported engaging a U-boat off Beach Haven on the day of the *Herbert L. Pratt* sinking, and newspapers told of a subsequent naval sortie to "give battle to the Hun." The *U-151* was long gone by the time the Navy arrived, however, and the trigger-happy warships instead fired wildly at phantoms. The scouring of the Jersey Shore by more than two dozen newly built subchasers over the ensuing weeks proved similarly fruitless.

The shark of 1916 had bitten clean through American naïveté about nature's predators that hunted from beneath the waves, and now the U-boats exploded the assumption that the Atlantic insulated the United States from attack. "It is imperative that the Yankees at home learn to know and appreciate us," declared a German newspaper in Cologne. The United States sat "on the other side of the big duck pond where one believes oneself safe," yet the Americans would now "feel the mailed fist on their necks" and learn "in their homes what war really is and what it means."

The *U-151* had not yet returned to port when the *U-156*, *U-140*, and *U-117* also set sail for the United States. The *U-156* seeded New York's approaches with mines, but did not act on headquarters' suggestion to bombard a Beach Haven shipyard, a Barnegat City railway, or an Atlantic City dock. One mine blew a hole in the cruiser USS *San Diego* (ACR-6) off Long Island on 19 July, killing six and sinking the warship in twenty-eight minutes. More than eight hundred Navy and Marine Corps survivors left afloat sang "The Star-Spangled Banner" and "My Country, 'Tis of Thee" until rescue arrived.

The *U-156* next cruised north to Massachusetts where a surreal episode transpired on 21 July. The Germans fired more than a hundred shells at ships sailing along the Cape Cod shore, causing several to land near the town of Orleans. The "Battle of Orleans" marked the first enemy attack on US soil since the Mexican-American War. Terrified bathers fled the beach while a Coast Guard surfboat rowed out to the damaged ships as shells screamed overhead. The *U-156* was eventually chased off by US Navy aircraft.

The *U-117* laid a minefield off central New Jersey in August that sank the Cuban freighter *Chaparra*, killing six, and the US freighter *San Saba*, killing her entire crew of thirty. After torpedoing the tankers *Sommerstad* and *Frederic R. Kellogg* off New Jersey, the *U-117* laid mines off Maryland and Delaware; these later sank the Navy cargo ship USS *Saetia* (ID-2317) and damaged the battleship USS *Minnesota* (BB-22). In September, the British Admiralty informed the US Navy that the *U-155*—formerly the *Deutschland*—and *U-152* were en route to the East Coast. The latter was tasked with laying mines off Atlantic City before hunting with torpedoes, but the boat was recalled in October.

The U-Kreuzers sank ninety-two ships off North America, killing 133 people, but this neither tied down US naval forces nor interrupted the flow of men and matériel overseas. "Every transport and cargo vessel bound for Europe sailed as if no such campaign was in progress," an official US Navy history stated. Most of the American Expeditionary Force embarked on troopships in Hoboken, New Jersey (giving rise to the slogan "heaven, hell, or Hoboken!"). The United States would land 2 million troops and 3.9 million tons of cargo in France by November 1918. "The Yanks are coming!" declared a popular patriotic song, and nothing above or below the waves would stop them.

Although the 1918 U-boat campaign along the East Coast proved strategically inconsequential, it foreshadowed more ominous developments to come. "To those who can see into the future, surely this is a warning of what later wars might bring," *U-151* officer Frederick Körner wrote after returning to Germany. "For the day will come when submarines think no more of a voyage across the Atlantic than they do now a raid across the North Sea." Körner concluded: "America's isolation is now a thing of the past."[16]

***

"OUR U-BOATS ACTIVE OFF THE USA!" trumpeted a Berlin newspaper on 6 June 1918, yet developments closer to home were troubling. The Spring Offensive reached the Marne River by late May, but weeks of heavy fighting had sapped the assault's momentum. It also ran headlong into fresh American troops eager for a fight, meeting fierce resistance and counterattacks by US Marine Corps and US Army units. Germany's exhausted armies ground to a halt in July. The Allies answered in August with a devastating counterstroke that inflicted staggering casualties while punching deep through German lines, and General Erich Ludendorff soon suffered a nervous breakdown.

Dire news from the Western Front and rumors of an impending mutiny in the High Seas Fleet had not yet reached the commander of the *UB-68* in the Mediterranean. He stealthily infiltrated a convoy southeast of Sicily in the early morning darkness of 4 October 1918 before torpedoing a British freighter and then quickly retreating. Undaunted and eager for another kill, he surfaced and pursued the convoy.

The German crew was preparing to attack from periscope depth when—for reasons that would never be determined—the *UB-68* suddenly lost longitudinal stability. Its bow dropped downward, standing the U-boat on its head as the interior lights went out, and began plunging uncontrollably into the depths. The commander yelled an order to blow water from the ballast tanks to lighten the boat, yet it continued to sink. The first watch officer shined a quivering flashlight beam on the depth gauge as its needle moved farther and farther to the right.

He looked away, unable to bear watching the gauge which showed death racing nearer by the second. Steel creaked and groaned under the increasing water pressure as the *UB-68* as it approached "crush depth," or the point at which the pressure outside the boat would implode its pressure hull. The pressure ruptured one of the buoyancy tanks with a loud *crack!* The commander was still barking orders when the depth gauge needle slowed, then stopped entirely.

The wobbling needle marked just over 300 feet as the *UB-68* hung vertically in the sea, then it started moving slowly to the left. The U-boat was rising, but the Germans' desperate attempts to halt its uncontrolled descent now left it too buoyant. Its ascent rapidly accelerated until the boat was rocketing upward in a manner the commander compared to "a stick plunged underwater and then suddenly released."

The U-boat breached the surface stern-first, a third of its length rising above it as propellers turned in midair. The stern then crashed downward against the sea, leveling the boat in the water and tossing the crew about the interior like a child's toys. The commander immediately heaved open the conning tower hatch. It was broad daylight, and the *UB-68* was surrounded. "Sirens were howling all around us, the merchant ships turned away and opened fire with the guns they had mounted on their sterns," he later wrote. "The destroyers, firing furiously, came tearing down upon me. A fine situation!"

The onrushing destroyers scored two hits, and the U-boat's interior began flooding. "I realized that this was the end, and I gave the order, 'All hands, abandon ship.'" The engineering officer remained behind to scuttle the U-boat to prevent its capture. He succeeded, but the boat's final dive took him and three others with it. The German commander shed his boots and heavy leather attire in the water and was wearing only a shirt, underwear, and one sock when he and the thirty-two other survivors were fished from the sea by HMS *Snapdragon*.

***

Three weeks after the *UB-68*'s sinking, rumors of an imminent naval mutiny proved more than idle hearsay. The High Seas Fleet had done little actual fighting while its best officers had been funneled into the U-boat force; morale and discipline consequently plummeted. The final straw was the 24 October 1918 order for the High Seas Fleet to sortie and engage the combined Allied battlefleets in a suicidal final melee—the Prussian "death ride" tradition at its most extreme. The enlisted sailors promptly revolted, sabotaging their warships and barricading themselves aboard. Many ran wild in Kiel, some cheering for President Woodrow Wilson.

The insurrection spread like wildfire, yet the U-boat crews remained loyal. The mutinous crews of two battleships surrendered when the *U-135*'s captain threatened to torpedo them. Three thousand mutineers attempting to storm a military prison were met by a formation of U-boat men armed with rifles and bayonets. The mob refused orders to halt, so the submariners opened fire, killing two. There were too few U-boat men to suppress the mutiny, however, and it soon spilled over into neighboring cities as civilians took up arms as well.

The German Empire's home front descended into anarchy while its armies were in full retreat. The Allies' "Hundred Days Offensive," its southern flank led by American troops, smashed through German lines in August and September 1918. By October, the Allies were advancing toward the Fatherland itself as the Central Powers collapsed on all fronts. Kaiser Wilhelm II abdicated the throne and went into exile, and the Great War ended on 11 November 1918 with an armistice that effectively constituted Germany's surrender.

Britain ordered the High Seas Fleet to sail to the Royal Navy base at Scapa Flow for internment, a final voyage that one German officer described as a "funeral procession." The warships were manned by skeleton crews and were intended to remain at anchor until being parceled off as victors' spoils, but the hated U-boats were to be handed over immediately. U-boat officers were thus denied the opportunity to scuttle their vessels in defiance, as the interned High Seas Fleet would do the following year.[17]

The first hours of peace found an assortment of Royal Navy ships anchored in the Bay of Gibraltar. Among the German prisoners of war (POWs) on one cruiser's quarterdeck was a thin and sullen naval officer who had once commanded the *UB-68*. Deeply depressed since his capture at sea five weeks earlier, his British interrogators had noted he "was very moody and almost violent at times, and it was very hard to make him talk at all." He even morosely claimed he was "done with the sea and with ships."

The 27-year-old officer heard celebratory fog horns and steam whistles sound across the bay. He watched as one British warship triumphantly raised a captured German flag upside-down. It all seemed too much to bear. His country was defeated, its leaders had seemingly proven themselves cowards and traitors, and he saw no future for U-boats.

At almost that same moment, news of the defeat reached a German infantryman at a hospital north of Berlin. He was recuperating from a poison gas attack on the front lines which had left him temporarily blind, and news of the Armistice was so distressing that he claimed to lose his eyesight again. "Everything went black before my eyes … [I] threw myself on my bunk and dug my burning head into my blanket and pillow," the soldier later wrote. "Since the day I stood at the grave of my mother, I had not wept … but now I could not help it."

The smoldering 29-year-old's grief would eventually devolve into something darker. Germany had not been defeated, he believed, but rather betrayed from within: "In these nights, hatred grew in me … for those responsible for this deed." It is likely that his account of immediate emotional anguish was more creative self-dramatization than fact. His thirst for revenge likewise may have developed not while brooding in the hospital, but instead over the ensuing months and years. In any event, history's dice of fate had already been cast.

The erstwhile *UB-68* commander spent ten months as a POW. He was greeted upon returning to Germany by *Korvettenkapitän* Otto Schultze, his former flotilla commander in the Mediterranean. Schultze was recruiting officers for the new German navy, a neutered revenant known as the *Reichsmarine*. In addition to prohibiting Germany from possessing U-boats, the Treaty of Versailles also limited the Reichsmarine to just 1,500 officers. Accordingly, Schultze wanted to retain only the best to serve as the nucleus around which the nation's naval strength might one day be restored.

"So, are you going to stay with us?" Schultze asked. The oberleutnant was unsure. He had become, as he described, "an enthusiastic U-boat man" firmly "under the spell of this unique U-boat camaraderie." Accordingly, only one question mattered. "Do you think we'll have U-boats again?" he inquired. "I'm sure we will," Schultze responded confidently. "Things won't always be like this." The officer elected to remain in the navy.

The captured U-boat officer's name was Karl Dönitz, and the hospitalized soldier's was Adolf Hitler. They had never met and, though born only two years apart, shared little in common beyond their native language. Hitler was an overwrought ideologue and idle dreamer from Austria whereas Dönitz was a hardworking and meticulous Prussian naval officer, yet they now shared the burdens of humiliation, anger, and an uncertain future.[18]

Twelve days of shark terror along the Jersey Shore in 1916 showed Americans what a single undersea predator was capable of, but those memories were quickly buried by the historic events of the two years that followed. The shark would eventually prove a harbinger of more than just the U-Kreuzers of 1918, however, when the entwining of Hitler and Dönitz's ambitions exploded off the US East Coast in a fiery second act in 1942. Compared to 1918, the carnage this unleashed was incomparable—and the stakes immeasurable.

CHAPTER THREE

The Gray Wolves

"A final 'Heil' to the Reich,
A final kiss to home we gave.
Give us who die on honor's field,
In honor, also, one last wave."
—Unknown U-boat sailor (1941)

The Great War left Germany destitute and demoralized. The Versailles Treaty of 1919 reduced its military to a token force and forced the country to both accept blame for the war and pay enormous reparations. The German Empire transitioned to a democratic republic, but the central government was weak and lacked popular support. The 1918 naval mutiny sparked left-wing uprisings across Germany that persisted into 1919 as the revolutionaries battled right-wing paramilitaries called *Freikorps* comprised partly of U-boat veterans. Violent unrest among political factions continued into the 1920s.

One faction was the National Socialist German Workers' Party, or "Nazis." Led by embittered former soldier Adolf Hitler, the Nazis railed against the "November criminals" responsible for the 1918 capitulation and espoused a pseudohistorical and pseudoscientific narrative of racial superiority. The Nazis claimed that Germans were the standard-bearers of humanity's "master race," and Hitler's messianic vision invoked the medieval Holy Roman Empire and the now-extinct German Empire by calling for a new imperial iteration: a "Third Reich." The Nazis graduated from street brawling to parliamentary politics, and Hitler's charisma and political maneuvering finally elevated him to absolute power in 1933.

Hitler styled himself the nation's *Führer*, or leader, but solidifying his control required building a coalition of power brokers and interest groups. The naval officer corps was conservative and disinclined toward radicalism, but the prospect of restoring Germany's fleet eventually earned the Nazis their support. This compromise was embodied by Admiral Erich Raeder. Placed in overall command of the Reichsmarine in 1928, Raeder continued serving as Germany's senior sailor under Hitler, who promoted him to the rank of grand admiral in 1939.

Raeder's stiff and pedantic style earned him the moniker "The Schoolmaster," and he held himself aloof from both his subordinates and the Führer. One officer stated that Raeder "rarely inspired enthusiasm, but instead solid respect," and another described him as "stuck in the old modes of naval thought." Raeder found Nazism brutish and crude (he protested the antisemitic violence of 1938's "*Kristallnacht*" directly to Hitler) and sought to keep the navy free of ideological influences. Devout National Socialists did lurk within Raeder's ranks, though some would not reveal themselves until later.[1]

***

Raeder held overall command of Germany's resurrected navy, but a very different personality led the *Ubootwaffe*, or U-boat force. Karl Dönitz (pronounced "*Der-nitz*") was born to middle-class parents near Berlin in 1891. Dönitz's conservative father was an optical engineer for Zeiss, and his mother died when he was 3. His father subsequently raised Karl and his brother "as rather one-sided Prussian children," as Dönitz himself wrote. He was a superb student, interested in geology and paleontology, but decided on a military career at a young age. He was serving on a light cruiser when World War I began in 1914 and transferred to the U-boat fleet two years later.

British POW records portray Karl Dönitz as despondent and guilt-ridden following his 1918 capture in the Mediterranean. The four men who went down with the *UB-68* appeared to him in dreams for years afterward. In an unpublished diary, Dönitz described seeing his chief engineer: "A damp trail of sea-water was your trace—the salt flood dropped from your hair and leathers."

Yet U-boat service had lost no luster in his eyes. "I was fascinated by the unique sense of comradeship," he later wrote. "Surely every submariner has sensed in his heart the glow of the open sea ... felt as rich as a king, and would change places with no man." Institutionally homeless in the postwar Reichsmarine, the years after his return to Germany saw him serve as a staff officer, lead a torpedo boat flotilla, and command a cruiser.

Forty-one years old when Hitler took power, Dönitz's thin physique and rigid posture conveyed a stature taller than his 5 feet, 9 inches. A receding hairline, narrow eyes, large forehead, and small mouth lent his face a somewhat unbalanced appearance. When his usually pursed lips did move, he spoke in a slightly nasal tone that conveyed blunt opinions. One U-boat commander characterized Dönitz as "lean in appearance, brief in his speech, and stern in his demands."

Dönitz was a perfectionist who lived frugally and was averse to flamboyant personas, despite his own command style often employing theatrical rhetoric. His severe bearing belied a good-natured sense of humor, and biographer Peter Padfield concluded that he displayed "the emotional insecurity of a much younger man." Dönitz also possessed a near-genius IQ of 138 and an inclination to discard orthodoxy in favor of writing his own rules.

A 1930 performance evaluation written by Wilhelm Canaris (later Hitler's military intelligence chief) stated that Dönitz was a "very ambitious" officer who "asserts himself to obtain prestige." Dönitz was indeed ambitious, but he was also deeply frustrated. He chafed at being under Erich Raeder's uninspiring thumb, later grumbling that "[Raeder] was the big chief and I was just the little man." The Great War had also left him captivated by the U-boat's potential, but the Versailles Treaty prohibited Germany from building or possessing them. The rise of National Socialism, however, was about to present the opportunity he sought.

Germany evaded the interwar prohibition on U-boats by conducting research and development under a front company in the Netherlands. New designs were sold to other countries and the resulting submarines were taken on sea trials by Reichsmarine personnel disguised as tourists. The Germans began "antisubmarine training" in 1933 while initiating a covert U-boat construction program. Four months after Hitler formally repudiated the Versailles Treaty in March 1935, the first new U-boats were launched. The Reichsmarine also took on the name *Kriegsmarine*, or War Navy.

Kapitän Karl Dönitz took command of the Kriegsmarine's first U-boat flotilla that same year. Although he would not be promoted to admiral until 1939, he was now Germany's most senior U-boat officer. "Body and soul I was once more a submariner," he recalled. His new role bestowed the title *Befehlshaber der Unterseeboote*, or Commander of Submarines. The acronym "BdU" also referred to the collective Ubootwaffe headquarters apparatus.[2]

German rearmament commenced in earnest in 1935, yet Dönitz's goals faced significant bureaucratic challenges. The Kriegsmarine was the least prioritized branch of the *Wehrmacht*, Nazi Germany's armed forces. The *Heer* (army) and *Luftwaffe* (air force) were better resourced and more politically favored, and most available naval resources went toward surface ships. Grand Admiral Raeder was part of Dönitz's challenge. A Battle of Jutland veteran nostalgic for the High Seas Fleet, Raeder saw U-boats as one part of a balanced fleet centered on capital ships. Hitler approved Raeder's grandiose but unimaginative plans in 1938 and assured him there would be no war with Britain until 1944 at the earliest.

Dönitz had drawn two naval lessons from World War I. The first was that challenging the Royal Navy

Admiral Karl Dönitz, May 1943. (German Federal Archives)

on its own terms was a fool's errand, and he consequently saw the colossal new battleships *Bismarck* and *Tirpitz* as a poor use of limited resources. The second lesson was that reliance on merchant shipping represented Britain's critical vulnerability. Bringing that nation to heel meant destroying the ships keeping it fed, fueled, and armed. "The U-boat," Dönitz concluded, "is the only means of defeating Britain."

By extension, he insisted that U-boats be employed exclusively for offensive operations against merchant shipping. He adamantly opposed using them for reconnaissance, coastal defense, and other tasks. "Their job is to sink as many ships as possible in the Atlantic," he insisted. "U-boats are not to be used for any other purpose."[3]

Nested within Dönitz's strategic paradigm was a tactical one based on existing doctrine for a different type of combat vessel. Despite the U-boat's defining characteristic being its ability to travel underwater, Dönitz wanted them to fight primarily on the surface. The deck and conning tower provided a "small and inconspicuous silhouette" that was difficult to visually identify at night, while their greater speed and maneuverability on the surface enabled "bringing the torpedo to a deadly short range." The U-boat would fight, therefore, using "the proven rules of torpedo boat tactics."

This was partly a response to a new submarine detection capability pioneered by Britain. Codenamed ASDIC, but better known as sonar (from "Sound Navigation and Ranging"), it functioned via a transducer on the bottom of a ship's hull that emitted pulses of ultrasonic sound waves. These bounced off an object to return an "echo," and the echo's strength and the duration elapsed before its return indicated the object's direction and distance. Sonar seemingly stripped submarines of their invisibility, leading the British Admiralty to declare in 1937 that "the U-boat will never again be capable of confronting us with the problem with which we found ourselves faced in 1917."

Sonar could only effectively detect submerged objects, however, and was largely useless against U-boats on the surface. Fighting like a torpedo boat also provided U-boat crews better visibility of their surroundings. Diving "renders you blind and helpless," cautioned the official tactical manual for commanders. A commander on the surface "continues to be able to take in the situation and retains his liberty of action" and should "only submerge when compelled to do so by direct pursuit." They were faster here too, the Royal Navy noting in 1940 that "the great advantage … is that the U-boat can escape at speed on the surface."

Dönitz also wanted his commanders to fight up close. German and British submarine doctrine emphasized submerged attacks from over a mile away—the naval equivalent of a sniper—which kept a submarine beyond sonar range and lessened the risk of its periscope being spotted. Dönitz dismissed this in favor of surface attacks from as close as 300 meters, with 600 meters as the optimum distance. Point-blank range reduced the risk that a torpedo would miss and, if it was spotted, allowed little time for evasive action.

U-boats of World War II attacked primarily during hours of darkness, the new German doctrine emphasizing "the difficulty of detecting the submarine at night on the surface due to its long and low silhouette." To the naked eye in darkness, the boat "disappears almost entirely in the water … Against the background of the sea alone, the conning tower is very difficult to make out." Commanders further reduced their odds of being spotted by trimming low in the water to leave only the conning tower visible.[4]

Nighttime surface attacks at close range were the bedrock of Dönitz's tactical centerpiece: the "wolfpack." A group of U-boats would ambush a convoy from multiple directions, overwhelming its escorts and sinking multiple ships in a chaotic melee before dispersing. Wolfpacks combined the element of surprise with the military principle of concentration of forces, enabling U-boats to achieve temporary local superiority against an enemy whose overall strength far outmatched Germany's. Here, finally, was the answer to the convoys that stymied the U-boats in 1917–18. Although Dönitz did not invent this concept (as he claimed), it was he who brought the theory into practice.

To locate convoys, a wolfpack would form a dispersed patrol line with 10–30 miles between U-boats, which acted as the prongs of a large rake that swept the sea at low speed. The first U-boat to sight a convoy radioed its location and heading to BdU, then stealthily shadowed the merchantmen while transmitting a radio homing signal. Meanwhile, Dönitz's headquarters vectored the other U-boats to converge ahead of the convoy along its expected route. Upon assembling the wolfpack, BdU would transmit: "ATTACK WHEN DARKNESS FALLS."

The wolfpack would pounce without warning from multiple directions. Steam and fire tore through the darkness as tracer shells stitched glowing trails across the waves and burning ships turned the sky a dull red. Men in the water pleaded for rescue as harried escorts raced past them to engage the attackers. The most successful U-boat commanders fought from inside the convoy itself, swerving between merchant ships which often scattered in panic. Dönitz frequently personally directed wolfpack operations from BdU headquarters ashore.[5]

***

Karl Dönitz understood that Imperial Germany's unrestricted submarine campaign of 1917 could have succeeded if enough U-boats had been available. Defeating Britain in the next war, he believed, required three hundred boats. This would enable one hundred to be on patrol at any given time, more than doubling the 1917 figure. In addition to sufficient numbers, Dönitz's strategy also sought specific capabilities from the next generation of U-boats.

He was vexed by his superiors' interest in resurrecting the bulky U-Kreuzers, and he saw little need for the new Type II boat, which was effectively a coastal submarine.

Dönitz knew that Raeder and the other admirals likely saw the Type IIs filling scouting and defensive roles and the U-Kreuzers conducting commerce raiding under prize rules, neither of which had a place in Dönitz's vision. He instead proposed two designs that balanced speed, maneuverability, range, and seaworthiness. Although Dönitz had no direct role in design or procurement during the interwar years, both of his desired models were in production by 1936.[6]

One of these two designs was the Type VII, and its VIIA and VIIB variants culminated in the famed Type VIIC in 1940. Measuring 220 feet long and 20 feet across at its widest, the Type VIIC had a submerged displacement of 857 long tons. The Type VIIC carried fourteen torpedoes, launched from four tubes in the bow and a fifth in the stern, and its agility and ability to dive quickly made it ideal for wolfpack operations. More than six hundred Type VIICs would be built, making it history's most-produced submarine.

The Type VII's larger counterpart was the Type IX, produced primarily in the IXB, IXC, and IXC/40 variants. These three models differed only slightly in size and were roughly 31 feet longer and 2 feet wider than the Type VIIC, with an average submerged displacement of 1,203 long tons. Their larger size enabled greater fuel capacity and thus longer range, space for twenty-two torpedoes, and a second stern tube. Intended for solitary operations in distant waters, Type IXs sank more tonnage per boat than the Type VIIs by exploiting weaker Allied defenses in the waters off South Africa, Texas, Trinidad, and elsewhere. Slightly poorer maneuverability and slower crash-diving made them less well-suited to wolfpacks.

The Type VII and Type IX boats were mechanically reliable, highly seaworthy (stable in rough seas), and able to range thousands of miles from port. Sleek and angular in appearance, they were also aesthetically similar. Overlapping capabilities meant each could perform the other's primary mission: a Type IX could conduct wolfpack operations and a Type VII could perform long-range solo patrols. For the war's duration, Type VII and Type IX variants would comprise nearly all of Germany's oceangoing attack U-boats.[7]

***

U-boats were technically "submersibles" rather than true submarines because they travelled primarily on the surface, but this was unrelated to German tactical doctrine. It instead reflected an engineering limitation, namely, that a combustion engine cannot be run while submerged because it requires a continuous flow of fresh air to ignite the fuel and ventilate the exhaust fumes. Consequently, and like all other submarines of that era, U-boats used diesel engines while on the surface and battery-powered electric motors while below it.

A surfaced U-boat was powered by a pair of supercharged four-stroke diesel engines with a combined 2,800 horsepower for the Type VII's six-cylinder engines and 4,400 horsepower for the Type IX's nine-cylinder versions. US Navy submarines used an intermediary electric motor, but a U-boat's engines turned the propeller shafts directly via friction clutches. An air intake duct aft of the bridge pulled fresh air through a trunking system into the engine room. Exhaust could be ventilated through the outer hull or used to blow water from the ballast tanks upon surfacing.

The diesel engines gave the Type VIIC a top speed of 17.7 knots, or 20.3 mph (1 knot equals 1.15 mph, and 1 nautical mile equals 1.15 statute miles). The larger Type IX was about a half-knot faster. Top speed was only used for brief sprints, such as when obtaining an ambush position or fleeing a destroyer. A Type VIIC making 10 knots with a standard fuel load had an operational range of 8,500 nautical miles. The Type IXC's range was 13,450 nautical miles while the IXB and IXC/40's legs were a few hundred miles shorter and longer, respectively.

A U-boat's top speed was significantly slower than a destroyer, and slightly slower than the fastest US Coast Guard cutter, though it could outrun subchasers and slower warships like Britain's Flower-class corvette. Troopships (whether purpose-built or ocean liners) were generally too fast to target, although a U-boat could outpace most freighters and tankers. Most merchant ships' top speed was 10–15 knots, enabling a U-boat to maneuver to a firing position ahead of its target or run down a fleeing one. A twin-rudder design also made them highly maneuverable.[8]

Despite greater speed and range while surfaced, a U-boat's ability to evade and attack from under the surface represented its most important attribute. As it prepared to submerge, the crew closed the air intake and switched from diesel to electric power. A Type VIIC running both "E-motors" at full power could make 7.6 knots submerged, the Type IX slightly less. This depleted a fully charged battery in roughly an hour. At 4 knots, the Type VIIC and IX could cover 80 and 63 nautical miles, respectively. Simultaneously running both diesel engines and both E-motors at full power was used to boost top speed for short sprints, and engaging one of each at lower speed enabled better fuel efficiency over long distances.

The electric motors also functioned as dynamos that recharged the batteries. While under diesel power, the spinning drive shafts charged long banks of batteries located beneath the compartments' deck plates. The lead-acid batteries weighed more than 40 tons and required six hours of travel to fully recharge. These represented a major hazard if the boat sustained significant flooding: submerging the battery cell terminals caused electrolysis to split seawater's sodium chloride (salt), producing lethal chlorine gas.

Even when using minimal battery power by lying motionless on the seafloor, air quality inside the pressure hull limited the time a U-boat could spend in the depths. The operative challenge was not oxygen depletion but rather carbon dioxide accumulation. This became deadly after about seventy-two hours, though it impaired cognitive abilities long before that. Even when using the air filtration system's CO_2 scrubber, the practical limit for remaining submerged was between twenty-four and thirty-six hours.[9]

A U-boat was built around a cylindrical structure called the "pressure hull" measuring approximately 15 feet across at its widest. Built of welded high-tensile steel, this was the innermost of two hulls and the strongest structure yet produced by marine engineering. Though the pressure hull was rated for a maximum depth of 656 feet, U-boats could and did venture deeper when required.

Catching a U-boat on the surface offered a chance to puncture its pressure hull with gunfire, rendering it unable to dive. Inflicting the same on a submerged boat could quickly drown its crew. The pressure hull's durability, however, meant that many boats were instead disabled by water ingress through the propeller shaft bushing, cooling water intake, and other weak points. Depth charges could also inflict enough damage to force a submerged U-boat to the surface. In these scenarios, crews seldom offered any resistance other than scuttling their boat to prevent its capture. Allied commanders usually plucked German crewmen from the sea as POWs if tactical circumstances permitted.

Around the pressure hull was a thinner outer hull which gave the U-boat its distinctive sharp bow, flared stern, and flat deck—a streamlined shape optimized for surfaced travel. The outer hull was not pressure-resistant and featured openings allowing water to flood the space between the two hulls. This prevented air pockets that could slow a crash dive or compromise the boat's buoyancy. The Type IX's outer hull fully encased the pressure hull in a double-hull design while the Type VII's outer hull only partly did so.[10]

Buoyancy was controlled by ballast tanks which featured flood doors on the bottom and vent valves on the top, creating an air lock. Opening the doors and vents allowed air to escape from the top while water flooded in from the bottom. The added water weight then caused the boat to descend. To ascend, high-pressure blow valves added compressed air to the tanks, forcing water out. The boat could also be steered dynamically to the surface using its hydroplanes to preserve available compressed air. After surfacing, engine exhaust blew the remaining water from the tanks.

The Type IX's main ballast tanks were all located between the two hulls, but one of the Type VII's was inside the pressure hull beneath the control room. Both models featured self-compensating fuel-ballast tanks that filled with seawater as fuel was depleted, eventually serving as normal ballast tanks once the fuel was consumed. The Type VII's smaller size meant that its fuel-ballast tanks bulged from the outer hull amidships. Apart from size, these "saddle tanks" were the primary externally visible difference between the Type VII and Type IX.

In addition to the primary ballast tanks, smaller auxiliary tanks were used to "trim" a submerged U-boat. One of the chief engineer's primary responsibilities, trimming refers to keeping the boat neutrally buoyant (neither rising nor falling) and on an even keel. This entailed adding or expelling water from the main and auxiliary tanks, shifting it between tanks using electric pumps or low-pressure air,

THE GRAY WOLVES • 47

and adjusting the angle of the hydroplanes. Sailors in the control room executed these tasks based on verbal commands from the chief engineer.

Attaining and maintaining the boat's trim was an art and a science which required tracking its changing weight as torpedoes were expended and fuel and provisions consumed. Trim was especially important at periscope depth to keep the periscope above the water without exposing the rest of the boat. Launching torpedoes from periscope depth upset the trim by making the boat thousands of pounds lighter. This required flooding the torpedo compensating tanks (two at the bow and one at the stern) immediately upon launch to prevent the boat from breaking the surface and revealing itself.

A U-boat on the surface moved like a conventional vessel: diesel engines or electric motors turned a pair of three-bladed propellers at the stern while two rudders steered the boat left and right. Diving and vertical movement in the water column was guided by two pairs of horizontal fins called hydroplanes located near the bow and stern. Forward propulsion caused water to flow over the planes, and tilting them steered the boat upward or downward.

A flat deck ran nearly the entire length of the U-boat. Made of hardwood planks for better foot traction, its edge was perforated with limber holes that allowed seawater to run off. Spare torpedoes were stored in the space between the upper deck and pressure hull. Crewmen entered and exited through the conning tower hatch on patrol; hatches in the deck itself were used only when in port or downloading spare torpedoes into the pressure hull. An 88mm naval cannon was mounted on the Type VII's foredeck while the Type IX carried a 105mm version plus a 37mm gun on the aft deck.

An oval-shaped conning tower amidships was topped with an open-air command station that served as the bridge. Ringed with a chest-high bulwark, or wall, the bridge was the commander's primary battle station when surfaced and featured a pedestal for mounting the optical device used for aiming torpedoes. A voice pipe led below deck, though orders were just as often shouted down the hatch, which was always kept open while surfaced. Attached to the bridge's aft end was a circular railing-bound platform called the *Wintergarten* which served as the antiaircraft gun station. Both the Type IX and Type VII boats carried a fully automatic 20mm gun here in 1942.

A jumping wire suspended between the bridge and the bow served as an antenna for sending high and medium frequency radio transmissions. The cable was anchored at the bow to a triangular metal frame with a sawtooth forward edge that served as a net cutter until its removal in the spring of 1941. Two more galvanized wires running from bridge to stern served as high and medium frequency receivers. A circular loop antenna on the bridge bulwark's starboard side enabled navigation by shore-based radio beacons and, on the bulwark's port side, a 4-foot rod antenna received very high frequency (VHF) broadcasts.[11]

A hatch on the bridge led down seven ladder rungs into the confines of the conning tower compartment. The attack periscope (one of two different periscopes) was operated from the aft portion of the tower compartment, and at its forward end was the helm for steering the boat while surfaced. An electromechanical targeting computer was mounted to the starboard bulkhead behind the ladder. This was the smallest of a U-boat's four pressure-resistant compartments. Eight more rungs down the aluminum ladder, which was slanted for sliding descents, led to one of the boat's three main compartments: the control room.

Measuring approximately 16 feet by 10 feet, the control room was packed with gauges, pipes, levers, and other hardware. The attack periscope column occupied part of the room's center. At either end of the room were water and pressure-resistant bulkheads featuring a hatch which led to either the U-boat's forward or aft compartment. Both hatchways were circular cut-outs not extending all the way to the deck ("knee-knockers," in American naval parlance). Above the forward and aft hatches was a red handwheel for opening main ballast tanks #5 and #1, respectively.

The "sky" periscope was operated from the control room's forward half. Also known as the observation periscope, its larger head was more easily sighted but also provided a view of the sky above. A few feet away, on the forward bulkhead to the right of the hatch, was the helm used for steering when submerged. Right of the helm, on the starboard bulkhead's forward end, were two stations where the hydroplane operators sat. Mounted on the bulkhead were gauges displaying the gyrocompass heading, plane angles, and other data.

Halfway down the control room's starboard side was an agglomeration of color-coded handwheels arranged in three columns, above which were more wheels and pipes. These were manifolds controlling the flow of compressed air and engine exhaust used to push water from the ballast tanks. Continuing aft along the starboard bulkhead, next was the main bilge pump used to remove water inside the pressure hull. In the aft starboard corner were the periscopes' hydraulic oil pumps.

At the base of the periscope column dominating the room's center was the "mother" gyrocompass linked to multiple repeater compass displays at the primary battle stations. On the overhead in the control room's aft portion were levers for venting main ballast tanks #2 and #4, plus handwheels for opening the air intake and diesel exhaust head valves. Other objects along the control room's port bulkhead included auxiliary pumps, a fathometer for depth soundings, and a chart table facing the tower ladder.

The four compartments (tower, control room, forward, and aft) could be isolated by sealing the hatches at either end of the control room. The three main compartments were subdivided into six rooms on a Type VII and seven on a Type IX. A U-boat's interior had no upper or lower decks and featured only a single passageway running from bow to stern with working areas on either side, like a train car. Rubber mats deadened the sound of feet against the deck. This was the entirety of the crew's living

Type IXC

Four Torpedo Tubes

Forward Torpedo Room

Pressure Hull

Outer Hull

Battery

Officers' Quarters

Galley

Petty Officers' Quarters

Captain's Quarters (port side),
Sound Room & Radio Room
(starboard side)

105mm Gun

20mm AA Gun

Periscopes

Conning Tower

Control Room

37mm
AA Gun

Deisel Engine Room

Electric Motor Room

Aft Torpedo Room

Two Torpedo Tubes

Type IXC
Length: 251.84 ft. (76.76 m)
Beam: 22.18 ft. (6.76 m)
Top speed: 18.3 knots (21 mph) surfaced,
7.3 knots (8.4 mph) submerged
Range at ten knots: 13,450 nautical miles (24,909 km)
Crew size: ~50

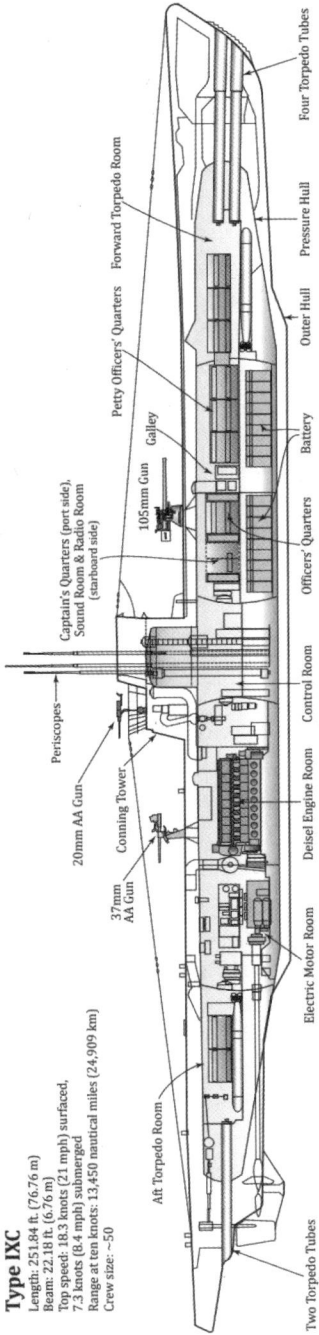

Four Torpedo Tubes

Tube Doors

Hydrophone Array

Hydroplane

Jumping Wire Antenna

Radio Direction Finder

Bridge

Conning Tower

88mm Gun

Sky Periscope

Attack Periscope

Wintergarten

20mm AA Gun

Fuel-Ballast Tanks

One Torpedo Tube

Rudders

Hydroplane

Type VIIC
Length: 220.14 ft. (67.1 m)
Beam: 20.34 ft. (6.2 m)
Top speed: 17.7 knots (20.37 mph) surfaced,
7.6 knots (8.75 mph) submerged
Range at ten knots: 8,500 nautical miles (15,742 km)
Crew size: ~45

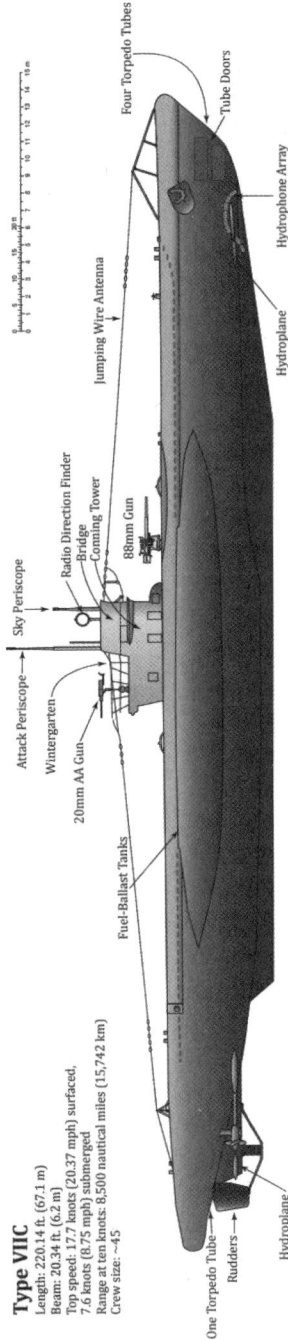

Type IXC internal layout and Type VIIC external view. (Custom art by Bob Pratt)

and fighting space: the bridge, the tower compartment, three main compartments, and one passageway.

Just past the control room's forward hatch, on the passageway's port side, was the commander's quarters. This comprised an alcove with a bunk, a small desk, several small lockers, the boat's safe, and a curtain which provided the only modicum of privacy aboard apart from the two toilets. Across the passageway from the commander's space was the radio room and, forward of that, the sound room where one of the radiomen manned the underwater listening system. Both rooms measured roughly 5 feet by 5 feet.

The passageway next led to the officers' mess, or "wardroom," and officers' sleeping quarters. It featured a wooden drop-leaf table for meals and a green leather cushioned bench that doubled as the chief engineer's bunk. There were two other bunks on the starboard bulkhead. The wardroom provided a pretense of normalcy with its oak paneling, lamp with a cream-colored lampshade hanging from the overhead, and white linen tablecloth.

The tower, control room, and officers' spaces were effectively identical between the Type VII and Type IX boats, but other aspects of their layout differed. On a Type IX, the next space forward of the wardroom was a tiny galley where food was prepared. Immediately forward of this was a longer room partitioned into quarters for the chief petty officers and junior petty officers. On a Type VII, the junior petty officers were berthed immediately aft of the control room, with the galley as the next space aft.

A U-boat had two washrooms, each containing only a toilet and sink, one of which was used to store provisions during the first half of a patrol. Both boats featured a washroom near the forward torpedo room door, though the location of the aft one differed between the Type VII and Type IX. The toilets could not be flushed when the boat was deeper than 80 feet, and a bucket scented with diesel fuel often sufficed for urination.

The forward torpedo room was the forward-most space on both the Type VII and Type IX. Hoists and chains hung from the overhead, and four large torpedo tubes protruded into the room's forward end. Known as the *Bugraum* (bow room) and nicknamed the "House of Lords," this dungeon-like environ doubled as the junior enlisted quarters. Here more than two dozen men shared 75 square feet with 23-foot torpedoes and much of the boat's provisions, although more space became available as both were used up. A total of a dozen folding bunks with thin mattresses were mounted to the bulkheads. Sailors also slept atop torpedoes, on deck plates, and in hammocks slung from overhead pipes.[12]

The control room's aft hatch on a Type VII led through a small utility room and into the junior petty officers' quarters, which had four bunks on each bulkhead. Next was an even smaller space with the galley on its starboard side. The galley featured a refrigerator, stove, kettle, two hotplates, and an oven. There was no junior-enlisted mess area, and a meal might be eaten sitting on a torpedo in the House of Lords. Opposite the Type VII's galley was another washroom, and the next space forward was the diesel engine room.

The Type IX's larger engines required shifting all berthing areas to the boat's forward half, and the control room's aft hatch therefore led directly to the diesel engine room. Here the passageway turned into an elevated walkway between the two engines. Even the smaller Type VII's six-cylinder diesels measured roughly 16 feet long by 9 feet tall. A U-boat's diesels were loud enough to completely defeat verbal communication, so flashing alert lamps indicated when the alarm or engine order telegraph was ringing.

Beyond the diesel engine room on both U-boats was the electric motor room housing the rectangular and quieter E-motors which powered the boat underwater. Also located here were two compressors that filled the high-pressure air flasks used to blow the ballast tanks and launch torpedoes. The diesel air compressor could only run while surfaced, making compressed air a finite resource if a U-boat was forced to submerge for an extended period. On a Type VII, the E-motor room's far end served as the aft torpedo room. The Type IX instead featured a separate aft torpedo room which also contained the second washroom and eight bunks for its slightly larger crew.[13]

The Allies recognized the U-boats' rugged and effective design after the Royal Navy captured a Type VIIC in 1941 and the US Navy captured a Type IXC/40 in 1944. Assessments considered them "well-built" and noted a strong pressure hull that enabled greater depths than Allied boats. The Type VIIC was quieter and more nimble than the US Navy's workhorse Gato-class submarine, and its large ballast tank vents, narrow superstructure and forward deck, and low forward hydroplanes led American officers to conclude the Type VII "is a quick diver." The same report stated that "the attack periscope was definitely the most impressive installation," being "beautifully engineered" and "the answer to an attack officer's prayer."

U-boats of World War II were neither fundamentally different from their predecessors nor demonstrably superior to Allied submarines. The U-boats' British equivalents had better submerged speed and range, and the American Gato-class boats were faster both atop and below the waves. The Allies found the U-boats cramped even by submarine standards and correctly deduced that this hindered reloading the tubes and downloading spare torpedoes into the pressure hull. The US Navy ultimately concluded that the U-boats were "conservatively designed" and that their engineering presented "little of interest."[14]

***

The U-boat itself was relatively uninteresting from a naval intelligence perspective because it was simple. Its workhorse variants were spartan and starkly functional machines that concentrated a significant amount of firepower within a rather small vessel. Dönitz did not exaggerate when he claimed that U-boats were "were very much less comfortable to live in than the submarines of other nations." American officers concurred when they concluded that the Type IX's berthing was "not up to minimum US naval standards." Crew comfort was absent from design priorities, Dönitz explained, "because they had been built on the principle that every ton of their displacement must be used solely ... for weapons, speed, radius of action."

An unpleasant life at sea reflected a U-boat's simplicity of purpose. Limited fresh water and a lack of bathing facilities meant that crewmen neither bathed nor shaved while on patrol. They became desensitized to a stench that combined unwashed bodies, cooking grease, human waste, and diesel. One officer wrote of being "the captives of our own smells." U-boat sailors' disheveled appearances often surprised Allied servicemen who captured them at sea. "They seemed an insignificant and unexciting lot," recalled British naval veteran Nicholas Monsarrat. "Was this really all that was meant by a U-boat's crew?"

Beards and shaggy hair were not the only distinguishing feature of a U-boat sailor on patrol. Generally free to wear whatever they considered practical, they sported an eclectic mix of attire. Captured British Army khaki battledress uniforms were popular, eventually being supplanted by German imitations made of gray-green denim. Engine room personnel commonly wore the naval-issue pale gray single-breasted leather tunic with matching trousers. Civilian-style shirts were common, along with parts of the Kriegsmarine-issued leather working uniform.

The only consistent attire was the commander's cap. A kommandant was iden-tifiable by his *Schirmmütze*, or peaked cap with a white crown. Officially intended for summer wear, Ubootwaffe tradition instead dictated that the commander wore the white crown whenever on patrol. Depending on an individual commander's choice of attire, this cap might be the only item distinguishing him from a common sailor. The white crown was typically worn without its wire stiffener, giving it a floppy appearance.

A Type IXC boat left port carrying 14 tons of foodstuffs. Limited space meant that hams and sausages hung from pipes, hammocks were filled with bread, crates of fresh vegetables were stacked in the officer's mess, and sacks of potatoes were wedged between torpedo tubes. This was the best quality food the Wehrmacht could provide, although fresh food spoiled quickly and everything became tainted by the boat's miasma. "The food was good," wrote one officer, "as long as you liked the taste of diesel."

The temperature on board varied depending on the surrounding water. It could be miserably chilly in colder seas, but warmer water like the Gulf Steam turned the pressure hull into a sweat lodge. Engine room temperatures could reach 122° Fahrenheit in southerly climates. Unlike American submarines, U-boats lacked air conditioning. Diving in warmer seas cooled the hull and caused condensation to fall like rain from the overhead.

"One's whole existence had to be adapted to the U-boat," wrote *U-333* commander Peter "Ali" Cremer. "Eating, sleeping, going on watch, all in the narrowest space, all in close physical contact, in the closest relationship with the steel hull." One *U-99* veteran fondly spoke of "a very familiar atmosphere. It's cozy, somehow." Outsiders rarely shared such sentiments. One war correspondent instead recounted "the heat, the stench of oil. Lead in my skull from the engine fumes ... I felt like Jonah inside some huge shellfish."[15]

***

The mythos surrounding the U-boats stemmed not from their engineering, but rather from the men who crewed them. The most important was the *Kommandant*, or commander, who held both the boat's success and the crew's lives in his grease-ingrained hands. "You are the brain of this steel beast," ace kommandant Günther Prien reminded prospective commanders. "One must think in iron and steel—or perish."

Admiral Dönitz recognized that his ambitious vision required cultivating a new generation of officers raised on his tactical and cultural paradigms and imbued with a bias for action. "Only those possessed of such a spirit could hope to succeed in the grim realities of U-boat warfare," Dönitz declared. "Professional skill alone would not suffice."

The most highly valued trait of a U-boat officer was tactical aggressiveness, and this was encouraged almost to the point of recklessness. Close-range attacks demanded aggressiveness, but so did lingering criticisms that the Kaiserliche Marine had been too risk-averse during World War I. "Attack and keep on attacking," one of Dönitz's fleet-wide orders demanded. "Do not let yourself be shaken off. If the boat is temporarily forced away or driven under ... try to get in touch again and once more ATTACK!"[16]

The Ubootwaffe's culture of tactical aggressiveness existed alongside a surprisingly progressive management style. Admiral Raeder summarized the Kriegsmarine's leadership philosophy as emphasizing "humane and intelligent treatment of all subordinates and a respect for the dignity of the individual." This was a consequence of the 1918 mutinies, which were attributed in part to an overly rigid and impersonal leadership culture in which officers lorded over enlisted men. Kriegsmarine officers were consequently taught to be dignified and demanding, yet approachable and personable.

The nature of serving on a U-boat, where a small crew lived and fought in the closest physical confines, engendered an even more egalitarian culture than that of the surface fleet. As the *U-564* commander explained, an environment where all ranks "lived so close together" and "shared the same fate" was necessarily also one where "everyone felt equally important." Some crews had a "coward on duty" tasked with critiquing the commander's decisions and voicing the crew's complaints. A commander could even be relieved if the crew objected to his leadership.[17]

The Ubootwaffe was, to a large extent, the organizational embodiment of Karl Dönitz himself. The public perceived him accordingly, and no officer on either side of the war would become more closely associated with the fighting force he led. Unsurprisingly, he attained archvillain status among the Western Allies; a 1943 *TIME* magazine cover depicted Dönitz's head as part of a U-boat conning tower at sea, his stern visage surrounded by periscopes shaped like fanged serpents. This portrayal was well-deserved. For the Western Allies, Dönitz was by far the most dangerous commander at Hitler's disposal.

Outsiders saw Karl Dönitz as steely and taciturn while acquaintances found him pleasant, yet quiet and unassuming. Germany's U-boat chief wore a third face, however, in the form of a charismatic persona that earned devotion from officers and enlisted men alike. "Not even legendary army commanders like Erwin Rommel or Heinz Guderian quite had Dönitz's touch," historian Peter Rust wrote. Dönitz addressed individual subordinates using the familiar *Du* rather than the formal *Sie*, and he referred to his men and their boats as his "Gray Wolves." They returned his paternal affinity with the monikers "*Vater Karl*" (Father Karl) and "*der Löwe*" (The Lion), and referred to themselves as "*Freikorps Dönitz*."

Father Karl provided his men the best available food, drink, accommodations, and recreation in port. At least one group of drunk U-boat officers sent him their bar tab—and he paid it. Dönitz personally greeted every boat returning from patrol and radioed married men on patrol about the births of children ("U-boat with a periscope" denoted a boy, "without a periscope" a girl). He also planned the unsuccessful escape of four officers from Bowmanville POW camp in Ontario, Canada.[18]

Dönitz cultivated the Ubootwaffe's image as an elite force, and he demanded it perform like one. When the *U-109* returned to port in May 1941, he confronted the kommandant before the crew had even been dismissed from formation. "Your patrol was crap, and you know it. Your seven thousand tons wasn't much," Dönitz admonished the *U-109*'s captain. Smiling wryly, he added, "But at least you brought the boat back. I suppose that's worth something."

The Ubootwaffe was an all-volunteer force when the war began. Medical requirements were strict, and the men earned nearly twice the pay of their surface fleet counterparts, yet a more effective recruiting enticement lay in the perceived prospect of swashbuckling adventure as part of an elite brotherhood. The public devoured this, too. When the crew of the vaunted *U-99* was captured in 1941, their British captors noted that they displayed "an exaggerated idea of their importance and dignity. These inflated opinions were no doubt due to the extraordinary degree of public adulation to which they had become accustomed."

The U-boat force also presented officers with opportunities for individual prestige. Although no official criteria denoted a U-boat "ace," sinking 100,000 tons of shipping earned the coveted Knight's Cross medal. An officer hungry for glory might suffer from "*Halsschmerzen*"—a sore throat—until a Knight's Cross was draped around his neck. The most successful commanders became celebrities, and photos of them grinning while wearing their uniform caps rakishly tilted further burnished their debonair images.

Günther Prien, Joachim Schepke, and Otto Kretschmer became the most venerated aces of the war's first eighteen months by collectively sinking 114 ships. Prien, a former merchant mariner, became the first propaganda icon in October 1939 after sinking the battleship HMS *Royal Oak* at Scapa Flow in Scotland. The *U-47*'s snorting bull emblem earned Prien the sobriquet "the Bull of Scapa Flow," Otto Kretschmer was dubbed "Silent Otto" and the "Tonnage King," and Joachim Schepke's chiseled good looks made him natural propaganda fodder. Kretschmer was the least flamboyant of the trio, although the British destroyer captain who defeated him considered Kretschmer "the most dangerous enemy of them all."

In addition to regime propaganda, the Ubootwaffe also had a more organic culture of its own. One facet was visible in emblems painted on conning towers, a practice Dönitz encouraged. Mickey Mouse adorned the *U-26*, a pair of demons made Erich Topp's *U-552* the "Red Devil boat," and the *U-201*'s snowman was a pun on the name of commander Adalbert Schnee (his surname meaning "snow"). Men commonly wore a miniature version of their boat's emblem pinned to their cap, and some conning towers also displayed the coat of arms of an adoptive city.

U-boat officers were drawn primarily from middle and upper middle-class Protestant families in northern Germany, and most were graduates of the naval academy located in the Flensburg district of Mürwik. Relatively few were commissioned from the enlisted ranks. The average age of a U-boat commander in 1942 was just shy of 27. Most held the rank of Kapitänleutnant, the third rung in the officer hierarchy, while others were one rank below (Oberleutnant) or above (Korvettenkapitän). Enlisted personnel tended to be working class and were more geographically diverse. The typical enlisted sailor in 1942 was in his early 20s and had a background in metalworking, machining, or electrical work.

Enlisted U-boat men displayed the same vices and irreverence as their Allied counterparts. Documents captured from the *U-570* included "parodies, skits, and poems, all of an unbelievably coarse and obscene nature," and Wehrmacht-issued brothel passes were found in enlisted POWs' pockets. One veteran told of how they "enjoyed an occasional fight" during booze-fueled rampages in French ports, particularly if another crew would "start bragging about how they had the best boat or the cleverest skipper." U-boat men operating from ports in the Far East also put their Axis partners to shame by carousing long after the Japanese drank themselves into unconsciousness.[19]

***

Dönitz was more openly supportive of National Socialism than many naval officers during Nazism's ascendancy and zenith. He enrolled his two sons, Klaus and

Peter, in the Hitler Youth before membership became mandatory. His ideological alignment seemingly remained within the upper threshold of his profession's mainstream, and he was not a party member. Though Dönitz believed in Hitler's vision, the U-boat chief's reputation in 1939 was that of a military officer rather than an ideologue—for now.

The Ubootwaffe's relationship with Nazism was complicated and evolved over the course of the war. It also became entangled with the postwar myth that Nazi Germany's military was a strictly professional institution untainted by ideology. Contrived by former German officers after the war, the pseudohistorical "clean Wehrmacht" narrative was tacitly endorsed by American, British, and German leaders to facilitate West German rearmament. The truth, however, is that the Wehrmacht was thoroughly infected with National Socialism. Germany's armed forces widely and systematically committed war crimes and assisted the Nazi Party's infamous *Schutzstaffel*, or SS, in perpetrating the Holocaust.

It is also true, however, that the Kriegsmarine was the *least* ideological of the Wehrmacht's three branches; Hitler once quipped that "I have a reactionary army, a National Socialist air force, and a Christian navy." The Kriegsmarine's relative political independence owed partly to Grand Admiral Erich Raeder, an old-fashioned conservative who tolerated Nazism for the purpose of restoring German pride and naval strength. The nature of the U-boat war also seldom involved occupying civilian areas or fighting "sub-human" Slavic enemies, thereby separating the Kriegsmarine from the opportunities for barbarism found by the Heer on the Eastern Front.

One key to understanding the U-boat officers lies in the Prussian military culture so deeply entrenched in the Wehrmacht. This inheritance from the "Iron Kingdom" imbued officers with the values of order, discipline, and duty. However, historian Ian Kershaw noted that "Prussian values were here a double-edged sword" because they pitted ethics and common sense against obedience to the state. "Whichever triumphed within an individual ... was a matter for conscience and judgement," Kershaw wrote. "It could, and did, go either way."

"Very few officers in the Ubootwaffe were 'steely Nazi fanatics,'" concluded historian Jordan Vause, and Peter Padfield described them as "more monarchical than fascist." Some U-boat officers were committed Nazis while a few were (quietly) avowed anti-Nazis, but most dwelled somewhere in between. The typical officer was a staunchly patriotic conservative imbued with what Admiral Raeder termed "disinterested service to the state," and they tended toward indifference regarding matters not directly affecting the armed forces. Enlisted men were even more ideologically tepid, Vause describing them as "probably as tolerant, and as unenthusiastic, about National Socialism as any man on the street."[20]

The war's three most famous U-boat aces—Joachim Schepke, Günther Prien, and Otto Kretschmer—aptly illustrated the Ubootwaffe's ideological spectrum. Schepke appears to have been a true believer, Jordan Vause characterizing him as "a willing idol and a good National Socialist." Schepke's memoirs also express more fanaticism than many comparable propaganda works. Prien's ideological leanings are less clear. The British translator of his memoirs described him as "unquestionably" sharing Hitler's worldview, though another historian concluded that Prien was "ruthlessly patriotic, but not a slavering Nazi."

Otto Kretschmer appears to have been the least ideological of the three; the destroyer captain who captured him in 1941 noted that Kretschmer "preferred to restrict himself to his duties and lament the mess politicians had made of things." A few U-boat officers were also remarkably forthright in their opposition to National Socialism. Reinhard "Teddy" Suhren's *U-564* was approaching the pier after a war patrol when Suhren asked through his megaphone: "Are the Nazis still at the helm?" When those on the pier replied affirmatively, Suhren elicited laughter by promptly reversing his engines and backing away.

Such open dissent was nonetheless rare, and Nazis in the Ubootwaffe were not hard to find. Moreover, their numbers and influence would grow as the war progressed. When the British offered whiskey to Otto Kretschmer's crewmen shortly after their capture, the second watch officer "haughtily refused his drink, pompously ordered the remainder not to drink with us, and ended with a Nazi salute and a '*Heil Hitler!*'"[21]

***

Most crews had four commissioned officers: the commander, chief engineer, first watch officer, and second watch officer. A U-boat's enlisted complement in 1942 averaged forty-one men on a Type VII and forty-eight on a Type IX. These were divided into *Seemänner* (seamen) and *Techniker* (technicians). Specialists such as photographers or war correspondents were sometimes taken on patrol. One correspondent was Lothar-Günther Buchheim, who used his experiences to write the novel-turned-film *Das Boot*. Doctors also accompanied some Type IXs to sea.

The techniker fell under the *Leitender Ingenieur*, or chief engineering officer. Addressed as "L.I." by the other officers, the chief engineer was responsible for propulsion, diving, trimming, and all other technical matters. He required encyclopedic knowledge of the boat's components and capabilities, plus what Buchheim described as "a special sense to anticipate the boat's every tendency to sink or rise." One chief engineer explained that his relationship with the captain "must be that of a good marriage." Though a commissioned officer, engineering officers followed a separate career track without the prospect of sea command.

The first watch officer was second-in-command and equivalent to an executive officer in the US Navy. Other officers addressed him using the phonetic abbreviation "*Eins-Vee-Oh*." Although the commander personally conducted submerged attacks using the periscope, the first watch officer led surface attacks from the bridge while the commander supervised. Below the first watch officer was the second watch officer, who was responsible for gunnery and radio communication. Some patrols also included an officer trainee (a "midshipman" in Anglophone navies).[22]

Below the commissioned officers were four senior enlisted sailors, or noncommissioned officers, equivalent to chief petty officers in the US Navy. They are sometimes referred to as warrant officers, although the Kriegsmarine phased out those ranks in 1936. The ranking enlisted man and often the oldest crewman was the *Obersteuermann*, or chief helmsman. "Obersteuermann" was both his billet and (usually) his actual rank. He delegated most steering duties and only manned the helm during particularly dangerous situations. The obersteuermann was also the navigator, utilizing a sextant and other instruments to determine the boat's position by measuring the angle between the horizon and the sun and planets.

The chief helmsman's immediate subordinate was the *Bootsmann*, or boatswain. Though boatswain was his billet, he often held the rank of *Oberbootsmann*. Addressed as "*Nummer Eins*" (Number One), the bootsmann maintained discipline within the seamen's department and typically operated the electromechanical targeting calculator during surface attacks. Two petty officers assisted him.

The other two senior noncommissioned officers belonged to the technical department. The *Elektro-Obermaschinist* and his team operated the E-motors and batteries while the *Diesel-Obermaschinist* led "*die schwarze Zunft*," or the Black Guild, in the diesel engine room. The latter duty was particularly unpleasant. Engine room sailors incurred hearing loss from prolonged exposure to the hammering pistons, reduced alertness from inhaling carbon dioxide, and heat-related rashes and boils.

Four radiomen called *Funker* handled communications: two *Funkmaat*, or radio petty officers, and two *Funkgast*, or basic radio operators. In addition to radio traffic and cryptography, they monitored the hydrophone, served as medics, and operated radar detectors during the war's latter half. They also acted as the boat's DJs by playing music records over the intercom while on patrol. The senior funker was responsible for typing up the commander's handwritten log (*Kriegstagebuch*, or KTB) for assessment and filing by BdU. Type IX crews in 1944–45 also included an *Oberfunkmeister*, or senior radio petty officer.

The *Mechanikermaat*, or torpedoman petty officer, was responsible for stowing, loading, and maintaining the boat's primary weapons. Two junior torpedomen called *Mechaniker* assisted him. The mechanikermaat was dubbed the "*Bugraumpräsident*," or bow room president, for being the only petty officer berthed with the junior enlisted in the forward torpedo room. Like other roles, the torpedomen's exact ranks varied slightly. Each crew also had a *Smutje*, or cook. Round-the-clock food preparation meant he was the only crewman not required to stand watch. The remainder of the crewmen were *Matrosen*, or basic sailors.

The metonym "Gray Wolves" came to denote both these men and the U-boats they crewed. Günther Prien wrote in 1940 that "man and machine are merged in the German U-boat" and this conceptual synthesis reflected the self-image of many sailors. "I felt

U-202 crewmen at Brest, France in 1941. (Deutsches U-Boot-Museum)

myself completely under the spell of the U-boat," veteran Herbert Werner recalled. "Its power had become an important component of my life, if not my very self."

More than forty thousand Germans served in the Ubootwaffe during World War II. Characterized by historian Lisle Rose as "complex and contradictory young men caught up in an age of crisis," they differed little from their British and American adversaries. For this reason, however, the Gray Wolves embodied something deadlier than the forest's baying pack canids or the ocean's leaden-eyed shark, and not only because they combined predatorial cunning with deadly weaponry. Whereas the shark or wolf is satiated by a single feast, men driven by a sense of duty will kill until rendered unable to persist.[23]

"Man," wrote philosopher Friedrich Nietzsche, "is the cruelest animal."

CHAPTER FOUR

A Tide of Steel

"Should enemy submarines operate off this coast, this command has no forces available to take adequate action against them, either offensive or defensive."
—Rear Admiral Adolphus Andrews, US Navy (22 December 1941)

"They do not understand the sea," Admiral Alfred von Tirpitz once lamented about the statesmen and army generals who drove Imperial Germany's policymaking. Little had changed between Tirpitz's era and the National Socialists' rise in the 1930s. Germany has historically been a land power, and Adolf Hitler's strategic outlook was decidedly continental. As Admiral Karl Dönitz wrote decades later, "To him, war at sea was something strange and sinister."

Germany was militarily and economically weaker (in relative terms) in 1939 than in 1914, and Hitler's failure to appreciate the maritime facets of national power contributed to his decision to plunge an unprepared Germany into another global conflict. Rearmament had prioritized surface ships over U-boats, and there were still too few of both. Despite assuring Grand Admiral Erich Raeder that Germany would not fight Britain for at least five more years, Hitler saw fate beckoning, and he would abide no delay.[1]

The dictator sought a rematch against France and Britain, but his most prized objective lay eastward. Hitler believed that Germany's destiny lay in the vast and fertile lands of Poland and the Soviet Union. After exterminating most of its Slavic and Jewish inhabitants and enslaving the remainder, the Nazis intended to repopulate this territory with German settlers to farm the land and extract its oil and other resources. An economically self-sufficient Reich impervious to blockade would then turn outward to the wider world. As Hitler declared in a 1933 speech, "No people have more right to the idea of world mastery than the German people."

After a secret agreement to divide Poland with Joseph Stalin's Union of Soviet Socialist Republics (USSR, or Soviet Union), Hitler began carving his dominion when the Wehrmacht stormed across the Polish border on 1 September 1939. World War II commenced in earnest two days later when France and Britain, which had pledged to defend Poland, declared war on Germany. War's outbreak heralded the onset of a six-year naval campaign of "unremitting ferocity," wrote Royal Navy veteran Nicholas Monsarrat, which would "live in men's minds for what it did to themselves and to their friends." The Battle of the Atlantic had begun.[2]

As in 1914, the United States remained neutral. This stemmed in part from memories of the 53,402 American servicemen killed in action during the Great War, but some domestic opponents to US involvement had more insidious motivations. "Friends of New Germany" was an American pro-Nazi organization founded in 1933 with the blessing of Hitler's regime, and its members included a German-born Lutheran pastor in New Jersey. He prominently displayed a swastika flag in his Newark church, which also hosted appearances by the *Ordnungs-Dienst* (Order Service), a uniformed paramilitary outfit modeled on the infamous Nazi brownshirts.

The organization rebranded itself as the "German-American Bund" in 1935, and membership eventually exceeded twenty thousand. The Bund operated three camp facilities and seven local chapters in New Jersey, where its activities led to brawls with groups like the Jewish-American War Veterans and American Legion. In 1941, nine senior Bund leaders were arrested at Sussex County's "Camp Nordland" for violating a law against promoting "race hatred" which the state government had passed specifically to target the Bund.[3]

New Jersey nonetheless seemed like a world away from Europe when war broke out in September 1939. Admiral Raeder had trusted Hitler's assurances that Britain would not take up arms on Poland's behalf, and he now lamented that the sailors of his woefully understrength fleet could only "show they know how to die gallantly." Karl Dönitz—who would be promoted to *Konteradmiral*, the lowest flag officer rank, less than a month later—similarly harbored no illusions about the difficulties ahead, yet the outbreak of war also presented Raeder's ambitious subordinate with a long-awaited opportunity.

"The U-boat is the only means of defeating Britain," Dönitz declared in a memo submitted to Raeder on the day Germany invaded Poland. He still lacked the means to this end, however. Dönitz was convinced that bleeding Britain to death would require three hundred oceangoing U-boats, but he possessed just fifty-six boats of all types in September 1939. Only forty-six were combat-ready, and twenty-four of these were the small Type II U-boats. That left just twenty-two medium Type VII and large Type IX boats.

Geography, too, continued to vex German naval ambitions. Like its prior incarnation as the Kaiserliche Marine, the Kriegsmarine had direct access only to the North Sea and Baltic Sea. The former was dominated by Britain while the latter was effectively a large lake that required passing through Danish waters to exit (and this only led to the North Sea). This situation would radically change in the summer of 1940, however, following a series of stunning victories on the European continent.

The need for secure access to Swedish iron ore contributed to Germany's invasion of Denmark and Norway in April 1940, but so too did Raeder's desire to base warships along Norway's long and craggy coastline. The battle for Norway was still raging when the pugnacious Winston Churchill became Britain's prime minister on 10 May—the same day that Hitler struck west. German forces sliced through

Holland, Belgium, and France, trapping Britain's expeditionary force against the English Channel at Dunkirk. Churchill's commanders evacuated their surviving troops, but France surrendered and Italy joined the war on Germany's side.

By June 1940, these victories had netted Germany an even greater prize than Norway's fjords: France's Atlantic ports. These were located along the Bay of Biscay, or large Atlantic inlet encompassing most of the western coastline of France and Spain. This "improvement in our strategically unfavorable geographical position," as Dönitz phrased it, enabled faster refueling and repair and eliminated the need to sneak around British home waters. Lorient, Brest, Saint-Nazaire, La Pallice, and Bordeaux quickly became major U-boat bases. Forced labor was used to construct massive concrete bunkers that served as bomb-proof U-boat garages, and Dönitz moved his headquarters to a château overlooking Lorient's harbor entrance.[4]

***

The Ubootwaffe largely adhered to prize rules during the war's first months. This was intended to preserve Hitler's options, as the 1936 London Naval Treaty banned unrestricted submarine warfare and he still hoped to force Britain to peace terms. Merchant ships could only be attacked without warning if they were confirmed to be armed, carrying troops, or guarded by warships. BdU announced that "so long as war against merchant shipping is governed by Prize Regulations, attacks are to be aimed at ships which … may be sunk without warning."

That meant naval vessels, and U-boats sank two prominent warships during the war's first weeks. In September 1939, the *U-29* sank the aircraft carrier HMS *Courageous* off Ireland. A month later, Günther Prien's *U-47* infiltrated the Royal Navy base at Scapa Flow and sank the battleship HMS *Royal Oak* before escaping the harbor undetected. The Scapa Flow raid was a major propaganda coup that made Prien an overnight celebrity in Germany. Yet the Ubootwaffe also lost the *U-27* and *U-39* during the war's first month. BdU did not know that both had been sunk because their torpedoes malfunctioned (exploding before hitting their targets), thereby altering British destroyers to their presence.

Nevertheless, Dönitz knew that picking off His Majesty's warships would never achieve his vision of strangling Britain into submission. When Hitler visited BdU headquarters on 28 September 1939, the admiral pleaded his case directly: "I have arrived at the conviction that in [the U-boats] we possess a means of striking England decisively at her weakest point." The Führer promised nothing, but the U-boat chief and his men reportedly impressed him.

Although Dönitz did not get his unrestricted campaign right away, Berlin incrementally loosened the rules of engagement over the following months. Finally, prize rules were discarded entirely in August 1940. Standing War Order 101 specified that all ships sailing under neutral flags were off-limits (they would remain so throughout the war), but any Allied merchant ship was now fair game.[5]

***

The Allied merchant fleets comprised thousands of tankers, freighters, colliers (a freighter that carried coal), ocean liners and smaller passenger ships, whale factory ships (repurposed as tankers), refrigerated vessels, tugboats, and more. These ships represented an array of business interests, and each country organized its merchant fleet differently. All were crewed by civilians referred to as "merchant seamen" or "mariners" to distinguish them from naval sailors. Their individual nationalities varied, regardless of which flag they sailed under, and roughly one in four British mariners were ethnically Chinese or Indian. Some women also worked aboard passenger ships, although freighter and tanker crewmen were almost exclusively male.

A majority of Allied mariners in 1939 sailed for Great Britain's Merchant Navy. This was the world's largest merchant fleet by tonnage, representing 17.9 million gross registered tons. The United States and Japan ranked second and third, respectively. Total Allied tonnage would be augmented the following year when Norway, possessing the fourth-largest merchant fleet, was pulled into the war. Canada and the Netherlands also contributed vessels, though an American law called the Neutrality Act prevented US ships from delivering cargo to belligerent nations.

King George V spoke glowingly of "my" Merchant Navy after the Great War, yet the seagoing equivalent of long-haul truckers made for unlikely heroes. A November 1939 *Daily Mail* article depicted the typical British mariner as "usually dressed rather like a tramp. His sweater is worn, his trousers frayed ... a cap is perched askew on his tanned face. He wears no gold braid or gold buttons: neither does he jump to the salute briskly." They also lacked the sentimental appeal of the armed forces. "Nobody goes out of his way to call him a hero or pin medals on his breast."[6]

The British applied the lessons of 1917 by implementing a convoy system soon after the war began. They also began conducting aggressive antisubmarine patrols, though this proved a poor use of limited resources because it tied down large numbers of ships and aircraft while destroying few U-boats. There were simply too many miles of ocean, especially considering that airborne radar was not yet available. Although a bitter pill to many officers spoiling for a fight, the Royal Navy acknowledged by the spring of 1940 that the greatest dividends would be earned guarding convoys rather than scouring swaths of sea in the hope of crossing paths with the enemy.

Convoys ran between different British ports and delivered cargo and troops to Gibraltar, Egypt, and West Africa, but the most crucial and most endangered convoys reached Britain from the Western Hemisphere via Canada. Departing every eight days from the Nova Scotia ports of Halifax and Sydney, up to sixty ships sailed in rectangular formations 2 miles long and 6 miles wide to present the shortest possible target from abeam. Merchantmen carrying flammable or explosive cargoes sailed at the formation's center, while those carrying the least volatile material occupied the "coffin corners."

Convoys required escort forces—destroyers, other medium-sized oceangoing combat vessels, and aircraft—all of which were in short supply. The fall of France in June 1940 left the Royal Navy overextended even as the nation braced itself for *Unternehmen Seelöwe* (Operation Sea Lion), the impending German invasion of the British Isles. The Royal Navy resorted to stopgap measures such as repurposing fishing trawlers as antisubmarine vessels and ocean liners as auxiliary cruisers.

Even so, only enough forces existed in 1940 to protect convoys within a few hundred miles of departure and arrival. Merchant ships therefore sailed largely undefended for most of the 2,400-mile journey across stormy Atlantic wastes which average more than 2 miles deep. Convoys eastbound from Canada could reach a British port in sixteen days, but an alternate destination was much nearer—a sinking ship can reach a velocity of 50 feet per second on its way to the bottom, impacting the seafloor in less than three minutes.

The Gray Wolves sent 345 merchant vessels on that final journey between June and December 1940, for a total Allied loss of 1.86 million gross registered tons. German sailors termed this "*die Glückliche Zeit*," or the Happy Time. Dönitz could still only maintain an average of thirteen U-boats on patrol, however, and the Happy Time saw eight of them sunk at a time when German construction was barely keeping pace with losses. The Allies nonetheless got the worst of it. They were losing ships at more than three times the rate of construction, and those still afloat were hunted by more than just aircraft and U-boats.[7]

The *Bismarck*, the largest battleship ever commissioned at that time, left port on its maiden voyage in May 1941 to conduct commerce raiding. Escorted by the heavy cruiser *Prinz Eugen*, the *Bismarck* was attempting a breakout into the Atlantic when the battlecruiser HMS *Hood* and battleship HMS *Prince of Wales* intercepted it south of Iceland. The ensuing heavyweight fight saw the *Bismarck* put a single 1,764-pound shell into the "Mighty Hood," triggering an explosion that obliterated the battlecruiser and killed all but 3 of her 1,418 crewmen. The vengeful British pursued the *Bismarck* over the next three days, twice almost mistakenly attacking USCGC *Modoc* while the US Coast Guard cutter was searching for survivors from convoy HX 126.

A torpedo bomber launched from a British aircraft carrier eventually damaged the *Bismarck*'s rudder, leaving the giant only able to steer in circles. Allied warships converged for the kill as the German commander radioed headquarters: "SHIP UNMANEUVERABLE. WE WILL FIGHT TO THE LAST SHELL. LONG LIVE THE FÜHRER." The Royal Navy's heavy guns then pummeled the *Bismarck* into a smoking hulk. Rescue of the enemy personnel was hastily terminated due to the threat of nearby U-boats, and only 116 of more than 2,200 German sailors survived the battle.[8]

The influence of Grand Admiral Erich Raeder entered a long decline following the last stand of the *Bismarck*, but the battleship's destruction was a minor loss compared to the Luftwaffe's defeat in the Battle of Britain during the summer and autumn of 1940. The Royal Air Force's triumph in home skies constituted Germany's first strategic setback and forced Hitler to indefinitely postpone Operation Sea Lion (a plan he had not been enthusiastic about, anyway). Now, as in 1917, the U-boat constituted Germany's final bid for success against the island nation.

This message did not sufficiently resonate in Berlin because Dönitz remained outside Hitler's inner circle of military officers. The Führer instead managed naval affairs through Admiral Raeder, who did not share his subordinate's single-minded fixation on U-boats. Raeder agreed that the Kriegsmarine's relative weakness necessitated targeting enemy merchant tonnage rather than seeking to engage the Royal Navy directly, though he envisioned surface ships playing a significant role as commerce raiders. Hitler, in any event, had already turned his attention east.[9]

Less than four weeks after the *Bismarck*'s demise, in June 1941, events pushed Winston Churchill and Joseph Stalin into an unexpected partnership when Hitler invaded the Soviet Union. The largest military offensive in history saw three million Wehrmacht troops and thousands of tanks and aircraft inflict staggering human and material losses against a reeling Red Army. Hitler considered Soviet annihilation a fait accompli, boasting that "the Volga [River] will be our Mississippi." In October, however, German forces advancing on Moscow received an unsettling taste of things to come when they found themselves under attack by American-built P-40 Warhawk fighters.

The first British merchant convoys reached the Soviet port of Arkhangelsk in August 1941, and they would soon utilize Murmansk as well. In October, Nazi foreign minister Joachim von Ribbentrop summoned Japanese ambassador Hiroshi Ōshima regarding reports of American tankers docking at the Soviet port of Vladivostok. Berlin did not yet fully appreciate this development's significance, but Ribbentrop had every reason for concern: the Americans had shipped the Soviets 400,000 barrels of high-octane aviation gasoline in August 1941 alone, and more was on its way. The last obstacle to Hitler's domination of continental Europe was being sustained by the same merchant tonnage that was supplying Britain.[10]

***

For both the Allies and Germans, "tonnage" was the Atlantic campaign's key metric. A warship's size is measured in tons of seawater displaced, but merchant ships in this era were quantified by "gross registered tons" in which 1 ton equaled 100 cubic feet of enclosed space. This meant cargo space plus passageways, crew quarters, and engineering areas ("tonnage" was therefore a misnomer since it referred to volume rather than weight). A ship's tonnage determined how much revenue it produced and what taxes and fees it incurred, but military and political leaders were instead concerned with the strategic implications of aggregate tonnage.

A nation's total merchant tonnage reflected its capacity to feed and arm itself, supply its allies, and transport armies by sea. The Germans learned this firsthand during World War I, during which their war effort and population suffered in large part because Germany's merchant fleet was effectively swept from the seas. Britain was even more dependent on merchant shipping than Germany, and this reliance had only grown during the interwar years. The Germans had calculated during World War I that supplying a single Allied soldier in the trenches required 5 gross registered tons of shipping per year, but this estimate had increased to between 7 and 15 tons by 1939.

Tonnage obsessed Admiral Dönitz, whose overarching strategy was to destroy ships faster than the Allies could build them. The amount of tonnage a U-boat commander sunk "was the only yardstick according to which he awarded praise and decorations," wrote *U-564* commander Teddy Suhren. Dönitz based his attrition strategy on a concept called "integral tonnage" that considered all merchant ships equally valuable targets, regardless of cargo, route, or nationality. "[Allied] shipping forms a single totality," he wrote in April 1942. "In this regard, it is immaterial where a ship is sunk. Once it has been destroyed, it has to be replaced by a new ship, and that's that."[11]

The Kriegsmarine calculated that shipyards in Britain and the nominally neutral United States could together build approximately 200,000 tons per month. Accordingly, the Germans concluded by 1940 that sinking 700,000 tons (roughly 140 freighters or 90 tankers) each month would seal Britain's defeat. This estimate may have been too conservative, as the British determined that 600,000 tons lost per month would effectively neutralize their capacity to fight on.

Yet the Gray Wolves were averaging only 171,294 tons per month as the war entered 1941. U-boats in the South Atlantic intercepted commodities from South America such as beef and copper while others patrolled the West African coast and Mediterranean, yet Dönitz's fleet still remained too small for his ambitious goals. Despite his agitation for more U-boats, their construction was hampered by a shortage of shipyard workers due to conscription while vehicle and aircraft production continued to receive priority for raw materials.

By June 1941, the Allies possessed enough escort vessels to guard merchant convoys for the entire transatlantic voyage. There were also more aircraft flying antisubmarine patrols. BdU responded by focusing its forces in the "air gap" southeast of Greenland. Known by the Germans as the "Black Pit," the air gap placed merchant ships in maximum danger because it was beyond the range of land-based air cover. Consequently, during the first half of 1941, this desolate stretch of ocean witnessed a dramatic shift in the nature of the Atlantic war.[12]

The Ubootwaffe conducted a few wolfpack attacks in 1940, but a steadily expanding U-boat fleet with ever more experienced officers meant that Britain felt their bite in earnest by March 1941. Wolfpacks bearing such names as "*Reisswolf*" (Shredder), "*Schlagetod*" (Death Blow), and "*Mordbrenner*" (Arsonist) sparked eleven major high seas battles that year. Convoys OG 71 and SC 26 each lost ten of twenty-two merchant ships, and the largest melee saw ten U-boats torpedo nearly one-third of SC 42's sixty-four merchantmen. The shepherds were also in danger—German torpedoes sank eleven convoy escorts in 1941.

Herbert Werner was a midshipman aboard the *U-557* during an attack against convoy OS 4 in August 1941. "Five torpedoes sliced toward the swaying phantoms," he wrote. "Red and yellow flames and a lava of molten steel were hurled into the air. We heard the hollow boom of collapsing bulkheads and the piercing shriek of falling masts. Hell reached a climax. Our faces glowed in the glare of the wild fire." Werner watched one vessel roll over as she "lifted her stern in her death agony" while another "collapsed like a pair of scissors ... Huge chunks of steel and debris splashed into the water around us." Within minutes, "a few burning planks were all that remained of three of Britain's ships."

For men left adrift after a sinking, the water's deadly cold made survival a matter of minutes. Their only hope was a designated rescue ship because the escorts were busy fending off an enemy attacking on multiple vectors. This presented an agonizing dilemma, one veteran stating that "in the absence of a rescue ship ... the escort group commander had an almost impossible decision to make."

Churchill's government had every reason for alarm in mid-1941. May saw 333,912 gross registered tons of merchant shipping sunk, then 301,620 more went down in June. By July 1941, U-boats had sunk 907 merchant ships (totaling 4.2 million tons) while additional vessels fell victim to Luftwaffe aircraft and Admiral Raeder's warships. The death toll for merchant mariners would exceed nine thousand by December 1941. This was not sufficient to cripple Britain outright, but annual imports fell from 50 million tons in 1939 to 42 million in 1940. Imports further decreased to just 31 million tons in 1941. This squeezed the nation's food supply, and even tea was rationed.[13]

Surface attacks partly negated Allied sonar, just as Dönitz had intended, but sonar had other limitations too. Water flow noise drowned out return echoes at speeds above 8 knots, exploding depth charges temporarily deafened it, and its narrow and conical beam limited the search area while creating a blind spot immediately forward of the searcher's bow. Sonar also could not easily differentiate U-boats from schools of fish, tide rips, and whales. German evasion tactics included diving deep beneath thermoclines, or places where the water column stratifies into layers which could trap or deflect sound waves.

Desperate for a tactical edge against the U-boats in 1940–41, the Allies complemented sonar with other tools. One low-tech solution was a parachute flare, or "star shell," which was launched into the night sky to strip the cover of darkness during a wolfpack assault. The burning flares cast battle scenes in an eerie glow as they drifted downward, though this proved a double-edged sword since they also illuminated the escorts and merchantmen.

What was needed most was radar (from "Radio Detection and Ranging"), the above-water equivalent of sonar. Instead of sound energy, radar emits pulses of radio waves through the air which bounce back upon hitting a solid object. A British breakthrough in 1940 produced centimetric radar which was first installed on warships and aircraft in March 1941. Though primitive and not always reliable, radar allowed convoy escorts to "see" German conning towers as the U-boats closed in at night.

The British also found a means of exploiting the wolfpacks' most glaring vulnerability. A radio signal's source can be triangulated, even if the message itself is indecipherable, and some in the Kriegsmarine questioned the wisdom of wolfpack tactics since they relied on radio communication. Dönitz accepted this risk based on his belief that transmitting in short bursts would sufficiently frustrate attempts to pinpoint a broadcast's origin. He knew shore-based listening stations were too distant to do so accurately, and he was convinced that this hardware was too large and heavy to be mounted on destroyers.

Two of these assumptions were proved wrong in the spring of 1941 when the first shipboard high-frequency direction finding (HF/DF, or "Huff-Duff") sets entered service. If one HF/DF-equipped destroyer intercepted a U-boat homing beacon or "short signal" message, then the direction of its source could be determined. Two or more interceptions, however, could provide a cross-bearing fix on its origin to within a quarter of a mile. The effectiveness of HF/DF was less than ideal, and there were relatively few sets available in 1941, but it proved a valuable supplement to sonar and radar.

Armed with these tools, the Royal Navy demonstrated in March 1941 that the Gray Wolves were made of the same flesh and steel as their prey. First, Günther Prien's *U-47* was depth-charged and sunk with all hands; British propaganda broadcasts subsequently taunted "Where's Prien?". Ten days later, Joachim Schepke's overconfidence ended his career when a radar-equipped destroyer ran down the *U-100* on the surface and rammed it. Schepke died gruesomely when the destroyer's bow crushed him against the periscope, and only a handful of his crewmen survived. Later that night, depth charges forced Otto Kretschmer's *U-99* to the surface where "Silent Otto" and most of his crew were captured.

May 1941 brought an even greater victory when the destroyer HMS *Bulldog* captured the *U-110* at sea. The Type IXB sank while under tow the next day, but only after the British obtained the most valuable intelligence it could provide. This windfall was not the *U-110* itself (a Type VIIC would also be captured in August), but rather what it carried aboard.[14]

German forces relied on a cipher machine called "Enigma," which the Kriegsmarine used to encrypt its radio transmissions with a naval code they named HYDRA. The Enigma machine itself resembled a typewriter with twenty-six keys mounted in a wooden box. Inside the machine were three rotors with twenty-six brass contacts, each wired to a different key. Pressing the key for a given letter passed a current through the rotors, which randomly assigned a different letter. Each keystroke also advanced one rotor by one contact, continuously altering the enciphering path as a message was typed.

The Enigma code was astoundingly difficult to break. Each individual letter represented one of 3×10^{114} possible permutations, more than the number of atoms in the observable universe. The code's multiple layers of complexity included swapping out the rotors and changing their sequence daily in accordance with instructions distributed by Kriegsmarine headquarters. Breaking the code required not only capturing or replicating an Enigma machine, but also knowing which settings were in use on a given day.

Yet Enigma was not unbreakable. Aided by Polish and French intelligence, British cryptographers at Bletchley Park in Buckinghamshire, England had broken the cipher by early 1941. It still required at least a week to decode a message, however, by which time it was of little military value. But the *U-110*'s capture provided both the machine and its rotors as well as the critical missing puzzle piece: documents detailing HYDRA's specific machine configurations. The ability to read German message traffic in almost real time now enabled the Royal Navy to route convoys away from wolfpacks.

Winston Churchill wrote that the Battle of the Atlantic was "a war of groping and drowning, of ambush and strategy, of science and seamanship," and it was even more challenging without the Americans in the fight. The beleaguered British-led alliance nonetheless leveraged sonar, radar, HF/DF, codebreaking, and hard-earned experience with increasing effectiveness as the year wore on. By the autumn of 1941, according to historian Lisle Rose, the Royal Navy had fought the U-boats to a "rough, brutal draw."

Other events also relieved pressure on the convoy routes. The *Afrika Korps* under General Erwin Rommel, dispatched to North Africa to bail out the faltering Italian army in early 1941, now found itself precariously squeezed by British Commonwealth forces. Raeder obliged Hitler's directive to relieve pressure on Rommel by deploying more U-boats in the Mediterranean and along the Gibraltar approaches even while his staff continued assigning boats to auxiliary duties like weather reporting. This came at the expense of Admiral Dönitz's tonnage war, and the U-boats had effectively abandoned the north-central Atlantic by December 1941.

The U-boat chief's frustration simmered. He believed that his Gray Wolves existed solely to destroy the merchant tonnage feeding Allied war industries, not as auxiliaries to ground campaigns. Waters off Gibraltar and in the Mediterranean were also within range of land-based aircraft and lacked sufficient space for U-boats to maneuver, ambush, and disperse. What Dönitz sought was a new frontier that was large, heavily trafficked, and poorly defended. He would not have to wait long.[15]

***

Isolationist sentiment in the United States held considerable sway in 1939–41. Polls indicated that four out of five Americans opposed entering the war, and songs like "The Yanks Are Not Coming" reflected distaste for another bloody overseas venture. Nevertheless, President Franklin Delano Roosevelt ("FDR") was sympathetic to the Allied cause and recognized the long-term threat posed by Germany, Japan, and Italy. The president warned the nation in December 1940: "If Great Britain goes down, all of us in the Americas would be living at the point of a gun."

In the interim, the threatened German invasion of Britain and "the deadly struggle of the U-boat war" had badly depleted British strength. "We were almost an unarmed people," Churchill later wrote, yet FDR's hands were tied because the Neutrality Act barred US firms from selling armaments to belligerents and prohibited shipping companies from arming merchant ships with defensive guns. Food and raw materials could still be exported, but only if paid for in cash and transported using the purchasing nation's own ships. London, however, was broke.

In addition to food, oil, and replacements for the equipment abandoned on Dunkirk's beaches, Britain also needed destroyers. Fortunately for Churchill, American isolationism was steadily eroding. In September 1940, FDR secured Congress' assent to loan fifty older "four-piper" flush-deck destroyers and ten Coast Guard cutters in exchange for leases to British possessions in the Western Hemisphere. These included an ideal location for a naval base in Argentia, Newfoundland. The US Congress finally approved the "Lend-Lease" Act in March 1941. A political victory for both Roosevelt and Churchill, Lend-Lease permitted the shipment of war-related cargo to Britain under payment terms left deliberately vague.

Isolationists protested loudly, yet polls indicated shifting American sympathies: 62 percent supported the "destroyers-for-bases" deal, and 71 percent supported Lend-Lease. FDR declared "the end of compromise with tyranny" and called on the United States to become the "Arsenal of Democracy" by using its "industrial genius" to "produce more ships more guns, more planes, more of everything." American manufacturers were soon deluged with orders. Although initial Lend-Lease shipments consisted largely of food and raw materials, British and Soviet forces were operating American-made aircraft and tanks in combat by December 1941.[16]

***

American policy in the Atlantic Ocean grew more assertive as the war entered its third year in 1941. In April, the United States extended its "Pan-American Security Zone" out to longitude 26° West, which lies more than halfway to continental Europe. US warships patrolled the zone while Washington declared that any belligerent warships entering it would be dealt with as "pirates" by patrolling US forces. US Marines arrived in Iceland in July to free up occupying British troops and, in November 1941, the US Coast Guard was temporarily shifted from the Treasury Department to the Department of the Navy.

In September 1941, FDR delivered a rhetorical broadside against isolationists claiming to be "in favor of freedom of the seas, but who would have the United States tie up our vessels in our ports." Roosevelt countered, "We propose that these ships sail the seas as they are supposed to." He struck the same note a month later by invoking Admiral David Farragut's famous quote from the American Civil War. "It can never be doubted that the goods will be delivered by this nation," the president declared, "whose Navy believes in the tradition of 'Damn the torpedoes, full speed ahead!'" Fighting words were fitting, especially considering that the US Navy and Coast Guard were increasingly finding themselves in active combat.

That same month saw American warships operating from Argentia, Newfoundland begin escorting eastbound convoys to a handoff point south of Iceland where Royal Navy escorts took over. One British officer recounted linking up with an American foray into the Atlantic: "Strange-looking destroyers, with long names often beginning with 'Jacob' or 'Ephraim,' would appear from the mist." Official neutrality aside, he remarked that "between Lend-Lease and this unobtrusive naval effort, [the Americans] were certainly doing their best round the edges."

They were indeed, and this incited frustration within the Ubootwaffe that only increased as 1941 unfolded. The United States had now laid claim to more than half the Atlantic, an edict backed by American destroyers and cutters patrolling far into the combat zone. Karl Dönitz's U-boat commanders watched with gritted teeth through periscopes and binoculars as these same "neutral" warships shepherded merchantmen to Britain while remaining off-limits to attack themselves. At the same time, British air patrols flying as far as 35° West were chipping away at the mid-Atlantic air gap, forcing the U-boats farther west—toward US forces.

The war's first brawl between German and American forces occurred in April 1941 when USS *Niblack* (DD-424) attacked the *U-52* after it approached the destroyer. In June, the *U-203* attempted to torpedo the battleship USS *Texas* (BB-35) but could not line up a shot. An irritated Hitler yanked the leash, but assured Admiral Raeder that he would never call a U-boat kommandant to account for mistakenly torpedoing an American ship. During meetings at Hitler's "Wolf's Lair" headquarters in East Prussia in July 1941, the Führer reiterated his intent to delay hostilities with the United States until after the Soviet Union's defeat. As Raeder noted, "After the eastern campaign, [the Führer] reserves the right to take severe action against the USA as well."

Escalations by both sides continued. The destroyer USS *Greer* (DD-145) and the *U-652* attacked each other in September, although neither inflicted any damage. FDR responded with a shoot-on-sight order against any Axis naval vessels found inside the security zone. On 17 October, a torpedo from the *U-568* severely damaged USS *Kearney* (DD-432) and killed eleven US Navy sailors. Two weeks later, 115 Americans perished when Erich Topp's *U-552* sank USS *Reuben James* (DD-245).

German attacks against several US Merchant Marine freighters also prompted calls to repeal the Neutrality Act clause which prohibited defensive weaponry on

US-flagged ships. FDR signaled his support in October 1941, declaring that "our American merchant ships must be armed to defend themselves against the rattlesnakes of the sea." Congress repealed Section 6 of the Neutrality Act the following month, and the US Navy began equipping the nation's merchant vessels with naval guns.[17]

***

Despite Hitler's wish to avoid antagonizing the Roosevelt administration, the Führer despised the United States. He had expressed measured admiration for American economic vitality and its German and Anglo-Saxon ethnic foundations earlier in his political career, yet his tone changed sharply in the 1930s. A polyglot republic based on individual rights embodied everything he detested, and the avowed anti-capitalist sneered at its bourgeois tradition of private enterprise. As he declared in 1942, "My feelings against Americanism are feelings of hatred and deep repugnance."

Much of Hitler's rhetoric disregarded the United States as a military threat. "I don't see much future for the Americans," he opined, "it's a decayed country." The Führer had convinced himself that no people so invested in their luxuries and lacking in martial discipline, let alone one he considered racially polluted, could defeat "Aryan" warriors. "I'll never believe that an American soldier can fight like a hero," he dismissively asserted nine days before the first U-boats reached the East Coast.

Yet Hitler had not entirely discarded his earlier awareness of America's potential as a global power. In his characteristically vacillating manner, he dismissed the United States as a near-term threat while also portraying it as the final obstacle to Nazi world mastery. Victory over Britain and the Soviet Union, Hitler believed, would set the stage for a third and final world war against the United States. By 1939, he even spoke of an eventual invasion of North America.

Although these grandiose schemes would remain only vaguely defined, they were already germinating. In 1940, Hitler referred to "the future war with America" and expressed his wish to bomb American cities using long-range aircraft based in the Azores. Herein was rooted part of the Führer's support within the Kriegsmarine, for a German multi-continental empire directed against the United States would naturally require a first-class fleet. One map produced by Raeder's staff showed the envisioned German "World Reich" in red arrayed against an American-led Anglophone dominion in blue. The scale of these ambitions amused General Franz Halder, Chief of Staff of the Army High Command. As Halder quipped in June 1942, "These people dream in continents."

Germany's alliance with Italy eventually expanded to include Japan. In September 1940, the dictatorships formalized their alliance as the Rome-Berlin-Tokyo Axis, better known to history as the "Axis Powers." Japanese militarism and racism earned Hitler's respect, and he pledged in April 1941 to "strike without delay" if Tokyo's actions incurred war between Japan and the United States. Four months later, the Führer couched their alliance in sweeping terms when he told Japanese ambassador Hiroshi

Ōshima that Britain and America represented existential threats to their respective nations. Hitler concluded, "This is why I think we must destroy them together."[18]

War between Japan and the United States was clearly imminent in 1941, though it was unclear how and where it would begin. The Japanese did not forewarn their German allies of their plan to attack the US naval base at Pearl Harbor, but news of the Hawaii raid elated Hitler. He reportedly slapped his thighs and jumped to his feet, exclaiming, "Finally!" Although Germany's alliance with Japan did not oblige either nation to enter a fight provoked by the other, the Führer seized the opportunity to dismiss any remaining pretense of goodwill toward the Americans. After all, the U-boats had already effectively been at war with the US Navy for several months.

Four days after Pearl Harbor, Hitler stood before his rubber-stamp legislature in Berlin to declare war against the United States. His rambling diatribe decried "a series of the worst crimes against international law" by US forces in the Atlantic and lambasted FDR as a "so-called president" and "paralytic professor" complicit in an "Anglo-Saxon-Jewish-Capitalist" conspiracy. "Germany, Italy and Japan," Hitler proclaimed, "will wage the common war forced upon them by the USA and England to a victorious conclusion."

Washington answered with its own declaration of war later that day. "Now at this very moment I knew the United States was in the war, up to the neck and in to the death," Churchill exuberantly wrote. "Hitler's fate was sealed. Mussolini's fate was sealed. As for the Japanese, they would be ground to powder," Churchill continued. "All the rest was merely the proper application of overwhelming force."

And therein lay the challenge. Applying this overwhelming force would require transporting millions of troops across the globe, but this was only one piece of a larger logistical and economic endeavor of unprecedented scale. Training and equipping those forces meant feeding workers, fueling tanks and planes and warships, running assembly lines around the clock, and more. These challenges, in turn, required moving millions of tons of cargo. As Churchill stated in a December 1940 letter to FDR, it was "in shipping and in the power to transport across the oceans" in which "the crunch of the whole war will be found."[19]

***

The American merchant fleet was constituted as the US Merchant Marine, a joint public-private enterprise encompassing all American-flagged commercial vessels capable of oceangoing travel. It comprised approximately 1,340 ships and 8 million gross registered tons in December 1941. The world's second-largest merchant fleet boasted first-class tankers, although its most numerous ships were the 1918-vintage Hog Island freighters now known as "rustbuckets." US Merchant Marine vessels would remain under private ownership and operation throughout the war while sailing under the direction of the War Shipping Administration (its corollary, the US Maritime Commission, oversaw shipbuilding).

American merchant ships in 1941 were crewed by fifty-five thousand civilian mariners. They ranged from teenagers to men as old as 70 and represented a range of ethnic and cultural backgrounds. Merchant crews were also racially integrated, unlike the armed forces. Many mariners were ineligible for the draft due to age or other factors, and 5–10 percent had a criminal record. The career mariners were "a tough bunch of guys" according to Hugh Stephens, who joined the Merchant Marine during the war. "The old-timers knew what they were doing. Us kids didn't, so we didn't know what to be afraid of."

A German admiral in World War I had dismissed American mariners as "the worst random conglomeration of riffraff that one could possibly imagine," and their public perception on the homefront in 1941 was ambivalent at best. Many associated them with boozing, brawling, and labor unrest. "The sailor from the merchant ships was in those days known to America as a bum," according to mariner Felix Reisenberg. Some servicemen "were very nasty to us if we tried to go into the USO clubs," Hugh Stephens recalled. As the *New York Times* noted, "Nobody steps up to the bar to buy them a drink. No moist-eyed old ladies turn to them in the subway to murmur 'God bless you.'"

American neutrality had protected the nation's mariners for more than two years, but the events of December 1941 now made this hardy working-class lot Karl Dönitz's number-one target. His designs against the US Merchant Marine, however, were more ambitious than seeking them out in the central Atlantic or the Western Approaches. "The hub of both shipbuilding and the production of armaments lies in the United States," Dönitz explained. "If, therefore, I go for the hub—and particularly the oil supplies—then I am getting to the root of the evil."[20]

***

"Whether or not Germany could have won the war," explained U-boat officer Herbert Werner, "she was certain to lose it if the gigantic production of American factories reached England in sufficient quantity." The United States already possessed the world's largest manufacturing output and highest per-capita worker productivity in December 1941, and wartime economic mobilization would leverage and expand these to astounding effect. American shipyards would build 151 aircraft carriers compared to Japan's 30, and American automotive plants would produce more tanks in 1943 than Germany did over the entire war. By 1945, two-thirds of the Allies' artillery, tanks, trucks, and aircraft were products of American factories.

It was not only American manufactured goods that Germany sought to immobilize. The United States and its neighbors also exported iron, coal, wheat, copper, and other vital commodities. Whether shipped to US ports as manufacturing inputs or to Canada where convoys to Britain assembled, all these cargoes needed to traverse East Coast shipping lanes. Breaking this link in the Allies' global logistical network meant immobilizing not only finished goods and raw materials from the United States, but also those of the Caribbean and Latin America. "The vast resources and wealth of this American hemisphere," declared FDR in 1940, "constitute the most tempting loot in all the round world."

One particular resource held paramount importance: "The terrible war machine must be fed not only with flesh, but with oil," Winston Churchill reminded the world in 1941. When the United States entered the war in December, it accounted for 63 percent of global crude oil extraction and 58 percent of refining capacity. The nation's most productive oilfields were in Texas and Louisiana, and many of its major refineries were located in New Jersey, New York, and Pennsylvania.

American oil was badly needed by Great Britain, which was consuming four tankers' worth of petroleum products per day. Because combat in the Mediterranean blocked the transit of Middle Eastern oil through the Suez Canal, the Gulf of Mexico and Caribbean basin were supplying nearly all of Britain's fuel by December 1941. Underlying this supply chain was a glaring strategic vulnerability: whether extracted in Venezuela or Louisiana (and whether refined in Aruba or New Jersey), nearly every barrel had to be shipped north along the East Coast. Much of this was hauled by tankers operated by American oil giants like Socony-Vacuum, Gulf Oil, and Standard Oil of New Jersey.

Severing this coastal artery would cut off the United States from its own oil supply. According to economist Alexander J. Field, "the eastern seaboard was as dependent on imports of petroleum and petroleum products by tanker as Great Britain." Seventeen East Coast states together consumed more than one million barrels per day in 1941, 90 percent of which arrived by tanker to ports such as Philadelphia, Baltimore, and New York. No pipelines connected oil fields to eastern cities, and railroads could supply only a fraction of demand. "The greater part of American tankers is used in coastal traffic, transporting oil from the oil region to the industrial area," Dönitz explained to Hitler. Accordingly, "the destruction of American oil supply vessels is of greatest importance to us."

Sinking tankers offered the additional benefit of impeding America's burgeoning shipbuilding effort because replacing them meant launching correspondingly fewer new tankers. "Her shipbuilding industry is located in the eastern states," Dönitz explained to Hitler. "Every tanker destroyed not only means one tanker less for carrying oil, but also represents a direct setback to America's shipbuilding program."[21]

Nested within the primary goal of cutting the East Coast maritime supply line was a secondary psychological objective. The Germans have historically ascribed considerable weight to the military significance of willpower, zeal, and other intangible variables. Historian Robert Citino wrote of "old Prussian traditions that emphasized the importance of spirit and will over crass material factors." Accordingly, BdU intended to instill shock and fear among ordinary Americans, not to mention leaving their homes without heating oil.

A U-boat offensive off North America would also support Germany's war against the Soviet Union on the Eastern Front. That campaign had been raging for six months, during which time German forces had destroyed nearly eighteen thousand Soviet aircraft and more than twenty thousand tanks, overrun factories, and captured the Ukrainian wheat fields that provided much of the Soviet food supply. Only the United States could make these losses whole, and American cargo was already arriving at Soviet ports in November 1941 when the Roosevelt administration formally extended Lend-Lease aid to the USSR. Likewise, and in time, U-boats would even stalk the Arctic approaches to Murmansk and Arkhangelsk.[22]

Throughout the war, BdU would continually shift its forces to wherever they could sink the most tonnage at the least risk to themselves. This was Dönitz's *Schwerpunkt* (a word he frequently used), a German concept of weighting a critical mass of combat power at a specific point in time and space. The US Navy already understood this. A January 1942 document stated that "the German has always been quick to discover the weakest link," and the next weak link was glaringly apparent: the nation's Atlantic coast presented "an excellent opportunity for Admiral Dönitz to reveal his gifts for improvisation."

The East Coast in late 1941 featured the world's most heavily trafficked shipping lanes and America's busiest ports. German intelligence accurately calculated that an average of 146 ships departed the United States for Britain each month while, concurrently, more than 100 sailed domestic routes between US ports each day. Wolfpacks would not be necessary because there were no convoys here. All ships instead traveled alone and unescorted, and those arriving via escorted convoys to Canada became vulnerable upon being routed independently to American ports.

Dönitz also recognized the advantages offered by North American geography. Immense distances made the coastal waters of the United States difficult to patrol, even while heavy traffic meant ships were easy to find. He also understood that shoals, shorelines, and currents funneled coastal shipping into bottlenecks at Cape Hatteras, the Florida Strait, and the entrances to the Delaware Bay and Chesapeake Bay. U-boats could therefore either prowl long stretches of ocean at will or haunt the chokepoints through which most of America's industrial output passed.

This would enable Dönitz to rapidly shift his schwerpunkt between the "immeasurable focal points of shipping, which we could now engage at will." The U-boats could rack up kills in one area before switching to another, staying one step ahead of the overextended Americans. "As the attackers, we held the initiative," Dönitz explained, "and by rapid switches of the main weight of our attack from one focal point to another we could confuse and surprise the enemy."[23]

In September 1941, Dönitz had requested advance notice of any German declaration of war against the United States. His intent was "to have my forces in position off the American coast" so that "full advantage could be taken of the element of surprise," but Japan's unexpected attack on 7 December left the admiral and his staff scrambling. Despite Hitler's assertion that "there's nobody stupider than the Americans," a sense of urgency permeated BdU headquarters in the days immediately following Pearl Harbor.

Despite littering the seafloor with the wrecks of 1,055 merchant ships between September 1939 and December 1941, the amount of tonnage destroyed by the Gray Wolves still fell short of Dönitz's objective of 700,000 tons per month. Their most successful months to date (October 1940 and May 1941) had destroyed only 342,204 and 333,912 tons, respectively. An all-out attack along the coast of an unprepared United States therefore represented a tantalizing opportunity, yet Dönitz recognized that American vulnerability would not last indefinitely. He wrote on 11 January: "We must take advantage of the situation before changes are made."[24]

Dönitz named his plan *Unternehmen Paukenschlag*. Though usually rendered as Operation "Drumbeat," a more nuanced translation reveals darker connotations. *Schlag* means a blow or strike, and *Pauke* refers specifically to a timpani drum. The timpani's deep and booming sound features in such works as Richard Wagner's Norse-themed opera *Der Ring des Nibelungen*, one of Hitler's favorites. A better translation may therefore be Operation "Thunderclap," evoking a sudden and jarring blow to the American psyche as the *boom, boom, boom* of explosions sounded offshore. It was Dönitz's theatrical flair par excellence.[25]

As the larger of the Ubootwaffe's two workhorse designs, the Type IX U-boats carried enough fuel to operate for up to three weeks off North America. Yet BdU possessed only twenty Type IXs, eight of which required overhauls or were otherwise unavailable. He requested all twelve available Type IX boats for Operation Drumbeat, but Kriegsmarine high command authorized only six (and mechanical issues would cause one to abort). Although just five U-boats would press the first wave of attacks against the United States, Dönitz contrived a plan of attack to compensate for his numerically small force.

Each U-boat would commence attacks in a different sector of North American coastal waters, and the sectors were arranged so that ships diverting from one area would find themselves in another U-boat's sector. "I further stipulated that the five boats would receive from me, by radio, the time and date at which they could simultaneously go into action," the admiral explained. A sudden assault spanning hundreds of miles would maximize psychological impact, make the U-boats appear more numerous, and overextend American naval and air forces. "We [U-boat crews] were supposed to take it to the piers of New York," boasted *Bootsmannsmaat* Peter Marl, "to hit the Yankees in the steamer lines."

The *U-123* was ordered to operate off New York and New Jersey, the *U-125* farther out to sea along this same section of coast, and the *U-66* off North Carolina. The *U-109* and *U-130* were to hunt off Canada and be prepared to shift south to American shores if conditions warranted. *Gruppe* (Group) *Paukenschlag* would operate concurrently with a separate force of twelve Type VII boats, designated

Gruppe Ziethen, which was dispatched to Canada to intercept convoys bound for the Soviet Union.

Ulrich Folkers' *U-125* was the first Gruppe Paukenschlag U-boat to depart Lorient, France on 18 December 1941. Reinhard Hardegen's *U-123* left on 23 December, Richard Zapp's *U-66* followed the next day, then the *U-109* under Heinrich Bleichrodt and *U-130* under Ernst Kals sailed on 27 December. Gruppe Paukenschlag thus began separate three-week, 3,000-mile voyages into the teeth of one of the worst Atlantic storms in fifteen years.

Weather stations in Iceland recorded gales over 90 mph, but the timetable forced the U-boats to sail most of the voyage on the surface. Mountainous seas bludgeoned them with such violence that they damaged decks and guns, and forward progress was impossible at times as the U-boats struggled not to be pushed backward. The same weather scattered six Allied convoys and drove two US destroyers aground, and Gruppe Ziethen suffered a fatality when a wave snatched the *U-701*'s first watch officer from the tower. In one Royal Navy officer's words, "anyone who really wants the North Atlantic to do its worst in winter should be qualifying for a lunatic asylum."[26]

***

Across the chessboard from BdU was the US Navy's Eastern Sea Frontier (ESF, technically the North Atlantic Coastal Frontier until 6 February). Established in July 1941, ESF existed to detect and destroy enemy forces from Maine to Florida out to 200 nautical miles offshore. Among ESF's subordinate commands was Third Naval District, headquartered in Manhattan and encompassing the coasts of Connecticut, the New York City region, and the northern half of New Jersey. Abutting this to the south was Fourth Naval District, headquartered in Philadelphia and responsible for southern New Jersey and the Delaware Bay. ESF also commanded Coast Guard assets since that service had been shifted under Navy control for the duration of the war.

Eastern Sea Frontier headquarters was on the fourteenth floor of the federal building at 90 Church Street in Lower Manhattan. Crowded with phones, switchboards, and teletype machines, its nucleus was an L-shaped operations room featuring large maps of the Atlantic Ocean and East Coast. Across the hall was the headquarters of Eastern Defense Command, its US Army counterpart, while the ESF commander occupied an office on the floor above. The Army Air Forces' First Bomber Command was located down the hall from ESF, although little formal integration existed between them.

The fifteenth-floor office was occupied by Adolphus "Dolly" Andrews, a 62-year-old rear admiral (two stars) from Texas. Described by a contemporary as "senatorial in port and speech," his stilted bearing wore thin on Secretary of War Henry Stimson, who considered him a "terrible old fusspocket." Yet Rear Admiral Andrews was also energetic, politically savvy, and well-connected in Washington. Not all his decisions over the coming months would prove wise, but his open-minded and flexible approach to the U-boat peril would prove him a far better asset than his immediate superior.[27]

Two weeks after Pearl Harbor, President Roosevelt promoted a flinty four-star admiral named Ernest King to the role of Commander-in-Chief, US Fleet (COMINCH). Admiral King would also absorb of the duties of Chief of Naval Operations in March 1942, cementing his authority over the entire naval service. A tall man with a Roman nose and cleft chin, the 63-year-old King certainly looked the part. The Navy's official historian characterized COMINCH as "a hard, grim, determined man," and FDR joked that he shaved with a blowtorch. As King reportedly remarked of his appointment, "When they get in trouble, they send for the sons-of-bitches."

ADM King was a heavy drinker with a volcanic temperament who tolerated neither dissent nor criticism, and his reputation for groping other men's wives led an otherwise admiring biographer to describe him as "lecherous." Although Roosevelt admired the irascible yet brilliant admiral, King privately dismissed the president as "slippery." COMINCH's list of critics was long. A British colonel found King "exceedingly narrow-minded" and "always on the lookout for slights," and General Dwight Eisenhower considered him "the antithesis of cooperation" and "a mental bully."[28]

Despite the outbound U-boats maintaining radio silence, the impending German assault had not gone undetected. The short status signal each Paukenschlag boat transmitted at 10° West, and the coordinating instructions radioed by BdU, were intercepted and decoded at Bletchley Park. The Admiralty's Operational Intelligence Centre began passing the Americans an ominous picture of twenty-one U-boats moving west. By the first week of January, Admiral King's headquarters was receiving daily updates about the enemy forces approaching North America.

The Enigma decrypts did not spell out German intentions explicitly, but a distress call from the *Cyclops* 316 miles east of Cape Cod on 11 January confirmed British suspicions. A report flashed the next day to Admiral King's office in Washington, D.C. warned of "a heavy concentration of U-boats off the North American seaboard." Several boats "approaching the American coast" were expected to "reach their attacking positions by 13 January." The early morning hours of 13 January then brought confirmation of "three or four" U-boats near 40° North, 65° West, a point 480 miles due east of New Jersey.[29]

As the reckoning drew nearer, Rear Admiral Andrews brooded over a large map on the wall at Eastern Sea Frontier headquarters. It portrayed the shipping lanes that lay on either side of a line of navigational markers (lightships in peacetime, now replaced by lighted buoys) dotting the coast. On any given day, approximately 125 merchant ships sailed this maritime turnpike linking the natural resources and industries of two continents.

The main southward coastal route began at the mouth of the St Lawrence River in Canada. This route skirted Nova Scotia, then passed between the Georges Bank underwater plateau and Nantucket Shoals before reaching Boston and then New York City. Here the Hudson River connects the continental interior to the largest and most geographically favorable natural harbor on earth. New York was also America's busiest port, averaging fifty daily arrivals and departures in November 1941.

Immediately southwest of New York City, across the Hudson River, lies New Jersey. The state is bordered by the Atlantic Ocean to the east, and the Delaware River runs along the Pennsylvania–New Jersey border to the west. The river empties into the Delaware Bay, which separates southern New Jersey from the state of Delaware. Dotting New Jersey's coast are summer destinations that include Atlantic City, Sea Isle City, Wildwood, and Cape May. The state's geographic position between New York City and the Delaware Bay meant that thirty to forty vessels passed the Jersey Shore each day.

Although New Jersey lacked any major ports of its own, its northern coast served as an extension of New York's harbor facilities. Wharves and warehouses crowded waterfronts in Perth Amboy, Bayonne, Newark, Jersey City, and Hoboken. Farther south along the Jersey Shore, coastwise traffic passed barrier islands broken by eleven major inlets. At roughly the midpoint of New Jersey's coast lay Barnegat City and its lighthouse, Barnegat Light. The state's coastline terminates at Cape May Point on the southernmost end of the Cape May Peninsula. Here the shipping lane branched off west into the Delaware Bay for ships headed to Philadelphia, Pennsylvania in addition to Wilmington, Delaware and Camden, New Jersey.

Eleven miles southwest of Cape May Point lies Delaware's Cape Henlopen, and the two peninsulas jointly constitute the Delaware Capes. Southbound ships continued past the Capes and along the Delmarva Peninsula where the borders of Delaware, Maryland, and Virginia meet. Another feeder at Delmarva's southern end led into the Chesapeake Bay. Farther south, traffic flow narrowed along North Carolina's coast between Cape Hatteras and Cape Lookout, where ships threaded the gap between the shallows and the stormy offshore zone where the Labrador Current meets the Gulf Stream. The lane diverged again at Florida's southernmost end to take ships either through the Florida Straits into the Gulf of Mexico or through the Old Bahama Channel into the Caribbean.

Merchantmen arriving from Britain to Canada via westbound convoys subsequently proceeded south, alone and independently, to load cargo at ports along the East Coast and beyond. On the way, they passed the three dozen ships departing each day from the Caribbean and Gulf of Mexico. This traffic comprised tankers hauling crude oil or refined petroleum products and freighters laden with manganese, bauxite, tin, foodstuffs, rubber, cotton, and phosphates. Accompanying them were ships arriving from the Far East after passing through the Panama Canal. Some northbound vessels were destined for US ports to feed their cargoes into stateside manufacturing plants and refineries while others sailed for Britain via Canada's Halifax or Sydney.

The large wall map at ESF headquarters in New York was bedecked with magnetic markers representing individual U-boats identified by Enigma intercepts. For the past two weeks, Rear Admiral Adolphus Andrews had watched the markers slide steadily from right to left across the map until they were now nearly atop the shipping lanes. Akin to watching the seconds before a train crash in slow motion, it left him vaguely nauseous. RADM Andrews knew that Dönitz believed the United States unprepared for a fight, but he doubted that his enemy counterpart realized just how pitiful America's coastal defense forces were.

When the Operation Drumbeat boats set course for North America in late December 1941, Eastern Sea Frontier possessed just twenty combat vessels to defend more than 1,600 miles of coastline. Seven were World War I-era subchasers, four were civilian yachts repurposed as armed patrol boats, and none were destroyers. The largest, a single Thetis-class Coast Guard cutter, was still more than 2 knots slower than a Type IX U-boat. "There is not a vessel available that an enemy submarine could not outdistance when operating on the surface," Admiral Andrews reported. "In most cases, the guns of these vessels would be outranged by those of the submarine."

The aircraft situation was hardly better. Andrews possessed only 103 planes, "a large proportion of which," he stated, "have no place in modern war." Fewer than one-third had any attack capabilities, most were limited in range to less than 1,000 miles, and none were "capable of maintaining long-range seaward patrols." ESF lacked any medium or heavy bombers, and ADM King's request for these would be denied in February. A single squadron of four blimps at New Jersey's Naval Air Station Lakehurst offered excellent patrol capabilities, but they were poor attack platforms.

The US Army Air Forces (USAAF, predecessor to the US Air Force) did have 139 additional aircraft assigned to coastal defense, but only 44 were bombers. The rest were unarmed observation planes, and maintenance issues prevented more than ten from flying at any given time. "[I] cannot too strongly emphasize," Andrews wrote to COMINCH, "the lack of sufficient air force on this Frontier to defend it properly and to patrol sea-borne trade along the coast." Army and Navy aircraft also operated under separate chains of command and interservice coordination was poor. Consequently, it was nigh impossible for one branch to obtain timely support from the other when a ship was a sunk or a U-boat sighted.

No portion of the paltry interservice team guarding the Atlantic coast was prepared for the oncoming storm. American inexperience would also cost lives when pitted against highly trained German crews already blooded in combat. Historian Samuel Eliot Morison, commissioned as a US Navy officer to document the war by experiencing it firsthand, painted a bleak portrait of the circumstances: "No more perfect set-up for rapid and ruthless destruction could have been afforded the Nazi sea lords."[30]

**

It was evident by 12 January 1942 that disaster was approaching the East Coast with alarming speed. Shortly before midnight, Britain's Foreign Office ordered all British merchant ships in North American waters to make for the nearest port. The tension in the air grew heavier at naval headquarters offices in New York, Philadelphia, Boston, and Norfolk. On 14 January, the malign timbre of Dönitz's timpani drum finally sounded at ESF headquarters when a report from the Navy blimp *K-3* reached 90 Church Street in Manhattan.

K-3 had been flying a routine patrol out of Lakehurst, New Jersey when the pilot sighted a triangular object extending above the water south of Long Island. Closer inspection revealed that it was not a sailboat, but rather the bow of a ship sunk almost vertically. This was the tanker *Norness*, torpedoed by Reinhard Hardegen's *U-123* upon its arrival off Long Island more than twelve hours earlier. Spotting a nearby raft occupied by several bedraggled men, the pilot turned into the wind and cut his speed to achieve a hover 50 feet above. The air crew struggled to hear the mariners over *K-3*'s engines, but one word was discernible: "Submarine."

Later that night, Long Island residents witnessed a fiery explosion 33 miles off Long Island's South Shore. Its source was identified after sunrise when an Army observation plane spotted the tanker *Coimbra*'s charred hulk awash. Calamity unfolded at a dizzying pace as reports of attacks and sightings poured into Eastern Sea Frontier. Another merchantman was torpedoed on 18 January, then four more within forty-eight hours after that. One ship disappeared without a trace off the Delmarva Peninsula, then another vanished off North Carolina.[31]

The Gray Wolves had arrived.

***

The hunting in the United States' front yard exceeded even Admiral Dönitz's expectations, with BdU headquarters noting that Gruppe Paukenschlag found "such an abundance of opportunities for attack that he could not possibly utilize them all." Reinhard Hardegen's *U-123* passed the Delaware Capes and put a torpedo into the freighter *Octavian* 70 miles south-southeast of Cape May just before dawn on 17 January. The Norwegian ship sank too rapidly to either transmit a distress message or launch lifeboats, and it maintained headway long enough that it appeared to sail itself beneath the waves.

Hardegen then thumbed his nose at the US Navy by cruising past the fleet anchorage at Norfolk, Virginia on the surface in daylight. South of Norfolk, the Germans found so many targets that it forced them to use their torpedoes selectively. "There's one—no, it's too small ... There, we'll take that one," recalled Horst von Schroeter, the *U-123*'s second watch officer. "Really totally crazy, that situation." It was "something I never experienced elsewhere during the entire war."

The *U-123* passed Richard Zapp's *U-66* off North Carolina as Zapp torpedoed the Standard Oil of New Jersey tanker *Allan Jackson* after midnight on 17/18 January, but the real slaughter occurred the next evening. It began when Hardegen sent the freighter *Norvana* to the bottom along with her entire crew of twenty-nine. Ninety minutes later, Zapp torpedoed the Canadian passenger ship *Lady Hawkins* with the loss of 251 lives. Two-and-a-half hours after that, the *U-123* blasted the *City of Atlanta* in shallow water from less than 300 yards away.

The *City of Atlanta* had scarcely touched the seafloor when Hardegen slipped astern of the tanker *Malay* and set her aflame with a barrage of 105mm shells. The *U-123* then swung north and torpedoed the freighter *Ciltvaira* just as Hardegen's radioman intercepted a message from the *Malay* reporting that she was still afloat and under power. Hardegen returned to the *Malay* by following the burning tanker's acrid smell and put a torpedo into her engine room. "It annoyed me that the tanker was underway again and I wanted to spoil his joy over it," his log remarked. "Blame yourself for sending a hasty report about being operational."

The U-boats found conditions off American shores "almost exactly those of normal peacetime," Dönitz wrote. Merchant captains sailed with their lights on while reporting their own positions over the 600-meter frequency. *U-103* petty officer Peter Marl recalled that "the whole area was full of singly traveling ships and there was no defense of any kind. That was hard to understand." Merchant captains finally put out their lights by the end of January, but their vessels' bulky shapes remained silhouetted against the fatal brilliance of coastal cities and highways. As *U-333* commander Peter Cremer observed, "On the East Coast they seemed to be asleep, to put it mildly."[32]

"The United States kept up the tall talk and left her coast unguarded," Hitler gloated. "Now I daresay that she is quite surprised." Operation Drumbeat was not a surprise, however, nor did it catch the United States as badly prepared as Rear Admiral Andrews' forces suggested. ESF possessed neither destroyers nor Treasury-class cutters, but the Atlantic Fleet possessed more than seventy destroyers and sixteen large cutters ready for action. One reporter spoke for many uneasy Americans on 20 January when he asked the president: "Where is the Navy?"

The discomfiting truth, which would remain obscured for decades, was that Admiral King ignored the reports of Gruppe Paukenschlag's approach and took no measures to prepare for the impending storm. On the night that Reinhard Hardegen's *U-123* arrived off New York City, at least thirteen combat-ready destroyers sat moored in Northeastern harbors. Seven were just a few miles away at Staten Island. But these were neither sortied to bloody Dönitz's nose nor assigned to antisubmarine duty with ESF. King knew that the U-boats had arrived, and yet, as a bewildered Reinhard Hardegen remarked decades later, "he did nothing."

King instead tasked nine of these destroyers to escort convoy AT 10, which was rushing a token force of US troops to Northern Ireland. Convoy AT 10 departed New York on 15 January and sailed almost directly over the *Coimbra* wreck, even dispatching two destroyers to pick up the tanker's survivors. The convoy passed within a few dozen miles of Ulrich Folkers' *U-125*, though neither the Germans nor Americans spotted the other. Six days later, four more destroyers left to escort troopship convoy BT 200 to the Pacific where, unlike Britain, American troops were indeed urgently needed.

It bears mention that AT 10 was a publicity stunt not of ADM King's invention and that he was under considerable pressure from both Roosevelt and the Army. However, King did not use his authority as COMINCH to either object to the plan or delay the convoy's departure, and his dutiful execution stripped much of the coast's remaining defensive capacity while sending thousands of US troops toward the known locations of U-boats. The two convoys' departures still left nearly sixty destroyers and sixteen cutters available, a dozen of which were patrolling the Gulf of Mexico and Caribbean, yet King refused to spare even one of these in the days immediately following the Germans' arrival.

Admiral King's failures would compound over the ensuing weeks. In addition to misallocating his limited forces, the purported Anglophobe was willfully deaf to the Royal Navy's hard-won and eagerly shared antisubmarine advice. Oddly enough, King had begun preparing for the impending U-boat threat while serving as Atlantic Fleet commander, only to inexplicably drop it from his priorities upon becoming COMINCH on 20 December.

After the war, British naval intelligence officer Patrick Beesly and historian Martin Middlebrook both deemed ADM King's negligence "criminal." His priorities were likely rooted in his focus on the Pacific Theater, where the prospect of fleet battles against the Imperial Japanese Navy offered a "real" war at sea. Whatever the explanation for King's decisions, no naval officer besides Karl Dönitz would bear more responsibility for the catastrophe now unfolding.[33]

Operation Drumbeat kicked off a months-long massacre deemed a "holocaust" by the Royal Navy's official historian. American historian Michael Gannon wrote that "for the United States, in terms of raw resources and material, Paukenschlag and its aftermath constituted the costliest defeat of World War II." It has also been dubbed the "Atlantic Pearl Harbor," yet the U-boats exacted a far greater toll off North America than the Japanese had in Hawaii. Moreover, as events in North Africa demonstrated, the stakes could not have been higher.

As the first five U-boats departed France for the US East Coast in December 1941, German general Erwin Rommel was facing disaster in the Sahara Desert. Both his Afrika Korps and his opponents badly required resupply, but fortunes shifted on 5 January when a convoy of Italian merchant ships delivered to Rommel fifty-five tanks, twenty armored cars, antitank guns, fuel, and other matériel. The reequipped Afrika Korps then smashed through British forces in Libya and captured Benghazi. As ESF staff noted in March 1942, "What is happening on the east coast of this country directly affects the fortunes of our allies across the sea."[34]

***

The Eastern Sea Frontier war diary, an official narrative summary of each month's events, reported for January 1942 that "the appearance of the enemy in such force gave little opportunity for warding off the blows that were struck so rapidly." An Army pilot unsuccessfully attacked the *U-123* off New Jersey on 15 January, but US forces were altogether impotent. The coastal zone was simply too large for so few Army and Navy assets to defend, a fact which the U-boats demonstrated "with mathematical exactitude." Without reinforcements, warned Vice Admiral Royal Ingersoll on 20 January, "I think we are in for a beating from the subs."

Although New Jersey's waters would become an active combat zone over the coming months, the storm largely bypassed the "Garden State" during its first fiery days. The assault commenced off New York City before shifting south where the *U-123* and *U-66* converged off North Carolina during the third week of January. The relative quiet ended abruptly on 25 January, however, when Army and Coast Guard forces heard an explosion off Atlantic City around 03:00. Another followed several minutes later, then Fourth Naval District's Inshore Patrol reported a third blast at 03:56. Some Jersey Shore residents were roused from their sleep by the explosions, awakening to the stark reality that the war had come home.[35]

Part II

CHAPTER FIVE

Varanger

25 January 1942
32 miles east-southeast of Wildwood, New Jersey
02:04

"Well, what do you think, captain?" second mate Wilhelm Wilhelmsen asked Captain Carl Horne as they stood on the bridge of the tanker *Varanger*. They were alone except for a crewman at the helm, or steering wheel. "It is what it is," the burly captain replied nonchalantly. He spoke without taking his eyes off the dark expanse of sea before them. "Can't say I've lost any sleep over it."

Captain Horne had spent twenty-seven years at sea, and this was not his first time sailing under threat of attack. "And you had no submarine trouble during the Great War?" Wilhelmsen inquired. Horne nodded. "That's a fact," he replied, his ruddy and clean-shaven face creasing into a smile. Wilhelmsen answered with a joke. "Maybe the *jævlene* don't want to tangle with you. You must scare them." Capt Horne chortled. "No, no," he replied with dismissive modesty. "Just lucky. Always have been."

Carl Horne did indeed feel lucky, despite being a de facto exile from his home country. Over the nearly two years since Germany's invasion of Norway, the 42-year-old had taken command of the tanker *Varanger* and married an American woman with whom he now had an infant daughter. Their house on Aldine Street in northeast Philadelphia, Pennsylvania was a long way from his hometown of Florø on Norway's western coast, yet it felt more like home than anywhere else.[1]

Norway's government, king, and part of its armed forces escaped to Britain before the country fell to the Wehrmacht, but they were not the only Norwegians resisting occupation from abroad. Carl Horne was one of thirty thousand mariners crewing one thousand Norwegian-flagged ships who found themselves unable to return home after the invasion. The government-in-exile requisitioned these vessels into national service, and the Norwegian Shipping and Trade Commission, or "Nortraship," was born. The world's largest shipping company, Nortraship managed about a third of its fleet from its American office at 80 Broad Street in New York City.

Norway has produced hardy seafarers since the Viking age, and its *Handelsflåten* (merchant fleet) was enormous relative to the country's population of just three million. Comprising one-fifth of global tanker tonnage in 1939, by 1942 its ships transported approximately 40 percent of the petroleum and 20 percent of the food sustaining Britain. Nortraship's losses were already dreadful, but its ability to keep the Allies fueled, fed, and equipped was of immeasurable value. Winston Churchill purportedly claimed that Norway's merchant fleet

Norwegian mariner at the helm in 1942. (Norwegian National Archives)

was "worth more than a million soldiers," and British parliamentarian Philip-Noel Baker was even more forthright. "Without the Norwegian merchant fleet," Baker wrote, "the Allies would have lost the war."

On the *Varanger*'s bridge, Wilhelmsen found Capt Horne's sober perspective heartening. The 31-year-old second mate took another sip of coffee. This was a sacrament in every merchant fleet, with even the engine room often having its own coffee machine. "You want any?" Wilhelmsen asked, gesturing with his mug. "No, but thank you," Horne replied, "I'm actually going to turn in for the night." The two shook hands. "*Sov godt, Kaptein.*"

Horne retired to his cabin as Wilhelmsen continued his duties on the bridge. Both were unaware they were presently being hunted, but this was not naïveté on their part. Every man on the *Varanger* could have been forgiven for presuming that New Jersey's waters were under American control. Yet they no longer were, and whatever faith Carl Horne or anyone else had in the US Navy's leadership was badly misplaced.[2]

***

The Navy's attempt to stonewall information about the first sinkings was undermined by the *Coimbra*'s fiery demise so close to shore ten days earlier, on 15 January. Rumors spread quickly, and the Navy publicly confirmed the attacks the following afternoon. The ensuing broadcasts and headlines announcing the arrival of "Nazi raiders" sparked widespread unease. However, unlike the frightened reaction to undersea predators stalking the coast in 1916 and 1918, there was little panic. Americans may have been more alarmed if they knew the true severity of the ongoing disaster, but Admiral Ernest King and Secretary of the Navy Frank Knox ensured that they did not.

Historian Ed Offley wrote that the first U-boat attacks off the East Coast "sparked what can only be described as a panic-driven coverup" in which Knox and King's disinformation obscured the scope and severity of the unfolding disaster. At the same time, far-reaching federal information control policies enacted on 15 January produced what one journalist described as "censorship thick as a Grand Banks fog [that] hid the facts of the battle." Official messaging was heavy on bluster and light on details, and the New Jersey Press Association criticized Knox on 9 February for the paucity of information from the Navy Department. Knox countered that it was necessary to hurt enemy morale. ADM King summarized his philosophy as: "Don't tell them anything. When it's over, tell them who won."[3]

Such tight control of information was unremarkable in the context of both world wars, but it also conveniently obscured Navy leaders' failure to meet the threat stalking the East Coast. This seemed to chafe against Rear Admiral Adolphus Andrews' intrinsic honesty. An 11 February press conference found Eastern Sea Frontier's commander grilled by reporters about the true status of the war offshore, including claims that "five or six" ships had been sunk off New Jersey. "Untrue," an irritated Andrews snapped, then delicately conceded that he was less than satisfied with the results of ongoing antisubmarine efforts.

Much of the scant information released to the public was farcical, such as a 23 January claim that US forces had "liquidated" multiple U-boats and that "some of the recent visitors to our territorial waters will never enjoy the return portion of their voyage." Six days later, Secretary Knox told reporters that "we are giving as well as taking," but his claim of sinking "fourteen undersea raiders" was off by a figure of fourteen. Reinhard Hardegen was thoroughly amused when he heard these news broadcasts aboard the U-123 offshore. "The Americans sank me every day," Hardegen recalled. "We were laughing … three times I learned by radio that I was sunk."

These untruths were only partly deliberate, being also fed by overly optimistic assessments by pilots and warship commanders. One example occurred on 28 January when a US Navy pilot patrolling the Canadian coast dropped a pattern of depth charges on the U-85 as it crash-dived. The pilot subsequently radioed headquarters to report "Sighted sub, sank same," and this laconic quip quickly garnered adulation from the New York Times and other outlets. The undamaged U-85, meanwhile, continued its patrol.

And so denial and obfuscation prevailed. Although it preserved Admiral King's image, many Americans correctly deduced that the disaster unfolding offshore was worse than bureaucratic vagaries revealed. As one article in *TIME* magazine cynically stated, "The sights and sounds which filtered through tight-lipped admissions by the Navy—torpedoes crashing into merchant hulls, the screams of young seamen frying in seas of oil—told the people all they needed to know."[4]

***

Not far from where Carl Horne's swaying cabin lulled him to sleep, another immigrant seafarer was just beginning his day's toil. Lodovico "Dewey" Monichetti was a grizzled and stocky 60-year-old from the Italian island of Ischia, located off Naples, who had fished off southern New Jersey for three decades. Monichetti's first stop after arriving via Ellis Island in 1911 was a train station where he showed the clerk all the money in his pockets and inquired how far it would get him. The answer was Sea Isle City, New Jersey.

He and his wife bought a $500 plot of land in the Back Bay area where they built a house, and Monichetti planted a fig shoot that he brought from Ischia in the backyard. He supported the family by selling his catch from a shack adjacent to the home. His fishing boat, the *San Gennaro*, left the harbor after midnight on 25 January alongside his friend Dominick Constantino in his boat, the *Eileen*. They passed together under Townsends Inlet Bridge before parting ways toward different spots along the cod banks offshore.

Night and morning intertwined as Monichetti's *San Gennaro* motored across the Atlantic's chop. Painted drab gray and measuring 32 feet in length and 6 feet at the beam, the aged but stalwart boat's hand-laid planks reflected years of weathering. The helm was her only enclosed portion, and Monichetti was accordingly grateful for the present mild conditions. Accompanying him were his 21-year-old son, John, and 52-year-old deck hand, Edward Elisano, both of whom were asleep.

They were still sleeping at 03:02 when a noise like thunder reverberated across the sea. Monichetti looked north, but sighted nothing. The noise repeated several minutes later. At 03:24, a third thunderclap was accompanied by a distant flash of light. "It lit up the sky," Monichetti recalled, although he "did not think much about it" at the time.

The fisherman's nonchalance notwithstanding, Monichetti suspected he knew the source of the sound and light show. Twice in the past two weeks he had reported sighting what he believed to be a U-boat. Although he suspected that his reports had not been taken seriously, Monichetti knew he had done his duty as a good citizen.

He awakened his son and deck hand upon reaching their destination, and the three men began paying out 100-yard fishing lines with hooks at 1-foot intervals. The noises and light in the distance "didn't change our plans for the day," Monichetti later explained. The Navy and Coast Guard could handle the Germans; the Monichettis had a living to earn.[5]

***

12 January 1942
49 miles northeast of Sydney, Nova Scotia
09:28

Operational conditions for U-boats along America's eastern seaboard were so permissive that German sailors soon dubbed the campaign the "American Turkey Shoot" and the "*Zweite Glückliche Zeit*," or Second Happy Time. Yet the fortunes of both war and the sea are fickle, and Korvettenkapitän Ernst Kals' first hours off North America had not left him particularly happy. Kals commanded the Type IXC boat *U-130*, one of the two Operation Drumbeat boats ordered to Canadian waters. But whereas the *U-123* and the two other U-boats in United States waters met little opposition, the *U-130* instead found the Canadians on full war footing.

Shortly before dawn on 12 January, the *U-130* reached its assigned patrol area near the Cabot Strait separating Nova Scotia and Newfoundland. Dawn found Kals on the bridge. The collar of a woolen turtleneck sweater was visible under a double-breasted, knee-length leather coat, and his matted hair was neatly parted under his white captain's hat. But Kals saw no ships, and the *U-130* was forced to crash dive at 09:28 when a twin-engine Bolingbroke bomber pounced from a clear sky. The boat plunged to 98 feet as the bomber dropped two depth charges. These rattled the Germans, but inflicted no damage. Kals' log noted that the close call was the fault of an inattentive man on bridge watch.

The bridge watch comprised four lookouts who were posted on a U-boat's bridge at all times while surfaced. Standing bridge watch was a life-or-death responsibility because failing to spot an enemy warship or plane in time could be fatal for all aboard. Admiral Karl Dönitz aptly described a U-boat crew as a *Schicksalgemeinschaft*—a community bound by fate. "If one crewman errs, if he fails as a lookout, improperly closes a valve, or forgets a seal," Dönitz declared, "he jeopardizes his boat's success, his life, and the lives of his crewmates. Thus is each dependent on the other, and is thereby sworn to one another."

The *U-130* crash-dived again upon sighting a pair of aircraft at 13:15, but fortune finally smiled a few minutes after sunset when a lookout sighted the Norwegian freighter *Frisco*. A full moon and clear sky left the sea's surface prohibitively bright, so Kals sprinted well forward of his target until drifting clouds darkened the scene. "*UZO auf Brücke*," ordered the first watch officer, Oberleutnant Hans Möglich. A moment later, a sailor brought an object resembling a bulky pair of binoculars through the hatch. Möglich grasped the apparatus with gloved hands and mounted it on the pedestal in the bridge's center. This was the *Überwasserzieloptik*, or UZO, a Zeiss-built optical device linked to the boat's targeting calculator and used for torpedo attacks on the surface.[6]

For a moving object to hit another moving object with a third moving object requires solving a relative motion problem. The slide rules used in World War I had since been superseded by a more advanced tool for computing attack trigonometry in the form of an analog targeting calculator mounted on the tower compartment's inside starboard bulkhead. The calculator used multiple data inputs to compute a firing solution, that is, the heading on which a torpedo would intercept the ship. The Siemens-built calculator was more sophisticated than its British equivalent, though not as advanced as the American one.

Aiming the UZO (or the periscope, for submerged attacks) at the target ship provided the first variable—the bearing from the U-boat to the target—which was automatically transmitted to the calculator. The first watch officer then called out the ship's speed and range, the U-boat's relative bearing from the ship ("target angle" or "angle on the bow") and the desired torpedo speed. These values were manually entered into the computer by the bootsmann. The calculator's electromechanical cams then computed the gyro-angle, or directional heading, that would steer the torpedo on a course intersecting that of the target.

The *U-130* was racing toward its attack position when the calculator produced the gyro-angle. Inside tube one, a spindle which had plugged itself into the torpedo now rotated a directional ring to match the gyro-angle. Launching the weapon would then set its gyroscope spinning on an axis oriented straight ahead. While hurtling through the water, a mechanism detected that the ring and gyroscope were not aligned, causing the torpedo's fins to adjust its course until the gyroscope matched the ring. The rudders then straightened out and would only move again for course corrections. This self-steering capability enabled a torpedo to turn up to 90 degrees, eliminating the need to aim the boat itself at the target.

The torpedo was shoved from tube one and detonated against the *Frisco*'s hull seventy-two seconds later. "Steamer heels over a bit to starboard," Kals wrote in the log, "otherwise no visible effect." This was likely attributable in part to the *Frisco*'s buoyant cargo of lumber she was carrying from Savannah, Georgia. The *U-130*'s radioman then reported that their target was transmitting a distress message. Kals explained in the log: "Considering the coast's proximity, I don't wait and fire the coup de grâce from tube five."

The second torpedo's impact caused flames to sprout near the *Frisco*'s stern. "Crew abandons ship in two lifeboats," Kals observed. "Eventually the whole ship is burning furiously." He also noted "the first beat of the drum" with satisfaction, unaware that Reinhard Hardegen had claimed Operation Drumbeat's first kill when the *U-123* sank the *Cyclops* twenty-four hours earlier. The *U-130* departed to the southeast, the glow of the burning *Frisco* remaining visible against the night sky for another hour.[7]

Described as "dashing" by one enlisted sailor, Ernst Kals was a 36-year-old native of Saxony with a slender face distinguished by a prominent nose. This was Korvettenkapitän Kals' second patrol as commander. He sank three ships on his first patrol only weeks earlier, but BdU had recalled him to port for undisclosed reasons. Setting out on patrol again eleven days later, only after opening his sealed orders did Kals learn that the *U-130* was bound for North America as part of Gruppe Paukenschlag.

It was not only Canadian vigilance that vexed Kals, as poor visibility repeatedly forced him to submerge to avoid stumbling across air or sea patrols. "I can't risk the boat in the bad visibility to similar surprises as yesterday or inevitable air attacks," he wrote on 15 January. Electric heaters fought a losing battle for warmth inside the boat while nighttime air temperatures as low as 5° Fahrenheit made bridge watch miserable. Kals noted that "the intense cold, for which our crew is poorly equipped, causes a great deal of difficulty."

The *U-130* was 34 miles off Sydney, Nova Scotia on 17 January when a lookout spotted another freighter. Kals misjudged its speed, causing his two torpedoes to miss, then the merchantman spotted the U-boat and fled. He gave chase, but ice on the deck slowed the U-boat and spurred him to attack again before the target was out of range. The ship then abruptly decelerated, causing Kals' second pair of torpedoes to miss. He scowled.

He was about to order the boat turned to fire the stern tubes when a destroyer appeared. It was just 330 yards off his port beam and bearing down fast, apparently intending to ram. The bridge watch's immediate one-word alert was the same in German as in English:

"*Alaaaaarmm!!*"

The jangling alarm bell signaled an imminent crash dive while those on the bridge piled through the hatch and slid down the ladder into the control room. Kals, still on the bridge, screamed an order to run one propeller forward and the other backward at full speed. This pivoted the *U-130* hard to port, causing the destroyer's bow to miss the boat by 10 yards. Dodging this blow bought the Germans another few seconds, but Kals spotted a second destroyer as he followed the last lookout down the hatch.

A U-boat was strictly an ambush predator. Its torpedoes required time to aim, its guns were entirely inadequate for facing warships, and it lacked armor. A kommandant who was attacked on the surface usually opted to crash dive. Sailors in the control room would tilt the boat's hydroplanes while flooding its main ballast tanks starting from the bow. At the same time, the engineering crew switched the boat to electric power while maintaining enough forward speed for water flowing over the planes to angle the bow downward. Type IX crews trained to a standard of putting 30 feet of ocean over the pressure hull within thirty-five seconds.

This chaotic but well-rehearsed process commenced before the bridge was even clear. Air intake and exhaust ports were cranked shut, diesels unclutched, and the electric motors engaged at full speed. "*Fluten!*" bellowed the chief engineer. *Flood!* Men turned valves and handwheels that caused air to escape the ballast tanks with a roar as the *U-130*'s bow cut sharply under the surface. Kals yanked the tower hatch closed behind him, meanwhile, a stream of men rushed past him toward the forward torpedo room to use their combined bodyweight to help push the bow downward.

Suddenly, a voice shouted: "Intake head valve won't close!"

Ice had jammed open the air intake's outboard inlet, and 8 tons of seawater now flooded through it as the boat submerged. This additional weight suddenly turned the dive into an uncontrolled plunge, and the *U-130* lurched sharply forward as every loose item rolled or slid toward the bow. Seconds later, it smashed into the bottom with an impact that hurled Kals and his crew about the interior as the boat skidded across the rocky seafloor.

"Off! Everything off!" Pumps, fans, ventilation fans, the air compressor—anything that generated noise was hastily powered down. Kals clenched his jaw as voices became whispers and the chugging engines above them grew louder. The *U-130* was only 157 feet below the waves, far too shallow to offer any protection from the depth charge attack they knew was imminent.[8]

Depth charges were cylindrical explosive devices detonated by a hydrostatic trigger upon sinking to a predetermined depth. Their purpose was to breach a submarine's pressure hull or damage the submarine badly enough that it was forced to surface. First deployed during World War I, it was sonar's proliferation during the interwar years that finally made them a potent weapon against submarines of all navies. Depth charges would eventually account for more than half of U-boats destroyed in combat. Known by the Americans as "ashcans," the Germans termed them "*wabos*" (from *Wasserbomben*, or water bombs).

They were relatively crude weapons. The US Navy's primary depth charge in 1942, the Mark 7, carried 600 pounds of TNT yet still needed to explode within 30 feet to reliably breach a U-boat's pressure hull. This limitation, coupled with the frequent ambiguity of sonar contacts, meant that Allied destroyers often saturated an area with dozens or hundreds of them. Depth charges often frayed men's nerves more severely than they damaged the boat, but their psychological effect was considerable.

Exploding depth charges were "like punches in the pit of the gut," wrote *U-333* commander Peter Cremer. Blasts would rock a U-boat violently as lights went out, gauges shattered, pipes burst, and seawater sprayed into the interior. Some compared the experience to being inside a metal drum as sledgehammers battered it. "There is nothing you can do, you just sit there and wait," one U-boat veteran explained. Cremer recounted enduring a seven-hour depth charge bombardment off Florida. "There were trickles [of water] everywhere … The minutes became eternity, all sense of time was lost."[9]

Aboard the *U-130*, eyes looked upward as the swishing of the destroyers' propellers, or "screws," swelled louder. They waited with trepidation for the *klatsch, klatsch, klatsch* of wabos splashing into the sea. Waxen faces turned toward Kals. "When the charges start to explode, everyone looks to the officers," one sailor explained. During one depth charge barrage, *U-99* commander Otto Kretschmer reportedly put on a display of indifference for his crew by reading a novel without realizing the book was upside-down. Erich Topp was told by a subordinate's wife that "my husband says that 'when it is very dangerous, I go into the pocket of my captain.'"

The enemy's pumps and auxiliary motors became audible above them as the screws' metallic singing reaching a crescendo. The first destroyer was crossing directly overhead, but there were no splashes. No thundering detonations bracketed the hull. The sinister mechanical chorus instead receded as both destroyers continued past. As Kals surmised, "One can assume that the ice froze up their depth charge racks."

The appearance of two more destroyers the next day prompted the *U-130* to crash dive again. Its rudder jammed momentarily during the dive, and damage to a stern hydroplane was causing a loud scraping noise. A harbinger of better fortune arrived that same day when a radio message from BdU authorized Kals to venture into American waters if desired. The *U-130* had already turned south when he replied with his chosen new operational area, fuel status, and current location: "SHIFT PATROL AREA TO GRID CA 54 AND 57. 145 CBM. BB 83. KALS."[10]

The *U-130* was going to New Jersey.

***

25 January 1942
34 miles east-southeast of Atlantic City, New Jersey
02:59

Second mate Wilhelm Wilhelmsen, on duty since midnight, looked out across a black expanse of sea as the *Varanger* continued her uneventful journey northward. The night was clear and a northeasterly breeze stirred only a slight chop across the placid ocean, yet the temperature hovered around freezing and it became quite dark after moonset around 01:20. Unlike American-flagged ships, the *Varanger* traveled in radio silence and with her side lanterns and foremast lantern extinguished. At their current pace, the ship would make New York City in less than twelve hours.

Built in Amsterdam in 1925, the *Varanger* measured 470 feet long and 9,305 gross registered tons. She had left the Caribbean island of Curaçao on 16 January carrying 85,425 barrels of fuel oil. Most oceangoing merchant ships of that era used oil-fired steam engines, but the *Varanger* and many other Norwegian ships ran on diesel. A single British-made Mark IV naval gun mounted on the bow distinguished the tanker from American merchantmen, most of which were not yet armed.

Norwegians comprised the majority of the forty *Varanger* crewmen, most of whom were asleep. Rounding out her complement were three Scotsmen, two Americans, and a dachshund puppy and his mother adopted by the crew in South Africa. The Norwegians included Wilhelm Wilhelmsen and the two others on watch. Manning the helm was 19-year-old Kåre Brevik while 29-year-old Harry Karlsen served as lookout outside on the bridge wing.

A tanker featured two major structures above deck. The midship house was usually slightly forward of amidships and contained the bridge in addition to quarters for the officers and radioman. The aft deck house was located near the stern and generally housed the remainder of the crew. On most tankers, two lifeboats were located on either side of each structure. The space below decks was mostly occupied by between seven and nine massive cargo tanks.

The bridge where Wilhelmsen and Brevik were standing watch was on the highest enclosed level of the midship house and featured large forward-facing windows. Karlsen's lookout post was on the "bridge wing," an open-air platform that ran in front of and on either side of the bridge. Unlike the bridge itself, the wing was exposed to the elements. So, too, was the "flying bridge" on the midship house's roof from where the ship could be helmed during daylight. Wilhelmsen and Brevik watched the sea slide past, both men unaware that Ernst Kals was watching them.[11]

Twenty minutes earlier, the *U-130* had been southbound when the bridge watch sighted the low and elongated shape of a tanker on a reciprocal, or opposite, heading. Kals could have identified her by name using the boat's copy of Erich Gröner's *Merchant Fleets of the World*. This annual publication listed every merchant ship afloat along with images of their external structure, flag of registry, gross registered tonnage, and other details (Bruno Weyer's *Handbook of Naval Fleets* provided an analogous reference for naval vessels). Kals did not bother because it was clearly "a larger-than-average tanker of about 9500 GRT." The *U-130* reversed course.

The Gröner and Weyer manuals were useful for determining a ship's speed, which was a critical variable for the trigonometry of intercepting it with a torpedo. Cruising parallel to the target was one method of estimating speed, and the *U-130* accelerated until it was running alongside the *Varanger*. Kals briefly held station half a mile off the tanker's port side. This was roughly the limit of visibility that night, and a moonless sky negated the need to place the moon on the target's far side. After clocking the *Varanger* at around 10.5 knots, Kals sped forward to position the *U-130* for an attack from abeam.

A ship is widest at its "beam," and to be "abeam" means to face a ship's length at a right angle. U-boat commanders preferred to attack from abeam or slightly forward of it, that is, between 60 and 90 degrees relative to the target's length. Kals therefore positioned himself well forward of the *Varanger*'s bow and oriented the *U-130*'s bow perpendicular to her track. "Slow ahead," he ordered, conscious of his own white wake atop a black sea. The oblivious tanker drew nearer, approaching at a right angle to the U-boat.[12]

Oberleutnant Möglich shouted the *Varanger*'s speed and range, plus the target angle, down the open hatch. In the tower compartment below, the boatswain turned dials to enter the data into the targeting calculator. Möglich issued another command, and the bootsmann flipped a switch that synchronized the calculator with the UZO and the boat's gyrocompass. The UZO now transmitted the bearing to the calculator, and two red lights indicated that its servomotors were churning through the math. Both red lights then went out and a single white light replaced them to indicate that a firing solution had been achieved.

The gyro-angle was automatically programmed into the selected torpedo's gyroscope. As the *Varanger* and the *U-130* each steered their respective courses, the calculator would continually update the firing solution so long as Möglich kept the ship in the UZO's crosswires. The other inputs—torpedo speed and running depth—appeared on a display panel in the forward torpedo room which indicated a running depth of 5 meters and a speed of 46 mph. The mechanikermaat manually applied the settings by quickly but precisely adjusting wheels on the tubes.

"*Folgen!*" the mechanikermaat reported, confirming the torpedo room's readiness to launch. The petty officer rested his palm on the manual lever in case the electric launch system failed. On the bridge, Korvettenkapitän Kals lifted his binoculars again. The *Varanger* was 1,100 yards away at 03:01 when Möglich issued the launch command. The one-word order translated to "away" or "c'mon," and evoked the medieval archery command "loose."

"*Los!*"

The G7a ("a" for air) was one of the Kriegsmarine's two primary torpedoes in 1942. Measuring 23.6 feet long and weighing 3,369 pounds, the G7a was powered by liquid fuel which used compressed air as an oxidant. This produced steam that fed a four-cylinder engine capable of moving the G7a 3 miles at its fastest speed setting. Its major shortfall was the exhaust vented from its tail end, which left a visible trail of bubbles pointing back to its source. At 03:01, however, not a soul aboard the *Varanger* spotted the G7a barreling toward them.[13]

Thirty-six seconds after launch, the torpedo slammed into the *Varanger*'s port side just forward of the bridge and 16 feet below the waterline. The impact triggered the G7a's detonator to initiate a chemical reaction that instantly transformed the warhead's explosives into an expanding sphere of superheated gas. This released a tremendous amount of energy in the form of a shockwave that punched through the steel hull plates and ruptured at least one cargo tank. From the *U-130*'s bridge, Kals observed a "medium high, white-gray explosion plume."

On the *Varanger*'s bridge, the blast threw helmsman Kåre Brevik and second mate Wilhelm Wilhelmsen toward the starboard bulkhead. "Alarm, sound it! Go!" Wilhelmsen shouted at Brevik. Mute with fear, the teenager shakily made his way toward the red alarm button on the aft bulkhead. Wilhelmsen grabbed the handle of the engine order telegraph, a circular brass instrument displaying various commands, and cranked its pointer to "STOP."

At the same time, Brevik's palm heel smashed the red button on the aft bulkhead. A shrill jangling like a schoolhouse bell filled the tanker's passageways and compartments. Wilhelmsen dashed toward the radio room as Brevik ventured outside to the flying bridge. There the helmsman found Harry Karlsen splattered with oil and gingerly regaining his feet. "*Er du skadet?*" Brevik asked as he offered a hand. *Are you hurt?* "I don't think so," a dazed Karlsen replied. "Let's go," Brevik urged. "Wilhelmsen's radioing for help right now."

Wilhelmsen was just stepping into the radio room when the ship lost electricity, plunging the *Varanger*'s interior into darkness. "*Faen i Helvete*," he swore upon confirming that power to the wireless telegraph was also out. The second mate grabbed the British Admiralty codebooks and messages and stuffed them into a lead-weighted sack before hurrying out. Wilhelmsen vacated the now-empty bridge for the main deck, where he launched the weighted sacks overboard before setting off to find the captain.

The explosion launched a slumbering Captain Carl Horne out of his rack and onto the floor, and he stumbled to the light switch as the pistons in his slumber-fogged brain started firing. A distinct odor indicated why his feet felt wet, and flipping the light switch revealed a layer of oil oozing from right to left across the deck as the ship began listing to port. "*Splitte mine bramseil …*" The alarm cut through the air as if to confirm this was not some terrible dream, but darkness returned seconds later when the electricity failed. His luck, it seemed, had finally run out.

Horne stepped outside into the evening chill and hastily assessed the situation. He knew that the hull's damage might not be enough to sink a compartmentalized vessel filled with buoyant oil. But that same cargo was both highly flammable and leaking from the tanks, threatening to immolate the *Varanger* and everything around her. Their attacker was also presumably lining up another shot, yet the ship's only means of defense had been knocked out when the explosion partly ripped the 4-inch gun mount from the deck.

"*Kaptein!*"

The *Varanger* crewmen were spilling out onto the deck in various states of undress when Capt Horne heard the voice of Arnfinn Krokeide, his first mate. Krokeide was mobile and coherent, but had sustained painful injuries to his ribs and jaw. Horne quickly relayed the order to abandon ship. The skipper had just departed when Wilhelm Wilhelmsen also found Krokeide. "No power to the radio, but I'm going to try one more time," Wilhelmsen reported. Krokeide, grimacing in pain, nodded and quickly briefed Wilhelmsen on the status of the lifeboats.

The No. 2 lifeboat, on the port-side boat deck, had been blown to splinters by the torpedo. The ship's list to port also prevented use of No. 4, located at the aft deck house on the same side, since it could be crushed if the *Varanger* capsized. "We'll have to take the starboard boats," Arnfinn Krokeide informed Wilhelmsen. "*Skynde deg.*" Hurry.

Tankers and freighters carried four lifeboats that each measured approximately 27 feet long and 8 feet wide. Typically wooden in 1942, one was usually equipped with an engine. Each boat was lowered by a pair of hand-operated metal cranes known as davits. On a tanker, lifeboats No. 1 and 2 were located on the starboard and port sides of the midship house, respectively. These were launched from the boat deck, usually located on the midship house's second level, just below the bridge. Near the stern, lifeboats No. 3 and 4 were located on the starboard and port sides of the aft deck house.

A frenetic but orderly evacuation was soon underway aboard the *Varanger*. The foredeck was broken upward at a sharp angle which forced men to crawl through gaps and holes to access the starboard side. Ship's cook Rolf Andersen snagged the two dachshunds, but the mother dog bounded from Andersen's arms and ran off.[14]

Kals and Möglich were watching from 700 yards away, their breath rising as clouds of vapor in the cold air. The kommandant could see the crew abandoning ship and knew that the tanker's engines had been stopped, yet it remained afloat. "Give him one more." A second torpedo careened toward the *Varanger* at 03:07, but both officers scowled as thirty seconds turned to forty, then fifty. "*Diese verdammten Aale …*" Kals muttered angrily, insisting in his log that "from a distance of 600 meters and on an absolutely stopped ship, only possible cause is a torpedo malfunction."

"*Noch Einen,*" Kals ordered. *Another one.*

After a second unsuccessful attempt to broadcast a distress call, Wilhelmsen departed the *Varanger*'s radio shack to find himself alone on the starboard boat deck. The No. 1 lifeboat was not in its davits. Looking down, he saw that it was nearly full and had just reached the water. Farther aft, Wilhelmsen sighted the similarly crowded No. 3 boat in the process of being lowered. He now had to descend to the main deck and use the rope ladder draped over the hull to reach the waterline.

Wilhelmsen's plans changed abruptly when the Germans' next blow fell at 03:13. Another torpedo smashed into the *Varanger*'s port side halfway between the midship house and stern, and Wilhelmsen immediately leapt from the boat deck as the foundering tanker convulsed. He plummeted through a layer of oil across the ocean's surface and into the 35° Fahrenheit water. The others quickly pulled the gasping and hyperventilating second mate into the lifeboat. Wilhelmsen was now covered head-to-toe in oil, as were numerous others.

The mariners expeditiously rowed the two lifeboats away as the *Varanger* went down by the stern. They had moved about 300 yards when a third explosion sounded at 03:24. The blast of the fourth torpedo and third impact resonated across the frigid sea as "a tremendous column of flames emerges from the ship," according to Kals. Flames illuminated the crew's shocked expressions as the *Varanger*'s stern sank to the seafloor 140 feet below, leaving her foreship protruding at an angle and partly veiled by smoke.

The *U-boat Commander's Handbook* stated that "it is better to destroy little than to damage much," and Eastern Sea Frontier had already noticed that U-boats frequently fired additional torpedoes at ships that were damaged but still afloat. ESF staff observed in January 1942 that "as many torpedoes were fired as necessary to sink a vessel or to prevent successful salvage." This was the *Fangschuss*, or killing shot from close range. BdU deemed this necessary to ensure a ship went to the bottom or was at least damaged beyond the possibility of salvage.

The three torpedoes' explosions were powerful enough to be heard and felt ashore, reportedly as far north as Beesley's Point. Tremors and rattling windows awakened residents in Sea Isle City, Wildwood, and Atlantic City. Fourteen-year-old Michael Davies was awakened in Sea Isle City when his bed shook. Several miles from the *Varanger*, fisherman Dewey Monichetti heard these same blasts as his commute to the cod banks continued. Glancing at his son and deck hand, he saw that both were still asleep.[15]

Not far from Monichetti, the merchant crew rowed west as they erected the No. 1 lifeboat's sail. Capt Horne wanted to put some distance between themselves and the wreck before starting the No. 3 boat's motor. Twenty minutes after shoving off from the wreck, a terrified shout from one of the Norwegians made their blood run cold:

"*Der borte! De kommer, tyskerne!*"

Every man turned still as stone, eyes wide and hearts pounding, as the *U-130* approached. Light from the burning *Varanger* backlit the U-boat, casting its contours in sharp detail as the muscular thrum of its diesel engines grew louder. Darkness and smoke obscuring the Germans on its bridge lent the vessel an air of otherworldly malevolence.

"*Alle sammen, vær stille! Ikke beveg deg!*" Captain Horne ordered. "Silence! Nobody move!" he added in English. Anxious murmuring dissipated, but fear remained palpable. Horne dreaded that one of his men might shout an insult at their assailants, and he wished to neither provoke the U-boat's crew nor make clear their intention to make for shore. "We didn't dare leave," Horne stated later, as he did not want "to give the submarine commander an excuse to shoot us." The *U-130* passed as close as 100 yards, but if the Germans saw their victims then they did not acknowledge them. The boat soon melded back into the night and disappeared.

Encounters of this sort between merchant crew survivors and U-boats were common along the East Coast in 1942. The effects of psychological stress on perception and memory, however, meant that these firsthand accounts were not always accurately remembered. The *Varanger* crew's imaginations unsurprisingly now ran wild, and they would later claim that two U-boats circled them like sharks for half an hour.

After the *U-130* melted away into the night, those in the No. 3 lifeboat tossed a towline to their companions in No. 1. A motor then revved to life as one set off to the west with the other in tow. The men could hear an airplane somewhere overhead. Capt Horne reflected on their luck: his entire crew had made it off the *Varanger* alive.[16]

***

22 miles east of Townsends Inlet, New Jersey
08:38

Dawn's first glimmers lightened the winter darkness shortly after 06:00, the sun rising an hour later. The three fishermen on the *San Gennaro* were pulling in their lines when something on the horizon caught Dewey Monichetti's eye. "What is it,

The *Varanger* after sunrise on 25 January 1942. (US National Archives)

pop?" asked Dewey's son John. Monichetti squinted. "Couple 'a sailboats ..." They had open tops and appeared crowded with people. He later recalled thinking, *I'll tell those poor devils they are too far out and might get into trouble and maybe lose their lives.*

More than three decades at sea told him that something was awry. It soon became clear that these were not sailboats, but rather lifeboats with sails erected. "*Ma-donna mia ...*" Monichetti's tone turned urgent. "John, Ed," he gestured without taking his eyes off the boats. "Get the towline."

Some of the *Varanger* men were so covered with oil that only the whites of their eyes were visible, and a few were only partially dressed. "We made a line, fast," Monichetti recounted. The fishermen took a few of the most injured aboard before making for shore at full speed, but pulling the two lifeboats slowed the *San Gennaro*'s progress. Help appeared when they encountered Monichetti's friend Dominick Constantino in the *Eileen*. Constantino took one of the two lifeboats in tow.

The *Varanger* was still standing on end after dawn, and a US Army Air Forces pilot from the 104th Observation Squadron in Atlantic City sighted the wreck's bow protruding from the surface at 10:10. He also sighted the *San Gennaro* and *Eileen*, which he misidentified as Coast Guard vessels, towing the lifeboats toward shore. Naval Air Station Lakehurst in New Jersey subsequently dispatched the Navy blimp *K-3* to the scene.

The *San Gennaro* and *Eileen* docked around noon near 43rd Street and Park Road in Sea Isle City, where more than a hundred curious locals gathered for a glimpse of the oil-stained *San Gennaro*. Coast Guardsmen transported the cold and exhausted *Varanger* crew to Coast Guard Station Townsends Inlet on Landis Avenue between 81st and 82nd Streets. Requests from the public to meet the survivors were denied, and one mariner who left the station via a basement door was quickly returned by the Coast Guardsmen.[17]

***

The *U-130* received a terse congratulatory message from headquarters that evening: "TO KALS. WELL DONE. BDU."

The commander described his crew's reaction as "intense joy in boat." He used his last torpedo to sink the tanker *Francis E. Powell* off Maryland on 27 January. The *U-130* was making its return transit when BdU arranged a rendezvous with Heinrich Bleichrodt's *U-109*, which was low on fuel. Kals transferred 5,020 gallons of diesel fuel to Bleichrodt on 6 February, and the *U-130* arrived at Lorient nineteen days later.

A kommandant faced each patrol's final ordeal alone. Shortly after returning to port, he would find himself sitting across a table from Admiral Dönitz, who reviewed the U-boat's logbook line by line. Vater Karl's feedback could be scathing—particularly if he identified insufficient aggressiveness—but he did not withhold accolades when he felt them deserved. Dönitz praised Ernst Kals' work off the United States and Canada as a "thoughtfully executed and successful patrol."[18]

***

One of the ship's two dachshunds was the only life lost in the *Varanger* attack, but the puppy Pluto survived thanks to the cook's quick thinking. Like his two-legged shipmates, Pluto was washed with kerosene to remove the oil from his body. Local woman Jennie Swing scrubbed the dog for an hour before his white paws and chest became visible again.

None of the crew's injuries were life-threatening, though several suffered from oil toxemia caused by swallowing and inhaling the ship's cargo. They were treated by local physician Dr Alexander Stuart, who deemed them "a tough gang." The most badly hurt was first mate Arnfinn Krokeide, who was hospitalized in Philadelphia with a broken jaw and bruised ribs.

The *Varanger* crew was lodged at St Joseph's Catholic Church on Landis Avenue. They devoured a meal prepared by Dewey Monichetti's wife, Rosina, and other South Jersey residents donated shoes and clothing. Local boy Michael Davies, who had been awakened the previous night when explosions shook his bed, arrived at St Joseph's for his altar boy duties to discover forty exhausted men dozing on cots in the church basement.

Reverend John McKechnie of Sea Isle City's Methodist church also visited the *Varanger* crew. "Where are you from, young man?" he asked a 16-year-old cabin boy from Scotland. "Clydebank, sir," the youth responded. McKechnie's face lit up. He, too, was from Clydebank. The reverend asked the cabin boy whether he knew his brother, Andrew. "I sure do, he lives just around the corner from my parents." The conversation revealed that some whom Reverend McKechnie knew in Clydebank had been killed by German bombs in March 1941.

Navy intelligence interviewed all survivors of enemy action in US waters, and Lieutenant Gilbert Countryman immediately drove from Fourth Naval District in Philadelphia to interview the *Varanger* crew. Norway's vice consul in Philadelphia arrived the following morning with two buses to take the crew to the immigration center in Gloucester City, New Jersey where they dined heartily alongside German and Italian nationals who had been interned after Pearl Harbor.

Reporters found Dewey Monichetti at his fish shack in Sea Isle City, and they were eventually permitted to interview the *Varanger* crew in Gloucester City. The survivors spoke freely about their experiences, though most were reluctant to provide their names due to family members living in occupied Norway. "We didn't know what was coming next," one stated while piling roast beef into his mouth. "An experience like this only makes them more determined to get another boat and return to sea," Capt Horne beamed. "They were all very cool and I was proud of them … the only regret, aside from the loss of the ship and cargo, was that one of our two canine mascots was lost."

Dewey Monichetti (right) and his son, John (left). (Courtesy of Joseph Bilby)

Horne politely answered questions from a horde of reporters. When they learned that he had sailed throughout the Great War without finding himself on the receiving end of a torpedo, one newsman asked whether he still felt lucky. "I've always been lucky," Horne replied with a smile, "and I'm glad my luck held out this time." He then excused himself to phone his wife.[19]

***

There was little luck to be found along the eastern seaboard in January 1942, however, and five more ships went down within forty-eight hours of the *Varanger* sinking. "A pattern for enemy attacks was clearly discerned as January ended," noted the Eastern Sea Frontier war diary. It was clear that "operations against submarines at this time are very different from those existing in the first World War." Unlike the U-Kreuzers, these were faster and bolder adversaries who "dashed in at night on the surface, delivered an attack, and retired at high speed on the surface."

On 22 January, ESF attempted to staunch shipping losses by pushing the shipping lanes farther offshore, away from the U-boats' shallow-water haunts. This accomplished nothing. Nine days later, shipping lanes were instead pulled as close to shore as safe navigation permitted and the Navy finally ordered coastwise merchantmen to sail with lights extinguished. "The answer to the problem of the submarine lay in a different direction," Rear Admiral Andrews posited as the maritime butchery continued into February. "But, as the month ended, there was little promise that the answer could be made in the foreseeable future."

The Allies were also about to lose their secret weapon against the Gray Wolves. On 1 February 1942, one week after the *Varanger* attack, the machines deciphering message traffic at Bletchley Park fell silent. The Germans had added a fourth rotor to the Enigma machine, supplanting the HYDRA cipher with a new version called TRITON. The Allies' window into enemy communications slammed shut.

Shore-based high-frequency direction finding stations could still indicate U-boats' approximate locations, but only when they transmitted. Even this provided merely a general idea of Ubootwaffe strength and movements. HF/DF was enough, however, to suggest that the worst was yet to come. On 9 February, British intelligence flashed another update to the US Navy: at least ten more U-boats were westbound across the Atlantic.[20]

CHAPTER SIX

India Arrow

"Reserve, I pray, one lusty cheer
For men whose names you never hear.
Who win no stripes and wear no braid,
But face great dangers unafraid.
Who take both peace and war in stride,
Who, when torpedoes strike, go overside
Perchance to be the lucky men
Who live to sail the seas again."
—Anonymous, "A Toast to the Merchant Mariner" (July 1943)

3 February 1942
59 miles southeast of Cape May, New Jersey
23:42

Nine days after Ernst Kals sank the *Varanger*, Kapitänleutnant Werner Winter watched a darkened freighter through the periscope while the obersteuermann counted off the torpedo's run time in seconds. Winter then heard and felt a gratifying *thump* as a white fir tree of water rose toward the gleaming moon, briefly veiling his target. The ship's lights turned on as it slowed to a halt, yet remained on an even keel in defiance of the 600 pounds of explosives which had just detonated against its hull.

"He's a stubborn one," Winter noted, using the German-language convention of referring to vessels as males when the name was unknown. The kommandant was addressing Oberleutnant Konstantin von Rappard, his first watch officer, who was crouched beside him at the torpedo data calculator. Winter removed his eye from the periscope. "*L.I.*, surface!" he shouted to the chief engineer. "Gun crews up!"

All U-boats in 1942 were armed with an artillery cannon on the foredeck and a 20mm antiaircraft gun on the wintergarten, or circular platform at the bridge's aft end. Type IXs, being larger, also featured a 37mm gun on the aft deck. Stowed inside the boat were Mauser M1934 handguns, MP 40 machine pistols, Karabiner 98k rifles, and up to four MG 34 machine guns. Although these small arms were seldom needed, the large guns mounted topside were utilized extensively. The *U-103* rose toward the surface as the gun teams retrieved ammunition from beneath the control room's deck plates. From the radio room, the funkgast reported a mayday over the 600-meter frequency:

SOS, THIS IS HPOC. 38° 05' NORTH, 74° 50' WEST, TORPEDOED, SINKING FAST. SOS, THIS IS HPOC. SINKING, PUTTING BOATS OUT NOW ...

The conning tower hatch clanged open and Winter emerged with a train of subordinates in tow. A full moon illuminated the bridge and deck, robbing steel and sea of their coloring and casting the entire scene in black and gray. The four men immediately following Winter assumed the standard lookout positions. The gunners emerged next, the first three manning the 20mm on the wintergarten. Three more gunners used the ladder rungs on the outside of the conning tower to descend to the aft deck where they began readying the 37mm. Others stood ready to shuttle ammunition from below deck. "Aim at the upper level of the deck house," Winter ordered. "He's chatty."

One sailor seated a stripper clip of twenty high-explosive shells in the 20mm while a second man cranked the elevation wheel that lowered the barrel into a horizontal position. A third pressed himself against two padded shoulder stocks and rotated the barrel toward the target. On the aft deck below, a man on the 37mm's right side leaned forward into a similar harness and traversed the barrel outboard. A man to his left loaded the gun while another man, in between them and directly behind the 37mm, squinted through its sighting device. Ammunition and actions *click*ed and *schlack*ed.

A verbal command was passed, then a deafening cacophony erupted as both weapons opened fire. Streams of green tracers spurted over the flat sea, their neon hue becoming more intermittent as the ammunition's sequence transitioned to alternating tracer and armor-piercing shells. The 20mm's muzzle spat four shells per second in disciplined bursts, the man operating its palm-lever trigger pausing only long enough for the loader to feed another magazine into the weapon.

Overlaying the 20mm's staccato bark was the booming percussion of the 37mm. A German squinting through an optical sight while adjusting a handwheel was not aiming the 37mm, but rather stabilizing it as the boat swayed. The shooter kept his body firmly pressed against the weapon's shoulder stirrups as he squeezed off glowing incendiary tracer shells at two-second intervals. The fully automatic 37mm deployed later in the war would frequently jam, but the *U-103*'s single-shot version cycled flawlessly as it hurled high-explosive projectiles more than twice the 20mm shells' weight.

The gunners aimed just aft of the bridge, where a merchantman's radio room was usually located. A furious maelstrom of metal ripped through the midship house; the mayday transmissions abruptly ceased. "*Feuer einstellen!*" The clamor abated, replaced by the sound of waves lapping against the *U-103*'s outer hull. Acrid smoke drifted past Winter on the bridge as he observed lifeboats detaching from the lightless ship. Though immobile and listing, it remained steadfastly afloat.

Each compartment or cargo space on a ship represents a separate pocket of buoyancy and, depending on the flooding's severity, even a badly damaged vessel can remain afloat. Another factor is cargo. An empty freighter is lighter and its air-filled cargo spaces are buoyant whereas heavy cargo like iron ore will cause a ship to sink faster. This particular freighter's distress transmission betrayed its identity as the Panamanian-flagged *San Gil*, a United Fruit Company ship carrying bananas to Philadelphia.

This made it no less desirable a target. Dönitz's strategy considered tonnage to be fungible, as a freighter hauling bananas to Philadelphia on one trip could easily carry aircraft parts or artillery shells to Murmansk on the next. Even sending fruit to the seafloor had strategic value considering that Florida citrus fruit constituted a significant proportion of the British population's vitamin C intake.

The crippled *San Gil* clung stubbornly to her remaining buoyancy, leading Winter to sarcastically remark in his log that "the steamer apparently floats on its cargo." He was loath to expend another torpedo and preferred to instead use the 105mm cannon to finish her off. His victim's distress call had included its location, however, and a relatively shallow depth of 130 feet would leave the *U-103* nowhere to hide if unwanted company arrived. Kapitänleutnant Winter grudgingly instructed Oberleutnant von Rappard to fire another eel.

Known as "fish" in the US Navy and Royal Navy, the Germans knew torpedoes as "eels" due to the coating of brown grease applied to reduce drag. Von Rappard set the torpedo to a running depth of 3.5 meters to hit the *San Gil* low on her hull, but a depth-keeping malfunction caused it to run shallow and strike just below the waterline. Winter scowled, but the cumulative damage was now sufficient to seal the ship's demise. The freighter slouched lower as its compartments flooded, and the *U-103* turned away on a southward heading as the *San Gil* slipped under the waves.[1]

***

6 February 1942
Jersey City, New Jersey

Two days after the *U-103* sank the *San Gil*, Amelia Proehl and her three daughters were preparing a welcome-home celebration at their house in Jersey City. The family's only son, 23-year-old Edward Proehl, was due home that day when the *India Arrow* made port. Edward's parents had initially been thrilled when he joined the Merchant Marine service. He had been unemployed when he registered for the draft in 1940, and going to sea seemed like an opportunity for valuable life experience and an honest wage. Edward's employment also exempted him from conscription since any mariner who went more than thirty days without sailing received a draft notice.

Yet a shadow hung over the Proehl home on Lincoln Street. This was no longer 1940, and the world was more dangerous for a young American man than it had been for a long time. In particular, the past three weeks' headlines about German raiders offshore had shifted their outlook significantly. Amelia Proehl looked at the clock, then again at the front door. *Shouldn't Eddie be here by now?*[2]

***

The US Navy publicly acknowledged ten sinkings along the East Coast from the U-boats' arrival on 12 January through month's end. In fact, twenty-two ships had been destroyed and one damaged (the tanker *Malay* limped back to port). Seventeen of these were attacked inshore of the boundary denoting Eastern Sea Frontier's 200-nautical mile limit. Most of January's 796 fatalities were merchant mariners, but 108 civilian passengers perished when the *U-66* torpedoed the passenger ship *Lady Hawkins* on 19 January. Nine more ships went down off Canada, killing 231.

January's fury slackened toward month's end as the Operation Drumbeat U-boats exhausted their torpedoes and reached the limit of their fuel. Any hopes for a reprieve, however, were dashed when February's first six days saw ten more ships sunk in the Western Atlantic. Six of these were sunk within ESF waters. Rear Admiral Andrews' staff at ESF correctly deduced what the ebb and surge in attacks indicated: the next wave of U-boats had arrived.

Drumbeat's success convinced Karl Dönitz that American waters presently represented the war's decisive theater. "If we engage all our Gray Wolves along the American coast," Dönitz argued, "we will be able to bleed enemy shipping to death." On 22 January, however, Hitler ordered every available U-boat north to thwart what he believed was an imminent Allied amphibious assault in German-occupied Norway. Dönitz was partly mollified the next day when the dictator's naval adjutant phoned naval high command to report that the Führer "had noted with great satisfaction the rising figures of sinkings off the American coast." The East Coast offensive would continue, albeit still with fewer forces than Dönitz wanted.

The admiral's frustration boiled as the ensuing weeks saw twenty U-boats cruising fruitlessly in the approaches to Norway, and he would later estimate that this saved half a million tons of Allied shipping. "Can anyone tell me what good tanks and trucks and airplanes are if the enemy doesn't have fuel for them?" Dönitz asked bitterly. "Yet the high command can't see it."

Although the "shortage of boats prevented us from taking full advantage of the opportunities" along the East Coast, Dönitz was determined to at least ensure "that this exceptionally favorable area was continuously occupied." The coming months would see a stream of U-boats departing French ports, with each boat being dispatched as soon as it was combat-ready. Three left during the first week of January and reached US shores just as the five Drumbeat boats were beginning their return voyages.[3]

***

2 February 1942
142 miles southeast of Atlantic City, New Jersey
03:32

One of the three U-boats that set sail for the United States in early January was the *U-103*, a Type IXB under Kapitänleutnant Werner Winter. The 29-year-old from Hamburg had commanded a Type II boat in the Baltic and North Sea during the war's first weeks before being transferred to BdU headquarters. His independent streak and receding hairline evoked a younger version of Admiral Dönitz, and *Vater Karl* himself had mentored him during Winter's ten months on staff duty. The younger officer leveraged this relationship to tactfully insist on another sea command, to which Dönitz eventually relented. Winter subsequently took command of the *U-103* in August 1941 and scored two sinkings on his first patrol.

Characterized as "a gentleman officer of the old school" by *U-103* crewman Peter Hansen, Werner Winter harbored quiet concerns about National Socialism and the coterie of vulgar mediocrities who had risen with Hitler's tide. He had gravitated toward Dönitz during his staff tour in part because the admiral appeared to embody traditional military virtues. Nazi influence on the Kriegsmarine was partly overt and policy-based, such as the 1934 expulsion of all Jews from naval service, but subtler effects stemmed from a political culture that tacitly rewarded vanity and egoism.

Few officers embodied this better than *U-123* commander Reinhard Hardegen. During the *U-103*'s westerly transit, Winter received three updates from Hardegen as the "Eins Zwei Drei" racked up eight ships sunk and one damaged off the East Coast. These reports provided actionable, real-time operational information to BdU and other boats, but Winter also knew that Hardegen was a braggart who reveled in trumpeting his successes to his peers.

Nazi egoism aside, the nature of submarine warfare in World War II meant that a U-boat captain's trade was an inherently personal one. "To a greater extent than in any other type of warship, officers and crew were simple extensions of the commanding officer's will," explained naval historian Peter Padfield, and Lothar-Günther Buchheim wrote that "every hit you scored was a kind of vindication of yourself to the crew." Divesting pride from duty was a greater challenge for some than others; ace commander Joachim Schepke's habit of exaggerating his scores led to the sarcastic term "Schepke tonnage."[4]

The *U-103* was 470 miles east of Atlantic City, New Jersey when a speech by Adolf Hitler was received via shortwave transmission. The 30 January address specifically extolled the Ubootwaffe, but the sound of the Führer's voice over the intercom disgusted at least one man aboard. Oberleutnant Oskar-Heinz Kusch was a lanky 23-year-old from Berlin and the only child of liberal middle-class parents. A talented artist, he wore his blond hair unusually long for a military officer and often sported a pencil mustache in port. Kusch's quiet demeanor belied a blunt outspokenness and irreverent sense of humor, both of which he used to disparage National Socialism.

"Concerning our present regime," he once told a pair of midshipmen, "you as higher educated human beings and prospective officers must be above such views." Oskar Kusch had entered the Kriegsmarine primarily because the *Gestapo*, the Nazis' infamous secret police, had placed him on a watchlist that effectively blacklisted him from civilian universities. A draft board officer noticed his sailing experience and recommended that he apply to the naval academy, which Kusch learned did not require the police certificate he was unable to obtain.

Kapitänleutnant Winter thought highly of his third-in-command. "An excellent officer," he wrote in Kusch's official performance evaluation. "He exhibits much heart and cheerfulness toward his subordinates, but at the same time a firm hand and determination ... in front of the enemy, he always demonstrates considerable tenacity and daring." Winter also credited him with "total dependability" and "unusual boldness." Kusch had been awarded the Iron Cross, Second Class in November 1941 and would receive the First Class award in six months' time.

Enlisted personnel also held Kusch in high esteem. Even Bootsmannsmaat Peter Marl, who by his own admission disliked most officers, wrote that "it was a pity there were not more of Kusch's type." The Austrian petty officer recalled how "Kusch inspired his men and never pulled rank or acted the conceited big shot. He cared deeply about the people serving under him." Marl also credited Kusch with one of the most valued military traits: "Even in tight situations, Kusch always kept his sense of humor."

For Kusch, naval service represented something of a refuge from the ideological poison that had corroded so many German institutions since 1933. His romantic sense of patriotism saw it as an opportunity to serve the Fatherland, with all the adventure and social respectability that entailed, for the price of only nominal genuflection at the National Socialist altar. Only the depth of Kusch's revulsion to Nazism was noteworthy, however—his ethical logic was not.

Kapitänleutnant Winter's uneasy reservations about National Socialism were more tempered than Kusch's disgust, but he shared his subordinate's perspective on military service. Neither man saw a contradiction between his worldview and his professional duties, as both believed that serving the nation imposed certain professional obligations regardless of who ruled in Berlin. Both Winter and Kusch would learn the depths of Nazi inhumanity firsthand before war's end, however, and one of them would pay dearly for it.[5]

The U-103 was 340 miles off Fenwick Island, Delaware in the pre-dawn darkness of 31 January when

Oskar-Heinz Kusch, 1943. (Deutsches U-Boot-Museum)

moonlight revealed a smudge of engine exhaust on the horizon. A freighter soon became visible. Kapitänleutnant Winter maneuvered ahead and submerged to attack beneath rough seas washing continuously over the periscope head. He fired a single torpedo, which missed. Another missed four minutes later, then a third. Winter smacked the periscope column in frustration, recalling how late U-boat ace Günther Prien once sarcastically asked how he could be expected to fight with a "wooden gun."

Technical issues plagued German torpedoes during the first half of the war, with one assessment during the conflict's opening weeks indicating that one in three were duds (US Navy submarines suffered similar problems). This was fortunate for Winston Churchill, who was aboard HMS *Nelson* in October 1939 when two eels launched by the *U-56* thumped harmlessly off the battleship's hull. Werner Winter had fired torpedoes at a Polish submarine and a British submarine in September 1939, but malfunctions thwarted both attacks.[6]

The Kriegsmarine identified two mechanical culprits. One was the torpedoes' depth-keeping mechanism; commanders widely reported firing eels that ran either too shallow ("surface runners") or too deep. Running deep was more widespread and more concerning because a surface runner would at least hit its target whereas running deep risked missing altogether. The Torpedo Directorate was initially reluctant to acknowledge the depth-control issue and opted to instead focus on the other failure point: the magnetic detonator.

During the war's first months, the Germans set their torpedoes to run 7–13 feet beneath a target ship's keel. The steel hull triggered the warhead's magnetic detonator as it passed underneath, and the resulting blast struck the target from below. This circumvented warships' belt armor and was particularly devastating against merchant vessels because it directed the shockwave against the keel, or lowest part of the hull. The explosion carved a large hole in the sea while heaving a ship partly out of the water. If it remained intact, this flexed its bow and stern downward. A ship could then fall back down atop the void, which left its midsection unsupported while flexing the bow and stern upward. No maritime engineering could withstand this immense stress, which could break ships in half.

Yet this counted for little if a torpedo did not reach its target or failed to explode when it did, as occurred countless times in 1939 and 1940. The "Torpedo Crisis" finally came to a head during the Norwegian campaign in April/May 1940 when three-quarters of U-boat torpedoes failed, sparking a scandal that saw several Torpedo Directorate officers court-martialed. In May, Dönitz ordered the magnetic detonators removed from service until they could be redesigned. This left only impact detonators, which triggered the warhead when the torpedo's nose struck a ship's hull.[7]

Mindful of fuel consumption, Werner Winter broke off pursuit of the freighter and resumed his original westward course. He contemplated transmitting the ship's course and location to BdU, but decided against it. It would be unwise to risk triangulation by American HF/DF considering he was unsure whether any U-boats were even near enough to act on such a report. The closest was Ernst Kals' *U-130*, which had sunk the tanker *Varanger* six days earlier, but Kals was 100 miles southeast and had no more torpedoes left.

The seas inauspiciously worsened as the *U-103* drew closer to American soil. Cold water splashing through the tower hatch rendered control room equipment damp and slimy to the touch. A few men suffered from seasickness, the "final exam" of any sailor. Oberleutnant Oskar Kusch's clothing was already wet at around 03:40 on 2 February when he assembled the men of his bridge watch and began preparing to go topside.

Wearing infrared goggles to adjust their eyes to the dark, the four lookouts each donned an oilskin, or long coat made of black rubberized material. They added rubber sea boots, black overtrousers, and a wide-brimmed hat known as a sou'wester. The lookouts pulled up their oilskin collars and tied their sou'westers under their chins, then Kusch led them up the conning tower ladder.

The first watch officer, second watch officer, and chief helmsman (obersteuermann) each led one of three bridge watches, or lookout rotations. The remainder of each four-man team comprised the bootsmann or one of his two petty officers as the *Brückenmaat*, or bridge mate, and two junior enlisted sailors. Each spent their four-hour watch facing away from one other while monitoring a 90-degree arc of sea and sky for threats or targets. The captain often accompanied them. The radiomen and engineering department did not stand bridge watch, instead manning their own watch rotations below deck.

Just before 04:00, Oberleutnant Kusch, Bootsmannsmaat Marl, and the two others climbed the ladder to the bridge where they found the current watchstanders eager to surrender their posts. Winds of over 25 mph whistled and howled, flattening oilskins against tired bodies and slashing at unshaven faces as breakers sprayed over the bridge. A dark expanse of white crests stretching in every direction lifted the *U-103* and smashed it down again, over and over, in an unceasing rhythm that rattled their bones. Freezing green waves, towering up to a dozen feet, left the four men gasping and white-knuckling the gunwale. The Atlantic's violence reminded them why they were tethered to the boat via heavy canvas belts. Four months earlier, all four of the *U-106*'s lookouts had been snatched by a rogue wave. They were never seen again.

Kusch and Marl were about halfway through their watch when the *U-103* reached the edge of the North American continental shelf shortly before sunrise on 2 February. They would soon observe searchlights shining from the US Army defenses at the Delaware Bay entrance. Marl recollected that "the whole sky was lit up by spotlights," sarcastically adding that "apparently the [American] soldiers had never heard about the war." The Atlantic seemed to greet the Germans' arrival with a bow of respect, the waves slackening to a chop of about 4 feet, yet the pale morning sun hid from them behind a callous gray sky. The *U-103* turned onto a northwesterly heading as heavy snowfall began.

Visibility fell from 3 miles to just 1 mile over the next four hours as a front of cold continental air mixed with evaporating seawater to create fog known as "sea smoke." The bridge watch nonetheless sighted a tanker off the port quarter at 10:25, and Kapitänleutnant Winter trained his binoculars over the whitecaps as the bridge itself pitched and heaved. "*Gut!*" he shouted over the noise of the waves and diesels. *Good!* He patted an approving hand on the shoulder of a lookout's salt-encrusted leather coat. "*Sehr gut!*" *Very good!*

The Germans maneuvered ahead of the tanker but lost sight of it by noon amid the driving snow and sea smoke. A northward heading only revealed more churning sea, but instinct told Winter his quarry could not be far. "Clear the bridge to dive!" he shouted. He had a specific solution in mind for reacquiring his target. Where eyesight failed them, sound might assist.[8]

One radio petty officer (funkmaat) and one basic radio operator (funkgast) were on duty at any given time. One funker was typically posted in the radio room, located immediately forward of the control room, where he transmitted and received messages in addition to encrypting and decrypting them using the Enigma code machine. He also listened in on merchant ships' message traffic; Allied convoys used the British Naval Cipher No. 3 and Allied Merchant Ships Code, but individual vessels along the East Coast transmitted unencoded messages. Nevertheless, one of the funkers' most critical responsibilities did not involve radios at all.

Water is more elastic and denser than air, and sound waves therefore travel farther and faster underwater. U-boats exploited this using a hydrophone array mounted on either side of the bow and wired to a listening set in the sound room. Technically "passive sonar," this is somewhat misleading because it did not "ping" its surroundings with sound energy like active sonar. This apparatus enabled the human ear to hear a ship's propeller from 12 miles away and a convoy from 60 miles. Mentally separating these sounds from background clutter like noises emitted by whales was a learned skill. An experienced funker could differentiate coal-powered ships from oil-powered ones, or distinguish the slow rumble of a merchantman's screws from the faster whirr of a destroyer's.

Winter was still in his dripping oilskin coat when his figure filled the doorway of the sound room, a cupboard-sized space with wooden walls to deaden outside noise. The funkmaat wore headphones and sat facing what resembled a large compass with a steering wheel below. Turning the wheel changed which portion of the array fed sound into the headphones while a pointer on the display indicated which direction was being listened to. The sailor rotated the wheel right, then left, then right again, his eyes darting from one side to the other. "*Horchpeilung* ..." the funkmaat whispered. *Sound bearing.* He squinted again.

"... one-four-zero."

The *U-103* surfaced and resumed its pursuit. Both diesel engines hammered as its bow sliced the waves, and the Atlantic retaliated by rolling the U-boat while an ashen sky poured a diagonal curtain of snow. Twenty minutes later, a smile formed under Winter's beard when the tanker reappeared 3.5 miles off the port beam. Although the German tactical paradigm stressed surface attacks, snow flurries and an overcast afternoon induced Winter to submerge because the periscope captured more ambient light than the UZO.

The bridge watch slid down the ladder into the control room where two of the lookouts took their seats at the hydroplane stations. "Clear the vents!" shouted the chief engineer as he assumed his usual standing position behind the planesmen. Winter secured the tower hatch while his crew shouted a succession of reports. "One ready!" "Two clear!" "Three, both sides ready!" "Four ready!" The engineering crew closed the air intake head valve and unclutched the diesels and the diesel-ober-maschinist yanked the engine order telegraph lever to signal readiness to dive.

"*Fluten!*" the chief ordered from the control room. Men around him immediately began turning handwheels and pulling levers to flood the ballast tanks. The air providing the U-boat's buoyancy escaped its tanks with a roar, and the forward hydroplanes were angled to force the bow downward. The world grew quiet as the diesels ceased pounding and crashing waves yielded to the gurgle of water rushing into the tanks. The Atlantic gave the conning tower a final slap as the *U-103* disappeared beneath it.[9]

***

Tankers were the Gray Wolves' most valued prey, and shipping lanes along the eastern United States were teeming with them. These included tankers operated by Socony-Vacuum Oil Company. The 1911 breakup of Standard Oil had produced Standard Oil Company of New York, or "Socony," and thirty-three other companies. Socony merged with Vacuum Oil in 1931 (decades later, a merger with Standard Oil of New Jersey would create ExxonMobil).

Socony-Vacuum's fleet included twelve "Arrow" tankers. New York Shipbuilding built eight of these in Camden, New Jersey. Bethlehem Steel's shipbuilding subsidiary launched four others at its yard in Quincy, Massachusetts. Among the four products of Bethlehem Shipbuilding was the *India Arrow*. Built in 1921 and sailing under a US flag, the *India Arrow* measured 468 feet long and 8,327 gross registered tons.

A merchant ship's stated nationality generally refers to its country of registry. Its crewmen might hail from multiple countries, but all thirty-eight mariners aboard the *India Arrow* were American citizens. Their tanker had departed Corpus Christi, Texas on 27 January carrying 88,369 barrels of crude oil. Sailing alone and unarmed, the *India Arrow* was scheduled to arrive at the northern New Jersey port of Carteret on Friday, 6 February.

Little about the aging *India Arrow* was noteworthy from an engineering perspective. Ship designs varied somewhat, but each tanker and freighter shared a similar layout and features with other vessels of its type. A tanker's forward-most compartment was used for dry cargo and sometimes crew quarters, immediately aft of which was the No. 1 cargo tank. Sequentially numbered tanks occupied the majority of the space below deck. Near the stern were engineering spaces housing the oil-fired boilers and steam engine. Aboard the *India Arrow*, the engineering crew lived above their working spaces astern while the deck crew occupied quarters in the bow. Cabins in the midship house were occupied by the captain, mates, radioman, and stewards.

The captain, or "master," of the *India Arrow* was Carl Johnson, a weathered 49-year-old from Staten Island who had already faced multiple lifetimes' worth of danger during his thirty-four years at sea. As the second mate on a freighter that sank in a storm off Cuba in 1916, Johnson had languished adrift for seven days. He then ferried cargo to Europe as a Navy officer during the Great War and was aboard the *Standard Arrow* in 1926 when it rescued twenty-three men from a sinking in New York Harbor. Considering this record, taking command of the *India Arrow* three weeks earlier had felt like an inconspicuous milestone.

He did not mind, his youthful appetite for adventure having long since been supplanted by the desire to spend time with his wife and three children. The *India Arrow* skipper wore his gray hair short on top and nearly buzzed on the sides, and he was plainly dressed in dark-colored utility pants and a button-down khaki shirt. Like U-boat sailors, merchant mariners generally wore whatever was sturdy and practical. Jeans were common. Only officers in the US Merchant Marine were issued uniforms, but these were not worn at sea.[10]

A merchant ship's officers were its "licensed" crewmen. These consisted of the captain, three mates, chief engineer, and up to four assistant engineers. The first mate aboard the *India Arrow* was 46-year-old Joe Davis from the Bronx. Ocean liners usually had a radio officer, as did many tankers and freighters later in the war, but most US Merchant Marine vessels in 1942 had a single unlicensed radio operator. A radio operator blurred the line between licensed and unlicensed since he messed with the captain and mates and his quarters were near to theirs. The radioman was 27-year-old Edward Shear from Hammond, Indiana. Shear was addressed as "Sparks," the Merchant Marine's ubiquitous moniker for any radioman.

The unlicensed crew was divided into three functional groups: the deck department, stewards department, and engineering department. The deck department was responsible for steering and navigation in addition to general nautical duties such as operating cargo winches, splicing rope, and standing lookout. The boatswain filled the role of a foreman or sergeant for the deck department. Below him were able seamen, then ordinary seamen. Dale Montgomery from Los Angeles, California served as the boatswain aboard the *India Arrow*, making him the most senior unlicensed crewman.

One of the deck department's able seamen was 21-year-old Charles Seerveld from Long Island. Seerveld's four years of shipboard experience included four cross-Pacific voyages aboard the *China Arrow*, and he joined Socony-Vacuum as a tanker crewman because it offered a monthly pay increase from $50 to $80. He found his *India Arrow* duties quite tolerable since he only worked daytime hours and had his own cabin. Also assigned to the deck department was able seaman Ernest Baldwin, Seerveld's childhood classmate.

A ship's stewards department performed such tasks as cooking and laundry (those who worked on luxury ocean liners were "jacket men"). One of the *India Arrow* stewards was Edward Proehl, whose family in Jersey City awaited his return in three days' time. Proehl worked alongside utilityman Nicholas Hetz, who handled the stowage of provisions. Born to Polish immigrants in Camden, New Jersey, Hetz had two brothers who were also tanker crewmen.

The boilers and steam engine were the domain of the engineering department. Firemen operated the oil-burning system, water tenders maintained the boilers' water levels, and oilers lubricated components. Machinist Fred Baker from South Carolina performed repairs and maintenance while general labor was carried out by wipers like 54-year-old Ira Buhrman of Maryland, a Marine Corps veteran of the Great War who had joined the Merchant Marine after Pearl Harbor because he was too old to reenlist. Overseeing the men laboring below decks was chief engineer Erich Suderow, a 55-year-old German immigrant whose wife described him as "more jealous of his acquired citizenship than if he had been born here."

The *India Arrow* crew also included a pumpman for operating the pumps and valves that moved the ship's liquid cargo. Many mariners preferred working tankers because they lacked bulky cargo requiring offloading via booms and winches. In peacetime, the biggest drawback to life as a "tanker stiff" was that the speediness of pumping out the cargo in port left little time for unwinding ashore. Increasingly, however, they were just grateful to reach shore at all.

There existed "an unstinting admiration of the men who sailed in oil tankers," wrote Nicholas Monsarrat. Tanker stiffs lived "on top of a keg of gunpowder. The stuff they carried, the lifeblood of the whole war, was the most treacherous cargo of all," he continued. "A single torpedo, a single small bomb, even a stray shot from a machine gun, could transform their ship into a torch."[11]

***

2 February 1942
110 miles southeast of Atlantic City, New Jersey
12:25

Winter tracked the tanker in his periscope's crosswires as it cut a zigzag pattern of 40-degree turns around a base course of 340 degrees. This defensive technique used irregular and unpredictable course changes to frustrate targeting calculations and prevent a submarine from obtaining a favorable attack position. Zigzagging also forced a submerged submarine commander to utilize his periscope more frequently, which slowed the boat and increased the probability of being spotted.

Aggressiveness, patience, confidence, and persistence were not the only makings of a U-boat ace. Putting a torpedo on target also required the spatial perception to accurately estimate distances and speeds and the quantitative acumen to quickly compute relative motion problems. Success and survival, moreover, demanded the mental dexterity to simultaneously update assessments and priorities, maneuver the boat, and react immediately to enemy attack. Unfortunately for the zigzagging tanker, Winter's mastery of these skills was beyond reproach.

The *U-103* was 2,000 yards from the tanker when Winter gave the order to fire. Two torpedoes were rammed from their tubes by a piston powered with compressed air, and both hit the target's starboard side. The tanker began burning as it slowed to a halt. Winter sighted human forms scurrying like ants across its deck. Down in the U-boat's radio room, the funker heard a distress call. "SSS, THIS IS WSEE, POSITION 38° 25' NORTH, 73° 00' WEST. GOING DOWN FAST. SSS, THIS IS WSEE …" A final message followed: "ABANDONING SHIP NOW GOODBYE."

Winter remained submerged as he circled to the tanker's starboard side and fired again. The shaft that set the gyro-angle failed to retract, however, causing the eel's propulsion system to run noisily inside the tube. A *whoosh* of compressed air filled the forward torpedo room a moment later, indicating that the "tube runner" had finally launched, but the delay caused it to miss. "*L.I.*, bring us up," Winter ordered, swallowing his intense frustration. "*Geschützbesatzungen*, stand by."[12]

All Type VII and IX U-boats in 1942 were armed with a naval artillery cannon mounted on the foredeck, just forward of the conning tower. The Type VII boats carried an 88mm gun while the Type IXs boasted a 105mm version. Commanders relied heavily on deck guns to sink ships during World War I, and shellfire was still occasionally used to sink merchantmen in 1942. Less than two weeks earlier, while the *U-123* was returning from its Operation Drumbeat patrol with no eels remaining, Reinhard Hardegen sank the *Culebra* and *Pan Norway* with gunfire alone. Both ships returned fire with their own weapons, hitting the Eins Zwei Drei several times but failing to penetrate its pressure hull. Nevertheless, the deck gun was more commonly used to finish off a damaged ship without using another torpedo.

The *U-103* surfaced into the gloomy winter afternoon at 13:15. Kapitänleutnant Winter was the first man to climb the conning tower hatch to the bridge. Following him were Oberleutnant von Rappard, then the other three lookouts, and finally the 105mm gun crew. The last man topside was Oberleutnant Oskar Kusch, the gunnery officer. Down in the control room, deck plates were lifted to access the shells stowed underneath.

Falling snow frosted leather and oilskin outerwear as Kusch's gun team clambered down to the foredeck. Working with disciplined haste, one man removed the 105mm's muzzle plug and another affixed the optical sight to a bracket on its left side. The others opened the small ready-use ammunition locker behind the gun, which revealed thirty-six shells sealed in individual cylindrical containers. A human chain formed inside the boat to pass more shells up from below.

Daylight negated the need to first mark the target with incendiary shells. The tanker languished only 400 yards away, but 4-foot seas continued rolling the *U-103*. Because a U-boat's instability made it impractical to give firing commands for individual shots, gun crews instead fired whenever their target fell into their sights. "Aim astern at the waterline," Kusch instructed. He sought to breach the hull at the engine room, a large compartment that could take a ship down if flooded. Snowflakes spiraled around them as Kusch watched his men ready the gun for action.

The aimer sighted in using the optic on the gun's right side while the layer traversed the barrel toward the target. Behind them, one of the two loaders unlatched and opened the breech, then the other loader slid a shell inside. When a sailor on the gun's left side yanked a lanyard, an ear-splitting roar sounded as the 105mm's muzzle belched flame. Two shots missed and threw up splashes of ocean before the third blew a hole in the hull near the stern. The layer traversed the barrel left. One blast followed another as one loader pulled each empty casing from the breech, then the other loader rammed the next shell home. Flames began licking from the tanker as Kusch's gun team reached a rate of one shell every four seconds.

Crewmen aboard the *U-103* soon observed the merchant crew rowing four lifeboats away from their burning ship. "We felt no hatred," *U-505* crewmen Hans Goebeler would explain years after the war. "It was like watching an automobile race: one loves to see a good crash, but at the same time hopes that no one gets hurt." Ace commander Otto Kretschmer characterized the U-boat man's trade as "grim but chivalrous warfare," though one imagines his victims held different opinions. Survivors left adrift were not discussed, however. "Not a word is said about the shipwrecked men," wrote Lothar-Günther Buchheim. "To speak of their fate is taboo."

Winter glanced up at the gray sky as the deck gun pounded the crippled ship. The *U-103* had already been stationary for longer than he preferred, and he presumed that the merchant crew had transmitted a distress call before abandoning ship. Seventeen shells hit before Winter resigned himself to expending another torpedo. The killing blow landed amidships with an explosion that sent flames hundreds of feet into the air. "Gigantic explosion," Winter wrote. "Ship capsizes to starboard in a few minutes." As the tanker entered its death roll, Winter's eye caught the name painted on the hull: *W.L. STEED.*[13]

***

4 February 1942
63 miles southeast of Atlantic City, New Jersey
18:49

The *India Arrow* maintained her northward course on the evening of Wednesday, 4 February under an obsidian slate of moonless sky. While eating a dinner prepared by Edward Proehl and the other stewards, one mariner elicited laughter when he joked, "Eat plenty, it may be your last meal." First mate Joe Davis took over as the duty officer on the bridge at 16:00 while able seaman Michael Kusy, another New York City native, manned the helm. Capt Carl Johnson joined them.

Those aboard the *India Arrow* were unaware that the *U-103* had been tracking them for almost ten hours. Werner Winter fired one torpedo at 13:12 which missed as a result of his own misjudgment. "Understeered due to large shooting angle and heel," he noted in his log. "I will not do that again."

U-boat officers learned to visually assess targets, and distinguishing a tanker from a freighter was not difficult. Besides being longer and lower, the placement of engine and boilers near a tanker's stern meant that its smokestack was farther aft (a freighter's engineering spaces were usually amidships). Most freighters also lacked the catwalks seen on tankers. Though flipping through the Gröner manual could reveal a ship's exact size and speed, an approximate visual estimate typically sufficed.

Visual assessments were used not only to identify a target but also to determine its speed and distance. Range could be estimated using the angle between the waterline and the bridge or mast. If unable to determine a target's speed by paralleling it, he could instead observe the bow wave's height or the wake's length relative to the ship's length. The hydrophone could also be used to count its propeller revolutions. These estimates required a knowledge of ship types and their capabilities, and Winter was experienced enough to deduce that the *India Arrow* was making about 10 knots.

The afternoon had since faded into a clear night with only a small sea running. The moon had not yet risen and Carl Johnson's tanker was entirely blacked out, yet Werner Winter could see his target with little difficulty. It was a benefit he owed to an ongoing American policy failure: the *India Arrow*'s outline was clearly etched into the bright Jersey Shore lights off her port side.

Bright coastal lighting from streetlights, advertisements, and automobiles still imperiled merchant ships even three weeks after the U-boats' arrival. "On a dark night, as the vessel passes down the coast, her hull is made plainly visible by the shore lights as she passes between [the lights] and the submarine," explained a Coast Guard report from March 1942. Some beachside New Jersey communities had responded positively to an Eastern Defense Command request that boardwalk lights be extinguished. As of March, however, no military or civilian authority had explicitly ordered a blackout anywhere along the East Coast. The notion also found opponents among civic leaders who cited the risks of increased crime and car accidents. Consequently, and in one reporter's words, Atlantic City remained "the most brilliantly lighted stretch of beach on the Atlantic Coast."

U-333 commander Peter Cremer recounted a shoreline so luminous that "we could distinguish the big hotels from the cheap dives." The U-boats did not even need to approach this close because the curtain of light reflected off low-lying clouds to create a glow visible many miles out to sea. "Against the footlight glare of a carefree new world were passing the silhouettes of ships recognizable in every detail and shape," Cremer wrote. "Here they were, formally presented to us on a plate: please help yourselves!"[14]

***

As Winter and von Rappard lined up the *India Arrow* in the UZO, Charles Seerveld lay reading on his bunk. Bert Palmer, a 31-year-old fireman from Long Island recently engaged to be married, was walking back to the engine room's sweltering heat after getting a glass of water. Capt Johnson was not zigzagging, though this would not have protected the *India Arrow* any better than the *W.L. Steed*. On his bunk near the bow, the ship's bell had just marked 19:00 when Seerveld felt "a terrific thump."

The torpedo's impact near the stern on the starboard side blasted a hole in the hull between the No. 10 tank, or farthest aft cargo space, and the ship's own fuel bunker. The breached tank immediately began disgorging oil onto the water's surface. Palmer's hydration break saved his life. Even if the explosion had not ruptured the bulkhead separating the fuel bunker from the engineering spaces, the men there had nowhere to go other than the aft deck—which was now engulfed in flames. Nobody from the engine room was seen again.

"We half-expected something like this," Charles Seerveld recalled decades later. "But, this early in the war, not many people knew what a torpedo felt like." Reaching the main deck, Seerveld saw a towering inferno near the stern. The prospect of abandoning ship frightened him as much as the fire because he was not a strong swimmer. Seerveld then abruptly about-faced and sprinted back to his cabin. He had forgotten his lifejacket.

Fred Baker was in the engineering crew's quarters near the stern when the torpedo struck the hull below him, and the blast dumped him unceremoniously from his chair. Quickly vacating his cabin, he found himself trudging through knee-deep oily water in the passageway. Although the torpedo hit the *India Arrow's* starboard quarter, Baker could feel the deck tilting to port.

The explosion violently shook the entire ship. On the bridge, Capt Johnson and Joe Davis staggered as Michael Kusy gripped the helm to avoid being knocked against the bulkhead. There was a brief moment of stunned silence as Johnson rushed to the window and quickly made the executive decision to abandon ship. "I'll check below," Davis shouted. He activated the alarm and grabbed his lifejacket. "Go," Johnson replied before turning his attention to Kusy. "You're relieved, kid. Get to your lifeboat."

Radio operator Edward Shear was also reading in his quarters when Werner Winter's blow fell. "Sparks" immediately sprinted to the radio shack which, as on most ships, was located immediately aft of the bridge. Shear fumbled the headphones on and began furiously tapping the telegraph key. Depressing and releasing the key opened and closed an electrical circuit to create a sequence of dots and dashes audible over the 600-meter frequency. Rather than "SOS," he used the new distress code "SSS" to specify a submarine attack:

SSS, THIS IS KDHP, TORPEDOED. SSS, THIS IS KDHP, TORPEDOED. SSS, THIS IS KDHP …

A radio station at Chatham on Cape Cod replied. "KDHP, THIS IS WCC, WHAT IS YOUR POSITION?" Shear did not know. "Captain! Where are we??" Johnson's reply was drowned out by the ambient chaos. "WHAT?!" Shear hollered before jumping to his feet and sprinting to the bridge. Cape Cod asked their position again. Shear returned a moment later just as the generator below decks flooded, cutting power to the interior lights and the wireless set. The hand-cranked auxiliary radio also proved inoperable. "Shit!"

Shear did not know that the Germans were eavesdropping. The funker seated in the U-103's radio room had heard the India Arrow's partial distress message, then Chatham's reply, and now another reply from Tuckerton, New Jersey: "KDHP, THIS IS WSC, WHAT IS YOUR POSITION?" Chatham repeated its message, but there were no further mayday transmissions. A third station now replied from Camperdown, Ontario. "KDHP, THIS IS VCS, WHAT IS YOUR POSITION?" The stricken India Arrow remained silent. As Winter's log observed, "The reply from Tuckerton Radio and Camperdown Radio for position remains unanswered."[15]

Charles Seerveld and Fred Baker emerged from below decks at about the same time. Pervading the cold air on deck was a medley of fear and confusion salted with anger. One man recalled that "we came up on deck swearing with rage." Chaos reigned, and Seerveld realized there was no point in going to his assigned lifeboat because there was only one boat left.

The No. 3 and No. 4 boats on either side of the aft deck house were engulfed in flames, and the No. 1 lifeboat on the starboard side was unusable because the ship's list prevented it from clearing the hull. This left only the No. 2 lifeboat on the port side, and first mate Joe Davis took charge of launching it from the boat deck on the midship house's port side. Seerveld and the others assembled on the main deck to board it once it was lowered down.

Radio operator Ed Shear abandoned the inoperable wireless set and donned his lifejacket, then spotted Capt Johnson alone on the starboard boat deck. The skipper had freed the gripes, or clamps, securing the No. 1 lifeboat to its chocks and was now turning a handle that raised and extended it outboard. If they could not launch it now, the captain reasoned, he could at least enable it to float free after the India

Arrow sank. "Sparks! Here," Johnson shoved the briefcase containing the ship's papers into Shear's hands. The incredulous radioman hesitated before unceremoniously tossing the briefcase into the lifeboat.[16]

On the port side of the midship house, Bert Palmer was assisting Joe Davis in launching the No. 2 lifeboat. They loosened the gripes and feverishly cranked the boat out over the deck's edge until it was hanging by two manila fiber ropes, or "falls," connected to the lifeboat's bow and stern. Two others climbed into the swinging wooden craft to ensure that its painter, or the line connecting the lifeboat's bow to the tanker, was led well forward with the slack taken up.

The *India Arrow*'s worsening list was causing the lifeboat to hang farther from the boat deck. This pulled taut the tricing pendant, or wire that kept the lifeboat close to the ship while being lowered. Davis and Palmer payed out the falls through the davits' pulley wheels until the boat reached the main deck below, then passed the frapping line around the falls and pulled the boat close enough for the others to embark below. "Pull!" Davis shouted to Palmer. "We gotta get it closer!"

Davis and Palmer made fast the frapping line around a cleat to hold the lifeboat in place. The first mate then looked over the edge while he and Palmer gripped parts of the ship as she leaned further to port. Davis saw the others finish boarding from the main deck below, then loosened the frapping line as he and Palmer prepared to belay again. "A little more slack," Davis yelled, "there we go! Ready ... now!" Pulley wheels squeaked as Bert Palmer and the first mate lowered the lifeboat.

Fred Baker and Michael Kusy reached the main deck to find twenty men packed into the No. 2 boat, leaving no space for them. Their only remaining option was to jump. Kusy dropped into the sea, followed by Baker and several others. Their plummets were short, as the port gunwale was now just 4 feet from the water. Ed Shear and Charles Seerveld leapt from the ship's starboard side.

The jumpers' lifejackets popped them back to the surface. Each immediately began swimming away from the *India Arrow* to escape the suction caused by seawater rushing into a sinking ship's interior. "Your chief concern should be to get clear of the ship's suction area," one manual for abandoning ship advised. "Few men caught within the suction area of a swiftly sinking ship ... have survived." Though suction's danger was greatly exaggerated, it pervaded fears about abandoning ship.

Michael Kusy and Fred Baker climbed onto a rectangular wooden cargo hatch cover floating off the port side. Looking back at the ship, they saw that the No. 2 lifeboat had just reached the water but had not yet gotten clear of the ship. Nevertheless, neither man realized that their ordeal was about to get much worse.

Joe Davis and the others in the No. 2 lifeboat were releasing the falls when the *India Arrow*'s list abruptly accelerated. Kusy and Baker watched in horror as the ship rolled uncontrollably to port and a frenzy of panicked shouts rose from the lifeboat. The midship house crashed down on top of it, snuffing out the voices and dragging the boat and its occupants into the depths. "I barely left the ship when it heeled over to port and trapped all the men in that lifeboat," Kusy later recounted. "I saw my buddies go down."[17]

A few minutes earlier, Charles Seerveld was shivering uncontrollably as he swam away from the burning wreck's starboard side. The *India Arrow* continued going down over the stern as her weight leaned precariously to port. Glancing backward, the able seaman spotted something in the fire's angry glow—the No. 1 lifeboat. Still attached to its davit by one fall, the boat rose and fell like a wooden mirage. Hope coursed through his shivering frame as he began splashing toward it.

Seerveld had nearly reached the lifeboat when the *India Arrow* entered her death roll. Unable to hear terrified shouts from the No. 2 lifeboat on the ship's opposite side, Seerveld inhaled sharply and pinched his nose as she capsized. No suction pulled him under, but collapsing onto her port flank caused the *India Arrow* to yank the lifeboat farther away from Seerveld. *If I die, you die with me*, she seemed to taunt. *Didn't you know that was part of the deal, Charles?*

Seerveld resumed sluggishly swimming toward the No. 1 lifeboat and eventually reached up and grasped its gunwale. His hands were so cold that he could hardly bend his fingers, but he succeeded in pulling himself up and tumbling into the boat. It was partially flooded, and he landed with a splash beside a briefcase. Someone had disconnected the fall attached to the bow, but the stern fall kept the boat hitched to the ship.

He had scarcely caught his breath when he heard a harried shout from somewhere nearby. "H-hey! … hey!" Someone was splashing toward him. "Who's that?" Seerveld shouted. "Sparks!" the voice replied. Just after Seerveld pulled radioman Ed Shear into the lifeboat, the lone fall went taut as the boat's stern was abruptly jerked toward the ship in a sudden movement that toppled both men. Water cascading into compartments and passageways was causing the *India Arrow* to settle further to port, and she was taking the lifeboat with her.

"Ah, shit!" Seerveld frantically struck the pelican hook joining the fall to the lifeboat, but the mechanism did not release the rope. The tanker's aft section was now submerged, the Atlantic hungrily lapping at the midship house to which the lifeboat was connected. The *India Arrow* continued pulling the two men closer until a metallic *clack* sounded as the fall finally disconnected. The boat drifted free.

Uneven flooding then suddenly caused the *India Arrow* to keel back to starboard. This sent a wave of oily water toward Seerveld and Shear, knocking them over again and flooding the lifeboat nearly to the gunwales. The surge did shove them away from the wreck, however, as if the dying giant had extended the pair a final gesture of mercy. A few moments passed before they heard a familiar voice shouting nearby, and they soon pulled Capt Carl Johnson into the lifeboat.

The stern's submergence extinguished the inferno there, but the cargo hemorrhaging from the tanker's punctured hull created an oil slick which had caught fire. The oil rose and fell as flames creeping across it gradually illuminated the winter night. In the light of the burning oil, the three men watched the bow rear higher into a moonless sky until the nearly 500-foot-long titan was almost vertical. Less than ten minutes after the warhead exploded, the *India Arrow*'s stern was scraping the seafloor 190 feet below while her bow protruded steeply from the water.

"We g-gotta f-find the others ..." Capt Johnson declared through clattering teeth, but their lifeboat was too badly flooded to use the oars. Nor could they hear much over the waves, fire, and the ship's tortured moans. The No. 1 lifeboat drifted out of the oil slick, but smoke prevented its three occupants from seeing any other survivors. Any hopeful thoughts they may have entertained were shattered seconds later by an explosion from the *India Arrow* only 100 yards away. A tongue of flame erupted from the wreck's bow.[18]

Sinking by the stern had left only the *India Arrow*'s foreship above water, but partly afloat meant potentially salvageable. Accordingly, Kapitänleutnant Winter elected to vent the air remaining in the bow section. The 105mm gunners ventured out to the *U-103*'s foredeck with Oberleutnant Kusch following.

Three sailors took positions on the right side of the deck gun, one behind the breech, and a fifth man on the gun's left side. The aimer, the forward-most man on the weapon's right side, looked through the optic while relaying instructions to the layer, who rotated the traversing and elevation wheels to align the 14-foot barrel with the burning ship. Behind them, one loader opened the breech and the other shoved a 105mm shell inside. "Gun ready!" the lead petty officer reported, lanyard in hand. "*Feuererlaubnis*," Oberleutnant Kusch replied.

Three hundred yards away, in the No. 1 lifeboat, Ed Shear saw a radiant orange flash as another 33-lb shell hurtled over the whitecaps. Upon striking the *India Arrow*, the impact depressed a wooden plunger in the shell's nose which shoved the firing pin backward into the primer. Another tongue of flames unfurled from the bow as Johnson, Seerveld, and Shear recoiled.

"Drop the oars!" Johnson bellowed. "Get down!"

Johnson presumed that the submarine crew was aiming at the tanker, but he also feared that attempting to row away might tempt them to test their gunnery skills on the lifeboat. Staying put, however, left them at the mercy of a dangerous geometry. The lifeboat's drift meant the *India Arrow* was now between them and the *U-103*, so any shell overshooting the wreck would come down in their vicinity. The trio huddled together in the oily water as the burning oil slick continued to spread and Shear peered over the gunwale.

Boom!

The oil fire had lifted the veil of darkness enough to reveal the *U-103* on the other side of the flames. The earlier attempt to sink the *W.L. Steed* had expended more than half the *U-103*'s ammunition, so Kusch's gunners now carefully aimed each shot. Each thunderous report of the 105mm gun was subsumed by the much-closer blast of each shell finding its mark.

BOOM!

The night grew gradually brighter as crackling flames spread across the sea. Now another, far ghastlier sound joined the cacophony. Johnson, Shear, and Seerveld blanched when it reached their ears.

"Oh my God."

Agonized screams were emanating from men trapped in the burning oil, their voices pleading and shrieking as flames enveloped them. The dense smoke obscuring the hellscape was a mercy for those in the lifeboat, for it prevented their eyes from bearing witness to what their ears heard. Shells continued pounding the wreck in a steady timpani beat that punctuated the ghoulish opera of their friends and shipmates burning alive. Johnson grabbed the other two men's lifejackets and pulled them closer. "Cover your ears," he told them. "It'll be over soon."

Below where Kapitänleutnant Winter was perched like a gargoyle on the bridge, Oberleutnant Oskar Kusch executed his gunnery duties with detached sobriety. The devout Catholic offered a silent prayer for those on his shells' receiving end. Seven hits and zero misses left the foreship perforated and burning before Winter decided she was mauled beyond the possibility of salvage. "*Das reicht*," he told Kusch. *That's enough.*

The *U-103* turned south at 19:20 as a full moon began its ascent into the sky. Winter cruised without particular urgency since he knew that his target had not succeeded in broadcasting its location. "It was the American tanker 'INDIA ARROW' of 8327 GRT," he noted in his log. "Now I have only three torpedoes left. Lean times."[19]

Fireman Bert Palmer had cheated death when the doomed lifeboat he helped launch proved too crowded to accommodate him. He then jumped overboard seconds before the ship capsized and swam clear of the oil slick. Fortune appeared to favor Palmer again when he sighted the lifeboat carrying Capt Johnson, Charles Seerveld, and Ed Shear. The Atlantic possesses many ways to kill a man, however, and Palmer was now struggling not to inhale water as he hyperventilated and the sea's fatal chill steadily eroded his capacity to resist. Palmer's smiling fiancée was flitting through his disjointed consciousness when he felt hands grab his lifejacket; Capt Johnson and the others hauled him into their lifeboat.

Johnson, Charles Seerveld, and Ed Shear succeeded in getting the No. 1 lifeboat mobile. Over the course of an hour they found Bert Palmer, Michael Kusy, Fred Baker, Dale Montgomery, and five others still alive. Using the coastal lights as a directional reference, the twelve *India Arrow* survivors began rowing west. The flaming sea still cast the attack scene in an eerie incandescence, and Capt Johnson's last view of the *India Arrow* was that of her bow jutting hideously from the waves.

Their misery was deepened by a freezing rain that turned at intervals to sleet. Despite seeing Atlantic City's lights reflecting off the underside of clouds in the western sky, their odds were bleak. The mariners were more than 50 miles from shore in a flooded and coverless rowboat in rough seas and winter temperatures. Worse still, Johnson and Shear knew that no rescue was on its way, leaving them to face the cosmically cruel prospect of a slow death within sight of the Jersey Shore's lights.[20]

Fifth Naval District received Shear's partial distress call, noting: "KDHP saying 'torpedoed,' but no position given." Eastern Sea Frontier knew only that the *India Arrow* had gone down somewhere "between Barnegat Bay and Sea Girt," but Socony-Vacuum's offices were closed for the evening. Bureaucratic confusion and red tape between the Army and Navy also hampered attempts to coordinate an air search. Socony-Vacuum's reply to the Navy around 13:00 the following afternoon stated that the ship should have been "about fifteen miles south" of the Winter Quarter Shoals lighted buoy, which was more than 70 miles southwest of the actual attack location.[21]

Inhibited by a waterlogged sail and a contrary wind, the lifeboat's twelve exhausted occupants gave up rowing after a couple of hours and eventually took down the sail to use as a blanket. Rain rendered futile their attempts to bail out the boat, and half of the group attempted to sleep while immersed in cold water. The other half kept watch for passing ships. They signaled two passing ships using the flare gun from the lifeboat's emergency supplies kit, but both steered away upon sighting the flares. Newspapers would later report that they feared a German ruse.

The *India Arrow* survivors bailed out the lifeboat in the morning and resumed rowing, only to fall afoul of a southeasterly current. The day passed without rescue and they endured another night adrift. Biscuits and fresh water from the emergency rations maintained their physical strength even as their morale eroded. Dawn on Friday, 6 February—the day the *India Arrow* was due to reach port—revealed a heavy fog that broke their spirits even further.[22]

Unknown to Captain Carl Johnson and his men, salvation was near at hand in the form of Frank Marshall. The 60-year-old Navy veteran lived on Carson Avenue in Atlantic City and earned his living fishing and operating a produce stand in Stratford. Marshall had steered his 24-foot boat, the *Gitana*, out of Absecon Inlet around 02:30 to check his pound nets offshore. Accompanying Marshall on his boat was another Atlantic City resident, 35-year-old John Shore of Fairmount Avenue.

The *Gitana* was chugging through the fog a few minutes past 06:00 that morning when Marshall and Shore sighted what appeared to be a signal flare roughly a mile off their port bow. Marshall steered toward the source of the flash and, twenty minutes later, found the *India Arrow* survivors. "Our ship's been torpedoed and we're probably the only survivors," Johnson stated with almost comical propriety. "Can you toss us a line and tow us to the nearest port?" "Tow, hell!" Marshall exclaimed. "We're taking you all aboard, come on."

The survivors were a pitiful sight. Covered in oil, several were unable to walk and most were barefoot except for two with feet so swollen that the fishermen had to cut their shoes off. The *Gitana* was slightly smaller than the No. 1 lifeboat, but it was dry and had a hot stove in the cabin. Marshall sped for the coast as John Shore served hot coffee and whiskey and the survivors smoked every last cigarette aboard. Capt Johnson refused any luxuries until his crewmen had been taken care of, and Shore eventually forced a cup of coffee into his hands. Johnson was shivering so badly he could barely hold it.

The *Gitana* reached Coast Guard Station Atlantic City, at the entrance to Absecon Inlet, around 09:00 that morning. None of the *India Arrow* crewmen were seriously hurt, though Johnson limped ashore on an injured foot and one steward with swollen legs required a wheelchair. Socony-Vacuum arranged to transport the tanker men to New York City, and boatswain Dale Montgomery accepted Bert Palmer's invitation to stay with his family on Long Island. After a hot breakfast at the Coast Guard station, the survivors all fell asleep.[23]

The twelve survivors' gratitude was overshadowed by the deaths of twenty-six shipmates. Six of nine stewards were killed, and only Fred Baker and three others remained of the 15-man engineering department. First mate Joe Davis drowned leading the No. 2 lifeboat, and Capt Johnson was the only officer who returned to shore. Among the fatalities was German-born engineering officer Erich Suderow. His wife told reporters that Suderow "knew what he was walking into, but insisted on doing his duty by his country."

Nicholas Hetz of Camden, New Jersey had recently informed his family that he expected to be home around 4 February, the same day the *India Arrow* was torpedoed. In Scranton, Pennsylvania, oiler Anthony Simon's widowed mother refused to accept Socony-Vacuum's designation of her son as "missing and presumed lost," insisting that he would be found alive. The mother of Ernest Baldwin, Charles Seerveld's former classmate, collapsed in grief while teaching Sunday school.[24]

***

The *India Arrow* was the third of four ships sunk during the *U-103*'s American patrol, but the sinking of the tanker *W.L. Steed* on the afternoon of 2 February was the deadliest. Despite her entire crew of thirty-eight surviving the attack itself, the merciless sea killed thirty-four of them as they drifted over the ensuing days. The sinking of the freighter *San Gil* around midnight on 3/4 February claimed two lives, and the Coast Guard rescued the other thirty-nine after sunrise.

Werner Winter's bloody work concluded sixteen hours after the *India Arrow*'s destruction when he pounced on her sister ship, the tanker *China Arrow*, off the Delmarva Peninsula. The *U-103*'s final torpedo crippled but did not sink her, so Winter shelled the *China Arrow* at the waterline until she went under 105 miles southeast of Ocean City, Maryland. All hands survived.[25]

U-boats ideally would not have to resort to shellfire at all, but the Torpedo Crisis and the resulting May 1940 switch to impact detonators had left the Ubootwaffe with dulled fangs. Magnetic detonation beneath a ship's keel achieved consistent and devastating effects by directing the explosive energy into its backbone, but impact detonation only blew a hole in the hull's side while diffusing part of the blast energy along the hull and into the surrounding water. The damage inflicted by impact detonation was therefore less consistent and more localized, and a single torpedo often proved insufficient to sink a ship.

Despite the evident unreliability of both the detonator and depth-keeping mechanism, the latter went unaddressed even as depth-keeping failures persisted into 1942. Torpedoes cause the most damage against the lowest parts of the hull, but German eels' tendency to run too deep and undershoot the target led many commanders to launch them at shallower running depths. These impacted higher on the hull, further reducing the destructiveness of impact detonation. Six days after Werner Winter's *U-103* reached the United States, however, *U-94* kommandant Otto Ites stumbled upon the depth-keeping issue's root cause during a routine inspection.

Ites noticed that excess air pressure had accumulated in one torpedo's balance chamber, or sealed space kept at sea-level pressure as a reference value. Using pressurized air to trim the boat and launch torpedoes also increased the overall air pressure on board, and a faulty seal had enabled the excess pressure to force its way into the balance chamber. This caused the torpedo to "think" it was running shallower than it was, thereby inducing the weapon to steer itself deeper. BdU determined that the phenomenon was widespread across the fleet. Its prompt resolution marked the end of the Torpedo Crisis, though a redesigned magnetic pistol would not see service until December 1942.

The Torpedo Crisis saved innumerable lives off the East Coast in 1942. Instead of the one-hit kills frequently achieved by magnetic detonation, U-boats averaged two hits per ship sunk. The five Operation Drumbeat boats collectively expended forty-eight torpedoes to sink twenty-five ships, only five of which were sunk with a single impact and no misses. The most inefficient attack was Reinhard Hardegen's sinking of the *Norness* off Long Island, which required five torpedoes: three hits and two misses due to running deep. This increased a merchant crew's odds of survival while also depleting an attacker's limited supply of torpedoes. Because a U-boat had to begin its return journey after expending all its eels, the "Second Happy Time" was only half as deadly as it could have been.[26]

***

Frank Marshall beamed with pride when interviewed by reporters. "Although I didn't get any fish," he stated, "I picked up the most valuable cargo my little boat has ever carried." To a man, the *India Arrow* survivors expressed determination to return to duty. Charles Seerveld would fulfill his vow to sail again, although "I never again slept without my clothes on, even in the tropics." Capt Johnson declared that "as soon as I get another ship, I'm going right out to sea again." The skipper added, "We're still mad. We knew we could expect anything out there, and we certainly got it, but that won't stop us."

At the Proehl family's home in Jersey City, Edward Proehl's expected time of arrival came and passed. An uneasy silence had settled across the house when a knock sounded on the front door. Three raps, curt and professional. *Not Eddie.* His mother felt as if her heart had dropped out and straight through the floor.

She opened the door to find a man in a Western Union uniform. "Telegram for Mrs Amelia Proehl," he said pleasantly. She shakily confirmed her identity and grabbed the message from the courier's hands. The words she read next would remain with her for the rest of her life:

SHIP TORPEDOED OFF JERSEY COAST. I AM SAFE. HOME TOMORROW.[27]

CHAPTER SEVEN

R.P. Resor

"Then men on ships about do stand,
And sadly watch her burn.
There is no way to lend a hand,
Just watch, and wait your turn."
—Robert Goodwin, "A Tanker's Hit," (August 1944)

26 February 1942
47 miles southeast of Atlantic City, New Jersey
14:16

"Anblasen!"

One hundred feet below the ocean's choppy surface, the Type VIIC boat's crew executed the order to begin purging seawater from the ballast tanks. A sailor at the manifolds on the control room's starboard bulkhead opened blow valves that allowed pressurized air to flow into the main ballast tanks. To ascend bow-first, these were opened in a cascading sequence beginning with the #5 ballast tank under the forward torpedo room. Hissing air was joined by the gurgling of ballast water being forced from the tanks. "Boat rises," the chief engineer reported. "Forward hard up, aft up five," he instructed the two planesmen. They pressed the electric push-button controls accordingly.

The *U-578*'s ascent slowed until it came to a crawl 60 feet below the surface. Behind the chief engineer and planesmen, Korvettenkapitän Ernst-August Rehwinkel extended the sky periscope, although he was still too deep to utilize it. His chief engineer then trimmed the boat by ordering water shifted between the auxiliary tanks, then the boat resumed slowly rising. An undulating sea and winter sky soon filled Rehwinkel's field of vision.

The captain draped his hands loosely over the sky periscope's handles as he visually swept the ocean's surface. In addition to seeing directly overhead, the sky periscope (also called the observation periscope) had a larger aperture that captured more ambient light than the attack periscope operated from the tower compartment. At the same time, a funkmaat in the sound room listened for engine noises using the hydrophone. Yet the Atlantic remained quiet, and Korvettenkapitän Rehwinkel saw nothing above them besides an empty expanse of rolling sea.

"Prepare to surface."

The engineering officer repeated the captain's order and the various stations reported in. "Diesels ready," "E-motors ready," "Bridge watch ready." Rehwinkel gave the order to surface before beginning to climb the conning tower ladder. Another small measure of air was added to the ballast tanks, and the hydroplanes were inclined to guide the *U-578* upward. The engineering officer counted off the dwindling depth before reporting: "*Turmluk ist frei ... Boot ist raus!*" The commander unlatched the conning tower hatch and heaved it open.

Rehwinkel squinted as he emerged into a gray winter afternoon and the lookouts quickly assumed their positions around him. U-boats typically remained on battery power briefly after surfacing in case a quick crash-dive was required. For this same reason, the *U-578* rode low in the water with its tanks partly full. Satisfied that they were safe for the moment, Rehwinkel shouted another order down the open tower hatch: "*Ausblasen mit diesel!*"

Both Germaniawerft engines thundered to life as a *Maschinenmaat* in the diesel room opened a valve that directed one engine's exhaust to the blowing manifold. This enabled another sailor in the control room to direct exhaust to the ballast tanks. A gurgling sounded as the fumes began purging the remaining water from the tanks.

There were no ships in sight. Impotent though American forces seemed, however, it was unwise to linger on the surface in daylight. Nineteen minutes passed before Rehwinkel gave the order to submerge again. The crew executed the surfacing process in reverse: air and exhaust ducts closed, diesels unclutched, E-motors engaged, tanks flooded. The deck and tower slipped under as the planesmen guided the *U-578* down to the seafloor.

Ten minutes after returning to the bottom, a voice summoned the kommandant. It belonged to the funkmaat listening to the hydrophone in the sound room. The radio operator heard the pulsing beat of a propeller in the distance. Although the sound was faint, it was clearly a large ship, and apparently northbound.[1]

***

18 miles east of Spring Lake, New Jersey
23:26

Ten hours later, John Forsdal was standing his lookout post at the bow of the tanker *R.P. Resor*. A half-moon in the clear sky above the able seaman cast an ethereal glow across the sea while a northwesterly breeze blew ripples across its surface and the swell rose and fell lazily against the hull. The New Jersey shoreline off her port side was brilliantly lit, and the lines etched around Forsdal's small and deep-set eyes shifted as he watched Manasquan, Sea Girt, and Spring Lake slide slowly past. The winter chill was tolerable, its silence nearly absolute. As the *R.P. Resor*'s bow cleaved the black Atlantic, Forsdal heard nothing apart from the engines' sonorous rumble and the bow wave's wet static.

John Forsdal, age 46, had spent the past twenty-eight years at sea. He survived two U-boat attacks during the Great War and subsequently emigrated from Norway to the United States, where he settled in San Francisco and became a citizen. Forsdal had joined the crew nine days earlier at Baytown, Texas. He wore earmuffs while a sweater and winter coat insulated his muscled torso, and atop the coat was a lifejacket made of cork and canvas. He wore his fine hair short around the ears but longer on top, and his weathered face bore several days of stubble. Forsdal was presently standing atop the forecastle, or elevated section of the deck at the bow.

Lookout duty, steering, and navigation were responsibilities of the deck department. Each watch consisted of an officer, two able seamen, and an ordinary seaman who stood duty in four-hour increments. The officer handled navigation, logbook entries, and communication with the engineering department. The three unlicensed mariners alternated between standing lookout, steering at the helm, and standby duty (which might include fetching coffee). The engineering department maintained its own watch rotation below decks.

Graham Covert, third mate aboard the *R.P. Resor*, was the officer in charge of the 20:00–00:00 watch on 27 February. Considered "an alert and competent officer" by Forsdal, Covert was from Long Island and had married just three weeks earlier. His father was a Navy officer in the Pacific theater and his two brothers had just enlisted in the Marine Corps. Besides Covert and Forsdal, the watch included a second able seaman whose name is lost to history. The fourth man on duty was 28-year-old Orville Hogard, an ordinary seaman (the deck department's lowest rank) from Texas.

Forsdal began his "trick at the wheel" when he took over the helm at 20:00. He noted how well the relatively new ship handled, her hydraulic telemotor transmitting the steering commands with smooth responsiveness. The other able seaman took over steering duty at 22:00, whereupon Hogard ventured out to the forecastle as lookout and Forsdal rotated to standby for an hour. An hour later, Forsdal donned his coat and earmuffs and went out to the forecastle to relieve Hogard.[2]

***

Measuring 435 feet long and 7,451 gross registered tons, the *R.P. Resor* was built in Kearny, New Jersey by Federal Shipbuilding and Dry Dock Company (a US Steel subsidiary). She shared a cutting-edge design with her identical sister, the *T.C. McCobb*, which made them the world's most famous tankers even before they were launched a few weeks apart in 1936. Purchased by Standard Oil Company of New Jersey, the sisters thereby joined the famed "Esso" fleet. This name stemmed from "S" and "O" for Standard Oil, a brand claimed by Standard Oil of New Jersey following the 1911 dissolution of Standard Oil Company.

Gracing the slipway first, the *R.P. Resor* was the first American-built ship featuring the Isherwood arcform hull for improved fuel efficiency. Other innovations included automatic boiler and turbine controls. Her steam turbines were more efficient than the reciprocating steam engines that powered most merchant ships, and she was highly maneuverable owing to the first contra-guide propeller ever installed on a new American vessel. She featured a single propeller like most merchantmen of that era. The buzz surrounding the *R.P. Resor* and *T.C. McCobb* in the late 1930s helped spur a global revival of tanker building that would prove immeasurably valuable in the war to come.

Seven days earlier, the *R.P. Resor* had departed Houston, Texas for Fall River, Massachusetts. In her cargo tanks were 105,025 barrels of Bunker C fuel oil used to power large ships and locomotives. It essentially constituted what remained after gasoline and other lighter fuels were refined out of crude oil. Commanding the *R.P. Resor* was Captain Fred Marcus, a 58-year-old Latvian immigrant and US Navy veteran with twenty-two years sailing for the Esso fleet.

The *R.P. Resor* commenced a zigzag course two days out of Houston, the legs of which became shorter after passing Miami. The tanker cut 15 degrees in either direction at 15-minute intervals as she began her transit north along the East Coast. In accordance with Navy directives, the *R.P. Resor* ran no navigation lights or running lights and her wheelhouse was blacked out.[3]

***

Zigzagging provided the crew of the *R.P. Resor* more peace of mind than safety, however. Sailing without lights on was similarly preferable to the alternative, but nor did this seriously impede a patient U-boat commander. This was especially true when coastwise traffic was starkly outlined against a brightly lit coast. Journalist Walter Lippmann lamented that "there's no use building ships without providing the means to protect them," yet the Americans had not exhausted every option for safeguarding shipping. In fact, Eastern Sea Frontier's war diary for February acknowledged that "there is one classic procedure to defend merchant shipping against submarine attacks," yet the US Navy was not utilizing it.

The British had been urging the Americans to institute a coastal convoy system for weeks. Their transatlantic cousins' refusal to do so seemed incomprehensible, and the Admiralty's Trade Division director increasingly struggled to remain polite about it. One British officer bemoaned "escorting convoys safely over to the American eastern seaboard, and then … [once the convoy disbands], finding that many of the ships thus escorted are easy prey to the U-boats." Norwegian mariners grew similarly embittered at transporting their cargo thousands of miles only for their ships to be blasted out from under them within sight of US shores. Britain's First Sea Lord personally petitioned Admiral Ernest King on 10 February, but COMINCH was unmoved.

The Royal Navy also eagerly shared the antisubmarine lessons learned so painfully during the previous war and again since 1939. American officers had established a liaison detachment at the Admiralty in August 1940, yet ADM King's Navy seemed wholly uninterested in the first weeks of 1942. COMINCH also purportedly groused that he hated "taking orders from a bunch of limeys." When King's deputy chief of staff informed a Royal Navy intelligence officer that the United States preferred to learn its own antisubmarine lessons, the British officer exploded in anger. "The trouble is, Admiral, that it's not only your bloody ships you're losing!"

Yet King was not opposed to convoying in principle. In fact, on 12 February he formally tasked Rear Admiral Adolphus Andrews with submitting an East Coast convoy plan for his approval. However, COMINCH was convinced that convoys without sufficient escorts would only offer the Germans more targets. He was not alone in this view. RADM Andrews concurred, and the ESF war diary reported that his district commanders all expressed, "in varying degrees, their opposition to the immediate introduction of the convoy system." They largely cited "the limited capacity of the defense forces assigned to the Districts."

On 26 February, Andrews submitted a letter to King recommending that "no attempt be made to protect coastwise shipping by a convoy system until an adequate number of suitable escort vessels is available." The convoy issue was effectively tabled because escort assets remained scarce, although King's stated conviction that "inadequately protected convoys are worse than none" was demonstrably false. British experience showed that even weak escorting forces often deterred solitary U-boats, especially close to shore where land-based air coverage was available.[4]

The US Navy instead opted for alternate approaches to protect merchant shipping. These included daylight-only travel "between such points as New York and Delaware Capes" and routing as much traffic as possible through the Chesapeake and Delaware Canal and Cape Cod Canal. In the interim, available combat vessels and aircraft were tasked with antisubmarine patrols despite British warnings that this was a prohibitively inefficient use of resources. RADM Andrews endorsed this approach, stating in February that convoys "should be introduced only if these remedies, when applied, prove inadequate."

While Andrews struggled to obtain destroyers for Eastern Sea Frontier, available air assets were also not being effectively employed. The Civil Air Patrol (CAP), a volunteer organization of civilian pilots established in 1941, offered the Army and Navy its services. "We may not sink any submarines," admitted Gill Robb Wilson, CAP founder and former New Jersey Director of Aeronautics, "but we might be able to frighten them into staying below the surface." If nothing else, he urged, this could "give our shipping a fighting chance." Andrews saw significant value in these "scarecrow patrols" and urged King to accept CAP's offer of assistance.

ADM King rejected the enthusiastic amateurs, citing only unspecified "operational difficulties," but the Army agreed to a 90-day trial period beginning in March. Sun Oil Company also led a fundraising effort which produced $45,000 to establish CAP airbases along the East Coast. Flying an eclectic variety of aircraft without pay, the Civil Air Patrol activated "Coastal Patrol Base One" at Bader Field in Atlantic City on 28 February 1942.

Karl Dönitz could hardly have hoped for an enemy course of action more favorable to his ends. After the war, U-boat officers would express bewilderment at how the US Navy failed to leverage Britain's antisubmarine experience. Historian John Lawton wrote that *U-404* commander Otto von Bülow "told me that many of his 'kills' in the early part of the war were managed because the American admiral did not believe that the British could teach him anything about the convoy system and protection."

While the Americans dithered, echoes of 1917 produced a sense of déjà vu at the British Admiralty. "History is repeating itself," an officer at the Royal Navy's headquarters in London wrote in January 1942. "Although we shall not win the war by defeating the U-boats, we shall assuredly lose the war if we do not defeat them."[5]

***

Although the *R.P. Resor* was sailing alone, the tanker carried at least one measure of reassurance in the form of a 4-inch/.50 naval gun. Manning the weapon fell to a nine-man US Navy detachment that augmented the ship's merchant crew of forty-one. Consequently, John Forsdal's vigil on the forecastle was augmented by a Navy sailor posted on the monkey bridge, or elevated platform on the flying bridge. Another Armed Guard stood watch at the gun recently installed on the aft deck.

The *R.P. Resor* was fortunate to have a weapon at all. Repealing the Neutrality Act's Section 6 in November 1941 allowed US Merchant Marine vessels to carry defensive armament, but a shortage of guns meant that most American merchantmen were still unarmed in late February 1942. Although the Esso tanker had been outfitted with a platform on the forecastle for a second gun, it was left bare due to a shortage of weapons.

"Fifty-seven of our Brothers went down with those ships," raged the Seamen's International Union newspaper on 2 February. "NOT ONE of our Brothers had so much as an air-rifle with which to protect himself against the enemy raiders ... A gun and a life raft is little enough to ask for, don't you think? Then what's the stall?" The radio officer aboard the *Ciltvaira*, torpedoed by the *U-123* on 19 January, hit a more optimistic note. "Our next ship will be armed. It'll be different then," he told reporters. "You'll see what we can do when the devils attack."

However, training American mariners as gunners was not a viable option. Whereas their British counterparts were employed by the Ministry of War Transport and kept on the payroll between voyages, American mariners were paid at a voyage's end and then released from service until they signed on for another trip. Lacking personnel to train in gunnery ashore, the Navy instead resurrected the Armed Guard.

The Armed Guard program was established during World War I to provide merchant ships with naval guns and sailors to man them. Though preferable in some ways to serving aboard a warship, more than six hundred Armed Guards would be killed in action in 1942 alone. Cynicism prevailed, and January's widely publicized "sighted sub, sank same" story led Armed Guards to joke that their motto was "sighted sub, glub glub."[6]

The lone gun's placement at the stern was not arbitrary, as US Navy guidance instructed mariners to steer away from an enemy to "force a stern chase." The bright moon above John Forsdal this evening improved a ship's odds because following a path of moonlight would put a U-boat commander in the horns of a dilemma. Pursuing while submerged meant the ship would outrun him, but pursuing while surfaced would present the merchantman's gunners with a well-illuminated target astern.

This required detecting a U-boat before it attained an attack position. John Forsdal was therefore not only watching for threats, but also listening for them. "If motor sounds are heard by lookouts," the Navy warned, "there is every likelihood that a surfaced submarine is maneuvering about the ship in order to take up a forward position for a torpedo attack." The sea around the R.P. Resor, however, remained silent.[7]

Near the stern, Coxswain Daniel Hey had just retired to his rack in the aft crew quarters. The 27-year-old was one of nine Armed Guard sailors aboard the R.P. Resor. The New York City native had been working for the Army Transport Service in Brooklyn when he joined the long line of volunteers at the recruiting office after Pearl Harbor. Hey was the detachment's senior enlisted sailor despite having been in the Navy for less than three months. Of average height with a muscular build, Hey typically wore his mop of curly dark hair slightly longer than Navy regulations permitted.

In lieu of traditional military ranks, US Navy enlisted personnel instead have "rates" which combine functional specialty and hierarchical rank into one title. Enlisted sailors in the Kriegsmarine and Royal Navy were similarly organized. Daniel Hey's rate was coxswain, a term which also refers to anyone steering a small boat. Coxswain fell under the boatswain's mate rating and was equivalent to a third-class petty officer. Why Hey's rank was not simply "boatswain's mate, third class" was entirely lost on him.

Coxswain Hey appreciated the camaraderie of a small detachment, theirs being just eight enlisted men under 27-year-old Ensign Charles Major. Navy brass, however, feared their sailors might be "influenced by the lack of discipline among merchant seamen." Foreseeing challenges regarding shipboard cohesion, the Navy sought to staff the Armed Guard program with officers "mature enough to avoid differences and bickering with merchant personnel." This represented the greatest challenge. Aboard the R.P. Resor, a chill between the mariners and sailors had lingered ever since Ensign Major's detachment boarded two weeks earlier.

Friction between Armed Guards and merchant crews was reported on nearly a third of armed merchant vessels in 1942, and the heartburn was mutual. Mariners chafed at having shipmates who were neither union members nor concerned with pay and overtime while Armed Guards resented the merchant crewmen's higher wages. Many Navy sailors were unaware their civilian counterparts only earned pay while their ship was in service—a mariner abandoning a sinking ship was off the clock the instant he hit the water.[8]

***

Although New Jersey's coastal lights were an entrancing sight from the *R.P. Resor's* forecastle, John Forsdal kept his gaze on the water. Spotting a submarine forward of the bow provided the best advance warning of an attack because it was likely at long range and had not yet launched a torpedo, but darkness was not conducive to seeing that far forward. Forsdal therefore focused his attention abeam because he knew that submarines of all navies preferred to attack from right angles for the widest possible target area. Sighting a U-boat here may be too late, but the Germans' habit of attacking from close range at night also meant a U-boat would more likely be spotted abeam than ahead. Forsdal directed most of his effort to watching the starboard beam. New Jersey lay off the port beam, and he doubted that any submarine commander was bold enough to stalk the shallows so close to shore.

It was off the port bow where Forsdal sighted movement at 23:27. A small, low-lying shape about 400 yards distant was approaching at about 30 degrees relative to the bow. Forsdal could not hear an engine over the noise of the *R.P. Resor's* bow wave, and all its lights were extinguished. Fishermen were a common sight at this hour, and Forsdal's primary concern was a collision. A tanker bowling over a fishing boat would mean both unpleasant legal consequences for Jersey Standard and likely the end of a fisherman's life.

Times were hard enough for fishermen, as catches were plummeting up and down the East Coast. "Torpedo and shellfire explosions have run the fish away," declared a Coast Guard chief petty officer in Virginia who was also a record-holding angler. "When the first torpedo exploded off the coast it probably killed every living thing within a quarter mile and a like distance in depth. It may be years before another fish will enter that area."

As the darkened fishing boat approached the *R.P. Resor's* bow, Forsdal about-faced and walked briskly to the bell at the forecastle's aft end. Glancing over his right shoulder as he walked, he saw the vessel's lights suddenly turn on. He discerned one green light and one red light, with a white light centered between them and about 5 feet above. It was perhaps 250 yards away and noiselessly drawing nearer.

Forsdal rang the bell twice before speaking into the voice pipe. "Small vessel about two points on the port bow, sir," he reported. The hollow reverberation of third mate Graham Covert's voice replied: "Aye aye." Fifteen seconds had now elapsed since Forsdal spotted the fishing boat. On the bridge, Orville Hogard turned the wheel in accordance with Covert's order. The *R.P. Resor* slowly shifted course to starboard.

Forsdal strolled back to the forecastle. He was still unable to see the approaching craft clearly. Its three lights, now about 45 degrees off the port bow, were too dim to reveal its hull or deck structures. The moon's position on the *Resor*'s starboard quarter also left the water off the port side cloaked in darkness. The lights winked off a few seconds later, and Forsdal paid them no further attention. A minute passed, then two.[9]

In the aft crew quarters, a hideous clangor of rending steel riveted through Coxswain Daniel Hey's veil of slumber as the *R.P. Resor* convulsed violently. The Armed Guard petty officer bolted upright in his rack. He took two seconds to digest what was occurring before hopping from the sheets. Around him stirred a commotion of groggy voices as other Armed Guards dropped out of bed and staggered into wakeful action. "Alright, let's go!" Hey shouted. "Grab your shit and get moving!" A fight, it seemed, had finally found them.

There was no confusion among the Armed Guards. The sailors moved with an intensity reflecting the ceaseless drills enforced by ENS Major. An Armed Guard detachment would ideally engage a U-boat *before* it attacked but, if the ship was already hit, then they were expected to return fire for as long as the tactical situation permitted. Official US Navy instructions were clear that "the ship must be defended with every means for as long as possible."[10]

On the forecastle at the moment of impact, John Forsdal felt the *R.P. Resor* spasm as a colossal explosion thundered against the port side amidships. The forecastle seemed to rise up and strike him, sending Forsdal tumbling across the deck. Deafened and stunned, he laid motionless for a few heartbeats while a wave of heat washed over him and a dawn-like illumination melted the midnight darkness. *Clang!* Something struck the deck beside him.

Burning pieces of the *R.P. Resor* were returning in the form of metal fragments and wood shards. *Thump! Clang!* Jarred back to reality, Forsdal scrambled under the empty gun platform. He waited there for one, two, three seconds. His chest heaved. The heat intensified. He heard flames roaring. When the apocalyptic squall abated, Forsdal warily emerged from under the platform. He could already tell that the ship was on fire, but what he now laid eyes upon beggared comprehension.

The midship house was engulfed by an enormous tower of flames that pierced the night sky with a cruel red-orange intensity. Forsdal could see no movement on the bridge, but he heard a nightmarish cacophony of screaming from farther aft. He pushed the horror from his consciousness as sweat poured down his brow from the heat. Forsdal could see two of the four lifeboats already burning since the boat deck was part of the midship structure, one level below the bridge.

That left only the two lifeboats at the aft deck house. Forsdal decided to venture closer to the midship house to determine whether there was any route past the flames to the stern. He had just descended from the forecastle to the foredeck when he sighted something on the surface 400 yards off the port bow that halted him in his tracks—a submarine. Its spectral profile showed no lights, yet it was illuminated by the fire's radiance and silhouetted by the shoreline's lights. Forsdal heard diesel engines as the submarine turned away, toward the coast.

Moving to the port side of the mast's rigging on the foredeck, the able seaman attempted to see beyond the firestorm amidships. He quickly concluded the stern lifeboats were not an option. The fire was clearly impassible and, in any event, Forsdal could not determine how far aft it stretched. As the advancing flames forced him back toward the forecastle, he realized that a liferaft was his last chance.

Forsdal decided to trade warmth for weight by hurriedly removing his lifejacket and heavy overcoat, discarding the coat, then donning the lifejacket again. Determining that the northwesterly wind was blowing the oil and fire off the tanker's starboard side, he moved to her port side and tripped the releasing gear which dropped a raft from its skids into the ocean below. He then located a line hanging over the side, swung himself over the railing, and began to lower himself. Descending hand-over-hand, he made slow and deliberate movements to avoid his palms slipping on the rope. Upon reaching the waterline, Forsdal inhaled deeply and released his grip.[11]

***

Half a mile from the *R.P. Resor*, several human shapes were crowded onto the bridge of the *U-578*. Four were sailors on bridge watch, who stood facing outboard. Two of these wore the *Pudelmütze*, or knit cap topped with a pompom, while the others had opted for the woolen version of the standard-issue side cap. Amid the four lookouts stood two figures clad in double-breasted gray leather coats. Visible atop both their heads were the contours of a naval officer's peaked cap.

Three minutes earlier, the pair of officers had watched anxiously for eighty-three seconds before an explosion thundered across the water. "An enormous tongue of flame" impaled the darkness as the *R.P. Resor* was "immediately engulfed in flames from stem to stern." A smile creased the face of Korvettenkapitän Ernst-August Rehwinkel. The 40-year-old from Hildesheim had served aboard the pocket battleship *Admiral Scheer* in 1936–37 during patrols and shore bombardments in support of Nationalist forces in the Spanish Civil War. One of the war's oldest U-boat commanders, Rehwinkel had lacked any sinkings to his name until now. "Finally the spell is broken and there is understandable joy in the boat," he later penned in the log.

The three weeks since the *India Arrow* sinking on 4 February had seen an additional fifteen merchant ships torpedoed off the East Coast while ten more merchantmen and a Free French corvette were sunk off Canada. Dönitz continued dispatching U-boats as they became available, and nine more departed occupied France for the United States between 3 and 23 February 1942. One of these was the *U-578*, a Type VIIC under Korvettenkapitän Rehwinkel.

The five Operation Drumbeat boats had all been Type IXs because BdU believed that the smaller Type VIIs lacked sufficient fuel to justify sending them farther south than Canada (New Jersey is approximately 700 miles farther from France than Newfoundland). Plans changed after the Gruppe Ziethen boats, dispatched to Canada in parallel with Gruppe Paukenschlag, proved more fuel efficient than BdU had expected. "Because the Type VIIC was intended as a wolfpack boat for pursuing convoys at high speed," Dönitz explained, "the planners had assumed a greater depletion of fuel than actually experienced in North American operations."

A total of ten Type VIICs had departed for the East Coast by the end of February. Commanders maximized their range by crossing the Atlantic at low speed using one engine and traveling submerged beneath foul weather. Some crews even took the initiative to repurpose some of their boats' drinking water capacity to carry additional fuel. Dönitz was both gratified and concerned, and issued "appropriate orders to put a curb on over-enthusiasm."[12]

From the bridge of the *U-578*, Korvettenkapitän Rehwinkel watched a reddish incandescence swell into a pillar of fire more than 150 feet high. Standing beside him was Leutnant Raimund Tiesler. A former deckhand on a Norwegian freighter, the 22-year-old from East Prussia was the *U-578*'s first watch officer. "He must have been full," Tiesler commented, and Rehwinkel's log would note that the *R.P. Resor*'s cargo was "apparently gasoline." This was an incorrect but logical conclusion since gasoline evaporates more readily and ignites at lower temperatures than fuel oils like Bunker C. This made gasoline-laden tankers more prone to fiery spectacles, though burning oil was hardly more merciful than burning gasoline.

Secret recordings of conversations between German POWs revealed that U-boat men spoke of combat almost exclusively in terms of tonnage destroyed and the type and quantity of ships sunk. Seldom did they speak of who manned these ships. Even so, a burning tanker could make a powerful impression. "The flames went up in a rush three hundred feet high at least, every color from white to black-blood-red … the ship looked like a slab of iron in a forge," one kommandant recounted. "It makes your blood run cold. God, I'd hate to be on board. But perhaps it's better that way. At least it's over in one go."

It did indeed seem over for the *R.P. Resor*, which Korvettenkapitän Rehwinkel concluded did not warrant another torpedo. "There is no doubt he is a total loss," he wrote. Rehwinkel also knew it would be imprudent to admire his infernal handiwork for long, especially a display as conspicuous as this. The *U-578* peeled away hard to port and departed.[13]

***

After climbing down the rope dangling against the hull near the *R.P. Resor*'s bow, John Forsdal eased himself into the bitingly cold water and instantly inhaled sharply: the first symptom of "cold shock." Cold water triggers a gasp reflex and hyperventilation in the minutes immediately following immersion. This causes water inhalation, particularly in rough seas, which drowns many immersion victims before hypothermia can kill them. Fortunately, his lifejacket and a calm sea together kept Forsdal's face clear of the water.

Teeth chattering, he desperately scanned for the liferaft he had dropped overboard. The raft was nowhere to be seen, but that was somehow not his most immediate emergency: inertia meant that the *R.P. Resor* was still making headway. Wracked by shivering and hyperventilation but terrified of being left behind by the still-moving ship, Forsdal splashed closer to the hull now sliding past him. He sighted barbed tongues of fire writhing on the tanker's deck above as they advanced toward the stern.

Forsdal succeeded in grabbing hold of the rudder post just as the stern was passing him, only to discover there was no safety there. The propulsion system was offline, but the *R.P. Resor's* forward movement was causing the water flow to turn her 17-foot manganese bronze propeller like a pinwheel. Although rotating slowly and getting slower, he could feel the *whump ... whump ... whump* of its whirling mass in the water with him. He was still catching his breath when one of its four blades grazed his abdomen. Between the screw's unnerving proximity and the flames above, Forsdal realized he could not remain here.

The *R.P. Resor* had nearly slowed to a halt when he let go of the rudder post and swam sluggishly to the ship's starboard quarter. Tilting his shivering body to look up, he saw the aft starboard lifeboat, No. 3, swung out over the hull by its davits. Indistinguishable outlines of human shapes were visible inside the wooden craft. A moment later, the bellow of a second large explosion sounded over the howling flames as one of the ship's cargo tanks violently ruptured. Realizing the imperative to get as far from the *R.P. Resor* as possible, Forsdal turned and began swimming east—into the open ocean.

Although his hyperventilation was subsiding, Forsdal had never felt colder in his life. His lifejacket and waterlogged clothing already made swimming laborious and exhausting, and he now found himself swimming through the fuel oil hemorrhaging from the *R.P. Resor's* hull. It formed a dense, tar-like layer over the water. Already exhausted, he felt himself growing heavier as oil accumulated on his skin and clothing. *Swim, goddammit ...* he willed himself. Forsdal soon heard his 11-year-old son's voice in his head. "*Daddy John!*" the voice exclaimed, using the boy's moniker for his father. "*Wow, that's a lot of oil, Daddy John ...*"

A glance backward at the ship's starboard side revealed a new threat: the fire had spread to the oil slick, setting the surrounding sea ablaze. Thick black smoke now rolled into the night sky as a menacing curtain of fire crept toward him. It felt as if Death himself were pursuing one able seaman John Jensen Forsdal of San Francisco. He continued to swim.[14]

***

Awakened at the other end of the ship from John Forsdal when the torpedo hit, Coxswain Daniel Hey stumbled out on deck and into a waking nightmare. The Armed Guard sailor froze in shock and horror upon witnessing the towering inferno that had enveloped the midship house all the way to the monkey bridge.

Hey saw no movement there besides the wispy yellow crowns of swaying flames. The blaze emitted a punishing wall of heat that smashed aside the winter chill, the temperature intensifying as the fire devoured the 4.4 million gallons of fuel oil in the tanks under his feet.

There would be no manning the gun—it was every man for himself. Hey joined a throng of panicked men running and stumbling toward the two lifeboats at the aft deck house. When Hey reached the No. 3 lifeboat on the starboard side, rated for thirty-two occupants, he found the boat crowded to the gunwales and already being lowered. The Armed Guard and three mariners instead scrambled to the No. 4 boat on the deck house's opposite side.

The four men frantically loosened the gripes securing the lifeboat to the chocks, but they were already out of time. The flames were advancing too rapidly. "We gotta jump!" one yelled. He leapt a moment later. Hey reflexively touched his lifejacket as he glanced over the deck's edge. He saw flames down there, too. The stifling air grew hotter, the night brighter. Another man went over the side. Moving to the deck's edge, facing the silent radiance of New Jersey's coastal lights, the coxswain followed suit and plummeted downward.

Hey narrowly missed landing on one of the other men as he plunged through the oily surface. Buoyed immediately upward by his lifejacket, the sailor popped up gasping and spitting fuel oil. The water was bone-chilling, but his face was assaulted by the same scorching heat he felt on deck. Fumes stung the four men's eyes as they bobbed amid the oil, pivoting in search of an escape from the fire encroaching from every direction.

Jagged flames burned a grim crimson as they eerily appeared to dance several inches above the oil slick, but this was not an illusion. A flammable substance's liquid form does not itself burn because a liquid's molecules are too densely packed to permit oxygen between them. Rather, only its vapor burns. The substance's rate of vaporization increases as the fire degrades it on a molecular level, feeding the blaze in a cycle that caused the flames around the *R.P. Resor* to spread like a prairie fire.

"There! Right there!" Hey shouted, pointing to a gap in the fire. He immediately began to swim for it. "Follow me!" His forward movement slowed as oil congealed on him, and adrenaline could not forestall the rapid onset of exhaustion. The air grew hotter as the flames marched closer. Somebody began to scream behind him, a visceral shrieking unlike anything Hey had ever heard. He did not look back. The gap ahead of him grew smaller, then smaller still.[15]

***

In the water on the opposite side of the *R.P. Resor*, John Forsdal felt like he was swimming through molasses. A War Shipping Administration safety manual warned that "swimming through oil is like swimming through mud," and this was particularly true of the dense and highly viscous Bunker C fuel oil bleeding from the cargo tanks.

Forsdal succeeded in putting about 50 yards between himself and the ship over what felt like 20 minutes, though he had lost all sense of time. This taxed his body to its limit, but he resisted the growing temptation to pause and catch his breath.

Water drains heat from the human body twenty times faster than air, and immersion in water as cold as that off New Jersey in February can be lethal within ninety minutes. A victim's core temperature begins falling immediately, and shivering commences as the body attempts to warm itself via involuntary movement. The redirection of blood from the extremities to the vital organs causes hands to grow rigid and numb. Grasping anything becomes increasingly difficult. Meanwhile, fluids congealing in the tissues impair the limbs' dexterity and make swimming even short distances a daunting endeavor.

He eventually heard a voice shouting indistinctly. "Hello?? ..." Forsdal yelled, his body jerking as he scanned the water. He started paddling in the approximate direction of the voice, which gradually grew louder. Just as he sighted what appeared to be another survivor in the water, Forsdal heard a second voice from a different direction. He recognized the latter as the *R.P. Resor's* radio operator.

"Sparks!" Forsdal hollered back. "Where are y-you?" The second voice replied. "I've g-got a raft ..." the unseen radioman announced. "Come over h-here so we can be together." It was the most heartening proposal Forsdal had ever heard, and he changed direction to swim toward the recognizable voice. A strange, life-or-death variation of 'blind man's bluff' ensued.

"Sparks?"

"I'm over here ..." the voice replied.

"Where are you?"

"Over here ..."

"W-where?"

"Here ..."

As the pair shouted back and forth, Forsdal's core temperature continued dropping. Swimming exacerbates heat loss because physical exertion increases blood flow near the skin, which allows the surrounding water to leach yet more of the body's warmth. Movement of the limbs pushes away this warmer water for colder water to replace it, accelerating the convection cycle.

Cold water exacted a deadly toll on German forces during their unexpectedly costly invasion of Norway in 1940. The most significant loss occurred when the Kriegsmarine cruiser *Blücher*, carrying eight hundred infantrymen plus a team of Gestapo agents tasked with capturing Norway's royal family, led an invasion force up the Oslofjord under cover of darkness. A Norwegian coastal battery unexpectedly hit the cruiser with several shells, then shore-launched torpedoes struck her hull. The *Blücher* capsized and sank, and the rest of the task force retreated.

This bloody nose, which bought enough time for Norway's government to escape Oslo, left hundreds of Germans afloat in the 36° Fahrenheit fjord. More than six hundred were killed, many by hypothermia. The Kriegsmarine nonetheless failed to appreciate convection's deadly effect until 1944, when men were instructed to instead avoid movement and rely on their flotation devices if shipwrecked.

In the fire's dim light, John Forsdal finally sighted 27-year-old Clarence Armstrong floating beside an empty raft with one arm hooked around its rope handhold. Forsdal wearily did likewise on the opposite side of the 10-by-10-foot wood square. He could discern none of the radioman's features. Only the ghostly contours of Armstrong's shoulders and head were visible, as if the Florida native had already shuffled off the mortal coil but had not yet been informed.

The *R.P. Resor* was now between their raft and the coast. The sea around the ruined ship sizzled as the fire continued marching outward across the oil slick, but the two men were far enough away to be safe for the moment. The unidentified third man had stopped shouting. Whoever he was, they did not hear his voice again. "Any … a-anyone else?" Forsdal inquired weakly to his companion. "I … d-don't know," Armstrong murmured.

Forsdal could feel the ocean sapping the warmth from his body and rendering him more sluggish by the minute. Summoning his last reserves of strength, Forsdal heaved himself atop the raft like a wounded harbor seal. "J-Johnny…" Armstrong implored feebly. "Please, Johnny, h-help me up onto the r-raft …" Forsdal attempted to roll over, but the cold and exhaustion rendered him paralyzed. His limbs felt like two-by-fours and he could not even extend a hand.[16]

***

Eighteen miles away, two Coast Guardsmen manning a coastal watchtower spotted an ominous glow on the horizon. They promptly called it in to Coast Guard Station Manasquan Inlet. Five miles south and five minutes later, a similar report reached the Shark River station. Chief Boatswain's Mate John Daisey, the ranking Coast Guardsman at Manasquan Inlet since 1935, quickly mobilized his men. Little did he know that the longest night of his life had just begun.

The *Asbury Park Press* depicted John Daisey as a "big, blustering man whose leather face, beaten by the winds and seas of the Atlantic and the Great Lakes, changes from a frown to a booming laugh in the twinkling of an eye." Highly decorated, his long career included a 1936 incident he considered his closest brush with death when heavy seas smashed his picket boat against the rocks and washed two other Coast Guardsmen overboard, but CBM Daisey saved both men and safely returned to port. "No matter what the ocean's like, no matter what I had to go through," declared one officer, "the one man I'd want to have with me is Daisey."

The hasty rescue force raced to sea piecemeal. Picket boat *CG 4344* got underway first, roaring seaward five minutes after fire was sighted. Aboard were Chief Boatswain's Mate John Daisey, Machinist's Mate 1st Class Thomas Evans, and Boatswain's Mate 2nd Class Oswald Etheridge. All were wearing watch caps and woolen coats over the Coast Guard surfman uniform. Motor lifeboat *4408* sped out of Manasquan Inlet fifteen minutes later while Shark River dispatched motor lifeboat *5177* and motor surfboat *4788*.

CG 4344 was a wooden-hull cabin picket boat measuring 38 feet long and featuring a mostly open cockpit with a small cabin. Motor lifeboats *4408* and *5177* were of the TR and TRS classes, respectively. These were roughly the same proportions as the cabin picket boats, but slower and with fully open cockpits. Type SR motor surfboats like *4788* were simply self-bailing wooden motorboats. The Shark River station also dispatched the civilian boat *Optimist II* (manned by her owner and several Coast Guardsmen). A second civilian craft, the *Doris May*, would also set out from Belmar with a crew that included Belmar's mayor, Leon Abbott.

CG 4344 skipped across the water as BM2 Etheridge pushed the picket boat to its top speed of 19 knots (20.9 mph). Navigation was simple, as the sinister reddish glare of the burning ship was visible for miles. They soon smelled the carrion stench of burning oil.

The chief petty officer was reminded of the old US Life-Saving Service which had rowed to the aid of imperiled mariners for decades before the Coast Guard was founded. Coastal rescue as a public service in the United States began in 1848 when Congress approved funding for the "preservation of life and property from shipwreck on the coast of New Jersey," and eight lifeboat stations were subsequently built along the state's shoreline. This evolved into the US Life-Saving Service, which was merged with the Revenue Cutter Service in 1915 to create the US Coast Guard. Rescuers like John Daisey still lived by the Life-Saving Service motto: "You have to go out, but you don't have to come back."[17]

***

Forsdal's mind reeled as he lay in the raft. The cold, the stench of burning oil, his stinging eyes, the crackling of encroaching flames … the entire experience was an assault on his senses. It felt even colder on the raft where the winter breeze afflicted him. "Wish I was back … in the water …" Forsdal slurred. "It's too damn c-cold up here …" Whether intended as a joke or merely idle commentary, it elicited no response from Armstrong.

Climbing onto the raft had, in fact, saved Forsdal's life for the moment. A victim is about halfway to losing consciousness after thirty minutes in water that cold. Spastic shivering becomes continuous and uncontrollable as the core temperature drops, and breathing and heart rate slow as the body shuts down circulation to the limbs to keep the vital organs warm. Confusion and disorientation begin, and the victim displays irrational and lethargic behavior. Hallucinations can occur.

Breathing becomes shallower and the pupils dilate as the heart rate grows erratic. Shivering ceases when the heat generated from burning glycogen can no longer offset the falling core temperature, and consciousness eventually fades as the body enters a hibernation-like stasis. The ordeal eventually concludes when the combined effects of increased blood pressure, lowered heart rate, and decreased oxygen cause heart failure.

A second cargo tank exploded, but Forsdal's heavy eyelids soon abruptly shot open upon perceiving a different noise—an engine. Unsure whether he was hallucinating, the able seaman undertook the agonizing and nigh-Herculean feat of rolling over onto his side. "Keep your chin up, Sparks ... they're here for us," Forsdal croaked as the engine noise grew gradually louder. Armstrong was silent.[18]

***

Even at top speed, it took *CG 4344* nearly an hour to reach the *R.P. Resor* from Manasquan Inlet. Chief Boatswain's Mate John Daisey, the Coast Guardsman commanding the picket boat, was no stranger to mortal peril. He had performed rescues in savage nor'easters, recovered flood victims in Pennsylvania, and survived at least two shootouts with smugglers on Lake Erie. Daisey had even cheated death while responding to the infamous 1932 fire aboard the ocean liner *Morro Castle*, which claimed 137 lives off Long Beach Island. None of this, however, had prepared Daisey for the sight now before him.

The 435-foot floating cauldron greeted the picket boat with hissing and crackling as steel contorted and sagged under the searing heat. The raging inferno lit the *R.P. Resor*'s surroundings with a flickering off-yellow hue as oil bled from a gaping hole in the hull, feeding a blaze that sprawled south from the wreck. Jets of flame burning a lurid red intermittently spouted from the wreck while fires inside the tanker burned so hot that the entire hull glowed a ghastly white.

Steering was made difficult by the thick layer of oil over the water, and the *CG 4344*'s propeller shuddered in protest as it choked on the *Resor*'s cargo. The rescuers' lungs convulsed in rejection of the poisonous air which sent them into fits of ugly coughing. An oil fire can burn hotter than 2,500° Fahrenheit, creating deadly clouds of dense smoke carrying sulfur dioxide and carbon monoxide along with soot and other particulates.

The oil fire was still spreading, and Daisey knew they were running out of time. "Closer! Bring us closer!" BM2 Oswald Etheridge complied, maneuvering from one oil-free spot to another while keeping about 30 yards from the blazing wreck. A harsh glare lit the three Coast Guardsmen's faces as they scanned the hellscape for any sign of life.

"Help! ..."

They barely heard the man's voice over the rasping inferno. "Stop the engine," Daisey ordered. "Chief, we ca—" "Stop the damn engine!" The engine's growl ceased as its oil-choked propeller gurgled into silence. "Help! ..." the feeble voice implored again. The chief petty officer pointed: "Over there."

As the picket boat ventured closer, the fire's light revealed a man floating in the water. He was so covered with oil that only the approximate shape of a human figure was distinguishable. The man's pleading grew weaker as *CG 4344* drew alongside. Daisey and Evans grabbed him, but it felt as if he weighed 400 pounds. "Holy shit! …" Daisey shouted for Etheridge's assistance.

Three pairs of hands now grabbed the oil-logged man, yet even their combined strength proved insufficient. The endeavor was rendered more arduous by the scorching air temperature; the glowing hull of *R.P. Resor* was radiating so much heat that *CG 4344*'s paint was blistering. Realizing that the man was too heavy to muscle aboard, Daisey and the others instead looped a rope around his waist to tow him clear of danger.

The engine roared back to life and the picket boat lurched forward, hauling the hapless survivor behind it. He yelped in protest as his head was forced underwater. "S-stop! … Stop!" the man begged. Daisey swore. "Move the line around aft!" The three Coast Guardsmen finally succeeded in hauling the man aboard at the stern.

Motor lifeboat *4408*, which left Manasquan Inlet minutes after *CG 4344*, arrived along with Shark River Station's *Optimist II*, motor lifeboat *5177*, and motor surfboat *4788*. Other rescuers appeared in the form of the Coast Guard cutters USCGC *Icarus* (WPC-110) and USCGC *Antietam* (WPC-128), the armed yacht *Zircon* (PY-16), the coastal minesweeper *AMc-200*, and the Navy subchaser *PC-507*. CBM Daisey hailed *5177* and shouted that the survivor had seen a fully loaded lifeboat cast off in the minutes after the attack. The other boat immediately sped off to search for it.

Motor surfboat *4788*'s propeller sputtered in thick oil as it approached the wreck to inspect a pair of rafts. Upon finding no signs of life, the Coast Guardsmen were attempting to retreat when their engine stalled. They were now stranded windward of the *R.P. Resor* as the fire crept nearer, and the surfboat's engine hiccuped and sputtered before finally roaring back to life. They escaped only yards ahead of the approaching blaze.[19]

***

On the other side of the flaming wreck, John Forsdal attempted to identify the source of the approaching engine noise. A searchlight scythed across the water. "Over here! …" Forsdal shouted hoarsely. His feeble supplications went seemingly unheard as the boat passed him, but it then cut a sharp turn and its light beam landed on Forsdal and Armstrong. Hope swelled in Forsdal's chest. The boat surged forward and then slowed again, putting the raft off its starboard side. He heard the voices of its crew, one of whom shouted something unintelligible. A circular white object trailing a rope then spun through the air and splashed next to the raft.

Forsdal moved on his stomach to the raft's side, grabbed the flotation ring, and hooked both arms through it. Just as he turned his head toward Armstrong, the line attached to the lifebuoy went taut, jerking Forsdal forward and off the raft. Immersion made him gasp again as he struggled to hold on to the lifebuoy. The vessel slowed again, but it still had more headway than the enfeebled and oil-slick mariner could manage. The ring was yanked from his arms and skipped away across the surface.

The boat sheered off into another turn as Forsdal splashed ponderously back to the raft. The few yards' distance felt like a mile, and the water felt warmer than the air. With rescue so close at hand, Forsdal decided against attempting to climb back onto the raft. He doubted that he possessed the strength for it anyway. Clarence Armstrong said nothing. He was no longer shivering.

Jets of flame intermittently streaked from the *R.P. Resor*'s hull as Daisey's *CG 4344* motored around to the starboard side. There he found the Navy subchaser *PC-507*, which had deployed a dinghy alongside John Forsdal's raft. The sailors were attempting to haul him into the dinghy by looping a rope under his armpits, but the oil weight thwarted the effort. All the while, the flames pressed their inexorable advance.

Daisey took the helm and deftly positioned *CG 4344* beside the raft, whereupon MM1 Tom Evans and BM2 Oswald Etheridge boldly climbed off the picket boat and onto the raft. Fumes and smoke left them coughing and nearly blind as they began pulling Forsdal from the water. An oil-covered victim weighs nearly three times his normal weight, and the two Coast Guardsmen were on the verge of passing out when they finally heaved Forsdal back onto the raft. Daisey then produced a knife, extended his bulky torso over the gunwale, and sliced Forsdal out of his clothing.

The three rescuers then "rolled him aboard like he was a sack of wheat," Daisey recounted. Forsdal collapsed to the *CG 4344*'s deck and spat out a mouthful of oil. Evans and Etheridge then fell in after him, both on the verge of vomiting. There was no Clarence Armstrong, the radioman having died and floated away shortly before

Left to right: Oswald Etheridge, Thomas Evans, and John Daisey are formally recognized for their actions on the night of 26/27 February. (*Asbury Park Press*, enhanced by Peter Shafron)

Forsdal's rescue. The mariner was wrapped in a blanket and brought into the boat's cabin to join the other survivor found earlier: Coxswain Daniel Hey from the Armed Guard detachment. None of the three men who went overboard with Hey survived.[20]

A Navy blimp, planes, and additional vessels arrived while CBM Daisey and his men scoured the scene until sunrise. Local volunteers and the Red Cross set up beachside hospital stations at Point Pleasant and Belmar, yet no influx of wounded men arrived. Of the *R.P. Resor*'s forty-one merchant mariners and nine Armed Guard sailors, only John Forsdal and Daniel Hey lived to see daybreak.

The *CG 4344* returned to Manasquan Inlet later that morning with Forsdal and Hey, who grinned as they were helped out of the boat. Point Pleasant's volunteer medical squad cleaned them of oil using kerosene and dressed them in clothing donated by local residents. A doctor noted that both had slight burns, but deemed them fit for interviewing by naval intelligence. Daisey and his men's torn and oil-sodden uniforms had to be thrown away. Forsdal discovered that his watch was stopped at 23:31, the precise moment he entered the water.

Forsdal was lodged at the Seamen's Church Institute of New York and New Jersey, an advocacy and welfare organization for mariners founded in 1834. "When you were swimming about in that heavy oil, what were you thinking about?" a reporter asked him. "I was thinking of my kids," Forsdal answered, "especially

Daniel Hey (left) and John Forsdal (right) at Coast Guard Station Manasquan Inlet. (Courtesy of Joseph Bilby)

my boy, Pinky, eleven years old … I thought, if Pinky could only see me now, he'd say 'Daddy John, you are awfully dirty.'" His experience being torpedoed in the previous war was mentioned. "They were gentlemen that time," Forsdal joked. "So, will you go back to sea?" "I guess so," Forsdal replied. "When I get a week off."[21]

***

Dawn revealed a pall of black smoke wafting north as Jersey Shore residents crowded the beaches to see the *R.P. Resor*, which was still burning. *Asbury Park Press* reporter E. Burke Maloney and six news photographers from New York chartered local fisherman Andrew Larsen's boat for an up-close view of the burning wreck. The boat encountered a corpse which they unsuccessfully attempted to retrieve using a rope. "So we reluctantly watched the dead sailor float away, bobbing up and down in the high waves," Maloney wrote. "No one said much for a while until there was a shout. 'There's another one!' We looked, and wished we hadn't. The seaman was burned horribly."

The scorched hulk was adrift 30 miles east of Lavallette, New Jersey when the newsmen's boat caught up with it. The "sickening and awful sight" left them in shocked silence. "We could see red tongues of flame" and "scarlet spurts of fire eating the long black hulk" amid "a blazing cauldron of oil," Maloney wrote. "It made us feel unimportant and useless as we surveyed the corpse of this 435-foot craft which a few hours ago had been throbbing with life."

"No one can close his eyes to the sight which greeted those on the beach last Friday morning," asserted an article in Belmar's *Coast Advertiser*. "New Jersey now knows that war is being waged in full fury." What the unnamed author saw from the beach clearly left an impression. "The devil himself would have given [the crew] time to get off," he declared. Another article in the same issue pointed out that "even in World War I, a sub commander gave his victims time to launch lifeboats, but not the underseas killer which trapped the *Resor*." The first author concluded: "The *Resor* sinking steels our hearts. It will be avenged someday, a day which can't come too soon."[22]

The fire had burned itself out by the following day when the tugboat USS *Sagamore* (AT-20) attempted to tow the wreck. Intense heat had contorted the hull, however, which caused it to take on water while under tow. The *R.P. Resor* was 36 miles off Seaside Heights when its stern bottomed out at a depth of 122 feet. Less than an hour later, and almost exactly forty-eight hours after the attack, the charred tanker rolled over and vanished.

The *R.P. Resor*'s fiery end would stand as one of the war's most stunning spectacles in American waters. Her sister ship would soon join her on the seafloor. Almost exactly a month after the immolation of her twin, the *T.C. McCobb* was spotted by an Italian submarine off northern Brazil. She fled, but the Italian boat gave chase and eventually sank her with shellfire and torpedoes. Thirty-four of thirty-nine crewmen survived.

The earlier sinkings of the *Allan Jackson* and the *W.L. Steed* made the *R.P. Resor* the third Esso tanker lost off the East Coast. These three attacks killed ninety-six Esso crewmen. "In their passing we have lost some of our closest friends," stated a eulogy published by the Jersey Standard Tanker Officers Association. They wore "no stripes or bars to show that war was their profession. It was not. Yet war came to them in its most tragic form as they followed their chosen work—the sea." The tribute was titled: "That This Nation Might Live."

Although 1942 was proving bleak for merchant mariners in general and tanker stiffs in particular, fearful odds had not deterred them so far. When a *New York Times* reporter asked a Norwegian survivor of the *Norness* if he would be returning to sea, the "blonde giant" grinned and replied, "Sure, I go!" A reporter visiting a crowded National Maritime Union hiring hall asked one mariner why he preferred being a tanker stiff. "Good dough," he replied nonchalantly. "You don't think about torpedoes. You figure that if one's got your number on it, that's too bad. If it hasn't, it won't get you."

The *R.P. Resor* burns offshore on 27 February 1942. The 4-inch gun is visible on the aft deck. (US National Archives)

Commendable flippancy notwithstanding, more mariners were finding their numbers on German torpedoes every day. The *R. P. Resor* was the thirty-fifth merchant ship and seventeenth tanker destroyed by U-boats in Eastern Sea Frontier territory. The actual damage was even worse, as this same period also saw twenty-five additional sinkings in the 200-nautical-mile strip of ocean immediately east of Eastern Sea Frontier's boundary. "One by one the comforting notions vanished," an editorial in *The New Yorker* reflected, "leaving behind them the pained, familiar feeling that this was not the way things were supposed to happen at all."[23]

***

John Forsdal's account of the attack established a narrative that would stand for more than eighty years. This version of events holds that the "fishing boat" that approached and briefly turned on its lights was the *U-578* baiting the *R. P. Resor* to turn, thereby providing a clear shot amidships. "While I cannot give any other explanation of the strange vessel," Forsdal attested, "there is no doubt in my mind from my experience as a seaman that it was a submarine."

This is not an outlandish scenario, yet available evidence instead suggests a conventional attack. The most telling evidence is in the *U-578*'s log, which indicates the presence of other vessels near the attack scene. Rehwinkel evaded "two illuminated fishermen" during his approach and observed "an approaching light" on the *R. P. Resor*'s opposite side. In his estimation, this was "apparently a destroyer or patrol vessel which was not seen before, probably just there by chance." After the torpedo hit, the latter "comes to the stern of the tanker to turn up and begin the hunt, however, he gives up after a short time."

This raises further questions. There are no records of any Navy or Coast Guard craft nearby and no documentation of any fisherman reporting such an encounter. Nor did John Forsdal or Daniel Hey report seeing any nearby ships. Rehwinkel's "patrol vessel" may well have been an optical illusion, but the presence of fishermen cannot be so easily discounted.

Distances specified in Forsdal's account also do not match German records. Forsdal claimed that the unidentified vessel approached to within 200–300 yards in the two minutes before the strike and, moments later, that he saw a U-boat 400–500 yards off the port side. Rehwinkel's log, however, states that the *U-578* was never nearer than 1,300 yards from the *R. P. Resor*. It should be mentioned that a Type VIIC did feature lights of the colors and approximate configuration that Forsdal described, although these were virtually never used on patrol.

Korvettenkapitän Rehwinkel had little incentive to employ a risky deception stratagem because he already enjoyed ideal conditions for an attack from abeam. Even if he had engaged in such a gambit, it seems unlikely that he would have falsified official records by omitting it from his log. Forsdal's narrative is therefore certainly plausible, though a preponderance of the evidence contradicts it.

Whether he torpedoed the *R.P. Resor* via trickery or not, Ernst-August Rehwinkel was brimming with optimism as he turned south after the attack and recorded an "expectation of additional ships" in his log. What the *U-578*'s commander and crew did not know is that a formidable opponent had just arrived in New York City with one mission: hunt down and destroy the U-boats. Only time would tell whether this foe would prevent Rehwinkel's next kill, but the clock was ticking.[24]

CHAPTER EIGHT

USS *Jacob Jones* (DD-130)

"To blow things to bits is our business (and Fritz's),
Which means there are mine-fields wherever you stroll.
Unless you've particular wish to die quick,
You'll avoid steering close to the North Sea Patrol."
—Rudyard Kipling, *Sea Warfare* (1916)

27 February 1942
90 Church Street, New York City
08:44

As thousands crowded the beaches to see the burning *R.P. Resor* on that Friday morning less than twelve hours after the attack, Lieutenant Commanders Hugh Black and Thomas Marshall stepped from the elevator at Eastern Sea Frontier headquarters in Manhattan. The 14th-floor office was crowded with staff officers, ringing phones, and wall charts marked with the coordinates of sinkings, merchant ships, and U-boat sightings. They were met briefly by Vice Admiral Andrews, then chatted with his chief of staff before being led to the operations room by Lieutenant Commander Louis Farley, the ESF operations officer.

Black and Marshall were the commander and executive officer, respectively, of USS *Jacob Jones*, a destroyer scheduled to commence patrolling the New Jersey coast later that morning. Hugh Black and his second-in-command left ESF headquarters feeling invigorated. LCDR Farley's briefing had made it clear that the patrol would not be a fishing expedition undertaken in the hope of a chance encounter with the enemy. The *Jacob Jones* was instead going out to pick a fight, and Navy intelligence knew just how to find one.[1]

***

The Pearl Harbor attack of 7 December 1941 had catapulted a wholly unprepared United States into global war. Isolationism and the Great Depression had fostered a military atrophy that President Roosevelt whimsically described as "a lack of naval butter to cover the bread," and multifarious challenges were exacerbated by the fact that both Germany and Japan wielded large and dangerous navies. Nor could FDR's administration realistically prioritize one adversary over another. As Secretary of the Navy Frank Knox told reporters on 28 January, "We can't take them one at a time when they're coming two at a time."

The nation's military fortunes offered "not a single ray of consolation," wrote journalist Westbrook Pegle. Imperial Japan, which had followed Pearl Harbor with a dizzying tide of conquests across the Asia-Pacific region, represented the most immediate threat. US forces had been overwhelmed on Guam and Wake Island, and the worst defeat in American history was unfolding in the Philippines. Ships and aircraft were consequently surged across the Pacific to bolster the crumbling strategic situation there, although not in time to save more than twenty thousand American troops in the Philippines from falling into Japanese captivity.

Although the US Navy's Atlantic Fleet remained a potent force even after dispatching reinforcements to the Far East, Admiral Ernest King kept its destroyers and cutters committed to transatlantic convoy escort and patrol duties far from the East Coast. King was also beholden to FDR, and his political patron's expectations and agreements with Winston Churchill impelled a significant American naval presence along the North Atlantic supply route. Politics and King's questionable allocation of forces therefore compounded a growing litany of operational demands. The consequences were disastrous. By February 1942, wrote historian Ed Offley, the US Navy "appeared to be coming apart at the seams."

The end of a bloody January brought little relief as Eastern Sea Frontier saw five more ships go down in the first five days of February. A desperate Rear Admiral Andrews shuttled between Manhattan and Washington, D.C. negotiating for more warships and aircraft. Higher and adjacent commands all seemed to be doing the same, and his command's war diary described February's haggling as "robbing Peter of a promissory note so that Paul could be paid with it." It became clear to Andrews that ESF faced a prolonged "shortage of every kind of ship and plane that could be used effectively against the U-boat."

The East Coast required warships with capabilities that large and unwieldy capital ships could not provide. Part of the challenge was the "Gun Club," or naval officers overly enamored with battleships and cruisers. In a March letter to Churchill, President Roosevelt lamented that the Gun Club had "declined in the past to think in terms of any vessel less than two thousand tons." Yet the president himself had both nixed the Navy's recommendation to produce more Treasury-class cutters and neglected to approve production of a "destroyer escort" designed specifically for guarding convoys.[2]

FDR's tenure as Assistant Secretary of the Navy led him to favor subchasers, and the first 110-foot wooden-hulled "SC" boats and 173-foot steel-hulled "PC" boats entered service in 1941. Subchasers were "one of Mr Roosevelt's fads," according to the Atlantic Fleet's Vice Admiral Royal Ingersoll. "He was a small-boat seaman himself and loved to cruise on little things." However, the new subchasers and the 200-foot "Eagle boats" left over from the last war both fell short of what the East Coast needed in February 1942.

Eastern Sea Frontier's ragtag fleet included four of the Navy's last remaining Eagle boats. One was USS *PE-56*, better known as the "*Eagle 56*," which operated out of Cape May, New Jersey. Rushed into production by Henry Ford in 1918, the Eagle boats were dismissed by an official Navy history as "square-built, slow, weak ... almost completely useless." The *Eagle 56* was "unlovely to look at and so slow that every time she dropped depth charges she had a hard time getting out of the way," wrote an officer at Fourth Naval District in Philadelphia, Pennsylvania. "Nonetheless, she was the best we had."

February at least brought two small reprieves. First, RADM Andrews was granted operational control of all 75 and 83-foot Coast Guard cutters on the East Coast ("cutter" refers to any commissioned US Coast Guard ship designed for an oceangoing, multi-mission role). He ordered these armed with 3-inch/.23 guns, .50 caliber machine guns, and "as many depth charges as practicable." These augmented ESF's two 165-foot Thetis-class cutters and one 125-foot Active-class cutter, which were currently his only vessels "capable of keeping the sea and taking offensive action against enemy submarines."

The second break was Britain's offer to send twenty-four antisubmarine trawlers manned by Royal Navy crews, a gesture intended to entice the Americans into implementing coastal convoys. Admiral King refused the trawlers only to relent around 13 February, though his opposition to convoys remained unchanged. Samuel Eliot Morison depicted the British trawlers as "rugged little coal burners, manned with tough and aggressive former merchant seamen," yet their mechanical reliability was dubious and their top speed of 10 knots was painfully slow.

Subchasers, armed trawlers, and small cutters were useful for observation, harassment, and rescue, but none were true submarine killers. Even King understood this. "The early months of 1942," he later wrote, demonstrated "that stout hearts in little boats cannot handle an opponent as tough as the submarine." ESF needed ships with the maneuverability to dodge torpedoes, the speed to chase down a fleeing U-boat, and the firepower to destroy it before or after it vanished into the depths. They also needed to be highly seaworthy and possess enough range to scour thousands of miles of ocean. What was needed, in other words, were destroyers.[3]

Recent events had siphoned dozens of destroyers that might otherwise have found employment with Eastern Sea Frontier. Fifty had been transferred to Britain in 1940, and eleven more were rushed to the Pacific after Pearl Harbor, yet this still left more than eighty destroyers and large cutters assigned to the Atlantic Fleet. Andrews pleaded with COMINCH for the permanent assignment of fifteen destroyers to his command, but King rebuffed him in January on the grounds that not even one could be spared.

Decades later, an Ernest King apologist would answer "Where was the Navy?" with the explanation that the Atlantic Fleet was busy "fighting the Battle of the

Atlantic." Yet, as historian Michael Gannon pointed out, there was no Battle of the Atlantic elsewhere in early 1942—the battle was off Florida, North Carolina, and New Jersey. Convoys to Britain lost only a handful of ships between January and April, meanwhile, Eastern Sea Frontier was averaging 1.85 sinkings per day. King's refusal to transfer even a single destroyer on a long-term basis to ESF until April represents, in Gannon's words, "a mystery that no amount of smoke will explain."

Rear Admiral Andrews finally won a small bureaucratic victory in late January when COMINCH granted him temporary use of a handful of destroyers. Seven patrolled the East Coast from 23 January to 5 February, but "none remained long enough in any one place to perform with complete effectiveness" and all seven were vacuumed away to the north-central Atlantic by mid-February. After several days without any destroyer coverage, four were temporarily detailed to ESF on 19 February. Two of these were assigned to patrol out of New York City: USS *Dickerson* (DD-157) and USS *Jacob Jones* (DD-130).[4]

***

The advent of torpedo boats in the late 19th century spurred the development of "torpedo boat destroyers," which eventually evolved into versatile medium-sized warships known simply as destroyers. Nicknamed "tin cans" for their thin hulls, destroyers were heavily armed and equipped with powerful engines that made them fast and maneuverable. They altogether evoked a famous declaration by Admiral John Paul Jones, father of the US Navy. "I wish to have no connection with any ship that does not sail fast," Jones wrote in 1778, "for I intend to go in harm's way."

German and British destroyers at 1916's Battle of Jutland had delivered high-speed torpedo attacks and screened for their respective battlefleets like seagoing cavalry. This role remained central to destroyer doctrine in 1942, but World War I had also revealed their suitability for a different mission. As the Eastern Sea Frontier war diary observed, the destroyer's combination of swiftness and hitting power made it "the deadly and traditional enemy of the submarine."

Few understood destroyer combat like Captain Donald Macintyre of the Royal Navy. "The hunt for, the stalking of, and the final killing of a U-boat had always seemed to me to be the perfect expression of a fighting sailor's art," Macintyre explained. "Contact with the enemy would be at close quarters, and the fight would develop finally into personal combat in which good seamanship might well decide the issue." Macintyre's seamanship was evidently good enough: he sank six U-boats, including Otto Kretschmer's *U-99*.

"There was a certain cachet to serving in destroyers," explained historian Jonathan Dimbleby. They were "sleek, fast, maneuverable and aggressive and … frequently exposed to the fatal firepower of more powerful enemy warships," which "bestowed on their crews an unmatched reputation for derring-do." John Steinbeck came to understand this while serving as a correspondent aboard one. "Battleships are like steel cities or great factories of destruction … Even cruisers are big pieces of machinery," the famed novelist wrote, "but a destroyer is all boat. In the beautiful clean lines of her, in her speed and roughness, in her curious gallantry."

Their crewmen, too, were a breed apart. Like the infantrymen of the Army and Marine Corps, tin can sailors took pride in their worse quality of life even while they griped about it. A penchant for off-duty rowdiness led one officer to deem them "the bane of the shore patrol," and, like U-boat crews, they enjoyed a degree of cohesion and camaraderie that larger vessels lacked. "On a destroyer, you know everybody, with their good sides and their faults. And everybody knows you," explained a crewman from USS *Borie* (DD-215), which sank in 1943 after a brutal point-blank gun battle with the *U-405*. "You can't sham on a DD. You gotta be a sailor, mister."[5]

USS *Jacob Jones* (DD-130) measured 314 feet long and, upon launch, drew 8.66 feet of draft and displaced 1,090 long tons. The destroyer's namesake was Commodore Jacob Jones, a Delaware native and hero of the Barbary Wars and War of 1812. Built by New York Shipbuilding on the Delaware River in Camden, New Jersey as one of 111 Wickes-class destroyers, she was commissioned too late for World War I and was later mothballed for eight years. By February 1942, the *Jacob Jones* was assigned to the Atlantic Fleet's Destroyer Division Fifty-four along with the *Dickerson* and *Roper*.

A Wickes-class destroyer was commanded from a small superstructure forward of amidships containing the bridge, radio room, and chart room. On the two decks below the superstructure were the officers' quarters and part of the enlisted quarters. On the third and lowest deck was the magazine where the ship's ammunition was stored. Aft of the superstructure were four smokestacks which lent DDs of her vintage the nickname "four-pipers." Between the second and third stack was the galley deck house. Below the galley were the two boiler rooms, then the two engine rooms were immediately aft of that. The remainder of the enlisted berthing was aft of the engine rooms near the stern.

Besides their stacks, the four-pipers had a distinctive "flush deck" design in which the main deck ran from bow to stern on an even plane, without a forecastle at the bow. This strengthened the hull at the expense of protecting the bridge and forward guns from heavy seas, which was worsened by a low bow. Other shortfalls included propellers situated too close together for tight maneuvering and a narrow stern that dug into the water and increased its turning radius. Four-pipers were also known for heavy rolling (side-to-side movement) and pitching (up-and-down movement), reflected by a sarcastic rhyme:

> Pitch, pitch your goddamn soul,
> The more you pitch, the less you roll.
> Roll, roll, you mean old bitch,
> The more you roll, the less you pitch.

No amount of pitching and rolling, however, could defeat a tin can sailor's bond with his ship. "Destroyer men from different ships, meeting on shore liberty, have only two general topics of conversation: their ships and their girls. They rank in that order," observed one officer in 1945. "He'll abuse his ship as the most uncomfortable, leakingest, buckingest crate that ever went to sea. But let somebody else pass unfavorable comment on her and he's up in arms." This could be seen in the *Jacob Jones'* nickname. The aircraft carrier USS *Lexington* (CV-2) was the "Lady Lex" and the battleship USS *New Jersey* (BB-62) was the "Big J," but crewmen of the *Jacob Jones* knew their destroyer simply as the "Jakie."

Although outdated by 1942, the Jakie was more than a match for any submarine. Her armament consisted of six 3-inch/.50 guns, six torpedo tubes, multiple .50 caliber machine guns, and dozens of Mark 7 depth charges. Each Mark 7 contained 600 pounds of TNT and could be rolled from racks on the stern or hurled up to 80 yards by a "Y-gun" launcher. The Jakie was also equipped with sonar, although not radar, and her top speed of 35 knots was nearly twice as fast as a surfaced U-boat.[6]

Commanding USS *Jacob Jones* was 38-year-old Lieutenant Commander Hugh "Dubie" Black from Oradell, New Jersey. A graduate of the US Naval Academy at Annapolis, LCDR Black served on a battleship and a cruiser, commanded a minesweeper, and trained midshipmen (officer candidates) at Harvard University before taking command of the *Jacob Jones* in April 1941. A teacher at Hackensack High School remembered Black as an "independent, trustworthy type of boy" with "considerable powers of leadership." The Annapolis yearbook humorously captured his sociability: "A groan, and from somewhere beneath a mound of sleeping paraphernalia there rises the larva of what Saturday night will transform into a butterfly of the most dazzling Spring variety." Black and his wife, Frances, had three children aged 10, 3, and 15 months.

Hugh Black had also proven himself eager to fight, conducting two depth charge attacks while running convoy escort out of Newfoundland in January. The first produced only "acres of dead herring and a cloud of hungry, squawking seagulls looking for a free meal," recalled Radioman 3rd Class Albert Oberg. Another attack in February similarly yielded no evidence of success. Two weeks later, after being assigned to ESF, the Jakie rescued fifteen survivors from the torpedoed Brazilian freighter *Buarque* off the Delmarva Peninsula.

The crew's next taste of combat occurred five days after the *Buarque* rescue, on 22 February, when the *Jacob Jones'* sonar pinged a suspected U-boat a dozen miles off Asbury Park, New Jersey. Lieutenant Commander Black unloaded his entire stock of fifty-seven depth charges on the sonar contact. Oil seeping to the surface led Black to report: "It is the opinion of the Commanding Officer, officers, and men of this vessel ... that the submarine was sunk." Although his superiors disagreed (correctly so, as there was no U-boat in the vicinity), they commended "a fine example of the persistent spirit so necessary in warfare."[7]

Hugh Black's ship was not the first to be named for Commodore Jacob Jones. The first USS *Jacob Jones*, hull number DD-61, was dispatched to Europe immediately after America's entry into World War I in 1917. The first *Jacob Jones'* wartime service, however, ended abruptly eight months later. The destroyer was off southwestern England in December 1917 when she crossed paths with Hans Rose's *U-53*, the same boat and commander which had unexpectedly visited Rhode Island and sank five ships off Nantucket in 1916.

The Americans spotted a pale streak of bubbles stretching toward them, but DD-61's evasive maneuvers did not prevent the *U-53*'s torpedo from finding its mark on her starboard side. The first *Jacob Jones* went down in eight minutes, and some of those who abandoned ship were killed moments later when the sinking ship's depth charges detonated beneath them. The forty-four survivors owed their eventual rescue to Hans Rose. The *U-53* commander "decided to let mercy prevail," as he later wrote, by radioing their location to Allied forces.[8]

Under Hugh Black's command on the second *Jacob Jones* were 148 other Americans. "We had good sailors on the Jakie," recalled Joseph "Paul" Tidwell, a 22-year-old fireman second class from Tuscaloosa, Alabama. Despite spending much of his time sequestered in the engineering spaces below decks, Tidwell was already considering making the Navy a career. Tidwell's engineering shipmates included 22-year-old George Pantall from Ohio, 22-year-old Thomas Moody from Kentucky, 25-year-old Richard Dors from Massachusetts, and 26-year-old John Merget from Virginia. Another of Tidwell's peers was the laconic and diligent Carl Smith, a water tender from West Virginia whose demeanor was unfailingly more even-keeled than their ship.

Overseeing the engineering department was Ensign Norman Smith from Vermont, the Jakie's assistant engineering officer and most junior officer. The independently minded and occasionally argumentative ensign's career had begun only weeks earlier when the Naval Academy class of 1942 graduated six months early. The Annapolis yearbook stated that the baseball team's captain "lives for baseball, the major leagues really lost a good bet to the Service

Paul Tidwell. (Courtesy of Eric Tidwell)

here." ENS Smith had avoided the label of a "Red Mike," or a midshipman too studious to pursue women; his class-mates conceded that he "occasionally used his smiling and witty way to charm the gals."

Adolph Storm, a 29-year-old apprentice seaman, was both one of the oldest and most junior sailors aboard. Only three months earlier, Storm had been manufacturing vinyl records at the Columbia Records plant in Connecticut, where he served as president of Local 237 of the United Electrical, Radio, and Machine Workers of America union. Pearl Harbor shifted Storm's perspective on where his ser-vices were most needed, and he joined the Navy the next day.[9]

Ensign Norman Smith. (US Naval Academy)

***

Lieutenant Commander Black and his executive officer reported to ESF headquarters a few hours before their DD left on patrol. Their mission brief revealed what naval intelligence had deduced about the enemy's operational patterns. Beyond the Jersey Shore's shallows, where sandbanks and shoals make inshore navigation hazardous, a gently sloping seafloor stretches for dozens of miles under shipping lanes marked with lighted buoys. Merchantmen here provided a plethora of targets. Daylight operations, however, left U-boats dangerously exposed because the relatively flat seafloor offered minimal topography to confuse sonar while affording little depth into which it could disappear if pursued.

The littoral zone drops deeper 50–70 miles offshore, where depths run 250–500 feet until meeting the continental shelf's edge. This drop-off's most prominent feature is the Hudson Canyon, one of Earth's deepest underwater valleys. Snaking northwest between 85 and 120 nautical miles off the Jersey Shore, the Hudson Canyon topographically resembles a tentacle reaching from the abyssal plain toward New York. Waters beyond the continental shelf plummet to more than 7,000 feet. Although far too deep for a U-boat to hide on the seafloor, such depths were ideal for evading enemy warships.

Underwater topography and traffic patterns therefore explained the U-boats' operational rhythm: they struck where ships were plentiful under cover of darkness, then retreated to deeper water as the sun rose. During daylight, they preferred targets farther offshore where air patrols and subchasers were seldom seen. U-boats usually concluded their nighttime hunts by descending to the bottom ("into the basement," as the Germans called it) to wait until sunset.

The *Jacob Jones*' orders were devised to exploit this. At night, LCDR Black's destroyer would patrol the line of lighted buoys along the coast between Barnegat Light and Cape May. When the sun was up, she would shift east and patrol along the 100-fathom curve that roughly marks the edge of the continental shelf. ESF's intent was to put the Jakie at the approximate place and time the enemy was expected to be. If he showed himself, he would have nowhere to run.[10]

***

The hours that U-boats along the East Coast spent lying motionless on the seafloor at depths between 100 and 400 feet were long ones for their crews. Lights were dimmed to preserve battery power while the mechanikermaat and his two junior torpedomen conducted routine torpedo maintenance. They first muscled the grease-covered, 1½-ton weapon from its tube and onto hoist rings suspended by chains from an I-beam overhead. They then unscrewed one plate near the torpedo's warhead and another near its motor and checked the gyroscope, depth-control pendulum, hydrostatic valve, battery, and other components.

Off-duty sailors could sleep, read books, or play cards, though gambling was usually prohibited. A permissive commander might allow them to listen to jazz on American radio stations. Reviled by the Nazis, the uniquely American genre was hugely popular among younger Germans. These idle hours were tedious nonetheless. "The boring routine began to grate on my nerves," one veteran recalled. He described with annoyance "trying to read with condensation water dripping on the pages of my English-language textbook, someone telling his old story for the tenth time, the same phonograph record playing for the hundredth time … this inactivity was a kind of slow psychological torture."

A lone U-boat was indeed lurking off the Jersey Shore on the morning of 27 February. Korvettenkapitän Ernst-August Rehwinkel had turned south after destroying the Standard Oil of New Jersey tanker *R.P. Resor* off Spring Lake the previous night, but his *U-578* did not hunker down on the seafloor to wait out daylight. The boat instead submerged and continued under electric power toward the Five Fathom Bank lighted buoy southeast of Cape May.[11]

***

As the submerged *U-578* crept south, Hugh Black's USS *Jacob Jones* got underway from Brooklyn Navy Yard at around 11:30. Baritone salutes of horns from passing vessels greeted the destroyer on her way down the East River. The Jakie was in open ocean, with the shoreline dropping away astern, when two radio transmissions were received. One was a Navy general advisory that all merchant ships between Nantucket and Cape Hatteras should make port before nightfall, and the other was a slight change of orders from Eastern Sea Frontier.

ESF directed Black's destroyer to divide the patrol area with USS *Dickerson* (DD-157). A fellow Wickes-class DD, the *Dickerson* sailed under Lieutenant Commander John Reybold, a Delaware native who had graduated from the Naval Academy with Hugh Black in 1926. ESF's orders specified that the *Dickerson* would patrol north of latitude 39° 10', which runs through Sea Isle City, while the *Jacob Jones* was to cover the Delaware Capes to the south.

This refers to New Jersey's Cape May and Delaware's Cape Henlopen. These two peninsulas flank the entrance to the Delaware Bay, a large estuary that connects the Atlantic Ocean to Philadelphia, Pennsylvania and the other industrial hubs along the Delaware River. Consequently, the Capes were heavily trafficked. Their strategic importance stretches back centuries, and it was from here that Commodore Jacob Jones departed on the voyage that saw his USS *Wasp* defeat HMS *Frolic* in one-on-one combat in 1812.

The Cape May Peninsula and its eponymous beachside town were among the nation's most popular summer destinations, and they also hosted numerous Navy and Coast Guard activities. These would soon include a dive bomber training facility designated Naval Air Station Wildwood, although construction would not begin until October 1942 when Hangar No. 1 was assembled from a wooden kit delivered by rail. Cape May's most important military station in early 1942 was the Navy's Section Base No. 9. Established in 1917 where an amusement park once stood at Sewell's Point, this was the operating base for Fourth Naval District's Inshore Patrol, which included the subchaser USS *Eagle 56*.

Hugh Black's *Jacob Jones* caught up with John Reybold's *Dickerson* early that afternoon, and ESF received confirmation they were southbound "in the direction of the Delaware Capes." The *Dickerson* would eventually double back to cover her designated zone north of the 39th parallel but, for the moment, the two warships constituted a long-overdue show of force.

Smoke became visible in the distance at around 15:30 as USS *Dickerson* and USS *Jacob Jones* approached the smoldering hulk of the tanker *R.P. Resor*. The intense heat of the previous night's inferno had buckled the wreck's hull, elevating its bow and stern. The destroyers orbited the smoking *R.P. Resor* like heavily armed swans while their crews crowded the decks to bear witness to a totem of American industrial strength now reduced to a smoldering funeral pyre.

Most of the onlookers were clad in the typical Navy sea uniform of blue denim trousers and the issued broad-collar jumper (minus the neckerchief) worn over a light blue chambray shirt. Those on deck included Ensign Norman Smith and Shipfitter 3rd Class Wilbur "Dusty" Rhodes. A gregarious and athletic 25-year-old from the Pennsylvania town of Mercer, Rhodes' usual joviality was thoroughly dampened by the grisly spectacle.

LCDRs Black and Reybold decided that the *Jacob Jones* would search for survivors around the *R.P. Resor* while the *Dickerson* resumed patrolling. Two hours of search patterns yielded no signs of life, and the tug USS *Sagamore* (AT-20) eventually arrived to tow the wreck. As the winter sun sank solemnly toward the shoreline and the *Sagamore* commenced recovery work, the *Jacob Jones* turned southwest in the direction of Cape May. At 19:56, Radioman 3rd Class Albert Oberg transmitted a message to ESF reporting that the destroyer was 21 miles east of Ocean City, New Jersey and resuming her patrol.

USS *Jacob Jones* followed the coast south throughout an evening that passed in darkened silence. Her hull sliced gracefully through a calm sea at 15 knots while the moon's cold glow lent the destroyer's lines and curves a hardness matching her lethal purpose. RM3 Oberg transmitted no further updates due to ESF orders for radio silence. The Jakie doubled back northward sometime after midnight, putting the coast of New Jersey off her port side.[12]

The ship spent the night at Condition 2, meaning a third of her crewmen were at their stations. Those on duty just before 05:00 included Paul Tidwell in the aft engine room and three lookouts posted topside. Two lookouts, Adolph Storm and John Struthers, were standing their posts on the roof of the galley deck house located just forward of amidships. Atop this structure were two of the ship's 3-inch/.50 guns.

Gunner's Mate 3rd Class Louis Hollenbeck, the third lookout, was above them in the crow's nest just aft of the superstructure. He wore a black watch cap and a woolen pea coat over the Navy-issue jumper, and the faded medium-blue of his denim trousers indicated the former battleship crewman's greater experience than some of his shipmates. He exhaled a fog of warm breath into the winter air while flexing a chilled hand on an M1919 .30 caliber machine gun. *What if we bag the sub that did that big tanker?* Hollenbeck wondered. *Boy, that'd really be something.*

Although pillowy clouds drifting across a hazy sky dulled the lunar light, overall visibility was good. The air temperature hovered around a chilly but tolerable 32° Fahrenheit while a northwesterly breeze ruffled the ocean sliding past the destroyer's hull. On the bridge, Lieutenant Commander Black's tense visage was shrouded in darkness. So, too, were his thoughts as the burned-out *R.P. Resor* loomed over his consciousness. The brooding skipper knew that the only recourse was to find the perpetrators and put them permanently on the seafloor.[13]

Where are you? Hugh Black wondered. *Where are you, you bastards?*

***

The bastards, as fate would have it, were not far away. The *U-578* was 28 miles southeast of Cape May at 04:25 when the bridge watch spotted USS *Jacob Jones* off the boat's starboard bow on a reciprocal course. Leutnant Raimund Tiesler, the first watch officer, now watched Korvettenkapitän Rehwinkel's square-jawed face as the kommandant did the tactical calculus. Tiesler knew Rehwinkel's blood was still hot from destroying the *R.P. Resor* less than thirty-six hours earlier, but was it hot enough to tangle with an American *Zerstörer*?

Warships were secondary targets for the Ubootwaffe. "Always the tonnage space first," one U-boat officer stated, "as that will be England's destruction." Attacking a destroyer was also a highly hazardous venture. All things being equal, a destroyer held every card against a U-boat—yet all things were not equal in the early morning hours of 28 February. The Americans had not spotted the *U-578*, giving the Germans the advantage of surprise. As the handbook for U-boat commanders emphasized, "He who sees first, has won!"

The aggressive mentality promoted by Admiral Dönitz was rooted in German doctrine's emphasis on individual commanders seizing fleeting opportunities for bold and decisive action. Technical and tactical skill "must be supplemented by … a war-like spirit and an audacious outlook," the handbook declared. "The weaknesses of the submarine must be offset by clever tactics, unscrupulous use, and obstinate persistence even when the chances of success appear slender." Attacking the destroyer would indeed be obstinate and audacious, and Ernst-August Rehwinkel made his decision accordingly. At 04:29, four minutes after spotting USS *Jacob Jones*, he ordered: "*Auf Gefechtsstationen.*" To battle stations.[14]

The *U-578* swung around to a parallel course while the UZO was brought topside. Leutnant Tiesler installed the optical device on its post with diligent haste, keenly aware they were one attentive American lookout away from being blown out of the water. "*Wir müssen uns beeilen*," Rehwinkel reminded him. *We need to move quickly.* The U-boat would be attacking from the east, and Rehwinkel wanted his eels in the water before the rising sun silhouetted the boat. He also wanted as much darkness as possible for a speedy retreat to deep water after the attack.

Pulses quickened on the *U-578*'s bridge as the U-boat hauled past the warship at top speed and began cutting a curving path toward the attack position. "Now I must just maintain low speed on the dog's curve," Rehwinkel's log noted, but this was not rhetorical flair on his part. The *Hundekurve*, or dog's curve, was a tactic for keeping a U-boat's bow facing the target to present the narrowest possible profile during a surfaced approach. Slow speed further cloaked the boat by reducing its bow wave and stern wake.

The Germans discerned the enemy's smokestacks, pilothouse, and guns in the waning moonlight, but the haze and angle of approach prevented a consensus regarding which type of warship it was. Tiesler asserted that it was a destroyer, but Rehwinkel disagreed. "*Nein*, he's a cruiser. Look at the superstructure and stacks. And he's too big for a *Zerstörer*. Check the Weyer manual if you don't believe me." The brückenmaat, or senior enlisted sailor on watch, concurred with the captain.

The distinction mattered because the draft, or depth between the waterline and the keel, was deeper on a cruiser. Maximum damage was achieved by hitting as low on the hull as possible, although setting the torpedoes to run too deep risked undershooting entirely. "It's very difficult to hit a destroyer," wrote Lothar-Günther Buchheim. "Shallow draft. Easily maneuverable."

"Flood tubes one, three, and five," Tiesler ordered. He would fire tubes one and three, keeping the stern tube ready in case a quick follow-up was needed. Two warheads would likely deliver a lethal blow, and it hedged against the risk of a malfunction or miss. The torpedoes' running depth was set at 3 meters. This was deep enough to prevent them from broaching the surface but shallow enough to maximize their effect by hitting low on the hull.

A torpedo's running depth was achieved by a hydrostatic valve located inside the balance chamber and connected to a spring-loaded piston. The spring's tension corresponded with a selected depth and, upon launch, the outside water pressure impinged on the valve. Too much or too little water pressure caused the torpedo's fins to tilt, steering it deeper or shallower. For greater stability, this mechanism was countered by a pendulum also connected to the fins. The torpedo nosing up or down would swing the pendulum in the opposite direction, which moved the fins to counteract the tilt.

The three tubes were loaded with G7e torpedoes. Whereas the G7a was propelled by an internal combustion engine, the G7e had a 100-horsepower electric motor powered by a lead-acid wet cell battery weighing 1,567 pounds. It was slower and required more maintenance than the G7a, but the G7e's tactical advantage was that its electric motor left no trail of bubbles pointing back to its source. This was vital for engaging a destroyer, particularly at close range—and Rehwinkel intended to grab the Americans by the belt before he struck.

The U-578 reached its firing position less than 900 yards off of the *Jacob Jones'* starboard bow at 04:54. Rehwinkel had overestimated the target angle, bringing the U-boat closer to the destroyer than intended, yet the Americans showed no indication of alarm. "Despite our favorable position, it is surprising that he does not see us," Rehwinkel's log noted. "He makes it easy for us."

"Target angle green six-five-zero …" Tiesler announced. Rehwinkel kept his eyes on the enemy as the first watch officer directed the attack. "Fire when ready, *Eins-vee-oh*," Rehwinkel instructed. Tiesler frowned in concentration as he centered the UZO's crosswires on the second of the ship's four smokestacks and slowly placed his right hand on the firing lever. Down in the control room, the obersteuermann's thumb rested on the button of a Junghans stopwatch as he listened to the first watch officer's voice from above.

"Tubes one and three, stand by! …"[15]

At that same moment, Fireman 3rd Class Paul Tidwell departed his duty station in the aft engine room to get sugar for his coffee. The moon dipping toward the western horizon signaled dawn's impending arrival as he ascended to the galley deck house located between the second and third stacks. Tidwell was in the galley at 04:58 when a titanic explosion rocked the destroyer.

The blast knocked Tidwell off his feet and sent him stumbling against a bulkhead while raising his hands to shield himself from the clattering pots and pans that rained down from the overhead. He felt the Jakie slowing to a halt, then another blast violently shook the ship five seconds after the first. A deathly silence followed. "I knew what it was right away," Tidwell recounted. "Sailors have dreams of being torpedoed, but this was a nightmare come true."

Machinist's Mates 1st Class Richard Dors and John Merget were in the No. 1 engine room when the torpedoes struck. Dors felt the ship immediately lose way after the first blast, then the second seemed to shove her backward. At that same instant, the engine room plunged into darkness. Merget groped for the throttle and closed it, and Dors was reaching for his lifejacket when a jet of brutally cold water nearly bowled him over. Merget and Dors joined the exodus of engineering personnel making their way topside.

A similar scene unfolded in the adjacent No. 2 boiler room. The first explosion threw Fireman 3rd Class George Pantall against an instrument panel, then the second one shuddered the deck beneath him. Trembling, he donned his lifejacket. "All I could think of was wanting to get out of there," Pantall recounted. Water Tender 2nd Class Carl Smith, however, appeared unperturbed.

Pantall and the others incredulously turned their attention to the unflappable West Virginian, who was watching his gauges as the pressure dropped rapidly. "Down to fifty pounds …" Smith remarked in his Appalachian drawl. Another moment passed before Carl Smith spoke again. "Alright, boys," he declared. "Go ahead up through the hatch." They needed no further prompting.[16]

The *U-578* peeled away hard to port after launching its pair of eels. Less than a minute later, an enormous explosion shook the boat while the sea around the destroyer reared up as if turned on its head. Fragments of piping and hull arcing through the air caused Rehwinkel and Tiesler to duck behind the bridge bulwark just as another thunderous blast marked the second torpedo's impact. A thick cloud of oily smoke dusted everyone on the bridge with soot. At the same time, nine strong detonations caused electrical failures aboard the U-boat. From the control room below, the obersteuermann shouted the torpedoes' run time. "Fifty-seven!"

The first torpedo struck the *Jacob Jones'* keel below the superstructure at 04:55. This set off the warhead's main charge of 617 pounds of hexanite, a TNT-based explosive boosted by powdered aluminum. The blast ripped open the destroyer's hull and ignited the contents of her forward magazine, sparking an even larger explosion on the lowest deck. Bulkheads bent and broke and riveted seams were wrenched apart within fractions of a second as the shockwave expanded aft through the lower decks and up toward the bridge. Lieutenant Commander Hugh Black was killed instantly, along with most of the ship's commissioned officers and all her chief petty officers.

The explosion sheared off everything forward of the boiler rooms as it lifted the Jakie from the sea amid a colossal tower of salt spray. The destroyer had scarcely settled back into the water when the second torpedo struck low on her hull near the stern, detonating under the crew quarters and blowing away much of the ship's aft 40 feet. What remained of USS *Jacob Jones* stopped dead in the water, the watertight bulkheads holding her afloat as the hull's mangled forward end spewed pitch-black smoke.[17]

In the crow's nest, seawater hit Louis Hollenbeck like a concrete wall as a ghoulish potpourri of metal, wood, and pieces of dead Americans rained across the ship. The spray had not yet settled when the ship spasmed from another massive explosion, this time farther aft. The crow's nest swayed precipitously for a moment before Hollenbeck peered over the edge. It took a moment to comprehend what he saw. The blast had amputated the Jakie's entire forward section: the magazine, forward crew quarters, and bridge were gone. Much of the ship aft of the engine room also appeared to have been destroyed. Small fires flickered across the deck.

Below Hollenbeck in the crow's nest and above Tidwell in the galley, Adolph Storm and 17-year-old John Struthers from Trenton, New Jersey were standing watch on either side of the galley deck house roof. Storm witnessed a sheet of flame erupt forward of the galley deck house just as the blast's concussion slammed him violently against the storage container behind him. He crumpled to the deck, although the splinter shield of the 3-inch gun in front of him blocked most of the debris. The ringing in his ears muffled another explosion near the stern. Storm used the gun mount to pull himself upright before finding John Struthers alive and intact on the other side of the deck house roof. Steam billowed from broken pipes as the pair shakily made their way down to the main deck.

Storm and Struthers reached the deck moments after Paul Tidwell emerged from the galley. The devastation that greeted them was breathtaking. The No. 1 stack was gone, the No. 1 boiler room was open to the sea, and the No. 2 stack had collapsed back onto the galley deck house. The force of the blast had peeled the hull grotesquely backward and rolled up part of the deck against the galley structure. Only the midship section, comprising the galley deck house and lifeboat davits above and the engineering spaces below, was still intact.

Immediately aft of the engine room was the crew quarters where Radioman 3rd Class Albert Oberg was asleep in the middle of three bunks at the compartment's forward end, his feet nearly abutting the fuel tank between the berthing area and the No. 2 engine room. The first explosion jarred Oberg awake, and the second threw him to the floor and killed the man in the bunk above him. The second blast fractured the fuel tank and a steam pipe as it crumpled the hull inward until a locker stopped it only inches from the end of his bunk.

The steam severely burned Oberg, but the oil sealed the wounds and he was scarcely aware of the burns at all. His clothing had also protected him; Oberg had complied with the standing order that all crewmen sleep fully clothed. A large hole had been torn in the port-side hull, and the compartment's aft end was now open to the sea. He numbly realized that he was the only man in the crew quarters left alive. Upon climbing out from the rack, he found himself in knee-deep water with still more coming in. Hearing voices topside, Oberg discovered that the stairwell leading up to the main deck was largely intact.

George Pantall, Richard Dors, and Tom Moody reached the main deck to find a scene of unfathomable devastation. The deck was slick with oil and covered in twisted metal and splintered wood. Small fires burned in multiple places and the air was heavy with an odor later described as carbide. "What happened? ..." one man asked repeatedly in bewildered shock.

After following Pantall to the deck, Carl Smith went immediately to the master valves and dutifully shut off the flow of fuel to the boilers. Whether abandoning a merchant ship or a warship, the boilers had to be extinguished to mitigate the risk of an explosion when cold water meets heated metal. Steam buildup in an unattended boiler can produce the same result. Another reason for powering down the engines was to ensure the propellers were not still turning while there were men in the water. His task complete, Smith joined the others at the lifeboat davits.

The sailors converging on deck displayed surprising discipline and composure, but Pantall was struck by how few there were. *Where is everybody?* There were only perhaps thirty-five men in total, and Pantall saw neither any chief petty officers nor commissioned officers until a horrifically injured figure staggered out on deck and collapsed.

It was Ensign Norman Smith. The 22-year-old officer's exposed skin was badly burned and the whites of his eyes had turned red. ENS Smith babbled incoherently through ragged breaths as he weakly grasped the arm of a sailor stooped over him, but his ruptured eardrums prevented him from hearing the enlisted men's reassurances. "It's okay, sir! You're gonna be fine! We're gonna get you out of here ..."

With no officers or chiefs to direct them, Shipfitter 3rd Class Wilbur "Dusty" Rhodes became the Jakie's man of the hour. The 25-year-old Pennsylvanian took charge of the remaining crewmen and organized an effort to launch the lifeboats. As Adolph Storm recounted, "Dusty Rhodes had taken command. He was just a seaman, but someone had to restore order and he did it."

Rhodes led a handful of sailors to one of the two intact lifeboats. The deck, however, was littered with debris and slick with oil that inhibited their feet from getting the traction necessary to launch the boat. They eventually cut the lifeboat's falls and moved to the other boat, only to find the davits smashed and the boat jammed onto its skids. Dusty Rhodes hammered it savagely with his fist as the others attempted to lift it, yet the boat refused to yield.

"All together on three, ready??" Rhodes shouted as he, too, grabbed hold of the lifeboat. "One, two—heave!" They grunted and strained, but there were simply not enough able-bodied men for the task. The waterline continued its advance up the wrecked destroyer's hull, toward the deck, as the Atlantic poured into its engineering spaces. "It's no goddamn good, Dusty!" Adolph Storm growled through clenched teeth as their party struggled to budge the lifeboat. Rhodes reached the same conclusion.

"The rafts! Get to the rafts!"

The 9-by-5-foot rafts were oval-shaped and covered with gray canvas, with rope handholds affixed to the outside and a slatted wood floor occupying the gap in the center. One was tossed over the starboard side, then someone threw a line to keep the raft from drifting away. One by one, the Jakie's crew jumped into the bitingly cold water and swam for it. Once a handful had hauled themselves on top, those on deck passed ENS Smith down to the raft. Still incoherent, he began screaming in agony.[18]

On the ship's port side, Richard Dors threw another raft overboard before dropping into the 38° Fahrenheit sea. John Struthers followed Dors over the side. They had just pulled themselves into the raft when they spotted Paul Tidwell swimming toward them. "It was cold, ice-cold water," Tidwell recounted decades after the war. "If you wanted to survive, you swam. I was pretty good." Dors and Merget helped Tidwell into the raft. One man on the Jacob Jones, however, was not yet ready to abandon ship.

"I wasn't going into that water without getting something warm in my stomach," Tom Moody later explained, so he went to the galley with George Pantall. "The coffee was there, but we couldn't find any cups. And there was no cream or sugar, so we drank it out of a ladle. It was hot. That was all we wanted." The duo then found a storage locker stocked with heavy underwear and each donned three layers. "That's a nice thing about the Navy," Moody later opined to reporters, "you get plenty of heavy underwear." When Moody and Pantall returned to the deck, they saw a raft off the starboard side crowded with at least a dozen men. Among them was Ensign Smith, whose agonized cries continued to haunt the desperate evacuation.

The tin can's flooding compartments created an artificial current that pulled the raft carrying Tidwell, Dors, and Struthers nearer to the maw of contorted metal where the bow had been. The trio attempted to wrest themselves free of its grasp using the paddles, but the raft was impossible to steer with three men on it. "Someone's gotta get off," declared Tidwell. He was about to volunteer when Dors spoke up. "I'll go."

Bracing himself, Dors rolled off the edge of the raft and swam laboriously back to the dying Jacob Jones. Climbing aboard was not difficult, as the gunwales were now even closer to the waterline and her mutilated forward end had gone under. Dors was attempting to cut another raft loose when he felt freezing water biting at his ankles.[19]

Radioman Albert Oberg and machinist's mate Rudolph Jacobsen launched a liferaft from the port side. Like Tidwell's raft, theirs was pulled to the forward end where it became snagged on jagged steel. Oberg and Jacobsen freed it, but lost their paddles in the attempt. By the time the whirlpool surrounding the ship had pulled their raft around its truncated forward end, Oberg and Jacobsen saw that her decks were now awash.

Dors, Moody, Pantall, and Storm all jumped over the side at about this time. The last thing Adolph Storm saw before going over the port side was Dusty Rhodes still giving orders on deck. Dawn crept in from the east as every man in the water splashed toward one of the three rafts. John Struthers reached the raft carrying Tidwell and Merget. Dors, Moody, and Pantall made a beeline for the raft crowded with fifteen men, which was closest to the ship. From the pitiable remnants of the DD's crew, a haggard voice spoke:

"She's gonna go."

A few men could still be seen on deck as USS *Jacob Jones* began her death plunge. The destroyer went down over the forward end and belched trapped air as she upended, the stern rising over the rafts in a parting salute that revealed the extent of the damage aft. Everything above her keel plates had been blasted away, and the propeller shafts now pointed skyward like bones. Those on the rafts watched the Atlantic swallow the maimed warship until the last of her gurgled out of sight. The Jakie was gone.

The sinking wreck's wash shoved away the raft carrying Albert Oberg and Rudolph Jacobsen just as a horrifying realization dawned on Oberg. He smacked Jacobsen's shivering arm beside him. "Pick your feet up!" the radioman screamed, lifting his own feet off the raft's slatted wood centerpiece. "PICK YOUR FEET UP NOW!" The machinist's mate appeared confused as Oberg tried to warn the others, but it was too late.

A ripple suddenly pulsed outward across the ocean's surface as something slammed into the survivors from below. It was like getting hit by a train. One geyser of water erupted after another, muffling a din of screams that lifted toward the breaking dawn. In a brutal mirror image of the first *Jacob Jones* in 1917, the ship's depth charges were detonating as she sank.

On dry land, the energy released by an explosion compresses air molecules as it radiates outward. This absorbs and dissipates some of the shockwave. The density difference between flesh and air then causes a victim's body to reflect some of the remaining kinetic energy. Even when an explosion on land is fatal, part of its destructive power is lost between the shockwave's source and its victim.

Unlike air, however, water is incompressible. The same principle that magnifies sound underwater thereby makes explosions deadlier by transmitting blast energy with greater intensity over longer distances. Because the human body is composed mainly of water, a shockwave actually passes through solid tissue without inflicting serious injury—but it violently compresses the body's air-filled spaces. Striking the survivors at more than 5,000 feet per second, the cascading shockwaves blew out eardrums, ruptured bowels, and collapsed lungs.

The concussions killed nearly everyone on the crowded raft, though the three men clinging to its handholds were more fortunate. Moody and Pantall were both blown out of the water, as was Dors, though he managed to keep his grip on the handhold. Pantall, weighed down by his extra layers of clothing, crashed back into the water and immediately sank, the wintry sea closing over him.[20]

The rumbling blasts and roiling waters gave way to the Atlantic's rhythmic chop as the grave of the *Jacob Jones* fell quiet for good. The living prayed while screams subsided to groans. Ensign Norman Smith, a month shy of his 23rd birthday, was finally silent. Louis Hollenbeck was one of the few occupants of the crowded raft to survive the depth charges. The other two rafts' occupants—Tidwell, Merget, and Struthers on one, Oberg and Jacobsen on the other—escaped serious harm. Moody and Dors each clung weakly to the crowded raft's handholds along with George Pantall, who was left exhausted and sputtering after nearly drowning.

Aided by his infusion of hot coffee, Tom Moody succeeded in mounting the raft. He then helped pull Pantall and Dors atop it. The explosions had blown out the wooden flooring, which forced them to either straddle the side or grasp the handholds. The minutes became an hour, then two hours. The sun marched higher into the morning sky as the most badly injured fell off the raft, or just released their weakening grasp and floated away.

Their short lives expired with the same stoic resignation that Kapitänleutnant Hans Rose witnessed in a dying crewman from the first *Jacob Jones*. "A few yards from [our U-boat] a man was struggling against death. I can see him yet," Rose wrote of one American sailor. "He looked over toward us, gave no cry for help, no cry of anguish, none of fear. Silent, resolute, heroic, he went down as we passed, dead for his country." One of the few to live through that February morning off Cape May spoke of their ordeal less poetically:

"They just died, one at a time, that's all."[21]

***

As the Jakie's own weaponry killed most of her remaining crew, USS *Eagle 56* of Fourth Naval District's Inshore Patrol was cruising off the Delaware Capes farther west. The morning muster had just been completed when an Army plane from the 104th Observation Squadron appeared overhead. The pilot waggled his wings as he passed overhead three times. The *Eagle 56* responded with signal flags, then the aircrew tossed an object into the sea which the sailors retrieved at 08:38. It was a message stating that the pilot had sighted shipwrecked men at 08:10 at 38° 37' North, 74° 32' West.

The *Eagle 56* immediately changed course, but sea conditions soured as the subchaser plodded southeast toward the open ocean. She found an empty lifeboat at 09:07 and located the first survivors fifteen minutes later. At 09:25, Section Base No. 9 at Cape May received a terse message from the subchaser: "AM PICKING UP SURVIVORS FROM USS JACOB JONES. DETAILS LATER."

The *Eagle 56* recovered twelve *Jacob Jones* crewmen from three rafts by 10:02. Among them was Carl Smith, the West Virginia water tender who had coolly attended to his duties in the first chaotic minutes after the explosions. The depth charges had pulverized Smith's body, and he died aboard the subchaser as the search for survivors continued. A raft with four bodies was also taken in tow, but the weather was worsening and all the survivors required urgent medical attention. The *Eagle 56*'s captain solemnly released the raft and made all possible speed back to Cape May.[22]

***

The *U-578* retreated southeast into deeper water as Korvettenkapitän Ernst-August Rehwinkel and Leutnant Raimund Tiesler debated which class of warship they had hit. Rehwinkel believed it was an Omaha-class cruiser, citing the catastrophic effect achieved by the torpedoes' 3-meter running depth as indicative of the Omaha-class' 6-meter draft. Rehwinkel was unaware that the *Jacob Jones* had been riding lower than her official draft of 8.67 feet (2.64 meters) because a boiler had recently been removed and her fuel tanks were nearly full.

Rehwinkel conceded his mistake when he realized that the recorded time between launch and impact was not fifty-seven seconds but rather 57 percent of a minute (thirty-four seconds). The warship had therefore been closer than he thought and appeared larger than it was. The misidentification might have saved the *Jacob Jones* if she had consumed more fuel or if the Germans attempted to hit the "cruiser" lower on its hull, in which case the torpedoes may have undershot the Jakie entirely.

The crew of the *U-578* heard "a continuous submarine hunt" in the direction of the Delaware Capes the next day, the log noting that "every 5–10 minutes there are detonations of depth charges in a series of two and more." Rehwinkel observed that they had "stirred up a hornet's nest," but the boat went unmolested. "Surveillance was meager, air reconnaissance light and inattentive."

The *U-578* cruised back into port at Saint-Nazaire, France on 25 March flying one white pennant and one red pennant. The former signified the sinking of a merchant ship, the latter a warship. Merchantmen were more strategically valuable although, as a measure of skill and daring, the Ubootwaffe generally considered a red pennant worth four or five white ones. Like all returning U-boats, the *U-578* was greeted at the pier by a band playing a jaunty tune, cheering girls, and likely Admiral Dönitz himself. His official evaluation deemed Korvettenkapitän Rehwinkel's patrol "well-executed."

An unrelated tragedy befell USS *Dickerson* less than three weeks after the *Jacob Jones* attack. The destroyer was patrolling off North Carolina on 19 March when a shell ripped through the chart room, killing LCDR John Reybold and three others. It was friendly fire: the jittery Armed Guard detachment on the freighter *Liberator* misidentified USS *Dickerson* as a U-boat. Eight hours later, a German torpedo sank the *Liberator*.[23]

***

The first loss of an American warship along the East Coast accelerated Cape May's transition to a full war footing. Air raid drills became routine and authorities prohibited such activities as fishing from bridges and photographing the beach. The Coast Guard even requested that civilians with horses help patrol the beaches "to protect the shores against invasion by submarine-borne spies and saboteurs."

Cape May resident Doris Branigan recalled "thousands upon thousands" of servicemen (her future husband among them) who flooded into the peninsula. Insufficient accommodations meant that "people were turning their closets into apartments. We used every square inch." The Navy eventually took over the luxury Admiral Hotel as both a headquarters and as housing for officers and their dependents.

Thirty-eight miles up the Jersey Shore, Atlantic City was undergoing what the *Saturday Evening Post* described as "the most amazing wartime change among American towns." A particularly heavy military presence in the beachside city known as "America's Playground" soon earned it the appellation "Camp Boardwalk." US Army soldier John Palmentieri recalled that "all you saw up and down the boardwalk was military uniforms … There were 2,000 guys doing calisthenics in Convention Hall and others on the beach."

One consequence of the USS *Jacob Jones* sinking would be carved from the sandy soil of New Jersey itself. The tragedy helped spur the construction of a canal across the Cape May Peninsula, a project which had been discussed intermittently for nearly a century. The 3.6-mile Cape May Canal was in operation by year's end, enabling ships to travel between the Delaware Bay and the Atlantic without transiting the open ocean off Cape May Point. It also provided faster access to the industrial centers of Philadelphia, Camden, and Wilmington.[24]

The Navy ultimately identified no lapses in judgment or planning to which the catastrophe could be attributed, concluding that "it is quite possible that the meeting between the destroyer and the U-boat was simply ill fortune." The timing, however, could not have been worse. "Obscure though the causes of the encounter may be, the result is well-defined: the loss, at a critical moment, of an efficient destroyer and a well-trained, experienced crew."

The destroyers that rotated through Eastern Sea Frontier patrol duty over the ensuing weeks included the Jakie's squadron mate, USS *Roper* (DD-147). Most of the Atlantic Fleet's seventy-plus destroyers operated elsewhere, however, and a daily average of twenty-four were allotted for transatlantic convoy escort despite these convoys losing only a single ship in the north-central Atlantic during March. U-boats destroyed or damaged thirty-one ships during that same month in ESF waters, where a daily average of fewer than two destroyers patrolled nearly 1,700 miles of coastline.

Even Admiral King's ally, President Roosevelt, was shocked to learn in late February that only seven warships were patrolling the East Coast. "This is a real disgrace," FDR fumed in a letter to the Secretary of the Navy penned two days before the *Jacob Jones* was sunk. Nor was any respite imminent, as a 5 March communiqué from Rear Admiral Andrews revealed. The message to Vice Admiral Ingersoll relayed the latest intelligence forecast: "Additional subs will reach this coast in two or three days."[25]

***

Of the 149 men aboard USS *Jacob Jones* when she sailed from Brooklyn Navy Yard, only eleven returned to shore the following day. Ten escaped death only by virtue of being at their watch stations amidships. Albert Oberg was the only survivor from the aft crew quarters, and no one survived from the forward quarters or bridge. As Louis Hollenbeck stated, "I'd either be in Hell or up above if I'd been off-duty at the time the torpedoes hit us."

"… And my boy?" asked LCDR Hugh Black's father when the Navy informed him that the *Jacob Jones* had been lost. Howard Black's worst fears were confirmed when he learned the bridge had been destroyed. "Well, that's where my boy would be, wouldn't it?" he concluded in words riven with grief. "If a torpedo demolished the bridge and that's where a commander would be, then I'm sure my boy was there." Before phoning his son's wife, he added, "I guess all hope is gone. But my boy was a fine sailor."

A memorial service for Hugh Black at the Episcopal Church of the Annunciation in Oradell, New Jersey drew nearly three hundred mourners. In attendance were Oradell's mayor, Black's childhood Boy Scout troop, and a choir of local women who sang "America, the Beautiful." At a Vermont service honoring Ensign Norman Smith, the minister's voice quavered as he recalled Smith's days as an altar boy and reflected that "no man can do more than to give his life for his country and his friends." He broke down in tears before he could finish the eulogy.

Peter Tarsa of Lowell, Massachusetts left a note for his Polish immigrant parents while home on leave two weeks earlier. "If you ever get a telegram about me being lost or killed, don't cry about it," the 20-year-old wrote. "Just remember I'm fighting for my country and whatever I do, dying or fighting, I'm happy because it's for my country." Five days after the sinking, John and Mildred Tarsa received a telegram:

THE NAVY DEPARTMENT DEEPLY REGRETS TO INFORM YOU THAT YOUR SON PETER WALTER TARSA APPRENTICE SEAMAN US NAVY IS MISSING FOLLOWING ACTION IN THE PERFORMANCE OF HIS DUTY …

The other fatalities included 17-year-old Roy Parker and his brother, 20-year-old Reed Parker. Lieutenant (Junior Grade) Benjamin Bronstein, the ship's doctor, was one of the country's first Jewish servicemen killed in action during the war. Also among the dead was the Jakie's unexpected hero, Wilbur "Dusty" Rhodes. The last living memory of Rhodes was that of Adolph Storm, who spotted the Pennsylvanian still leading the evacuation in the ship's last minutes. "He got order on the boat and stood by giving directions," Storm told reporters. "If there's ever a guy who should be given a plug, it's Dusty Rhodes."

"As soon as the doctors let me go, I hope to get on a destroyer again," Water Tender 2nd Class Woodrow Roussell informed reporters at Philadelphia Naval Hospital. "Maybe we can reverse the situation this time." Adolph Storm similarly had no plans to return to his labor union duties any time soon. He, too, wished to serve aboard another destroyer. Storm told the newspapers:

"I've got a job to do."[26]

CHAPTER NINE

Gulftrade

"Dirty, rust-streaked, squatty tankers,
Decks awash on lonely way,
Filled with hell-brewed chain lightning,
Lifeblood of the battle fray,
Floating coffins on the oceans,
Prey of lurking submarines,
Ah, the brave may quake in spirit,
Shudder, safe in shoreside dreams."
—Anonymous, "Tanker Seamen!" (17 March 1944)

10 March 1942
14 miles southeast of Manasquan, New Jersey
00:36

Ten days after the *U-578* sank USS *Jacob Jones*, a solitary vessel curtsied deferentially as it pushed through mountainous nighttime seas. It rolled or pitched at each wave's blow before invariably settling back on its keel for the next. The darkened shape, which seemed pitifully small amid the turbulent expanse of ocean, crested each wave and then plunged down its opposite slope, where the Atlantic rewarded its persistence by hurling itself violently against her hull and deck. Battered but undeterred, the vessel shrugged off each assault as winds continued to buffet her with a spite that felt almost personal.

This was the US Navy's *Larch* (YN-16), currently on patrol between Manasquan Inlet and the Barnegat lighted buoy. On her bridge stood Lieutenant George Coale, a Washington, D.C. native and former Naval Academy swimmer. The weather left the *Larch*'s 36-year-old commander neither concerned nor seasick, at least as far as his crew could tell. If Coale was in anything less than optimal condition, then his countenance betrayed nothing. It inspired confidence in Gunner's Mate 3rd Class Victor Downey, who was battling creeping nausea.

Launched in July 1941, the *Larch* was an Aloe-class net tender measuring 163 feet long and displacing 569 long tons. She lacked the "USS" designation because she had not yet been formally commissioned. Her most distinctive feature was a double bowsprit (two "horns") jutting from the bow at a 45-degree angle like an insect's mandibles.

Each horn functioned as a crane with an electric winch and 1,800 feet of wire capable of lifting 22 tons. Although built to lay and maintain antisubmarine nets rather than hunt submarines, the *Larch* was crewed by thirty-eight Navy sailors and armed with a 3-inch/.23 cannon, two .50 caliber machine guns, and depth charges. As far as the beggared Eastern Sea Frontier in March 1942 was concerned, that was good enough.[1]

While the *Larch* patrolled between Manasquan and Barnegat, USCGC *Antietam* (WSC-128) covered Barnegat to Atlantic City. Measuring 125 feet in length and displacing 232 long tons, the *Antietam* was an Active-class cutter designed for counter-smuggling operations along the outer line of patrol during Prohibition. They were highly versatile and reliable, despite a propensity for rolling in heavy seas which made the *Antietam* a miserable ride on the night of 9/10 March.

Launched in 1926 on the Delaware River in Camden, New Jersey, the *Antietam* was built by the same New York Shipbuilding subsidiary as her fellow Active-class cutters. She had been repainted from her usual peacetime white to naval gray after the Coast Guard was placed under Navy authority in late 1941. The USCGC *Antietam*'s armament of a single 3-inch/.23 gun and depth charges was adequate for her assigned mission of hunting U-boats, yet the enemy remained elusive.[2]

***

Because Admiral Ernest King still refused to implement coastal convoys, Eastern Sea Frontier reported that roving patrols remained "the fundamental defensive measure" during March. This approach, however, had neither sunk nor even seriously damaged a U-boat. The British Admiralty explained to the US Navy's Admiral Harold Stark that the futility of patrolling was "one of the hardest of all the lessons of the war to swallow" because "[going] to sea to hunt down and destroy the enemy makes a strong appeal to every naval officer." As one Royal Navy veteran later reflected, "We ourselves had travelled a long and hard road, and had wasted much effort in hunting for U-boats since 1939." Even President Wilson recognized this in 1917 when he compared antisubmarine patrols to "hunting hornets all over the farm."

The US Navy admitted that relying on patrols in lieu of convoys was "the inevitable resort of inferior numbers," and it was ineffective for precisely this reason. Even the ESF war diary acknowledged that antisubmarine patrols "can be really successful only when carried out by forces in such overwhelming numbers that complete coverage is possible." Destroyer Division Nineteen's commander concurred. "While patrolling operations of this type are of some value," he observed, "the submarine menace on our Atlantic Coast can be defeated only through the operation of a coastal convoy system."

In addition to U-boats, patrolling ships and aircraft also searched for any indication of the covert Axis resupply ships which naval intelligence believed were operating incognito in American waters. In three days' time, on 13 March, USS *Dahlgren*

(DD-187) would hail two fishing trawlers "displaying unusually bright lights turned off and on" 55 miles off central New Jersey. When the trawlers failed to respond, ESF ordered they be "located and watched by aircraft because of strategic sub area." Nothing would come of the incident, however, just as nothing ever seemed to.

It was 21:05 that night when Third Naval District received a report of a "vessel flashing light at another vessel 5 to 15 miles off Mantoloking [New Jersey]." District headquarters tasked the *Larch* and the Eagle boat USS *PE-48* (*Eagle 48*) to investigate. Aboard the *Larch*, Lieutenant Coale summoned the crew to "general quarters," or battle stations, at 20:23. This catapulted the net tender into full combat readiness, but the event proved a false alarm when the merchantman was hailed and identified as the American freighter *A.L. Kent*. General quarters was secured, and the *Larch* resumed her patrol.

LT Coale was on the bridge at forty minutes past midnight when the crew's attention was seized by a small white-orange light that appeared unexpectedly on the horizon. The distant speck glimmered against a dark sky as watchstanders swung into action. Coale had issued his orders by the time it winked out a minute later. The bow and its protruding pair of cranes swung to the heading on which the flare had been seen, and GM3 Downey felt the *Larch* tremble as she accelerated to flank speed.

Minutes later, a report from USCGC *Antietam* beeped through the radioman's headset. *This is the real thing*, LT Coale realized when his radioman recited the message. The boatswain's whistle sounded over the *Larch*'s intercom at 00:55, heralding the order to make ready for action. A voice spoke next:

"General quarters, general quarters. All hands, man your battle stations …"[3]

***

The fates of the *Larch* and *Antietam* had intersected with that of the *Gulftrade*, one of several merchant ships plying New Jersey waters on the night of 9/10 March 1942. The Gulf Oil Company tanker had been plodding north from Port Arthur, Texas carrying 80,000 barrels of Bunker C fuel oil. Manned by thirty-four Americans, the *Gulftrade* measured 429 feet long and 6,676 gross registered tons. She was a 1920 product of the Sun Shipbuilding and Drydock Company shipyard in Chester, Pennsylvania, located along the Delaware River a few miles south of her homeport of Philadelphia.[4]

The *Gulftrade* was 4 miles off Barnegat Light when Rolland Johnson took over the engineering watch at 20:00 on 9 March. Naked bulbs lit the sallow faces of three unlicensed crewmen under Johnson's charge. In addition to an officer, each engineering watch comprised a fireman for feeding the boilers, an oiler for lubricating engine bearings and changing out steam injectors, and a wiper for general tasks. Located near the stern on the lowest deck, the engine room and boiler room jointly constituted a single large space crowded with pipes, valves, auxiliary systems, and the propeller shaft. Three 16-by-20-foot Scotch marine boilers occupied its forward end.

Standing over a dozen feet tall, near the compartment's aft end, was the *Gulftrade*'s triple-expansion reciprocating steam engine. Oil-fired boilers converted fresh water to steam which was piped into the engine where it expanded inside the cylinders, driving the pistons in an up-and-down motion which turned the propeller shaft. Steam that passed through all cylinders was captured as vapor and re-condensed for another run through the system. Triple-expansion steam engines were typical for merchant ships of that era, with warships featuring more powerful turbo-electric and steam turbine engines.

In addition to keeping the propeller turning, Rolland Johnson's engineering crew contributed to the *Gulftrade*'s safety in several ways. Commands relayed from the bridge (for example, reversing the engines) via the engine order telegraph demanded immediate execution since an imminent collision might afford only seconds to react. Another duty was minimizing the amount of smoke produced because a submarine could see engine exhaust from 20 miles away under ideal conditions. This required maintaining proper oil temperature and pressure, changing the sprayer plates, and cleaning the burners. The engineering watch was also responsible for shutting down the engines during an abandon-ship scenario. In addition to risking a boiler explosion, a running engine could spew burning fuel through fractures in the hull or deck.

Engineering mariners toiled in dim and sweaty conditions below the waterline, not unlike the U-boat sailors who hunted them. Few in the deck department envied their counterparts below decks. Engineering departments and deck departments tended to regard each other in critical terms, as reflected by a wartime poem by engineering officer Robert Goodwin:

> The engineers work in the grease and the heat
> Boy, take it from me, it's no fun,
> Sweating and swearing, trying the job to complete,
> While out on deck the mate suns.

Dynamics between the "underground savages" and "deck apes" ranged from friendly rivalry to mutual hostility. In fact, tension existed between and within shipboard departments throughout the Allied merchant fleets. Disputes on American ships were often settled using boxing gloves. "Everyone has their place in the pecking order," Merchant Marine combat veteran Hugh Stephens would explain eighty years later. Because merchant ships lacked the Navy and Coast Guard's rigid hierarchy of ranks, Stephens explained, understanding one's role within the crew was more challenging. "But one person has to have the final say," he continued, "and that's the captain."[5]

As Rolland Johnson assumed responsibility for the engineering watch at 20:00, the deck department's four-man watch also changed over on the bridge. Third mate Valentin Alvarez took over as duty officer while quartermaster George Parks manned the helm. Two other unlicensed crewmen took up lookout and standby duties. Joining them was Captain Torger Olsen, a heavyset 56-year-old Norwegian immigrant. A storm warning was in effect from the Gulf of Maine to Cape Hatteras, and the *Gulftrade* was making 10.5 knots through heavy seas whipped by winds topping 40 mph.

A quiet tension prevailed on the bridge as the clock marched toward midnight, but neither the weather nor the Germans constituted the most imminent threat. The danger at hand stemmed instead from the Navy's directive that all merchant vessels sail with their lights off. This meant no white running lights on the foremast, mainmast, and stern, and no red and green navigation lights on either side of the bridge. Although this made merchantmen less obvious targets, sailing in total darkness greatly increased the risk of collision.

This was hardly an abstract concern for Capt Olsen, especially since the night's weather impeded visibility. Jeopardy became manifest at around 23:00 when the watchstanders briefly glimpsed two southbound ships in their immediate vicinity. Both were fully darkened and unnervingly close to the *Gulftrade*. One was less than 500 yards off the tanker's port bow, while the other was hugging the coast several hundred yards off that ship's starboard quarter. It was unknown whether either had seen the *Gulftrade*.[6]

The inertia of a fully loaded ship of the *Gulftrade*'s size and speed entailed a stopping distance of about half a mile, and a collision could unleash a degree of kinetic violence rivaling the destructive power of a torpedo. New Jersey alone had seen four such accidents so far in 1942. Just five days earlier, a collision had claimed six lives and sank the freighter *Gypsum Prince* at the Delaware Bay entrance. These mishaps also obstructed shipping lanes with hazards that risked further accidents; the subchaser USS *Eagle 56* lost a propeller when she smashed into the *Gypsum Prince*'s submerged wreck.

In January, Eastern Sea Frontier had attempted to reduce U-boat attacks by pulling the shipping lanes as close to shore as safe navigation permitted. Because this left little safety margin between the lanes, collision-wary merchant captains responded by ignoring them altogether. On one day in February, fifteen out of thirty vessels in Sixth Naval District waters were found outside the specified lanes. ESF added a 2-mile buffer between the lanes in March, yet captains still sometimes disregarded them.

"The seafaring man … is a rugged individualist," stated a War Shipping Administration manual, and Samuel Eliot Morison observed that "in the merchant marine there is a sturdy independence which, in time of war, becomes a fault." On 21 March, a patrol boat aimed its searchlight beam on a merchant vessel and signaled "WHAT SHIP?" only to receive the reply "SHUT OFF THAT GODDAMN BRIGHT LIGHT." Eastern Sea Frontier also noted one particular captain who "rarely complies with routing instructions" and "is of the considered opinion that he knows a good deal more about navigation than the United States Navy."[7]

Although the *Gulftrade* was within the shipping lane, so were the other lightless shapes lurching through the stormy waters around them. Third mate Valentin Alvarez looked to Captain Olsen, who found himself in a dilemma. Remaining darkened would risk colliding with a nearby ship, but their Navy routing instructions also advised that "late information reveals that submarine activity exists South of Long Island, off the New Jersey Coast, and in the vicinity of Wimble Shoals." The skipper was finally tipped toward a decision a few minutes after 23:00 when a red flare arced into the sky forward of the *Gulftrade*'s bow.

"Hard right rudder!" Olsen thundered.

"That's a sub, cap'n!" George Parks exclaimed as he frantically turned the wheel to starboard. "You *see* a sub??" Olsen demanded, craning his neck and squinting. "No—I mean it's a decoy, cap'n! He wants us to get broadside so he can sling a torpedo at us." Parks' words betrayed tangible fear, but the captain realized that his quartermaster was merely jittery. "Well, we're keeping clear of it no matter what it is," Olsen declared. He ordered Parks to steer west of the flare's origin.

Olsen then issued a different order to third mate Valentin Alvarez. "Val, put the lights on. Foremast and navigation," he instructed. "Thank you." The skipper had finally concluded that a collision represented more immediate danger than an attack. Alvarez dutifully turned on the 20-watt bulb on the foremast and the red and green navigation lights on either side of the bridge. Capt Olsen soon retired to his quarters.

The watch changed over again less than an hour later. First mate Martin Tammick, a flinty 58-year-old from Boston, arrived on the bridge shortly before midnight to assume watch officer duties from Valentin Alvarez. The third mate briefed Tammick on the other ships sighted nearby and Capt Olsen's decision to turn on the lights. The first mate was wary, but understood the skipper's reasoning. "For how long is he planning on leaving us lit up?" Tammick asked. "I guess that's a good question," Alvarez replied. "I'll ask."

Alvarez found Olsen at his desk at 23:56. A mariner for thirty years and a captain for sixteen, the captain of the *Gulftrade* was wearing a beige long-sleeve collared shirt buttoned all the way up. His captain's hat lay atop the documents spread across his desk. "Martin's got the watch, captain. I'm about to turn in, but I told him I'd ask how long you planned on leavin' the lights on."

"Where we at, again?"

"Barnegat," the third mate replied. "New Jersey."

That's fifty miles from New York, Olsen reflected Most importantly, central New Jersey was 300 miles north of the waters now known as "Torpedo Junction." The captain frowned contemplatively. "Leave 'em on till we're well north of Barnegat." Olsen nodded to himself as if confirming his own decision.

"Yeah ... it's too damn crowded out here."[8]

***

It is unknown whether Torger Olsen disregarded the routing instructions' warning of U-boats "off the New Jersey Coast" or simply forgot. What is known, however, is that the operative factor in Olsen's decision to show his lights was that the *Gulftrade* had already passed the most dangerous part of the voyage. Known as the "Graveyard of the Atlantic" even long before the war, one stretch of coast would result in 55 percent of all East Coast U-boat attacks occurring off one state: North Carolina.

Roughly 150 miles off North Carolina's Cape Hatteras, the cold and southward Labrador Current converges with the warm and northward Gulf Stream. This produces fog and heavy seas which force ships to hug the state's coast, though venturing too far inshore risked encountering the shoals and shallows that have wrecked countless vessels over the centuries. Consequently, all north-south traffic along the East Coast was canalized into a 100-mile-long bottleneck between Cape Hatteras and Cape Lookout. The continental shelf here was also quite narrow, providing U-boats a speedy retreat to deep water.

This confluence of factors made North Carolina's coast the deadliest stretch of ocean on earth by March 1942. Night after night, coastal residents heard sounds of gunfire drifting shoreward as fires burned against the eastern sky. Ships destroyed while running this gauntlet in March included the *Dixie Arrow*, sister ship of the *India Arrow*, which burned fiercely while drifting along the coast like the *R.P. Resor* off New Jersey the previous month. March also saw *U-124* commander Johann Mohr add seven wrecks to Torpedo Junction's growing underwater cemetery. Mohr radioed his successes to BdU in the form of a poem which rhymed in German as well as English:

A HUNTER'S THANKS FOR OPEN SEASON!
OFF CAPE LOOKOUT, THE NEW MOON'S NIGHT
BEHELD AN EERIE TANKER FIGHT.
POOR ROOSEVELT! HIS LATEST SCORE
WENT DOWN BY FIFTY THOUSAND TONS.

Even braving rougher seas farther offshore did not save the passenger ship *City of New York* on 29 March, and her Armed Guard detachment fired shells at the *U-160* while the passengers abandoned ship. These included Desanka Mohorovicic, the pregnant wife of a Yugoslav consular official. She later went into labor in a crowded lifeboat tossed by 15-foot waves. Fortunately, a surgeon happened to be in the lifeboat. Although the doctor had broken ribs and possessed only a first aid kit, a healthy baby boy was taken aboard the destroyer USS *Roper* when three of the four lifeboats were found the following day. The destroyer's name honored naval officer Jesse Roper, and Desanka chose her newborn son's name accordingly: Jesse Roper Mohorovicic.[9]

The *City of New York* was only the second passenger ship sunk off the East Coast, but tankers were being destroyed at four times their rate of construction. Attrition rates indicated that half the Allied tanker fleet could be sunk by year's end, meanwhile, a tanker stiff's life expectancy was falling by the day. By 31 March

1942, the death toll for tanker crewmen in the Americas reached 1,374. "Might as well advertise for suicides," one shipowner remarked after losing eight of his twenty tankers. Journalist Alistair Cooke wrote of "a melancholy tune being picked up every night … from the wireless messages of oil tankers going down off the coasts of New Jersey, Delaware, and the Carolinas."

The destruction of sixty-eight tankers in the Western Hemisphere during the first three months of 1942 threatened the United States with what one columnist described as "the greatest problem of transportation and supply … ever faced by any nation at war." Petroleum shipments to US ports in March were 40 percent below demand while British fuel reserves fell to just two months of fuel oil and five weeks of gasoline. The Roosevelt administration's Petroleum Industry War Council bluntly warned that the U-boat offensive threatened to deny America "enough fuel to carry on the war," and that the year 1943 may well be "intolerable." Someone at Eastern Sea Frontier penned a wry response:

"Intolerable the future might be, but the immediate present is bad enough."[10]

***

10 March 1942
4 miles southeast of Barnegat Light, New Jersey
00:01

"A full belly too, look how he sits!" Kapitänleutnant Viktor Vogel shouted over the roaring sea as another wave hissed over the *U-588*'s foredeck. Neither Vogel nor Leutnant Walter Wichmann appeared phased by the cold brine sloshing in the sleeves of their oilskins. "Let's get to it!" Vogel exhorted. Wichmann's feet squelched in flooded sea boots as he turned to speak into a bowl-shaped metal fixture on the bridge bulwark's inboard side. "*UZO auf Brücke*," reverberated down the voice pipe.

The bridge continued to sway as the *U-588* pounded up and down through white foam boiling atop the wave crests sweeping the seascape, and Vogel lowered his binoculars and reached out both hands to steady himself. The bow and stern tanks were flooded to sit the boat deeper in the water, providing the screws more bite and mitigating the stern's tendency to jump the waves. Exhaust ports sputtered and coughed as the Atlantic smothered them before retreating across the deck and pouring overboard through the limber holes.

Another wave dumped itself down the open conning tower hatch as the UZO was brought up. Kapitänleutnant Vogel helped to steady the targeting optic as Wichmann mounted it on its post. The 29-year-old kommandant then glanced at his Alpina KM-592 wristwatch, the dial of which was coated in radium salts and zinc that imbued a pale green glow. It indicated five minutes past midnight.

Four weeks earlier, the *U-588* had departed La Pallice, France carrying a Type VIIC's standard loadout of fourteen torpedoes. Four had been loaded in the forward torpedo tubes, with four more on the torpedo room's deck and two beneath it. Another eel was loaded in the stern tube, with a spare on the aft torpedo room's deck. The last pair had been stowed in pressure-proof canisters between the pressure hull and foredeck. Downloading these into the pressure hull was labor-intensive and left the boat vulnerable, but Vogel had been able to do so before entering Eastern Sea Frontier waters.

Kapitänleutnant Vogel was running short of opportunities to expend his last six eels because his 13,240 gallons of remaining fuel put the *U-588* at the end of its operational tether. The inexplicably lit tanker's appearance was therefore particularly timely, albeit unexpected. Typically, only neutral ships still sailed fully illuminated along the East Coast in March 1942. These invariably carried markings that conspicuously indicated their neutral country of registry, but Vogel discerned no such identification on this tanker.

Leutnant Wichmann pressed his face against the UZO's rubber eyepiece and clamped an arm tightly around the pedestal as the bridge teetered. The first watch officer began methodically reciting commands and data points which were answered and echoed from below the open hatch, all voices shouting over the thundering waves and clangor of diesel pistons. Viktor Vogel again gazed across the churning sea at the lighted ship. *What were you thinking, my friend?*[11]

***

It was 00:40 when the *U-588*'s torpedo smashed into the *Gulftrade* between the mainmast and midship house. Plates buckled as the warhead blasted through the hull and ripped open the No. 5, 6, and 7 tanks, splattering their viscous cargo across the ship. This did not catch fire, but the fuel oil inside the tanks was instantly set alight in a pillar of fire that reached up through the fractured deck. In addition to tearing up much of the main deck, the blast caved in the aft part of the midship house and splintered the No. 1 lifeboat like matchwood.

Captain Torger Olsen was working on payroll documents at his desk when the room imploded around him. Portholes shattered, the door crashed inward, and part of the overhead caved in. The lights also cut out, the *Gulftrade*'s interior going pitch-black as Olsen felt steel bones bending and breaking. Shaken but unharmed, he groped his way out of the room and down the passageway.

The captain stepped out onto the bridge wing and beheld a sight even worse than he had feared. The catwalk between the midship house and aft deck house had been torn away, and sections of decking were wrenched nearly upright around a yawning chasm from which a towering column of fire emanated. The flames nearly reached the top of the 96-foot mainmast and were sighted by Jersey Shore residents 4 miles away. A wave that extinguished the inferno seconds later brought Olsen little solace, as he now grasped the full extent of his ship's damage.

The blast had torn the *Gulftrade* nearly in half. The fissure from which the inferno had sprouted was not a hole in the deck, but rather a rapidly widening gap between the tanker's forward and aft sections. Waves crashed over the gunwales as Olsen felt the ship's sinews straining; piping and sections of hull still holding her tenuously intact squealed in protest as the Atlantic shoved each half of the *Gulftrade* independently of the other.

Looking toward the stern, on the other side of the chasm, he saw the indistinct shapes of men emerging from the engineering department quarters in the aft deck house. He knew there would be additional men ascending from the engine room below. Capt Olsen knew there was nothing he could do for them at the moment. As the *Gulftrade*'s last tendons broke asunder in an ugly discord of squealing and cracking, the ship's master turned and made for the bridge. Panic coiled tightly in his chest as he cursed himself for putting the lights on. *What have I done?*

Olsen found Martin Tammick on the bridge while radioman William Meloney, a 24-year-old from Atlantic City, New Jersey discovered that the explosion had demolished the radio shack. The engine order telegraph and phone connections had been severed, but proof of life arrived from below decks when the engines were powered down. In fact, the entire crew had escaped harm owing to the torpedo striking amidships at the cargo tanks rather than farther aft, near the crew quarters and engineering spaces.

Tearing the *Gulftrade* in half, however, had also separated Olsen and eight others on the forward half from the twenty-five men on the stern half. The tanker's halves now drifted apart, waves tossing each with more violence than the whole. The buoyant cargo in the intact forward tanks appeared to be keeping the forward half afloat, but the officers present—Capt Olsen, first mate Martin Tammick, second mate Ed Johnson, and third mate Valentin Alvarez—unanimously decided to abandon ship. The others voiced no protests.

Olsen and able seaman Jesse Farrow made their way to the boat deck on the midship house's port side. Violent seas and a deck slippery with oil made launching the No. 2 lifeboat a daunting task, but the pair succeeded in lowering it to the main deck where the others boarded. Olsen and Farrow next lowered the boat to the water before the able seaman began a harrowing descent down the wood-and-rope "Jacob's ladder," which slid side-to-side against the hull as the lifeboat's seven occupants watched Farrow descend toward them. The oil congealing on the water proved a blessing by calming it enough to safely board the lifeboat, and the captain quickly followed Farrow down the wooden rungs.

Once all nine men from the *Gulftrade*'s forward half were inside the No. 2 boat, they tripped the pelican hooks securing it to the davits. Upon casting off from the ship's forward half, however, they quickly discovered that the oil slick prevented full oar strokes. Their open-top wooden craft soon drifted clear of the oil only to be rewarded with the full brunt of the Atlantic's acrimony. Each assault of wind and water seemed to cut to the bone. Capt Olsen looked toward the *Gulftrade*'s stern half. It was now even farther away, and he could no longer see human shapes moving about on its deck.[12]

***

There were at least two other vessels (in addition to the *U-588*) in the *Gulftrade*'s immediate vicinity at the time of the attack. The freighter *Jonancy* was steaming southwest along the shoreline approximately 1,000 yards from the *Gulftrade*. At the same time, a smaller ship was on a southward heading between the *Jonancy* and *Gulftrade*. This placed it about half a mile from each when the torpedo struck the *Gulftrade*. Olsen's crew struggled to see the smaller ship due to its size, yet its identity was fortuitous: the Coast Guard cutter *Antietam*.

The three ships' crews had only glimpsed one another so far, but this changed abruptly at 00:40 when an ugly orange flash split the darkness 500 yards off USCGC *Antietam*'s port bow. So near was the blast that the Coast Guardsmen heard the sharp *crack!* of its shockwave outrunning the sound of the explosion itself. This rocked the *Antietam* 15 degrees to starboard, causing crewmen to stumble as a hail of debris splashed around the ship. The towering inferno aboard the *Gulftrade* briefly illuminated the stricken tanker before breaking seas smothered the flames.

General Quarters was called, the bell clanging as feet drummed the decks and the cutter radioed an alert to all ships and stations. The net tender *Larch* and USS *Eagle 48* were soon inbound while a motor lifeboat commanded by Ensign LeRoy Howell set out from Coast Guard Station Barnegat. One motor lifeboat each was also dispatched from Coast Guard Stations Bonds and Little Egg.

The *Larch* was the nearest backup, but Lieutenant George Coale's net tender was still nearly two hours away. That left the *Antietam* as the *Gulftrade*'s only hope for the moment. The crew readied the 3-inch/.23 gun, machine guns, and depth charges as her General Motors diesels roared and the bow angled seaward. True to the Coast Guard motto of *Semper Paratus*, or Always Ready, USCGC *Antietam* was en route within sixty seconds.[13]

***

One of the men sighted by Captain Olsen on the stern half was the *Gulftrade*'s chief engineer, Guy Chadwick. Having been asleep in the aft deck house, Chadwick rushed barefoot out on deck where he immediately slipped on oil. He landed on his tailbone while others exiting behind him similarly slid and stumbled. Chadwick recovered himself and gingerly made his way to his assigned lifeboat, No. 3, only to find it hanging by one fall as the other fall dangled against the hull. Presuming that overeager shipmates had already botched its launch, he led the others to the No. 4 boat on the port side.

The 46-year-old engineering officer soon realized, however, that no lifeboat could remain upright for long in these sea conditions. Others reached the same conclusion, and a dispute arose at the davits about whether to abandon ship as twenty-five men shouted over the wind and waves. Guy Chadwick, the ranking crewmen on this half of the *Gulftrade*, found himself at odds with his own deputy. Second assistant engineer Rolland Johnson and seventeen others wanted to abandon ship. "You won't last ten minutes out there!" Chadwick yelled. "And what happens if that sub finds you??"

Chadwick grabbed Johnson by the shoulders, his calloused hands seizing fistfuls of chambray shirt and canvas lifejacket. He pulled his subordinate closer so that they would not have to shout in front of the unlicensed crewmen, but the younger man's determination was unshakable. "You can stay. I'm leaving," Johnson declared. "And I'm taking whoever wants to go with me." The chief engineer stared back at him for a moment. "Alright," Chadwick finally relented. "Alright, c'mon then. We'll help you launch the boat."[14]

***

While Rolland Johnson's group prepared to abandon the stern half, USCGC *Antietam* was speeding toward the dismembered *Gulftrade* at high speed but with ample caution. Her crew scanned the heaving sea for any sign of an enemy they knew was near at hand. They did not know whether the U-boat was making a run for it or lining up another shot, but a lookout's warning soon revealed the answer: "Torpedo on the port bow!!"

Two independently powered screws made the *Antietam* highly maneuverable, but her crew had only seconds to react. The engine was thrown into reverse at full power, the lookout watching in impotent terror as the torpedo hurtled toward them. "Brace for impact!" The eel hurtled nearer—and missed, passing less than 50 feet forward of the bow. The naval equivalent of being grazed by a bullet instantly whetted the Coast Guardsmen's desire for retaliation. Leaning to port as her bow swung east, the *Antietam*'s streamlined form stood off into the night to respond in kind.

Not far away, the sea battered Capt Olsen's party in the No. 2 lifeboat while wind shrieked across wavetops littered with debris from the *Gulftrade*. Olsen now regretted the decision to abandon ship, but deliverance found them. The nine men had been adrift for about thirty minutes when USCGC *Antietam* materialized. She had sped off in search of a fight after the torpedo's near-miss, but failed to catch her elusive attacker's scent.

Adrenaline coursed through survivors and rescuers alike as the *Antietam* maneuvered amid the wreckage to the lifeboat. The Active-class cutter's low sides, designed for launching boarding parties during Prohibition, enabled the Coast Guardsmen to quickly haul aboard Olsen, Alvarez, Tammick, and the others. As the *Gulftrade*'s halves continued drifting apart, the cutter's crewmen sighted moving human shapes and a flashlight beam on the stern half. The *Antietam*'s grumbling General Motors engines swelled to a roar as she set off in pursuit.[15]

***

Guy Chadwick opted to remain aboard the *Gulftrade*'s stern half along with six others: the first and third assistant engineers, two firemen, a wiper, and an able seaman from Texas named Leonard Smith. The only man not from the engineering department, Smith seemed noticeably more jittery than the others. Rolland Johnson and seventeen others left in the No. 4 lifeboat, which Chadwick's party struggled to launch due to oil on the deck. The engineering officer slipped again, and the lifeboat was waterborne by the time he recovered himself.

After watching the sea hungrily pull the No. 4 lifeboat away from the wreck, where the night's darkness devoured it, the mariners sat on the aft deck. The *Gulftrade*'s forward half was still visible, but only barely. The stern section's interior lighting was somehow still functioning, enabling the two other assistant engineers to venture down to the engine room and close the valve that admitted seawater as coolant. Five minutes had passed when one man sighted a swaying shape approaching from out of the gloom.

"Hey! Hey, a ship! Right there, look!"

***

Aboard the *Larch*, LT George Coale was on the bridge a few minutes before 02:30 when a large form loomed out of the darkness. It soon became distinguishable as a tanker or, rather, half of one. "Mother of God, look at that ..." one sailor exclaimed. Waves hideously rolled the wallowing half-ship as its deck leaned at a 45-degree angle. Coale saw no signs of life, however, because net tender had encountered the *Gulftrade*'s now-abandoned bow section. "Bring us around the other side," the *Larch*'s commander ordered. "Keep your distance."

***

"Look, right there!" shouted one of the seven mariners on the *Gulftrade*'s stern half. Elbows and feet thumped against the deck as Guy Chadwick and the others stood. "Comin' toward us! Ya see it? They're here for us!" Chadwick felt a surge of hope. What materialized from the darkness was not the *Larch*, however, nor was it the *Antietam*. It was the *U-588*.

The baleful throb of diesel pistons heralded a lightless shape that emerged from the nighttime murk and waves like a sea monster from some bygone era. The *U-588* passed between the *Gulftrade*'s severed halves and within 100 yards of the petrified men, foam tumbling at its bow as an 88mm deck gun became visible. The U-boat did not seem large by oceangoing standards, yet it appeared unnaturally steady, as if heavily weighted in the keel. A bolt of fear paralyzed the mariners. *Maybe the jig's up, then*, Chadwick thought.

"Get down!" he bellowed. "Get behind something and stay low!" Metal drums would hardly stop machine-gun bullets, but he did not know what else to do. Perhaps, he reasoned, whatever remained of them could be scraped off the deck by the Coast Guard for a proper burial. However, it took only seconds for fear to morph into anger. The first obscenity flew at the U-boat, then another, as the sluice gates opened for a torrent of the foulest prose in the seafarer's vernacular. One survivor would later tell of "names you couldn't print," but the *U-588* offered no response.

As it passed through the channel separating the tanker's severed halves, a beam of light suddenly sliced through the darkness—from the *Gulftrade*. A man had inadvertently activated a flashlight, the beam of which fell across the conning tower, revealing for a split second an emblem of two roosters facing beak-to-beak. The men's ire immediately turned inward.

"Shut it off!"

"I'm trying, I'm sorry!"

"SHUT IT THE FUCK OFF!"

The beam jerked across the foredeck and deck gun before the light finally turned off. "Holy shit you just killed us," one man spat. "I swear to God I'll—" Chadwick's stentorian voice interrupted him: "Shut. Up." The others fell silent while the U-boat seemed to linger; it felt as if the Germans were deliberately taunting them. Chadwick, at once defiant and resigned, stood again and muttered, "Fuck it." The others looked over in confusion as he disappeared below decks.

The U-boat was still visible two minutes later when he returned with a pack of cigarettes. He distributed them to the others. A few of the men were still hurling profanity at the *U-588*. The men sat on the aft deck and smoked as the U-boat's malevolent profile finally melted back into the darkness. The diesel engines' pulsating growl steadily receded until they heard only crashing waves. Taking a long pull on a Chesterfield cigarette, Chadwick looked toward the *Gulftrade*'s forward half. It was barely visible now, and there were no signs of life on board.[16]

***

Aboard USCGC *Antietam*, Capt Olsen and the eight other survivors from *Gulftrade*'s forward half were draped with blankets and led below deck. Olsen had just gratefully accepted an offer of coffee when he felt the cutter accelerate. She then abruptly decelerated and shuddered as her engines began whining in protest. It sounded and felt as if the *Antietam* were choking.

Among the floating wreckage from Captain Olsen's bisected tanker was a mooring line which had just fouled the *Antietam*'s port screw. The cutter resumed quaking and lurched forward at half speed. Olsen heard a commotion of voices and swearing. The *Antietam*'s skipper attempted to pursue the tanker's stern half using only one engine, but when this proved futile he ordered a radio message transmitted to Lieutenant Coale's *Larch*.

Nine minutes after the *Larch* encountered the *Gulftrade*'s abandoned forward half at 02:25, LT Coale received a message from the *Antietam*. The cutter reported sighting an indeterminate number of survivors on the stern half, last seen drifting in the general direction of the Barnegat lighted buoy. The transmission also effectively passed the rescue baton to the net tender since the *Antietam* could not maintain sufficient speed on a single propeller. For the men on the *Gulftrade*'s aft deck, the *Larch* was their last hope.[17]

***

"I'm not gonna tell you again, Smith!" Guy Chadwick bellowed. "Sit. Down!" Able seaman Leonard Smith would hear none of it. "We're dead if we stay here," Smith insisted. He grew increasingly hysterical. "What happens when that sub comes back? Or when this half a damn bucket sinks out from under us?" He stamped his foot on the deck for effect. Voices rose in dispute, but Smith remained determined to jump overboard and swim. To where, he could not say.

"Listen to me, Leonard—*LISTEN*, goddammit!" The others fell silent when Chadwick seized their attention. His tone then softened. "That temperature will kill you in no time, and that's if you don't drown first." He scanned the others' faces before turning again to the distressed young Texan. "Let's stick with the ship as long as she sticks with us, okay?" Smith hesitated a moment. "Y-yeah. Okay," he conceded, sitting down again.

The minutes ticked by. Another hour passed. The floating wreck's forward list increased while it drifted northeast. Johnson's party had taken the only lifeboat, leaving them little recourse if and when the *Gulftrade* decided to no longer "stick with them." Its list was severe enough by 02:40 that the screws were out of the water. Twenty minutes later, the mariners were fashioning a makeshift raft when they again heard engine noise over the shrieking wind and crashing waves. One man strobed the flashlight beam in the universal Morse code pattern for "S.O.S." as the noise grew louder.

Gunner's Mate 3rd Class Victor Downey had never felt more exhilarated in his life. Watching through salt spray and past the *Larch*'s horns, Downey spotted a faint light flashing a looping rhythm of three short blinks followed by three long ones. He soon discerned figures waving from the half-tanker's aft deck. The tanker survivors cheered and whistled as the *Larch*'s sashaying form took sharper lines. "When the rescue boat showed, I never saw anything that looked so good in my life," Chadwick later recounted. "I hollered as much as the kids."

Nevertheless, they were running out of time. The stern section's worsening list was gradually tipping them toward the water, as if the *Gulftrade* were shrugging them off in slow motion. Lieutenant George Coale positioned the *Larch* directly behind and beneath the stern, then the mariners on the tanker's aft deck tossed a rope to the Navy crew. Hopes of shimmying down to the *Larch* were soon dashed, however, when the heavy seas prevented it from being pulled taut.

How are we gonna get those fellows off that thing? Coale wondered. The wreck's continuing drift, its slanting deck, and the raging seas made rescue a daunting challenge. He considered putting the *Larch* gunwale-to-gunwale with the *Gulftrade*, but that position would be difficult to hold and the wreck could keel over on top of them. For the mariners to jump to the *Larch* risked putting them in the water, but deploying a dinghy would only add new hazards.

LT Coale watched another abortive attempt to suspend the rope between the ships. *There has to be a better way*, he thought to himself. *If only we had something other than a damn net tend—* His eyes suddenly widened as a spark of ingenuity struck him, and his next orders stunned everyone on the bridge. The watch officer stared incredulously. "Sir? ..." Unwavering, Coale repeated the order.

The stranded tanker stiffs watched the *Larch* crewmen toss the line away, then the ship reversed its engines. It backed away before maneuvering around to the wreck's starboard side. The Navy ship then aimed her odd-looking bow directly at them, as if she were about to ram the *Gulftrade*—which is precisely what Lieutenant Coale did. Engines revved as the *Larch* accelerated and slammed her double bowsprit against the tanker's messroom, creating a bridge between the two ships. A voice amplified by megaphone cut through the stormy din:

"Attention: climb onto the horns and move across to our vessel. This must be done now ... I say again, climb onto the horns and move across to our vessel ..."

Waves continued assaulting the *Larch* as her horns ground and smashed against the *Gulftrade* and Coale's helmsman struggled to hold the ship in position. For the mariners, a new dilemma manifested itself: although the *Larch* offered salvation on the other side of the horns, any man who went overboard while crossing them was as good as dead. One misstep or large wave was all that eternity required. Metal clanged as waves lifted and dropped the two ships. No one from the merchant crew moved.

"I say again, climb across the horns to our vessel ..."

The impasse was broken by a petty officer aboard the *Larch*. "Let's get over there, let's go!" the sailor shouted. "C'mon! I'm goin' over, who's with me?" In a spontaneous act of courage later lauded as "immediate and without orders," several of LT Coale's men formed an impromptu boarding party that began crawling across the double bowsprit to the *Gulftrade*.

Kapok lifejackets scraped against metal as GM3 Victor Downey and the others painstakingly inched upward and outboard along the horns, pausing only when the Atlantic wound up another haymaker. The first man on each horn soon reached the tanker's hull. From above them, the mariners individually began making short but harrowing descents down the falls into a *Larch* sailor's waiting grasp. Within less than ten minutes, the Navy crew brought all seven tanker men to safety. At Coale's signal, the helmsman deftly pulled the *Larch* away from the *Gulftrade*'s now-abandoned stern half.

For the next half hour, the *Larch* searched for the men who had abandoned the stern half in the No. 4 lifeboat. When no trace was found, both the *Larch* and USCGC *Antietam* turned for port. Sixteen survivors of the *Gulftrade* (nine on the *Antietam* and seven on the *Larch*) arrived after daybreak at Section Base No. 8 at Tompkinsville, Staten Island.[18]

***

Boats dispatched from Coast Guard stations along the coast were combing the vicinity of the *Gulftrade* attack before the survivors had even reached shore. The morning's search also coincided with one of the Civil Air Patrol's first-ever antisubmarine flights. This was the first CAP mission flown from Atlantic City's Bader Field, which still comprised only a gravel runway and two hangars. The aircraft's two civilian pilots encountered half of the tanker fifteen minutes into their patrol, and later sighted an empty lifeboat, but Rolland Johnson and the seventeen other missing men were never seen alive again. The *Gulftrade*'s logbook washed up on an Atlantic City beach eight days later.

The consequences of turning on the *Gulftrade*'s lights left Torger Olsen ravaged by guilt. "I saw we were up to Barnegat and I thought they shouldn't be able to get us anymore. I suppose we must have made a fine target," he ruefully told one reporter. "All I wish is that they would put me aboard a Coast Guard cutter so I could go out to sea and hunt the sub that sank my ship." Gulf Oil Company evidently judged him less severely, as they would soon grant Olsen command of the tanker *Gulfbelle*.

The *Gulftrade*'s forward half grounded 4 miles east-southeast of Barnegat Inlet, with the bow angled 30 feet above the water. The forward half was visible from shore until settling just under the surface. "Surely a sunken ship is as sad as any of the sad sights of war," Navy ensign Ellis Sard reflected of the partially submerged wrecks littering the coast. "It brings a melancholy chill ... if you ever need proof that a ship is living, look at a sunken one."

The tanker's stern sank in 90 feet of water 10 miles northeast of the bow. Being hazards to navigation, both were marked with buoys. The stern was wire-dragged, or knocked down using a chain or cable suspended between two tugboats, to a depth of 50 feet the following year. The forward section was reduced by dynamite in 1944.[19]

The *Gulftrade* incident illustrates a lesson about the psychology of critical stress incidents. Despite claims from the USCGC *Antietam* crew of seeing a torpedo cross the cutter's track and narrowly miss the bow, the *U-588* never fired a torpedo at the *Antietam*. Viktor Vogel's log instead stated that "because it is not clear what type of patrol vessel it is, [I] set off to the east," and his torpedo launch reports indicate no such attack. Yet the Coast Guardsmen were not lying, but rather experiencing errors in perception and memory commonly induced by high-stress, life-and-death scenarios.

Available records also seemingly shed no light on the flare which the *Gulftrade* crewmen sighted roughly ninety minutes before the attack. Neither USCGC *Antietam*'s report nor a statement provided by the *Jonancy* captain mention seeing a flare despite both ships' proximity to the attack. Capt Olsen also omitted mention of the flare from an affidavit signed two days later. The *Larch*'s report does mention a distant light which is identified as a flare, although this was likely the short-lived fire aboard the *Gulftrade*.[20]

The stern half of the *Gulftrade* adrift. (US National Archives)

***

January 1942 had seen seventeen ships sunk within 400 nautical miles of the East Coast, then twenty-two more went down in February, and gruesome new depths of calamity in March destroyed thirty-four ships along the eastern seaboard. These attacks killed 524 merchant mariners, 164 Allied military personnel, and 15 civilian passengers while sending 206,486 gross registered tons of shipping to the bottom. This amounted to 47 percent of all tonnage destroyed by U-boats worldwide in March; Canadian and Caribbean waters accounted for most of the remainder. It was the Allies' worst month at sea to date.

Maritime insurance firms ceased writing policies. In less than three months, shipowners' claims totaled $1.36 billion in 2023 dollars, wiping out more than two decades of profits. U-boat commanders continued to relish the easy hunting, Kapitänleutnant Erich Topp comparing it to shooting hares while another komman-dant joked that he was part of the world's largest ship-scrapping effort. At least one German sailor taunted survivors by shouting: "Send the bill to Roosevelt!"

Off Torpedo Junction, newborn Jesse Roper Mohorovicic and his mother were rescued when the Navy found three crowded lifeboats on 30 March, the day after the *City of New York* sinking. The fourth boat, however, drifted north unobserved. It held thirteen mariners, a 21-year-old Armed Guard named John McInnis, and six civilian passengers who included a woman and her young daughter, Miriam. Bodies were pushed overboard as survivors succumbed to dehydration and exposure over the ensuing days. "Please don't throw my mummy in the water," Miriam tearfully begged McInnis when her mother died. He obliged, but died himself shortly thereafter. Twelve days after the sinking, Miriam and the ten others still alive were sighted by the Navy blimp *K-4* and subsequently rescued 90 miles east-southeast of Atlantic City, New Jersey.

The ongoing slaughter left East Coast beaches strewn with dead fish, sodden lifejackets, and pieces of decking and lifeboats. The shallows where children played in warmer months now produced bloated corpses while oil scum marred the sand. Bill Manthorpe, later a career US Navy officer, would recall his mother using turpentine to clean his feet after visiting the beach at Ocean City, New Jersey.

"All hope that the Germans would be unable to carry out a sustained attack along this coast vanished," Rear Admiral Andrews lamented during March. The month proved so devastating that even the typically unflappable Admiral King admitted that "the submarine situation on the East Coast approaches the desperate." So many U-boats were patrolling America's eastern seaboard that they remained largely absent from the north-central Atlantic and British Isles. A spokesman in London told reporters that "our end of the battle … is going pretty well." He then added, "but the United States' end is not so hot."

Admiral King had privately acknowledged the necessity of costal convoys by 12 February, but its implementation had been deferred due to inadequate escort capacity. Continuing carnage forced the Navy to another decision point on 6 March, at which time the convoy system was again postponed "until such time as suitable forces were available," according to ESF's war diary. Although the decision was King's, it was based on RADM Andrews' recommendations for escort strength submitted on 26 February. While those escorts were being amassed, Andrews turned his attention to the plan's next iteration.

Only hours before Viktor Vogel's torpedo hit the *Gulftrade* on 9 March, a proposal was submitted to COMINCH titled "Suggested Atlantic Coastal Convoy Plan (if and when suitable escorts are available)." King approved the final plan on 2 April and directed the Sea Frontiers to begin preparing for convoy operations. Merchant shipping in American waters would finally sail in coastal convoys—but not yet, as the Navy required more than five weeks to meet its self-imposed escort requirements. Something else was needed to staunch the losses of ships and lives in the interim.[21]

***

The Americans' fundamental challenge lay in the asymmetry of pitting a numerically inadequate force against a highly mobile enemy across an enormous battlespace.

"The initiative must always lie with the submarine," ESF staff noted. "The U-boats can, with relative freedom, determine the time, location, and method of attack," then disappear before significant firepower could be brought to bear against them. What the United States needed was a means to position that firepower where a U-boat could be expected to show itself. Surface and air patrols could only achieve this by sheer luck, and the convoy system was not yet ready, but March saw the Navy employ an alternative approach.

It was President Roosevelt in January who first proposed using "Q-ships" along the East Coast. These were seemingly defenseless merchant vessels armed with hidden guns and crewed by naval sailors. Intended to lure an unwitting U-boat to its destruction, the British had used Q-ships during World War I with mixed success and high casualties. Ever eager to please his political benefactor, King tasked Andrews with putting FDR's suggestion into action.

The Navy secretly acquired the freighters *Evelyn* and *Carolyn* and commissioned them as USS *Asterion* (AK-100) and USS *Atik* (AK-101). Dummy deckhouses with hinged trapdoors concealing four 4-inch/.50 guns were installed, and their cargo holds were filled with lumber for buoyancy in case the hull was breached. Other weaponry included depth charges, machine guns, rifles, sawed-off shotguns, and hand grenades. Disguised as the *Carolyn* and *Evelyn*, the Q-ships both left port for their first patrols on 23 March 1942.

Three days later, USS *Atik* was 340 miles east-southeast of Norfolk, Virginia when she encountered the *U-123* under Reinhard Hardegen, back for his second American patrol. Taking the bait, Hardegen fired a torpedo that blew a hole in the *Atik*'s hull. The lumber kept the Q-ship afloat while the crew maintained the ruse by launching a lifeboat and transmitting a mayday. Tuckerton, New Jersey's wireless station received the transmission: "SSS, LAT 36°00 NORTH LONG 70°00 WEST, CAROLYN, BURNING FORWARD, NOT BAD."

Hardegen was approaching to finish off the "*Carolyn*" at close range when trapdoors and tarpaulins suddenly fell away, revealing heavy guns and depth charge launchers. A storm of gunfire erupted as American shells bracketed the *U-123* while bullets perforated and ricocheted off the outer hull and tower. The boat was retreating at flank speed behind a cloud of smoke when a bullet shredded the leg of a German midshipman on the bridge. He quickly lost consciousness and died an hour later on the wardroom table. Seething with rage, Reinhard Hardegen returned to the damaged Q-ship and put another torpedo into her engine room.

So much secrecy surrounded the Q-ships that the Navy did not realize something was amiss until the following morning. USS *Asterion* raced to her sister ship's last reported position, but no trace of USS *Atik* or her 141-man crew would ever be found. The *Asterion* would patrol uneventfully as the *Evelyn* until the Q-ship program was shelved the following year.[22]

CHAPTER TEN

Toltén

"I tell you naught for your comfort,
Yea, naught for your desire,
Save that the sky grows darker yet
And the sea rises higher."
—G. K. Chesterton, "The Ballad of the White Horse" (1911)

13 March 1942
23 miles south-southeast of Seaside Heights, New Jersey
12:52

The midday sun shined indifferently on the body of an adult male sprawled across a wooden raft swaying atop the malignant sea. The human form appeared to be another of the previous night's harvest of corpses, though he was very much alive. The man was not yet convinced of this, however, the shock and exhaustion of the preceding twelve hours leaving him only marginally cognizant.

He weakly opened his eyes, but the searing sunlight was unbearable and he quickly closed them again. The man grimaced and moved an arm over his face. His parched throat was agonizing. He dimly wondered whether he was in Purgatory or, assuming he was still alive, whether he would be found. Or perhaps he could just finally die and be done with it, like the others. He was too weary to prefer one scenario over another.

The ship's loss was a blur. The man could remember emerging on deck to find sheer chaos. He vaulted over the gunwale, felt the painfully cold shock of hitting the water, then ... *what happened after that?* Then he had found the raft. He vaguely remembered someone else on the raft with him, but he knew neither who he had been nor where he had gone.

The sun was passing its apogee when the man heard a rhythmic mechanical sound that grew gradually louder. *Chug-chug-chug-chug-chug-chug.* An engine. His eyes opened again and he gingerly rolled his aching body over to confirm that he was not hallucinating. The man weakly held up one hand to block the sunlight as the gray hull of a warship became visible. He heard voices speaking in English: "Hey, he's moving!"[1]

***

11 March 1942
Chesapeake Bay, Maryland
17:32

Sunlight waned as the Chilean freighter *Toltén* left Baltimore in her wake. "He's on his own now," remarked Captain Aquiles Ramírez Bárcena to his second mate. The topic at hand was Guillermo Ortega Flores and his failure to return to the ship for departure, possibly due to the time-honored seafaring tradition of consuming an immodest volume of alcohol. Ramírez was loath to leave one of his crew behind, but the *Toltén* needed to get to New York.

Two years earlier, the Chilean government seized five Danish merchant ships stranded in Chile following Germany's invasion of Denmark. Their crews were forcibly disembarked and the ships granted to Chile's largest shipping firm, the *Compañía Sudamericana de Vapores* (CSAV, or South American Steamship Company). The 280-foot-long freighter *Lotta* was thereby renamed the *Toltén*. Built in the Danish port of Ålborg in 1938, she was the most modern of the five ships despite being fairly small at only 1,858 gross registered tons. The *Toltén* featured a bow and hull strengthened for impact with floating ice, although the ship's derricks, winches, stanchions, and masts lent her a utilitarian profile little different from other freighters.

Aquiles Ramírez Bárcena (Chileans carry both parents' surnames), age 41, had sailed for CSAV since graduating as a star student from Chile's merchant marine academy. His attainment of the title "Captain of the High Seas" in 1938 made him the country's youngest merchant captain. A born seafarer who hated paperwork, Ramírez possessed wide shoulders and a broad, clean-shaven face. When CSAV sought a captain for the *Toltén*'s first voyage, he was at the top of the list.

Ramírez had a knack for cultivating loyalty and admiration in a way that few skippers could. His personal touch included a collection of amusing sea stories and a habit of inviting crewmen to play dominoes, and he was known to chide: "you must work, friends, but you also must live!" Ramírez also indulged

Captain Aquiles Ramírez Bárcena. (Courtesy of Aquiles Ramírez Astudillo)

his favorite hobby by improvising a carpentry workshop aboard ship. He and his wife, Lucy, had four children, the youngest only a few weeks old.

The younger man with neatly combed, wavy hair conversing with Capt Ramírez on the bridge was Norman Pugh Cook, the *Toltén's* 28-year-old second mate. His father, Ernest Pugh, had emigrated from Britain to Chile in 1906 and was followed thereafter by his wife, Mabel Cook. Norman Pugh was the first of their three children. After Mabel's untimely death from cancer, Ernest married Ida Gillmore and had two more sons.

Norman Pugh did not come from a maritime family tradition, but he had attended the Chilean naval academy at his father's encouragement. Two years after graduation, marriage and the birth of his daughter induced Pugh to leave the navy in search of better economic prospects. The couple called their daughter by her middle name, Mabel, in honor of her grandmother. Pugh loved Mabel "to pieces," his grandson would state decades later. Norman Pugh was not previously acquainted with Capt Aquiles Ramírez or anyone else aboard, but the second mate quickly ingratiated himself with his new shipmates.[2]

***

5 March 1942
23 miles southeast of Halifax, Nova Scotia
05:34

"*Los!*"

Leutnant Adolf Schönberg's command to fire echoed down the voice pipe. Beside him, Kapitänleutnant Otto von Bülow watched through his Zeiss binoculars as a lone freighter pushed through an ill-tempered gray sea under a sky just beginning to lighten from the nearing dawn. The boat jolted as a G7e torpedo was ejected from tube two, and von Bülow mentally calculated how long it would take the eel to reach its target. The ship was crossing his bow at a range of 545 yards and a speed of 4 knots, so running time should be … 30 seconds, give or take.

Whump! Twenty-nine seconds later, von Bülow heard a dull and somewhat muffled explosion. *Coal, maybe?* The ship's lights went out as she began settling by the stern, and von Bülow watched as the merchant crew winched a lifeboat toward the sea. His radio room reported picking up their distress call, and he soon spotted a second lifeboat.

The attack was another milestone in Otto von Bülow's litany of firsts. The 30-year-old was the first kommandant of the *U-404*, which was also his first sea command. Now the ill-fated American freighter *Collamer*, bound for Murmansk in the Soviet Union, had become his first sinking. The distress message and nearing dawn, however, meant it was time to conclude business. "*Noch Einen,*" von Bülow instructed.

The party crowding the conning tower watched the coup de grâce hit under the bridge with a thunderous explosion that collapsed the hull inward, breaking the freighter in half. Bow and stern each tipped vertically before plunging steeply downward. Otto von Bülow's *U-404* then turned toward Cape Sable, leaving two crowded lifeboats marking the *Collamer*'s grave.[3]

***

Second mate Norman Pugh was still surprised to find himself at sea again. He had worked for his father's business after leaving the Chilean navy, and had recently changed careers again by accepting a job at Chile's embassy in Canada. Pugh was slated to begin his new role on 1 May 1942, and would therefore be relocating to Canada with his wife and daughter in only a few weeks' time. As their move drew nearer, Pugh sought every opportunity to spend time with friends and family in Chile. This, by accident of fate, was how he found himself aboard the *Toltén*.

When Pugh met a group of friends for dinner on 3 February, those present included the unfamiliar face of CSAV's vice-president. Upon learning of Pugh's naval background, the CSAV executive subjected him to an aggressive recruitment pitch. "We really need officers to crew the requisitioned ships," he explained, referring to the newly acquired Danish vessels. Pugh was reluctant. He cited his impending relocation to Canada in addition to the fact he had never worked on a merchant ship, his only seafaring experience being his two years of navy service.

The shipping executive would hear none of it. "You'll be back before the first of May, gringo," he assured him dismissively. Pugh hemmed and hawed, but the proposition was enticing. He eventually concluded that the voyage would be a minor adventure that could earn some cash to help establish his family in Canada. By the meal's conclusion, Norman Pugh had agreed to sign on for a single voyage.

The *Toltén* set sail from Valparaíso two days later, on 5 February 1942. The port city was draped in fog and an unseasonable chill that morning, the Pacific washing lazily through its iconic bay under a gray sky. It evinced Valparaíso's nickname of "Pancho," the diminutive form of "Francisco," which referred to the city's resemblance to San Francisco, California when viewed from the sea. The *Toltén* next stopped for a

Norman Pugh Cook. (Courtesy of Sergio López Pugh)

few hours at Chile's port of Tocopilla to load a cargo of potassium nitrate before resuming her course along South America's Pacific coast toward her first destination: Baltimore, Maryland.

The voyage's first days were uneventful, but a dark cloud of foreboding seemed to hang over the ship's 29-man crew. The chief steward cryptically confided to his wife that he felt this would be his last voyage, and the ship's accountant unsuccessfully requested to be excused from the voyage. During a brief stopover by the *Toltén* in Panama, the accountant inexplicably mailed his life insurance policy and personal effects back to his wife in Valparaíso.[4]

***

The Panama Canal is less than 50 miles long, but to Captain Aquiles Ramírez it may as well have been a thousand. West of the canal, the Pacific coast of Latin America felt like an extension of his home country: familiar, and untainted by death. Yet the war continued to spread like a cancer, and the *Toltén*'s exit through the canal's east end into the Caribbean brought Ramírez and his crew into its newest theater of combat.

The raw materials extracted throughout Latin America and shipped north made the Caribbean's confined waters a major thoroughfare of copper, rubber, manganese, and other essential industrial resources. The region's exports included 40 percent of global demand for bauxite, which was smelted into the aluminum used to build aircraft. Much of Latin America's bauxite was shipped through Trinidad, also a waypoint for South Africa-bound traffic.

The most important resource in the Caribbean basin, however, was oil. Venezuelan crude was brought by tankers to refineries on Aruba, Curaçao, and Trinidad. These islands together constituted the world's largest concentration of refining capacity, producing a daily average of half a million barrels of gasoline and other petroleum products. Nearly all of this was shipped north by sea to East Coast ports or transatlantic jumping-off points in Canada. This was of paramount importance to America's most critical ally. Most oil reaching the US East Coast originated from Texas and Louisiana, but the Caribbean accounted for more than 60 percent of Britain's oil consumption in early 1942.

The island refineries also produced 100-octane aviation gasoline, a new fuel produced by the "catalytic cracking" process pioneered by Sun Oil in Paulsboro, New Jersey. This fired high-compression aircraft engines with up to 30 percent greater power and improved a plane's climb rate, high-altitude performance, and maneuverability. Demand for 100-octane fuel was insatiable; a large Allied bombing raid over Germany could consume 10,000 gallons. Much of this was refined at an Aruba refinery operated by Standard Oil Company of New Jersey that produced 210,000 gallons per day.

The Germans recognized multiple vulnerabilities in the supply chain by which Caribbean oil fueled Allied tanks, bombers, and ships. U-boats could torpedo the tankers bringing crude oil from Venezuela to the islands, hit tankers carrying refined fuel to the East Coast, or use their deck guns to bombard the refineries themselves with incendiary shells. The war consequently metastasized again in February 1942 with the first blows of a Caribbean U-boat offensive to complement the continuing assault along the East Coast.

The seas around Aruba, Port Lucia, Trinidad, and the Bahamas saw thirty-three ships go down by 15 March. Italian submarines in the Caribbean sank another sixteen by month's end, and a second wave of U-boats left port before the first had returned. These losses further reduced Allied tanker tonnage and would destroy 22 percent of their bauxite fleet by May. Dönitz noted: "Once again, we had struck them in a soft spot."[5]

***

The Caribbean therefore no longer insulated Latin America from the war, but nor had these states' policies been entirely passive. Nearly every Latin American government had broken diplomatic relations with the Axis Powers by March 1942 except for Chile and Argentina. Germanophile and fascist sentiments existed in both countries, and a group calling itself the National Socialist Movement of Chile had attempted a coup in 1938. As *TIME* magazine observed, "The dominant groups in Chile are sharply split on foreign policy."

Some in the capital city, Santiago, described the nation's pragmatic foreign policy as reflecting "the good sense of Chile." In addition to domestic tensions between pro-Allied and pro-Axis factions, however, economic considerations also influenced Chile's prudent neutrality. Exports of copper and other goods to Nazi Germany ceased in 1939 only when trade became physically impossible, and President Juan Antonio Ríos wanted to avoid spoiling a potential postwar trade partnership. "Chile has not yet decided who will win the war," remarked the US State Department in an April 1942 memo.

In turn, Nazi Germany and Fascist Italy pledged that their navies would not attack Chilean ships so long as they prominently displayed their nationality and sailed with lights on at night. A large Chilean flag was therefore painted on each side of the *Toltén*'s hull. Chilean naval directives issued to merchant captains emphasized that, in the eyes of both Axis and Allied forces, "every neutral ship travelling darkened … is considered suspicious and can be considered belligerent."

Neither Axis nor Allied policies targeted neutral merchantmen, yet their crews still faced considerable danger (neutral Ireland's merchant fleet would remember 1939–45 as "The Long Watch"). The British Foreign Office tallied 253 neutral ships sunk during the war's first year alone. These were misidentified by U-boats or by Allied forces hunting German blockade runners and covert resupply vessels. Chilean ships steaming north to American ports passed charred corpses and drifting wreckage while their radio operators heard pleas for assistance over the 600-meter band. Hitler's war was creeping closer to the United States' southern neighbors, prompting some to observe that "the war is already in Latin America."[6]

Laboring deep within the hull of the *Toltén* shielded her engineering crewmen from most of the deck department's harrowing experiences. The firemen working under Scottish-born chief engineer Peter Wright Stuart included 37-year-old Julio Faust Rivera and the double-surnamed Luis Gárate Gárate. The latter was a last-minute addition, having been hired the morning of departure to replace a fireman who did not show up.

Sailing under a neutral flag meant that the *Toltén*'s engineering department was largely spared what Nicholas Monsarrat described as "the cold-blooded hazard involved in working below decks" on Allied merchant ships. Engineering departments suffered the Allied merchant fleet's highest fatality rates because U-boats tended to aim for their primary workspaces. The boiler room and engine room represented "huge halls" with "no partitions," noted German war correspondent Lothar-Günther Buchheim. "If they take a hit, they can fill quicker than any other compartment." Once this cavernous space is flooded, "no ship can be kept afloat."

Nicholas Monsarrat wrote that a direct hit would leave men working below decks with "perhaps ten seconds to get out as the water flooded in." Scalding steam would billow from smashed piping around them as boilers threatened to explode upon contact with freezing water thundering in. Electric power usually went out, turning the engineering spaces into a lightless hell where men pushed and shoved one other in frenzied desperation. "Those ten seconds, for a dozen men fighting to use one ladder in the pitch darkness," Monsarrat reflected, "would mean the worst end to life that a man could devise." Only after making it up the stairs was survival a possibility, assuming the ship was not already capsizing or entering its death plunge.

Engineering duty in Allied merchant fleets "seemed to demand a special category of nervous endurance," and their shared jeopardy engendered closer bonds than in the deck department. "The engine room guys knew they had no chance if a torpedo hit," American mariner Hugh Stephens explained. "It was much more closely knit because they knew they had to rely on each other."[7]

Capt Ramírez seldom slept when his ship and crew were imperiled, and he grew more physically weary the farther the *Toltén* ventured into the war zone. He bore the responsibility for his ship's safety with utmost solemnity, and he knew that mistaken identity during wartime was a real danger. Neutral Brazil had already suffered three ships sunk by U-boats and another by an Italian submarine. The *U-94* would sink another Brazilian vessel, the *Cayrú*, off New Jersey on 9 March.

Ramírez nonetheless placed considerable trust in the chivalry and diligence of his counterparts in the world's navies. His grandson would characterize him as "a gentleman of the sea, faithful to the old maritime traditions, who trusted in its laws." He believed it unlikely that any naval commander would deliberately attack the neutrally flagged *Toltén*, and that even one ruthless enough to do so would at least abide by prize rules. "The crew is always given ten minutes to abandon ship," Ramírez reassured the *Toltén*'s jittery accountant. In such a scenario, they would "lose nothing but their neckties."[8]

***

5 March 1942
20 miles off southeastern Nova Scotia
23:55

"Kommandant auf Brücke!"

Eighteen hours after sinking the *Collamer*, the *U-404* was continuing south when Kapitänleutnant von Bülow was summoned to the bridge. The commander, who was wearing a plaid shirt with its collar pulled through an old gray sweater, donned his sheepskin jacket before climbing the ladder in the center of the control room. He squeezed past two sailors smoking cigarettes in the tower compartment below the open hatch. Reaching the bridge, von Bülow aimed his binoculars at a vessel on a reciprocal course to his own.

Its dark and narrow shape rose and fell like the *U-404*. He discerned a low deck structure, lack of masts, and slender bow carving a narrow V-shaped wake that clung to its hull. "One of ours, by the looks of it," he announced. "Port fifteen, slow ahead," he ordered. "Blinker to the bridge … *Geschützbesatzungen*, stand by."

A funkgast emerged with the signal lamp, and its shutters clanked as he strobed a coded signal in Morse code at the approaching submarine. A correct, albeit misspelled, reply winked back. The *U-404* issued the challenge again, but the other boat did not respond further (it was the *U-96*, the setting for the novel and film *Das Boot*). The two U-boats passed each other in silence like assassins groping through the dark. The kommandant remained topside with the bridge watch for a while longer.[9]

Otto von Bülow's piercing gaze exuded an air of intensity befitting his aristocratic lineage; the von Bülow family has for centuries produced generals, fighter pilots, scholars, and statesmen. Even South Dakota governor

Otto von Bülow after returning from patrol. (Deutsches U-Boot-Museum)

and US senator William J. Bulow counted among the *U-404* commander's extended kin. Their martial heritage may have been preordained, as their name stems from an archaic word meaning "staff of the commander." The von Bülow coat of arms portrays a knight's helmet over a shield emblazoned with fourteen bezants (gold coins). The heraldry of England's Duchy of Cornwall portrays fifteen, purportedly a nod to a 15-bezant ransom which a von Bülow paid to free a captured Cornish knight during the Crusades.

This led to an unexpected remark from Adolf Hitler aboard the cruiser *Deutschland* in the years before von Bülow joined the Ubootwaffe. Upon learning von Bülow's pedigree, the Führer told the nervous young officer that he would one day make him "King of Cornwall," with all its lands as his fiefdom. Von Bülow would never be certain how serious the dictator's comment was, but he never forgot shaking Hitler's hand—a "cold, clammy, rubbery" appendage with a weak grip.

Otto von Bülow was the son and grandson of naval officers and had never considered a career other than the navy. Entering *Marineschule Mürwik* before German rearmament began in earnest, his class of seventy-eight midshipmen was selected from more than five thousand applicants. His last name had helped his odds for admission. Although the Kriegsmarine was highly meritocratic, candidates were also admitted based on their perceived sociopolitical compatibility with the naval officer corps' conservative yet cosmopolitan culture.

Von Bülow had transferred to the U-boat force in April 1940. It was a career change that his father never would have considered, as the elder von Bülow was a product of the High Seas Fleet in a time when the battleship reigned supreme. The Kriegsmarine's upper echelons were populated with holdovers from this era. Like Grand Admiral Erich Raeder, many still dreamed of great battlefleet confrontations like 1916's Battle of Jutland.

Resentment toward the Ubootwaffe simmered among many senior officers. The operational and physical demands of "the War of the Kapitänleutnants" had relatively little need for senior officers, and Dönitz quipped that the old guard preferred capital ships because they "couldn't parade a band across the deck of a U-boat." Von Bülow knew how much stubbornness and pride was involved, but he also knew that whatever dreams of a mighty battlefleet outlived the monarchy had gone down with the battleship *Bismarck* in 1941. Theirs was a war of the wolves now.[10]

Five days before the *Toltén* departed Baltimore, a funkgast was standing his watch in the *U-404*'s closet-sized radio room. He was wearing headphones over his right ear only, leaving the left uncovered to hear the commander, when his boredom was interrupted by staccato beeping that heralded a shortwave message from BdU. An experienced radioman could mentally decipher plaintext Morse code in real time like spoken language, but even a U-boat funker heard this transmission as merely a nonsensical sequence of letters. Only after transcribing the letters and keying them into the Enigma cipher machine did the message become intelligible:

IF FUEL PERMITS, OPERATION IN THE LARGE SQUARE 'CA' IS APPROVED.

Kapitänleutnant von Bülow read the message before summoning his obersteuermann and first watch officer to the chart table in the control room. The latter was Leutnant Adolf Schönberg, whose face looked even younger than his twenty-three years. Schönberg appeared wearing a grayish-green single-breasted denim jacket with rank insignia on its shoulder straps. The obersteuermann's frayed dark blue reefer jacket completed their sundry assortment of attire. All three stooped over the 1870G Nord-Atlantischer Ozean map in the control room.

The *U-404* was currently in BB 7772, a 6-square-mile area south-southeast of Nova Scotia. Rather than latitude and longitude, the Kriegsmarine divided the globe into squares identified by two-letter codes. Digits appended to a grid square referred to a smaller square within it. Von Bülow scanned the map until he found grid square CA. The East Coast ran diagonally through CA, the northern half of North Carolina in its bottom-left corner and Boston in its top-right. He began thinking out loud while tracing his finger along the map.

They would proceed south from BB 7772 to … CB 1, east of Cape Cod, then track west to CA 3. The *U-404* would follow the coast southwest from there while skirting CA 2, which encompassed the greater New York City area. "You can say hello to your kindergarten," von Bülow quipped to Leutnant Schönberg, referring to his birthplace of Suffolk County on Long Island. The first watch officer's family had been among those expatriates who returned to Germany during the interwar years. "My teachers never liked me much, *Herr Kaleun*," a smirking Schönberg replied. "I doubt they'd think much better of me now."

Von Bülow moved his finger south through CA 2 until stopping on CA 5. This square consisted largely of ocean, but its top-left corner contained most of New Jersey's coastline plus part of Philadelphia in neighboring Pennsylvania. The captain tapped his finger on CA 5 and looked. The obersteuermann nodded in concurrence as his eyes flitted across the map. "*Gut*," von Bülow declared. "*Sehr gut*. Then let us take a trip to …" He found a coastal city 68 miles northwest of the square's center.[11]

"… Atlantic City."

***

The *Toltén* reached Baltimore on schedule, and the crew secured the lifeboats to their chocks to prevent them from hitting the derrick while it lifted the saltpeter from the ship's cargo holds. They enjoyed a couple of days' respite ashore, though Guillermo Ortega failed to return to the ship for reasons unknown. Prior to departing for their next destination, New York City, Capt Ramírez reported to the harbormaster for routing instructions. Accompanying him as his interpreter was chief engineer Peter Wright.

The routing instructions specified a northward route along New Jersey's coastline and advised keeping as close to shore as possible and making port before sunset. Any ships sailing during hours of darkness, the orders decreed, must extinguish all lights. Ramírez raised no objections, which elicited confusion from Wright. "You're keeping the lights on, right?" the engineer asked during their walk back to the pier. "*Por supuesto*," the captain replied. *Of course.* "They give everyone the same general instructions, as I understand. It doesn't change our rights and obligations as a neutral vessel." Wright still appeared uneasy. "Don't worry about it," Ramírez reassured him. "*Vámonos a New York y despues a casita.* Easy day."

With her cargo holds empty, and minus one crew member, the *Toltén* departed Baltimore at around 17:15 on 11 March. Reaching New York required passing through the Chesapeake & Delaware Canal that traverses the neck of the Delmarva Peninsula, connecting the Chesapeake Bay and Delaware Bay. According to the harbormaster's office, clearing the canal at least one hour before dawn would enable them to reach New York by sunset.

Second mate Norman Pugh watched Maryland's Eastern Shore passing the *Toltén*'s starboard side as she steamed north through the Chesapeake Bay on the evening of 11 March. The freighter did not clear the Chesapeake & Delaware Canal until around 08:00 on the morning of 12 March, however. This brought the *Toltén* into the Delaware River nearly two hours after sunrise, meaning she would not make New York before sunset.

Now sailing in daylight, Ramírez's ship followed the river south until it opened into the Delaware Bay. The Cape May Canal would not be completed until December, so traffic departing the Delaware Bay still needed to pass between the Delaware Capes (Cape May and Cape Henlopen). Radio operator Reinaldo Poppenberg Quintero broadcast the Chilean ship's position as she approached the Capes that afternoon. Entering the open ocean at approximately 14:45 on 12 March, the *Toltén* turned north to begin the final leg of her journey to New York. *Almost halfway home*, Norman Pugh reflected.[12]

The Chileans turned on their lights and navigation lights as the sun dipped toward the horizon off their port beam and Wildwood, Avalon, and Sea Isle City slid past them. At around 21:45, the *Toltén* was 8 miles off Long Beach Island when a lookout shouted an alert that startled Capt Ramírez and everyone else on the bridge. An unknown vessel was speeding toward them from out of the darkness—it was USCGC *Antietam*, the same cutter that had responded to the *Gulftrade* attack less than forty-eight hours earlier. From the crew quarters, fireman Julio Faust heard an electronically magnified voice booming somewhere topside.

The *Antietam* slowed as she neared, bow toward the *Toltén*, while Capt Ramírez descended to the main deck. He was joined there by engineering officer Peter Wright, who listened intently as a Coast Guardsman on the cutter's bow issued an order via megaphone. "*Están dando jugo …*" Wright muttered. He translated the Americans' order for Ramírez. The captain's English may have been rudimentary, but he did not need his interpreter to deduce the gist of their demand.

The *Antietam* was ordering Ramírez to extinguish his ship's lights. He attempted to explain that his neutral flag entitled the *Toltén* to sail fully illuminated, but the Coast Guardsmen insisted that all vessels were required to travel with lights off. Moreover, they warned, any ship refusing to comply with US Navy or Coast Guard orders was liable to be fired upon. Behind the American holding the megaphone, Ramírez could see several men manning a large gun mounted to the cutter's deck. The implication was clear: *this is not a suggestion.*

The Americans' threat hung in the chilly air as Wright looked with concern to Capt Ramírez. The brutal dilemma compelled him to choose between making the *Toltén* a target for submarines or risking the *yanquis* shooting at him. Even if their threat was a bluff, the Coast Guard could still board and confiscate his ship. A moment of tense silence passed before Ramírez conceded. "*Bien,*" he told Wright with a resigned sigh. "*Diles que las apagaremos.*"

They would turn the lights off.

Ramírez and Wright watched the *Antietam* depart. "*Que se vayan a la chucha …*" the engineering officer spat. *El capitán* was silent. Facing danger in the performance of his duties was one thing, but being forced at gunpoint to endanger his crew was another matter entirely. He was mulling over their predicament when an idea struck him. He summoned the ship's officers, and Norman Pugh listened intently as Captain Ramírez began to explain his intentions.

In the hours that followed, the *Toltén* continued her course north while Ramírez led a tense vigil on the bridge. The ocean was calm, the sky moonless and black. Reinaldo Poppenberg remained at the wireless station. The ship's only radioman, he typically manned his post until 02:00. Norman Pugh was also on the bridge. The 28-year-old wore a cream-colored turtleneck sweater with geometric designs knitted by his wife, Raquel, the wool's warm hug serving as a reminder of their forthcoming new life in Canada. He imagined Mabel speaking English like a native.

Pugh found reassurance in the presence of Aquiles Ramírez, who exuded the quiet confidence of a man whose years at sea had not gone untested. The captain had once helped avert disaster after a storm disabled his ship and left it adrift for two days off the Chilean coast, and even his first name (the Spanish form of "Achilles") evoked stalwart courage. However, and notwithstanding his confidence that they would reach New York safely, Ramírez felt unsettled as he watched shadows squirm eerily across the *Toltén*'s deck. He knew it was going to be a very long night.[13]

***

The German account of what transpired that evening suggests that Captain Ramírez did not fully comply with USCGC *Antietam*'s order that the ship darken. Otto von Bülow's version of events begins at 23:37, when his bridge watch sighted a pinpoint of light 14 miles off Seaside Park, New Jersey. Its faint glow was rendered more conspicuous by the night's darkness, which was so impenetrable that von Bülow would remember it more than thirty years later.

The *U-404* approached to find the partly illuminated *Toltén* steaming a zigzag course. "No side lights, no steaming lights, no stern light," the commander's log noted. "Only two faint deck lights on the stern." U-boat commanders were always on the alert for a trap, but von Bülow's intuition detected no ruse. "Well, *Herr Kaleun?*" Leutnant Schönberg asked. "*Ja, ja,*" replied von Bülow. "Let's start the show."

The order "*Auf Gefechtsstationen!*" stirred the control room and torpedo rooms into a flurry of activity. The *U-404* commenced its attack run by accelerating on a course parallel to the *Toltén* while the UZO was brought topside and mounted on its post. "One eel," von Bülow instructed, extending an index finger; firing single torpedoes was a tactic popularized by Otto Kretschmer and his motto of "one torpedo, one ship." In the forward torpedo room, an order marched through the voice pipe: "Ready tube one for surface firing."

Leutnant Schönberg adjusted a small lever to brighten the reticle while the UZO fed the bearing to the target into the calculator. He shouted the target angle, range, and speed down the open hatch, adding: "Position changing!" Below him, in the tower compartment, the boatswain turned dials on the calculator's face to input the data. The target was cutting a zigzag pattern of 30–40 degrees around its base course, but this only meant that the first watch officer would have to refine the data inputs before catching it between pivots.

The *U-404* overtook the freighter on its port side, crossed its bow diagonally, then cut two right angles. "Running depth two meters!" Schönberg hollered over clattering diesel pistons. The target was now only a few hundred yards away, the *U-404*'s bow aligned perpendicular to the *Toltén*'s length. "Target angle green zero-eight-zero!"

"*Steht!*" the bootsmann yelled back. *Set!*

"Target speed ten!"

"*Steht!*"

"Range six hundred!"

"*Steht!*"

"*Folgen!*" Schönberg yelled as he swiveled the UZO to keep it aimed at the target. The boatswain in the tower flipped the switch that engaged the relay linking the calculator to the UZO, which began transmitting the bearing from the *U-404* to the *Toltén*. The first watch officer replied: "*Lage laufend!*" This cued the petty officer to engage another switch, and the calculator's red lights lit up to indicate that the gyro-angle was being calculated. A torpedoman in the forward torpedo room unlocked the hand firing levers at the tubes.

The zigzagging ship was due for another pivot to starboard, but the *U-404* was now so close that this would require turning off sharply and pursuing it again. The calculator's servomotors were still buzzing. "*STEHT??*" Schönberg thundered. The calculator's red lights went out and a single white light replaced them. "*Steht! Lage null-acht-null!*" the bootsmann finally replied. "Tube one, ready??" The bugraum answered via the voice pipe: "Tube one, ready!"

"*Rohr eins, LOS!*" Schönberg bellowed and punched the trigger. The boat recoiled as a single G7e leapt from its tube. "*Torpedo laeuft!*" a voice from the bow reported as the eel streaked forward. The helmsman then put the rudders hard over, and the *U-404* peeled away in a looping turn onto a heading opposite the target's.

Traveling 634 yards in 40 seconds, the torpedo struck the *Toltén* amidships on her starboard side between the engine room and No. 3 cargo hold. The blast, which churned a white volcano of water higher than the mainmast, wrenched the hull open and ignited the nitrate particulate in the cargo holds. Night turned briefly to day as von Bülow and Schönberg witnessed a "heavy detonation with a bright, fiery glow." The ravaged vessel slid to a halt, red and orange flames adorning the decks as water poured through her shattered hull. The spectacle's brutal finality evoked one U-boat officer's reflection of a similar scene: "This was the death of a ship."

The explosion was so powerful that von Bülow surmised the ship was carrying munitions, but this thought was interrupted when its lights suddenly turned on, revealing a large Chilean flag painted on the hull. Von Bülow's heart skipped a beat. "*VERDAMMT!*" he struck the bulwark in anger as the freighter's wailing alarm became audible. "Why did the damn fool have his lights off??"[14]

Aboard the *Toltén*, the fire illuminated a nightmarish scene as water pouring into her interior caused the ship to list rapidly to port. The blast had severely compromised her structural integrity, and bulkheads creaked as the ship threatened to split in half. Those alive amid the bedlam surged toward the boat decks, but the lifeboats were not hanging from their davits ready for loading—they were still restrained in their chocks where they had been set before unloading in Baltimore. Men frantically manipulated wire lashings and turnbuckles while the *Toltén* made haste toward the seafloor.

It quickly became clear there was no time to get the boats swung outboard, loaded, and lowered, so the desperate Chileans turned instead to the rafts. Men clambered across the deck and dropped overboard, one by one, into the black ocean below. One man swam to a raft and clumsily pulled himself onto it, and the raft jerked a moment later as a gasping shipmate also heaved himself on. The first man inched over to grant his companion more room, but he would remember little else of those violent and chaotic minutes.

The *U-404* cruised away on a southwesterly course as an odor that von Bülow described as celluloid wafted over the surface. "All quiet on the 600-meter band," Schönberg noted. "Not surprising, he went quick," the commander replied. "Poor bastards." In the light of the ebbing flames, von Bülow watched as the mangled ship "breaks apart and goes steeply into the deep." The Atlantic devoured the *Toltén* in less than six minutes. With her receded the voices of the surviving crew, which dwindled pitiably until they, too, were gone.[15]

***

13 March 1942
23 miles east-southeast of Seaside Heights, New Jersey
12:52

Twelve hours after the *Toltén*'s destruction, the man sprawled on the raft lifted his upper body and turned to look at the approaching vessel, lifting a hand to shield his eyes from the sun. The ship's hull was painted a dull gray like a warship, and he heard voices speaking in English over the engine. Large, black lettering on the hull read: U.S. COAST GUARD.

The man on the raft was fireman Julio Faust Rivera, the *Toltén*'s sole survivor. He was first spotted by an Army plane at 08:34, and Third Naval District subsequently dispatched USCGC *Antietam* and the minesweeper *AMc-200* while Naval Air Station Lakehurst deployed three blimps. A blimp sighted Faust again around noon shortly before the *Antietam* located him.

The *Antietam* and *AMc-200* recovered a lifeboat with five bodies in the general vicinity of Faust's raft. In their pockets were "Z-card" identity documents revealing them as crewmen from the tanker *Gulftrade*, torpedoed two nights earlier. Rescuers also found the body of Reinaldo Poppenberg, the *Toltén*'s radio operator. Faust and the six bodies were transferred to the net tender *Larch*, which brought them to Section Base No. 8 at Tompkinsville, Staten Island.[16]

***

The *Toltén* sinking sparked shock and condemnation in Chile, where it also inflamed tensions between pro-Allied and pro-Axis camps. The newspaper *La Unión* invoked a "national feeling of indignation … Chile has maintained an honest neutrality and the injury is therefore more cruel and unjust." Labor leader Bernardo Ibáñez denounced "the criminal action of the cowardly fascist corsairs," and enraged citizens chanting "*Abajo con el eje!*" ("Down with the Axis!") smashed windows at the Nazi-sympathetic newspaper *El Chileno*. Domestic support for neutrality persisted despite the outrage, and political sensitivities even led some publications to avoid stating that an Axis submarine was believed responsible.

Not all Chileans accepted the official explanation of the ship's loss, the magazine *Vea* asking: "Who is to blame for the wreck of the *Toltén*?" Rumors abounded in Chile that the Americans or British intentionally sank the ship to draw their nation into the war. Sole survivor Julio Faust told Chilean and Peruvian reporters that he suspected the United States of deliberately making the ship a German target. Chile's defense minister repudiated this as "absolutely false … in Faust's official statement he has not expressed similar and whimsical inventions." The naval chaplain who presided over the memorial service criticized "street interpretations" which accused the United States—"a great friend of Chile"—of nefarious intent.[17]

Chile's foreign minister summoned the ambassadors of Germany, Japan, and Italy. The Axis diplomats expressed regret, but stressed that the *Toltén* would not have been attacked if her lights had been on. The Nazis also insinuated that an American or British submarine may have been responsible, but ultimately offered to pay indemnity to the Chilean government. No payment was ever made. BdU staff absolved Otto von Bülow of blame. The *U-404* encountered another Chilean ship off Atlantic City three days after the *Toltén* sinking. Because the ship was fully lit with markings visible, von Bülow did not attack.

American historian Clay Blair, a US Navy submarine veteran of the Pacific war, would interview the former *U-404* commander in 1987. "This was the Chilean government's first contact with the realities of the war. And they didn't know what to do," von Bülow told Blair. "They thought that if the US couldn't protect them so close to America, what could they do for [Chile]? So they stayed out of the war."

Berlin was confident that Chile would maintain its neutrality. "The new foreign minister, who is friendly to the US, will not be able to put through anything with which the new president disagrees," German leadership concluded. "[The president] will not tolerate breaking off relations with the Axis under any circumstances." The tragedy nonetheless irreparably soured Chilean public opinion against Germany, and Chile severed diplomatic relations with the Axis Powers ten months later. The nation never formally entered into hostilities against Hitler's government, although Santiago would issue a token declaration of war against Japan in April 1945.[18]

Chilean investigators concluded that the disaster was a direct consequence of American insistence that the *Toltén* extinguish her lights. The United States embassy in Santiago responded by blaming Capt Ramírez. American officials insisted that neutral vessels were not required to report for routing instructions as Ramírez had done in Baltimore. By doing so, they asserted, he had obliged himself to adhere to US lighting restrictions and obey all orders from US naval forces.

Chile countered that Ramírez had not voluntarily reported to the harbormaster for routing instructions. The investigation cited testimony from four other Chilean merchant captains who claimed that American port authorities had attempted to force them to accept routing instructions, but all had refused. The Chilean captains reportedly experienced no further pressure, and were instead informed that this meant sailing at their own risk. All subsequently reached their destinations without hindrance.

The United States also claimed that USCGC *Antietam*'s "order" on the night of 12 March was only a recommendation. However, in addition to Faust's testimony to the contrary, Norman Pugh's half-brother would conclude that "it does not seem logical that Captain Ramírez or the officer on duty would carry out the order to darken." As Kenneth Pugh Gillmore emphasized, Ramírez understood that putting out the lights would make the *Toltén* "a possible target for attacking submarines."

Finally, USCGC *Antietam*'s patrol report curiously lacks any information regarding the cutter's operations on the night of 12 March. A document titled "Cruise Report, 8 March to 14 March, 1942," submitted by the cutter's commander three days after *Toltén* attack, provides at least a paragraph-length narrative for each day—except for 12 March. This entry instead states only: "Patroling area Manasquan to Barnegat, As before [sic]," and the entries for 12 and 13 March show evidence of alteration.[19]

***

Norman Pugh Cook's family was among those devastated by the sinking. His wife, Raquel, was forced to seek employment to provide for their 4-year-old daughter, Mabel. They would struggle financially for years. Seven-year-old Kenneth Pugh Gillmore was too young to fully understand why his brother Norman never returned home, but the tragedy's effects would shape much of the rest of his life.

Two families experienced apparent miracles, however. Guillermo Vera Gatica was believed dead until he reappeared in Valparaíso on 28 March, having been absent for the *Toltén*'s departure from Valparaíso on 5 February because he had signed on to the *Huemul* instead. His spot aboard the doomed ship was filled at the last minute by Luis Gárate Gárate.

The second man to return from the dead was Guillermo Ortega Flores, who was left behind in Baltimore two days before the ship's loss. The exact circumstances of Ortega's absence are lost to history, and accounts differ between drunkenness, illness, or desertion. While in the United States, Ortega attended the funeral of radioman Reinaldo Poppenberg Quintero at St Stephen's Catholic Church in Brooklyn. Reinaldo Poppenberg, the only *Toltén* crewman whose remains were ever recovered, was buried at St John's Cemetery in Amityville, Long Island.

A memorial service for the twenty-eight mariners was held at the Church of the Holy Spirit in Valparaíso on 23 March. The city's bishop and Chile's senior naval chaplain jointly officiated the highly emotional event. Public turnout was enormous, and the eulogy by chaplain Julio Barrientos Ruz moved many attendees to tears:

> "They were ordered to sail with lights off, and our flag went dark, as if to cover itself in mourning, or perhaps not to witness the nocturnal sacrifice of so many of His children ... Ignorant of so much sinister detail, we only know that within a few moments everything had disappeared ... a maritime beast, painted black as a night ghost, mortally wounded them ... Their pain is tempered by the Christian hope that God, infinitely merciful, has welcomed into His bosom the souls of our dear victims. Lord, give them eternal rest, and may the eternal light shine for them."

Writing in 1975, Chilean maritime historian Ariel Sandoval Hernández reflected on the choice forced on Captain Ramírez by USCGC *Antietam*. "These questions are difficult to answer conscientiously," Sandoval wrote, "especially for those who have not been faced with this distressing dilemma." Only after the war did Otto von Bülow's log reveal that the Chilean captain had partly defied the Americans' order:

two of the *Toltén*'s lights were showing when the Germans sighted her. In the end, Aquiles Ramírez Bárcena had chosen to protect his crew.[20]

***

The appalling losses along the eastern seaboard in March 1942 were partly a consequence of Admiral Ernest King's arrogant obstinacy. COMINCH had opposed coastal convoys for weeks only to finally change his mind that month, yet on 19 March he rebuffed another British plea for coastal convoys in American waters. In fact, planning for this operational pivot was already underway even before King formally approved the convoy plan on 2 April. The first East Coast convoys would not sail for another six weeks, however, because Admiral King's endorsement carried a critical stipulation.

Despite ample contrary evidence, King and other Navy leaders believed that convoys lacking anything less than ironclad escort protection would merely present the Germans a convenient buffet of targets. COMINCH therefore decreed that no convoys would sail until the Navy had amassed what it deemed to be sufficient escort forces: thirty-one destroyers and forty-seven cutters and subchasers. Coastwise traffic was thus left at the Gray Wolves' mercy in the interim, and the slaughter continued apace.

ADM King's intransigence made him "perhaps the most disliked leader of World War II," according to historian John Ray Skates, and his many detractors included an obscure Army brigadier general named Dwight Eisenhower. Although he would not take command of all Allied forces in the European Theater until November 1942, Eisenhower's role in strategic planning at the War Department meant that he clearly recognized the consequences of Ernest King's dereliction of duty. As Eisenhower penned on 10 March, "One thing that might help win this war is to get someone to shoot King."[21]

The list of COMINCH's failures that were costing lives included a brightly lit coast which continued to silhouette merchantmen offshore. William Meloney of Atlantic City, the radioman who survived the *Gulftrade* attack three days before the *Toltén* was hit, voiced his opinion to reporters on 18 March. "Tell 'em the lights on the coast are the greatest menace we have," the 24-year-old angrily told the *Philadelphia Inquirer*. "And tell 'em the lights off Atlantic City are the brightest all along the way."

The US Navy, however, reported that public opposition to a coastal blackout persisted. "Squawks went up all the way from Atlantic City to southern Florida that the tourist season would be ruined," Samuel Eliot Morison wrote after the war. "Ships were sunk and seamen drowned in order that the citizenry might enjoy business and pleasure as usual." Rear Admiral Andrews lambasted blackout resisters as "selfish, greedy, and unpatriotic." This narrative, which would stand for decades as a sort of blood libel against coastal residents, would nonetheless earn historian Joseph Bilby's appellation of the "Greatest New Jersey War Myth."

Contradicting these claims are records from the war cabinet of Governor Charles Edison (son of inventor Thomas Edison), which portray New Jersey residents as generally cooperative regarding light-suppression measures. Additionally, orders issued by the Army and Navy were often unclear or contradictory. Allegations of selfish recalcitrance by the public conveniently deflected blame away from the Navy, and this was almost certainly not a coincidence. This narrative originated from the Navy itself in 1942 and was echoed after the war by Samuel Eliot Morison, the historian granted an officer's commission and tasked by FDR with writing the Navy's combat history as it was being fought. It is worth noting that Morison's expansive body of work consistently paints an adulatory portrait of Admiral Ernest King—whose support was indispensable to Morison's task.

Unsurprisingly, ultimate blame for the deadly luminosity along the East Coast lay with King himself. He insisted that a blackout was not necessary, rejecting the idea again on 14 March 1942. COMINCH instead favored a "dim-out" that would entail only the "suppression of lights showing to seaward."

TIME magazine stated that New York City's urban sprawl ("the greatest concentration of light in all the world") simply "blinked out," yet achieving the dim-out took several weeks. Up and down the Jersey Shore, boardwalk lights went out and the eastern halves of streetlight bulbs were darkened using black paint mixed with aluminum. Theater marquees, neon signs, and searchlights at Atlantic City's Convention Hall went dark. As the *New York Times* reported, "Some beachfronts are blackened out so effectively that the eastward facades of homes and hotels loom grotesque and blank against the western star-glow."

The US Army's Eastern Defense Command enforced the dim-out in conjunction with local authorities, but the policy's results proved less than impressive. Automobile headlights were still visible, and patrol vessels noted that ships were still silhouetted as far as 25 miles offshore. An Army assessment two months after the dim-out went into effect reported that a "hazy backdrop of light" still rendered the shoreline "a shooting gallery." Evidence that Admiral King's Navy did not take the issue seriously was visible on Cape May, where thousands of exterior lights on the seaward side of Section Base No. 9 remained lit each night.[22]

***

On the night after the *Toltén* sinking—the same day Admiral King refused the proposed blackout—the *U-404* encountered the American collier *Lemuel Burrows* 9 miles off southern New Jersey. The ship was hard to miss. Kapitänleutnant von Bülow noted that she was "distinguished before the lights of Atlantic City," one survivor bitterly recounting that "it was lit up like daylight all along the beach." A torpedo hit amidships and the collier slowed to a halt while bleeding steam into the sky.

Most of the crew abandoned ship in two lifeboats as another torpedo from the *U-404* heaved the *Lemuel Burrows*' stern out of the water. The stern then crashed down, swamping the lifeboats and drowning more than a dozen men. After hitting the collier with a third eel, the U-boat approached the survivors. A voice shouted a question in impeccable English: "Hey, you there, what is the name of your ship?" The speaker (likely Leutnant Schönberg) repeated the question, but no one responded. Fourteen of thirty-four crewmen survived.

Lawrence Sullivan, third mate aboard the *Lemuel Burrows*, had spent his entire adult life aboard ship. The 42-year-old lived in Boston with his mother, to whom he had recently confessed that he believed it only a matter of time before a torpedo found him. On 17 March, Sullivan's body washed ashore at Wildwood, New Jersey.

Three weeks after the *Toltén* and *Lemuel Burrows* attacks, Captain Bjarne Sand guided the freighter *Chr. Knudsen* out of New York Harbor. Capt Sand was no stranger to peril on the high seas, having been the second mate on one of the five ships sunk by Hans Rose's *U-53* off Nantucket in October 1916. Twenty-six years later, on 8 April 1942, the *Chr. Knudsen* left New York laden with a cargo of nitrates and began her journey on a southward course along the Jersey Shore.

Little is known of what transpired after the ship's departure besides the approximate time and location of her voyage's abrupt end. At some point on the night of 9/10 April, the *Chr. Knudsen* crossed paths with Oberleutnant Eberhard Greger's *U-85* roughly 80 miles off Atlantic City. The Type VIIB boat loosed two torpedoes at the Norwegian ship, then a brilliant orange flash lit the darkened sea. The *Chr. Knudsen* sank too quickly for a distress transmission, taking her entire crew to the bottom. The *U-85* resumed its course south.[23]

***

The Germans continued savaging shipping on America's doorstep, but events a month after the *Toltén* attack demonstrated that the Grey Wolves were not invincible. USS *Roper* (DD-147), a Wickes-class destroyer which had served alongside USS *Jacob Jones* in Destroyer Division Fifty-four, assumed the Jakie's patrol duties in March. The mission was personal for the men of the *Roper*: many had lost friends on the *Jacob Jones*, and her captain had graduated from Annapolis with Lieutenant Commander Hugh Black. Six weeks after the Jakie's destruction off Cape May, the night of 13/14 April found USS *Roper* patrolling off the Outer Banks through waters teeming with bioluminescent plankton.

The destroyer's wake glimmered eerily behind her as she felt her way through the darkness using a British-built radar set, a tool the *Jacob Jones* had lacked. A blip appeared on the radar display shortly after midnight, then the hydrophone operator heard screws turning too fast for a fishing boat. USS *Roper* went to general quarters. She had caught the scent of Eberhard Greger's *U-85*, the same boat that sank the *Chr. Knudsen* off New Jersey four days earlier. As the *Roper* closed to 700 yards, Greger fired a torpedo from the stern tube. A fluorescent blue streak stretched toward the *Roper* as the eel hurtled toward her and narrowly missed, passing harmlessly along the port side.

Now only 300 yards ahead of the destroyer, the *U-85* cut hard to starboard just as the *Roper* fixed the U-boat in her searchlight and opened fire. Bullets clanged off the conning tower and a 3-inch shell punctured the pressure hull, prompting the Germans to hastily scuttle the boat and abandon ship. Some made it into the warm sea while others were cut down by furious American fire. Most of the 46-man crew made it overboard alive, though the *U-85* took Eberhard Greger to the bottom.

Unsure whether the U-boat was truly out of the fight, the *Roper* plowed through the knot of floating survivors and dropped eleven depth charges on the wreck. This killed all the men in the water, and the Americans subsequently recovered twenty-nine bodies. The first destruction of a U-boat in American waters was as brutal as it was poetic. Not only had the *Roper* avenged the *Jacob Jones*, but the *U-85* was the same boat erroneously claimed as sunk by a Navy pilot in January's "sighted sub, sank same" incident.[24]

CHAPTER ELEVEN

Persephone

"O Trinity of love and power,
Our brethren's shield in danger's hour,
From rock and tempest, fire and foe,
Protect them wheresoe'er they go."
—US Navy Hymn

24 May 1942
9 miles southeast of Virginia Beach, Virginia
07:40

Five hundred feet over the Atlantic Ocean, Lieutenant Alfred Cope watched waves breaking over the partly exposed shipwreck below him. Cope was wearing a khaki one-piece flight suit, the same A1 boots used by bomber crews, and an uninflated "Mae West" lifejacket (named for its resemblance, once inflated, to the Hollywood star's bust). A fleece-lined leather jacket was draped over the back of his seat. Cope steered slightly east, putting the wreck off *K-6*'s port side. The forlorn steel cadaver was the *Tiger*, a Socony-Vacuum tanker torpedoed in shallow water two months earlier.

"How long you think that thing's gonna sit there?" asked his copilot, one of nine other Navy personnel aboard *K-6*, from the seat beside him. "I dunno," Cope replied. "I'd think if they were gonna salvage it then they woulda done it already … I guess she's a total loss." His eyes lingered on the wreck. "That's a hell of an insurance claim," he added.

Lieutenant Cope was a Pearl Harbor attack survivor and former submarine officer now serving as a naval aviator, but he was not piloting an airplane. *K-6* was instead one of five airships, or blimps, assigned to Airship Patrol Squadron Twelve (ZP-12) at Naval Air Station Lakehurst in New Jersey. *K-6* had taken off from Coast Guard Air Station Elizabeth City, North Carolina at 06:35 and was now proceeding north along Virginia's shoreline. LT Cope's orders were to rendezvous with a convoy departing the Chesapeake Bay and "give the most practical coverage possible" during its transit north.

The morning sun cast sharp rays of light through the gondola's large plexiglass windows as *K-6* approached the Chesapeake Bay. At 08:10, *K-6*'s radio operator made contact with the convoy assembling below. A caravan of one freighter and nine tankers soon began its trek north. *K-6* was off Atlantic City a few hours later when *K-4*, another ZP-12 blimp, appeared on an opposite course. The two crews waved as the airships passed.

"Hey," LT Cope seized his radioman's attention upon sighting a tanker lagging behind the other ships. "Hail slowpoke down there and ask why he's draggin' ass." Two enormous engines located just outside the gondola's windows made an airship "damn noisy," according to one veteran, so Cope passed his order over the internal communication system. Using Morse code and politer phrasing, *K-6*'s radio operator transmitted Cope's inquiry over the convoy's designated frequency:

"HPFT, WHY ARE YOU OUT SO FAR?"

HPFT was the call sign for the *Persephone*, a Standard Oil of New Jersey ("Esso") tanker, and the ship's response was prompt: "DRAFT 30 FEET. FOLLOWING INSTRUCTIONS FROM ARUBA." The radioman relayed the reply, and Cope shrugged in response. "Alright, I guess."[1]

***

14 May 1942
5 miles outside Rastenburg, East Prussia
15:03

"From the point of view of operational cost, our U-boat operations in the American area are justifiable," Admiral Karl Dönitz continued. He was standing, his slim frame facing a small seated audience. "Sinkings from 15 January through 10 May amounted to 303 ships, or a total of …" Dönitz's briefing continued while six pairs of eyes watched him from around an oak conference table. Two pairs of eyes belonged to army generals, three more to naval officers. The sixth belonged to Adolf Hitler.

The location was Hitler's *Wolfsschanze*—Wolf's Lair—headquarters, located deep in a tract of dense forest that left it perpetually enveloped in gloom. The afternoon sun cast a modicum of brightness into the meeting room, though all its windows faced north to avoid the direct sunlight that Hitler detested. The entire facility was still being fortified and expanded, and the room's wood paneling and rattan chairs hardly resembled the windowless bunkers that would constitute the Wolf's Lair's primary working areas later in the war. Dönitz pitied the Heer and Luftwaffe officers who comprised most of the staff here. His army and air force peers despised the isolated and melancholy site, and the admiral himself looked forward to returning to his own headquarters.

This afternoon's briefing marked one of Dönitz's first direct interactions with Hitler, and the U-boat chief punctuated his presentation with measured pauses as the dictator took stock of his stoic and calculating poise. Dönitz's eyes were "rather close together and extremely alert," historian John Toland would write after meeting him. "His mouth was smallish and he had unusually large ears that seemed to be constantly collecting information."

Dönitz was also assessing Hitler. Despite claiming after the war that he had minimized his contact with the Führer to "disengage myself from his power of suggestion," his actions over the next three years would tell a different story. The facts instead suggest that Dönitz saw something else in the dictator's malevolent gaze: the opportunity to advance his vision of an ocean in flames, and a license to indulge the darker inclinations of his own nature.

"As shown here, the monthly tallies of tonnage sunk have increased for four consecutive months ..." He was hitting every note Hitler wanted to hear. The Führer's increasing interest in the Ubootwaffe since the American campaign began four months earlier had not gone unnoticed by the Befehlshaber der Unterseeboote, whose influence by 1942 was ascendant at the expense of the politically obtuse Grand Admiral Erich Raeder. The mystique Dönitz cultivated around the Gray Wolves also likely struck a personal chord with Hitler, who had his own penchant for lupine imagery.

Admiral Dönitz segued into a cursory and dismissive overview of US antisubmarine operations. He voiced his prediction that the Americans would soon organize a convoy system along the East Coast, but expressed confidence this would not staunch the volume of tonnage being sent to the bottom. "As long as their escorts are inexperienced," he assured his audience, "we will be able to attack the convoys in the usual manner, even in shallow waters."

He went on. "The total tonnage the enemy can build will be about 8.2 million tons in 1942, and about 10.4 million in 1943," Dönitz stated. "That would mean that we have to sink approximately 700,000 tons per month to offset new construction." Only incremental sinkings beyond this figure could erode the Allies' existing transport capacity, he specified, adding the disclaimer that these figures took Allied propaganda at face value. "Our experts doubt that this goal can be reached, and they estimate that the enemy can build only about 5 million tons in 1942."

Hitler listened intently as Dönitz's nasal voice marched through statistics of tonnage sunk and tonnage yet to be sunk. The dictator had once bemoaned that "my generals know nothing of the economic aspects of war" and, though a strategic dilettante, his appreciation of this domain (if not his understanding) was altogether keener than theirs. Accordingly, he valued Admiral Dönitz's fixation on starving the engines of Allied industry.

The Führer generally did not get on well with the Heer's generals, and his grievances went beyond operational matters. They were too aristocratic for his taste, too insufficiently awed by his vision. And yet, despite this U-boat admiral being cut from the same substrate as the army generals, he perceived much about Dönitz's character that his stodgy counterparts lacked. Hitler saw ambition and ruthlessness—and loyalty, in all the ways he demanded it. He saw great potential in him.

"All in all," Dönitz continued, "the tanker losses will have an ill effect on American industry in the eastern states, and thus on shipbuilding ..."[2]

***

13 May 1942
16 miles north-northeast of Asbury Park, New Jersey
10:04

Less than twenty-four hours before Dönitz briefed Hitler at the Wolf's Lair, an object emerged from the sea off northern New Jersey. Gray and resembling a metal pipe protruding an arm's length above the water, the object rotated slowly around its vertical axis. It paused, then began to rotate in the opposite direction. Thirty feet below the surface, Kapitänleutnant Gerd Kelbling was at the periscope station in the *U-593*'s conning tower compartment. He was seated on a bicycle-type seat attached to a thick metal column, which his knees straddled. The helmsman, a few feet forward of the kommandant, was presently the tiny space's only other occupant.

Kelbling pressed the periscope's right foot pedal, and hydraulics whirred as the column rotated smoothly counterclockwise, panning his view of the world above. He lifted his foot to stop rotating and, with his left hand, tilted a lever that extended the periscope slightly higher. The commander then depressed the opposite pedal with his left foot, and his view of the Jersey Shore panned to the right. Kelbling traversed his line of sight north along the coast, then south, and north again. He intermittently engaged a switch that toggled between the periscope's two magnification settings.

He saw, for the fourth consecutive day, nothing.

The Type VIIC boat *U-593* had reached the United States coast three days earlier, on 10 May, after a 20-day journey from Saint-Nazaire. Another U-boat had reported merchant traffic off central New Jersey, yet Kelbling found only empty sea. He had next proceeded northeast toward New York by following the Hudson Shelf Valley. Gouged from Earth's crust by glacial movement during the last Ice Age, the shelf valley is the offshore continuation of New York's Hudson River. It runs southwest from Ambrose Channel to the continental shelf's edge, where it merges with Hudson Canyon.

Frequent air patrols limited the *U-593*'s surfaced travel to nighttime only, and the boat crash-dived to avoid

U-203 commander at the attack periscope in the conning tower compartment. (Deutsches U-Boot-Museum)

a plane on the morning of 11 May. Propeller noises that afternoon enticed Kelbling to periscope depth, where he spotted only a destroyer with a *Luftschiff*, or blimp, cruising overhead. He put the *U-593* back on the bottom.

Kelbling ran north along the 20-meter line on the evening of 11/12 May, keeping the relative safety of the Hudson Shelf Valley's deep water beneath him. He spent another day on the seafloor before venturing north toward Long Island, then west toward Ambrose Channel, then south again toward New Jersey. The search pattern revealed nothing. The situation was, as a U-boat sailor once remarked, "about as productive as milking mice." Impatient and annoyed, Kelbling ordered the *U-593* back to the bottom to pass another sunny day on the seafloor.

Born in Silesia, a region of eastern Germany that would become Polish territory after the war, this was 26-year-old Gerd Kelbling's second patrol as a commander and his first to the United States. He had commanded the minesweeper *M 89* until it was sunk by a British mine in 1940, then took over the *M 6*. Kelbling subsequently transferred to the Ubootwaffe in January 1941 and became the *U-593*'s first commander on the same day that a mine sank the *M 6*. Though known as a strict disciplinarian, Kelbling was well-liked by his crew.

On this morning, 13 May, the *U-593* was lying 184 feet below the surface 16 miles off Asbury Park when the funkmaat monitoring the hydrophone heard propeller noises. Rising to periscope depth, the *U-593* motored slowly at a depth of 17 feet as Kelbling anxiously scanned the sea. He found it empty once again, and the U-boat returned to the bottom at 10:10 to wait out daylight.

The *U-593* later surfaced under cover of darkness and dodged fishing boats while heading south toward Barnegat Light. Kelbling submerged in the early morning hours to listen for screws. Hearing nothing, he turned southwest at 05:55, hoping to make as much progress toward the mouth of the Delaware Bay as the encroaching dawn would permit.[3]

***

25 May 1942
Naval Air Station Lakehurst, New Jersey
04:23

Twenty-eight miles away, and ten minutes after Gerd Kelbling put the *U-593* on the seafloor, the airship *K-4* took off from Naval Air Station Lakehurst in Ocean County, New Jersey. Commanded by Lieutenant Charles Becker, *K-4* flew southeast over Manchester and Berkeley Townships, then over the brackish waters of Barnegat Bay, which spans 42 miles of the state's central coast. Becker then passed Long Beach Island before turning south to follow the shoreline toward Cape May, unknowingly cruising just a few miles west of the *U-593*.

Like Al Cope, who had flown *K-6* up from Elizabeth City the previous day, LT Becker was also assigned to ZP-12 at NAS Lakehurst. This was the birthplace of the

Navy's "lighter-than-air" program in 1921 and, as the site of the 1937 *Hindenburg* disaster, Lakehurst was also where the age of commercial airship travel had abruptly ended. The Navy would eventually establish fifteen airship squadrons, but ZP-12 was the only one upon its activation in January 1942. Its five airships had averaged 225 hours of monthly flight time since then, and their duties had recently begun transitioning from patrol to convoy escort.[4]

Manufactured by Goodyear, the K-type airship (or "King ship") was the Navy's lighter-than-air workhorse and history's most-produced airship. Its helium-filled rubberized fabric envelope measured 249 feet long by 63 feet wide, suspended beneath which was a 42-by-9-foot gondola manned by ten Navy crewmen. On either side of the gondola were gasoline-powered, 550-horsepower engines which turned a pair of three-bladed propellers.

"The best answer to U-boats on the coast is the blimp," *TIME* magazine declared in June 1942. Indeed, airships were superb antisubmarine platforms due to several capabilities which airplanes lacked. The K-type could fly continuously for up to forty-eight hours, hover as low as wavetop height, and operate in weather that grounded conventional aircraft. Slow enough to keep pace with convoys, blimps could also make 78 mph when needed. At least one airship pilot amused himself by taking an airplane pilot aloft and then cutting the engines: this would induce a fatal stall in a plane, but a blimp just kept rising—along with its terrified passenger.

A blimp's high endurance, low speed, and ability to loiter forced any nearby U-boat to submerge for an extended period. After the war, Admiral Dönitz himself would admit to a US Navy airship veteran that they were "very disturbing to U-boat activity." Though poorly suited for attacking U-boats, airships did possess offensive weaponry. The K-type was armed with four Mark 17 depth charges (two in an internal bomb bay and two more on external racks), a .50 caliber machine gun mounted in a turret above the cockpit, and a .30 caliber gun that fired from an aft window.

Airships could also absorb an impressive amount of damage. Alfred Cope would soon command a squadron which included *K-74*, a blimp that engaged the *U-134* in a fierce nighttime gun battle off Florida in July 1943. *K-74*'s machine guns and depth charges damaged the U-boat before German gunfire finally brought the airship down. The entire air crew survived the battle and ensuing crash, though one was killed by a shark while awaiting rescue. *K-74* is the only US airship ever lost to enemy action.

Becker's orders on 14 May were to rendezvous with a convoy assembling at the Delaware Capes and escort it north to New York. Some of its ships had been part of the prior day's convoy which Lieutenant Cope's *K-6* escorted from the Chesapeake Bay. At 06:55, *K-4* arrived just in time to see the first ship of the convoy appear south of the Five Fathom Bank lighted buoy. Other escorts appeared in the form of three Coast Guard cutters, a few smaller patrol craft, and several Army bombers.

The convoy emerged slowly, like an immense yet benign python, as *K-4* maintained its holding pattern over the Delaware Bay channel.

The ten men suspended in the sky enjoyed a stellar view. A large wraparound forward window enabled the cockpit's occupants to see 180 degrees of clear sky while the others gazed down from windows paneling both sides of the gondola. A blimp in strong winds pitched and rolled like a ship, but this morning's agreeable weather meant the crew could make coffee while they waited for the convoy to depart. *K-4* did not have to wait long, and the convoy was northbound from the Capes by 07:00.

"What's up?" Becker asked upon noticing his copilot leaning toward the instrument panel with a frown. "We're down five gallons on the port side ..." Becker looked at the engine oil gauge. "Well I'll be damned, huh," he remarked before speaking over the internal voice system. "Call base and let 'em know we got a leak, yeah?" Lakehurst's reply inquired about the severity of the leak and whether *K-4* needed to abort, and Becker responded that he would attempt a slower cruising speed and report back. He throttled the engines down to 1,400 rpm. "Let's keep an eye on that gauge."[5]

***

Lacking the quantity of escorts that Admiral King decreed were necessary for convoy defense, Eastern Sea Frontier instead enacted an interim solution in April 1942. The "Bucket Brigade" used available naval and air assets to shuttle groups of vessels from one anchorage to another while hugging the shoreline and sailing only during daylight. They sheltered overnight in the Chesapeake Bay, Delaware Bay, and protected shallow water anchorages established by the Navy where sufficient natural harbors were lacking.

Neither the merchant mariners nor the American public were privy to the statistics, but the Bucket Brigade had yielded remarkable results. ESF had seen only two merchant ships torpedoed during the first half of May (although the sinkings of one American and one British patrol vessel killed 106 servicemen). Moreover, attacks had declined despite more enemy presence than ever: the number of U-boats within 400 nautical miles of American shores reached a wartime peak of seventeen on 20 May 1942.

ESF continued amassing convoy escort forces during April and the first half of May. On 14 May—the same day Dönitz briefed Hitler at the Wolf's Lair—the first coastal convoy set sail when twenty-five merchantmen left Hampton Roads, Virginia for Key West, Florida. Shepherding them were seven escort vessels: two destroyers and two subchasers from the US Navy, one cutter from the US Coast Guard, and two antisubmarine trawlers from the Royal Navy. Shore-based blimps and planes augmented the surface escorts. The long-awaited implementation of convoying did not represent a seismic shift in coastal operations, however, because the Bucket Brigade had by this time already matured into a de facto convoy system.

Convoys emptied the shipping lanes just as they had in 1917, BdU headquarters noting on 17 May that "Boats which are lying immediately along the coast and off the main ports report no traffic." Dönitz was chagrined, albeit unsurprised, when the first coastal convoy sightings trickled in. U-boats sighted few ships at all along the East Coast during May 1942 until Gerd Kelbling's *U-593* reported "very heavy spasmodic traffic on the coast of New Jersey" on 27 May.

***

As *K-4* floated above the convoy, Captain Helge Quistgaard stepped out onto the bridge wing of the tanker *Persephone*. Clad in a khaki utility shirt, he squinted and shielded his eyes to behold nearly two dozen ships stretching toward the horizon. Quistgaard would have been braving this route at night and alone only weeks earlier, but now the *Persephone* was steaming at the tail end of twenty ships guarded by blimps and bombers overhead and naval vessels on their flanks.

The route between the Delaware Bay and New York, which ran the entirety of the Jersey Shore, was the second leg added to the nascent East Coast convoy system. The first convoy sailed this route on 15 May, the day after the inaugural Chesapeake Bay–Key West convoy. The Jersey Shore convoys were guarded by a pair of 83-foot Coast Guard cutters because neither Third nor Fourth Naval Districts possessed any destroyers. Air cover was therefore particularly important, and the convoy did not sail when conditions were not conducive to flight operations. The Jersey Shore route was also watched by Civil Air Patrol volunteers flying from Coastal Patrol Base One in Atlantic City, New Jersey and Coastal Patrol Base Two in Rehoboth Beach, Delaware.

The *Persephone* had enjoyed favorable weather and a northeasterly trade wind since sailing from Aruba ten days earlier with a cargo of 80,000 barrels of fuel oil. She anchored in the Chesapeake Bay overnight on 23/24 May before steaming north with the morning convoy under the watchful eye of Lieutenant Alfred Cope's *K-6*. After anchoring overnight in the Delaware Bay, she was now en route to New York. One of the convoy's slower ships, the *Persephone* steamed near its tail end. *K-6* had admonished Quistgaard the previous day for lagging behind the convoy's main body, but he preferred scolds above to enemy submarines below.[6]

Measuring 8,426 gross registered tons and 469 feet in length, the twin-screw *Persephone* was launched in 1925 in Kiel, Germany by the same Friedrich Krupp Germaniawerft shipyard that now produced U-boats. Although built for the German-American Petroleum Company, Standard Oil of New Jersey leveraged its majority shareholder status in 1935 to transfer these tankers to its own shipping subsidiary, Panama Transport Company. Jersey Standard replaced their German crewmen with other nationalities in 1939. Most of *Persephone*'s thirty-seven crewmen were now Danish, the ship herself sailing under a Panamanian flag.

Helge Quistgaard was born and raised in Copenhagen, Denmark and studied in Britain before immigrating to the United States in 1939 and marrying an

American woman. Quistgaard had spent more than half his life at sea but, at age 40, he was still relatively young for a merchant captain, many of whom worked into their late 60s or beyond. Recent occupational hazards had nonetheless catalyzed a shift in his perspective. Though Quistgaard lacked any concrete plans for a career change, the idea had crossed his mind with increasing frequency as of late. As he well knew, any mariner who was not fearful these days was either foolhardy or lying.[7]

The death toll for merchant crewmen in Eastern Sea Frontier waters stood at exactly 1,450 by 1 May, and total Western Hemisphere fatalities numbered approximately twice this figure. "Burn to death, drown, be blown to bits when the torpedo hits the engine room, starve to death in a lifeboat," one mariner told a reporter. "Any way you look at it, you're a gone sucker."

Ever-present peril grated on men's nerves. "No fooling though, it's a queasy feeling to be shadowed by those bastards," one mariner remarked. Hugh Stephens, who joined the Merchant Marine in 1943 and saw heavy combat in Mediterranean and Arctic waters, expressed a similar sentiment seventy-eight years later: "You're such a doggone target. You were standing there like a pigeon in the feeding lanes." A Canadian mariner captured the fatalism that took root. "You knew you were goin' to get it, you could sense it," he remarked. "[Ships] were afire, there were a lot of bodies around … we said, 'Well, it's goin' to be our turn.'" His ship was torpedoed days later.

Men now went to sea "schooner-rigged," that is, taking only the essentials and leaving their valuables for safekeeping at a union hall or the Seaman's Church Institute. Some had their identifying information tattooed on their legs. "You sleep with your clothes on," one stated. "Well, I don't exactly mean sleep. You lie in bed with your clothes on." Their conduct ashore reflected their anxiety, one first mate reporting that "they all got drunk in port and were hard to handle." By May 1942, these combined factors had brought the US Merchant Marine to a crisis point. As the US Navy noted with growing concern, mariners "were not only hard to handle, they were increasingly hard to find."

Morale in the Allied merchant fleets was eroding as the death toll climbed. One captain reported that it had become "impossible to keep a good crew on board." Of particular concern were engineering crewmen, whose numbers grew thin as many found less hazardous employment ashore. Although ostensibly a labor issue rather than a military one, the fact that men were remaining ashore because they preferred not to die led the Petroleum Industry War Council to conclude that the solution lay in the armed forces' domain. Unless the Navy could put the U-boats in check, one merchant captain asserted, "shipping would cease and he himself would wind up in a morgue."

Adolphus Andrews, who retained command of Eastern Sea Frontier following his promotion to vice admiral (three stars) on 1 May, appreciated the strain that war imposed on these civilians. "The bravery, patience, and skill of the merchant seamen have been put to the test within the dangerous waters of the Frontier," his headquarters acknowledged in March. "The courage required to take vessels through waters where shipmates have perished, and the masts of sunken ships stand as warning tombstones, is apparent."

Yet mariners were not the only casualties. The US Navy had suffered 311 men killed in action along the East Coast as of 1 May 1942. Most were lost either when Ernst-August Rehwinkel ambushed USS *Jacob Jones* or when Reinhard Hardegen turned the tables on USS *Atik*. Armed Guards comprised the remaining thirty-two US military fatalities, and 205 servicemen from four other Allied nations had also been killed. Uniformed casualties expired no better or worse than their civilian counterparts. "Some men died well ... Some men died badly," wrote Nicholas Monsarrat. "Other men just died."

Capt Quistgaard was not yet frightened off. Still, the notion of a career on dry land was something to ruminate on. Maybe he could even start his own business. This was America, after all.[8]

***

The *U-593* spent the night of 13/14 May on a southeasterly course while avoiding New Jersey fishermen. It was warm enough that Kapitänleutnant Kelbling wore only the greenish *Päckchen* denim jacket with matching trousers but, to his chagrin, that same warmth left the sea awash with bioluminescent plankton. The *U-593*'s screws painted a glowing swath of ghostly blue light in their wake as tiny dinoflagellates flitted beneath the surface like sparks in the night air. Diving to listen at 04:30, the Germans heard nothing and surfaced again.

Lights may have glowed beneath the sea, but the Jersey Shore had become darker when the East Coast dim-out enacted in March was expanded 15 miles inland in April. "The gloom of the beachfront is fascinating and romantic, if a bit spooky," a *New York Times* editorial remarked. Describing the newly lightless shore as a place where "friends are recognized in the dark by their voices," the article reminded frustrated locals that activities like golf, hiking, and tennis were "still beyond the interference of the Axis." So, too, was swimming. "There has been no case of a bather cracking his skull by diving on a submerged U-boat."

Gerd Kelbling's ineffectual hunt went on as the nearing dawn of 14 May warned of the imminent termination of his operational freedom. Civil twilight, when the sun has risen far enough that artificial illumination is no longer needed, was in full effect by 05:51. Four minutes later, the *U-593* surfaced 70 miles off Barnegat Light. Kelbling was reticent to concede yet another fruitless evening, but a lookout finally sighted masts in the distance. "*Achtung!*"

The *U-593* maneuvered ahead of the target before submerging. Creeping to within 600 yards, Kelbling loosed a pair of eels that impacted almost simultaneously against the bow and amidships. He resisted the urge to shout exuberantly as the explosions threw two columns of water skyward over the ship, but only once they receded did his error become apparent. "*Gottverdammt!*"

He now discerned a red square with a white cross painted on the hull—it was the *Stavros*, registered in neutral Switzerland. The sun had prevented Kelbling from spotting her markings earlier, to include "SWITZERLAND" emblazoned on the upper edge of the hull where the white lettering had previously appeared to be part of the superstructure. There was no value in waiting to see if the ship sank, so Kelbling retreated on a northeasterly course. In fact, there had been no fatalities aboard the *Stavros*, which reached New York City later that day with the assistance of two tugboats.[9]

***

25 May 1942
5 miles southeast of Wildwood, New Jersey
09:17

Farther ahead of the *Persephone*, the Navy airship *K-4* cruised above the convoy. The loose train of merchantmen hardly resembled the box formation of the transatlantic routes, but clear weather enabled *K-4* crew to see more than 5 miles in any direction. *K-4* plodded between the front and rear of the convoy at a speed just under 30 mph and an altitude of 250 feet.

Like a submarine's hydroplanes and rudders, an airship featured separate controls for vertical and horizontal movement. Operating both was fatiguing since it required all four limbs, particularly at lower speeds when the rudders and elevators lost much of their bite. The pilot therefore typically handled elevation while the copilot steered with the rudder. The airship's rigger (responsible for maintenance and repairs) manned the .50 caliber turret located between and above the pilots. The cockpit's fourth and final occupant was the bombardier, who sat between and below the pilots at a curved plexiglass window.

Becker radioed NAS Lakehurst again at 09:20 to report no further oil loss at the slower cruising speed. Lakehurst authorized *K-4* to stay with the convoy, but advised Becker that Lieutenant Frank Trotter's *K-3* would relieve them after investigating a U-boat sighting off the Delmarva Peninsula. LT Becker wondered if the Germans had figured out that no convoys yet covered the 137-mile stretch between the Chesapeake and Delaware Bays. Ships instead dashed along Delmarva individually and during daylight while air patrols flew overhead.

At 14:45, Becker's radio operator heard Lakehurst order LT Trotter's *K-3* to relieve Becker's *K-4* as soon as possible due to the oil leak. Charles Becker sighed and shook his head. "I shouldn't even have called it in." *K-3* was already airborne, however, and *K-4* needed to return north anyway, so it mattered little either way.[10]

***

14 May 1942
106 miles east of Beach Haven, New Jersey
16:41

The *U-593* cruised northeast toward open ocean after attacking the Swiss ship. Kelbling transmitted a mea culpa to BdU: "NAVAL SQUARE CA 5344, 2 HITS ON ZIGZAGGING SWISS. COURSE 310°. NEUTRALITY MARKINGS NOT RECOGNIZED AT 500 METERS." Embarrassing though it was, other commanders had committed worse sins.

The weather was fair, but a hazy sky left Kelbling uneasy since he knew that the *Stavros* attack had likely drawn aircraft to the area. He put the *U-593* into the basement at noon to wait for the haze to burn off. The boat surfaced at around 16:00 under a sky no less hazy than before, but Kelbling elected to remain surfaced as he cut a northeasterly course.

The U-boats had found little to fear in American skies during the first months of the Second Happy Time; Eastern Sea Frontier had possessed only fifty-three planes with attack capabilities as of 31 January. The US Army Air Forces had possessed twice that figure in bombers, though maintenance issues kept more than half of these grounded. USAAF aircraft also fell under an Army chain of command frequently out of sync with the Navy and, in any event, the services' combined air strength was still insufficient to effectively patrol such a large expanse of ocean.

By the time the *U-593* arrived in May, however, ESF's aerial fleet numbered 167 naval planes in addition to ZP-12's five airships at NAS Lakehurst. Overall flight hours had quadrupled since January. The naval aviators flew in conjunction with an enlarged US Army Air Forces fleet which included A-29 Hudson light bombers and B-25 Mitchell medium bombers. April 1942 also saw the first deployment of aircraft-mounted radar that allowed air patrols to detect surfaced U-boats at night.

Unity of command was achieved in late March when USAAF coastal air units were placed under Navy operational control. So was the Civil Air Patrol; the Navy finally accepted the civilian pilots' assistance on 6 March. The Jersey Shore was now covered by CAP aircraft flying from Atlantic City and Rehoboth Beach, some of which would soon be armed with depth charges and (more commonly) 100-pound demolition bombs deployed via jury-rigged ordnance racks.

Arrogance inhibited Admiral Dönitz's appreciation of how quickly the operational environment was changing, and he persisted in deriding American tactical acumen. He assured Hitler at the Wolf's Lair on 14 May that "the American fliers see nothing," but Dönitz's smug disdain was badly misplaced. Off the New Jersey coast some 4,300 miles away, on the very same day that Dönitz spoke those words, Captain Maurice Fitzgerald of the US Army Air Forces most definitely saw something.[11]

That afternoon found Captain Fitzgerald piloting a B-25A Mitchell medium bomber 200 feet over the water 116 miles east of Atlantic City. The sky was largely clear, although haze limited visibility. It was 16:41 when CPT Fitzgerald spotted a narrow, white blemish across the water. "Hey, you see that? Twelve o'clock, about a mile and a half." His copilot's reply was tinged with excitement: "Yes I do …" Twenty-two seconds later, with the object half a mile away, the pilots discerned a telltale V-shaped wake trailing behind a low-lying vessel making about 9 knots.

"Well hello, there."

Adrenaline coursed through Fitzgerald's limbs as he accelerated to 200 mph. Ten seconds later, he saw water spray up around the sub. "He's going under!" shouted his copilot. Water churned as the U-boat nosed down and the sea swashed across its foredeck. As Fitzgerald hurtled over the waves, he discerned tiny figures atop the tower growing both larger and fewer as the Germans poured down the hatch.

"*ALAAAAAARRMM!!*"

The bomber was ninety seconds out when the men on the *U-593*'s bridge watch spotted it, and now they tumbled down into the control room as the bellicose roar of American radial engines intensified. An abrasive metallic ringing sounded from the alarm bell and the helmsman cranked the engine order telegraph pointer to "DIVE," prompting the engineering crew to disengage the diesels and activate the E-motors. Vents banged open and the bow began cutting under. Kelbling, the last man down, wheeled tight the hatch's locking mechanism behind him. "*Schnell auf tiefe gehen!*" he screamed. *Go deep quickly!*

In the B-25's nose, the bombardier cranked a lever that opened the bomb bay doors, then flipped the depth charge arming switch. CPT Fitzgerald could see the U-boat turning to starboard, its forward deck now submerged. The B-25 was at a right angle to the sub's long axis, but he had no time to swing around to attack from the stern or bow. Fitzgerald suddenly had an epiphany: the submarine blowing its tanks had broken the surface tension, meaning he could attack from low altitude without the depth charges skipping across the surface like pebbles. He pushed the yoke down further.

The brückenmaat stumbled to his station at the bow hydroplane controls while another lookout rushed to the aft plane controls beside him. Men shouting "*Warschau!*" rushed past them toward the bow to serve as human ballast, each grabbing the forward hatchway's upper lip and swinging his body through. The planesmen turned the manual control wheels while other sailors grasped levers and hung their entire body weight from them. Air escaped the tanks with a *whoosh* as water rushed in from below, and the aft-most tank was vented last for a steeper descent. "*SCHNELLER!!*" Kelbling thundered. *FASTER!!*

The seconds felt to Kelbling like an eternity, but they ticked by entirely too quickly for Maurice Fitzgerald. He pressed his throat microphone closer. "Two depth charges, on target, deploy at will!" His eyes boring a hole in his fleeing quarry as its conning tower disappeared, CPT Fitzgerald pulled back hard on the yoke, leveling off just 25 feet over the water. Only the U-boat's stern bustle, or sculpted sheet steel forming its pointed tail, remained visible. The instant the target was lined up in the bombsight, the B-25's bombardier stabbed a switch that released a pair of round-nosed Mark 17 depth charges.

The *U-593* had now disappeared beneath the roiling sea. The first Mark 17 splashed a few yards to starboard of where the tower had been seconds ago, the second landing 20 feet farther. Kelbling's crew heard the splashes overhead. "*Wabos!*" The 325-pound weapons traveled another 50 feet laterally as they sank, then detonated nearly in unison with a hollow boom. Men were tossed against bulkheads as the blast shoved the U-boat over onto its port side. Lights flickered and steel ribs moaned as the rumbling explosions melded into the sizzling noise of water rushing back into the hole ripped in the ocean.

The sea spouted two fountains as Fitzgerald banked his B-25 left for another attack run. He now approached at 20 degrees relative to the sub's initial bearing, lining up the bomber's nose with his unseen enemy's bow. He had seen the U-boat turning to starboard as it dived, so even overshooting again would still put the depth charge over the bastard's stern. The bombardier released a third and final depth charge in almost the same spot as the first.

Fitzgerald threw his plane into a climbing turn as his copilot scoured the water below. "Oil, we got oil!" The pilot looked down to see a dark stain spreading across the water. "Hot damn!" Fitzgerald shouted, triumphantly slapping a gloved hand against the yoke. "Debris too, you see that??" the copilot asked. Three orange or reddish-brown rectangular objects were bobbing below.

"Yeah. Looks like wood."

A formal analysis of Captain Fitzgerald's attack would conclude that the third depth charge "probably detonated within lethal range." In fact, this explosion inflicted less damage than the first two, which only blew off some of the deck's wooden planking. Under the surface, the TNT's thunder dissipated and left only labored breathing and the indifferent hum of the *U-593*'s E-motors. "Cycle and close all vents," the chief engineer ordered as the commander exhaled deeply. Kelbling then spoke: "Depth forty meters. Both ahead slow." Fearing that his luck was exhausted for now, he elected to remain submerged until well after sunset.[12]

***

The *U-593* meandered fruitlessly off the Jersey Shore over the next four days, ranging between 6 and 125 miles offshore. The boat was on the seafloor off Sandy Hook on the afternoon of 18 May when the *swish-swish-swish* of approaching screws was heard. The noise grew louder until its source stopped almost directly overhead, then the Germans heard the clanking rattle of a chain as an anchor hit the seafloor a few yards aft of the U-boat's stern. By sheer coincidence, a new lighted buoy had been deployed almost directly above them. Kapitänleutnant Kelbling exploited the noise to camouflage the *U-593*'s hasty retreat.

That night, Kelbling fired a pair of eels at a passenger ship 7 miles east-northeast of Monmouth Beach, New Jersey. Both missed their target. The *U-593* surfaced two nights later to repair a jammed air intake valve, only for a destroyer to appear 900 yards away. The boat crash-dived, whereupon it was battered by six well-placed depth charges that crushed the spare torpedo canisters under the deck and damaged the compass. The destroyer passed overhead repeatedly while pinging the sea with sonar, but the *U-593* eventually surfaced and escaped at flank speed.

Kelbling's frustration intensified as his fuel supply dropped below 18,500 gallons. Still armed with eight torpedoes, he formulated a new plan on the night of 23 May. Traffic in and out of New York seemingly followed a consistent schedule, so why not choose

Gerd Kelbling. (Deutsches U-Boot-Museum)

a spot along their usual route and let his prey come to him? That would mean attacking in daylight, but it was a risk he was now willing to take. The *U-593* would proceed close inshore—"*unter die New-Jersey-Küste*," he wrote in the log—and wait.

Just prior to sunrise on 25 May, the boat came to rest near the Barnegat lighted buoy. Traffic patterns farther north along the Jersey Shore led Kelbling to conclude that ships southbound from New York likely passed here around 08:00, and those steaming north probably did so around 13:00. Swells around the buoy pushed the *U-593* along the seabed, eventually forcing an annoyed Kelbling to instead ascend to periscope depth and troll back and forth at low speed.

The kommandant's prediction proved accurate at around 09:05 when he spotted four tankers, two freighters, and a few smaller ships. All were southbound and hugging the shore just over a mile ahead. They sailed "partly alone at large intervals, partly in groups" and were under "heavy air escort"—including another damn luftschiff. Kelbling sighted no destroyers, though he presumed there were subchasers or other escorts somewhere nearby. His pulse quickened.

The struggle to find targets, which now led Kelbling to attack despite the presence of air escorts, illustrated how convoys endangered U-boats in a way that antisubmarine patrols seldom could. Dispersing warships and planes to patrol a vast area of ocean had previously enabled the Germans to seek undefended merchant ships at will,

but co-locating them with the merchantmen inverted this dynamic by compelling a U-boat to place itself at the point of maximum danger. Sir Peter Gretton, who commanded the destroyer HMS *Wolverine* in 1942, explained that convoys forced the enemy "either to fight on your own ground and on your own terms, or to remain impotent." Rather than being a purely defensive tactic, convoying was instead "the essence of offense."[13]

The *U-593* crept west, toward Barnegat Light, until it was less than 600 yards from the convoy. Below the submerged U-boat's keel was just 10 feet of water. "Flood tubes one through five," Kelbling ordered. Men in the forward and aft torpedo rooms quickly opened valves that filled the tubes with water; this came from the compensating tanks below their feet because taking on outside water would disrupt the boat's trim. This was unavoidable when launching torpedoes, however (firing a pair of G7e eels immediately subtracted 7,068 pounds from the U-boat's weight). The chief engineer offset this buoyancy increase by immediately adding seawater to the compensating tanks from outside the boat. Otherwise, the boat risked breaching the surface in view of the enemy.

"Stand by for submerged firing from one through four," the kommandant spoke from the attack periscope. He would use tube five, in the stern, as his backup shot (six was already empty). Drawing a bead on several vessels overlapping one another tantalizingly, he estimated the range to the ships, their speed, and the angle between their heading and his own line of sight. Kelbling relayed these figures verbally to the bootsmann, who cranked them into the calculator. Its servomotors started turning.

"*Lage ist laufend …*"

Although a U-boat could fire a "fan" in which a single launch discharged multiple torpedo tubes, Kelbling instead launched four individual eels at 10:15. They all missed, and his log blamed the targeting calculator. He then immediately pivoted and fired tube five at a tanker. This also missed. The failed attack went undetected, but also left all six tubes empty. Kelbling remained submerged as he retreated farther offshore to load his last three torpedoes.

In the forward torpedo room, heavy rails suspended by chains from the overhead were lowered and fastened to each torpedo. Five sweating sailors used pulleys to hoist the weapon to chest height, coated it with grease, then used handwheels to crank it forward into the tube. A pneumatic steel piston was seated against the eel's tail before shutting the breech door. This air-driven rod (rather than direct impingement by pressurized air) shoved the torpedo from the tube during submerged attacks, preventing bubbles from revealing the U-boat's position. US Navy submarines instead used a bubble-catching device.

It took an hour to load the three remaining torpedoes. Finally, at around 13:00, an exasperated and silently desperate Kelbling began slinking back toward Barnegat for a final attempt at redemption.[14]

***

25 May 1942
6 miles northeast of Barnegat Light
15:08

As Gerd Kelbling prepared to deploy his last three torpedoes, the blimp *K-4* rounded the convoy's lead ship. LT Charles Becker looked west where the afternoon's visibility provided a clear view of the shoreline off the convoy's opposite side. Less than 3 miles away, he saw the low-lying spit of sand and scrubby vegetation—technically two barrier islands, broken by Barnegat Inlet—that frames Barnegat Bay.

K-4 was cruising south along the convoy's seaward side at 15:10 when someone shouted: "Woah, hey, smoke! We got smoke!" At almost the same instant, Becker spotted an ominous black cloud billowing from the convoy's tail end less than four miles away. It was hard to miss against the glassy sea and clear sky. Becker began issuing rapid-fire orders.

The airship's copilot adjusted their course as he reached down beside his seat and cranked the elevation wheel forward, angling the fins that tilted the airship's nose down. *K-4*'s rigger climbed the ladder between the pilots to man the gun turret while the radioman transmitted a hurried report to Lakehurst. Every available pair of eyes scanned the water for any sign of a periscope, the gunner traversing the .50 caliber barrel across its full 120-degree arc. "And here we go ..." Becker announced with gusto as he gripped the throttle. The engines' roar intensified as he pushed them to 2,200 rpm—oil leak be damned.[15]

***

Less than five minutes earlier, the *Persephone* was 2.5 miles due east of Barnegat Light. Second mate Anton Andersen was on duty along with an able seaman at the helm and an ordinary seaman on the flying bridge. A few men were sipping coffee in the messroom while the ship's third engineer led the four-man engine watch below decks. Capt Helge Quistgaard lay asleep in his quarters.

He was shaken awake at 14:58 when the first of Kelbling's two torpedoes smashed into the engine room's starboard side. Quistgaard bounded from his rack and was reaching for his lifejacket when the second blow struck the No. 8 tank. The *Persephone* shuddered as the captain stumbled against a bulkhead. Collecting his mental bearings, Quistgaard again propelled himself forward.

The *U-593* had fired two torpedoes in quick succession from just over a mile away. The moment the second eel left the tube, Kelbling retracted the periscope and sheered away sharply to the northeast. The muffled thunder of two underwater explosions sounded three minutes and twenty seconds later, and his crewmen cheered as the boat's slow underwater retreat continued. Kelbling cautiously waited a few minutes before extending the periscope.

He saw black smoke enveloping the tanker, which appeared dead in the water. A few small patrol boats were already orbiting the wreck and an airship drifted above. *Well, that didn't take long.* Considering how flat the sea was and how many American eyes were now scouring it for any sign of him, he quickly lowered the periscope again. Two more peeks above water were enough to convince him that "the sinking of the steamer is likely."[16]

Not far away was *CGC-159*, a 75-foot "six bitter" Coast Guard cutter based out of Cape May which had been escorting a different convoy when the torpedo struck the *Persephone*. The small cutter's commander immediately changed course toward the black spire billowing from the stricken tanker. At that same moment, less than 3 miles away, Ensign LeRoy Howell sprinted out of Coast Guard Station Barnegat, threw himself into the driver's seat of his car, and slammed the door. Engines revved and tires squealed as ENS Howell tore out of the parking lot.

On the *Persephone*'s bridge, second mate Anton Andersen and two other men witnessed a tongue of flame flash from the punctured hull as a black geyser of oil splattered across the main deck and midship house. Mercifully, the cargo did not ignite, but flooding in the engine room made the ship lumber to a halt as she settled by the stern against the shallow bottom. Within seconds, the *Persephone* had been reduced from a marvel of modern industry to dead weight.

Anderson did not know where Capt Quistgaard was—or whether he was alive—and did not want to delay the evacuation due to the risk of fire. The second mate gave the order to abandon ship. The wireless set was not functioning, although this mattered little considering they were surrounded by rescuers, in daylight, less than 3 miles from shore. The second mate then led a group to the starboard boat deck as the sea began sprawling across the aft deck, activating an emergency raft that automatically released itself. Three mariners who had been drinking coffee in the messroom jumped overboard and swam for the raft.

The speedy evacuation left Capt Quistgaard the last living man aboard the *Persephone*. Finding the bridge vacant, he attempted to contact the engine room. There was no response. He moved to the starboard boat deck and looked down to see the No. 1 lifeboat, waterborne, with seven men inside and Anton Anderson in command. He also saw a raft crowded with mariners about 100 yards beyond the lifeboat. That still left more than a dozen men unaccounted for.[17]

Nevertheless, circumstances could have been worse. His ship was not burning, and the shallow water meant that her stern was already resting on the bottom. Her foredeck and midship house remained above water.

Quistgaard made his way to the port-side boat deck and began to launch the No. 2 lifeboat by himself. He alternated between the two davits, paying out each fall a few feet at a time, as he winched the lifeboat haltingly toward the water. The captain then descended to the main deck, unrolled the Jacob's ladder against the hull, and climbed down to the lifeboat. He then disconnected the falls, only to realize that he could not row it by himself. Quistgaard sat slumped on the cross-thwart with a sigh.

The immobilized *Persephone* photographed from the Navy blimp *K-4*. Captain Helge Quistgaard is visible on the boat deck in a white life jacket. (US National Archives)

***

"Let's go, let's go!" Ensign LeRoy Howell thundered at the harbor a few blocks west of Coast Guard Station Barnegat. Most of Howell's men had been conducting routine maintenance when the ensign's car screeched into the parking lot. By the time Helge Quistgaard was lowering his lifeboat, the station's Coast Guardsmen had their orders. The boats at the pier bobbed and swayed as men clambered aboard with arms full of equipment. Picket boat *CG-4304* tore out of Barnegat Inlet with ENS Howell in command, followed closely by *CGR-871* and *CGR-882*.

***

Six minutes after sighting the smoke, the airship *K-4* reached the crippled *Persephone* to find the cutter *CGC-159* already at the scene. Becker circled the wreck clockwise, floating south over Andersen's No. 1 lifeboat and around the *Persephone*'s submerged aft section. A *K-4* crewman stood ready to drop an inflatable raft, but most of the survivors were either on the raft off the port side or in the No. 1 lifeboat off the starboard side. One man was in the water swimming toward the raft.

Four minutes after *K-4* reached the *Persephone*, ENS Howell's *CG-4304* arrived from Barnegat Inlet. *CGR-871* reached the scene less than sixty seconds after that, then *CGR-882* another minute later. The former peeled off to retrieve the swimming man as Howell directed *CG-4304*'s coxswain toward a raft in the water ahead.

Above them, in *K-4*'s cockpit, Lieutenant Becker transitioned his focus from saving lives to taking them. "So, I wanna say the tin fish came from about … three points forward of the starboard beam? Maybe four?" He pointed. "I reckon so," his copilot concurred. "And his course to get out of Dodge is …" Following his intuition, he extended his hand east-northeast. Becker nodded in agreement. "Very rude of a guest, to show up shooting like that," he quipped as his companion turned the wheel to aim *K-4* northeast. The copilot replied: "Let's see if we can't teach him some manners."[18]

Below *K-4*, Howell and the others in *CG-4304* brought aboard the raft's seventeen occupants. *CGR-871* had just retrieved a man from the water when a Coast Guardsman spotted someone partway up the side of the *Persephone*'s smokestack. They approached and found a naked man clinging to the ladder rungs with a pair of jeans clutched in one hand. He was taken onto the picket boat where he explained in broken English that, at the time of the attack, the jeans had been hanging on a hook with $300 in one of the pockets. Though newspapers did not print his choice of expletive, the man reportedly boasted that no "Nazi ******s" would separate him from his hard-earned wages.

Off the *Persephone*'s starboard side, *CGR-882* retrieved second mate Anton Andersen and six others from the No. 1 lifeboat. *CGC-159* approached the No. 2 boat, where a melancholy Capt Quistgaard sat alone. No sooner had the Coast Guardsmen brought Quistgaard aboard than *CGC-159* raced off—but not back toward land.[19]

The 83-foot *CG-477* was already running search patterns. Around the same time that Quistgaard was picked up, the cutter got a sonar contact about 1,000 yards north of the Barnegat lighted buoy. Its crew rolled a single depth charge off the stern, then accelerated to clear the blast before turning sharply back and deploying another. The cutter repeated this attack four more times.

The submerged *U-593* was slinking away to the northeast when the Germans heard the rumble of *CG-477*'s six depth charges. The blasts were well astern: close enough for attention, but not alarm. Kapitänleutnant Kelbling briefly considered checking his surroundings with the periscope before deciding that, for the moment, discretion was the better part of valor. Hotter pursuit might have seen him resort to "silent running," which achieved the optimum balance of silence and speed by turning the screws at 90 rpm. This moved the U-boat at roughly 2 knots (2.3 mph), with all auxiliary systems secured for minimal noise. Kelbling instead ordered the screws to turn at 233 rpm, and the *U-593* crawled away at 6 knots.

Five US Army bombers combed the area as *CG-477* deployed depth charges and *CGC-159* ran search patterns. Meanwhile, the airship *K-4* scanned the search zone's perimeter using a magnetic anomaly detector (MAD). Capable of sensing the magnetic signature of large metallic objects, MAD had been derived from oil prospecting technology and was so secret that the Germans did not know of its existence. At approximately 16:20, just as Lieutenant Frank Trotter's *K-3* arrived on scene, a Douglas B-18 Bolo bomber dropped a pair of depth charges that were both duds.[20]

With Capt Quistgaard aboard, *CGC-159* hunted the U-boat for the better part of two hours. Despite the exhilarating experience, the deaths of a still-undetermined number of his men left him sullen. He held up a hand to block the sun's glare as he scanned the surface. Payback represented the only solace at hand, and Quistgaard strained his eyes in the hope of spotting the afternoon sun glinting off a periscope lens. Neither he nor the Coast Guardsmen sighted anything, however, and *CGC-159* abandoned the search at around 17:20.

Turning shoreward snapped Quistgaard out of his brooding silence, and he looked across the water at his ship. The *Persephone* was immobilized and halfway underwater, yet there was no fire, and the water was too shallow for her to sink much further. Quistgaard made his way to the patrol craft's commander, who appeared to be half his own age. "Excuse me!" he shouted over the engine noise as he pointed at the *Persephone*. "Would you be able to return me to my ship? Just for a few minutes." The Coast Guardsman looked incredulous. "What? Why?" The Dane answered: "I'd like to get the mail."

A quick assessment of the situation put his request in a more reasonable light, and *CGC-159* soon pulled alongside the *Persephone*. Quistgaard and several Coast Guardsmen boarded and retrieved twenty-three bags of mail and the ship's papers. *CGC-159* then started for shore under a setting sun.[21]

Ten minutes after LT Trotter's *K-3* arrived, Becker's *K-4* obtained a MAD contact in the search area's northeast corner. MAD contacts later in the war were usually confirmed by dropping a sonobuoy, which featured a miniature hydrophone and radio transmitter that enabled an aircrew to hear below the ocean's surface. Developed by Radio Corporation of America in Camden, New Jersey and first tested in Barnegat Bay, the first air-deployable sonobuoy would not enter service for another few weeks.

K-4 came to a hover as LT Becker used the foot brake to hold the elevator flaps in position and the rigger depressed the .50 caliber's barrel toward the ocean. A marking device loaded with bronze powder was dropped from the gondola, then *K-4* crossed the spot four times. Whereas a sonar operator listened for the Doppler shift—rising or falling tones indicating that a contact is getting nearer or farther—MAD required assessing multiple readings against a visual reference to determine whether the contact was moving (if stationary, it was likely a shipwreck).

"We might just have him, fellas," LT Becker announced with relish. "Bombardier, staaaand by …" he instructed with a flourish. Between and below the pilots, the bombardier turned a knob to arm the depth charge as *K-4* lifted 600 feet over the yellowish smear of bronze powder on the water. At Becker's command, the bombardier pulled a lever that released the 325-pound depth charge.

The weapon cast a spray of seawater when it crashed through the surface, then a much larger and more violent fountain followed when it detonated seconds later. The ocean smoothed itself again to reveal a slight track of oil, although Becker's copilot suggested this might be from *K-4*'s own leak. Comparing Kelbling's log with ZP-12's records suggests that *K-4*'s MAD contact could have been the *U-593*, but the German log notes only *CG-477*'s depth charges, indicating nothing else within an hour of *K-4*'s attack. LT Becker's airship obtained no further contacts.[22]

A daylight attack so close to shore provided a stunning scene for coastal onlookers. The faculties at Seaside Park Grade School and Barnegat City School led their students to the beach, where they witnessed the crippled *Persephone* as smaller vessels, airships, and planes swarmed around her. The Barnegat City First Aid Squad rushed to the Coast Guard station where they were joined by Mrs Mabel Dodd, a nurse and the wife of local physician Dr William Dodd.

Three Coast Guard boats returned to the Barnegat station between 15:30 and 16:30, delivering twenty-seven survivors ashore. Two went back to the *Persephone* to search for the nine crewmen still unaccounted for, but they returned with only an empty lifeboat in tow. Captain Helge Quistgaard, the last to reach shore, rejoined his crew around 19:00.

***

After a submerged egress to the northeast, the *U-593* surfaced that night under a moon that left the sea "bright as day." Kapitänleutnant Gerd Kelbling suspected that aircraft were still hunting for him, so he submerged again until moonset. The Germans were 171 miles east-southeast of Cape May the following morning when the bridge watch spotted an aircraft carrier escorted by two destroyers and an air patrol. Armed with one remaining torpedo, Kelbling trailed the carrier, but was forced to crash dive when a plane changed course in his direction. He gave up the pursuit after a few hours.

On the morning of 30 May, the *U-593* encountered a lifeboat carrying survivors from the Dutch freighter *Polyphemus*. They had been adrift since being torpedoed by Ernst-August Rehwinkel's *U-578* four days earlier, and Kelbling's crew gifted them bread and a flask of rum. With approximately 11,220 gallons of fuel remaining, the *U-593* started its return voyage to Saint-Nazaire on 1 June.[23]

***

The events of 25 May killed nine men aboard the *Persephone*. Three of the four engineering crewmen on duty died when the first torpedo struck the engine room, four more were killed in the aft crew quarters, and Quistgaard concluded that the two remaining victims were "presumably killed by debris." Six days after the attack, a Coast Guard foot patrol along the beach found the body of a fair-haired man with

"Nordic features" and wearing jeans. The deceased was identified as 46-year-old Karl Sundberg from Sweden, the *Persephone*'s electrician.

The twenty-eight survivors were clothed and fed by the Coast Guard, and six of the most badly injured were taken to Royal Pines Hospital in Pinewald, New Jersey. Immigration officials and Fourth Naval District intelligence officers visited the men during their overnight stay at Coast Guard Station Barnegat, and the survivors departed for New York City in the morning on a bus chartered by Standard Oil of New Jersey. On 8 June, US Coast Guard headquarters received a letter from Jersey Standard praising Ensign LeRoy Howell and the other rescuers.

The partially submerged wreck of the *Persephone* sat in full view of the beach—less than 2 miles from the *Gulftrade*'s still-visible forward half—until August, when it broke in half while under tow. The aft section sank in 50 feet of water less than 3 miles northeast of the attack site and was marked with a buoy. Struck by passing ships more than once, it was eventually reduced by explosives and wire-dragged to a depth of 39 feet. The forward section was towed to New York where 21,000 barrels of oil were pumped out. The *Persephone*'s largely undamaged midship house was removed in 1943 and installed on the Esso tanker *Livingston Roe*, which had recently suffered a fire in Brazil.[24]

***

More than five months of dreadful losses did not stop thousands of merchant mariners from going to sea. "I tell you, any guy who keeps on shipping these days has got bubbles in his think-tank," one joked the day before setting sail again. Some survived one sinking, signed on with another ship, then were torpedoed again. The Boston Seaman's Club founded a "40-Fathom Club" for those who had survived a sinking, and a sign over a barroom table in Halifax, Canada read: "RESERVED: SURVIVORS ONLY."

Seeking to better understand the merchant mariners, *Harper's Magazine* reporter Helen Lawrenson ventured into a dingy bar in Manhattan where she met "Low-Life McCormick," "Screwball McCarthy," "No-Pants Jones," and other mariners. Most had been torpedoed at least once. They swilled "vast and formidable quantities of beer" while singing obscene sea ditties, antics which only further endeared them to Lawrenson. She found the mariners "intensely patriotic, casually fearless, and wise … they were the most truly sophisticated men I have ever met."

They were also earning the respect of their uniformed counterparts. "Into the seaports came exhausted, unnerved men, oil-smeared and half-naked. Many wore dirty bandages over horrible burns," one Navy veteran wrote. "Few asked for more than a drink or a cigarette. In ordinary times many of them might be drifters, troublemakers, drunks, and brawlers," yet they showed "great courage" and "a common defiance." As the Eastern Sea Frontier war diary for April 1942 summarized, "Ships went down and lives were lost, but other ships and men took their places to keep the cargoes moving up and down the coast."[25]

Crew of the tanker *Malay*, which made port under her own power after being shelled and torpedoed by the *U-123* in January 1942. (US National Archives)

***

Gerd Kelbling was not the only U-boat commander who found ceaseless frustration off the East Coast in May 1942. The *U-352*, a Type VIIC commanded by 31-year-old Hellmut Rathke, encountered little apart from "bees" (enemy aircraft) and empty stretches of unnervingly shallow water. Kapitänleutnant Rathke was an authoritarian officer and impetuous Nazi disliked by his crew, and he still had no sinkings to his credit. Desperation presumably clouded his judgment on the afternoon of 9 May when he sighted the 165-foot USCGC *Icarus* (WPC-110) 24 miles south of Cape Lookout, North Carolina.

At almost that exact moment, the Thetis-class cutter's sonar operator received a "mushy" sonar echo off the port bow. This raised little alarm until an explosion 200 yards astern churned the water a muddy brown—the *U-352* had fired a torpedo which malfunctioned, veering downward and detonating on the seabed. Rathke attempted to elude the sonar's piercing gaze by lying motionless on the bottom, but the sea was too shallow to hide, and USCGC *Icarus* quickly retaliated by bracketing the *U-352* with a pattern of five depth charges.

Ping! Ping! Ping! Sonar waves chirped loudly amid a cascade of deafening explosions that destroyed the periscope, disabled both E-motors, and killed the first watch officer in the tower compartment. Rathke screamed orders as the boat lost its trim and the bow tilted upward, dragging the stern against the white sand below. The Americans attacked again, and the next salvo of blasts knocked the battered U-boat onto its port side. The *Icarus* pivoted and deployed a third pattern of depth charges, then a fourth.

The Coast Guardsmen suddenly saw a dark shape burst through the surface 1,000 yards off their starboard bow. Fearing that the Germans intended to man their guns, the *Icarus*' commander ordered his crew to open fire. The 3-inch/.23 cannon thundered and machine guns chattered furiously as Rathke's crew spilled out of the conning tower hatch. The first 3-inch shell ricocheted off the U-boat's deck, then another passed narrowly overhead. Six direct hits followed, one of which severed a maschinenmaat's leg.

The cutter ceased firing, and the *U-352* sank five minutes after it had surfaced. "Remember your duty!" Rathke yelled as his stunned crewmen floated in the Gulf Stream's warm cerulean waters. "Say nothing! Tell them nothing!" The commander used his belt as a tourniquet for the maschinenmaat who had lost his leg, but the 20-year-old became the crew's fifteenth and final fatality.

USCGC *Icarus* arrived in Charleston, South Carolina the following morning and turned over thirty-three POWs to a waiting contingent of military policemen from the Marine Corps base at Parris Island. The first U-boat crewmen captured off the East Coast were subsequently interrogated at length. Reports described Hellmut Rathke as "conspicuously arrogant," and his insistence that Adolf Hitler was a "genius" did little to endear him to his captors. Rathke also admitted that he "did not like operating in water as shallow as that off the United States coast," remarking with exasperation: "Thirty meters of water—what could I do?"[26]

CHAPTER TWELVE

Berganger

"No movie, no newsreel, no happy end,
Death sits and waits just down the bend.
I'm saying my prayers, my gun is so hot,
Don't say I'm scared, I know that I'm not,
All of my fear is now just a rage,
I'll make some history, if only one page."
—George X. Hurley, US Navy Armed Guard, "Saga of the Murmansk Run" (1943)

2 June 1942
256 miles east of Atlantic City, New Jersey
11:32

Seven days after Gerd Kelbling hit the *Persephone*, Ernst-August Rehwinkel did not mind the summer rain pelting his face and neck on the *U-578*'s bridge. The precipitation was the closest thing to bathing he had experienced in nearly a month. He was standing amid four lookouts who wore sunglasses with circular lenses and leather side shields, although it was overcast enough that the commander left his hanging about his neck. Korvettenkapitän Rehwinkel's gaze remained fixed ahead as the *U-578*'s bow split the ruffled water and the sea scalloped over its foredeck like a tidal rock.

The *U-578*'s current pursuit had kicked off forty minutes earlier when the bridge watch spotted a faint plume of exhaust on the horizon. "Come to zero-nine-zero!" Rehwinkel shouted down the hatch. "Both ahead full!" The tanks were fully blown, seating the *U-578* high in the water to maximize speed, and the hull vibrated as both screws took a harder bite of the water at nearly 500 rpm. Thrashing screws carved a swath of foam astern that quickly dissipated as the Atlantic wiped clean the boat's tracks. "The earth encourages each man's belief that it will treasure the traces of his existence for all time," wrote Lothar-Günther Buchheim. "The sea offers no such illusion."

Rehwinkel hollered the target's heading and approximate distance to the obersteuermann in the control room. The smudge against the overcast midday sky disappeared a few minutes after being sighted, but the *U-578*'s chief helmsman was at the chart table plotting the respective courses of both predator and prey. Even losing sight of the ship would not prevent its interception. "He's making at least fifteen knots," observed Oberleutnant Claussen. "*Ja*," Rehwinkel concurred, "he's making us work for it."

This was Korvettenkapitän Rehwinkel's second patrol off the American coast. His first patrol saw him turn the Esso tanker *R.P. Resor* into a blazing inferno and annihilate the destroyer USS *Jacob Jones* off Cape May less than forty-eight hours later. He lost an asset upon returning to port, however, when Leutnant Raimund Tiesler was diagnosed with a pelvic fracture requiring an extended recuperation. Oberleutnant Emil Claussen subsequently replaced Tiesler as first watch officer.

His previous patrol's successes had come not a day too soon, as Rehwinkel was a decade older and a rank higher than most U-boat commanders. He did not know how many more patrols BdU would afford him before relegating him to shore duty. A famous German general once stated that "a staff officer has no name," yet such was the inevitable fate of even the greatest U-boat aces—those who survived their sea command, anyway.

Rehwinkel intended to increase his odds of surviving to see a desk job by keeping his distance from the American coast on this patrol. Summer's longer days meant shorter nighttime prowling hours, and the newly instituted coastal convoy system had sharply reduced inshore targets. He also understood that the US armed forces now exercised a more robust presence there than in February and March. Merchant traffic in deeper water therefore seemed more promising, and hunting farther offshore offered the possibility of attacking in daylight with relative safety, in addition to greater depth for evasion.

The *U-578* was 640 miles off the Delmarva Peninsula late on the afternoon of 26 May when the bridge watch sighted the Dutch freighter *Polyphemus*. Rehwinkel completely demolished its aft section with two G7e torpedoes, and the surviving crew quickly abandoned ship. The ship was leaning over her bow when the U-boat approached to question the crew. Among the sixty-two men in the water were fourteen from the Norwegian tanker *Norland*, which had been torpedoed by the *U-108* six days earlier.

Rehwinkel intended to dispatch the languishing *Polyphemus* with his 88mm gun, but she saved him the trouble by going down over the stern during his brief interrogation. With the ship now taking her cargo of wheat and wool—and fifteen men who had been asleep in the aft crew quarters—to the bottom, the Germans gave the survivors cigarettes and indicated the direction of New York. Rehwinkel's display of chivalry aside, his log entry ridiculed the merchant captain as "a typical fat Dutchman" (specifically describing him as *vollgefressener*, which evokes overindulgence during times of scarcity).[1]

Despite Admiral Dönitz's instructions in late 1939 to "rescue no one and take no one with you," U-boat crews still frequently assisted survivors in mid-1942. "The humane treatment of shipwrecked seamen was a matter of course," claimed *U-333* commander Peter Cremer. "They were not enemies anymore, but simply shipwrecked, and had to be helped as far as possible." This would become rare in the war's second half, however, due partly to the repercussions of an incident that transpired in September 1942.

The incident was the *U-156*'s sinking of the British ocean liner *Laconia* off West Africa. Upon realizing there were hundreds of civilians and Italian POWs aboard, the *U-156*'s commander draped a Red Cross flag on his foredeck and broadcast an unencoded message to nearby Allied forces before rendering assistance. He signaled his non-hostile intent to a passing US Army bomber, but this did not prevent the American pilot from attacking. Unable to dive quickly due to survivors on deck and lifeboats in tow, the *U-156* barely escaped.

Dönitz reacted by issuing the "Laconia Order," which decreed that "all efforts to save survivors of sunken ships … must stop," including "handing over food and water." Such assistance, he decreed, "runs counter to the elementary demands of warfare for the annihilation of enemy ships and crews." Its vague phrasing contrasted with the direct and unambiguous verbiage that typically characterized his orders, and its implications generated considerable unease. "BdU cannot give you such an order [to shoot survivors] officially," one flotilla commander told his U-boat commanders. "Everyone has to handle it according to his own conscience."

Six days after sinking the *Polyphemus*, rain beaded on steel as Rehwinkel continued closing the distance between the *U-578* and the distant merchant ship. The temperature down in the control room was a bearable 86° Fahrenheit, although the U-boat's engine room was less comfortable at 97°. The freighter crept back into view around 11:40, now close enough that both masts were discernible. Rehwinkel changed course to maneuver ahead. Their target melted from sight again just before noon, reappeared, then disappeared once more.

"Steer two-nine-zero," Rehwinkel ordered.[2]

***

2 June 1942
245 miles east of Atlantic City, New Jersey
11:58

Unaware of the *U-578* closing in from the southeast, Captain Normann Nymann watched raindrops trickle down the bridge window as a steady but mild wind slanted their tracks along the glass. The 47-year-old native of Telemark, Norway had commanded the freighter *Berganger* since October 1941. It was the third ship he had captained for the Norwegian Shipping and Trade Mission, or "Nortraship," which operated the Norwegian merchant fleet for the Allied cause.

Built in Amsterdam in 1932, the *Berganger* measured 456 feet long and 6,826 gross registered tons. Her 8,200-horsepower engine enabled a top speed of 15.5 knots, slightly faster than most merchantmen of her vintage. In the nearly full cargo holds were 48,000 bags of coffee, 1,000 bales of cellulose fiber, and 1,100 liters of sunflower seed oil. She was crewed by forty-four men (most Norwegian) and carried three passengers: a British married couple and an Argentine saloon girl.

The *Berganger* had left Buenos Aires, Argentina carrying 5,320 tons of dry cargo. She loaded 3,623 additional tons in Santos, Brazil before setting course for Boston with a scheduled arrival of 16 May. Capt Nymann guided his freighter north, keeping well clear of the perilous East Coast littoral and maintaining radio silence. The *Berganger* steered the Royal Navy's No. 30 zigzag pattern, which entailed course changes every sixth and ninth minute. The *Berganger* sailed alone because ships capable of 14 knots or faster were exempt from sailing in convoys.

By June 1942, Eastern Sea Frontier's coastal convoy system had expanded to three routes: Chesapeake–Key West, New York–Delaware Bay, and New York–Halifax. The Navy noted that "the enemy revealed himself as extremely reluctant to attack convoys," and only four ships in convoy were sunk that month. Vice Admiral Andrews reported with cautious optimism that there existed "tangible grounds for hope that the most disastrous period of submarine warfare on this coast is now over." Although the strategic outlook was indeed brighter, danger still abounded.

The *Berganger*'s voyage had seemingly passed without incident only because Nymann and his crew were unaware how narrowly disaster had missed them. They had been spotted at 19:11 the previous night by Oberleutnant Amelung von Varendorff's *U-213*. The U-boat pursued the ship after one torpedo missed it, von Varendorff confessing in his log that "I cannot bring myself to let the freighter, which is superior to me in speed, go." He finally relented 44 miles later after four more eels missed, and the *Berganger*'s journey proceeded with not a man aboard the wiser.

The watch changed over at noon. The two officers on duty on the bridge, Capt Nymann and first mate Sverre Høvik, turned over their posts to second mate Finn Jensen and third mate Anton Eik. Ordinary seaman Arnold Steffensen took over the helm while radioman Tor Wigdel manned the wireless station. Capt Nymann retired to his cabin to sleep.

Included in the noon changeover was the stern lookout position manned by 29-year-old Johan Vidnes. His eyes were weary from gazing for hours across the barren sea, and he happily turned over his silent vigil to Olaf Brevik. Vidnes' duties left him too much time to wonder about his parents, or last year's harvest, or whether his family even had enough to eat. Although a seafarer by trade, and surrounded by fellow Norwegians aboard the *Berganger*, he had never felt farther from home.[3]

Johan Vidnes' *fedreland* no longer even belonged to Norwegians. As the Wehrmacht descended on Norway in April 1940, King Haakon VII refused Nazi demands to appoint a new government under Vidkun Quisling (a collaborator so reviled that his surname would become an international byword for "traitor"). During the invasion's first hours, Quisling broadcast an order for all Norwegian merchant ships to make for German-controlled waters. The king countermanded this with an order to make for British-controlled ports instead, and every skipper opted to obey the king. Hitler demanded King Haakon's capture, but Norway's badly outmatched forces delayed the Germans long enough for the royal family and government to escape to Britain.

Norwegians are known for their agreeable and dispassionate nature, but the king's defiance had electrified his people. In occupied Norway, his personal emblem appeared scratched into the sides of German troop trains, chalked onto Gestapo vehicles, and painted on public buildings. Coins bearing the crest were discreetly worn as jewelry, and Norwegians embraced a slogan popularized by King Haakon himself: "*Alt for Norge*" (All for Norway).[4]

***

Two hours after Johan Vidnes assumed his post at the *Berganger*'s fantail, the *U-578* had nearly reached its attack position. Korvettenkapitän Rehwinkel stooped over the open hatch. "*L.I.,*" he addressed the chief engineer. "Bring us to periscope depth."

The bridge watch hurried down the ladder, the port-quarter lookout assuming the helmsman's position in the tower compartment as the others continued down to the control room. The starboard-quarter lookout and brückenmaat took their posts at the hydroplane stations, and the chief engineer stood behind them. Rehwinkel secured the hatch and sat at the attack periscope in the conning tower. To his right, the dials of the torpedo calculator lit up as Oberleutnant Claussen activated the apparatus.

Pounding diesels gave way to humming E-motors as the *U-578* slipped under the surface. Using the periscope required maintaining perfect trim at a precise depth, and the chief engineer carefully eased the boat into position at a depth of exactly 44 feet under the surface. "Forward up five, aft up five," the engineering officer instructed. "Close flood valves, close vents, slow ahead."

"Come to heading one-one-zero," Korvettenkapitän Rehwinkel ordered in the conning tower compartment. The helmsman complied as the kommandant spoke another order into the voice pipe. "Ready all forward tubes for submerged firing, stand by for fan shot from one and three." The order passed like an echo through the boat as Rehwinkel put the *Berganger* in the periscope's crosswires. "*Achtung, computer …*" The first watch officer stiffened at his cue.

Rehwinkel verbally relayed the ship's speed, the angle between the U-boat and the target, and his chosen running depth for the torpedoes. Claussen loaded the values into the rectangular box on the bulkhead before engaging the electromagnetic coupling that passed them to its computational mechanism. "*Lage ist laufend …*" The calculator buzzed faintly as its components churned through the math. "*Steht,*" Claussen reported when it produced a gyro-angle. "*Lage null-neun-zwo.*"

As the *U-578* stalked nearer, the calculator continually updated the gyro-angle in each torpedo and the dispersion angle by which they would spread across the target's length by the end of the run. Over the whirr of the periscope's hydraulics, Claussen heard the captain make an annoyed smacking sound with his lips. "Zero-four-zero," he directed. Rehwinkel had misjudged the "dog's curve," putting the *U-578* farther from the ship than he intended.

"Stand by for fan shot from one, three, and four," Rehwinkel ordered, erring toward caution by electing to fire a spread of three torpedoes rather than two. The *Berganger* soon changed course. "Correct distance one thousand, angle left zero-nine-nine." Claussen replied: "*Steht.*" Below them, the chief engineer prepared to flood the forward compensating tanks to offset the imminent release of several tons of weight from the forward tubes. At the bow tubes, a torpedoman rested his hands on two firing levers and his leg across the third in case the electrical firing mechanism in the tower compartment failed.

Rehwinkel wanted to hit the zigzagging ship before it veered off its base course again. "*Bugraum?*" his voice reverberated through the pipe. "*Folgen!*" the mechaniker-maat responded, then the commander spoke again. "*Rohr eins, drei, vier—Los!*" The *U-578* flinched three times as the eels leapt from their tubes at 2.3-second intervals.[5]

As each G7e torpedo streaked forward, water resistance turned a two-bladed impeller located atop a truncated cone on the warhead's nose. This cone was the impact pistol, and the impeller rotated a shaft running through the pistol's length. The shaft's rotation aligned the firing pins with the booster charge and seated the electric detonators in their sockets, arming the warhead after 150 yards. A head-on impact would detonate it, and four metal prongs around the pistol would accomplish the same for a glancing blow.

At 14:29, ninety-eight seconds after leaving its tube, one of the *U-578*'s three torpedoes slammed into the *Berganger*. The impact rammed the drive shaft backwards, impinging the firing pins against the detonators and closing the electric circuit. This set off the booster charge—11 ounces of pentaerythritol tetranitrate—which triggered the 617-pound hexanite main charge. This sequence unwound the warhead's energy in a fraction of a second, gouging a wound across the port-side hull where the engine room adjoined the No. 3 cargo hold. Inside the *Berganger*'s engineering spaces, the noise of pounding pistons suddenly yielded to the chilling roar of seawater pouring into the engine room. All four men working there were either killed instantly or in the seconds that followed.

Rehwinkel heard a second detonation, though he observed only one through the periscope. The third torpedo was a clear miss and the hydrophone operator heard its motor fade away into oblivion. Rehwinkel observed smoke billowing from amidships as his target heeled over to port, its bow swinging likewise as the ship appeared to enter a lazy turn.[6]

***

"*Å fytti hælvette!*"

Second mate Finn Jensen swore as the bridge rocked with the ship, but his reaction wasted no time. "*Hardt styrbord!*" he ordered helmsman Arnold Steffensen.

Reaching for the engine order telegraph, Jensen shoved both levers all the way forward: full speed ahead. The "Merchant Marine 10 Commandments," which the US War Shipping Administration would publish in 1943, reflected the longstanding imperative of taking every possible measure to save one's ship. The very first commandment exhorted mariners under attack to "Fight the ship through. Your responsibility—your best bet."

Jensen dispatched third mate Anton Eik to lead the evacuation. The second mate next moved to the red alarm button on the aft bulkhead and smashed it seven times with his fist, finishing with a longer eighth ring. An abrasive, metallic jangling filled compartments and passageways as he repeated the pattern twice more. At the same time, radioman Tor Wigdel frantically tapped out a stream of distress calls. "SSS, THIS IS LCXB," Wigdel transmitted. "39° 25' NORTH 69° 50' WEST, TORPEDOED, SINKING. ABANDONING SHIP NOW. SSS, THIS IS LCXB …"

In the crow's nest on the swaying foremast, 21-year-old Hans Vingen composed himself before descending to the deck. He felt the ship listing as he retrieved the three rafts that supplemented the four lifeboats. Vingen hauled each raft across the deck and dropped them overboard before proceeding to the boat deck. Most freighters carried all four lifeboats at the midship house, but the *Berganger*'s configuration was similar to a tanker's, with two lifeboats at the midship house and two near the stern.

Capt Nymann materialized amid the mayhem on the bridge just as someone below decks started shouting a report through the voice pipe. The voice, elevated over the chilling noise of seawater thundering inside the hull, reported that the engine room was flooding and those on duty there were likely dead. Nymann could see the ship's dire condition from the bridge, too. She was listing to port and already down noticeably by the bow. The captain cupped his hand around the pipe's conical cover and shouted, "Get out of there, now!"

The captain of the *Berganger* was not the only man whose slumber was interrupted by the attack. A bleary-eyed Johan Vidnes rushed to his assigned place of duty, the ship's list forcing him to mind his footing as he passed others appearing on deck. At the stern, Olaf Brevik was staring intently through his binoculars when he heard rapid footfalls behind him. Brevik's eyes were alight with nervous excitement when he turned and sighted Vidnes, who was winded but wearing a visage of grim determination. "*La oss gå?*" Brevik asked. *You ready?*

"Been ready for a long time, my friend," Vidnes replied.

On the bridge, Arnold Steffensen was dismissed now that his duties at the helm were no longer required. Second mate Finn Jensen and the radioman were the last two to depart the bridge. On his way out, Jensen stuffed the ship's classified documents into a lead-weighted sack and heaved it overboard.[7]

Three minutes after launching its torpedoes, the *U-578* surfaced more than 1,000 yards off the *Berganger*'s port beam. The tower hatch opened and Korvettenkapitän

Rehwinkel emerged, followed by Oberleutnant Claussen and the bridge watch. After them would follow the 88mm gun crew queuing in the control room. Only Rehwinkel and Claussen had made it topside when something suddenly shrieked through the air overhead. A white geyser erupted off the boat's starboard quarter. "*Alaaaarrmm!!*"

From the *Berganger*'s aft deck, Olaf Brevik saw the 4-inch shell throw water skyward on the far side of their target. "Too high!" Brevik shouted. "Drop fifteen meters!" Vidnes feverishly cranked the elevation wheel on the left side of the Mark IV 4-inch/.50 gun. Arnold Steffensen, who had joined the two gunners once his duties at the helm were complete, rammed another shell into the breech. He then jammed his fingers into his ears just before Vidnes fired again. "Right there! Dead-on!" Brevik yelled. "Give him another!"

The Germans spilled chaotically back down the *U-578*'s ladder while the alarm bell's grating clangor commenced. As each man's feet slammed against the control room's deck plates, other sailors' hands brusquely pulled him aside to make room for the next man. The ocean washed over the foredeck as another shell screamed toward them. Rehwinkel was about to drop into the hatch when, from only yards away, he felt a shattering crash and heard the yowl of high-tensile galvanized steel breaking. He ducked and covered his head, nearly falling through the hatch headfirst. Seconds later, Rehwinkel slammed the hatch shut behind himself.

Johan Vidnes and Olaf Brevik were not merchant mariners—not anymore, anyway. They were gunners of the Royal Norwegian Navy. Vidnes had been aboard a merchant ship off South America when Hitler conquered Norway, and subsequently enlisted in his country's navy-in-exile in Canada. He and Olaf Brevik then trained as gunners at Camp Norway in Nova Scotia. When Ernst Rehwinkel unwittingly provided Vidnes and Brevik a fleeting opportunity to hit back, they had not hesitated.[8]

The British Admiralty had unambiguously declared that "no merchant vessel should ever tamely surrender to a U-boat." Gunners were taught that "a U-boat on the surface is particularly vulnerable to gunfire," but speed was crucial. "Open fire immediately once the U-boat is sighted … it is imperative to get your blow in first." Vidnes and Brevik's counterparts in the US Navy's Armed Guard program were taught that "damage to the upper part of the pressure hull of a submarine, or to the control mechanism for diving, prevents a submarine from submerging." Damaging a U-boat with a single gun from a ship that was already sinking was a tall order, but defiance was duty.

Each thunderous report from the gun hurled a 31-pound shell at 2,177 feet per second. Though the Mark IV was a British gun in service since 1911, an ESF staff officer noted its destructive power after a similar shell killed the USS *Dickerson* commander in a March 1942 friendly fire incident. The Navy officer remarked that "it is extraordinary what a single four-inch shell can do to a destroyer if it lands in a vulnerable place"—and the *Berganger* gunners knew that every part of a U-boat was a vulnerable place.[9]

"Quick, quick, he's going under!" Rain pelted the trio at the gun as Steffensen fed another shell into the breech and Vidnes shoved it closed. The 14-foot-long barrel deafeningly belched a tongue of flame as it slung a third shell downrange. This shot appeared to be dead-on, but the U-boat had nearly disappeared. "Keep sending 'em!"

Arnold Steffensen's entire body was trembling with adrenaline. The 23-year-old civilian had never imagined himself battling a submarine. Eight decades after the war, American mariner Hugh Stephens would recount helping his ship's Armed Guards load the guns under Luftwaffe attack in the Mediterranean. "You become somebody else," Stephens explained. "You almost become an animal, because you've got to kill him before he kills you."

The trio fired three more shells at the turbid sea marking where the submarine had retreated. "Did we hit him??" Steffensen asked excitedly. "That second one's a good bet ... but I'm not sure," Brevik replied, lowering his binoculars. "But we definitely made the *tyskerjævler* flinch." An exuberant Steffensen grabbed Vidnes' shoulder, raised his other hand in a fist, and yelled *"Alt for Norge!"* triumphantly across the waves. There was no real triumph to be had, however, and the *Berganger*'s deck was now tilting even further. It was time to go.[10]

***

In the *U-578*'s control room, Rehwinkel scowled as he removed his hat and ran his fingers broodingly through unkempt hair. His anger was not directed at the enemy, however. The *U-103* had once torpedoed a British freighter in 1941, prompting its crew to abandon ship. The U-boat began shelling the "abandoned" ship, but it suddenly started shooting back. The gunners had rowed to her opposite side and re-boarded. "That was very brave of them," *U-103* petty officer Peter Marl later wrote.

The *U-578* commander's ire was instead directed inward: he had seen that goddamn gun through the periscope before he surfaced. He cast a sidelong glance at Claussen. "And *that* is how complacency kills," Rehwinkel stated wryly. "I draw the conclusion that the crew still believes their ship will float," Rehwinkel explained in his log. "Therefore I decide to shoot a coup de grâce from tube II."

"L.I., periscope depth. Slow ahead on both," Rehwinkel instructed before climbing the ladder back to the tower compartment. "Forward up twenty, aft down five." The planesmen seated in front of the chief engineer pressed the control buttons to steer the U-boat gently upward. "Twenty-five meters ..." The engineering officer eyed the depth gauge as he eased the steel shark to periscope depth. "Twenty ... seventeen ... fifteen ... Close valves and vents and prepare to trim."[11]

***

The torpedo's explosion destroyed the *Berganger*'s No. 2 lifeboat, the only one with a motor. The No. 3 boat swamped and drifted loose when the crew attempted to launch it, and two men jumped overboard to recover it. That left two lifeboats on opposite sides of the ship.

Capt Nymann divided the ship's complement in half, with his group boarding the No. 1 lifeboat on the deck house's starboard side. Johan Vidnes found himself in the other group, led by first mate Sverre Høvik, which boarded No. 4 on the stern's port side. Vidnes helped lower the boat to the waterline before descending the rope ladder to board it. He and the others then released the falls and began rowing speedily away from the foundering *Berganger*.

The No. 4 lifeboat had only cleared the hull by a few yards when Rehwinkel's coup de grâce struck at 14:48. Vidnes' lifeboat rocked as the dark shape of a torpedo rocketed 9 feet underneath it and into the *Berganger*'s port side at the No. 5 cargo hold. The explosion ripped a large fissure which began flooding the cargo hold. At the same time, the shockwave radiated through the ship, rupturing seams and deforming bulkheads as the Atlantic thundered down passageways and into compartments.

The explosion deafened Johan Vidnes as his lifeboat lifted and the ocean dropped away from its gunwales. He perceived himself rising in slow motion before realizing that he was tumbling through the air. Sea replaced sky as the world inverted. Vidnes violently hit the water, the impact contorting his body as he plunged through the surface.

His lifejacket promptly buoyed him upright. Gasping and wiping salt water from his eyes, Vidnes collected himself and looked around. The lifeboat's twenty other occupants had also been thrown headlong across the sea, injuring third mate Anton Eik's leg but leaving them all otherwise unharmed. They individually swam back to the No. 4 lifeboat, which had landed right-side-up but was damaged and partially flooded. Four climbed in to bail it out while Vidnes and the others grabbed hold of its gunwale and floated.[12]

Two minutes after the second torpedo strike, the survivors witnessed the death of the *Berganger*. The freighter went down over the bow, the chorus of screeching and grinding steel reaching a crescendo as the stern lifted until it was pointing skyward at nearly 90 degrees. Vidnes and the other crewmen stared in disbelief at the 456-foot ship standing on her head. The *Berganger* seemed to pause and shudder for a moment before the sea resumed devouring it from the bow. The ship disappeared slowly at first, then quickly, plowing nose-first into the depths as she vanished entirely.

Most U-boat crewmen did not visually witness an attack. An engineering sailor could survive the entire war without ever seeing a ship sink. What was not seen, however, was frequently heard instead. "The noise is frightful," one U-boat commander wrote. Wolfgang Hirschfeld, an *Oberfunkmaat* aboard the *U-109*, wrote of hearing the "groaning, grinding sound" for the first time. "That's the sound of a ship dying," a more experienced crewmate explained. "The noise is the water pressure bursting the bulkheads."

The crew of the *U-578* heard a dissonant chorus of groaning steel as the *Berganger* began her voyage to the seabed some 7,000 feet below. The wreck achieved a downward velocity exceeding 25 feet per second as the ambient pressure passed 2,200 pounds per square inch. Bulkheads and fuel tanks crumpled around air pockets, ejecting debris into her slipstream as the ship's death rattle receded into the abyss. The *Berganger* collided bow-first with the seabed moments later, the impact wrenching bulkheads and decks apart under a billow of silt in a place where no light had ever shown.[13]

***

Johan Vidnes was clinging to the No. 4 lifeboat five minutes later when an apprehensive clamor swept through the survivors. He turned to see the *U-578* approaching as the throaty, pulsating noise of diesel engines grew louder. Its deck extended from bow to stern and was broken by an oval-shaped tower amidships and, just forward of that, a naval cannon. Connected to the tower's aft end was a circular platform where a single antiaircraft gun was mounted. The gun was presently unmanned and its barrel locked upward at a 45-degree angle.

The tower bulwark's upper edge seemed to stand a dozen feet above the deck, over which Vidnes could see the faces of six or seven Germans. Most of them wore a military-style side cap, the type without a brim that lays flat when not worn. A man clad in a forest-green twill jacket with matching trousers was snapping photographs. Another German wearing a white tank top climbed down the ladder rungs on the tower's side and made his way aft along the deck. The disheveled figures were a far cry from what Vidnes had imagined. They exuded confidence and professionalism all the same, and their demeanor conveyed neither malice nor friendliness.

Germaniawerft diesels dropped to a hoarse rumble as the *U-578* slowed to a halt beside the No. 4 lifeboat. Among those on the bridge stood a figure clad in a khaki British Army field uniform. A red-checkered civilian shirt was visible over the top button of a waist-length tunic tucked into a pair of slightly baggy matching pants. One survivor would tell naval intelligence officers that he had a "movie-type beard." His ensemble was unadorned by rank or insignia, yet his authority was suggested by his age and the fact he was the only one wearing a white sea captain's hat.

Ernst Rehwinkel leaned forward over the bridge bulwark. "*Spricht irgendwer Deutsch?*" he shouted. Most stared wordlessly at him. A few shook their heads. "English?" Rehwinkel inquired. "Yes," a lone voice answered. It was Høvik, the senior officer present since Capt Nymann's boat was still some distance away. "I just need some informations," Rehwinkel replied matter-of-factly. "What is the ship's name?" "*Berganger*," Høvik replied. "And your flag?" "*Norge.*" The U-boat captain next asked the *Berganger*'s tonnage. Høvik's answer was a lie, but Rehwinkel only nodded again.[14]

As Rehwinkel grilled the first mate, Vidnes discreetly studied the U-boat. A modest beam and sharp bow lent it a streamlined appearance, and a seemingly fresh coat of paint rendered the hull and tower a pale gray and the deck a darker shade of gray. He presumed that the former made it less readily visible by surface ships and the latter better camouflaged it from aircraft. Emblazoned on the conning tower's starboard side was an image of a snorting bull.

He saw a jumping wire which ran from the tower to the bow, then two more between the tower and the stern—at least, there should have been two aft wires. The German who had climbed down to the deck was attempting to repair one which had evidently been severed. Vidnes also spotted damage to the metal plating where the wooden deck terminated near the stern. He smirked at the confirmation that at least one of their shells found its mark. *Sincerest regards from King Haakon, din jævel.*

Rehwinkel now questioned Høvik about their ports of departure and destination, appearing surprised when Høvik mentioned transiting the Cape Cod Canal. "And what carries your ship? The cargo?" he asked. Høvik told him. "You make a radio message for help?" "No," Høvik lied.

Ernst Rehwinkel did not respond, instead looking over and past the lifeboat. He then turned his head and spoke something to the others before looking back down at the lifeboat. "Good luck to you all," he said, tipping the brim of his cap. The idling engines grunted to life, swelled, then receded as the *U-578* made its exit toward the northwest.

The No. 4 boat proved too damaged to be of further use, leaving insufficient lifeboat space for all forty-three survivors. Capt Nymann reluctantly approved leaving thirteen of the strongest men behind on the two rafts, which were soon lashed together along with the damaged lifeboat. The two serviceable boats hoisted sails and set off.[15]

Nearly forty-eight hours later, at 12:55 on 4 June, the destroyers USS *Madison* (DD-425) and USS *Plunkett* (DD-431) were proceeding from Boston to Cape Henlopen when they encountered floating debris. Five minutes later, the *Madison* spotted thirteen men on a pair of rafts lashed together with an empty lifeboat. The destroyer recovered the survivors, among whom were Johan Vidnes, Olaf Brevik, and Sverre Høvik.

USS *Plunkett* discovered an empty lifeboat at 14:45 which Høvik confirmed was from the *Berganger*. The *Madison* took Høvik, Vidnes, and the others to Norfolk, Virginia, where they learned that the empty boat's occupants had been rescued by the Norwegian freighter *Bañaderos*. The fishing boat *Mary J. Landry* found Capt Nymann's group 14 miles off Block Island that night and brought them to New Bedford, Massachusetts. The forty-three survivors were reunited six days later in New York City.

The *Berganger* was not the only ship to fight back against a U-boat off New Jersey. On 23 April, a battle fought 106 miles off Beach Haven saw the Norwegian freighter *Reinholt* exchange more than fifty shells with the *U-752*. The Germans fled when a pair of destroyers arrived, and the *Reinholt* limped to New York for repairs.[16]

Gunner and dog on a Norwegian ship, 1943. (Norwegian National Archives)

***

Korvettenkapitän Rehwinkel's final log entry for the patrol stated that "the conditions off the US coast were significantly different than in February/March 1942." In contrast to February, when Rehwinkel torpedoed the *R.P. Resor* and USS *Jacob Jones*, there were now fewer solitary merchantmen and more patrolling warships. By 29 June, Eastern Sea Frontier's fleet had expanded to 150 combat vessels. These included thirteen Coast Guard cutters of 125 or 165 feet, fifty-seven smaller cutters, eighteen British armed trawlers, and ten destroyers. A daily average of just two destroyers had patrolled the East Coast in March, but this had increased to six destroyers per day by May.

Aircraft were becoming a greater menace by the day, but destroyers remained the greatest threat to U-boats in mid-1942. High speeds and shallow drafts rendered them difficult to hit with impact-detonated torpedoes, and their compartmentalized designs enabled some to survive torpedo strikes; USS *Blakeley* (DD-150) remained afloat even after the *U-156* blew off her bow in May 1942. Nevertheless, global operational demands still left far too few destroyers along American shores—or anywhere else, it seemed—to put the Gray Wolves in check.

June 1942 was the Allies' most disastrous month at sea since the war began. The Ubootwaffe destroyed 127 merchant ships worldwide that month, obtaining their highest-ever tally of 609,255 gross registered tons of merchant shipping. Ten additional merchantmen were damaged. However, though June represented the pinnacle of Dönitz's successes to date, that same month also brought a discomfiting revelation that called his entire tonnage strategy into question.

By June 1942, German intelligence reports suggested that the scale and maturity of America's shipbuilding program had been significantly underestimated. Dönitz told Hitler in May that "I do not believe that the race between enemy shipbuilding and U-boat sinkings is in any way hopeless," but he emphasized the need to sink ships "as quickly as possible … whatever we sink today [in 1942] counts more than what we may sink in 1943."

Regarding both shipbuilding and destroyers, Dönitz believed that part of the solution lay in a redesigned magnetic fuze. Restoring this capability would make torpedoes more destructive by detonating beneath a ship's keel rather than against its hull, and more forgiving to aim because physically impacting the target was not required. This would help offset American shipbuilding by increasing the tonnage sunk per U-boat, in addition to providing a more effective weapon against destroyers. Their devastating effects would also cause ships of all types to sink more rapidly, denying gunners like Johan Vidnes and Olaf Brevik a chance to hit back.

Faster sinking offered another, even more ruthless dividend. Merchant mariners "won't be able to save themselves due to the rapid sinking of the ship," Dönitz explained to Hitler in May 1942, and more dead mariners "will no doubt make it more difficult to man the many ships America is building." Hitler had already realized this. In January of that year, he told Japanese ambassador Hiroshi Ōshima that he favored "killing as many of the crew as possible. Once it gets around that most of the seamen are lost in the sinkings, the Americans will have great difficulty enlisting new people."

The battle along the East Coast had clearly passed an inflection point, but two new German plans were already underway. One of these operations was a product of Dönitz's headquarters, and three U-boats tasked with executing it left port between 18 and 20 May. The other scheme originated from more shadowy corners of Hitler's war apparatus. While naval intelligence officers interviewed the *Berganger* survivors in New York, two additional U-boats were westbound across the Atlantic carrying special cargoes. This plan did not aim to sink ships, however. The Nazis instead intended to land their next blow on American home soil.[17]

CHAPTER THIRTEEN

Rio Tercero

"With sloping masts and dipping prow,
As who pursued with yell and blow
Still treads the shadow of his foe,
And forward bends his head,
The ship drove fast, loud roared the blast,
And southward aye we fled."
—Samuel Taylor Coleridge, "The Rime of the Ancient Mariner" (1798)

13 June 1942
Amagansett, New York
00:28

Boatswain's Mate 2nd Class John "Jack" Cullen whistled as he strolled through the fog, the beach's packed sand muting his footfalls to a dull crunch. The night of 13 June 1942 found him walking a routine 6-mile foot patrol along Amagansett Beach on Long Island's South Shore. The flashlight in his left hip pocket was of little use in such dense fog, though he also carried a flare gun loosely in his right hand. Visibility was 20 feet at best, and the first day of the new moon phase meant there was no moonlight.

The fog and impenetrable darkness together lent the night an aura of vague foreboding, but nothing presently troubled Jack Cullen. The 21-year-old from Manhattan, soon to be described by *The New Yorker* as "a thoroughly wholesome, typically American boy," was born to an Irish immigrant mother and a Great War veteran father. His boyish features and slightly chubby face contrasted with an athletic physique under his single-breasted "surfman" uniform (the only Coast Guard uniform not also worn by the Navy). Cullen left his Macy's deliveryman job two days after Pearl Harbor to join the Coast Guard, which assigned him as a "sand pounder" for the Coast Guard Beach Patrol.

Prior to the Coast Guard's establishment in 1915, the US Life-Saving Service patrolled the nation's beaches to provide immediate assistance if a ship in distress was sighted. Long Island's congested and hazardous southern coastline had kept rescuers busy for decades. Beach patrols were resurrected after Pearl Harbor to detect landings, sabotage, and other enemy activity along the coast. Of particular concern were rumors that Axis agents were communicating with U-boats from the beaches, and that German sailors were venturing ashore for resupply.

The sand pounders were only intended as a tripwire to enemy incursions. The actual shoreline defense was tasked to Army units like the New Jersey National Guard's 113th Infantry Regiment, which guarded New York City and the Jersey Shore. Pearl Harbor's immediate aftermath saw the regiment's rifle, machine gun, and antitank companies rushed to defensive positions at Cape May, Eatontown, and Sandy Hook's Fort Hancock. The 52nd Coast Artillery Regiment's guns were also emplaced at Fort Hancock to guard New York's approaches. The installation of remote-controlled flamethrowers on the causeway linking Sandy Hook to mainland New Jersey had even been proposed that spring.[1]

BM2 Cullen began his patrol toward Montauk at Long Island's eastern end when he departed Coast Guard Station Amagansett ten minutes after midnight. He heard waves gently breaking on his right. On his left, dunes and scattered high grass separated the beach from the coastal road and its cottages and fishing shacks. Cullen walked close to the surf where the wet sand's firmness enabled him to make better time. Decades later, he would recall humming Jimmy Dorsey's 1941 hit, "Tangerine":

> When she dances by,
> Señoritas stare and caballeros sigh.
> And I've seen,
> Toasts to Tangerine
> Raised in every bar across the Argentine …

Twenty minutes into his patrol, Cullen was striding along the waterline when he unexpectedly sighted an object ahead of him in the surf. He glimpsed movement and heard hushed voices and splashing. Slowing his pace, Cullen aimed his flashlight beam only to turn it off immediately upon realizing it could not penetrate the fog. Approaching closer, he saw the indistinct shape of an inflatable raft. Two men clad in bathing suits or shorts stood in ankle-deep water beside it while a fully clothed third man stood at the water's edge. All three looked at him.

"What's the trouble?" Cullen called out, his tone authoritative but friendly. None of the three men responded. He felt the hair on the back of his neck stand up. The fully dressed man suddenly started advancing toward Cullen. "Who are you??" the patrolman demanded. There was no response, and his heart rate accelerated as the figure approached. Cullen raised his flashlight again, prompting the man to freeze in place and finally speak: "Wait, are you the Coast Guard?"

"Yessir, and you are? …" Cullen replied. The man was more clearly visible now. Clean-shaven and thin, he stood about average height and had abnormally long arms. He wore a brown fedora, a red woolen zip-up sweater, a gray coat, and some sort of grayish denim pants that appeared to be wet. "We're fishermen from Southampton. We, ah, ran aground." His speech was faintly tinged with a foreign accent that Cullen could not place. The fog seemed to thicken around them. "Okay. What are you gonna do, then?" Cullen replied. He took a small step backward.

The question seemed to catch the thin man off guard. "We'll, ah … we'll stay here until sunrise," he replied. "That's four hours away," Cullen pointed out. "You all should come up to the station till then, c'mon." He gestured for them to follow. The men looked at one another. The thin man complied, but took only a few steps before halting. "I'm not going with you," he abruptly declared. "Sir—" irritation rose in Cullen's voice as he turned and reached for the man's arm.

"Now wait a minute," the stranger angrily interjected as he yanked his arm away from Cullen. "You don't know what's going on here. How old are you? Have you got a father and mother? I wouldn't want to have to kill you." The threat stole the words from Cullen's mouth. His legs grew weak and his heart felt like it was trying to pound its way free of his chest.

Cullen's attention snapped to his left when he detected movement in his peripheral vision. A fourth man appeared from behind Cullen wearing only swimming trunks and dragging a duffle bag. The bag man started speaking in a foreign language, whereupon the thin man immediately cut him off. "Shut up, you damn fool!" he snapped in English.

Germans. Cullen felt immediately lightheaded. *But were they coming, or going?* "What's … in the bag?" he asked, summoning every ounce of courage he could muster. "Clams," replied the bag man in a heavy accent. "Yeah, that's right," the first man added. Cullen knew there were no clam beds for miles. "Everything's fine," the stranger told his companion with the duffle bag. "Go back down with the others and stay there." Turning his attention back to Cullen, his tone became conciliatory. "Hey, why don't you just forget this whole thing? Here, I'll give you some money and you can go have a good time."

The man fished two $50 bills from his pocket. "Here's some money. A hundred dollars." "I don't want it," Cullen replied indignantly. "Then take three hundred," he reached again into his pocket. The patrolman's head was spinning as two realizations dawned on him. The first was that a show of naïveté might offer his best chance of survival, and the second was that his story might not be believed without evidence. "Take it," the man demanded. "Okay," Cullen finally replied. When he accepted the wad of bills, the man suddenly removed his hat and took a step closer.

"Now take a good look at me," he ordered, his demeanor hardening again. He aimed his own flashlight upward and switched it on. "Look into my eyes." Cullen hesitated, terrified that the stranger might somehow hypnotize him. "Look at me," the stranger repeated. Cullen met his gaze. The light eerily illuminated the man's narrow face and a gray streak in his slicked-back hair. His eyes appeared attentive yet somehow dull, and his expression was oddly flat. It was as if he were some humanoid creature masquerading as Joe Fisherman from Long Island.

"I'll be meeting you in East Hampton sometime," the man threatened. "Do you know me? Would you recognize me if you saw me again?" He leaned closer, the muscles around his eyes tensing. When Cullen did not answer, his interrogator repeated the question in a sharper tone. "… No," the patrolman finally replied. "No, sir. I never saw you before in my life."

The answer seemed to satisfy him. "My name's George John Davis," he stated. "What's yours?" "Frank Collins," Cullen lied in response. The man calling himself Davis said nothing. Cullen began to slowly walk backward, sand crunching beneath his feet as fog again subsumed the strangers. He backpedaled until a grassy dune caught his heel mid-step and caused him to stumble backwards. Jack Cullen hastily recovered, pivoted, and set off running faster than he ever had in his life.[2]

***

22 June 1942
103 miles east of Atlantic City, New Jersey
06:41

Nine days after Jack Cullen's confrontation on Amagansett Beach, Captain Luis Scalese stepped out onto the *Rio Tercero*'s bridge wing. He brushed a hand over his dark hair as he watched a gentle southwesterly breeze ruffle the shimmering blue water under a clear sky lit by the morning sun. There were far worse days to be at sea. Allied merchant captains seldom wore a uniform aboard ship, but Scalese's mustache and black hair were complemented by a long-sleeved tunic with a high collar clasped at his throat and epaulettes that each featured an anchor and four gold stripes.

Luis Scalese and most of his forty-one crewmen were from Argentina, one of only two Latin American countries that still maintained normal relations with the Axis Powers. Termed "prudent neutrality," Argentina's position reflected the divided opinions of its populace. The nation's longstanding ties with Britain resulted in considerable pro-Allied sentiment within the major political parties, intellectuals, and media outlets (the Nazi-financed newspaper *El Pampero* being a notable exception). The army wished to maintain neutrality, however, and President Roberto Ortiz likely feared a coup if he aligned Argentina with the Allies.[3]

That the *Rio Tercero* sailed under an Argentine flag was historically noteworthy. Argentina had possessed no state-sponsored merchant fleet until just nine months earlier, the economy having instead relied on other nations' shipping to carry Argentine imports and exports. Great Britain accounted for more than half of Argentine exports—particularly cereals and meat—in 1939, but the war had severely reduced British traffic to Argentine ports.

In addition to a sharp decline in export revenue, Argentina lacked the warehouse capacity to store the backlog of agricultural and livestock products bound for foreign markets. The United States also declared an embargo on Argentina to pressure Buenos

Aires to break relations with the Axis. These events made it clear that Argentine interests demanded an Argentine merchant fleet, and the government consequently established the *Flota Mercante del Estado* (State Merchant Fleet) in October 1941.

The new fleet was outfitted by appropriating twenty-six foreign ships interned in Argentine ports. One of these was the Italian-flagged *Fortunstella*. Built in Hebburn, England in 1912, she measured 400 feet long and 4,864 gross registered tons. A coal-fired engine evidenced her age, as most merchant ships built after World War I were powered by fuel oil. The *Fortunstella* was renamed the *Rio Tercero*, and Captain Luis Scalese became one of the first "*gauchos del rudder*" (rudder cowboys), a reference to the famed horsemen of the South American highlands.[4]

To avoid being fatally misidentified like the Chilean freighter *Toltén* three months earlier, the *Rio Tercero*'s neutrality markings were conspicuously displayed. Thirteen Argentine flags were painted on the ship: five on each side of the hull, one on a wooden sign on the aft deck, one on the No. 4 hatch cover, and one over the bridge. The large hull flags occupied more than half the distance between the waterline and deck, and "RIO TERCERO" and "BUENOS AIRES" were painted in large block lettering three times on each side of the hull.

The *Rio Tercero* offloaded a cargo of cereals in New York City before taking on "general cargo" that included textiles, newsprint, asbestos fiber, and nine cases of clocks. Her crew of forty-one was joined by one passenger, Argentine medical doctor Francisco Arambarri. The ship left New York on 21 June 1942 for the return journey to Argentina, and sunrise the following day found the *Rio Tercero* continuing southeast at 9.5 knots toward the deep waters beyond the continental shelf.

The deck department and mates enjoyed an overcast and cool day, but conditions were less pleasant under the waterline. The No. 3 cargo hold adjacent to the boiler room served as the coal bunker, inside which a wiper clenched a damp rag between his teeth while he labored in the glow of a portable electric lamp. His shovel dirtied the dusty and dimly lit air as he dumped coal into a chute which deposited it on the boiler room deck. The bare-chested fireman then scraped the coal from the deck with his own shovel and pitched it through a boiler's open fire doors. The water tender, meanwhile, monitored gauges and periodically adjusted valves to maintain proper water levels in the boilers.

Capt Scalese was making good time in part due to his freedom to steer a straight course, unlike his zigzagging Allied counterparts. It was another unremarkable day at sea for the crew of the *Rio Tercero*, but far more sensational events were unfolding back on the American homefront.[5]

***

Jack Cullen's encounter on Amagansett Beach nine days earlier inadvertently compromised Operation Pastorius, a plot to infiltrate saboteurs into the United States. It was orchestrated by the *Abwehr*, Germany's military intelligence bureau.

The Abwehr was led by the enigmatic Admiral Wilhelm Canaris, a U-boat veteran of the Great War described by one historian as "perhaps the most unusual [officer] in the German service." The plot was named for Franz Pastorius, who founded America's first German settlement at what is today the Philadelphia neighborhood of Germantown.

Operation Pastorius entailed the *U-202* landing one team of four saboteurs on Long Island, New York and the *U-584* landing another team near Jacksonville, Florida. Armed with false identities, cash, and explosives, the saboteurs had orders to conduct "sabotage attacks on targets of economic importance for the war" and "stir up discontent and lower fighting resistance" among the American populace. Their list of targets included a Philadelphia cryolite plant, Hell Gate Bridge, aluminum plants in three states, two hydroelectric power plants, and locks on the Ohio River. They were also ordered to bomb Jewish-owned businesses.

The plot was not without precedent. In July 1916, agents of the German Empire planted bombs at an ordnance depot on Black Tom Island in Jersey City, New Jersey. The bombs set off more than a thousand tons of explosives bound for the Western Front. The blast killed four, shattered windows for miles, and even damaged the Statue of Liberty (the statue's torch was thereafter permanently closed to tourists). Six months later and 9 miles away, German operatives set fire to a munitions factory in Lyndhurst, New Jersey. Another colossal explosion resulted, although a quick-thinking switchboard operator enabled an evacuation that saved countless lives. Twenty-five years later, in 1941, the FBI's arrest of thirty-three German agents effectively wiped out Nazi intelligence operations in the United States.

The eight agents chosen for Operation Pastorius were all German-born men who had lived in the United States during the interwar years. Two were naturalized American citizens and peacetime US Army veterans. Most had been members of the German-American Bund, the notorious homegrown Nazi movement. None had experience in covert operations, so Admiral Canaris' organization put them through a crash course in explosives, firearms, hand-to-hand combat, and espionage tradecraft. They sang the "Star-Spangled Banner" ad nauseam and read American newspapers, but taking notes was forbidden. All critical information was instead memorized.

The only written information the saboteurs would take to America were the names and addresses of three US residents who could assist the operation. One of these individuals was a saboteur's pro-Nazi uncle in Chicago. Another was a different team member's close friend from the Bund in New York City. The third name was a Lutheran clergyman in New Jersey. The list was written in invisible ink on a handkerchief carried by the leader of each team.

The stranger who menaced Jack Cullen on the beach was the leader of the Long Island team, 39-year-old George Dasch. Journeying to the United States as a stowaway in 1922, he worked odd jobs in New York and Chicago and served thirteen months in the US Army Air Corps. He left behind his ill American wife when he returned to Germany in May 1941. Assigned the cover identity of "George John Davis," Dasch's fictional birthplace of San Francisco was chosen to exploit that city's 1906 fire as an explanation for his lack of a birth certificate.

Operation Pastorius found little enthusiasm within BdU. Admiral Dönitz and most of his officers were "averse to embarking these individuals in U-boats," according to Günter Hessler, a BdU staff officer and Dönitz's son-in-law. As Hessler explained years later, BdU staff feared that "some of them were not actuated by patriotic motives" and, if caught, would divulge secrets in order "to save their own skins."[6]

When the *U-202* left port on 27 May 1942, Kapitänleutnant Hans-Heinz Linder informed his crew via the intercom that their four passengers were on a special mission. They were to be treated with respect, he ordered, and no questions were to be asked. Linder himself had not even been told the details of the agents' mission. In any event, he was more concerned with getting them off his boat as soon as possible.

Multiple issues beset the Type VIIC during its outward voyage. An enlisted sailor was stricken with appendicitis approximately nine days after departure, but little could be done beyond providing morphine and ice. On 9 June, Linder was admonished via radio by BdU: "BOAT IS NOT PROCEEDING AT ECONOMICAL SPEED. BAD FUEL UTILIZATION!" That same day saw the *U-202* pass under heavy fog which blocked the sun and stars, forcing Linder to navigate by dead reckoning as he passed Nova Scotia and steered toward New York.

Shortly before 19:00 on 12 June, the *U-202* reached the eastern end of Long Island, New York. Navigation here demands utmost caution due to shoals, currents, fog, and heavy traffic that make Long Island's South Shore one of the nation's most treacherous shorelines. Seven miles off Amagansett Beach, Kapitänleutnant Linder laid the *U-202* on the seafloor at a depth of 75 feet. The four saboteurs waited anxiously as pebbles and seashell fragments, swept up by the ocean swells, ticked quietly against the outer hull.

The *U-202* surfaced after sunset into a moonless and foggy night. Linder followed a heading from the gyrocompass as he crept northwest under electric power, keeping the boat trimmed so low that only its conning tower was above water. Visibility was less than 100 yards and ambient noise was virtually absent. Linder heard little besides the buzzing E-motors, and the fog meant that he heard the sibilant murmur of waves breaking against sand before he could see the beach. The *U-202*'s keel finally scraped softly against sand at 22:52. Linder whistled, and his crew quickly went into action.

The Germans speedily loaded an inflatable dinghy with several duffle bags and four wooden boxes containing dynamite, time fuzes, and detonators. Two armed sailors would accompany them to the beach before returning with the raft. Dasch's team wore khaki Kriegsmarine working uniforms with black boots and swastika-emblazoned caps; if captured prior to changing into civilian attire on the beach, the uniforms would ostensibly classify the saboteurs as POWs rather than spies.

The kommandant issued the agents an unambiguous directive in the event they ran into trouble on the beach. Anyone interfering with the landing, or merely stumbled across the scene, was to be immediately overpowered and brought back to the *U-202*. A towline was attached to the dinghy, and Hans Linder watched his two crewmen row the saboteurs toward shore until they vanished into the fog.[7]

***

22 June 1942
101 miles east of Atlantic City, New Jersey
06:48

Nine days after the Nazis waded ashore on Amagansett Beach, the Argentine freighter *Rio Tercero* was proceeding south along New Jersey's southern coast when a G7e torpedo hurtled at 35 mph into her starboard side. The explosion's shockwave, and the momentum of the water shoved before it, punched through the hull and shattered its plating into fragments that perforated the engine room like jagged metal buckshot. Displaced water then rushed back in against the hull, prying the puncture larger as a jet of water blasted into the ship with enough force to tear off limbs. A cacophony of rending metal melded with the thundering of the Atlantic surging through the hull, and a boiler exploded when cold sea met red-hot steel. The four engineering crewmen on duty never had a chance.

In the radio shack by the bridge, radioman Roque Volpe frenetically tapped out a looping mayday. "SOS, THIS IS LOII, TORPEDOED, 39° 15' NORTH, 72° 20' WEST. SOS, THIS IS LOII ..." The messages flooding the ether were received by the Amagansett radio station. A prompt reply beeped through Volpe's headset. "LOII, THIS IS WSL ..."

Captain Luis Scalese ordered a hard change of course toward New Jersey's coast. Despite knowing it was likely futile, he was determined to do everything in his power to save the *Rio Tercero*. The ship's bow swung west as he stepped out on the bridge wing and quickly scanned the sea. Their assailant remained unseen. Two minutes later, as the deck slanted precipitously beneath him, Scalese grabbed the ship's log and departed the bridge for the last time.

Chaos swirled around Dr Francisco Arambarri, the ship's sole passenger, as he tended to an injured fireman. "You'll be fine, *no te pasa nada*," Arambarri reassured the mariner. "You'll be dancing *dos por cuatro* in no time." The mariner was not badly hurt, but even the doctor could tell that the *Rio Tercero*'s wound was fatal. "*Bueno, vamos*," Arambarri intoned, helping the patient to his feet. "I'll have another look in the lifeboat, okay?"[8]

***

13 June 1942
Coast Guard Station Amagansett, Long Island, New York
00:57

After the unnerving confrontation on the beach, Boatswain's Mate 2nd Class Jack Cullen sprinted back to the two-story, cottage-style building which had served as the station since 1902. Cullen burst through the front door and immediately began unloading a barely coherent stream of words at BM2 Carl Jenette, the petty officer on duty that night. A perplexed Jenette stood slowly. "Hey, Cullen, buddy ..."

Jenette's eyes grew wide when Cullen produced a wad of cash from his pocket. "Germans. On. The beach!" Cullen finally exclaimed, thrusting out a trembling hand filled with cash. A dumbfounded Jenette took the money and looked back up at Cullen. "Okay, pal ... now, again, from the top." Cullen inhaled deeply and started recounting the experience. "Oh boy," Jenette replied when Cullen finished. "This is big."

Jenette phoned their superiors and mustered the three other Coast Guardsmen on duty. They then opened the weapons locker and armed themselves with M1903 Springfield rifles. "You don't have to come with us if you don't want," Jenette told Cullen, speaking as he pushed a stripper clip of .30-06 rounds into his rifle's internal magazine. "No way," Cullen replied, chambering a round in his own weapon. "I'll go."

Arriving at the beach at 01:05, the five Coast Guardsmen began advancing slowly through the fog with rifles raised. Jack Cullen was staring intently down the iron sights on his Springfield, sweeping its barrel horizontally as he took long, careful steps. "Can't see shit out here ..." someone muttered. The soft static of breaking surf grew more audible. Jenette sniffed the air. "You guys smell that?" "Yeah," another man replied. "Diesel." They pressed cautiously forward.

"*Psst.*" Jenette tapped Cullen's arm before speaking in a whisper: "Show us where you were earlier." Cullen paused and scanned his immediate vicinity, then the others followed him deeper into the fog. "See the footprints? I was talking to the first guy here, then another guy appears from that way." Cullen pointed. "He was dragging a—" In that instant, a loud mechanical growl suddenly resonated from somewhere beyond the veil of fog. They froze in shock as the sand vibrated beneath them. Whatever its source, it could not be farther than a few hundred feet. Five quivering rifle barrels pointed seaward. "Jesus, what the hell is that??" The noise seemed for several moments to strain itself toward a crescendo before ceasing altogether.

Whatever was transpiring, Carl Jenette realized, was beyond five Coasties' ability to handle. He knew there was a detachment of the 113th Infantry just 5 miles down the beach—this was their time to shine if there ever was one. Their own Coast Guard superiors would arrive at the station at any minute, so Jenette and another man returned while Jack Cullen and two others remained at the beach. Moments later, the sand under Cullen's feet quaked again as the ominous engine noise resumed.[9]

***

"*Scheisse! … Scheisse!*"

Six hundred feet away from the armed Coast Guard party, a stream of profanity drifted up through the *U-202*'s conning tower hatch. While Kapitänleutnant Linder and his crew were waiting for the dinghy's return, the ebbing tide had swung the U-boat parallel to shore while waves pushed it farther toward the beach; the keel settled firmly into the sand. Fog prevented the Germans from noticing the situation, and only upon attempting to depart did they realize that the U-boat was stuck. Linder immediately ordered the ballast tanks flooded to prevent the boat from being pushed further ashore.

"*L.I.!*" he shouted down the hatch moments later. "Blow the tanks, then full astern on both motors!" The chief engineer acknowledged the order before issuing his own: "*Anblasen!*" There followed a loud *whoosh* and gurgling noises, then the E-motors' humming began. When this proved futile, Linder ordered the tanks flooded once more. The next attempt saw the ballast purged again before the diesel engines roared to emergency speed in reverse, their thunderous bellow causing the commander to grimace. Amagansett Beach still held fast to the *U-202* while its screws spun impotently, shaking the beach under Cullen and Jenette less than 300 yards away.

"*Eins-vee-oh …*" The sea foamed against the U-boat's hull as Linder turned to Oberleutnant Christian Reich. "I need you to ready the boat for demolition and have Hille prepare the final message to BdU." The kommandant's tone was hushed and rapid. "Don't transmit yet. That'll be the last thing we do." He left the rest of the statement unspoken. "*Jawohl, Herr Kaleun,*" Reich replied soberly before climbing down through the hatch.

An hour passed. Linder's crew succeeded in orienting the bow away from shore by running one screw forward and the other in reverse, yet the *U-202* only settled further into the sand when low tide's arrival at 02:14 left insufficient water to float it. Sunrise steadily approached as the tide returned agonizingly slowly. The dissipating fog soon revealed car headlights and a house facing the beach. Linder also discerned a radio tower east of the house, about 200 yards from the U-boat. A dog was barking loudly. Soon, anyone out for a morning stroll would behold 220 feet of German steel laid out like a dead whale.[10]

***

Nine days later and 101 miles east of Atlantic City, a stampede of Argentine mariners aboard the *Rio Tercero* converged on the two port-side lifeboats. "*Vamos, dale!*" the boatswain shouted. *Let's go, c'mon!* The freighter's crewmen found themselves in a race against time as the *Rio Tercero* made haste to her grave and they endeavored not to accompany her. A mariner named Justino Aguilar lost his footing and fell overboard from the port-side boat deck. "*Apúrense!*" Scalese yelled to the others. *Hurry up!* He waved their attention back to the davits; they could do nothing for Aguilar up here. "Get these boats launched, now!"

The lifeboats reached the water within three minutes. It was not a moment too soon, as the *Rio Tercero* was quickly disappearing beneath a seething gyre. "*Ayuda!!*" Aguilar implored desperately. *Help!!* His voice was riven with panic as he struggled to keep his face above water, his anguished pleas growing increasingly unintelligible.

"There is a legend that every vessel has a tremendous suction that draws everything down within a radius of a hundred yards," a War Shipping Administration safety manual stated in 1943. "This is definitely an exaggeration." Aguilar was, however, at the mercy of a sinking ship's physics: not suction, but aeration. Flooding compartments pull water inside while expelling air, rendering surface water turbulent and frothy. This makes it less dense, and anything floating on it therefore becomes less buoyant. A victim may perceive that he is being "pulled" under, but it may be more accurate to say that he is falling.

Those in the lifeboats hurriedly disconnected the falls and began rowing toward Aguilar. They watched in horror as his gasping face submerged again, clawing hands following his head under. This time, Aguilar did not come back up. The sea around the *Rio Tercero* sizzled as she continued settling by the stern. The Argentine freighter tilted her bow toward the azure sky, as if surrendering, then slid backward into the depths.

Only rolls of newsprint bobbed where the *Rio Tercero* had been moments ago, but Capt Scalese allowed his crew no time to contemplate either the swiftness of her demise or the five men she took to the bottom. The survivors put the lifeboats alongside each other and started to lash them together. The genteel Dr Arambarri could not help feeling out of place among three dozen hardy mariners. Although the doctor had kept his head so far, he knew their ordeal was not over.

Five minutes after the *Rio Tercero* disappeared, Dr Arambarri was jolted back into the moment when men around him began to shout and point. "*Miren, por allá!*" Palpable fear swamped both boats. "*Allá están!*" Three hundred yards away, a dark shape was rising from the sea.

A tower-like structure breached the surface first. At its aft end was a railing-bound platform with a fearsome-looking gun mounted in its center. Another, even larger gun was mounted forward of the tower on a flat deck which ran the length of the boat. The deck was about 20 feet wide amidships and tapered to an angular bow that gave the U-boat a lean, predatory appearance. Dr Arambarri had always envisioned a submarine as some sort of steel whale, but this more closely resembled a shark.

The sea sluiced through slots in the deck's edge as the submarine seated itself atop the sea like an ordinary ship, its deck about 3 feet above the water. It then seemed to exhale with a loud *ssshhhh!* Water sprayed upward along its hull. Bearded faces appeared over the tower's bulwark. The grumble of diesel engines began. Rolls of floating newsprint bumped off the U-boat's hull as it steered toward the lifeboats, its sharp bow cutting the placid sea like a knife.

"We surface. We show ourselves, the treacherous fish rearing its head," Lothar-Günther Buchheim reflected about the *U-96* encountering survivors of a ship it had just sunk. "What can they be feeling … when our streaming tower emerges suddenly in an eddy of frothing water, when the tip of our bow pierces the surface, when the gray shark plows up a ring of foam? … Hatred? Horror? Paralysis?"

The *Rio Tercero*'s survivors likely felt a mix of all three. "*Tranquilo!*" Scalese yelled as the U-boat approached. "Nobody speaks but me! Is that clear?" Every man sat still as stone as thirty-five pairs of eyes watched their captain. The afternoon sun glinted off the gold stripes and anchors on Scalese's epaulettes as Arambarri watched him sit rigidly upright and lift his chin. The captain inhaled deeply.

Looking back toward the submarine, the doctor saw a half-dozen Germans crowding an open-air chariot bridge atop its conning tower. One wore what might be described as a sea captain's hat with a rumpled-looking white crown. The man in the white hat leaned over the bulwark and shouted a question in English.

"Who is the captain?" demanded Kapitänleutnant Hans-Heinz Linder.[11]

***

The *U-202*'s attempt to escape from Amagansett Beach nine days earlier finally succeeded after three excruciating hours. The crew used the last compressed air to blow the tanks one final time, then connected both diesel engines and both E-motors to the propeller shafts. "*Dreimal Äusserste Kraft!*" Both propulsion systems went to full speed three times while the rudder was frantically jerked from side to side. Each surge of torque wrenched the boat incrementally further seaward. Finally, at 03:10, the *U-202* broke free on the fourth attempt.

Cheers broke out as the Germans felt water under the keel again and the sea slid past the hull with a comforting hiss. Linder slapped the bulwark in relief and spontaneously embraced Oberleutnant Reich. It was "the utmost and final time for us to get away," he later remarked in the log. "Otherwise we could march in tomorrow's Flag Day parade in New York!"

"Make ready for diving," the commander ordered as the boat turned onto a southeasterly heading. Linder thought little more about Dasch's team on the beach; he was just relieved to not be in American handcuffs. The *U-202* submerged as the first rays of dawn broke over the South Shore.[12]

***

"Who is the captain?" Linder repeated. The *U-202* was nearly close enough for the *Rio Tercero* survivors to touch. Scalese raised his hand like a schoolboy. "*Yo soy el capitán*," he announced. "English?" Linder shouted. "*No*," Scalese shook his head. "*Français?*" the kommandant then asked. Scalese replied in the negative again. Linder conferred with his men momentarily before returning his attention to Scalese.

"Please, come aboard fast," Linder instructed in English, gesturing to make his intentions clear. "You only." A pair of Germans descended ladder rungs built into the side of the tower. The Argentines used the oars to propel the tethered lifeboats until one boat's wooden gunwale thumped against the *U-202*'s hull.

Dr Arambarri's dread did not negate his curiosity, and he found himself discreetly studying the submarine as Capt Scalese climbed onto its deck. The doctor noticed a white hedgehog painted on the conning tower's starboard side. On the tower's front was a coat of arms comprising two stone towers behind a wall, beneath which was the word "INNSBRUCK" in white lettering. A few feet aft of the hedgehog emblem, Scalese ascended the rungs on the tower's side and reached the bridge to find himself within arm's reach of the *U-202* commander.

Hans-Heinz Linder stood roughly 6 feet tall with a well-built physique, blonde hair, and a month's worth of beard growth over a ruddy complexion. His eyes appeared tired but alert. Linder wore khaki working pants with suspenders, a gray sweater, ankle boots, and a cap which sat canted on his head. Its brim was covered in dark blue cloth and edged with gold embroidery. Centered on the black band above the brim was a roundel of red, white, and black rings inside a wreath of gold oak leaves. Adorning the white crown above the roundel was a gold eagle-and-swastika emblem, and pinned to the roundel's left was a metal version of the same hedgehog emblem painted on the tower.

"Welcome," Linder greeted the Argentine captain as he gestured to the open hatch at their feet. "The guest … first." Scalese glanced down warily before answering with a compliant nod. From one of the two lifeboats, Dr Arambarri watched him dip out of view, followed by the German captain. They left behind four lookouts on the tower who watched the horizon impassively through dark-tinted glasses.[13]

An overpowering stench assaulted Capt Scalese as he descended the aluminum ladder into the stale and sour air of the *U-202*'s interior. It smelled like a school locker room inside an auto repair garage situated next to a garbage dump. He also caught a whiff of what smelled like citrus-scented cologne as the ladder's first seven rungs brought him into a tiny compartment occupied by a lone young man who studied the merchant captain with intense curiosity. Scalese spotted an engine order telegraph, what appeared to be the periscope station, and other devices of functions unknown.

The next eight rungs led him down into what seemed like the U-boat's nerve center. The compartment's port and starboard bulkheads were covered with valves, gauges, levers, and other instruments. Pipes and more levers crowded the overhead. An enormous vertical cylinder, which Scalese guessed was the periscope housing, dominated much of the room's center. Much of the starboard bulkhead consisted of a bank of color-coded handwheels. Against the port bulkhead and immediately adjacent to the ladder was a chart table with a map spread out across it. Scalese noticed that the map was marked with a line roughly matching the *Rio Tercero*'s course.

The pale and unshaven Germans stared at him. They were young, Scalese being clearly the oldest man in the control room. One was clad in a filthy white undershirt and light gray leather trousers. Two wore military-style officer caps like the captain's, albeit with a blue crown instead of a white one. Most of the men's headgear displayed the same metal hedgehog pin that Linder wore.

Reaching the bottom of the ladder after Scalese, Linder retrieved a well-worn book titled *Die Handelsflotten der Welt*. He flipped through it as Scalese saw illustrations of merchant ships along with information about each. Linder pointed to an image that closely resembled the *Rio Tercero*. "You, *ja*? Your ship?" It was indeed, but the name listed was *Fortunstella*.

Scalese shook his head. "*Anteriormente, era la Fortunstella*," he replied. "*Un barco italiano.*" Linder squinted and tapped his forefinger on the page again. "Say me the name of your ship." The merchant captain's face creased as he struggled to assemble an answer Linder might understand. "*Ella solía ser llamada la Fortunstella*," Scalese gestured as he spoke. "*Pero se convirtió en el Rio Tercero.*"

Linder frowned and put the Gröner manual aside. It was unclear whether he had understood Scalese's explanation or had simply abandoned this line of questioning, but the interrogation continued. "You make a transmission? On the radio?" Scalese shook his head. "*No*," he lied. Linder next asked the location of the ship's papers. "*En el barco*," the Argentine responded, pointing down to indicate they had gone to the bottom with the *Rio Tercero*.

Capt Scalese did still have the ship's log in his possession, which he surrendered. The Argentine captain was stunned when the submarine commander responded by offering him a bottle of cognac and a pair of shoes. "For you," Linder stated. Scalese hesitated before accepting them with a nod of gratitude. "*Gracias.*" The *U-202*'s captain said something to one of his men before turning back to Scalese and gesturing at the control room ladder as if to say, "after you."

Back in the lifeboat, Dr Arambarri's mind spun with frightening possibilities as five minutes passed, then ten. *Was the captain a hostage? Were the devils torturing him?* The others whispered as they worked the paddles to keep the lifeboats against the sub's hull. The four German lookouts on the tower above them, each wearing sunglasses that resembled goggles, remained fixed like statues and paid the survivors no attention.

Fifteen minutes after Scalese vanished inside the metal beast, his crew stirred when he appeared again on its bridge. The German in the white cap followed, and the survivors spotted a bottle and a pair of shoes in the captain's hand. Scalese said nothing as he crossed the U-boat's deck and climbed back into one of the lifeboats.

The survivors pushed their lifeboats away from the *U-202* as its engines growled. Capt Scalese kept his eyes on the U-boat's bridge, where he saw Linder disappear down the hatch. Four other Germans emerged, their movement suggesting that each was carrying something. Two narrow, cylindrical objects appeared over the bridge bulwark's edge. Dark and metallic. The sailors pointed them at the lifeboats.

Machine guns.

Terrified voices immediately rose from the lifeboats. Scalese felt dizzy. The machine guns' muzzles stared mutely, like a pair of lifeless eyes, as two Germans lifted the weapons' rectangular metal covers and the other two placed gleaming belts of ammunition atop them. Capt Scalese numbly heard someone praying the Lord's Prayer.

"Padre nuestro, que estás en el cielo. Santificado sea tu nombre …"

Clack! The sailors closed the covers over the ammunition belts.

"Venga tu reino. Hágase tu voluntad, en la tierra como en el cielo …"

Shlick-shlack! They racked the charging handles.

"Danos hoy nuestro pan de cada día, y perdona nuestras ofensas …"

Scalese was hyperventilating, his eyes wide but unseeing, yet he held his shoulders back. He knew that some of his crew would be looking to him in their last moments.

"No nos dejes caer en tentación, y líbranos del mal …"

Scalese did not hear the low-pitched noise in the distance at first, but he did notice a sudden flurry of movement on the U-boat's bridge. Germans shouted unintelligibly as the monotone noise grew louder. The machine guns disappeared.

"Amén."[14]

The droning noise swelled into the guttural, thumping snarl of aircraft engines as the survivors turned around to behold a twin-engine US Army bomber swooping out of the haze behind them. The Argentines erupted in raucous cheers as the gull-winged aircraft raced toward them at 160 mph. *"Vamos, carajo!"* They waved eagerly. *"Bájalo!!"*

The B-25B Mitchell banked sharply to approach from astern as the *U-202* accelerated away from the lifeboats, the sea arcing over its bridge as the bow tipped downward. The plane's bomb bay doors opened as the *U-202*'s tower followed the bow under, then the aft deck, and finally the stern bustle. The bomber was hot on Linder's heels, its engines thrumming louder as it dropped to 300 feet over the water. Just as the conning tower disappeared, three cylindrical objects fell from the Mitchell's bomb bay and splashed in a line along the now-submerged U-boat's axis.

The bombardier, however, had accidentally dropped inert practice depth charges. Second Lieutenant Hugh Maxwell, the bomber's 26-year-old pilot, threw the B-25 into a sharp turn and roared back toward the roiled patch of ocean where the enemy had just disappeared. Ecstatic shouting continued. As Maxwell crossed the U-boat's estimated track at a 40-degree angle, the bomber's fuselage emptied four Mark 17 depth charges. The weapons splashed at 15-foot intervals in a row centered about 60 yards beyond where the *U-202* submerged.

Three seconds passed before a white disc bloomed under the surface. It expanded as three additional, overlapping circles appeared. Each disc widened into a pale crater that rose from the surface as a dome while a waterspout erupted angrily from its center. The four nearly synchronous explosions produced a single protracted rumble that shook the lifeboats while their occupants cheered themselves hoarse. "*Qué golazo!*" Men whistled sharply. "*Vamos! Haganlos mierda!*"

Having discharged all his ordnance, 2LT Maxwell returned the mariners' gratitude with a tip of his wings. Before low fuel forced the pilot to turn for shore, Dr Arambarri watched an air crewman toss a pair of lifejackets from the plane. The intrigued survivors maneuvered the boats to retrieve them. Pinned to one lifejacket was a handwritten note:

"We're sorry as hell we couldn't do as good a job to the submarine as it did to your boat."[15]

***

Eastern Sea Frontier dispatched the subchaser USS *PC-503*, the armed yacht USS *Niagara* (PG-52), the British antisubmarine trawlers HMS *Lady Rosemary* and HMS *Northern Chief*, and two more aircraft. The tugboat *John R. Williams* was also sent from Cape May. Not long after the B-25 departed, a Navy blimp passed overhead and dropped a supply of hot dogs. The rafts were spotted again by an Army plane at 16:02.

The lifeboats drifted 13 miles over the next ten hours. They were finally located at 18:20 by the *PC-503*, which towed the boats until transferring them to the cutter USCGC *Navesink* (WYT-88). From the *Rio Tercero*'s complement of forty-two men, thirty-seven reached New York alive. Speaking on a Spanish-language CBS broadcast, Captain Scalese expressed his "heartfelt thanks" to "the Air Force and the Navy of the United States."

Luis Scalese and his crew were convinced that the *Rio Tercero* had been deliberately targeted. They insisted that "the identity of the ship could not have been mistaken due to plainly visible neutrality markings," according to a US Navy report which also described them as "vehement" in their "extreme animosity against the German commander." A memorandum from the Third Naval District commandant to Admiral Ernest King's office likewise stated the Argentine crew was "fighting mad and definitely anti-Axis!"

The *Rio Tercero* survivors were flown back to Argentina where they arrived on 4 July. Scalese's wife, sister, and brothers met him at the airport. Intense media attention required police to shepherd them through the airport to a caravan of vehicles waiting outside.[16]

***

Like the Chilean reaction to the *Toltén* sinking three months earlier, anger in Argentina escalated into riots. Buenos Aires residents pelted Germany's embassy with rocks and bottles, and police were deployed to protect German-owned homes and businesses. Public opinion regarding neutrality remained divided, however, partly because many Argentines were of German or Italian descent. Claims circulated that the *Rio Tercero* was attacked because Scalese had reported a U-boat sighting to American forces. "I believe that this rumor came from our own Foreign Ministry," claimed *Rio Tercero* radioman Roque Volpe, "to calm popular anger" and "avoid retaliation against German interests in Argentina."

The *Rio Tercero* was the second Argentine ship hit by U-boats, the tanker *Victoria* having been damaged off Virginia by the *U-201* in April. Scalese's statement that the submarine was named "Innsbruck" inadvertently weakened Buenos Aires' demands of Berlin when the Nazis responded that U-boats carried only numbers, not names. German officials did not divulge that "Innsbruck" and the coat of arms on the tower represented the *U-202*'s adoptive city.

Behind closed doors, however, Kapitänleutnant Linder's superiors were displeased. BdU's Operations Division assessed that the incident "is considered to have seriously impaired the relations between Germany and Argentina." Although describing Linder's mistake as "excusable," they concluded that its diplomatic consequences were "highly undesirable under the present circumstances." Argentina would nonetheless remain neutral until Buenos Aires issued a mostly symbolic declaration of war on Germany and Japan in March 1945.

Neither Argentina nor Chile would join the war in any meaningful way, but German offenses against Latin American countries did not go entirely unanswered. Mexico joined the Allies when U-boats sank two Mexican tankers in May 1942, and Brazil followed suit after Hitler elected to punish their pro-Allied policies with a U-boat offensive later that year that killed more than six hundred Brazilians. Of all the Latin American nations, only Mexican and Brazilian forces would fight in combat overseas.[17]

***

George Dasch's team of Nazi agents fled Amagansett Beach only minutes before Jack Cullen returned with four other armed Coast Guardsmen. The standoff on the beach left them even more nervous and quarrelsome as they ventured inland on foot. "They're looking for us and it's all your fault, George," Richard Quirin spat. "You should have killed that guy on the beach. Or else the rest of us should have done it."

They caught a train to Manhattan and arrived that morning to find 2.5 million people crowding the streets for the "New York at War" parade. The Nazis wandered amid unwitting onlookers who cheered when 150 merchant mariners, all of whom had survived being torpedoed, passed carrying a banner that read: "AXIS SUBS DON'T SCARE US—WE DELIVER THE GOODS."

The four saboteurs checked into two Manhattan hotels and immediately began spending their cash on luxury goods, fine dining, alcohol, and prostitutes. When Dasch confessed to Ernst Burger (the man Cullen saw dragging the duffle bag) that he wished to turn himself in, Burger broke down in tears and revealed that he was already planning to do so. This was a relief to both men, as the Abwehr had authorized them to kill any teammate who jeopardized the operation. Dasch and Burger agreed to surrender themselves and betray the entire operation to the American authorities.

Before they could do so, the *U-584* landed the second team at Ponte Vedra Beach, Florida on 17 June. These men proved more committed to their mission, and team leader Edward Kerling made it to New York City where he linked up with a friend from the Bund at Pennsylvania Station. On 23 June, the pair traveled to the Rahway, New Jersey address of a man known to them only as "Pastor Krepper." German intelligence had indicated that Krepper could provide safehouses and forged identity documents, but the seditious churchman was not home that day. None of the saboteurs would succeed in linking up with him.

George Dasch took a train to Washington, D.C. on 19 June and went to FBI headquarters, where initial skepticism was dispelled after he opened a briefcase containing $82,350 in cash. He also revealed the invisible ink on his handkerchief. FBI agents who searched Dasch's briefcase were intrigued to find two small metal emblems shaped like hedgehogs: souvenirs from the *U-202*. The ensuing manhunt put all eight German saboteurs in custody by 27 June, and the foiled plot was made public by FBI director J. Edgar Hoover that same day.

A military tribunal handed down a 30-year prison sentence for George Dasch and a life sentence for Ernst Burger, but their cooperation saved their lives. The other six German agents were sentenced to death and went to the electric chair on 8 August 1942. The FBI also opened an investigation on Carl Krepper, the New Jersey pastor

Mugshots of the Operation Pastorius saboteurs. George Dasch is in the top-left corner. (US National Archives)

whose name and address were found in the saboteurs' possession. Boatswain's Mate 2nd Class Jack Cullen was awarded the Legion of Merit, one of the US military's highest decorations, for his "keen presence of mind and discerning judgment in a grave emergency."[18]

The Amagansett incident led to the establishment of a separate, armed Beach Patrol division within the Coast Guard. The "sand pounders" also soon used horses to patrol beaches along the Jersey Shore and elsewhere. Another species of four-legged Americans joined them in August 1942 via the "Dogs for Defense" program, which allowed families to loan their dogs to the military. Canine training began at a Brigantine, New Jersey park before moving across the Delaware River to Philadelphia, Pennsylvania. More than three thousand dogs would eventually serve with the Beach Patrol.[19]

***

Although the *Rio Tercero* sinking garnered relatively little attention at Eastern Sea Frontier, numerous irregularities raise troubling questions about Hans-Heinz Linder's decisions that day. The first is his demonstrably false claim that the *Rio Tercero* bore no neutrality markings. A Coast Guard photo taken a week prior to the attack shows "RIO TERCERO" and "BUENOS AIRES" in large white lettering three times on her port hull. Five Argentine flags are also painted on the same side, and both German and Argentine accounts describe the afternoon's overall visibility as "good."

Even if he somehow did not distinguish the ship's markings from a distance, Linder must have seen them upon approaching close enough to observe that the starboard lifeboats were empty in their davits, as stated in his log. Yet he denied there were any markings at all, writing that "steamer does not even have a flag, additionally no special markings." He repeated this claim in a transmission to BdU: "TODAY A STEAMER PROCEEDING INDEPENDENTLY SUNK. ARGENTINE 'RIO TERCERO', EX 'FORTUNSTELLA' … WITHOUT FLAG AND NEUTRAL MARKINGS."

Linder therefore must have realized the *Rio Tercero*'s identity before she sank. His claim that he only learned this from questioning Capt Scalese seems like a preemptive attempt to defuse this accusation. The act of bringing Scalese aboard (rarely done during World War II) could even have been a charade to convince the merchant captain that the attack was in error, although this is entirely speculation.

Another incongruity stems from the *Rio Tercero*'s log, surrendered by Capt Scalese, which detailed the freighter's voyages since the beginning of 1942. Linder's subsequent transmission to BdU mentioned the ship's "Cyclic traffic New York–Buenos Aires" and listed the five trips, their dates, and ports of departure and arrival. His reason for reporting this information is revealed by the next sentence: "This steamer seems to me to operate clearly in enemy service." Linder seems to be framing his actions as ethical and reasonable, even if not legal.

The incident also presents an even more disturbing question: did Linder intend to massacre the *Rio Tercero* survivors? Captain Scalese and Dr Arambarri were adamant that the Germans were about to riddle the lifeboats with bullets and vividly recounted how four sailors with two machine guns were interrupted by the bomber's nick-of-time appearance. The survivors' elation at their deliverance was also attested by the *U-202*'s log, which mentions the Argentines "all waving enthusiastically" at Second Lieutenant Maxwell's B-25. Regardless of Linder's actual intentions, the Argentine perception of an imminent massacre meant that their terror was very real.

This is unlikely, however, as there is only one confirmed instance of a U-boat shooting survivors during World War II (by contrast, US Navy submarine crews machine-gunned shipwrecked Japanese personnel in multiple instances). When the *U-402* sank USS *Cythera* (PY-26) off North Carolina and took her two surviving crewmen back to France as POWs, the Germans were shocked when one of the Americans asked why they had not been murdered in the water. Even three months after Dönitz's "Laconia Order" emphasized the need to "annihilate" merchant crews, his staff warned officers that "the killing of survivors in lifeboats is inadmissible." As a 1942 manual reassured Allied mariners, "more likely than not, you will find that enemy sailors will give you the same treatment they would expect to receive."

The machine guns seen in the moments preceding the bomber's arrival might have been a defensive measure against just such a threat, and Linder's gifts of shoes and liquor also seem to refute any murderous intent. The *U-202* commander had nonetheless already committed a war crime by deliberately attacking a neutral ship, and it is not out of the question that he intended to erase the evidence by eliminating the witnesses.[20]

The *Rio Tercero* six days before her sinking. (US National Archives)

***

Kapitänleutnant Hans Linder described the B-25's depth charges as "well-placed," but they detonated too shallow to damage the *U-202*. He tempted fate again eight days later when he sank the passenger liner *City of Birmingham* while it was under escort by the destroyer-minesweeper USS *Stansbury* (DMS-8), but the boat escaped with only minor damage from the escort's depth charges. Linder's subsequent return voyage to France saw him refuel at sea from another Kriegsmarine vessel. This was not one of the several German tankers that served as covert resupply ships (contrary to US Navy suspicions, these never operated off North America). In fact, the vessel that refueled the *U-202* was not a surface ship at all.

April 1942 saw the Kriegsmarine deploy the Type XIV "U-tanker." Dubbed "*Milchkühe*," or milk cows, the U-tankers were purpose-built resupply boats one-third larger than a Type IX and lacking torpedo tubes. Their extra space was used for provisions, spare parts, a machine workshop, and a bakery, plus a doctor and other specialists. Most importantly, they carried spare torpedoes and 134,260 gallons of extra diesel fuel. Giving just 10 percent of this fuel more than doubled the duration that a Type IXC could spend in the Caribbean. Ten U-tankers would eventually be launched, and their ability to extend the attack boats' range immediately opened up new hunting grounds.[21]

Dwindling successes along the East Coast led Admiral Dönitz to again seek easier targets, and the war reached the Gulf of Mexico in early May. Within days, U-boats swarming off the Mississippi River delta were sinking three of every four Allied tankers departing Texas and Louisiana ports. Forty-one ships were destroyed in Gulf Sea Frontier waters during May 1942, a tally worse than any single month suffered by Eastern Sea Frontier. The Gulf proved such a bountiful hunting ground that one U-boat, after refueling from the U-tanker *U-459*, detoured from the Caribbean to join the feeding frenzy.

This was the *U-103* under Kapitänleutnant Werner Winter, the same boat and commander that sank the *India Arrow* off New Jersey in February. Also aboard was Oskar-Heinz Kusch, Winter's talented and staunchly anti-Nazi second watch officer. When the *U-103* torpedoed the freighter *Ogontz* on 19 May, a 17-year-old Armed Guard sailor refused to abandon ship "until I get one shot at that sub." The teenage gunner succeeded in firing a single 4-inch/.50 shell (which missed) just before the *Ogontz* capsized, killing him.

The Germans pulled two survivors onto the *U-103*'s deck. The men were greeted by Werner Winter, who was tanned and wearing khaki shorts. He gave them cigarettes and treated a gash on one man's head. "Are you American boys?" Winter asked. "Sorry we had to do this, but this is war."[22]

CHAPTER FOURTEEN

John R. Williams

"As long as the Third Reich wishes to send submarines into the Frontier, some ships
will be sunk, whatever the forces arrayed against them."
—Eastern Sea Frontier War Diary (June 1942)

24 June 1942
Cape May, New Jersey
16:05

A radiant sun glowed over the Delaware Bay entrance less than forty-eight hours
after the survivors of the *Rio Tercero* were rescued. Somewhere overhead, between
the bay and the sun, a solitary airplane hummed through the late afternoon sky.
Newspapers lay ruffled on desks and tables as residents of southern New Jersey and
eastern Delaware went about their daily routines.

"RUSSIANS FALL BACK AT KHARKOV," announced the *New York Times*
while Harrisburg, Pennsylvania's *Evening News* reported the recent Japanese landings
in Alaska with the headline "JAPS ESTABLISH SECOND TOEHOLD ON
ALEUTIANS." The *Philadelphia Inquirer* declared that the "U-BOAT MENACE
MUST BE SMASHED," evoking the 1916 shark attacks by portraying Uncle Sam
fishing as a dorsal fin labeled "The U-boat Shark" cruised past.

Nor was the Alaska invasion the only attack against America's western flank.
Submarines of the Imperial Japanese Navy torpedoed several ships off California
and Hawaii in the weeks following Pearl Harbor. The Japanese submarine *I-17* also
shelled an oil field near Santa Barbara, California on 23 February, sparking panicked
invasion scares along the West Coast, and the *I-25* similarly bombarded an Oregon
military base on 21 June.

But not all the news in June 1942 was so dire. Four of the six Japanese aircraft
carriers that had attacked Pearl Harbor were lured into a trap near Midway Island
on 4 June, and the savage air battle that followed saw US Navy dive bombers
reduce all four flattops to burning hulks. Camden, New Jersey's *Courier-Post*
tempted readers on 22 June with details about "HOW U.S. BLASTED JAP
WARSHIPS IN MIDWAY BATTLE" on the same day that New York City's *Daily*

News boasted that "JAPS ROARED IN, STAGGERED AWAY AT MIDWAY." On this summer afternoon, however, Admiral Karl Dönitz was about to remind Americans on both sides of the Delaware Bay entrance just how near at hand the nation's enemies were.

They heard his latest missive before they saw it. Sound carries long distances over water because the ocean cools the air immediately above it while the sun heats a layer of warmer air above that. Because warm air bends sound waves, sounds originating on the surface do not dissipate upward but are instead reflected down to reverberate out across the water. It was a few minutes past 16:00 on 24 June when the dull thunderclap of an explosion was heard on both Cape Henlopen and Cape May. A few coastal residents looked upward for rainclouds. After six months of war, however, others knew better. They instead looked out across the water separating the two peninsulas.

The droning noise overhead was the Wright Cyclone engine of an O-47 aircraft from the Army's 104th Observation Squadron, which flew antisubmarine patrols out of Atlantic City. Although the lieutenant at the O-47's controls could not hear the blast, he quickly spotted its aftermath. He radioed base as he banked the single-engine plane toward a point 12 miles south-southeast of Cape May, where an ominous plume of smoke was rising from the sea.[1]

***

Admiral Dönitz had long predicted that favorable conditions along the East Coast of the United States would not last indefinitely. "One of these days the situation in the American zone will change," he told Hitler during the naval briefing at the Wolf's Lair on 14 May 1942. "Even at this time, everything points to the fact that the Americans are making strenuous efforts to prevent the large number of sinkings."

That assessment was delicately understated. Three days later, the BdU war diary would report: "Attacking conditions on the north coast of America, from Cape Fear to New York, have been extremely unfavorable since 20 April. Boats lying immediately off the coast and off the main ports report no traffic." Dönitz himself would later write that "the number of ships sailing independently also decreased. There was a general tendency for ships to sail together in batches, with the result that, when one batch had passed, the sea remained empty for a long while." By May 1942, "it was only off the coast of Florida that conditions remained favorable."

Yet Dönitz's optimistic messaging to Hitler instead emphasized the Americans' purported lack of tactical acumen. Patrol vessels along the East Coast "are manned by inexperienced crews and do not constitute a serious threat at present ... [they] are traveling too fast most of the time even to locate the U-boats, or they are not persistent enough in their pursuit with depth charges," he assured the Führer. "In any case, our U-boats, with their greater experience in warfare, are mastering these countermeasures."

Again, the truth was more troubling. "By the end of April ... antisubmarine defense measures in the immediate vicinity of the American coast were becoming more efficient," Dönitz later wrote. "Antisubmarine forces, both at sea and in the air, had been very considerably strengthened." BdU staff observed on 30 April that U-boats near United States shores "are constantly forced underwater by numerous sea and air patrols and have no chance to operate on the surface and charge their batteries."

The Befehlshaber der Unterseeboote was reluctant to concede that events were playing out as he had predicted. "I therefore decided to continue operations in American waters," he later explained, resolving himself to "meeting the changes in the situation ... with appropriate tactical counterstrokes." He had a specific counterstroke in mind: a new operational approach, using a different weapon. Dönitz presented the plan to Hitler during the 14 May meeting at the Wolf's Lair. The Führer voiced no objections.[2]

***

Even if Allied intelligence had been blind to Dönitz's latest gambit, it would not have taken the United States by surprise. As early as January 1942, Eastern Sea Frontier headquarters had recognized the enemy's propensity to "react to the altered conditions with his usual resiliency" and, "whenever his operations were bringing diminishing returns, [to] shift both the method and location of the attack." The Americans also correctly deduced the next method of attack—if not its specific targets—and these suspicions were soon confirmed.

The first corroboration came in April when a US Army intelligence asset in occupied France reported the nature and approximate timing of the new German attack. ESF took the information seriously, noting that the source's "previous predictions had usually been borne out by events." The asset subsequently reported the delivery to Dönitz's flotillas of the exact weapon the Americans suspected would be employed. Another key piece of information originated from a source within the Chilean shipping firm Compañía Sudamericana de Vapores. The source informed US officials that the German ambassador, presumably seeking to avoid a repeat of the *Toltén* incident, had advised Chile of the impending operation and recommended that CSAV ships avoid New York Harbor.

Vice Admiral Adolphus Andrews issued a preliminary warning on 9 June 1942 specifying the nature of the threat and warning that it "may be encountered in Atlantic coastal waters in the near future." Copies of the written advisory were delivered to the post office on 13 June. Once again, however, Admiral Dönitz was one step ahead. By the time Andrews penned his letter, the three U-boats tasked with executing his plan were already en route to the East Coast. Each was armed with a weapon not yet employed on this side of the Atlantic—not during this war, at least.[3]

***

U-boats of the Kaiserliche Marine laid fifty-seven mines along the East Coast during the closing months of World War I in 1918. The mines were deployed in clusters near the entrances of the Chesapeake Bay, Delaware Bay, and New York Harbor. These sank the cruiser USS *San Diego* and five other ships, damaged the battleship USS *Minnesota*, and were still being found months after the war ended. Over a century earlier, during the War of 1812, American forces employed a primitive mine in an attack against HMS *Ramillies* in a Connecticut harbor. The British commander decried this "cruel and unheard-of warfare" and threatened to "order every house near the shore to be destroyed" if such operations continued.

Whether on land or at sea, mines are a primarily psychological weapon. Their second and third-order effects are more valuable than whatever casualties or material damage they inflict, as their actual or suspected presence is enough to restrict movement of enemy assets. A comparatively small volume of ordnance, if carefully deployed, can therefore achieve major operational and strategic effects.

Termed "infernal machines" during the 19th century (and, confusingly, known as "torpedoes" until the 1870s), mines were known in the Kriegsmarine as "roses," "seaman's eggs," and "ocean onions." Regardless of their nomenclature, mines were a means to attack shipping with an economy of force. "Even a few mines laid immediately off the busy entrances to New York (Delaware Bay, Philadelphia, Baltimore, Washington, Norfolk) are likely to lead to success," BdU asserted. "Mine countermeasures are sure to be few." The Germans also intended to divert American naval assets away from the shipping lanes and toward the harbor entrances.

Dönitz had already demonstrated a keen eye for America's strategic pressure points, and the Delaware Capes was near the top of his priorities. Here only 11 miles lay between New Jersey and Delaware, and the shipping lane itself was barely a third of that. Blocking the Capes would immobilize US industrial output at piers in Philadelphia and Wilmington, where it was of no use to the British and Soviets. Additionally, this would exacerbate existing logistical pains. "Production had outstripped transportation," noted *TIME* magazine on 1 June 1942. "At one East Coast port, forty thousand military trucks waited and waited for ships to carry them." Mining harbor entrances could keep them there for longer still.

Although the Kriegsmarine had a few purpose-built minelaying boats (the Type VIID), any attack U-boat could deploy mines from standard torpedo tubes. The minelaying operation was therefore assigned to three Type VII boats: the *U-87* under Joachim Berger, the *U-701* under Horst Degen, and the *U-373* under Paul-Karl Loeser. Each was tasked with mining the entrance of a different East Coast harbor.[4]

The tool for the job was the TMB mine. This was a magnetically fuzed "ground mine," meaning it lay on the seafloor until being triggered by a metallic object passing overhead. Although generally reliable, its overly sensitive magnetic trigger sometimes sank vessels smaller than its intended targets. Maximum destructive effect required the TMB to be laid at a depth of 80 feet or shallower, and the coast offered no shortage of suitable locations. BdU noted a suitably shallow strip,

10–40 miles wide, that spanned much of the seaboard "from Fire Island lightship (E. of New York) to Cape Canaveral." Furthermore, "practically all the large ports … are in this sector of the coast."

Although the bay entrances were conducive to mining, tactical conditions here dramatically increased the operation's risk. In addition to being heavily trafficked and patrolled, shallow depths would leave a minelaying boat badly exposed. "Thirty-six feet of depth is no proposition for a U-boat," *U-701* commander Horst Degen wrote years later. "One could as well have put her in an aquarium for easily catching her." BdU consequently timed the operation to coincide with June's new moon to maximize the darkness available for concealment.

The three U-boats set sail from different French ports. Paul-Karl Loeser's *U-373* departed La Pallice on the night of 18 May, Joachim Berger's *U-87* left Saint-Nazaire the next evening, and Horst Degen's *U-701* sailed from Lorient the night after that. The *U-87* and *U-701* were bound for New York Harbor and the Chesapeake Bay, respectively. Loeser's *U-373*, armed with seven torpedoes and fifteen TMB mines, set course for the Delaware Bay.[5]

***

A TMB mine is loaded onto the *U-373*, May 1942. (Deutsches U-Boot-Museum)

Flowing more than 300 miles from its source in New York's Catskill Mountains, the Delaware River winds south along the New Jersey–Pennsylvania border through what in 1942 was one of America's largest concentrations of industry. The Lehigh Valley on its west bank was home to Bethlehem Steel, one of the nation's premier manufacturers. On its east bank, the New Jersey city of Trenton was a major hub of ordnance and chemical production. Trenton was also where the Continental Army famously defeated a German mercenary force after George Washington led his troops across the river on Christmas Night in 1776.

Farther south, the river passes through Philadelphia, Pennsylvania. The third-largest hub of American war production, the city produced tanks, jeeps, and other heavy equipment. It was also home to the Frankford Arsenal (the military's sole producer of rifle and machine-gun ammunition), and the Philadelphia Naval Shipyard. This shipyard built the battleship USS *New Jersey* and fifty-two other warships. Not far away, William Cramp & Sons Ship and Engine Building Company also launched cruisers, submarines, and merchant ships.

A few miles downriver from Philadelphia lies Chester, Pennsylvania. Here the Sun Shipbuilding and Drydock Company shipyard would expand to twenty-eight slipways, making it the world's largest shipyard by 1945. Two of every five American tankers built during the war were products of "Sun Ship," with most being the new turbine-driven T2 design. In addition to ships, Pennsylvania produced 31 percent of the nation's steel and one-fifth of its total wartime industrial output. The state is nonetheless effectively landlocked, the Delaware River and Bay constituting its only ocean access.

In addition to ships and manufactured goods, the United States would provide 86 percent of the Allies' high-octane aviation gasoline and 80 percent of their overall fuel. Crude oil was shipped from the Caribbean and Gulf of Mexico through the Delaware Capes for processing at sites like Sun Oil's refinery in Marcus Hook, Pennsylvania. Located 4 miles downriver from its subsidiary's Chester shipyard, the Marcus Hook refinery would produce more aviation fuel than any other on earth during the war. Philadelphia also hosted Atlantic Refining Company and Gulf Oil Company facilities, which together achieved a peak output of 2.9 million gallons per day.

Across the river from Philadelphia lies Camden, New Jersey. The Radio Corporation of America produced communication and radar equipment here, but shipbuilding dominated the city's industry. New York Shipbuilding's facility in Camden would become the world's most productive shipyard by war's end. Naval construction along the waterfront was not new, and both USS *Jacob Jones* (DD-130) and her similarly ill-fated predecessor were built here.

South of Philadelphia and Camden, the river reaches the port of Wilmington, Delaware. Here the Hercules Powder Company produced explosives and the Dravo

Corporation shipyard would build fifteen "destroyer escorts," a new warship design intended specifically to fight submarines. Wilmington was also a major point of debarkation for supplies bound for China, Britain, Russia, North Africa, and other far-flung battlefronts.

Past Wilmington, the Delaware River empties into the Delaware Bay, a large estuary enclosed by New Jersey's Cape May to the north and Delaware's Cape Henlopen to the south. Prior to the Cape May Canal's completion in late 1942, the Capes represented the only access to the Atlantic for the factories, refineries, and shipyards lining the Delaware River. Blocking this chokepoint would force cargo to be redirected overland to other, already busy ports and prevent the ships built and repaired in Delaware River shipyards from reaching the sea at all.[6]

BdU was not the first adversary to recognize the Delaware Bay's importance. During the American Revolution, control of the Delaware River and Bay meant control of Philadelphia. Patriot forces accordingly blocked the only direct maritime access to the city by building Fort Mifflin on the river's Pennsylvania side and Fort Mercer on its New Jersey side. A British incursion up the river in 1777 was thwarted when submarine inventor David Bushnell floated explosive kegs downstream at British ships. The "Battle of the Kegs" killed several Royal Navy sailors and forced the fleet to withdraw.

The U-Kreuzers' mining of the Delaware Capes in 1918 further underscored their strategic importance, but it was not until World War II that fixed fortifications were constructed to guard the bay entrance. Congress and the War Department approved an expansion and modernization of American coastal defenses in 1940, and thus Fort Miles was born. This layered network of defenses sprawled across nearly 200 miles of coast and featured reinforced bunkers housing thirty-two heavy guns by 1944, the largest of which could put a 2,100-pound shell into a ship 26 miles away. Supporting the guns was a network of thirteen fire-control towers complemented by powerful searchlights.

The fortifications themselves spanned both Cape Henlopen and Cape May. In New Jersey's southernmost dunes, Fort Miles' Battery 223 was established just a few hundred yards from the Cape May lighthouse. The battery's two 6-inch guns were housed in a T-shaped bunker of reinforced concrete designed to withstand a direct hit from naval guns or aircraft. Cape May would also host the four 90mm guns of Anti-Motor Torpedo Boat Battery Seven.

Two of Fort Miles' observation towers, towers No. 23 and 24, were built on Cape May. Seventeen feet wide and supported by creosoted beams buried deep in the sand, the towers served as Battery 223's eyes and ears. Tower No. 23 was located at Sunset Beach, on Cape May's western shore, while tower No. 24 faced the Atlantic 3 miles up the beach from the guns.

Fort Miles' guns were manned by the 261st Coast Artillery Regiment; the unit's soldiers mostly hailed from Delaware. Some artillerymen on Cape May were lodged at the Saint-Mary-by-the-Sea convent at 101 Lehigh Avenue until permanent barracks were completed, while others occupied tents. "Boy, it was cold in those tents. I'll never forget that," veteran Hank Branagan would recall. Manning the guns twenty-four hours a day was also tedious. "Sometimes the commander would come back from town drunk and pull the alert signal," Branagan recounted. "I think he was trying to keep us on our toes."

Neither Battery 223 nor Anti-Motor Torpedo Boat Battery 7 would be operational until 1943. Few of Fort Miles' heavy guns, in fact, were yet in service in June 1942. The only operational Cape May defenses were four towed 155mm guns located on the site that Battery 223's bunker would soon occupy. Traversing emplacements for the 155mm guns called "Panama mounts" were complete by 15 June.[7]

Not all of Fort Miles' defenses were on land. Spanning 8,000 yards across the bottom of the shipping channel at the Delaware Bay's entrance were two belts of defensive mines. Numbering 455 in total, they were wired for command detonation from shore to allow routine traffic to pass safely over them. The mines were intended as the last line of defense against an enemy fleet attempting to break into the bay.

Foremost in the imaginations of Fort Miles' planners were the German battleships *Bismarck* and *Tirpitz*. The fortifications represented the primary line of defense if these giants attempted to bombard the Philadelphia Naval Shipyard and its nearby oil refineries. Military planners' worst-case scenario saw the battleships spearheading an invasion fleet, as the Delaware Bay offered an enemy landing force a short route to Washington, D.C. Although far-fetched to modern imaginations, and recognized as highly unlikely even in 1940, the prospect of invasion was less outlandish than it may seem.

Documents uncovered by historian Holger Herwig in 1970 would reveal that Kaiser Wilhelm II's German Empire had toyed with plans for an invasion of the United States. Proposed landing sites for German troops included Manhattan, Long Island, Cape Cod, and the Chesapeake Bay. Some plans utilized Cuba or Puerto Rico as a springboard. In 1900, the German naval attaché in Washington, D.C. recommended "a ruthless and merciless attack against the trade and industrial centers" of New York, New Jersey, and Pennsylvania. "Here is the heart of America," another officer concurred, "and here the United States can be attacked and forced into peace the easiest." World War I had shelved these fantastical schemes, but they remained a subject of interest to officers like Karl Dönitz, who studied them during the interwar years.[8]

***

A foreshadowing of the impending chaos occurred on 11 June 1942, just as Dönitz's three minelaying U-boats were beginning their operations along the coast. The Esso tanker *F.W. Abrams* strayed off course in rough weather southwest of Cape Hatteras and triggered an American mine. The captain, believing he was under attack, attempted to beach his ship. In doing so, he steered further into the American minefield and set off two more mines. There were no fatalities, but the crippled *F.W. Abrams* fully sank a few days later.

Dönitz's mines claimed their first victims off Virginia Beach four days later. On the afternoon of 15 June, coastal convoy KN 109 was approaching the Chesapeake Bay from the south when it unknowingly entered the minefield sown by Horst Degen's *U-701* three days earlier. The first mine holed the tanker *Robert C. Tuttle*, causing chaos to sweep the rest of the convoy. The tanker *Esso Augusta* broke formation and triggered a second German mine, leaving her damaged but afloat, and the escorting destroyer USS *Bainbridge* (DD-246) depth-charged a sonar contact which inadvertently set off a third mine.

As beachgoers watched Coast Guardsmen bring ashore the body of the *Robert C. Tuttle*'s assistant engineer, three more ships were approaching the Chesapeake Bay from the south. The tugboat *Warbler*, escorted by the British armed trawler HMS *Kingston Ceylonite*, was towing a freighter torpedoed the previous month. A warning arrived too late to prevent one of Degen's mines from detonating under the *Kingston Ceylonite*, shattering the trawler and killing eighteen of thirty-two Royal Navy sailors aboard.

And still failures continued to accrue. ESF dispatched minesweepers the next morning to clear the area around buoy 2CB, which marked the Chesapeake Bay channel entrance, but the collier *Santore* was sunk the following morning by another of Degen's mines. It was later discovered that the minesweepers failed to clear east and northeast of the buoy.

Once again, the U-boats had America playing defense. Three ships were sunk, one damaged, and twenty-two lives lost. Minesweeping and traffic redirection also restricted movement in and out of the Chesapeake Bay, including the major US Navy base at Norfolk, Virginia. Eastern Sea Frontier admitted that "from the German point of view, this had been a highly successful venture at relatively cheap cost."[9]

***

10 June 1942
43 miles east-southeast of Cape May, New Jersey
21:08

Oberleutnant Paul-Karl Loeser made a final pass through the *U-373* to verify that the scuttling charges were set and the Enigma machine disassembled, with its four encoding rotors hidden throughout the boat. Tonight's stakes were too high to leave anything to chance. The U-boat had spent the preceding hours on the seafloor at the doorstep of the United States, and now Loeser was about to venture, on the surface, toward one of its most heavily defended harbors.

Loeser re-entered the control room. "Periscope depth," the 27-year-old kommandant ordered. Compressed air hissed as it partially purged the ballast tanks and lifted the *U-373* off the muddy seabed. The chief engineer eased the *U-373* upward until it was slowly trolling at a depth of 44 feet as the diesel room crew made one engine ready to cruise and prepared the other to blow the tanks after surfacing. In the control room, Loeser hung his hands from the sky periscope's handles and slowly rotated his view of the world above.

Loeser broke the silence moments later. "Stand by to surface," he announced, retracting the periscope. "Boat ready to surface," the chief engineer reported. "Bring us up, *L.I.*, both ahead slow." There was no need to expend valuable compressed air by blowing the tanks since the boat could be steered upward using the dive planes. "Forward up ten, aft up five," the chief engineer instructed. His voice counted off the depth as Loeser ascended the tower ladder. "Eleven meters, ten, nine … *Turmluk ist frei, Boot ist raus*. Equalize pressure." The commander whirled the tower hatch's locking wheel and heaved it upward. "Tower hatch open," he reported.

Loeser emerged on the bridge alone as the lookouts waited just below on the ladder. The *U-373* remained on electric power in case a crash-dive was required. The captain's voice sounded again: "Bridge watch up." Lookouts scrambled up the ladder as the diesel engines thundered to life. The air intake was deliberately left closed, causing the engines to pull a cool and refreshing breeze through the open hatch that purged the stale miasma which had accumulated during their long hours on the seabed.

The crew savored the fresh air below as Oberleutnant Loeser took stock of the warm summer night. A sullen shroud of fog hung across a silent and calm sea while a slight northeasterly breeze gently rolled its placid surface. The clear sky lacked a betraying moon, leaving the *U-373* cloaked in darkness.

A close friend of *U-202* commander Hans-Heinz Linder, Paul-Karl Loeser's first three patrols as a U-boat commander had totaled seventy-three days at sea without a single success. Finally, his fourth patrol sank the Greek freighter *Mount Lycabettus* 363 miles southeast of Nova Scotia and the British *Thursobank* 323 miles off Delaware. Loeser also held a personal appreciation for what mines were capable of. Two months after he was transferred off the *U-40*, a British mine sunk the boat and killed all but three of its 48-man crew.[10]

The *U-373* had enjoyed an uneventful voyage from La Pallice. On 31 May, the bridge watch spotted a submarine which an exchange of recognition signals revealed as Horst Degen's *U-701*. The U-boats pulled abreast and Loeser and Degen conversed briefly via shouting before parting ways. A transmission from BdU on the afternoon of 8 June stated: "BERGER, DEGEN, LOESER: EXECUTE TASK AT EARLIEST ON NIGHT OF 11 JUNE, FURTHER DETAILS TO FOLLOW ON 9 JUNE." A shorter follow-up message was received the following day: "COMPLETE TASK AS SOON AS SITUATION IS FAVORABLE. NO FURTHER RESTRICTIONS."

Loeser's orders did not require entering the Delaware Bay itself, which was prohibitively shallow and blocked by antisubmarine nets. Shoals and shallows on the New Jersey side of the bay entrance force traffic to pass farther south, near Cape

Henlopen, where depths run between 50 and 150 feet. Merchant ships and naval vessels therefore entered and exited the Delaware Bay via a channel measuring only about 3 miles across.

The target area lay astride the shipping lane and measured 5.6 miles by 4.8 miles. Designated "Overfalls Place" by BdU due to nearby Overfalls Shoal, the zone's top-right corner lay 9 miles southwest of Cape May and its bottom-left corner was five miles east of Dewey Beach, Delaware. BdU ordered Overfalls Place to be "extensively fouled with mines" at depths between 49 and 72 feet and at least 1,100 yards apart.

Loeser's priority was to confirm that he had, in fact, reached Overfalls Place. The U-373 crept slowly forward through the fog as its crew took depth soundings and the circular direction-finder antenna on the bridge picked up a signal from the Overfalls radio transmitter that merchant ships used for navigation. Both the depth and beacon fix told him that the boat was precisely where it needed to be.

"I think we've found our spot, Otto," Loeser declared to Oberleutnant Otto-Ulrich Blum, his first watch officer, who stood beside him on the bridge. The two were equal in rank, though Loeser wielded a commander's authority. "This fog could make things thorny," Blum observed. "Nothing says we can't wait another day." Loeser frowned in contemplation. Blum's caution was not unreasonable because the fog increased the risk of stumbling across an American surface patrol, but another twenty-four hours might not yield any improvement.

Each passing moment brought Paul Loeser closer to American soil than he had ever been. During his first American patrol in March, he had passed flashing red beacons beckoning fishermen into Absecon Inlet at Atlantic City. He soon also sighted a searchlight marking the Delaware Bay entrance, but changed course to the east shortly thereafter. Fog or not, Loeser resolved that there would be no turning back this time. He justified his decision in the boat's log: "In the belief that a more favorable opportunity will not arise, I decide to deploy."[11]

Loeser changed course slightly to aim the U-373 toward the western end of Overfalls Place. Down in the forward torpedo room, sailors flooded the tubes and released the locking bolt that secured the first of the three mines in tube one. At 22:41, Loeser began scattering his "roses" 4.5 miles east of Rehoboth Beach. A jolt of compressed air ejected the first TMB mine, which landed quietly on the muddy seabed 48 feet below as the U-373 turned sharply to port. The boat proceeded half a mile southeast before dropping the next mine.

Just as the second mine left the tube, a lookout spotted a blinking light through the fog. Loeser sighted a one-second flash, then a four-second pause, followed by another flash. He exuberantly slapped Blum's arm in vindication. "Na, schau mal einer an!" Loeser exclaimed with satisfaction. Would you look at that! "Buoy 1HC." They were in exactly the correct spot.

The U-373 dropped its third mine less than a mile after the second. Having now left three "ocean onions" in a southeasterly row, Loeser ordered a 90-degree turn and dropped his fourth. Maintaining a speed of 10 knots, the U-boat deposited mines at intervals of 1,000–2,800 yards in a northeasterly zigzag pattern.

The TMB mine was a 7.5-foot-long cylinder with rounded ends weighing 1,631 pounds and carrying an explosive charge nearly twice the size of a torpedo's. Ejecting each mine released a spring-loaded safety bar from the top of its aluminum casing, which unlocked the booster charge release mechanism and the spindle of a hydrostatic clock. As the mines sank, increasing water pressure seated the booster charge over the detonator and activated a 60-hour arming delay. The mines would remain inert until this expired to frustrate minesweeping operations and allow the device to settle into the seabed. After sixty hours, the arming cycle would prime the TMB for detonation by the first metallic object passing overhead.

The mines were released at depths of 47–72 feet. No current was running, enabling each TMB's stabilizing fins to steer it downward to precisely its intended location. The entire undertaking took seventy-two minutes. After discharging the last mine at 00:53, Loeser sought to put distance between himself and the coast to reload his now-empty tubes with torpedoes. The *U-373* turned southeast at 16 knots, leaving fifteen countdown timers ticking at the bottom of the channel.[12]

***

Following his 9 June warning of imminent minelaying, Vice Admiral Andrews penned a formal advisory to ESF's subordinate commands. The letter revealed that "recent information indicates that enemy submarines before proceeding to the US are loading mines," and directed that "every possible effort should be made to sweep the approaches to our principal harbors and to make exploratory sweeps of our coastal sea lanes." At 10:41 on the same day that the letters were delivered to a New York City post office, the first of Paul Loeser's mines armed itself on the bottom of the shipping channel.

What the Germans did not know, however, is that heavy guns and remote-detonated minefields were not the Delaware Capes' only defenses. Two unseen tripwires also guarded the bay entrance. One comprised three JM-4 sonobuoys anchored to the seafloor that listened for intruders, and the other was a pair of cables made from rubber-coated lead, steel, and copper which spanned the seabed beneath the channel. A steel hull passing above these magnetic "indicator loops" generated an electric current received by a galvanometer ashore.

Loeser's surreptitious stopover took the *U-373* dangerously close to the sonobuoys and directly over one of the indicator loops, immediately betraying his presence to American forces. Citing "strong reason to believe sub activity in vicinity of Delaware Capes," Eastern Sea Frontier closed the bay entrance shipping traffic. Eastern Defense Command's Philadelphia/New York sector went to heightened alert while Fourth Naval District began intensively scouring the bay entrance between McCrie Shoal and Overfalls Shoal.

Navy minesweepers clearing a channel for shipping located several of the *U-373*'s mines. Two minesweepers each located and safely exploded a German mine on the afternoon of 17 June, and a third was neutralized the following day. A fourth would be revealed in six days' time, but this "rose" would not be found by a minesweeper.[13]

***

Operated by Moran Towing Company, the *John R. Williams* was a steam-powered tugboat contracted by the Navy for salvage and rescue work. She was an unremarkable vessel measuring 137 feet long and just 396 gross registered tons. The *John R. Williams* was crewed by eighteen men under Captain Leroy Allen, who had worked his way up from deckhand over many years. The tug had been gainfully employed for the past six months due to countless torpedo-damaged ships and lifeboats requiring towing, not to mention collisions and groundings caused by navigating without lights.

Another such mishap transpired on 24 June 1942 when a merchant convoy, fearing they had entered the *U-373*'s minefield, scattered near Fenwick Island Shoal off southern Delaware. This caused the British freighters *Fort Binger* (recently repaired after a gun battle with Victor Vogel's *U-588* in the Gulf of Maine) and *Port Darwin* to run aground on the shoal. The convoy proceeded without them as the *John R. Williams* stood out from Cape May at 12:05 to assist.

The ever-valiant *Fort Binger* freed herself from the shoal and continued north under her own power. When the tugboat arrived at 14:40, Captain Allen discovered that the *Port Darwin* had also recovered herself. This scenario was not uncommon; the *John R. Williams* had been dispatched to tow the *Rio Tercero*'s lifeboats two days earlier only to be recalled. By 16:00, the *Port Darwin* was steaming north toward Cape May under escort by the patrol boat USS *YP-334* while the *John R. Williams* followed at 11 knots.

The tugboat was 13 miles south-southeast of Cape May Point when 28-year-old assistant engineer Harold Jorgensen stepped out on deck and took a deep breath of fresh ocean air. He spotted engineering officer William Lacoy, a fellow Staten Island native, sitting on the hawser rack at the stern and chatting with unlicensed crewmen Homer Pendleton and William Balfour. Jorgensen strolled toward them, oblivious to the needle that was beginning to twitch on the seabed just forward of the bow.

The "dip needle" at the center of the TMB mine's detonation mechanism was held horizontal by a set of gimbals and springs and functioned like a compass laid on its side. As the *John R. Williams* passed above the mine, the hull's magnetic field swung the needle's magnetized end until its opposite end touched a metal contact. This closed a circuit that allowed the battery's electric current to reach the detonator.[14]

"Hey Bill," Jorgensen began, "not sure if you saw earlier but—"

Fifty-one feet below the keel, an exothermic chemical reaction instantly converted 1,279 pounds of hexanite into a dense sphere of gas hotter than 5,000° Fahrenheit. Its heat vaporized the nearest water while the expanding shockwave pushed the rest aside, forming a steam void beneath the tugboat. The blast energy was magnified by reflecting off the seabed before hitting the keel at more than 20,000 feet per second, blowing out the bottom of the engine room and instantly killing fourteen men.

The buoyant gas bubble ascended as it attained its largest size, then contracted as the ocean's weight compressed it back to critical pressure. The bubble briefly oscillated, unleashing further pulses of energy before finally yielding to the surrounding water pressure by collapsing from the bottom. Water rushed into the void from below, lifting a pillar of water from the boiling ocean into a summer afternoon. The *John R. Williams* dropped into the steam void as it caved in around her, the sea closing over the mangled tugboat.

Harold Jorgensen heard only a loud ringing noise as he realized that he was no longer aboard the tugboat, but rather looking down on it from above. The blast had launched the four men on the aft deck into the air, but gravity quickly reclaimed both them and the tug. Jorgensen plummeted downward while the *John R. Williams* dropped into the void as it collapsed around her. "She didn't settle and sink," according to William Balfour, "she just disappeared in a flash and there was nothing left of her."

Her four surviving crewmen each plunged into the sea along with pieces of the tugboat. "We went down in the water and I thought I'd never get to the top again, I was so long coming up," one recounted. Jorgensen burst through the water and inhaled sharply. Gagging and spitting oil, he spotted William Balfour nearby. Only an oil slick and scattered debris marked where the *John R. Williams* had been moments earlier.

Sighting a mattress from the crew's quarters bobbing in the water, Jorgensen swam to it and pulled himself onto it. Catching his breath and composing himself, he traded the mattress for the tug's air intake vent which floated nearby. "Hey! … Hey! …" Balfour called. He directed Jorgensen's attention to Homer Pendleton, who had pulled himself onto a liferaft blown clear of the tug. Balfour elected to stay put as Jorgensen let go of his air intake and swam to Pendleton's raft.

The men soon looked upward as a plane from the 104th Observation Squadron flew overhead, the pilot having sighted the column of smoke. They spotted the approaching USS *YP-334* minutes later, and the Navy men brought aboard Jorgensen, Pendleton, and Balfour. The patrol boat then fished a stunned but alive William Lacoy, the engineering officer, from the water. There were no other survivors.

The *YP-334* transported the four survivors to Beebe Hospital in Lewes, Delaware. Less than two hours after the explosion, a fisherman found the bodies of Capt Leroy Allen and able seaman Simeon Cronk. Eastern Sea Frontier concluded that the *John R. Williams* had strayed outside the channel swept through the minefield "either through ignorance or inattention." Coincidentally, the loss occurred less than 2 miles from where a German mine had crippled the tanker *Herbert L. Pratt* in 1918.[15]

***

The Navy quarantined and swept the vicinity of Overfalls Shoal in the aftermath of the *John R. Williams* sinking. A fifth mine was located and safely detonated on 26 June. The ten others were never located, and it is likely they eventually drifted, or "walked," out of the channel. In any event, the mines automatically disarmed themselves sixty days after going live.

The *New York Times* reported the possible destruction of a submarine 3 miles off Barnegat several days after the tugboat's loss. The article suggested that "this may have been the sub that planted the mines," yet this was wishful thinking. Paul-Karl Loeser sank no further ships, but Dönitz credited him with a "well executed" patrol following his return to France on 8 July.

The *John R. Williams* was the sole victim of the *U-373*'s minefield, and the *U-87* had even less success. News that a neutral ship carrying Axis diplomats was pending departure from New York Harbor caused BdU to change the *U-87*'s target zone to Boston, with a 25-mile strip of New Jersey's coastline as the secondary zone. On the night of 11/12 June, the *U-87* laid four TMC mines (a more powerful version of the TMB) in Boston Harbor's North Channel and two more in the South Channel. These sank no ships, and the US Navy found one near Stellwagen Bank ten days later.[16]

Only the mines laid off Virginia Beach by Horst Degen's *U-701* achieved significant success. After sowing the mines, the *U-701* torpedoed three merchant ships and ambushed the patrol boat USS *YP-389* southeast of Cape Hatteras on the night of 19 June. This initiated a running gun battle in which the US Navy crew valiantly returned fire and dropped depth charges in their wake as they retreated, but the Germans' 88mm and 20mm fire blasted the patrol boat to pieces. Six of her twenty-four crewmen were killed.

Degen's success ended off North Carolina on the afternoon of 7 July when Second Lieutenant Harry Kane of the US Army's 396th Bomb Squadron spotted the telltale narrow wake of a submarine from his A-29 Hudson bomber. Pouncing at 220 mph, he released three depth charges seconds after the *U-701* submerged in water clear enough that Kane could still see the boat when his ordnance splashed. Two depth charges straddled the *U-701*, and its compartments began flooding as the U-boat came to rest on the seafloor.

The *U-701* crewmen donned Dräger-made *Tauchretter* devices. This combination rebreather/inflatable lifejacket was worn when abandoning ship on the surface because it prevented water inhalation in heavy seas, but Degen's crew utilized the Dräger device for its primary intended purpose of escaping a sunken submarine. At least eighteen Germans made it to the surface, but only the *U-701*'s commander and six other badly sunburned and delirious men remained alive when a Coast Guard seaplane recovered them more than forty-eight hours later. When Second Lieutenant Kane visited Horst Degen in the hospital, the *U-701* commander greeted him in English: "Congratulations, good attack."

The thirty-six mines laid in June 1942 sank only three ships and damaged three more. "It is fortunate for us that the Germans chose an initial operation of relatively small scale," ESF concluded, while conceding that the mines "did achieve success out of all proportion to the effort expended." Yet the mines failed to significantly impede traffic at any of the three harbor entrances, and the attempt had cost BdU a U-boat and its crew.

The minelaying also taught the Americans valuable lessons at a relatively low cost. "[The Germans] have, in the long-term view, succeeded only in placing us on our guard against any future and more elaborate mine laying projects," ESF staff wrote. Mines that later appeared off Charleston, Jacksonville, and the mouth of the Mississippi River failed to achieve even fleeting success, but not all German minelaying operations in the Americas were so bloodless. A minefield sown by the *U-214* off the Panama Canal's eastern end likely sank the Gato-class submarine USS *Dorado* (SS-248) in October 1943. All 77 US Navy personnel aboard were killed.[17]

***

"Our submarines are operating close inshore along the coast of the United States," Admiral Dönitz gloated during an interview by the *Völkischer Beobachter* on 4 August 1942. "Bathers, and sometimes entire coastal cities, are witnesses to ... the red glorioles of blazing tankers." His boasting was not yet hollow. With his fleet's reach extended by the U-tankers, operations intensified in the Caribbean and Gulf of Mexico. Corpses and burning hulks littered Gulf shores as June 1942 became the Battle of the Atlantic's deadliest month to date. During that same month, a 7-mile stretch of beach south of Asbury Park, New Jersey became marred with so much oil that the state government requested federal assistance to clean it.

However, the schwerpunkt of Dönitz's offensive was only shifting south because the once-rich East Coast hunting grounds were now barren. ESF's April losses totaled twenty-five ships, but this plummeted to eight in May. Fifteen went down in June, then just four in July. Despite sixteen U-boats patrolling within 100 nautical miles of the United States in June 1942, the "Great American Turkey Shoot" was quickly winding down.

By summer's end, a fully resourced and interlocking convoy system linked all major ports between Florida and Nova Scotia. It concurrently expanded south. The Caribbean would remain perilous for some time, but convoys halted the devastation off Texas and Louisiana by September. That same month, New York City began to supplant Halifax as the primary jumping-off point for transatlantic convoys. Eastern Sea Frontier's war diary described America's coastal shipping lanes as "a single link in the great chain binding together the US and our allies" and, by August, that link was cast in steel.[18]

Events in North Africa soon demonstrated this chain's importance. Italian merchant ships had enabled a German victory here in January 1942, but it was Allied merchantmen that tipped the scales in July and August. Churchill's plea to FDR for "all the Sherman tanks you can spare" resulted in tanks being rushed from northern New Jersey to Brooklyn, then hurriedly loaded onto seven merchant ships.

Six survived the sprint across the Atlantic and around the Horn of Africa to Egypt where they offloaded 300 tanks, 100 howitzers, and 13,000 tons of ammunition. Re-armed British Commonwealth forces then checked Rommel's advance toward the Suez Canal at the decisive Second Battle of El Alamein.[19]

During the summer of 1942 and beyond, peril still abounded off North American shores—but now for the U-boats. The *U-402* limped home after being damaged in an air attack off North Carolina on 14 July, but the fates of less fortunate crews were communicated only by cold silence: the *U-215* was off Boston when its radio transmissions abruptly ceased on 3 July, the *U-701* fell silent four days later, then the *U-576* stopped reporting in the week after that. Finally, on 19 July 1942, BdU withdrew the last U-boats from East Coast waters.

In a radio broadcast to eight days later, Dönitz cautioned his countrymen against "exaggerated hopes" in light of the "harsh realities of the U-boat war." His reedy voice lacked its usual optimism, and his tone evoked the sober assessments that his enemies had expressed behind closed doors at Eastern Sea Frontier six months earlier. Dönitz warned the German people that "more difficult times lay ahead of us."

***

TIME magazine declared that summer that "the U.S. had been licked all along its Eastern seaboard," and the butcher's bill was staggering. U-boats had destroyed 194 merchant ships and six naval vessels within 400 nautical miles of the United States between January and August 1942. Forty-two additional ships were damaged. These attacks killed 2,688 merchant mariners, 416 US servicemen, 176 servicemen from other Allied nations, and 146 civilian passengers. Ensign Ellis Sard described cruising through the aftermath along the East Coast in January 1943. "We passed our first wreck, then another, then another," Sard wrote. "The masts of the wrecks poked above water … it was quiet and sad, and a little spooky."

The "Second Happy Time" also left wounds on the still-nascent American war machine; Samuel Elliot Morrison asserted that the U-boat offensive was "as much a national disaster as if saboteurs had destroyed half a dozen of our biggest war plants." One in four US Merchant Marine tankers were now on the seafloor, and Britain's volume of imports (50 million tons in 1939) would fall to just 23 million tons by December. But it was over, and U-boats would make only sporadic and ineffectual incursions into American waters after the summer of 1942. The Battle of the Atlantic, however, was far from finished.[20]

The late summer and autumn of 1942 saw Admiral Dönitz redeploy his forces to the north-central Atlantic, where the air gap still left convoys beyond the range of Allied aircraft. This could have been mitigated by the US Navy's available "Very Long Range" variants of the B-24 Liberator bomber, but Admiral Ernest King would delay this until April 1943. Worse yet, the four-rotor Enigma cipher instituted in February remained unbroken in late 1942. Codebreaking is also a two-player game.

Germany cracked both the Allied Merchant Ships Code and Naval Cipher No. 3 by mid-1942, and losses surged as wolfpacks intercepted one in every three convoys bound for the British Isles.

The Ubootwaffe set another record in November 1942 by sinking 112 merchant vessels in addition to five troopships, two destroyers, and an escort aircraft carrier. Merchant shipping destroyed in November totaled 684,723 tons, putting Dönitz within striking distance of his 700,000-ton monthly goal. Sinkings in the Atlantic were compounded by those in the Mediterranean and elsewhere. U-boats and Luftwaffe aircraft decimated convoy PQ 17 in the Arctic Ocean during July 1942, and only eleven of its thirty-five ships reached Soviet ports. Ultra-long-range Type IXD2 boats began stalking the Indian Ocean in November.

The rise of a new figure within the Nazi inner circle also enabled German shipyards to launch more U-boats at a faster pace. Hitler had appointed 37-year-old Albert Speer as minister of armaments and war production in February 1942, and his organizational talents soon achieved considerable success. Speer also forged an effective partnership with Admiral Dönitz. The Reich was launching approximately twenty-five U-boats per month by August 1942, bringing the admiral's long-sought fleet of three hundred boats closer to reality. With both sides feeding ever more steel and blood into the Atlantic as 1943 approached, the stage was set for the U-boat war's fiery climax.[21]

CHAPTER FIFTEEN

Pan Pennsylvania

"Only later, with experience and maturity, did we learn that one who saves lives is as
heroic as one who kills the enemy."
—*Maschinenobergefreiter* Hans Goebeler, *Steel Boat, Iron Hearts* (1999)

9 March 1944
476 miles southeast of Reykjavík, Iceland
20:08

"Scotch, Scotch. This is Virgil. Come back, Scotch."

Once again, there was no reply to the transmission. On the flying bridge of the destroyer escort USS *Joyce* (DE-317), Lieutenant Commander Robert Wilcox lowered his binoculars and glanced at his radioman. "Still nothing, sir," the enlisted Coast Guardsman reported. Wilcox looked out again across the choppy sea as clouds passing over the moon intermittently revealed the angst painted across his face. *Goddammit, Ken, where are you?* Echoing between his ears was the last voice transmission from his friend and colleague, Lieutenant Commander Kenneth Phillips: "This looks like the real thing."

Ken Phillips, commander of USS *Leopold* (DE-319), had excitedly spoken those words over the radio only minutes earlier. Seconds later, a light had appeared 6,000 yards ahead of the *Joyce* as the *Leopold* launched a pair of star shells to illuminate her surroundings. They bloomed with a flickering luminescence that tore a hole in the night, and the shooting started immediately. LCDR Wilcox and his crew heard the *Leopold*'s guns booming in the distance as points of light marked tracer shells zipping across the wavetops.

Then it all stopped. USS *Joyce* was racing toward the fray at flank speed when the *Leopold*'s gunfire ceased as abruptly as it had begun. The star shells' parachutes eased them down into the frigid sea, yielding the sky again to darkness. The *Joyce* repeatedly attempted to contact the *Leopold* using the "Talk Between Ships" (TBS) system, a VHF radiotelephone for short-range voice communication, but her hails had gone unanswered.

Wilcox now ordered a visual message flashed to the *Leopold* via signal light. Lamp shutters clattered as Morse code was strobed across the foreboding sea, yet no reply winked back through the inky night. The Task Group 21.5 commander, who had overheard Wilcox's unanswered hails over the TBS, now also attempted to raise the *Leopold*. "Scotch, Scotch. This is Virgil," the voice from USS *Poole* announced. "Come back, Scotch." The only response was hissing static.

"Sir, radar says the *Leopold*'s slowed to six knots." Wilcox frowned. *Why would Ken slow down? And why did he stop shooting?* He felt dread taking root in the pit of his stomach. Something was very wrong.

Still unable to see the *Leopold* through his binoculars, Wilcox demanded an update from his antisubmarine officer, Lieutenant (Junior Grade) John Bender. The younger officer informed the commander that his section still heard nothing on the hydrophone, not even the *Leopold*'s screws. Moments later, however, Wilcox's worst fears were confirmed when LTJG Bender's sound hut reported that the hydrophone operator could now hear an unsettling dirge of groaning and squeaking noises.

Someone on the flying bridge took the Lord's name in vain when USS *Leopold* finally came into view at 20:15. The *Joyce*'s sister was dead in the water and jackknifed, her fantail elevated above the horizon. A blast hole amidships stretched from the waterline to the main deck, and her bow was canted to starboard at an angle suggesting the violence with which her back had been broken. The gruesome tableau was the most sickening thing Bob Wilcox had ever seen.

He heard whistles and shouts from the *Leopold* survivors as they came into view. Figures waved from the maimed warship's decks while others were huddled on rafts and in lifeboats, their wraithlike forms appearing small and indistinguishable in the moonlight. Many were afloat by their lifejackets as the Atlantic battered them and its deathly cold drained the life from their bodies.

LCDR Wilcox's heart was beating against his ribs and his mouth felt dry. Words escaped him, and he took a sharp and shuddering breath before finding his voice again. He knew that whoever hit the *Leopold* could have the *Joyce* lined up at that very moment. Stopping to rescue the survivors may well mean joining them. Yet Bob Wilcox was a Coast Guardsman: saving lives was his vocation.

"Advise Virgil of the situation," Wilcox ordered his radioman. "Flash priority, immediate assistance requested." The *Joyce* was zigzagging toward the survivors when LTJG Bender suddenly shouted through the voice pipe. "Sound contact, bearing two-eight-zero!" Bender's hydrophone operator switched on the speaker, and a sinister mechanical growl filled the air. It sounded quite different from the whine of a G7e which Wilcox had heard in training, yet the mechanical palpitation of a torpedo propeller was unambiguous. *Some new weapon?* Bender added in rapid-fire: "Whatever it is, it's headed right at us."

"I have the conn," Wilcox declared, taking direct command of steering. Faced with the most agonizing decision of his life, Wilcox ordered the engines to flank speed and the rudder hard over. USS *Joyce* veered away from the *Leopold*'s desperate survivors, the sharp turn leaning his ship to port as Wilcox aimed a megaphone at the men in the water:

"We are dodging torpedoes! God bless you, we'll be back!"[1]

***

17 March 1944
490 miles south-southeast of Cape Farewell, Greenland

Nineteen months after Germany abandoned its East Coast U-boat offensive, Kapitänleutnant Klaus Hänert was seated in the *U-550*'s wardroom watching ersatz coffee slosh in the porcelain mug in his right hand. The fingers of his left hand were pensively rubbing the tawny stubble marking him as a rare specimen who shaved while on patrol. The tepid coffee mirrored the waves which had rolled the *U-550* unceasingly since commencing weather reporting duty two weeks earlier. This entailed taking barometric measurements from the bridge every few hours, and sea conditions had been altogether unpleasant. Even listening to music was difficult because heavy seas kept knocking the needle out of its groove.

Klaus Hänert grew up in the German coastal city of Flensburg, where he spent his youth sailing and swimming long distances in the Baltic Sea. After graduating from Mürwik, where his father taught engineering, he earned a stellar reputation on two destroyers and Admiral Raeder's staff. He joined the Ubootwaffe in January 1942 and served aboard the *U-68* in the Caribbean and South Atlantic before being selected to command the *U-550*. One of four children, the war years had claimed both of his brothers.[2]

Hänert completed U-boat commander school in May 1943, the same month that marked both the climax and the irreversible turning point of the U-boat war. A series of convoy battles during the first four months of 1943 culminated in the first week of May when convoy ONS 5 was swarmed by fifty-seven U-boats from four wolfpacks. The outnumbered escorts, however, held the wolves at bay for seven consecutive days and nights. Seven U-boats were sunk in exchange for just thirteen merchant ships.

The wolfpacks' failure to destroy ONS 5, which marked the Battle of the Atlantic's long-awaited turning point, also coincided with the first week of "Black May." Germany lost forty-four U-boats that month, a staggering figure that left even Hitler aghast. "This can't go on!" the Führer interjected during a meeting with Dönitz on 14 May 1943. Among the 1,834 German fatalities of Black May was the admiral's son, Leutnant Peter Dönitz, killed when the *U-954* went down with all hands on 19 May.

By 1943, Allied technological superiority left the U-boats nowhere to hide. Improved and expanded radar capability, including radar-equipped aircraft that seemed to lurk behind every cloud, forced them to stay submerged as long as possible. Every radio transmission risked triangulation by high-frequency direction finding equipment. Radar and HF/DF jointly represented checkmate for the wolfpacks,

Klaus Hänert as a midshipman (left) and Kriegsmarine officer (right). (Courtesy of Wolf Hänert)

which relied on radio communication and surface travel. As Dönitz bluntly informed Hitler during Black May, "The enemy's new location devices are, for the first time, making U-boat warfare impossible."

The truth was even worse than Dönitz knew. Although adding a fourth rotor to the Enigma machine had locked out Allied cryptographers in February 1942, they again broke the code ten months later. Deciphered Enigma transmissions enabled the Allies to route convoys around danger while vectoring "hunter-killer groups" which hunted down and destroyed U-boats one by one. Each hunter-killer group comprised multiple destroyers or destroyer escorts and one escort aircraft carrier. Built by adding a flight deck atop a merchant ship hull, these "Jeep carriers," or "baby flattops" could bring American and British air power anywhere U-boats operated.[3]

Dönitz's tonnage strategy had also failed. In September 1942, Hitler dismissed the prospect that American shipbuilding "comes anywhere near what propaganda would have us believe," but it did, and ship construction finally outpaced losses by the end of that year. The Ubootwaffe sank a monthly average of 474,357 tons of shipping in 1942, but revised German calculations indicated the need to destroy at least 1.3 million tons per month in 1943. The first four months of 1943, however, averaged only 353,653 tons.

It simply was not enough. The Allies were building approximately one million tons of shipping per month by mid-1943. Most construction occurred in the United

States, where 158 vessels were launched in July of that year alone. All tonnage sunk since 1939 had been replaced by December 1943 and, by 1944, the United States was launching an average of one ship every six hours. "The capacity of American shipyards was totally underestimated," U-boat commander Peter Cremer wrote after the war. "They built them faster than we could sink."

German losses during Black May were so steep that Dönitz withdrew his U-boats from the Atlantic for the duration of the summer to outfit them with radar detectors, homing torpedoes, and other new technologies. He also conducted a secret referendum in which U-boat personnel overwhelmingly voted to continue the campaign. Bitter tides resumed upon their return in September 1943, with sixty-three more U-boats destroyed by year's end, then an additional fourteen failed to return in January 1944. When the *U-550* left port on 6 February 1944 for Klaus Hänert's first patrol as commander, he knew that the odds stood decidedly against he and his crew ever stepping foot ashore again.[4]

Replacing these losses also skewed the crews younger. "The chiefs of staff must know why they are sending out such children on the U-boats," Kriegsmarine correspondent Lothar-Günther Buchheim cynically opined. "At that age, they don't yet have anything to lose. A boy knows nothing of love, knows not what it is to die." Although Hänert's moniker of the "Old Man" was a traditional term of respect for a U-boat kommandant, his 26 years of age also made him the *U-550*'s third-oldest crewman.

Black May was one of several German catastrophes in 1943. The loss of the entire Sixth Army at Stalingrad in February was followed by the Afrika Korps' capitulation in May. The Red Army then defeated the Wehrmacht in July at the Battle of Kursk, history's largest tank-versus-tank engagement. The millions slain fighting the Soviets in the east included Knight's Cross recipient Karl Hänert, Klaus' brother. Feeding the bulk of Germany's combat power into the meat grinder of the Eastern Front also primarily left depleted and second-rate units to shoulder the burden of repelling the impending Allied landing in France.

Nor were civilians spared the war's horrors. As Hitler's armies retreated, fleets of American and British bombers were steadily reducing German cities to rubble with round-the-clock bombardments. Hänert had been in Hamburg in July 1943 when Allied firebombing incinerated thirty-seven thousand people along with much of the city, and he returned from the bomb shelter to find his hotel had burned down. Allied bombing would ultimately kill more than 350,000 German civilians. "Almost everyone had family members who had been killed in the bombings," asserted U-boat enlisted veteran Hans Goebeler. "We wanted to avenge ourselves against the gangsters who had brought about their deaths."[5]

Standing just over 6 feet tall and possessing a lean physique, light-brown hair, and blue eyes, the *U-550* kommandant looked like he had stepped out of a propaganda poster. Klaus Hänert was no Nazi, however, being instead cut from the older and more dignified Prussian officer tradition. "Isn't there anyone who will shoot *Herr* Hitler?" Hänert had rhetorically asked close confidants more than once.

The Third Reich's worsening fortunes only hardened the faith of Hitler's most fervent acolytes. Among these was Karl Dönitz, who devolved into a strident Nazi ideologue as the war progressed. Although the extent to which this malignancy had been latent under his earlier veneer of professionalism is unclear, he had revealed himself as a true believer by 1943. "In comparison to Hitler, we are all very wretched pipsqueaks," Dönitz declared in August of that year. "Anyone who believes he could do better than the Führer is stupid."

Dönitz's loyalty finally elevated him to Hitler's inner circle in January 1943. The promotion was a consequence of a December 1942 incident in which German warships sortied to attack convoy JW 51B in the Arctic but suffered an embarrassing defeat. An infuriated Hitler subjected Grand Admiral Erich Raeder to a tirade lasting more than an hour, and Raeder subsequently resigned as Kriegsmarine commander-in-chief. Hitler replaced him with Dönitz, whom he promoted to grand admiral and lauded as "a National Socialist through and through … he keeps the Kriegsmarine free of bad influences."

Raeder had attempted to keep the Nazis at arm's length from the Kriegsmarine, but Dönitz conversely declared that "ideological conviction is obligatory … it is utter nonsense to say the soldier or officer must be non-political." The stiff-armed Nazi salute replaced the traditional military one, and new U-boat officers were increasingly better versed in ideology than seamanship. Nor was this entirely forced on the navy by the Party. Nazism also gained traction within the Ubootwaffe as the more traditional pre-war generation of U-boat officers was killed off and younger, more heavily indoctrinated ones ascended the ranks to replace them.

Although the Nazis still disgusted many U-boat officers, they invariably considered this immaterial to their professional obligations. "It was the duty of a military officer to fight," historian Jordan Vause wrote. "Ideological disagreements, even if they seemed irreconcilable, did not excuse insubordination." Some clung to fantasies that Germany could be spared from both the Nazis and the Allies. One oberleutnant hoped for a "negotiated peace" which could "bring National Socialist power to an end … without a wholesale surrender and destruction of Germany." As Vause ultimately concluded, "The charitable view is that the U-boat commander was neither malicious nor doctrinaire, but that he was as ill-informed, as misled, and as self-denying as anyone in Germany."

The U-boat men's loyalty and willingness to fight nonetheless remained unbroken. "We got the feeling that someday we would die together from the Americans and the Russians, but we had given our oath. That's a bad soldier, who forgets he put up his three fingers," Hans Goebeler stated in 1982. "We were all just young boys doing what we saw as our patriotic duty." And it was duty, above all else, that drove Klaus Hänert.[6]

***

Kapitänleutnant Hänert absentmindedly rapped his hand against the white tablecloth as Oberleutnant Gutram von Lingelsheim-Seibicke held court in the wardroom. The *U-550* commander paid little attention to his 22-year-old first watch officer, being instead preoccupied with the message he would soon deliver to his crew. BdU had informed Hänert that the *U-550's* weather reporting duties had concluded. They were finally an attack boat.

Hänert's silent contemplation was interrupted when a dinner of *Kommissbrot* dark bread and canned beef laced with soybean filler was placed in front of him. He looked up to see 20-year-old *Matrosengefreiter* Albert Nitsche, who wore a loose-fitting blue pullover with gray leather trousers. "*Danke schön,*" Hänert thanked him with a smile. "*Sehr gerne, Herr Kaleun,*" Nitsche replied deferentially. The commander's response evidenced the warmth that lay beneath his reserved demeanor.

"How are you doing, Nitsche?"

The events of 22 February remained vivid for all aboard, particularly Nitsche. Sixteen days into their patrol, a Canadian PBY Catalina seaplane south of Iceland spotted the *U-550* on the surface in daylight. The grating alert that sounded was not a ringing bell signaling a crash-dive, but rather a siren heralding a fight. The gun crews rushed to their stations as Oberleutnant Lingelsheim-Seibicke swerved the *U-550* to port, aiming the stern at the enemy plane to provide the gunners a clear line of sight.

The seaplane dropped from 3,000 feet as it bore down on the U-boat's starboard quarter. Albert Nitsche pressed his body into the 37mm's shoulder stirrups and began firing. The double 20mm guns behind him thundered with even greater fury, the four barrels each spitting three shells per second. Dark puffs of flak bloomed in the afternoon sky around the Catalina, which veered off into a wide arc at 1,500 yards while the *U-550* kept turning. A deadly pirouette ensued as the foes circled once, twice, three times.

A PBY Catalina was as slow and ungainly as it was lethal, and Nitsche was still slinging flak when the bird of prey turned sharply and began diving at the *U-550's* port beam. Placing the crosshairs over its cockpit, he depressed the trigger. *Click.* Jammed. The seaplane closed in, skimming 50 feet over the waves as the 37mm gunners frantically attempted to clear the jam. The Canadians now started firing their own guns. Nitsche heard the *twang* of bullets striking steel, then the muffled sound of them hitting something softer behind him.

He heard the oberleutnant screaming an order to get below deck. Nitsche tore himself from the 37mm and joined a mad scramble that left behind a dead man on the wintergarten. The Canadian aircraft released four depth charges that landed in a row off the U-boat's starboard side. Water thrown by the blasts knocked one man overboard as the others scrambled down the hatch. Nitsche did not look back. It was his 20th birthday.

The two men lost in the attack were 18 and 20 years old, and one had been a guitarist whose singing and strumming had provided precious interludes of levity for the crew. Nobody pondered the fate of the man swept overboard. A fatally cold swath of ocean curves from Northern Europe past Iceland and Greenland to the northeastern United States. Even with a lifejacket, the temperature will kill a man within a couple of hours.[7]

This was the first war patrol for Johann "Hans" Rauh, a brewer's son from Munich with a stocky build, dark hair, and boyish features. He had turned 19 aboard the *U-550* six weeks earlier. As a *Mechanikergefreiter*, his primary duties were handling and maintaining the torpedoes. Rauh was close friends with Albert Nitsche, finding Nitsche's impish sense of humor a welcome tonic to the drudgery and terror of their daily existence.

Rauh was clad in a working jacket and matching trousers made from gray-green sailcloth-type fabric as he sat with his back against a bulkhead in the forward torpedo room. Like many of his crewmates, he wore canvas shoes to mitigate footfalls that could be heard by enemy hydrophones. In the radio room, *Funkmeister* Hans Zwemke had the record player plugged into the intercom. "*Eine Insel aus Träumen geboren*" drifted through the boat's squalid interior:

> Sailor, sailor, take your heart in both hands,
> When your ship anchors in Hawaii.
> Sailor, sailor, your voyage is over,
> If your heart doesn't resist the spell …

Marika Rökk's dulcet voice abruptly terminated. The denizens of the House of Lords, or forward torpedo room, looked warily at the intercom speaker. Rauh's hope that the rough seas had knocked the gramophone needle off the vinyl was dashed by a brief screech of acoustic feedback. Then the Old Man spoke.

"*Achtung*," Klaus Hänert's voice reverberated through the boat. "*Hier spricht der Kommandant*." Rauh stared apprehensively at the intercom. "We have new orders. The *U-550* will proceed southwest, to American coastal waters." There was a pause. "This crew has been tasked with bringing the war to America itself. The enemy will fear the Gray Wolf once again. I have the utmost confidence that each of you will do your duty." The word "duty" hung heavily in the fetid air.[8]

"*Westwärts*, my boys, and long live Germany."

***

15 April 1944
New York Harbor
16:06

"Like steaming through soup," grumbled Captain Delmar Leidy as he squinted into the heavy bank of fog enveloping New York Harbor. Beside him stood chief radio officer Mort Raphelson. The pair were on the bridge of the American tanker *Pan Pennsylvania* as convoy CU 21 left New York for Londonderry, Northern Ireland. Also on the bridge was Lieutenant (Junior Grade) John Melican, a 28-year-old Holy Cross alumni from Massachusetts who commanded the ship's Armed Guard detachment.

A variation of the T3 tanker design, the *Pan Pennsylvania* was the first of five sister ships launched in Norfolk, Virginia in 1943–44. One of the largest tankers on earth, she measured 501 feet long and 11,017 gross registered tons. She was powered by two steam turbine engines geared to a single propeller shaft and capable of 20 knots, a blistering speed for a tanker of her size. Additionally, the *Pan Pennsylvania* had teeth in the form of a 3-inch/.50 gun on the bow, a 4-inch/.50 gun on the stern, and multiple 20mm guns. Lacking a boat deck at the midship house, the ship instead carried two of her four lifeboats on standalone davits slightly aft of it.

The *Pan Pennsylvania* was laden with 140,000 barrels of 80-octane aviation gasoline in her tanks and seven B-25 Mitchell bombers lashed to her foredeck. In command was Captain Delmar Leidy, a stocky 42-year-old with heavy eyebrows and a toothy smile. Augmenting Leidy and his forty-nine mariners were LTJG Melican and his thirty Armed Guard sailors, bringing the total complement to eighty-one. Significant proportions of both the merchant and Navy crews were on their first sea voyage.

Captain Leidy was all eyes and ears as the *Pan Pennsylvania* maneuvered out of the foggy harbor. Fog was common in the springtime when warm and wet air settled over cold water, but it merited special caution. A ship in the New Jersey/New York region in 1944 was seven times more likely to be sunk by a collision than a torpedo. The coastal minesweeper *AMc-200*, which responded to the *R.P. Resor* and *Toltén* attacks, sank only weeks later from a collision off Wildwood, New Jersey. Eighteen months later, and farther north along the Jersey Shore, thirty-eight Navy sailors died when USS *Murphy* (DD-603) was cut in half by the tanker *Bulkoil*.

CU 21 was one of 1,462 convoys that sailed from New York City during the war, and New Jersey's role as an extension of New York's port facilities had only increased since 1942. Bayonne was a major staging point for combat vehicles, other cargo was loaded directly onto ships from rail cars at Craven Point, and bulk fuels from refineries in Bayonne and Elizabeth were pumped onto tankers like the *Pan Pennsylvania*. More than 1.3 million servicemen would pass through Camp Kilmer (named for a New Jersey poet killed in the Great War) near New Brunswick, one of the state's three major staging bases for troops headed overseas. Much of the men and matériel passing through New Jersey and New York were bound for Britain in preparation for the long-awaited Allied landing in occupied France.[9]

Convoy CU 21 consisted of twenty-nine merchant ships plus HMS *Premier*, an American-built escort carrier being transferred to the Royal Navy. Guarding the convoy were the six destroyer escorts of Escort Division 22, designated Task Group 21.5 for the mission. Four of these guided the convoy out of New York Harbor: USS *Harveson* (DE-316), USS *Gandy* (DE-764), USS *Kirkpatrick* (DE-318), and USS *Poole* (DE-151). The other two, USS *Joyce* (DE-317) and USS *Peterson* (DE-152), waited off Sandy Hook, New Jersey to take up positions at the convoy's rear.

The convoy's two columns snaked their way southeast through the swept channel bisecting the minefield guarding New York, finally clearing it around 20:00. The commodore elected to postpone assuming the normal formation of six columns until morning, as the fog and darkness were dangerous conditions for dozens of ships to be jostling positions. Metal would be bent either way, as it turned out. The freighters *Aztec* and *Sag Harbor* collided at 20:34, and USS *Peterson* left the convoy to escort them back to port.

As the *Pan Pennsylvania* and the rest of convoy CU 21 emerged from the minefield, the escorting destroyers worked like a well-oiled machine. The alertness on their bridges was more than standard vigilance. Though U-boats had seldom made their presence known along the East Coast since 1942, Bob Wilcox and his officers knew that the enemy was stalking these waters at this very moment.

The North Atlantic was ringed by more than forty HF/DF stations on two continents by 1944, and this network had recently detected two U-boats approaching North America. Dubbed "Red George" and "Red Fox," Eastern Sea Frontier focused on tracking Red George because its earlier departure meant it would reach the East Coast first. HF/DF could not triangulate the boat's exact position, however, and the latest ESF estimate only placed Red George in "the general area within 600 miles east of Cape May, New Jersey."[10]

***

15 April 1944
Somewhere east-southeast of New York City
22:13

As convoy CU 21 was departing New York, "Red George" emerged from the depths. The Type IXC/40 boat's exterior indicated how much had changed since 1942. Its foredeck was bare, most 88mm and 105mm deck guns having been removed in 1943 when surface attacks became prohibitively dangerous. Two dual-20mm guns on the wintergarten had replaced the single 20mm, and a second platform known as the "bandstand" had been added immediately aft of, and slightly below, the wintergarten. On the bandstand was a fully automatic 37mm in lieu of the single-shot version formerly on the Type IX's aft deck. The bridge also now featured an antenna for detecting Allied radar.

Kapitänleutnant Klaus Hänert climbed through the tower hatch. He was followed by a train of men bundled in attire ranging from Kriegsmarine-issue pea jackets to scarves knitted by their mothers. Hans Rauh, having barely tasted fresh air for weeks, deeply inhaled the chilly springtime night. A clear, starlit sky and gently rolling sea were a welcome reprieve from the north-central Atlantic's stormy oblivion, but these were not what captured the men's attention.

No comprehensive East Coast blackout had been implemented during the deadliest months of 1942. Nevertheless, a strict dim-out in full effect by June of that year now left New York's urban sprawl visible only as a faint glow on the western horizon. Even so, the Germans were awestruck. The enlisted sailors cycled through turns topside to savor a cigarette and contemplate the distant electric luster, and Hans Rauh found himself wondering if he might one day see New York up close and under happier circumstances.

Their trek toward North America had been nerve-wracking. Radar detector alerts spurred repeated crash dives that depleted most of their battery power and nearly all their compressed air, and westward progress was further slowed by crossing both the Labrador Current and Gulf Stream. Few U-boats had ventured this close to United States shores since the "Second Happy Time" in 1942. Six days ago, however, BdU authorized the *U-550* to proceed inshore of the 100-fathom curve—into American home waters.

Hänert had already decided where the *U-550* would operate. He knew that tankers loaded fuel at refineries in Pennsylvania and New Jersey before assembling in New York to join convoys. The commander also understood that, upon leaving the safety of New York Harbor, these convoys maintained a fairly predictable eastward heading for about 250 miles before disappearing into the vastness of the open Atlantic. He would therefore go close inshore, south of Long Island, and let the enemy come to him.

The *U-550* kommandant was unaware that American forces were actively hunting him. Nor did he know that the *U-856*, designated "Red Fox" by the Americans, had already been destroyed. Hounded by aircraft from the escort carrier USS *Croatan* (CVE-25) during its approach to North America, depth charges from the carrier's escorting warships eventually forced Red Fox to the surface 630 miles east of Seaside Heights, New Jersey. The *U-856* sank, and twenty-eight of fifty-five crewmen survived as POWs.

On the bridge with Kapitänleutnant Hänert and Oberleutnant von Lingelsheim-Seibicke were two other officers. One was 22-year-old Oberleutnant Hugo Renzmann, the *U-550*'s chief engineer. A large man, Renzmann was slightly taller than Hänert and possessed wide shoulders, a thick neck, and deep-set eyes. Renzmann and Hänert were not particularly close on a personal level, but they had developed an effective professional synergy.

The other officer was Friedrich Torge, a 25-year-old *Marineoberassistenzarzt*, or naval doctor. Physicians were assigned to long-range patrols as the war progressed, though the Kriegsmarine eventually recognized that the medical service could not sustain such high casualties. Enlisted men disliked it for superstitious reasons. Whenever a doctor came aboard, one veteran recalled, "we knew we were in for some heavy action." Fate had not even ordained Torge to be here. He had used a forged medical document to circumvent the fact that his dentures (the result of a horse riding accident) technically disqualified him from U-boat service.

Torge and Hänert had become good friends, each man seeing something of himself in the other. Torge was a pastor's son who joined the Kriegsmarine to pay for medical school because the other option was joining the Nazi Party. "The Kriegsmarine and the swastika," Torge assured his family, "are mutually exclusive." But as he beheld the lights of the world's most powerful nation, with death poised to strike at any moment, the doctor realized just how little such self-justifications mattered.

Kapitänleutnant Hänert gazed wordlessly at the American coast. The night veiled his prominent, straight nose and high cheekbones that tapered down to a sharp jaw. One gloved hand rested in a pocket of his double-breasted leather coat. The other lifted a cigarette to his lips, its dull ember glowing in the darkness. His voice finally broke the silence to address the chief engineer.

"*L.I.*"

"*Ja, Herr Kaleun?*"

"Let's watch the air supply ... I don't want to get jammed up again. Let me know when the batteries are fully charged, then you can take us into the basement." Hänert looked down at the luminescent dial of his Siegerin wristwatch. "*Und dann warten wir,*" he added. *And then we wait.* He turned to Friedrich Torge with a smirk. "As for you, *Herr Doktor* ... well, if I need your expertise then things have gone terribly awry." Torge laughed. "Just say the word, *Herr Kaleun.* I've got you."

Hänert took another drag on his cigarette. Acrid and bitter, it was a far cry from the Brazilian cigars he preferred. The *U-550* commander decided to permit his crew a few more minutes of fresh air. Considering everything the Fatherland had asked of them, and everything he now asked of them, it felt like the least he could do.[11]

***

16 April 1944
223 miles east of Point Pleasant, New Jersey
07:52

The following morning found Lieutenant Commander Robert Wilcox on USS *Joyce's* flying bridge. Clad in a visored uniform cap and double-breasted reefer jacket, he puffed a pipe of Heine's Blend tobacco as a white mustache of brine tumbled against the bow. Under an overcast sky and atop a heavy well, USS *Joyce* kept station 2,700 yards behind the convoy's main body while USS *Gandy* guarded its port flank. USS *Peterson* was 5 miles astern, making top speed to rejoin them after escorting the two damaged ships back to New York the previous night. Wilcox looked at his watch. In a few minutes, the convoy would begin to ponderously transition from two columns to the standard six-column formation.

Raised in Baltimore, Bob Wilcox followed in his late father's footsteps by attending the US Coast Guard Academy and was now married with a 4-year-old son. The energetic and intelligent 30-year-old was strikingly handsome, his fine features and slicked-back blonde hair lending him an almost cinematic presence. Privately, however, his dignified and confident air felt like a façade. Wilcox was a haunted man, the ghosts of USS *Leopold* hanging around his neck like an albatross.

Thirty-nine days had passed since that night south of Iceland. The *Leopold* had left the convoy to pursue a radar contact and was 3 miles from the *Joyce* when her star shells revealed the *U-255* crossing her bow. The *Leopold*'s gunners immediately opened fire as the *U-255* crash-dived and retreated into the depths, but not before its harried commander loosed a T5 *Zaunkönig* at his pursuer.[12]

Known as the *Zerstörerknacker*, or "destroyer cracker," the Zaunkönig was an acoustic homing torpedo first deployed in 1943. Featuring both a magnetic and impact detonator, it steered itself using two hydrophones specifically calibrated to seek the distinct noise of a destroyer's fast-whirling propellers. This guidance capability made aiming less important and enabled a U-boat to quickly launch one in the enemy's general direction while crash-diving. Although mechanically unreliable and far less deadly than BdU believed, the Zaunkönig finally provided U-boats a means to strike back against their tormentors.

True to his promise to the men of the *Leopold*, Wilcox returned after evading the torpedo that disrupted his first rescue attempt. Intelligence reports indicating a wolfpack in the area, however, led Task Group 21.5's commander to not detach any additional destroyer escorts. The *Joyce* was on her own.

Anguished shouting and pleading from the *Leopold* survivors again filled the chilly air as the *Joyce* returned to her mangled sister ship. "Net floating off the port side, men waving!" a petty officer shouted. "All stop!" Wilcox ordered. "Get those two on board, now!" Wilcox recognized one of the two survivors on the net as Lieutenant Pete Cone, the *Leopold*'s executive officer. A lively thrill-seeker from a prominent Virginia family, Cone was a good friend of Wilcox. The pair had enjoyed more than a few gin and tonics together in port.

Men on the *Joyce* tossed lines which LT Cone and the other man managed to loop around themselves. Wilcox could see the terror and desperation etched into his friend's face. *Please don't leave again, Bob*, Cone's eyes seemed to beg. *Please don't leave me here to die.* What happened next would weigh on Wilcox for the rest of his life. A lookout sighted another incoming torpedo, which LTJG Bender's sound hut immediately confirmed.

Wilcox now found himself facing another excruciating decision with only seconds to act. Seeing that Cone and his companion were at least secured to the *Joyce* by ropes, Wilcox ordered: "All ahead flank, left full rudder!" As his ship veered away, the lines went taut—then broke. Horrified, Wilcox watched the two men recede into the blackness as the *Joyce* sped away.

USS *Joyce* saved only 28 of 199 men aboard the *Leopold*, making the night of 9/10 March 1944 the worst combat loss in the Coast Guard's history. Among the dead were Lieutenant Commander Ken Phillips, Lieutenant Pete Cone, and all the rest of the officers. Wilcox maintained his composure in the immediate aftermath until he could steal a moment alone in his cabin. There he had finally wept, his tall frame wracked with sobs.

Two weeks later, a board of inquiry praised the *Joyce's* prompt and courageous actions that night, but this brought Wilcox little consolation. He still saw Pete Cone's face every time he closed his eyes. A Coast Guardsman's prime directive was to save lives at sea, yet the men of the *Leopold* had spent their last shivering moments waiting in vain for the *Joyce*. Wilcox was left plagued by guilt as undeserved as it was crushing, and he knew that all the gin and tonics in the world could not lighten it by an ounce.[13]

***

The six shepherds guarding convoy CU 21 were technically not destroyers but rather destroyer escorts, as indicated by their "DE" hull numbers. Depicted by war correspondent Ernie Pyle as "rough and tumble little ships," the first DEs were commissioned in April 1943. Edsall-class destroyer escorts displaced 1,200 long tons, yet were half as costly as "fleet" destroyers and could be built in three months. This led crewmen to joke that "DE" stood for "destroyer, expendable." Although the 306-foot-long warships were relatively slow by naval standards, their top speed of 21 knots was more than sufficient for keeping pace with merchant convoys.

A DE boasted three 3-inch/.50 guns, two mounted forward and one aft. Augmenting these were ten autocannons, typically a double 40mm Bofors plus eight 20mm Oerlikons mounted in pairs. These fired high explosive, armor piercing, tracer, and incendiary shells. Destroyer escorts also carried depth charges, deployable by K-guns or stern racks, and a devastating forward-firing spigot mortar system known as the "hedgehog." Their arsenal even included blunt force in the form of a reinforced bow designed for ramming.

The typical destroyer escort was manned by 185 enlisted men and 12 officers. Most enlisted crewmen were in their late teens or early 20s, and most officers were younger than 30. Many crewmen were poached from the Armed Guard program, but thirty-seven DEs were manned entirely by Coast Guardsmen. One was 19-year-old Collingwood Harris from Manasquan, New Jersey. An attempt to impress a girl led Harris to Camden to join the Marine Corps in 1943, but the Marine recruiter had already met his daily quota. The Coast Guard recruiter was still taking volunteers, and thus Harris found himself a radarman second class aboard USS *Peterson*.

The original six destroyer escorts of Task Group 21.5 (*Joyce, Peterson, Poole, Kirkpatrick, Harveson,* and *Leopold*) were sister ships in the truest sense, and not only because all were manned by Coast Guardsmen. All six were Edsall-class DEs constructed in Texas by Consolidated Steel and commissioned within days of one another. The *Leopold's* loss had therefore been like losing a sibling. Their late sister's replacement was USS *Gandy*, a Navy-manned Cannon-class DE on her first combat mission.

Task Group 21.5 felt more than just bereavement. White-hot anger also simmered, in addition to fear of an enemy who seemed to be everywhere and nowhere at once. "It was not apparent that Germany had not won the war," Collingwood Harris explained years later. "Our perception was that the sea was alive with submarines ... There was some kind of mysterious invincibility that the Germans were supposed to have."

Lieutenant Commander Wilcox had first tasted combat aboard USCGC *Modoc* (WPG-46) prior to America's formal entry into the war. The *Modoc* had been assigned to the Greenland Patrol in May 1941 when the cutter's crewmen found themselves witnesses to the legendary duel between the Royal Navy and the battleship *Bismarck*. The experience, which included several close calls for the *Modoc*, underscored the disquieting reality that war was pulling Bob Wilcox inexorably closer.

Wilcox hated the war. He hated how it chewed up human lives without mercy or dignity, and he hated what it required him to do. He had joined the Coast Guard to save lives, not take them. Yet equally fundamental to the fabric of Robert Wilcox was duty, and his country had called on him to do a job. He had further obligations, too. As USS *Joyce* split the swells on that gray April morning, Wilcox found his mind drawn to a letter he received from his wife, Alice, shortly before the *Leopold* incident:

"Bob, please be careful."[14]

***

16 April 1944
228 miles east of Point Pleasant, New Jersey
08:05

In the *Pan Pennsylvania*'s messroom, chief radio officer Mort Raphelson lifted the biscuit off his plate and inspected it. The 22-year-old had come to believe that the simplest things could make or break one's day at sea, and he had high hopes for a decent breakfast. Food aboard ship was typically hit or miss but, now and again, a man was surprised.

Raphelson was a jovial Philadelphia native with a slim build and dark hair. His parents had forbidden him from attending the US Merchant Marine Academy even after he aced the entrance exam, and he languished as an insurance salesman until they relented. Raphelson subsequently attended the US Maritime Service Radio Training School in Boston in 1942. The intervening months had taken him to Britain, South America, and India.

Raphelson's eyes lit up in approval upon taking a bite of the biscuit. *Maybe it's gonna be a good trip*, he mused. The radio officer had just taken a second bite when the entire *Pan Pennsylvania* suddenly quaked violently. Porcelain shattered as plates and men were thrown off seats and tables. A catastrophic boiler malfunction was the first possibility that entered his mind, but this was reflexive denial. He knew in his gut what was unfolding, in part because this was not his first experience under attack.

Convoy HX 228, which departed New York for Liverpool on 28 February 1943, had been Mort Raphelson's first transatlantic voyage. The convoy was ambushed southeast of Greenland by wolfpack *Neuland*, and the freighter immediately starboard of Raphelson's tanker caught two torpedoes and exploded. The destroyer HMS *Harvester* recovered several dozen survivors only then to be torpedoed herself.

Raphelson knew he had to get to the bridge. Dashing out of the messroom, he was assaulted by steam pouring from ruptured pipes. Now doused in sweat, he backtracked and made for the hatch leading outside to the stern. Raphelson was going to have to take the scenic route.[15]

***

Minutes earlier, and not far away from where Raphelson's breakfast was interrupted, Funkmeister Hans Zwemke was slumped in his seat in the U-550's sound room. His headphones sat askew on his head, leaving his left ear uncovered, as he languidly turned the wheel that activated different groups of hydrophone receivers. The boat had been laying on the seafloor since the previous night. It briefly rose to periscope depth three hours earlier when Zwemke heard propellers, but Kapitänleutnant Hänert saw nothing through the fog. The boat returned to the bottom.

Nearly three hours passed before an indistinct noise emerging from the ocean's eerie static pulled Funkmeister Zwemke upright in his seat. "*Horchpeilung!*" Hänert's lanky frame appeared in the doorway. "*Aus dem Westen,*" Zwemke added in a whisper. *From the west.* He pushed the other headphone on and focused again on the indicator needle sweeping across the compass rose in front of him. He adjusted the wheel slightly. "Maybe … five kilometers."

Hänert patted Zwemke's shoulder approvingly before stepping back into the control room and addressing chief engineer Hugo Renzmann. "*L.I.*, periscope depth." Air was squeezed into the ballast tanks as the E-motors started droning. "Forward up ten, aft up five," Renzmann directed. Hänert and the helmsman squeezed past him and climbed the ladder to the conning tower compartment. Bootsmannsmaat Paul Lennemann joined them in the tower and took his post at the torpedo data calculator beside the attack periscope.

Renzmann adroitly halted their ascent at a depth of 60 feet. Its screws whirled slowly as it trolled at 2 knots; a U-boat could not hover because water needed to be moving over the planes to keep it stable. Silence was nonetheless paramount, so the U-550 crept forward at a walking pace. Hänert tilted his white captain's hat backward, pressed his right eye to the eyepiece, and extended the periscope. The U-boat then resumed slowly rising, the periscope's head lifting surreptitiously into a gray morning as Hänert peered into the world above—and his heart leapt into his throat.

The morning sun had burned away the fog like a rising curtain to reveal a large convoy bearing down on the U-550 from the west. At its front cruised an aircraft carrier with planes crowding its flight deck. Hänert could see a dozen merchant ships behind it, with more following. One destroyer accompanied the carrier while two more held station on the convoy's flanks, and Hänert knew that others likely lurked out of sight. Although they seemed oblivious to his presence, he had to act quickly. The convoy was too fast to pursue while submerged. If it got past him, the opportunity would be gone.

The periscope's controls were slick with sweat as he panned his view to the aircraft carrier 45 degrees off their bow. It was 1,000 yards away and closing quickly. Hänert heard his own pulse hammering against his skull: *tha-thump, tha-thump, tha-thump*. He ordered all four bow tubes flooded. *Nein, nein* … The carrier was already too far across their bow. His jaw muscles flexed.

The *U-550* was now inside the eastbound procession of ships. They were forward and aft, starboard and port, merchantmen and escorts alike oblivious to the fox in the hen house. Hänert panned his view further west, then abruptly stopped.

In his crosswires was the biggest tanker he had ever seen. The massive ship was riding low in the water, and he could see several B-25 bombers on its foredeck. The sight of the aircraft made Hänert's eyes narrow as an atypical flash of anger passed over him. His mind's eye saw the charred corpses of children in Hamburg and his mother and sister running to the bomb shelter in Flensburg as sirens wailed. This hairline fracture in the captain's stoicism vanished as quickly as it appeared, returning him to the task at hand. This tanker's cargo would fuel no aircraft, he resolved, and those bombers were going only one place: down.

Hänert's voice betrayed none of the anxiety boiling inside him as he ordered the crew to prepare for a fan shot from tubes one, three, and four. He relayed the target data to Bootsmannsmaat Lennemann beside him, and the 23-year-old boatswain turned the calculator's dials accordingly. Down in the control room, Obersteuermann Walter Hauffe's thumb waited over the button of a stopwatch. Lennemann watched a single white light replace the calculator's two red lights. "*Folgen!*" The forward torpedo room reported likewise.

Klaus Hänert stepped over fate's precipice with a single command. "*Los!*" The boat flinched three times, and he inhaled sharply when the final eel was away. *Run,* his inner monologue screamed. *Now.*

Hänert suddenly felt the boat wobbling and rising. "*Ich kann es nicht in dieser Tiefe halten!*" shouted Oberleutnant Renzmann from the control room below. The sudden release of more than 10,000 pounds had left the *U-550* dangerously buoyant, putting them at risk of breaking the surface in full view of the American destroyers. Hänert thundered: "DIVE, *L.I.*, NOW!"

He slid down the ladder without his feet touching a single rung as sailors began feverishly turning levers and wheels in the control room. A musky, single-file train of denim, leather, and unwashed bodies rushed past them toward the forward torpedo room. As the *U-550* fell away into the depths, Hänert gazed at the stopwatch in Obersteuermann Hauffe's hand. "*Fünfzehn Sekunden,*" Hauffe reported. *Fifteen seconds.*

Simultaneously, Renzmann's voice marked the *U-550*'s descent: "Twenty meters!" The trio of eels continued speeding toward the unwitting tanker above, meanwhile, the grinding metallic orchestra of the approaching convoy's engines and screws grew louder. Hauffe's eyes remained on the stopwatch. *"Zwanzig Sekunden ..."* Obersteuermann Hauffe's voice fell into an alternating cadence with Renzmann's as the engineering officer counted off the increasing depth. "Forty meters!" The rumble of a single explosion suddenly sounded from the surface. Hänert's eyes went wide. *A hit.*

Unlike the early war years, no cheering sounded from the bow where Hans Rauh and Albert Nitsche were squeezed against their crewmates as human ballast. The *U-550* continued dropping deeper as Oberleutnant Renzmann worked to trim the boat and slow its descent. The bottom drew nearer.

"Eighty meters!"

Their downward plunge terminated with a series of jarring blows that violently shook the boat as its keel gouged a deep rut into the seabed. With the *U-550* now motionless at a depth of 330 feet, the crew quickly turned off motors, pumps, and anything else that produced noise. Bootsmannsmaat Lennemann ushered non-essential men to their bunks to minimize carbon dioxide accumulation, and they were soon as still and silent as the dead. In the aft torpedo room, Hans Rauh stared at the overhead while the wounded tanker emitted a disquieting chorus of creaks and groans.[16]

***

One of the *U-550*'s three torpedoes found its mark on the *Pan Pennsylvania*'s port-side hull, blasting a 40-foot hole in the No. 8 tank and rupturing the No. 7 tank. Seaman 1st Class Patrick DiAgosto, an Armed Guard sailor manning a 20mm gun above the impact site, was killed by the explosion. Gasoline and seawater poured into the engine room, but sheer luck prevented an even worse outcome: the No. 8 tank, three-quarters empty, was the only tank not full.

LTJG John Melican vaulted off his rack and rushed to a porthole. Peering outside, he observed a torrent of red-tinted gasoline hemorrhaging from an enormous gash ripped in the port-side hull. *That's bad.* He bolted topside, where he sighted a jagged fissure stretching across three-quarters of the deck. Panic had seemingly gripped the merchant crew. Although this was nearly as concerning as the explosion damage, Melican's responsibility was the guns.

He shouted an order to aim the forward 3-inch/.50 gun to port. If their assailant dared to show himself, then Melican intended to put a shell right between his goddamn eyes. Billowing steam obscured the gunners' view, however, and they saw nothing besides the water's reddish tinge from the ship's high-octane cargo bleeding into the sea. Melican jogged toward the bridge and across a deck that was already slanting as the *Pan Pennsylvania* leaned on her wounded flank.

At the same time, chief radio officer Mort Raphelson was taking a circuitous route to the bridge. The alarm screeched its grating one-note tune as he ascended the stairwell and began crossing the aft deck. The radio officer could feel the ship's heading change as Captain Leidy swerved the wounded tanker to clear the convoy's path. Raphelson was rounding the aft deck house a moment later when he sighted a pair of mariners lowering the No. 3 lifeboat, which was occupied by several men.

What are they doing? There had been no order to abandon ship. The *Pan Pennsylvania* was also still making 13 knots, much too fast to safely launch a lifeboat. Moments after Raphelson passed the davits, one of the lifeboat falls suddenly payed out too quickly, dumping the boat's occupants into the water where they were pulled toward the whirling propeller. Bloodcurdling screams followed.[17]

***

On the seafloor below them, Funkmeister Hans Zwemke turned the hydrophone's pointer wheel left, then right, then left again. Kapitänleutnant Hänert again appeared in the doorway. "*Zwei Zerstörer,*" Zwemke whispered. His eyes returned to the directional needle as he kept turning the pointer wheel, breathing through his teeth. "*Nein …*" Zwemke paused. "*Drei.*" *Three destroyers.* But these were convoy escorts, not a hunter-killer group. *Maybe they won't stick around long.* Hänert patted Zwemke on the shoulder and returned to the control room. He took long and deliberate steps, placing his feet on the deck as softly as possible.

Oberleutnant Hugo Renzmann was waiting for Hänert in the control room. "*Wir stecken fest, Herr Kaleun,*" the chief engineer reported in a hushed tone. *We're stuck.* The *U-550*'s hard landing on the seafloor had plowed it deep into the mud. "We'll have to blow all the tanks," he continued. "It's the only way." Hänert frowned. That would create noise and bubbles. "Alright. Get ready … but stand by for now. I want to see how much longer our friends up there hang around."[18]

***

"Bridge to engine room, this is the captain … hello??" Capt Delmar Leidy slammed the phone back onto the receiver. The engine order telegraph went similarly unanswered. He ordered the whistle sounded in the hope that the engine room would hear it and shut down the propulsion—assuming they were still alive. Leidy next strode to the bridge wing. Looking down, he saw that the No. 3 lifeboat was no longer in its davits. "God dammit!"

Leidy moved to the bridge wing's port side and looked aft, where he sighted men attempting to launch the No. 1 lifeboat. "PUT IT BACK!" he barked. Heads swiveled toward the captain. "You did NOT receive an order to abandon ship!" Leidy roared, his face reddening. "Put the goddamn boat back and get back to your stations!" He shook his head in dismay. *What the hell has gotten into this crew?*

Though determined to save his ship, Leidy was stubborn and not foolish. He turned to his engineering officer. "Go down below and see if there's anyone trapped who we might still be able to help," he instructed in a hushed tone. "And check everything you can. Watertight doors, cargo spillage, the engine room … I need to know how fucked we are."[19]

***

More than 300 feet below, the *U-550* crewmen spoke only in whispers and moved with mincing steps. Hänert was hunched over the chart table in the control room. Despite the enemy's presence above them, the U-boat's prospects for escape were less dire than they might seem. Lying motionless on the bottom makes a submarine difficult to distinguish from the clutter of echoes produced by sound waves bouncing off the seabed. "In certain circumstances," the *U-boat Commander's Handbook* advised, "a temporary stationing of the submarine on the bottom of the sea is also likely to be successful as a protective measure."

But the destroyers prowling overhead could saturate the ocean with high explosives on a whim, and Hänert's instinct was to escape while he still had enough battery power to do so. He knew that the edge of the continental shelf, where the seafloor drops away to thousands of feet, lay just 15 miles south. Getting over that precipice would enable the *U-550* to dive below its official maximum depth of 656 feet, stressing the pressure hull to its limit but putting them beyond the reach of depth charges. Making a run for it would forgo the seafloor's camouflage, but Hänert knew that another oceanic phenomenon was also protecting them.

Between the *U-550* and Task Group 21.5 lay a thermocline, or separation between a cold layer of water and a warmer layer above it. This phenomenon occurs when varying temperature and salinity cause the water column to stratify into layers of differing density. Thermoclines inhibit sonar's effectiveness by bending sound energy sharply downward, trapping it between layers, or deflecting it prematurely back to the surface. Hänert recognized that the thermocline could shield their escape, but first they needed to get free of this damned mud.[20]

***

"General Quarters, General Quarters. All hands, man your battle stations …"

An electric tension permeated the air aboard USS *Joyce*. The General Quarters alert blared through the intercom as her Fairbanks Morse engines roared and Coast Guardsmen, clad in blue denim working uniforms and olive drab M1 helmets, scurried to their stations. The *Joyce* had been tasked to rescue the stricken *Pan Pennsylvania*'s crew. Unlike the *Leopold* incident, this time Wilcox had backup in the form of USS *Peterson* and USS *Gandy*, which were ordered to screen for him. The other three destroyer escorts remained with the convoy while Wilcox dashed toward the *Pan Pennsylvania* with the *Peterson* and *Gandy* at his heels. LTJG John Bender, meanwhile, was in the sound hut adjoining the *Joyce*'s flying bridge.

In the sound hut, the hunt for their unseen enemy was already underway. Sonarman 2nd Class Nelson Allen was seated at the QGB sonar console while another sonarman monitored the plotting displays. Allen's brows were furrowed as he methodically scoured one sliver of sea at a time. He transmitted a pulse of ultrasonic energy into the depths, then listened. Hearing no return, he manually rotated the transducer another 5 degrees and pinged again. Likened to searching for a black cat in a pitch-dark room using a narrow flashlight beam—while the cat is moving around—the hunt relied on Allen's ability to hear slight variations in the pitch of the return echo.

Lieutenant Commander Wilcox appeared in the sound hut doorway. "Mr Bender, what do we have?" The diligent New Jersey native, who had left Princeton University to join the Coast Guard, pivoted attentively as the two enlisted men remained engrossed in the search. "Nothing yet, sir," Bender replied. "Sound conditions are awful, there's all sorts of stratification down there." Wilcox's blood was up. This was not his first combat experience, but he had never felt anything like this.

"I want this guy, gentlemen."[21]

***

The air around the *Pan Pennsylvania* was taking a reddish hue from the gasoline vapors, and Mort Raphelson was panting and coughing by the time he reached the bridge. The engineering crew had reversed and secured the engines, but no evacuation was underway. LTJG Melican was outside on the flying bridge shouting to one of his 3-inch/.50 gun crews when Raphelson got Leidy's attention.

"Cap'n, I—" *BOOM!* Raphelson was interrupted by a shot fired by Melican's gunners to alert nearby ships. "Already hailed the commodore and the escort commander on the TBS," Leidy interjected. *Well, okay then.*

"Respectfully, we really ought to consider—," Leidy was already shaking his head, "—abandoning ship—," Raphelson continued despite seeing he had already lost the skipper, "—before we get hit again." He grew more insistent. "Have you been down there? We're in a bad way." Leidy appreciated his radio officer's concern, but he was not ready to give up his ship. "We're still afloat, Mort. We're not going anywhere for now."

The engineering officer returned from below decks. He reported that the steam line to the blower was broken, the No. 8 tank was flooded with seawater, and the bilge pumps and engine room were flooding with gasoline. Worse still, that gasoline was burning. The *Pan Pennsylvania* was now a massive firebomb with a lit fuse made even more deadly by gasoline's volatility. Its fumes were also steadily incapacitating the crew; every man aboard was now bleary-eyed and coughing. Accepting the gravity of the situation, Captain Leidy finally issued the order to abandon ship.

The captain disposed of the classified documents while LTJG Melican led the evacuation. As the remaining merchant crewmen converged on the No. 1 lifeboat, Melican tripped a pelican hook that released a liferaft for his surviving Armed Guards. He held its painter line and walked it to the *Pan Pennsylvania's* bow where he tied it off. "Let's go, folks." Melican spoke with a cool confidence, but he felt lightheaded and his throat was sore. "All ashore that's—," a brief fit of coughing seized him, "—goin' ashore …" Several Armed Guards jumped into the heaving, blood-red water and swam to the raft.

Captain Leidy was in his quarters when Melican appeared in the doorway. "People are getting woozy from the gas out here, captain. We gotta get moving before this whole thing blows." Leidy hardly needed the reminder. "I'll be right there." The *Pan Pennsylvania*'s list was approaching 30 degrees when Melican returned to the deck. He found that his Armed Guards had launched the No. 1 lifeboat, but the raft was drifting away because the painter had broken.

Melican ordered every man still on the *Pan Pennsylvania* to the last lifeboat, No. 2, which hung from its davits over the rougher waters on the windward side. Leidy, Melican, and Raphelson were winching it downward when surging waves below the lifeboat caused nerves inside it to break. Two men panicked and tried to leap back onto the deck. Neither made it. The horrified officers watched as the pair instead plummeted into the water, where they quickly succumbed to the gasoline fumes. The lifeboat had just reached the water when disaster struck again. A swell threw Seaman 1st Class Richard Price from the boat and smashed his head against the ship's hull, killing him.

Leidy, Melican, and Raphelson were still reeling from the No. 2 lifeboat catastrophe as they prepared to depart via one of the remaining liferafts. Leidy was the last man off the tanker. The three officers, plus a handful of others, shoved off in the raft around 08:45. Waves were washing over the abandoned *Pan Pennsylvania*'s foredeck as Melican slowly cut the raft's oars loose. He handed one to a mariner and another to an Armed Guard.

But the men only held the oars weakly in their hands. Their eyes were glassy and vacant and they made no attempt to row. Melican spoke, but his words came out slurred. His head pounded and his throat burned. Looking around groggily, he dimly realized that they were all intoxicated by the gasoline fumes. Swells pushed the raft away from the tanker as its occupants stared blankly at one another, at the sea, and at their abandoned ship.[22]

***

USS *Peterson* speedily weaved an irregular, jagged course to the attack scene as she swept the area with sonar. Fingers twitched on triggers at the prospect of payback for USS *Leopold*. Obtaining a sonar contact at 08:46, the voice of the *Peterson*'s commander sounded over the net: "Proceeding to attack."

Below the *Peterson*, Hans Rauh and Albert Nitsche looked upward as they breathlessly listened to the throbbing screws overhead. Zwemke was listening on the hydrophone in the sound room when he heard six splashes in quick succession as *Wasserbomben* rolled from USS *Peterson*'s stern racks. "*Wabos!*" The depth charges' blasts jarred the boat, but their triggers were set too shallow. Hänert exhaled.[23]

***

It was 08:50 when USS *Joyce*'s crew sighted the *Pan Pennsylvania* and the yawning wound carved from her hull. Survivors huddled in two lifeboats and two rafts floated nearby. In the sound hut just forward of the flying bridge, LTJG Bender's sonarmen methodically swept the sonar beam across the depths five degrees at a time. The transducer on the *Joyce*'s keel projected a beam that was powerful but narrow, making the aim-ping-listen process a painstaking one. Upon obtaining a return echo, the beam would be held on the contact while the ship steered toward it. The sonarmen would track its course and speed while the U-boat swerved to throw off its pursuer and show the narrowest possible profile.

"I've got … something," reported SO2 Nelson Allen. "But it's mushy." Bender radioed a request to the bridge: "Check bearing two-seven-zero at range two-five-zero-zero yards." The bridge replied that the *Pan Pennsylvania* was at 270 degrees. Sonar waves rarely follow a direct path, instead returning via multiple angles from different sources, particularly when a thermocline interferes. The *Joyce*'s sonar was apparently getting a return from the hull of the crippled tanker ahead. He requested another check bearing and was again informed that it was the *Pan Pennsylvania*. Bender shook his head in exasperation.

***

Thirty minutes after abandoning ship, the stupefied *Pan Pennsylvania* survivors spotted USS *Joyce*'s superstructure over the wavetops. LTJG Melican heard a voice over a megaphone instruct them to "remain in the general vicinity." The Armed Guard officer was too impaired by the fumes to reply, but lucid enough to wish he could sarcastically ask where the Coast Guardsmen expected they might go.

The *Joyce* drew alongside the raft. Her crew draped a cargo net over the hull and tossed lines to keep the survivors from drifting away before helping the groggy mariners and sailors climb the net. The destroyer escort retrieved Capt Leidy, Mort Raphelson, and thirteen other merchant crewmen, plus LTJG Melican and fifteen other Armed Guards.

Assisting the rescue was USS *Peterson*. Disregarding a potential inferno from the gasoline slick and the imminent likelihood of depth charges, the *Peterson*'s Chief Electrician's Mate Stuart Goodwin and Motor Machinist's Mate 3rd Class David Stephenson spontaneously jumped overboard to help get men aboard. Collingwood Harris would recall that the tanker's survivors "seemed to be somewhat bewildered … it wasn't like what you see in the movies."

The *Peterson* recovered the second lifeboat's twenty-two occupants by 09:33. The destroyer escort set the empty boat adrift and made a wide sweep toward the second raft, taking its three men aboard by 09:43. The last of the fifty-six survivors were recovered just as a voice crackled through the TBS: "Make all possible speed, *Joyce* is about to attack."[24]

***

"Rig for silent running," Kapitänleutnant Hänert whispered. He was looking upward despite there being nothing to see but cold metal. The commander could only hear a single set of destroyer screws, which Zwemke's headphones confirmed. This was their chance. "Now, *L.I.*!"

Hans Rauh and Albert Nitsche felt the electric propulsion kick on. Pumps, the compressor, the rattle of pressurized air in the piping … Hänert winced at how loud it all sounded. The muck beneath the U-boat's keel resisted for several agonizing seconds before the boat heaved once and the familiar sensation of submerged movement returned. The *U-550* had wriggled free.

Yet it was also too buoyant from the extra lift required to pull them loose, and Renzmann now scrambled to halt their ascent and trim the boat. Hänert and Bootsmannsmaat Lennemann both climbed into the tower compartment, where Obersteuermann Hauffe was already at the helm. "Come to one-six-zero," Hänert ordered as he sat at the periscope. "Ninety rpm on both." As the *U-550* turned south, the captain issued another order which a chain of whispers relayed forward and aft: "Flood tubes two and six. Open tube doors."

Like carrying a handgun with a round chambered, U-boats in 1944 kept one or two Zaunkönig homing torpedoes (the same type that sank USS *Leopold*) ready for immediate launch. "BdU wanted us to keep a 'sting in the tail,'" one officer explained. The weapon's ability to follow the sound of a warship's screws also meant it could be launched "blind," or without calculating a firing solution or even seeing the target. The *U-550* had one Zaunkönig in tube two at the bow and another in tube six at the stern. If the *Amerikaner* wanted a fight, then Hänert could give them one.

Unease washed over Rauh and Nitsche in the aft torpedo room. Rauh reached under tube six and turned a valve to open the connection to the compensating tank. Another sailor then opened the low-pressure air feed, causing water to gurgle into the tube until the click of a lever falling into place confirmed that the pressure was equalized. Next, a handle was cranked which opened the tube to the sea and exposed the torpedo's black, bullet-shaped head.

The lone destroyer escort audible when Hänert decided to make a run for it was USS *Gandy*. What the Germans did not know, however, is that the *Joyce* and *Peterson* were also overhead. Their screws had been silent because they were recovering the surviving merchant crewmen and Armed Guards, and Funkmeister Zwemke had not heard their auxiliary machinery humming over the noise of the *Pan Pennsylvania*'s death throes.

But he heard them now. Zwemke swiveled the hydrophone wheel as turbines revved to life at the surface and propellers began whirling angrily. "*Heilige Scheisse* …" he swore breathlessly. Lifting off the bottom had forfeited the acoustic camouflage provided by both the thermocline and the seabed, leaving the *U-550* completely exposed. The radioman frantically turned the wheel left and right as he discerned three destroyers converging on the boat. His composure began to crack. "*Scheisse! … Scheisse! …*" Every man aboard the *U-550* now heard the *swish-swish-swish* of screws growing louder. One of the three hunters was closing in while its sonar beam scythed through the depths.

Ping …

The sonar's metallic chirp made the hair on the back of Hans Rauh's neck stand up. *Ping …* "All ahead full," Hänert whispered. The commander's expression remained carved out of stone, but his insides felt hollow and each burst of sonic energy seemed to chill him to the marrow.

Ping … Ping … Ping …

The longest seconds of fifty-four lives ticked by as the acoustic pulses grew louder, their intervals shorter. Pings hitting the hull soon acquired a tangible quality, like sand thrown against a tin roof. Albert Nitsche felt them in his teeth and bones. Hans Rauh could now hear the rhythmic thumping of machinery above them as a funeral chant of thrashing screws swelled louder.[25]

Ping! Ping! Ping! Ping!

***

Crewmen on USS *Joyce* were helping the last *Pan Pennsylvania* survivors up the cargo net when Wilcox heard LTJG Bender from the sound hut: "Contact!" Though the younger officer's familiar cadence sounded hollow through the voice pipe, his excitement was palpable. Wilcox materialized in the sound hut doorway a moment later. "Range and bearing?" he asked. SO2 Allen did not look up; the metallic ringing in his headphones was growing sharper by the second. "Range one-eight-zero-zero, bearing three-two-zero," Bender replied as he turned around. "Sir," his face was alight with satisfaction, "that's a sub."

The *Joyce* shifted direction, her hull trembling as she accelerated to 15 knots. "We have something good," Wilcox announced over the TBS. Bender reported: "No Doppler, echo's sharp. Target moving slightly left." Wilcox knew that his adversary was moving at a crawl to stay quiet as he attempted to retreat into the safety of the pelagic abyss, but the *Joyce* was gaining rapidly as she covered 500 yards per minute.

"Range seven hundred!" Bender exclaimed. Wilcox ordered a 5-degree course change to lead the target slightly as his crew readied the depth charges on the aft deck. The *Gandy*, cruising off her starboard beam, turned east to follow behind the *Joyce* for her own attack. "Contact dead ahead, range close!"

Because a sonar beam was conical and its transducer could not be raised or lowered, a sonar contact fell progressively lower within the beam as the searching vessel closed the distance. Eventually, just before the searcher overtook its quarry, the contact ceased to return an echo altogether. The *Joyce*'s acoustic searchlight held fast to the contact until it disappeared from sonar 120 yards forward of the bow. *I've got you*, Bob Wilcox relished coldly. *I've. Got. You.* His next order had been welling inside him for thirty-nine days:

"Fire."

Thirteen Mark 9 depth charges rolled from the *Joyce*'s stern racks at 09:53. Unlike the old "ashcans" used in 1941–42, the newer Mark 9 had fins and a teardrop shape within a cylindrical cage for faster sinking on a stabler trajectory. Its main charge consisted of Torpex, a mixture of RDX, TNT, and aluminum powder yielding 50 percent more explosive force than the TNT used in the older Mark 6 and 7 designs. Two of the *Joyce*'s depth charges failed to deploy, but the other eleven splashed along with a canister of green dye to mark the location. Their fins spun each depth charge as it hurtled downward through the water column.

Five seconds later, the *Joyce*'s thin hull quaked when the first three thudded in the depths. Wilcox watched a trio of overlapping circles bloom and contract as they broke the surface, each upsurge reaching its apogee as explosive gases rushing upward sent a jagged plume of water erupting from its center. Water was still hanging in the air when four more explosions flowered, then another three, and finally the last and shallowest depth charge. Creamy-looking deep water poured to the surface in the *Joyce*'s wake as Wilcox radioed the dye marker's bearing to the *Gandy* for her attack run.[26]

***

Less than sixty seconds earlier, Hänert slid down the ladder into the control room as the terrifying swishing of propellers neared a crescendo. From the surface sounded a sudden crunching noise, followed by a series of splashes. "*Wabos!*" Zwemke croaked. The others hardly needed the warning; they had all heard the *Joyce*'s ashcans splashing like lilies on a grave. *Klatsch, klatsch, klatsch* … Zwemke ripped off his headphones as Hans Rauh and Albert Nitsche's pallid faces looked upward. Every free hand gripped hatchways, bunks, and pipes.

Five seconds later, the first three depth charges detonated with an abominable roar. Shards of glass and sparks burst from instruments as the inferno enveloped the boat. The lights flickered and went out, plunging the compartments into darkness just as four more depth charges exploded. Their individual blasts formed one prolonged, ear-splitting cascade of thunder that hurled men against bunks and bulkheads. Steel moaned in protest as the hull and frames flexed and the deck plates were blasted out of alignment beneath Hänert's feet.

Three more wabos were hurtling downward. As each sank, the increasing water pressure extended a bellows inside its trigger mechanism. One depth charge landed on the U-boat's aft deck with a chilling *thud* before rumbling off the deck's edge. The bellows of all three trigger mechanisms then tripped the release of their spring-loaded firing pins. *Click!* The pins plunged into the primers, and the hellish thunder resumed.

In the aft torpedo room, Rauh and Nitsche reflexively ducked each time the boat spasmed. A jet of bitterly cold water suddenly struck them as the Atlantic's sinister ingress began. More water spurted through a breach in the diesel engine room. A final depth charge's detonation heralded the hideous concert's intermission. It had lasted just twenty seconds, but Hänert felt like he had aged a decade. The sea around the boat fell silent except for the receding singing of their attacker's screws.

Bedlam reigned inside the *U-550*. "Get the main bilge up!" Renzmann's voice carried over the hiss of leaking air and seawater spraying into the compartments. Overlaying the stench of urine was the pungent odor of diesel; either a fuel tank or line had ruptured. "Damage reports, now!" Flashlight beams flitted over shattered gauges and trickling water as Renzmann pushed his way aft through shadowy figures moving like ghosts in the gloom.

Leaking fuel was the least of their problems. "*Wie schlimm ist es??*" Hänert shouted when his soaking wet chief engineer reappeared. "Everything from the diesels aft is flooding!" Renzmann reported, both men yelling over the ambient noise. "*Hecktorpedoraum* has it worst, severe water ingress at the E-motors and diesels too!" Hänert took a deep breath just as the emergency lighting turned on. He now knew there would be no return to port. Even if the flooding could be staunched before it drowned them, they would all choke to death once it engulfed the batteries and produced chlorine gas.

Their war ended here; it was only a question of how. Regulations and tradition both permitted surrender, despite Dönitz recently fuming that "there is no such thing as raising a white flag in the Kriegsmarine." A commander should instead choose "dying with honor" so long as he retained the means to fight ... and the *U-550* still had two Zaunkönig anti-destroyer torpedoes ready for launch. Hänert could take a destroyer escort or two with him before he and his crew all "bit the seaweed." It would incur a steep and final price, but fighting was his duty.

Yet Hänert also had another duty. This obligation was not spelled out in any secret orders from lunatics in Berlin, but it was the moral imperative of every military commander and every sea captain: to bring one's men home alive. As Renzmann watched the Old Man's face expectantly, and terrified teenagers plugged leaks under flickering lights around them, Hänert made his choice. He had upheld his duty to the Fatherland, and now he would uphold his duty to his crew. No one else had to die today.

He responded to Renzmann with an uncharacteristically oblique order. "We have to go up!" Hänert yelled over the tumult, "or we all die!" The statement of fact was directed as much at himself as at Renzmann, who only nodded. "*AUSBLASEN!*" the chief engineer yelled. They were going up.

"*Klar bei Tauchretter!*" someone shouted as the damaged *U-550* began rising. It ascended unevenly, first by the stern and then the bow. "Twenty meters! ..." Renzmann hollered over the clamorous disarray. "Ten meters! ..." Gear rolled fore and aft. "*Boot ist raus!*" The boat heaved as it gracelessly reached daylight. Hänert immediately began climbing the conning tower ladder to the main hatch, one hand clutching the wardroom tablecloth as an improvised white flag.[27]

USS *Joyce* continued north, away from the smear of green dye, as the *Gandy* closed in from the east. Bob Wilcox was watching through his binoculars when a dark shape suddenly burst through the surface 2,000 yards astern. The U-boat's pointed bow pierced daylight at an angle amid a storm of bubbles. A short tower and two platforms bristling with guns followed. The boat leveled off and settled deeply in the water, as if not fully buoyant.

For the rest of his life, Wilcox would describe this sight as his proudest moment. LTJG Melican later wrote that the *Joyce*'s crew sounded a "great yelling as the bow of the submarine broke the surface." Wilcox, Harris, and every other American present could scarcely have imagined such a climactic unveiling. Here was the amorphous phantom that had killed their friends on the *Leopold* and haunted every night's sleep since, all the while seemingly lurking beneath every wave. They had found their monster, and they had dragged it into the light.

As the wounded boat revealed itself, Klaus Hänert was grimly climbing the rungs to the tower hatch. It was his boat. His crew. His duty. He knew that the Americans, unaware of his intentions, were poised to blow the *U-550* out of the water unless he could signal his surrender first. The Old Man reached the top of the ladder, where his trembling hands turned the hatch's locking wheel and heaved it open. An ashen sky filled his view, as if to warn him that he was already too late. Just as he was reaching through the hatchway to pull himself up to the bridge, all three destroyer escorts opened fire.

Enemy shells ripped through the conning tower, instantly killing Walter Hauffe and Paul Lennemann at their stations. Gore splattered across the tower compartment's confines as Lennemann was torn nearly in half. On the ladder a few feet above them, shrapnel tore into the right half of Hänert's body and lacerated his face, shoulder, and leg. He lost his grip and plummeted 14 feet to the control room deck.

USS *Joyce*, still on a northward heading, blasted away with her aft 3-inch/.50 and 40mm guns. USS *Peterson*, about 3,000 yards behind the *Joyce* and with the U-boat off her port bow, let loose with 3-inch and 20mm fire. On a roughly perpendicular track was USS *Gandy*, her forward 3-inch/.50 guns thundering as she raced directly toward the U-boat.

Captained by LCDR Bill Sessions, the *Gandy* had been sprinting due west for a depth charge attack when the *U-550* appeared 500 yards off her starboard bow. "Right full rudder, come to three-two-zero!" Sessions roared. "Open fire and stand by to ram!" Guns blazing, the *Gandy* raced between the *Joyce* and *Peterson* on a beeline for the enemy, the *Peterson*'s torrent of gunfire abating just long enough for Sessions to cross her bow. Several hundred yards to their north, the *Joyce* entered a looping turn to steer back toward them.

The *Pock-Pock-Pock-Pock!* of automatic fire overlaid booming 3-inch guns as the *Gandy* charged at 15 knots, her bow aimed at the *U-550*'s conning tower. The *Gandy*'s bow missed the tower and instead smashed into the outer hull farther aft, shearing off the U-boat's stern bustle. Steel screeched as the destroyer's keel rode up and over the outer hull. "Left full rudder!" The *Gandy* splashed back down and sheered hard to port, her gunners delivering a punishing broadside as she sped past.[28]

Chaos reigned inside the *U-550* as the American gunfire punched fist-sized holes through the conning tower. The barrage abated only long enough for the impact of the *Gandy*'s bow to violently throw the Germans about the interior. The odor of leaking diesel fuel grew stronger as blood from the two eviscerated petty officers dripped down from the tower compartment onto men crowding the control room below. Flooding forced Hans Rauh, Albert Nitsche, and others to abandon their positions in the aft compartment. They retreated to the control room and secured the hatch behind themselves.

Hänert winced as Oberleutnant von Lingelsheim-Seibicke helped him upright. His own blood streamed down his face, he could not see out of his right eye, and the loud ringing in his ears rendered the surrounding din barely audible. The shouting and gunfire all sounded strangely muted, as if he were very far away. Lingelsheim-Seibicke's face was only inches from his. As Hänert's uninjured eye watched his subordinate's lips moving, he realized his first watch officer was speaking to him: "*HERR KALEUN!*"

Hänert's consciousness plunged back into the present. "*Herr Kaleun! Wir müssen die Männer aus—*" The captain cut him off. "*Ich weiss!*" he rasped. *I know!* He clasped the oberleutnant's arm and shakily regained his feet. His next order was largely a formality at this point, but his authoritative timbre carried it all the same: "Prepare to abandon ship!"

The *Gandy* sped past the wallowing U-boat after ramming it, her guns spitting a storm of high explosive and incendiary shells as she continued north. The *Joyce* had doubled back and was now approaching from the north; Wilcox's gunners opened up the moment the *Gandy* cleared their line of fire. Each *boom!* of the *Joyce*'s 3-inch/.50 cannons slung a 13-pound shell at 2,700 feet per second as streams of tracers crossed the wavetops and misses sowed foaming spouts around the U-boat. "The thing that would stick in my mind," recounted Collingwood Harris, "is that the firing was very intense."

Pock-Pock-Pock-Pock! The staccato hammering of automatic weapons intensified when USS *Peterson* resumed shooting, trapping the U-boat under withering fire from three directions. The odor of burnt nitrocellulose propellant clung to the *Peterson*'s decks as her 40mm and 20mm gunners unloaded at the cyclic rate. She was charging forward at 20 knots. As the destroyer escort's starboard hull passed close alongside the *U-550*, her K-guns barked, hurling a pair of depth charges set to detonate at 30 feet. The *Peterson* veered hard to port as they exploded under the Germans' keel.

The *Peterson*'s point-blank depth charges flung men violently about the *U-550*'s interior, interrupting their efforts to add extra layers of clothing. Each man also donned a Dräger rebreather over his white lifejacket. Dr Torge put on his red-and-white Red Cross armband, pocketed his schnapps flask, and hastily devoured a packet of butter to boost his energy for the swim ahead. The crew formed a line stretching from the control room into the forward torpedo room as the junior enlisted pushed and argued. Officers and petty officers took their places at the line's end.

Using his good arm, the captain grasped von Lingelsheim-Seibicke by the lifejacket and pulled him closer. "You'll have to lead them out!" Hänert shouted over the *clang*s and *zing*s of shells striking the boat. Hänert and Renzmann would be the last ones off, as they had one final duty to attend to. "*Jawohl, Herr Kaleun!*" Lingelsheim-Seibicke replied. "But not yet!" Hänert added, wincing again.

BOOM! Another shell passed through the tower's inch-thick steel like wet paper. *Pock-Pock-Pock-Pock!* The compartments were continuing to flood. Time was running out, but Hänert knew they would be cut to pieces if they tried to abandon ship now. He gazed ruefully through the open hatch at the gray sky.

The veterans of 16 April would never agree on what happened next. At 10:03, as the vengeful trio of warships blasted away, Wilcox sighted what he believed to be a flare rising from the *U-550*'s open conning tower hatch; LTJG Melican's report would mention a "white light." The surviving Germans would always deny firing any signaling device, and it was most likely a tracer deflecting off the U-boat's hull. Whatever it was, the *Joyce*'s commander seized the opportunity to halt the slaughter.

"CEASE FIRE!" Wilcox bellowed. "Cease fire! They're surrendering!"[29]

The Germans felt the torrent of gunfire slacken. At least one of the American warships was still shooting, but Hänert knew they had to either abandon ship now or accompany the *U-550* to the bottom. "Now! Go!" Hänert clapped von Lingelsheim-Seibicke on the shoulder and the first watch officer began clambering up the ladder. "Follow *Eins-Vee-Oh!* Quickly, boys!" The queue shuffled forward.

The guns of the *Joyce* and *Gandy* fell quiet, but the *Peterson*'s did not. Adrenaline mixed with rage over USS *Leopold* instead manifested itself in the continued fury of the *Peterson*'s guns. "Finally, the order came to cease fire," Harris recalled. "Nobody ceased firing, and the guns kept firing and the orders had come in screaming, 'Cease fire, cease fire!'" Harris remembered one gunner in a state of "hysterical euphoria" who gleefully shouted: "Did you see that? I shot his head off!" "Those twin 40s were going 'kaboom,' rhythmically pounding away. I guess that order was given five or six times before the guns began to let up. They didn't just stop."

Lieutenant Commander Wilcox felt a disturbingly familiar knot in the pit of his stomach as he watched the U-boat crew spilling from the conning tower hatch while the *Joyce* approached. He knew that stopping to recover them would make the *Joyce* a sitting duck. What if "Red George" was part of a wolfpack? Yet he also knew the Germans would not last long afloat. The water was too cold and too rough.

But few of the destroyer escort crewmen were eager to risk their necks for the men who had just blasted the *Pan Pennsylvania*, particularly if the Germans had friends nearby. "Nobody was taking any chances," Harris explained. "I thought that this [U-boat] was one of many that were out there." Nor did regulations demand the rescue of enemy personnel, the Navy having decreed that a ship's "commanding officer should be able to judge for himself. At no time should he sacrifice his ship to get [enemy] survivors." Wilcox's tactical intuition told him to go. The *Joyce* could be in another U-boat's sights at this very moment, and the convoy was sailing away minus half its escorts.

Bob Wilcox was watching Hänert's men jump overboard when he made his decision. He had left men to die in the frigid Atlantic once before—he would not do so again. Saving lives, after all, was his duty. Although Wilcox could not save Pete Cone, Ken Phillips, and all the others lost with USS *Leopold*, he could save these men—his enemy—right now. Nobody else had to die today.

"We are picking up survivors," he announced over the radio. "Don't trust him," warned the *Gandy*'s captain. The *Peterson*'s skipper added: "Look out, he may try to take down a few Yankees." Wilcox's reply demonstrated that compassion had not compromised the callous armor that war builds around a man's heart. "If this son of a bitch torpedoes me," Wilcox stated, "I hope you kill every goddamn one of them."[30]

In the U-boat's control room, a final pair of canvas shoes passed Hänert's head as their owner ascended the ladder, leaving the commander and chief engineer as the last living men aboard. The water was now more than knee-deep. At the high-pressure blowing manifold on the starboard bulkhead, Renzmann began opening the individual valves to add the remaining compressed air to the ballast tanks. "That should buy you a few more minutes. Don't wait for me," he added, looking back. "Alright," the captain replied after a moment. "I'll see you topside."

Hänert's injuries made exiting the boat a challenge. He laboriously mounted each ladder rung, climbing past the dead men in the tower until reaching the hatch. Outstretched hands assisted him past the missing top rung and into daylight. Off the *U-550*'s port side, the half-blind kommandant could see three dozen bobbing white lifejackets dispersed toward USS *Peterson*. The American ship was a long way off, but it had been the nearest vessel when von Lingelsheim-Seibicke led them out. The zerstörer circled at a distance, her guns finally silent.

The fifteen remaining Germans were huddled on the platforms awaiting the approaching USS *Joyce*. Albert Nitsche stood near the 37mm gun at the bandstand's aft end. He watched Kapitänleutnant Hänert limp across the wintergarten and down to the bandstand, offering encouragement with a smile on his bloody face. Hänert patted Hans Rauh on the back before halting and putting his back to the railing and his hands on his hips. It was everything he could muster to remain upright. As the *Joyce* drew alongside, Hans Rauh spotted Americans wielding Thompson submachine guns like he had seen in the movies. One was snapping photographs.

One of the Americans looking back at Rauh was Lieutenant (Junior Grade) John Melican. A British officer wrote of a similar scene that "it was odd, and infinitely disgusting, suddenly to see this wicked object, the loathsome cause of a hundred nights of fear and disaster, so close to them, so innocently exposed." It is not known

Last men off the *U-550*. Hans Rauh is visible on the bandstand with his head turned toward the camera. Klaus Hänert stands behind Rauh with his hands on his hips. Albert Nitsche is at the bandstand's aft end, facing the camera. (US National Archives, photographed by CPO Emmett O'Hara)

if Melican felt disgust at the sight of his flesh-and-blood foe, but it evoked nothing in the way of fear. He instead reported that Hänert's crewmen "appeared numb and cold, some were bloody and lacerated, others appeared helpless and unconscious."

Likewise, the U-boat itself now hardly seemed the malevolent steel shark of Melican's imagination. It was perforated with shell holes, only the tower and gun platforms remaining entirely above water as the gray sea eddied over its deck. The guns, which the Germans had made no attempt to use, were locked in their upright diving positions. The drowning *U-550*'s equilibrium continued deteriorating, its deck seesawing forward and aft as if trying to shake off the last of its crew.

Off the U-boat's opposite side, the *Pan Pennsylvania* was billowing smoke into the gray Sunday morning sky. Errant shellfire had set the tanker "ablaze from the stern to the bridge, ammo bursting from the after magazine," as Melican described. He turned his attention back to the Germans. With the Coast Guard crew at battle stations, LCDR Wilcox tasked the *Pan Pennsylvania*'s surviving Armed Guards with handling the POWs that the *Joyce* was about to retrieve.

"It's time to leave, boys!" Hänert shouted as the Coast Guardsmen draped a cargo net over the side of the *Joyce*'s hull. "I'll see you all in a few minutes!" One by one, Rauh, Nitsche, and the others climbed over the bandstand's railing and dropped into the deathly cold sea.[31]

Below them, Oberleutnant Renzmann worked with diligent haste to scuttle the boat by opening its ballast tank vents. Flooding from the battle damage had reached waist height, but an American boarding party could potentially keep the boat from going under (the US Navy would capture the *U-505* this way seven weeks later). Renzmann turned the red wheel over the control room's aft hatch, then pulled four red levers on the overhead. He next sloshed to the control room's forward end and opened the final main ballast tank using the wheel over the forward hatchway.

With all flood valves now open, Renzmann pointed his flashlight beam down the passageway toward the House of Lords. "*Ist da noch wer??*" he shouted. No response followed. Satisfied that he was leaving behind nobody alive, the chief engineer moved to the conning tower ladder and climbed.

Upon squeezing his large frame through the hatch, Renzmann saw an American destroyer 15 yards off the starboard side. Off the port side, and much farther away, he could see a tanker in flames. Between the U-boat and the tanker, USS *Peterson* was orbiting the scene. Most of the *U-550* crewmen were afloat off the port side, between the U-boat and the distant *Peterson*. Some were on small inflatable rafts while the remainder floated amid the waves.

Kapitänleutnant Hänert and Dr Torge were the only others still aboard when Renzmann emerged. They were standing at the bandstand's railing watching the remainder of the crew, seemingly a dozen men, swim sluggishly toward the nearer American destroyer. The chief engineer joined the captain and doctor on the bandstand. "It's done," he reported.

The *U-550* with the *Pan Pennsylvania* burning in the background. (US National Archives, enhanced by Peter Shafron)

He knew that the Hänert likely wished to be the last man off the *U-550*, so he did not delay. Renzmann swung his legs over the railing and dropped into the water. "Friedrich …" Hänert prompted. Dr Torge feared that perhaps his friend would not follow him, but he did not protest. Hänert watched the doctor splash and begin swimming toward USS *Joyce*. He looked once more off the U-boat's other side, where most of his crew was swimming toward USS *Peterson*, before facing the *Joyce* again. The Old Man grimaced in pain as he gingerly swung one leg at a time over the railing. He inhaled deeply, then dropped off the edge.[32]

The frigid water sucked the breath from Hänert's lungs and he immediately coughed and sputtered, the cold shock rendering him unable to control his breathing. His wounded right arm and leg were of only marginal use. Cold degrades even the fittest swimmer's performance, and Hänert's years of long-distance swims in the Baltic now seemed woefully insufficient. Exertion brought increased blood flow to his skin, which enabled the 40° Fahrenheit water to sap his body heat even more rapidly.

Despite making slow and painstaking progress toward the *Joyce*, he was growing weaker by the second. Shrapnel had left his lifejacket in tatters, and he felt progressively heavier as it disintegrated. Hänert's strength was ebbing only yards from the destroyer escort's hull when a rope suddenly splashed into the water before him. Summoning a final reserve of vigor, he grasped it, only to find he was too weak to pull himself closer to the *Joyce*. As Hänert coughed and sputtered again, he felt someone grab his shoulder from behind. "I've got you!" a familiar voice shouted. "I've got you, Klaus!" It was Dr Torge.

LTJG Melican's men aggressively searched the gasping German survivors as Hugo Renzmann peered over the deck's edge. He saw Torge use the last of his energy to loop a rescue line around their commander. "I wrapped myself in that rope," Hänert would tell his son years later. "I made up my mind that if the Americans wanted their rope back, they would have to pull me in with it."

Hans Rauh was struggling to climb the net when a Coast Guardsman extended a helping hand. Grasping it, he looked up in surprise at the first black person he had ever met. The mechanikergefreiter had barely reached the deck when several Americans angrily grabbed fistfuls of his wet clothing. Shouting unintelligibly at him, they dragged Rauh's limp body from the edge and searched him with an intensity bordering on violence. Kapitänleutnant Hänert and Dr Torge were the last men to be rescued, their depleted strength forcing the Americans to muscle the pair's waterlogged weight aboard the *Joyce*. Hospital corpsmen tended to the wounded as Dr Torge passed around the flask of schnapps.[33]

The *U-550*'s final dive began at 10:34 as Renzmann watched the bow tilt upward. Though bittersweet, the sight at least imparted the satisfaction of knowing that American hands would never touch his boat. The *Joyce*'s Coast Guard crewmen and the *Pan Pennsylvania*'s Armed Guard detachment were occupied with the POWs, but the *Gandy* and *Peterson* erupted in cheers as the vanquished *U-550* sank. As

Ensign Bill Stanback recounted seventy years later, "You would have thought we had just won a football game."

The three dozen *U-550* crewmen led into the sea by Oberleutnant von Lingelsheim-Seibicke remained strung out in the direction of USS *Peterson* as the pitiless sea deadened their cries for help. *"Kameraden! ... Bitte, Kameraden!"* The glowering steel shepherd was unmoved by their pleas. Neither the *Peterson* nor *Gandy* would retrieve any German survivors, who were left behind with the burning and abandoned *Pan Pennsylvania*. None were seen alive again, though American forces would find six bodies over the following weeks.

Still unsure whether other U-boats were nearby, the destroyer escorts made three more depth charge attacks after the *U-550* went under. Wilcox eventually determined that the U-boat wreck was responsible for the sonar contacts, and they finished chasing ghosts shortly before noon. The victorious *Joyce*, *Gandy*, and *Peterson* finally formed up three abreast and turned east to rejoin the convoy.[34]

***

The events of 16 April 1944 killed fifteen merchant mariners and ten Armed Guards. The destroyer escorts suffered no fatalities, although the *Peterson*'s gunfire wounded four on the *Gandy*. The thirteen *U-550* crewmen retrieved by USS *Joyce* were the only Germans to survive. Among them were Klaus Hänert, Hugo Renzmann, Friedrich Torge, Hans Rauh, Albert Nitsche, and Hans Zwemke. One of them, 21-year-old Heinz Wenz, died of his injuries aboard the *Joyce* a few hours later. The burning *Pan Pennsylvania* went keel-up near the attack site, where her aft third broke off and sank. The remainder drifted north for two days before being sunk by aircraft.

In five furious minutes, Task Group 21.5 expended thirty-seven armor-piercing 3-inch shells and nearly two thousand 20mm and 40mm shells, divided between tracer and incendiary. The DEs also deployed nineteen depth charges. No shells or torpedoes were fired by the *U-550*. "The utmost credit goes to LCDR Robert Wilcox [and] the officers and men of the USS JOYCE," wrote LTJG John Melican. The *Joyce*'s actions "could not have been carried out with greater precision and efficiency." According to Melican, Wilcox and his crew had embodied the Coast Guard motto of *Semper Paratus* (Always Ready), "in the highest sense of the phrase."

The officer and enlisted POWs were segregated aboard the *Joyce*. Hans Rauh, Albert Nitsche, and the other enlisted POWs formed an unlikely bond with their captors over the ensuing days. The Americans gave their prisoners clothing and cigarettes, and both sides spoke of homes, families, and girlfriends. Rauh and the others expressed disappointment upon learning they were being taken to Britain rather than to the United States.

After the DEs returned to their stations with the convoy, LCDR Wilcox went to the cabin where his enemy counterpart was stowed. Klaus Hänert's right eye was now bandaged, and he was sitting on the edge of a neatly made rack as he watched Wilcox through his uninjured eye. The two officers were only three years apart in age and both were tall and fair-haired. Hänert's unpolished English would prove sufficient for he and Wilcox to converse during the voyage to Northern Ireland but, presently, the Coast Guard officer had unfortunate news for his ranking POW.

"I'm sorry to tell you that your sailor, Wenz, he just died." Hänert was silent for a moment before replying. "Thank you, commander." He expected his captor to depart, but Wilcox instead proposed something unexpected.[35]

***

17 April 1944
Somewhere in the western Atlantic
11:03

"They that go down to the sea in ships, that do business in great waters; These see the works of the Lord, and His wonders in the deep ..."

Coast Guardsmen and Navy sailors stood on one side of Heinz Wenz's body, U-boat men on the other. Between them stood Lieutenant Commander Robert Wilcox in his dress blues, a Bible in hand as he recited chapters 27 and 103 from the Book of Psalms: "Thou preparest a table before me in the presence of mine enemies ..."

A cool breeze carried his words across the surreal gathering. Clear weather and a placid sea contrasted with the previous day's tempestuous gloom. An American flag was draped incongruously over the 21-year-old's body. No other flag was available. As Hänert watched in silence, a German poem crossed his mind:

> There are no roses on a sailor's grave,
> No lilies on an ocean wave,
> The only tribute is the seagulls' sweeps,
> And the teardrops that a sweetheart weeps.

A rifle detail fired three salvos of seven shots into the air when Wilcox finished reading. The board where the deceased lay was then slanted toward the sea, Wenz's body slid out from beneath the American flag, and Klaus Hänert watched as one more young man was consigned to the depths.[36]

***

26 April 1944
Londonderry, Northern Ireland
09:02

Decades later, Collingwood Harris would vividly recall how Londonderry's port at Lisahally sat ensconced by hills lush with the green brilliance of an Irish springtime. Three thousand miles from his native New Jersey and ten days after the *Pan Pennsylvania* attack, Harris and a handful of other Coast Guardsmen were looking down at the pier from USS *Peterson*'s flying bridge. Below them stood twelve Germans in a formation of two rows.

Klaus Hänert stood in the front row and farthest to the right, his light-brown hair neatly parted. He wore sunglasses for his injured eye and a Coast Guard-issue sweater with the collar of a khaki shirt pulled through its neck. Hugo Renzmann stood on his left, then Dr Torge. At the left-most end of the back row stood Hans Rauh and Albert Nitsche. Their hair was longer than ever, though they were now clean-shaven.

The loss of forty-four of his fifty-six men left Hänert numb, his dignified bearing straining under the weight that his shoulders now bore. And yet, despite almost impossible odds, here stood twelve where there ought to be none. It is unknown whether he ever afforded himself due credit for this unlikely accomplishment, but the decades of life ahead of these men and their descendants would prove testament to their commander's honor. He had done his duty.

An audience of American servicemen had gathered. On all sides of the formation, US Marines clutching M1 Garand rifles stood ready to take them into custody. Onlookers' furtive chatter dissipated as a lone figure emerged, striding toward the formation. Tall, blonde, and handsome, the American officer moved with a liveliness

U-550 survivors in Londonderry. Front row, left to right: Klaus Hänert, Hugo Renzmann, and Friedrich Torge. In the back row, Hans Rauh stands second from the right. (US Navy photo courtesy of Eric Wiberg & Mark Munro)

in his step that had been absent for many weeks. A single command from Klaus Hänert boomed across the pier. *"Ach-TUNG!"*

The twelve prisoners snapped smartly to attention. Robert Wilcox halted in front of the POWs and faced them. "It was rather an interesting scene in a sort of chivalrous or gallant way," as Collingwood Harris described it. *"Besatzung ... Ordnung!"* The prisoners rendered a crisp military salute, with Hänert taking one large step forward before saluting. He ignored the pain in his wounded shoulder as he held his fingertips against his brow. Wilcox returned the salute, and a dozen hands snapped back to their trouser seams.

The USS *Joyce* commander extended his hand. Hänert grasped it firmly. "Good luck," Wilcox stated. "Fair winds, commander," the *U-550* commander replied. Although Bob Wilcox could not see Klaus Hänert's eyes behind the sunglasses, one wonders whether each man saw something on his counterpart's face. It was, perhaps, the faintest trace of a smile.[37]

Part III

CHAPTER SIXTEEN

Wolfsdämmerung

"So the U-boat force fought with what it had, and in the last year of the war it
accomplished little but self-destruction."
—Oberleutnant Herbert Werner, *Iron Coffins* (1969)

23 April 1945
5 miles southeast of Cape Elizabeth, Maine
12:13

The wake behind the green buoy dissipated as the subchaser towing it slowed to
a halt. It was a chilly day with a clear sky and Maine's rocky coast visible in the
distance. On the opposite end of the towline was the subchaser USS *Eagle 56*, the
same ship that rescued the USS *Jacob Jones* survivors off Cape May more than three
years earlier. Damaged a few weeks later when she hit a submerged shipwreck at the
Delaware Capes, she was returned to service by cannibalizing another Eagle boat for
parts. The twilight of the subchaser's career now found her towing a cylindrical green
target buoy for Navy and Marine Corps pilots based at Naval Air Station Brunswick.

All sixty-two men aboard the *Eagle 56* knew that Nazi Germany was on the
brink of surrender, and none would have been surprised to learn that Adolf Hitler
had only days left to live. The Battle of the Atlantic was effectively over, the U-boat
peril now mostly spoken of in the past tense. As one 21-year-old crewman recently
wrote to his sister in New Jersey, "What could be safer than Portland Harbor?"

Lieutenant (Junior Grade) John Scagnelli, a 25-year-old former collegiate
swimmer, was asleep below decks when he was awakened by his head slamming into
a bulkhead. The explosion which hurled him from his bunk also broke the ship in
two, heaving both halves upward amid a plume of water and steam that rose 200
feet skyward. Dazed and bleeding profusely from the scalp, Scagnelli clambered
topside as the dying ship rolled toward her flank.

Machinist's Mate 2nd Class Johnny Breeze was preparing to jump from the
stern when MM3 Oscar Davis grabbed his arm. "Breezy, a sub, look! Look!" Breeze
sighted the unmistakable shape of a conning tower some 500 yards away. "It seemed
like a submarine surfaced," Gunner's Mate 3rd Class Lawrence Edwards recalled.
Several survivors would report witnessing something painted in red and yellow on

the tower. The U-boat was only visible for a few moments before vanishing beneath the calm afternoon sea.

Scagnelli, Breeze, and roughly twenty others leapt into the 42° Fahrenheit water under a billowing cloud of smoke and steam. The aft section of the *Eagle 56* tipped fantail-up and decamped for the seafloor within two minutes. Ten minutes after that, the subchaser's other half aimed its bow toward the New England sky and similarly departed. Those crewmen left alive—only thirteen would return to shore—watched the savior of the USS *Jacob Jones* survivors disappear in an upheaval of oil and bubbles as the hull's large white "56" slid beneath the waves.

The *Eagle 56*, one of the Battle of the Atlantic's last casualties, followed more than two years of relative quiet in Eastern Sea Frontier and Gulf Sea Frontier waters. The Ubootwaffe damaged or destroyed only ten ships here in 1943 and three in 1944. Of these, only the *Pan Pennsylvania* was hit anywhere near New Jersey. Until the *Eagle 56* attack, 1945 had seen just two merchantmen sunk and one damaged within the Sea Frontiers. Although the Gray Wolves would not return to the Jersey Shore in force during the Reich's bloody final days, the killing along the East Coast was not yet finished.[1]

***

The U-boats' defeat in American waters in 1942 was followed by their irreversible loss of the wider Atlantic during 1943. BdU was forced to abandon wolfpack tactics altogether by mid-1944, the last surviving U-tanker resupply boat was sunk in June of that year, and the last U-boats in the Mediterranean were destroyed by September. Herbert Werner, a mere midshipman in 1941, had since become a battle-hardened kommandant. He described a January 1945 encounter with five new U-boat commanders preparing for their first patrols. "I looked at them," Werner wrote, "and I saw dead men."

Grand Admiral Karl Dönitz continued sending U-boat crews to their deaths under the premise that the campaign diverted Allied resources from other fronts. Dönitz biographer Peter Padfield wrote that the grand admiral was "convinced, like Hitler, that willpower and fanaticism would make up for numerical or technical inferiority." Historian Robert Citino described this "overreliance on will and determination" as "a ticket to oblivion." He compared it to "a kind of *Täuschungsmanöver*—a vast deception operation, but this time you wound up fooling only yourself."

In March 1945, Dönitz exhorted his men to sink "as many ships as possible for the Anglo-Saxons in total disregard of the risk," citing Japanese troops' battle to the death on Iwo Jima as an example for Germans to emulate. Once a tactical innovator with a clearly defined and ostensibly viable strategic vision, Dönitz's war had devolved into an agonizingly protracted *Totenritt*, or death ride. This was the Prussian tradition of the all-or-nothing final counterattack "no matter how dim the prospects," explained Robert Citino. "It existed in a realm beyond rational discourse or sober reflection."

Obersteuermann Helmut Klotzch shouts for rescue after the *U-175* is sunk by USCGC *Spencer*, 17 April 1943. (US National Archives)

Morale in the Ubootwaffe nonetheless remained "unimpaired to the bitter end," noted Winston Churchill. "Our crews sailed out obediently, even optimistically, on ludicrous missions that ended in death," wrote Herbert Werner. For some, betting one's life on patrol became preferable to visiting the rubble-strewn cities they called home. "At least [aboard the U-boat] everything was in its place, I knew where fore and aft lay," one stated. Notwithstanding the Gray Wolves' willingness to continue the fight, their perspective grew salted with fatalism. A message scrawled on a naval barracks wall in 1945 declared: "More than a U-boat sailor one cannot be."

Their continued loyalty and willingness to fight was partly a legacy of the High Seas Fleet mutiny in the closing days of World War I. German military historian Sönke Neitzel explained that senior naval officers remained "ever conscious of the shame of the sailors' rebellion of 1918." According to Admiral Erich Raeder, "every senior officer in the Kriegsmarine silently swore that there should never again be a November 1918."[2]

Admiral Dönitz was described by one subordinate as a "fey and gloomy figure" by the war's final months, and he grew ever more disconnected from his men as he slipped further into Hitler's orbit. The Führer declared that "I regard [Dönitz] as my best man," and one observer described the odd couple spending ever-greater lengths of time "together under four eyes." Their melding of mind and purpose continued even as their outward differences grew more apparent, the ramrod-straight admiral's martial presence contrasting with the hollow-chested dictator's increasingly stooped posture and shuffled gait.

Hitler fed on Dönitz's unflagging optimism, will to victory, and uncritical endorsement of the Führer's self-image as Germany's man of destiny. He also valued one of his few subordinates who did not cater to his tantrums and impulses. Dönitz, in turn, fastened himself to an idol who rewarded his ambition and quelled his insecurities while indulging his military predilections. Through this toxic symbiosis, wrote Peter Padfield, "each reinforced the other's cosmic delusions."

The admiral's star rose as Hitler's relationship with the Heer continued to sour. The Führer's mistrust toward the army was seemingly validated on 20 July 1944 when he narrowly survived a bomb planted by a cabal of army officers in a crowded conference room at the Wolf's Lair. The virtual absence of naval officers among the conspirators (a notable exception was spymaster Admiral Wilhelm Canaris) further burnished Hitler's opinion of the Kriegsmarine. So, too, did Dönitz's vocal Nazism. "I would rather eat dirt than see my grandchildren grow up in the filthy, poisonous atmosphere of Jewry," the grand admiral declared in August 1944.

Dönitz also quashed any dissent within his own ranks, railing against "complainers who voice their own wretched and miserable opinions." Any man in the Kriegsmarine who "becomes the least bit shaky in his loyalty to the National Socialist state and the Führer," he warned, would be "called to account" without mercy.[3]

***

One such "complainer" was Oskar-Heinz Kusch, the anti-Nazi oberleutnant on Werner Winter's U-103 when it sank the India Arrow off New Jersey in February 1942. The following year saw him take command of the U-154, thereafter dubbed the "U-Sunshine" for Kusch's easygoing attitude. His flotilla commander was Fregattenkapitän Ernst Kals, the former U-130 captain who torpedoed the Norwegian tanker Varanger. Kusch led the U-154 on two arduous combat patrols to Brazil, but ceaseless American air attacks were not the only threat to his life.

Oberleutnant Kusch's hatred of National Socialism had grown more vocal by 1943, but the U-154's three other officers were committed Nazis. Conflict simmered with particular intensity between Kusch and first watch officer Ulrich Abel. Kusch received the Kriegsmarine's authorization to marry in December 1943, yet remained unaware of how much danger he was in. The sword fell the following month when Abel formally accused Kusch of sedition and cowardice, and Ernst Kals dutifully placed Kusch under arrest.

The allegations presented at Kusch's court-martial included a claim that the devout Catholic had removed a portrait of Hitler from the wardroom because "we don't practice idolatry here." Abel and the other accusers also alleged that Kusch had denied the threat of "world Jewry," compared National Socialists to tapeworms, and claimed that Hitler's ranting and raving saw the Führer pull down curtains and roll around on the floor. Charges for cowardice were dropped, however, once it became clear that Kusch's personal performance in combat was impeccable.

The trial was a charade, and historian Jordan Vause wrote that "only Kusch himself rose above the tawdry mess." He did not deny many of the accusations, instead claiming that his words had been misconstrued and that irreverent humor was part of the Ubootwaffe's cultural fabric. Former *U-103* commander Werner Winter testified in Kusch's defense, yet a combination of Nazi bile and sensitivity stemming from the 1918 mutiny sealed the 26-year-old officer's fate. Kusch showed no emotion when the judge declared him guilty and sentenced him to death.

Werner Winter leveraged his personal relationship with Dönitz to plead for a retrial, but Winter's onetime mentor was determined to make an example of Kusch. "[Dönitz's] widely advertised bond with his men seems to have failed completely," Jordan Vause observed. Kusch penned a letter to his father hours before his death. "Life could have been wonderful, but a senseless fate has torn it to pieces," Kusch wrote. "I shall be your faithful son for ever and ever eternally. Yours, Oskar." When asked in front of the firing squad whether he had any last words, he responded: "No, nothing." Oskar-Heinz Kusch's life then ended with a volley of bullets at 06:32 on 12 May 1944.

Dönitz's callous and uncompromising stance regarding the young officer's fate is telling, especially considering that the admiral had lost his own son, Peter, almost exactly a year earlier. It would not be the family's last casualty. On the day after Kusch's execution, the elder of his two sons was killed on a torpedo boat in the English Channel. Klaus Dönitz's body later washed ashore in France.[4]

***

As the war turned in the Allies' favor after 1942, the Nazis placed ever-greater hope in an array of high-tech weapons projects. Among these were the V-1 cruise missile and V-2 ballistic missile ("V" for *"Vergeltungswaffen,"* or vengeance weapons). New U-boat designs to replace the obsolete Type VII and IX also held high priority, but their lengthy development demanded an interim solution. The spring of 1944 therefore saw the first operational use of the *Schnorchel*, a tube for air intake and engine exhaust that enabled a U-boat to remain submerged for an entire patrol. However, it also limited the boat's speed to about 5 knots and was visible to both radar and the naked eye. The schnorchel ultimately only slightly improved a U-boat's odds of attack and survival.

The twilight of defeat also saw Germany deploy the world's first true submarines (as opposed to submersibles). The Type XXI and XXIII *Elektroboote* featured a streamlined hull packed with batteries that enabled twice the submerged speed of existing U-boats and greatly extended underwater range. The elektro-boats greatly concerned the British and Americans, though their potential was negated by their appearance only in 1945. An even more revolutionary design, the hydrogen peroxide-fueled "Walter boats," never saw combat. The victorious Allies would use the Type XXI, XXIII, and Walter designs to develop the first generation of Cold War submarines.[5]

***

Just as United States forces in the Pacific and European theaters effectively fought two different wars, Nazi Germany faced the Soviet Union in Eastern Europe and the Anglo-American-led Western Allies everywhere else. Yet it was the plains of Eastern Europe—the keystone of Hitler's envisioned World Reich—that became its grave. Of the 5.3 million German military fatalities during World War II, approximately 4 million were killed fighting the Soviets on the Eastern Front. This stark reality, however, tells an incomplete story about the Allied Powers' individual contributions to victory.

Despite significant geographic and political distances between the Western Allies and the Soviets, Anglo-American economic and naval strength enabled them to cooperate strategically to an extent never possible between Germany and Japan. Consequently, and despite decades of Soviet and Russian propaganda, the Western Allies were by no means a mere supporting act for the Red Army. More truth can instead be found in the oversimplified, albeit not entirely inaccurate, adage that the war in Europe was won by "British intelligence, American steel, and Soviet blood."[6]

Soviet battlefield victories after 1942 were, in large part, a result of the enormous volume of weapons and supplies received from the United States. By 1945, one in five Red Army tanks was an American-made M4 Sherman and one-third of its unarmored vehicles were Ford jeeps and Studebaker trucks. The United States also provided the USSR with 12,004 aircraft, 58 percent of its aviation fuel, and 53 percent of its explosives. Soviet premier Nikita Khrushchev's memoirs claimed that his nation would have been defeated without American aid. "No one talks about this officially," Khrushchev added. Even legendary general Georgy Zhukov admitted as much in a conversation secretly recorded by the KGB: "It cannot be denied that the Americans sent us matériel without which we could not have formed our reserves or continued the war."[7]

Much of the cargo that reached the Soviet Union and Britain was hauled by a new merchant ship design. Antiquated freighters built at Philadelphia's Hog Island during the previous war were supplanted after 1941 by "Liberty ships." Dubbed "Ugly Ducklings" by FDR, these British-designed merchant vessels were mass-produced in US shipyards using welding in lieu of riveting for faster production with less steel. A total of 2,710 Liberty ships were launched. A similar approach produced 523 tankers, the majority being the standardized T2-SE-A1 design first built for Socony-Vacuum in 1941/42. The American output of Liberty ships and tankers collectively represents the greatest feat of mass manufacturing ever seen.

The Liberty ships played a key role in Operation Overlord: the landings at Normandy, France in June 1944. By month's end, the Allies had put ashore approximately 850,000 troops, 148,000 vehicles, and over 500,000 tons of supplies. Hundreds of merchant vessels accompanied the landing fleet across the English Channel and shuttled supplies over the ensuing days as V-1 missiles hurtled overhead toward London. The ships'

Armed Guard sailors stayed gainfully employed fighting torpedo boats, shore batteries, and the handful of Luftwaffe aircraft that dared show themselves.

The human and material colossus transported by Allied merchantmen for the Normandy operation was an astounding spectacle. American war correspondent Ernie Pyle, who visited Omaha Beach after the first landings, wrote that "men and equipment were flowing from England in such a gigantic stream that it made the waste on the beachhead seem like nothing at all, really nothing at all." Stunned German POWs beheld the spectacle "as if in a trance," Pyle wrote. "The expression on their faces was something forever unforgettable."

Admiral Karl Dönitz ordered every available U-boat thrown at the Allied armada off Normandy, yet even BdU's war diary acknowledged that "for those boats without a schnorchel, this means the last operation." The order was so suicidal that Dönitz's operations chief disobeyed it by instead dispatching only schnorchel-equipped boats in the Channel itself. It mattered little either way. From 6 June until 31 August, the once-vaunted Gray Wolves destroyed just ten merchant ships and nine landing vessels for the price of twenty U-boats sunk and nearly a thousand crewmen killed or captured.

Advancing Allied armies also captured or cut off the French ports which the Ubootwaffe had relied on since 1940. The US Army's VII Corps captured Brest, and American and Free French forces reached the outskirts of Lorient. Only Brest and Bordeaux were captured, however. Lorient, Saint-Nazaire, and La Pallice all remained in German hands until war's end, albeit under siege and largely useless as U-boat bases. The Ubootwaffe consequently shifted to German and Norwegian ports.[8]

Merchant shipping weaponized American industrial strength, and this enabled the liberation of continental Europe by providing the Allies with decisive quantitative and qualitative advantages. This has contributed to the myth that the Wehrmacht was simply overwhelmed by Allied numbers rather than bested by skill of arms, yet the facts show that US forces in 1944–45 outfought their German adversaries in every domain of battle. Hitler and Dönitz had sneered at American combat prowess in 1942, but one Wehrmacht general would concede that the American fighting man proved himself "a very worthy, well-trained, and physically tough opponent."[9]

***

By 1944, Dönitz was "not fighting with his head, but with his blood … not like a rational commander, but as a National Socialist," according to Peter Padfield. Likewise, Hitler was determined that the Third Reich would not fall without taking the greatest possible number of lives with it. As armaments minister Albert Speer recounted, "In a kind of delirium [Hitler] pictured … the destruction of New York in a hurricane of fire." He envisioned "skyscrapers being turned into gigantic burning torches, collapsing upon one another, the glow of the exploding city illuminating the dark sky." Around this same time, moreover, one resident of the greater New York City area was working to make this nightmarish vision a reality.

Carl Krepper was a short and unassuming man who emigrated from Germany in 1909. Ordained a Lutheran minister in Philadelphia the following year, Krepper became a US citizen and earned a degree from Rutgers University. He spent most of his American years ministering to congregations in New Jersey, where he also became an ardent Nazi and joined the German-American Bund's predecessor organization. When Krepper returned to Germany in 1935, his stateside connections to other German immigrants and Nazi sympathizers brought him to the attention of the Abwehr, Admiral Wilhelm Canaris' military intelligence division. He was recruited and subsequently returned to the United States as an enemy agent in 1941. Pastor Krepper required no U-boat to reach the United States: as an American citizen, he took a normal passenger ship.

Krepper was living in Rahway, New Jersey when the FBI began investigating him after Operation Pastorius imploded in June 1942. His name and address had been turned over by saboteur George Dasch, and an FBI sting operation in Newark apprehended Krepper in December 1944. The treacherous preacher had been unable to link up with the agents landed by U-boat in 1942, nevertheless, the threat of a Nazi attack on US home soil loomed conspicuously over Carl Krepper's trial in February 1945.[10]

A few weeks earlier, in late 1944, reports had begun percolating through intelligence channels of a plan to strike American cities using V-2 missiles launched by U-boats. One source stemmed from Germany's second and final saboteur infiltration attempt. The *U-1230* covertly landed two agents—a German citizen and an American traitor—on the coast of Maine in November 1944. In an echo of Operation Pastorius, the scheme fell apart when the American surrendered himself to the FBI. Alarm bells soon went off, however, when the American-born double-turncoat told his interrogators about U-boats "fitted with a special rocket-firing device ... to be used against the Eastern Coast of the United States."

The Nazis did, in fact, intend to attack the United States using missiles launched by U-boats. Mayor Fiorello LaGuardia triggered public anxiety in December when he invoked the specter of missiles hitting New York City, and a Navy press conference a month later stated that an attack by these "robot bombs" was "not only possible, but probable." In January, Albert Speer boasted in a radio address that missiles would "fall on New York by February 1st, 1945."

The alarm reached a fever pitch by 2 April 1945 after Enigma decrypts revealed that seven U-boats, designated *Gruppe Seewolf* (Group Sea Wolf), were westbound with orders to "attack areas in the American coastal zone." The threat of a last-ditch revenge attack killing American civilians prompted Operation Teardrop, the war's largest hunter-killer effort. Four escort carriers and more than forty destroyers assembled in two blocking lines and swept eastward to flush out the U-boats before they reached their missile launch positions. The wolves bit back, sinking USS *Frederick C. Davis* (DE-136) with 115 lives lost, but the Teardrop forces destroyed five Seewolf boats between 15 April and 5 May.

Four U-boats went down with all hands, but the *U-546*'s captured crew experienced the wrath of men fearing imminent terror bombing of their own families. When the POWs denied knowing of any missile attack, US Marines beat them with truncheons and threatened to use "the Russian methods." Additional coercion, described only as "shock treatment" by Navy records, eventually rendered the *U-546* kommandant unconscious. But the POWs were not lying, and British intelligence had been rightly skeptical about the threat: Germany's missile project was still in the prototype phase. Yet Operation Teardrop destroyed only five U-boats—where were the other two?[11]

***

Dönitz visited Hitler's bunker every day until 20 April 1945, when Kriegsmarine headquarters staff fled Berlin only an hour ahead of Soviet forces. The admiral relocated with his officers to Plön in northern Germany, but other rats were abandoning the sinking ship. Luftwaffe chief Hermann Göring was stripped of all titles and banished from the Nazi Party on 23 April after attempting to assume leadership of what remained of Hitler's empire. The same fate befell SS chief Heinrich Himmler days later when Hitler learned of his attempts to negotiate with the Allies. Dönitz was in Plön on 30 April when a telegraph arrived from Hitler's bunker: "FRESH TREACHERY AFOOT … FÜHRER EXPECTS YOU TO TAKE INSTANT AND RUTHLESS ACTION AGAINST TRAITORS."

Composer Richard Wagner's operas played over the radio as the Reich's final reckoning loomed. These were Hitler's favorites and had partly inspired the theatricality of the Nazis' public image in the 1930s. Wagner's operas were steeped in Germanic mythology and told of titanic struggles, betrayal, heroic death, and rebirth. His magnum opus culminates with the *Götterdämmerung*, or Twilight of the Gods, an apocalyptic final battle that sees the hero treacherously slain and the world destroyed to be born anew.

Hitler's own Götterdämmerung arrived in April 1945 as the Soviet noose closed around Berlin. On 29 April, he married his longtime girlfriend, Eva Braun, in a perfunctory ceremony in his Berlin bunker. He then dictated a final will and testament that named his successor but consisted largely of a rambling diatribe against the Jews. The document also included a swipe at the Heer in the form of Hitler's wish that the army learn to be as loyal as the Kriegsmarine.

Red Army troops were only a few blocks from the *Führerbunker* by the following afternoon when the newly married couple bid farewell to a few devotees and retired to Hitler's study. Braun sat at one end of the sofa, drew her knees to her chest, and bit a capsule of potassium cyanide. It is not known whether he waited for her agonized convulsions to cease before he sat at the sofa's opposite end and placed a cyanide capsule between his teeth. He pressed the barrel of a 7.65mm Walther pistol against the side of his head, then simultaneously bit down and pulled the trigger.

Several hours later, Dönitz was with Albert Speer at Plön when a message from the bunker left him stunned: "THE FÜHRER APPOINTS YOU, HERR GROSSADMIRAL, AS HIS SUCCESSOR." A subsequent and final telegraph confirmed Hitler's death, but *Reichspräsident* Dönitz had little time to process his unexpected promotion to head of state. He first needed to deal with Himmler, who arrived at Plön that evening with an entourage of SS troops. Dönitz's own bodyguard detachment consisted of U-boat sailors led by former *U-333* commander Peter Cremer. The U-boat men hid in the trees around the building while Dönitz, with a loaded pistol concealed beneath documents on his desk, informed the erstwhile *Reichsführer-SS* that he had no use for him. Himmler departed after daybreak.

That same day, 1 May, Dönitz broadcast a radio address to the nation. Excerpts from Wagner's operas prefaced his announcement that Adolf Hitler had died "a heroic death" while "fighting to his last breath against Bolshevism." Dönitz then stated: "The Führer has appointed me as his successor. In consciousness of the responsibility, I take over the leadership of the German *Volk* at this fateful hour ..."[12]

***

The U-boats sent to America's coast amid the Reich's death rattles included the *U-853* under Oberleutnant Helmut Frömsdorf. After sinking the subchaser *Eagle 56* off Maine on 23 April 1945, Frömsdorf crept south, using the seafloor's uneven topography to hide from sonar. The ability to charge his batteries from periscope depth enabled him to elude US forces as the *U-853* rounded Cape Cod and entered Rhode Island Sound, although a Coast Guard frigate did briefly detect him. "CAN HEAR ELECTRIC MOTORS AND BLOW OF TANKS," the frigate reported. "SIGHTED SMOKE ON SURFACE FROM NO VISIBLE SOURCE ... PRESUMED TO BE ENEMY SUBMARINE USING SCHNORCHEL."

The *U-853* was still making its way south on 4 May when BdU broadcast a message: "ALL U-BOATS. ATTENTION ALL U-BOATS. CEASE FIRE AT ONCE. STOP ALL HOSTILE ACTION AGAINST ALLIED SHIPPING. DÖNITZ." Another followed. "MY U-BOAT MEN," it began, "YOU HAVE FOUGHT LIKE LIONS. AN OVERWHELMING MATERIAL SUPERIORITY HAS DRIVEN US INTO A TIGHT CORNER FROM WHICH IT IS NO LONGER POSSIBLE TO CONTINUE THE WAR. UNBEATEN AND UNBLEMISHED, YOU LAY DOWN YOUR ARMS AFTER A HEROIC FIGHT WITHOUT PARALLEL." It concluded, "LONG LIVE GERMANY."

A subsequent order to sail for the nearest Allied port would not be broadcast until 8 May, but the ceasefire's implications were clear. "The murdering had finally come to an end," wrote Oberleutnant Herbert Werner. "My death in an iron coffin, a verdict of long standing, was finally suspended. The truth was so beautiful that it seemed to be a dream." What neither the Allies nor the Germans knew, however, was that one final battle remained.[13]

It has never been conclusively determined why Helmut Frömsdorf did not comply with Dönitz's ceasefire order, and his own sister would later express bewilderment at his actions. He either failed to receive the message, willfully disregarded it, or believed it an Allied ruse. Perhaps the *U-853*'s previous narrow escapes (which earned it the nickname "*Der Seiltaenger*," or the Tightrope Walker) convinced the 24-year-old commander that the boat could survive seizing a final measure of glory. Whatever Frömsdorf's reasoning, the last U-boat in American waters would go down fighting.

At 17:40 on 5 May, thirteen days after sinking USS *Eagle 56* and five days after Adolf Hitler's death, the *U-853* torpedoed and sank the freighter *Black Point* 3 miles off Point Judith, Rhode Island. Eleven mariners and an Armed Guard were killed. Frömsdorf then remained submerged as he retreated toward East Ground, a steep shoal a dozen miles southeast that could hide him from sonar. Two Navy destroyer escorts and a Coast Guard frigate on the opposite side of Block Island quickly responded, and ten other warships soon joined them.

The *U-853*'s most likely escape route was not hard to deduce. Lined abreast and trailing noisemaking homing torpedo decoys, the improvised hunter-killer force began sweeping south from Block Island's northern tip at 20:10. The shallow water and flat seafloor left nowhere to hide, and sonar soon pinged a contact creeping along the bottom while hydrophones heard the faint beat of propellers.

The Navy's USS *Atherton* (DE-169) and the Coast Guard's USS *Moberly* (PF-63) attacked with depth charges and hedgehogs. Due to explosions defeating their sonar and the Germans maneuvering to shake off their pursuers, the Americans lost contact with the *U-853*. They relocated it lying silent and motionless 120 feet below, and another attack brought oil, bubbles, and debris to the surface. The sonar contact then started moving again.

Frömsdorf's doggedly persistent retreat achieved no escape from the Americans' wrath. The sonar contact finally halted after midnight, but depth charges and hedge-hogs continued pummeling the U-boat for hours. At dawn, the blimps *K-16* and *K-58* arrived from New Jersey's NAS Lakehurst and fixed the motionless *U-853*'s position using MAD gear before conducting their own attacks. USS *Atherton*'s commander stated: "I don't think there's a hull that took a bigger beating during the war."

A sonobuoy deployed by *K-16* transmitted what Navy records describe as "a rhythmic hammering on a metal surface" followed by "a long, shrill shriek" until they were "lost in the engine noise of the attacking surface ships." The deluge of high explosives did eventually unlace the *U-853*'s steel seams, but evidence suggests that some of Frömsdorf's crew were alive for most of the savage 16-hour bombardment. "By then, they may have gone insane," one U-boat veteran later remarked.

Yet the *U-853* crew's final hours, like their commander's motivations, would remain forever shrouded in mystery. Floating debris recovered at the scene included Dräger rebreathers, a sou'wester coat—and a Kriegsmarine officer's cap. "What ambitions burned in its owner's mind cannot be known," a Navy press release reflected.

The "Battle of Point Judith" concluded around midday on 6 May, and Navy divers confirmed Der Seiltaenger's demise that afternoon. One diver attempted to access the control room but found it blocked by the corpses of the crew. Even in death, they permitted the enemy no entry. Before bringing the body of 22-year-old Herbert Hoffmann to the surface as evidence of the kill, the diver glimpsed something red and yellow in his peripheral vision. Emblazoned on the conning tower was a red horse with a golden mane and tail, below which was painted "U 853."[14]

***

On the morning of 14 May, eight days after the *U-853*'s last stand, two destroyer escorts arrived off the Delaware Capes with an unexpected guest: the *U-858*. The Type IXC/40 was one of two Gruppe Seewolf boats to survive Operation Teardrop's dragnet. The warships escorted the U-boat past the wreck of USS *Jacob Jones* (DD-130) to Section Base No. 9 at Cape May. The Germans were sent across the bay entrance to Fort Miles, and the *U-858* was later taken to the Philadelphia Naval Shipyard for analysis. The *U-805*, the last surviving Seewolf boat, similarly arrived under escort at Portsmouth, New Hampshire the following day.

In the days immediately following Hitler's death, Dönitz relocated his shoestring government to Germany's naval academy in the Flensburg district of Mürwik. Accompanying him were a coterie of staff that included former *U-123* commander Reinhard Hardegen in addition to *Marine-Infanterie* units comprised of repurposed Kriegsmarine sailors. Among these units' officers were U-boat commanders Paul-Karl Loeser (*U-373*) and Otto von Bülow (*U-404*). When US Army general Dwight Eisenhower refused a negotiated surrender, Dönitz authorized General Alfred Jodl to sign the formal capitulation at Eisenhower's headquarters on 7 May 1945. World War II in Europe was over.

Dönitz, Speer, and Jodl maintained the façade of a government over the ensuing days while furnishing SS officers with false identities as naval personnel (the Auschwitz camp commander became boatswain's mate "Fritz Lang"). Finally, on 23 May 1945, British forces placed Dönitz and his staff under arrest. "There have been few more satisfying pictures than these," proclaimed a British narrator over newsreel footage of them being led away with hands on their heads. Particular relish was reserved for Dönitz, the narrator dismissing the onetime archvillain of the high seas as "the rat-faced little admiral." When asked upon his arrest whether he wished to make a statement, the final Führer was laconic.

"Words," Dönitz replied, "would be superfluous."[15]

***

Between 1939 and 1945, U-boats in all oceans destroyed 2,764 Allied and neutral merchant ships for a total of 13.84 million gross registered tons. Britain's Merchant Navy and Norway's Nortraship suffered 30,248 and 3,670 killed, respectively. The US Merchant Marine suffered 9,521 fatalities for a per-capita death rate of 3.9 percent. This exceeded every branch of the US armed forces (the next highest was the Marine Corps at 2.94 percent killed). More than sixty thousand mariners from all Allied nations perished. Most merchant fleet losses were inflicted by German naval and air forces due to Japanese doctrine's emphasis on attacking enemy warships.[16]

U-boats destroyed 216 ships of all types within 400 nautical miles of the United States' Atlantic and Gulf coasts during World War II. Forty-seven more were damaged. Fatalities from these attacks numbered 2,868 merchant mariners, 793 Allied military personnel, and 146 civilian passengers. These figures do not include the ships and lives lost off Canada, South America, and the Caribbean islands.

Globally, U-boats destroyed 285 Allied naval vessels, 45 of which were amphibious ships or landing craft. Fifty-nine naval ships were damaged but returned to service. These attacks killed 2,100 US military personnel and 16,221 from other Allied nations, excluding Armed Guards and other gunners aboard merchant ships. USS *Jacob Jones* and USS *Leopold* were among thirty-four United States naval ships sunk by U-boats. Other American losses included six destroyer escorts, four destroyers, and one escort carrier.

The US Navy's Armed Guard program suffered 2,085 killed out of 144,970 assigned to more than 6,000 merchant ships. Armed Guard sailors earned five Navy Crosses and seventy-five Silver Stars, and their cynical "sighted sub, glub glub" joke was replaced by a well-earned pride. "We may not be the fanciest outfit in the world," one Armed Guardsman bragged in 1945, "but show me another gang of salesmen, farmers, newspapermen, teachers, and lawyers that's knocked off as many U-boats and planes."

Although the Gray Wolves exacted a dreadful toll from the Allies, they paid a staggeringly high price in return. Of the 1,167 U-boats commissioned by Nazi Germany, 757 were lost from all causes. Most of these were sunk by Allied warships and aircraft, and more than half went down with all hands. Approximately thirty thousand U-boat sailors were killed in action during the war. Another five thousand were captured at sea. Exact casualty figures remain subject to debate, but historians agree that over 60 percent of the Ubootwaffe's total manpower strength perished—a proportional fatality rate scarcely rivaled in the history of modern war.[17]

Lisle Rose wrote that the Battle of the Atlantic was "carried out on a particularly cruel sea of brutal winds," yet the preceding accounts of destruction and survival off the Jersey Shore were largely forgotten, except by those who survived them and the families of those who did not. These harrowing ordeals were largely overshadowed by other wartime events, the losses of these ships being of little individual significance amid a war that destroyed entire fleets, armies, and cities. Like the ocean smoothing over a vessel's wake, the passage of years would only further erode their places in the world's collective memory. Nevertheless, the legacy of war along New Jersey's coast can still be felt in the 21st century—if one knows where to look.[18]

CHAPTER SEVENTEEN

Bones in the Ocean

"Scatter flowers on the waves,
There our fathers found their graves,
Brothers, sons, and husbands sleep,
Strew your garlands o'er the deep.
Ebbing tides of summer day,
Bear these blossoms on their way,
North and east to bank and coast,
Where they lie whom we love most."
—Mary Brooks, "Scatter Flowers on the Waves" (1915)

22 July 2011
38 miles southeast of Cape May Point, New Jersey

With one hand on the double-braided polyester line rope, the naval officer tilted his body to the right and tapped the low-pressure valve button in his left hand. He heard only air gurgling from his buoyancy control vest and the loud rasp of his own regulator. The world around him was otherwise silent. The sea was dark and chilly despite the hot summer day above, and the sun's rays progressively dimmed as he followed the line, hand over hand, into the depths. He looked upward to the other man holding on to the line above him.

His companion held up one hand with his thumb and forefinger pressed together and the other three fingers extended. The naval officer returned the gesture, then glanced at the device on his wrist. The digits on its screen read: 72. *More than halfway there.* Reaching up, he pinched the mask around the bridge of his nose and exhaled gently to equalize the pressure in his inner ears. The ambient pressure here was more than three times that at the surface.

The solitude allowed him to contemplate what his grandfather experienced here, the pulverized flesh and rent steel ... little wonder "Gramps" seldom talked about it. As the pair of divers passed 100 feet, a dark shape gradually materialized from the blackness below. Little remained of the once-proud vessel, yet her ghostly outline was still recognizable. Even with the regulator in his mouth, a smile formed across the naval officer's face.[1]

***

This final chapter requires a shift in tone on the author's part, owing to multiple intersections between myself and the legacies of these events. Researching and writing this book afforded me countless interactions with characters' family members, shipwreck discoverers, and even a 99-year-old Merchant Marine combat veteran. Each phone call, email, and text message reminded me why I had undertaken this effort. The preface explained that this story is ultimately a human one, so it seemed fitting to conclude this story with the surviving characters' later lives and how the events they experienced still echo in the 21st century.

The Allied merchant mariners who rightfully constitute the centerpiece of this story included the quarter-million "heroes in dungarees" who served in the US Merchant Marine. "The stuff had to go overseas," one proudly stated. "We were the only ones who could do it, and we did it." Yet the Merchant Mariners' service only began to gain wider appreciation in the 1970s, and their civilian status left them ineligible for the G.I. Bill and other benefits afforded to military veterans. Finally, in 1988, the federal government formally granted veteran status to all American mariners who served at sea during World War II. Unbeaten in two world wars, the United States Merchant Marine continues to sail the globe today.

The first monument dedicated to American merchant mariners was erected at the Sun Oil (now Sunoco) refinery in Marcus Hook, Pennsylvania. The Sun Seamen's Memorial commemorates those killed aboard the tankers built upriver in Chester by Sun Shipbuilding. The 9-foot bronze statue portrays a mariner with a duffle bag over his shoulder gazing east toward the Atlantic. Its 1949 dedication saw a wreath laid by a Philadelphia woman whose son was killed on the *J.N. Pew*. The memorial stands at what is now the Marcus Hook Industrial Complex.[2]

Doomed survivors from the *Muskogee*, 22 March 1942. (*Berliner Illustrirte Zeitung*, enhanced by Peter Shafron)

A memorial to all Merchant Marine and Armed Guard personnel was dedicated in 2005 at Wiggins Waterfront Park in Camden, New Jersey. Located adjacent to the battleship USS *New Jersey*, its centerpiece is a 12-ton bronze propeller donated by a local scrapyard and refurbished by volunteers and the South Jersey Port Corporation. Another memorial dedicated in 1991 at New York City's Battery Park portrays three mariners on a liferaft. A fourth man, reaching toward them from the water, is submerged at high tide each day. The sculpture is based on a photograph of survivors from the *Muskogee* taken by a photographer on the *U-123*. None of them were seen again.

Nortraship veterans faced a similar struggle for recognition after the war, but their service eventually found its rightful place in Norway's national pride. A 2014 poll by the newspaper *Verdens Gang* voted the unnamed *Krigsseiler*, or war sailor, as the "most important Norwegian" of the preceding two centuries. New York's Battery Park features a memorial to those killed from the 706 Norwegian merchant vessels lost to enemy action.[3]

***

The *U-Boot-Ehrenmal Möltenort*, or Möltenort U-boat memorial, is a red brick tower topped with an eagle and surrounded by walls engraved with the names of each U-boat crewman lost in both world wars. Located near Kiel, it was rededicated in 1954 to honor all those killed by submarine operations. The nearby Laboe Naval Memorial, which memorializes all German naval personnel lost at sea, stands 236 feet tall and is said to resemble a conning tower or a Viking ship's bow.

U-boat historian Axel Niestlé wrote that "in the end, the majority of German U-boat crews paid the utmost price for their failure to recognize the real face and intentions of their fanatic political and military leadership." Those who did survive returned home forever changed. "All around me was emptiness," Peter Cremer reflected upon returning to Hamburg's ruins. "Most of my comrades were no longer alive, the years of my youth had gone." Gottfried König stated: "Today I am appalled that young men could have fought, sunk ships, and destroyed lives with such ease and thoughtlessness."

Of the many firsthand German accounts of the U-boat war, few are as visceral as Herbert Werner's 1968 memoir *Iron Coffins*. Werner's parents and sister were killed in an Allied bombing raid in 1944, and he eventually moved to the United States. He politely declined to discuss his experiences when New Jersey wreck diver Richie Kohler phoned him in the early 1990s. As Werner wrote in his memoir, "My recollections are still uncomfortably vivid and will remain so, I am afraid, until their pressure is lifted by my demise."

New Jersey Historical Commission director Marc Mappen wrote that the U-boat sailors "were brave men in a wicked cause," though Peter Padfield accorded them somewhat more virtue. "I am persuaded that, with exceptions as in all navies, and despite their youth and pernicious indoctrination, they fought honorably from the beginning." Michael Gannon agreed, while clarifying that this "concedes nothing to the odiousness of the cause for which [they] fought." Timothy Mulligan provided perhaps the most succinct and fitting characterization by concluding that the U-boat sailors were "neither sharks nor wolves." They, like their victims, were simply men.[4]

***

In June 1942, a journalist expressed hope that "the time may be close at hand when the [Roosevelt] administration will be called to sharp accounting for the poor showing in meeting the submarine menace on our Eastern Coasts," but no one ever was. Admiral Ernest King instead retained the role of COMINCH and, in December 1944, became one of only four Navy officers ever promoted to the five-star rank of Fleet Admiral. King also demanded a court-martial for Captain Charles McVay, commander of the heavy cruiser USS *Indianapolis* (CA-35) when it was sunk by a Japanese submarine in 1945. Convicted of negligence in a trial now considered a travesty of justice, Charles McVay's exoneration came only decades after his suicide.

Declassified documents cast a damning portrayal of ADM King's malfeasance during the darkest days of 1942. Among his fiercest critics are historians Michael Gannon, Peter Padfield, and Ed Offley. "All the strings ended in King's hands," Gannon declared, and Jonathan Dimbleby wrote that "only his most indulgent supporters have since sought to exonerate him." These include Clay Blair, who blamed FDR for many of King's apparent failures. Yet even if Ernest King has been unfairly maligned, admitted Evan Mawdsley, the first half of 1942 "was not his finest hour."[5]

***

In November 1945, the Allies convened a military tribunal in the German city of Nuremberg to prosecute senior leaders of the Nazi Party and Wehrmacht. The defendants included Erich Raeder, the Kriegsmarine's commander-in-chief from 1928 until Karl Dönitz's ascension in January 1943. Dreams of employing an immense battlefleet for world conquest earned "The Schoolmaster" no sympathy from Peter Padfield, who wrote that "Raeder and his staff stand revealed as crude, simple, and humorless as villains of a comic strip seized with a master plan to hold the world to ransom." Raeder's image would remain more hapless than malevolent, yet his role in planning Hitler's conquests earned him a sentence of life in prison.

Karl Dönitz faced the same three-count indictment as Raeder, which he dismissed as "typical American humor." The charges were crimes against peace (waging wars of aggression), war crimes, and conspiracy to commit both. On the charge of crimes against peace, however, Dönitz was ruled not guilty. The tribunal concluded he was "not one of the top group until later in the war" and was "performing strictly tactical duties" prior to 1943.

Part of the war crimes charge against Dönitz hinged on the "Laconia Order" that prohibited aiding survivors because victory demanded "the annihilation of enemy ships and crews." Prosecutors claimed that these last two words ("*und Besatzungen*") constituted a veiled directive to massacre shipwrecked men. One U-boat officer testified that "we were convinced that Admiral Dönitz meant that," and Padfield concluded that "the presumption must be that [shooting survivors] was what Dönitz had intended for." Although the judges found insufficient evidence of murderous intent, they declared that "the orders … deserve the strongest censure."

The tribunal also charged Dönitz with violating the 1936 London Naval Treaty by waging unrestricted submarine warfare. His lawyer parried this with an affidavit by US Navy Fleet Admiral Chester Nimitz detailing how American submarines had similarly ignored prize rules while sinking more than eleven hundred Japanese merchant ships (the United States destroyed most of Japan's merchant fleet by war's end). Dönitz's lawyer argued that the US Navy had *not* violated international law, and therefore neither had Dönitz. His client was consequently ruled not guilty of that offense. "It was written down forever that submarine warfare cannot be carried on without inhumanity," journalist Rebecca West subsequently reflected, "and that we have found ourselves able to be inhumane."[6]

Dönitz was not indicted for crimes against humanity despite coordinating with the SS to use concentration camp inmates as slave labor. He also maintained that he had been unaware of the extermination camps and the Nazis' broader genocidal policies until after Germany's defeat, yet Dönitz's alleged horror at these crimes was only for public display. Following a trial witness' deeply disturbing testimony about the Holocaust, Dönitz's lawyer asked his client, "Didn't anybody know anything about these things?" Dönitz merely shrugged and continued eating his lunch.

The onetime Befehlshaber der Unterseeboote was nonetheless found guilty on two of three charges and sentenced to ten years in prison. This was the least severe punishment handed down at Nuremberg, and Padfield concluded that "both Dönitz and [Albert] Speer were fortunate to escape the gallows." This relative leniency appalled Oskar-Heinz Kusch's father. "The verdict passed in Nuremberg is far too lenient for some of these criminals," he fumed in a letter to former *U-103* commander Werner Winter. "Every one of them should have been hanged without exception."[7]

The convicts served their sentences at Spandau prison in West Berlin. Albert Speer observed that Raeder "treats Dönitz with the condescension of a superior officer, which particularly irritates him," and the two bickered frequently while imprisoned. A letter from Dönitz's son-in-law reported that polling ranked him equal to General Erwin Rommel in public esteem, but this disgusted Dönitz, who considered Rommel a traitor for his involvement with the July 1944 assassination conspirators. Dönitz displayed no remorse while in prison and continued expressing loyalty to Hitler, leading Speer to conclude in his diary that "he is unable to see the magnitude of the horror." Dönitz purportedly believed that Speer would be released early from his 20-year sentence because "the American Jews would make sure of it," but both served their full prison terms. Raeder was released after nine years due to poor health.

Jordan Vause concluded that Dönitz's claim of being merely a sailor has "collapsed into dust," and even onetime disciples like Erich Topp and Ernst-Günther Unterhorst recognized the darkness of his true nature. "If we speak of Dönitz," wrote the latter, "we speak of brutality, human destruction, [and] barbarism as a result of … National Socialism." Dönitz's purported ignorance of the Holocaust, too, was a lie. He had been a keynote speaker at the infamous Posen conference in October 1943, at which Heinrich Himmler revealed the ongoing mass murder of Europe's Jews. Peter Padfield concluded that "charity is an appropriate response" toward many Germans swept up in the Third Reich's madness—but, for Karl Dönitz, "charity has no place."

Historian Eric Rust noted that "Dönitz's charisma proved stronger than his many failures," and his apologists' success in whitewashing his image meant that "Der Löwe" remained popular among both U-boat veterans and his more credulous former foes. Dönitz lived the rest of his life quietly near Hamburg, where he penned a detailed but entirely self-exculpatory memoir. It was not until 1974 that he learned the Allies had broken the Enigma code. A BBC interview team that visited his home the year prior found "an austere old man … dapperish but rather frail," his eyes "peering out suspiciously from inside his skull as if haunted by the past." Karl Dönitz died in 1980 at age 89, unrepentant to the last.[8]

***

Lingering injuries from Reinhard Hardegen's 1936 plane crash finally ended his seagoing career after the *U-123* returned from its second American patrol in May 1942. He oversaw homing torpedo development and led a provisional infantry unit in 1945 before winding up with Dönitz's short-lived administration in Mürwik. His eventual release from captivity took eighteen months because the Allies confused him with SS war criminal Paul Hardegen. The *U-123* was scuttled at the pier when the Wehrmacht abandoned Lorient in 1944. After the war, the "Eins Zwei Drei" was salvaged and returned to service as the French submarine *Blaison* until it was decommissioned in 1959 and scrapped.

Hardegen was the war's twenty-fourth most successful U-boat commander in terms of merchant tonnage sunk. After the war, he started his own oil trading business and served thirty-two years in Bremen's parliament as a member of the Christian Democratic Union. An avid swimmer and golfer, he once quipped: "Now I sink putts, not ships." Although he reinvented himself as a businessman and civic leader, Hardegen never entirely shed his famous swagger: the license plate of his BMW read "U123."

In 1986, Hardegen received an unexpected phone call from an American historian and author in Florida. The caller was a former Roman Catholic priest named Michael Gannon who, not long after, would visit Hardegen in Germany.

Gannon found the former ace commander "gaunt, pale, and haunted-looking," but also energetic and eager to share the memories that became Gannon's acclaimed 1990 book *Operation Drumbeat*. The gregarious elderly German accompanied Gannon on a promotional tour of the United States to "show Americans that the enemies of yesterday are friends of today." The war's first U-boat commander to reach the United States, Hardegen was the last one alive at the time of his death in June 2018 at age 105.[9]

***

Although rumors lingered along the Jersey Shore and elsewhere that U-boat crewmen had come ashore to visit movie theaters and dance halls, and that U-boats sneaked up rivers, none of these tales contain any truth. Much like the shark attacks of 1916, however, memories of 1942's offshore carnage faded until few Americans in the 21st century are aware it happened at all. "People don't realize how close that war was to home," wreck diver Steve Gatto told the *Cape May Star and Wave* in 2011. Yet physical remnants of the war still exist along the Jersey Shore today, and not all of them are underwater.

The Navy turned over Section Base No. 9 to the Coast Guard in 1946. It thereafter became US Coast Guard Training Center Cape May, which today serves as that service's only basic training facility for enlisted recruits. Not far away is the bunker that housed Battery 223's heavy guns. It still exists less than 500 yards from Cape May Lighthouse and was added to the National Register of Historic Places in 2008. Long threatened by erosion, *Atlas Obscura* noted that the waterline's encroachment "gives the impression that the bunker is steadily moving out to sea as the years pass."

The two Fort Miles fire-control towers built on Cape May are also still standing. Visitors to tower No. 23 at Sunset Beach can ascend to its sixth floor where a clear day offers a 12-mile view. On the peninsula's other side, tower No. 24 was incorporated into what is today the Grand Hotel of Cape May and can be seen protruding from the hotel's roof. The Cape May Canal, ushered into being by the USS *Jacob Jones* sinking, continues to serve recreational boaters.

Naval Air Station Lakehurst, where Airship Patrol Squadron Twelve was based, remained in service after the war. Located 13 miles southeast of Trenton, NAS Lakehurst became Joint Base McGuire-Dix-Lakehurst in 2009. It serves as the headquarters for the Civil Air Patrol's New Jersey Wing, representing roughly 1,600 of the nation's 66,000 CAP volunteers. The Lakehurst Historical Society conducts tours which take visitors to the enormous blimp hangars and the site where the German airship *Hindenburg* met its fiery end in 1937. These and other remnants of World War II in New Jersey can be experienced without getting one's feet wet, but the war's most captivating physical legacy lies offshore.[10]

***

Drawing a line extending 200 nautical miles northeast from Sandy Hook and another 100 nautical miles southeast from Cape May, then connecting them with two more lines, produces a region that can fairly be termed "New Jersey waters." Plotting wartime coordinates reveals that twenty-three merchant ships, one US Navy destroyer, and two U-boats went down here during World War II. Extending the seaward boundary a few miles east adds another U-boat (*U-550*) and merchantman (*Pan Pennsylvania*). These twenty-eight sinkings claimed the lives of 421 merchant mariners, 169 Allied servicemen, and 149 U-boat sailors. Thirteen vessels were sunk in this zone during World War I.

These are today among more than a thousand shipwrecks along the Jersey Shore, collectively representing a maritime historical heritage almost unrivaled in the United States. "A wreck is probably within a mile or so of where you're standing on any beach," New Jersey diver and historian Dan Lieb remarked in 2015. He was speaking with a reporter who would later intrigue readers with an article about how "Atlantic City and Cape May are convenient gateways to a sprawling, unseen graveyard."

These wrecks (a few of which were sunk as artificial reefs) represent more than just sightseeing for divers. Maritime archaeologist Keith Muckelroy stated that a shipwreck is "a single event in time that becomes part of a dynamic environment," and New Jersey's wrecks constitute an important facet of the state's underwater ecosystem. Their wood and metal provide algae and other small organisms with a stable substrate higher in the water column, where more nutrients are available. This attracts fish which use crevices and debris to hide from predators. Wrecks are consequently bountiful fishing spots. Fishermen note the coordinates of "hangs" where their nets snag obstructions, and numerous wrecks have been discovered this way.[11]

Wider availability of scuba diving equipment and training in the 1960s fostered the birth of a small but devoted subculture of wreck divers in the Northeastern US. Pioneers like Mike de Camp, John and Evelyn Dudas, John Chatterton, and Gary Gentile all cut their teeth off the Jersey Shore between the 1960s and 1980s. Some of the first divers to use trimix (a blend of helium and regular air) did so to reach deep wrecks off the state's coast in the 1990s. "The New Jersey guys took it to a new level," diver Morgan Bodie stated in 2015. "They showed everybody else 'we are the studs.'"

This type of scuba diving was particularly dangerous in its nascent years as divers wielding hammers and crowbars explored Northeastern wrecks well below recreational depths. This laid the groundwork for what is now known as "technical diving," or recreational diving beyond normal risk thresholds. Hobbyists and explorers with a piratical dash, they identified long-lost wrecks while salvaging priceless artifacts amid intense rivalries with other groups of divers. Not all survived their exploits. John Dudas of West Chester, Pennsylvania died in 1982 on the wreck of the 1918 U-boat victim *Sommerstad*. His widow Evelyn continued pushing underwater boundaries for decades and operated a West Chester dive shop until 2016.

By the 21st century, New Jersey wreck diving had evolved beyond its early status as a daredevil niche sport. Dive boats and shops now serve all experience levels, and wreck divers here remain obsessive. "I don't think people are as hardcore in any other state," stated one diver who regularly travels from Texas to dive Jersey Shore wrecks. This pride is hardened by the Garden State's murky water, frigid bottom temperatures, and strong currents. According to longtime Jersey Shore diver Gene Peterson: "If you do ocean wreck diving in New Jersey, then you are in a class by yourself."

Wrecks offer opportunities for spearfishing and photography, yet it is their stories that draw the most devoted visitors. "We're history buffs," declared Steve Gatto, "and this is history." Few understand this better than New Jersey lawyer and technical diver Joe Mazraani. "New Jersey wreck diving isn't just a legacy of shipwrecks, it's a legacy of people," he explained. "These are stories of people who lived and died aboard the ships we dive and the people who've devoted their lives to discovering and diving them. It's the intersection of these two lines of history that makes what we do and where we do it so special."[12]

The physical remnants of the U-boat war are not immune to forces of man and nature. Damage from the explosions and fire that sank these ships was often compounded by subsequent dynamiting and wire-dragging. Decades of saltwater corrosion and marine life are continuing the wrecks' deterioration, and these stresses are exacerbated by gillnet fishing and bottom trawling. Fishing activities constitute the greatest near-term threat to New Jersey's wrecks, many of which are adorned with nets, chains, and monofilament.

Artifact recovery and preservation is therefore a vital historical service because these items will otherwise eventually be buried forever under shifting sands. "You're not recovering treasure, you're actually preserving treasure," explained Gene Peterson, who has brought up more than a thousand artifacts. These and other items recovered by divers are displayed at museums across New Jersey and neighboring states.[13]

Sadly, a few unscrupulous divers over the decades have not afforded these sites the respect they deserve. Multiple individuals have taken German sailors' bones from the *U-853* off Rhode Island. One dive shop owner removed a bone in 1990 and only returned it when John Chatterton, a world-famous New Jersey wreck diver and discoverer, threatened to inform newspapers about his ghoulish souvenir. In the 1970s, New Jersey diver George Hoffman shamelessly desecrated the tomb of more than one hundred Americans when he pilfered the USS *Jacob Jones* wreck for copper piping to sell as scrap. Hoffman smugly boasted: "It was worth 48 cents per pound. Used a hacksaw."[14]

Although the world wars left a considerable historical and ecological inheritance along the East Coast, the seabed holds more than just marine habitats and rusted tombs. Oil washing ashore in 1967 led Representative James Howard (D-NJ) to recommend a formal reassessment of the environmental hazard these wrecks posed, and Coast Guard divers subsequently surveyed the *Varanger*, *R.P. Resor*, *Gulftrade*, and *Coimbra*. The survey concluded that none posed an immediate hazard and that this was likely true of other tanker wrecks.

Lingering concerns about ecological time bombs on the seafloor led the US Congress in 2010 to fund another assessment by the National Oceanographic & Atmospheric Administration. "We're starting to see significant corrosion," a resource protection coordinator for NOAA's National Marine Sanctuaries program explained. "Vessels that weren't totally torpedoed didn't break apart and may have intact fuel tanks." Scott Wahl represented the city of Avalon, New Jersey at NOAA's 2011 conference on the topic in Baltimore. "Without a clean environment, we [in Avalon] don't have an economy," Wahl stated. "Preventing spills from shipwrecks isn't just a cost, it's an investment."

Two years after NOAA's final report in 2013 identified forty-two wrecks of concern, satellite imagery revealed an oil slick 85 miles east of Sea Bright, New Jersey. Its source was the tanker *Coimbra*, sunk by Reinhard Hardegen's *U-123* in January 1942. Consequently, 2019 saw one of the largest salvage operations ever undertaken in US waters. State and federal agencies worked with contractors to deploy divers and remote vehicles that successfully pumped 476,000 gallons of oil from the *Coimbra*.[15]

The war also littered the East Coast seabed with unexploded ordnance. The scallop boat *Snoopy* was off North Carolina in July 1965 when her net inadvertently brought up a German torpedo which exploded and killed eight of twelve men aboard. A New Jersey fishing boat found a live warhead 2 miles off Barnegat Light eight years later, and a half-mile area of Point Pleasant Beach was evacuated in 1985 when a fisherman returned with part of a torpedo netted 10 miles off Manasquan Inlet. October 2022 brought another reminder of this hazard when a trawler's net hauled up a Mark 6 depth charge a few miles from the *U-853* wreck off Rhode Island.[16]

***

Fourteen U-boats were sunk within 200 nautical miles of United States shores, although the exact whereabouts of the *U-857* and *U-879* wrecks remain unknown. Two U-boat wrecks lie due east of the Jersey Shore and a third was sunk off the Delmarva Peninsula. Eight are at diveable depths, though four are only accessible to technical divers. The *U-352* off North Carolina and the *U-853* off Rhode Island are both frequently dived. With these fourteen U-boats perished 665 German sailors, most of whom are entombed within. These wrecks remain the property of the German government. U-boats are also legally protected by the Sunken Military Craft Act of 2004, which recognized all US and foreign naval vessels sunk in combat along American shores as war graves. They can be visited, but not disturbed.[17]

There were thought to be only thirteen U-boats off the United States until September 1991, when several New Jersey wreck divers investigated a local fisherman's report of a "hang" 60 miles off Long Beach Island. They were shocked to discover a Type IXC/40 U-boat 230 feet below the surface, and nowhere near any known U-boat wreck. Full of bones, the boat had clearly met a violent end: the pressure hull over the aft torpedo room had been breached, and the outer hull and most of the pressure hull on the control room's port side had been blown away.

Richie Kohler and John Chatterton, formerly rivals in the fiercely territorial world of Northeast wreck diving, joined forces to solve the mystery. They scoured the "U-Who" for evidence with a trusted clique of fellow divers, three of whom died while diving the wreck. The divers eventually found a knife engraved with a sailor's name which suggested the boat's identity, but definitive proof eluded them. The six-year mystery was finally solved in 1997 when a venture into the diesel engine room produced a metal tag bearing the boat's name. The *U-Who* was the *U-869*, previously believed sunk off Morocco.[18]

But how did the *U-869* meet its end? The Navy and Coast Guard concluded that USS *Koiner* (DE-331) and *Crow* (DE-252) sank the boat when they attacked a sonar contact on 11 February 1945. Although the punctured pressure hull near the stern is consistent with depth charges and hedgehogs, the damage amidships appeared too catastrophic for either weapon. The pressure hull's jagged edges are also bent outward, suggesting an internal explosion.

Chatterton and Kohler theorized that the *U-869* was hit by its own T5 Zaunkönig homing torpedo. At least two other U-boats were sunk by "circle runners," and the placement of the Zaunkönig's fuze behind the warhead caused it to burn toward the target, providing more penetration and possibly explaining the gaping hole and evidence of an internal blast. This theory is further supported by the lack of debris or bodies produced by the DEs' attack. Compelling arguments against the circle-runner explanation nonetheless persist, and a Navy and Coast Guard reassessment in 2005 formally credited the kill to USS *Koiner* and USS *Crow*.

The *U-869* story was the subject of Robert Kurson's 2004 bestselling book *Shadow Divers*, which sparked broader interest in Northeast wreck diving. The mystery's conclusion also brought a measure of solace to the relatives of the fifty-six men whose bones are strewn about its interior. Among these relatives was the *U-869* commander's son. Only 3 years old when his father died, he kept a handwritten letter which his 27-year-old father, Hellmut Neuerburg, left for him in 1945:

> Soon, daddy will have to go out to sea with his U-boat and our most ardent hope is that we will all see each other again soon at home in good health and in peaceful times. Then the sun will shine again on you, my children, and especially on your parents who live only with and for you, and indescribable happiness will make our life again worth living.[19]

***

Most of the twelve vessels most prominently featured in this book—six tankers, three freighters, a tugboat, a Wickes-class destroyer, and one U-boat—have been explored by divers. Several are well-known dive sites, though the scant remnants of the *Persephone* and *John R. Williams* are all but forgotten today. Neither the *Berganger* nor *Rio Tercero* have been located as of this writing, although both are too deep to dive.

Tracing the later lives and fates of this story's characters was often unsatisfying. Most of these real-life individuals vanished into the fog of history, although a few family members of survivors and fatalities have actively preserved the memory of their relatives' experiences. The obscurity of so many characters highlights another facet of their extraordinary stories, for friend and foe alike were simply ordinary people in extraordinary circumstances.

Mike Monichetti is the grandson of Lodovico "Dewey" Monichetti, the Italian immigrant fisherman who rescued the crew of the Norwegian tanker *Varanger* after it was torpedoed by Ernst Kals' *U-130* in January 1942. During my conversations with Mike in 2021 and 2022, he told me that his grandfather was "intensely proud of being an American" and held a "lifelong pride for helping rescue those guys." Mike's uncle, John, who first sighted the *Varanger*'s lifeboats, later served as a tank mechanic under General George Patton. Another of Dewey's sons, Mike's father, survived intense combat as a merchant mariner in the Mediterranean. Dewey "did what he loved most," fishing, until his death in 1968.

Dewey's fish shack in Sea Isle City still stands across the street from where he offloaded the *Varanger* survivors at 43rd Street and Park Road, and the Monichetti family still resides in the homestead next door. The large fig tree adorning the home's backyard was once the fig shoot that Dewey brought from Italy in 1911. The family has become a fixture of Sea Isle City in the decades since the war, and Mike has declined numerous offers for the property. The spot where Dewey's fishing boat, the *San Gennaro*, offloaded the *Varanger* survivors that January morning is now the site of Mike's Seafood, owned and operated by Mike Monichetti.[20]

U-130 commander Ernst Kals' next patrol took him to the Caribbean, where he shelled a refinery on Curaçao, and he was awarded the Knight's Cross in September 1942. Eight weeks later, 105 American servicemen perished when he sank three American troopships during the Allied landing in Morocco. Kals turned over command of the *U-130* in January 1943 to assume leadership of Second U-boat Flotilla at Lorient. Two months later, USS *Champlin* (DD-601) sank the *U-130* with all hands.

Kals served in Lorient through the Allied siege from the summer of 1944 until Germany's surrender, during which time he was severely wounded by a landmine. He subsequently spent thirty-three months in French captivity. The legacy of the sixteenth-highest scoring U-boat ace is nonetheless irreparably marred by his role in the Oskar Kusch affair. Despite being the accused's immediate superior, he neither sought leniency (as Werner Winter did) nor even visited Kusch while he awaited execution. Ernst Kals died in Emden in 1979.[21]

The *Varanger* sinking was one of the few U-boat attacks in American waters with no fatalities. It was "the biggest thing to ever happen in Sea Isle City," stated

364 • KILLING SHORE

resident Mike Davies in 2006. Age 14 at the time, Davies was awakened by the offshore explosions and then unexpectedly encountered the *Varanger* crewmen in the basement of St Joseph's Church later that morning. "Absolutely I remember it," he stated, "my bed shook. It was that strong."

The *Varanger* herself sits 34 miles east-southeast of Sea Isle City at a depth of 140 feet. The wreck is upright and has long been considered one of New Jersey's most picturesque. Her helm was recovered by divers from Skip Galimore's boat *Aquanaut* in the early 1970s. Jeff Barris described the *Varanger* wreck as "enormous and quite breathtaking" in 2000, though much of its skeletal structure has since collapsed. The site is also subject to strong currents. It is known by fishermen as the "28 Mile Wreck."[22]

***

Werner Winter, the *U-103* commander who sank the *India Arrow* in February 1942, sailed again in April for a patrol to the Caribbean and Gulf of Mexico. He concluded his sea command in July with a total of fifteen ships sunk before taking command of First U-boat Flotilla in Brest, France in July 1942. Winter was in this billet when Brest was cut off by Allied armies advancing into Brittany in the summer of 1944, and he was taken prisoner when the US Army captured the port in September. The *U-103* was scuttled at the pier in Kiel in May 1945 and later broken up for scrap.

Like many former Kriegsmarine officers, Winter served in the West German navy after its establishment in 1956. This third iteration of the German navy exists today as the *Deutsche Marine* but is also known informally by its Cold War name, the *Bundesmarine*. The US Navy provided West Germany several surplus Fletcher-class destroyers, and Winter commanded the former USS *Anthony* (DD-515) as the *Z-1*. Werner Winter died in Kiel in 1972.[23]

Winter was profoundly impacted by the fate of Oskar-Heinz Kusch, his second watch officer for both of the *U-103*'s patrols to American waters. "For me, this marked the beginning of my inner turn away from National Socialism," he stated after the war. In postwar correspondence with Kusch's father, Winter praised his late subordinate as "an excellent young officer and an outstanding human being." The elder Kusch expressed appreciation for Winter's sentiments and shared his righteous anger toward those who had "condemned to death a completely blameless young person whose character was far superior to theirs."

"I still consider it my damned duty and obligation," Kusch's bereaved father told Winter in 1946, to ensure "that his murderers, including Dönitz ... are brought to their just and well-deserved punishment, and I would set heaven and hell in motion for this." Chief accuser Ulrich Abel went down with the *U-193* in April 1944, but Kusch's father filed a criminal complaint against the judge who sent his only child to the firing squad. A trial convened in 1949 saw Winter testify and several of Kusch's former enlisted sailors attend, but the judge was acquitted on the grounds that his ruling had been a technically lawful application of military justice.

Few tragedies better capture the moral dilemma faced by decent Germans beset by the Nazis' madness. Oskar Kusch embodied the clean professionalism so often undeservingly attributed to the Wehrmacht as a whole, and his murder by that very institution illustrates the price of integrity in a society poisoned by ideology. *U-552* commander Erich Topp considered Kusch one of Germany's greatest heroes and urged his memorialization in the manner of the July 1944 assassination conspirators. Topp, the war's third-highest scoring ace, also candidly admitted that he had not possessed the courage that Kusch displayed.

Oskar Kusch's story did not become widely known until after German reunification in 1991. His legal record was finally wiped clean five years later, and today he is honored by a memorial in Kiel and a street adjacent to his execution site that bears his name. Peter Hansen, who served under him aboard the *U-103* and *U-154*, published a book about Kusch's story in 2005. The modern German armed forces have preserved Kusch's memory as a shining example of moral courage.[24]

The Socony-Vacuum tanker *India Arrow*, sent to the bottom by Winter and Kusch's *U-103* in February 1942, sits upside-down in 190 feet of water 63 miles east-southeast of Cape May. Although infrequently dived due to its depth, it is considered one of the most impressive wrecks in the region. A massive propeller rises more than 20 feet off the bottom and visibility is often excellent. Brandon McWilliams described swimming through the *India Arrow* in 2007: "It was so wide open, and the ceiling (keel) so high, that it was like being in a huge dark cathedral … Here and there, rust holes allowed emerald green light to filter through and at points along the center line you could look port and starboard and see out both sides of the wreck."[25]

***

The wreck of the Esso tanker *R.P. Resor*, destroyed in a spectacular inferno by Ernst-August Rehwinkel's *U-578*, is today one of New Jersey's best-known dive sites. Sitting 35 miles east-southeast of Seaside Heights at a depth of 130 feet, the wreck is contiguous and its stern remains largely intact as of 2022. The 4-inch gun that Daniel Hey and the other Armed Guards never had the chance to fire is still mounted on the aft deck, where it points down toward the rudder. Long sections of piping can be used to navigate to and from a debris field known for an abundance of lobsters. Atlantic Divers, one of New Jersey's premier dive shops, considers the *R.P. Resor* "the most spectacular wreck off the coast for advanced divers."[26]

***

The *U-578*'s sinking of USS *Jacob Jones* (DD-130) less than thirty-six hours after the *R.P. Resor* was the third-deadliest U-boat attack off North America. Lieutenant Commander Hugh Black of Oradell, New Jersey was honored by the 1943 commissioning of USS *Black* (DD-666). His executive officer and the ship's doctor were similarly honored with USS *Marshall* (DD-676) and USS *Bronstein* (DE-189), the latter of which helped sink two U-boats in 1944. A third *Jacob Jones* was also commissioned bearing hull number DE-130. Unlike her two predecessors, she survived her war.

USS *Black* served until 1969. She provided naval gunfire support to US troops in Vietnam in 1966, at which time a reservist named J. Dennis Black served as her antisubmarine officer. The son of Hugh Black, he was only three years old when his father was killed in action off the Delaware Capes. "There was no other ship for me," Lieutenant (Junior Grade) Black told *The Naval Reservist* magazine. "It had to be this one."

A US Navy investigation in 1945 bafflingly concluded that a spontaneous boiler explosion sank the *Eagle 56*, not a torpedo from the infamous *U-853*. This verdict denied her forty-nine fatalities and thirteen survivors the Purple Heart medal until her sinking was finally recognized as a combat loss in 2001. New England-based Nomad Exploration Team located the USS *Eagle 56* wreck—with boilers intact—off Cape Elizabeth, Maine in June 2018. Four years later, a team of British divers found the first USS *Jacob Jones*, sunk by Hans Rose's *U-53* in 1917, off southwestern England in August 2022.

Fireman 2nd Class Joseph "Paul" Tidwell from Alabama was one of the eleven survivors of the second USS *Jacob Jones* rescued by the *Eagle 56* off Cape May. He retired from the Navy as a master chief petty officer, then worked at a shipyard and taught diesel engine technology at a trade school, where he took pride in ensuring that each of his students found employment. Paul Tidwell eventually moved to Florida, having developed a lifelong aversion to the cold after the events of 28 February 1942.

For Tidwell, memories of that day remained uncomfortably raw. "He never talked about it," his son Jim recalled. "We asked him a couple of times, but he didn't say much." Paul's grandson Eric became interested in his grandfather's experiences and eventually became a naval flight officer for F/A-18 Super Hornet fighters. In 2011, an upcoming assignment to Japan inspired Commander Eric Tidwell to make a special trip while "Gramps" was still alive: Eric was going to dive the wreck of his grandfather's ship.[27]

The venerable USS *Jacob Jones* was located in 1967 by divers John Dudas and Bill Scheibel. The bow section, sheared off by the *U-578*'s first torpedo, lies 28 miles southeast of Cape May at a depth of 110 feet. The larger aft section sits another 7 miles farther offshore at 130 feet. Diver George Hoffman located the bridge sitting upright in the sand in 1972. Although her torpedo tubes are still loaded, little of the Jakie is recognizable as a warship today. Technical diver Gary Gentile described USS *Jacob Jones* in 1990 as "plastered all over the seabed."

Atlantic Divers owner Gene Peterson offered to support Eric's venture at no cost. Paul Tidwell's three children accompanied their wheelchair-bound father to Cape May, where the family gathered ashore at fire-control tower No. 23. After seven decades of silence, the 91-year-old veteran "suddenly opened up," his grandson recalled. The memories that Paul Tidwell shared in his Alabama drawl included a remark to a *Philadelphia Inquirer* reporter: "That water was cold."

The family remained ashore while Atlantic Divers took Eric Tidwell out to the wreck aboard the boat *RV Explorer*. During the twenty-two minutes Eric spent on the Jakie, he knelt momentarily on the seabed beside her for an impromptu moment of reflection. "I kind of laid my hands on it," he described. "It was quite a day."[28]

***

U-578 commander Ernst-August Rehwinkel—who sank USS *Jacob Jones*, in addition to the *R.P. Resor* and *Berganger*—did not long outlive those who died by his torpedoes off New Jersey. The *U-578* disappeared in August 1942 while transiting the Bay of Biscay off western France. Its sinking was for years attributed to an attack by the Royal Air Force's No. 311 (Czechoslovak) Squadron on 19 August, but this was eventually determined to have been against a different U-boat. The *U-578* is one of sixty-three U-boats lost under circumstances that remain unclear.

A stroke of luck spared one *U-578* officer from Rehwinkel's fate. First watch officer Raimund Tiesler, who loosed the mortal blows against the *Jacob Jones* and *R.P. Resor*, was transferred off the boat after its first American patrol due to an injury. Tiesler was commanding the *U-649* when it sank after colliding with another U-boat, and he later survived the sinking of the *U-976* by a pair of DH.98 Mosquitos from the Royal Air Force's No. 248 Squadron. In the 1990s, he became close friends with the navigator of the British plane who sank his U-boat in 1944. Raimund Tiesler died in Herdecke, Germany in February 2000.[29]

***

Captain Torger Olsen was wracked with guilt over making the *Gulftrade* a target of the *U-588* by turning on his lights to avoid a collision off Barnegat. Gulf Oil Company subsequently gave him command of the tanker *Gulfland*, and Olsen was sailing off West Palm Beach in October 1943 when another tanker, the *Gulfbelle*, smashed into his. The impact and ensuing inferno killed most of the crewmen aboard both ships, including Torger Olsen.

The forward half of the *Gulftrade* sits 5 miles southeast of Barnegat Light under 60 feet of water. Another tanker was damaged in 1950 when its keel struck the wreck, which was thereafter dynamited again. The bow section's twisted debris has yielded many artifacts—and at least one unexploded hedgehog bomb—over the years, but is seldom dived today. The *Gulftrade*'s stern half lies about a dozen miles northeast of the bow and 15 miles southeast of Seaside Heights. One of the Jersey Shore's most intact war wrecks, it featured penetration points and up to 20 feet of relief as recently as 2019. Its 90-foot depth, upright position, and easily navigable contours make it readily accessible to intermediate divers, and the *Gulftrade*'s aft section is among the state's most popular dive sites. Both halves of the wreck offer rewarding spear fishing and lobstering.

Five months after the *Gulftrade* attack, the Canadian destroyer HMCS *Skeena* and corvette HMCS *Wetaskiwin* attacked Viktor Vogel's *U-588* with depth charges in the north-central Atlantic. Vogel evaded them, but was again detected by sonar the next morning. Another bombardment produced a powerful underwater detonation. The Canadians soon observed a glistening oil slick with debris and human remains as the *U-588* sank thousands of feet to the seafloor.[30]

***

The freighter *Toltén*, torpedoed by Otto von Bülow's *U-404* with the loss of all but one crewman, was the only Chilean vessel lost during the war. The grandson of second mate Norman Pugh told me that Norman's father, Ernest, "never overcame the death of his eldest son." Before dying less than three years later, Ernest warned Norman's younger half-brother, Kenneth, not to seek a career at sea. Yet saltwater runs in the family's veins, and Kenneth Pugh Gillmore instead became one of nine Pughs to serve in the Chilean navy after the war. He specialized in antisubmarine warfare, which remained important during the Cold War due to the Soviet submarine threat.

Kenneth Pugh Olavarría is the son of Kenneth Pugh Gillmore and the nephew of Norman Pugh Cook. He, too, joined the Chilean navy and eventually retired as a three-star admiral. "I remember him training me as a child to be a sonar operator," the younger Kenneth proudly told me. "He taught me to 'ping, rotate five degrees, then listen.'" Pugh Olavarría expressed his gratitude when I sent him Otto von Bülow's attack sketch which portrays the *Toltén* zigzagging when she was hit. "I know that my father, as an officer specializing in torpedoes and antisubmarine warfare, would have been very proud to know that his brother was correctly maneuvering the ship." At the time of our conversation, Kenneth Pugh Olavarría was in his fifth year representing Valparaíso in the Chilean senate.

Kenneth Pugh Gillmore remembered his father's search for closure regarding the circumstances around Norman's death, and unanswered questions troubled Kenneth for decades. Had the *Toltén* been deliberately sunk by Allied forces? And, if not, did Captain Aquiles Ramírez turn off his lights based on a recommendation or an order? As Senator Pugh told me, "My dad spent many years trying to decipher what happened to his brother."

He found his answers by the time he died in 2021 at age 86. Kenneth Pugh Gillmore learned that Norman's ship had indeed been sunk by Otto von Bülow's *U-404* and that USCGC *Antietam* had almost certainly ordered—not recommended—that Ramírez extinguish the *Toltén*'s lights. "That gave him peace of mind," Senator Pugh told me. "By clearing up any doubts about who was responsible for the attack, he finally reconciled himself with his brother's death."

Sergio López Pugh, Norman's grandson and Senator Pugh's nephew, spoke of the tragic aura that hung over his mother, Mabel, and the rest of the family. "I never met any of my grandfathers and, as a child, I always wished that I could have had a grandpa," Sergio shared in polished English. "Now that I'm an adult and I read about him in your text, I realize I missed much more than I ever thought." At the time of this writing, Sergio López Pugh was a reserve Chilean Marine Corps officer in his nineteenth year of service.

Aquiles Ramírez Astudillo, the grandson of *Toltén* captain Aquiles Ramírez Bárcena, worked as a shore employee for Compañía Sudamericana de Vapores. He has a keen interest in the *Toltén* story and was a generous source of information for this book. The photos and documents he shared included a biographical essay he penned in 2012 which stated that "we always remember our grandfather as an example of '*La Vida Recta*' [the straight life] and patriotic values." This tribute carries even greater significance considering that Captain Ramírez did everything possible to protect his crew by keeping his ship partly illuminated. His grandson wrote:

> Like a good captain, Aquiles Ramírez went down with his ship when it was treacherously wounded in the darkness of night. The sea that he conquered, and that had rocked him since he was a child, today serves as his impenetrable burial shroud. Captain Ramírez, always present in the hearts and minds of his crew, lived on in those of his friends. By embodying what it means to be a man and a gentleman, it was a legacy that he fully earned.[31]

Today, the *Toltén* lies 15 miles east-southeast of Seaside Heights at a depth of 95 feet and is one of New Jersey's most frequently dived wrecks. The Chilean ship's remains are low-lying but contiguous, though the bridge lays in the sand about 40 feet from the hull. The collapsed foremast is visible between the boilers and bow, the engine can be seen amid a debris pile aft of the boilers, and the steering quadrant was prominently visible as recently as 2019.

Otto von Bülow and the *U-404* set out on another East Coast patrol less than two months after the *Toltén* attack. Later that year, he sank the destroyer HMS *Veteran* and was personally awarded the Knight's Cross with Oak Leaves by Hitler after mistakenly reporting that he had sunk the aircraft carrier USS *Ranger* (CV-4). Von Bülow turned over command of the *U-404* in July 1943 to Adolf Schönberg, the Long Island-born first watch officer who had launched the torpedo at the *Toltén*.

Eight days after Schönberg assumed command of the *U-404*, an Anglo-American force of three B-24 Liberators picked up the boat on radar in the Bay of Biscay. Schönberg's men damaged all three aircraft with 20mm fire. The boat transmitted an incomplete message, "ATTACKED BY AIRCRAFT," just as the wounded third bomber drove the attack home. The *U-404* went down with all hands.

Von Bülow briefly commanded a Type XXI elektroboot in the spring of 1945 before leading an ad-hoc infantry unit, and war's end found him in Mürwik along with Dönitz's administration. Like many former U-boat officers, he joined the Bundesmarine in the 1950s. Von Bülow and former *U-550* engineer Hugo Renzmann traveled to Charleston, South Carolina in 1960 to take command of USS *Charles Ausburne* and sail it back to West Germany as the *Z-6*. He expressed regret about the *Toltén* sinking in a 1975 letter to New Jersey wreck diver Tom Roach. Otto von Bülow died in Hamburg in 2006.[32]

***

Helge Quistgaard, the Danish captain of the *Persephone*, became a United States citizen in 1950. He opened his own maritime inspection business in Philadelphia and worked part-time as a port captain in New York City. Quistgaard died in King of Prussia, a suburb of Philadelphia, in 1979. The unsalvaged portion of the *Persephone* is dispersed across a sandy bottom at a depth of just 50 feet, though the once-popular dive site is seldom visited today.[33]

Gerd Kelbling, who torpedoed the *Persephone* in daylight off Barnegat, commanded the *U-593* on sixteen war patrols. He sank a US Navy minesweeper and two landing ships in the Mediterranean in 1943, killing 120 Americans. Kelbling's luck ran out in December of that year when he provoked the wrath of the destroyers USS *Wainwright* and HMS *Calpe*, which battered the *U-593* with depth charges for thirty hours. "It was hell," Kelbling recounted. "I didn't even have time to feel scared … you're thinking all the time, 'this is the end.'"

The flooding *U-593* began to rapidly lose buoyancy. A petty officer blew the last of the compressed air into the tanks, but the boat continued plummeting and passed 750 feet as it approached crush depth. Kelbling was in waist-deep water in the control room when, at the last moment, the chief engineer managed to get the E-motors running at half speed. The *U-593* then limped to the surface where Kelbling and his entire crew were captured. "It was a miracle that we survived," he admitted.

Reuters interviewed an elderly Kelbling six days after the Russian submarine *Kursk* sank in 2000. "I can understand better than others what those Russian sailors suffered," Kelbling said. "When you're on the bottom and can't do anything, it's a terrifying situation psychologically." Kelbling died in Ammersee, Upper Bavaria, in 2005.[34]

***

The wreck of the Argentine freighter *Rio Tercero* lies roughly halfway between Hudson Canyon and Toms Canyon, near the continental shelf's edge. The depth here is between 500 and 1,000 feet. The *Rio Tercero*'s exact location has not been determined as of this writing.

The *U-202*, which torpedoed the *Rio Tercero* in June 1942 after delivering the Operation Pastorius agents ashore, was sunk by the Royal Navy almost exactly a year later. Thirty of the 48-man crew were captured. Hans-Heinz Linder was not aboard at the time, having been previously transferred to First U-boat Flotilla staff in Brest, and thereafter to a training command in Latvia. Linder died in a Soviet air attack in September 1944.

Coast Guard beach patrolman John "Jack" Cullen, who encountered the Nazi agents on Amagansett Beach, spent the rest of the war making appearances at war bond drives, parades, and warship launches. Cullen later entered the dairy industry and shared his story with the Coast Guard's Oral History Program in 2006, five years before his death. Coast Guard Station Amagansett was restored to its original appearance and added to the National Register of Historic Places in 2018. Today it serves as the Amagansett US Life-Saving & Coast Guard Station Museum.

The six Nazi saboteurs executed in August 1942 were buried in unmarked graves in pauper's cemetery in Washington, D.C. George Dasch and Ernst Burger, who avoided the electric chair by betraying the operation to the FBI, were deported after the war and died in obscurity. Intelligence chief and World War I U-boat commander Admiral Wilhelm Canaris (who noted Dönitz's ambition in a 1930 performance evaluation) was, in fact, already plotting against the Nazis when he was tasked with planning Operation Pastorius in 1942. Canaris, whose Operation Pastorius had landed saboteurs by U-boat in New York and Florida in 1942, was arrested after the July 1944 assassination attempt and hanged in Flossenbürg concentration camp in April 1945. The physician present reported that Canaris died "firm and like a man."

Pastor Carl Krepper, the German immigrant and US citizen who worked as a Nazi agent in New Jersey for three years, was convicted of multiple federal offenses in March 1945 and served six years in prison. His subsequent request for a pardon was denied. Krepper passed his final years in Massachusetts where he died in 1972 at age eighty-eight. No one claimed his ashes, which were interred with others in an unmarked grave.[35]

***

Two world wars left New Jersey's seabed replete with mysteries, one of which was discovered 60 miles off Atlantic City in 1992. Gene Peterson spent years trying to identify the ship. He recovered its brass helm in 1994, yet nothing seemed to shed any light on whose grave sits 165 feet under the surface. It was not until 2007 that Glasgow University archives in Scotland linked the helm's serial number to the long-defunct manufacturer John Hastie and Sons. More than six decades after being torpedoed by the *U-432*, the ship regained her name: *Miraflores*.

Relatives of the thirty-four men lost with the British-flagged *Miraflores* expressed their appreciation to Peterson. Robert Bing of Houston, Texas was 4 years old when his father, an able seaman, disappeared along with the ship in February 1942. Bing searched for years for information about his father's fate before stumbling across news of the discovery, and he soon visited Gene Peterson's home in New Jersey where he touched the helm of his father's ship. Robert Bing Jr's journey was complete and, in a very real sense, so was his father's.

Rustin Cassway and several other New Jersey divers solved a similar mystery in 2018 after recovering a boiler plate from a wreck found at 227 feet. The Norwegian Maritime Museum used the plate to identify the wreck as the *Octavian*. Long believed torpedoed off Canada, the Nortraship freighter had instead been sunk by the *U-123* south of Cape May on 18 January 1942. The divers traveled to Oslo to donate the plaque to the museum and meet relatives of the seventeen *Octavian* mariners lost in the sinking. "It closes the story," Cassway stated, "and brings the ship home to Norway where it belongs."[36]

***

The events surrounding the torpedoing of the tanker *Pan Pennsylvania* on 16 April 1944 hardly seemed memorable except to those who experienced them. Like other World War II veterans, the Americans and Germans who lived through that day hoped to put difficult memories behind them as they entered an uncertain postwar world. In time, however, many found peace through embracing, not locking away, the events of that fateful morning. The final part of their story nonetheless remained unwritten, and it would take a New Jersey diver in the 21st century to finally conclude it.

Mort Raphelson, the *Pan Pennsylvania*'s chief radio officer, settled near his hometown of Philadelphia where he married and raised four children. He earned two degrees from Villanova University and worked for twenty-six years as an electrical engineer for Radio Corporation of America in Camden, New Jersey. A diehard Phillies fan, he spent much of his spare time on fishing boats in the Delaware Bay. Raphelson died in March 2016.[37]

USS *Joyce* captain Robert Wilcox served thirty years in the US Coast Guard, yet he always considered the *Joyce* "my ship." His son, Dick, remembered his parents' "pretty raucous" parties, and his granddaughter, Kimberly Wilcox Joshi, recalled her grandfather's fishing lessons and "wicked sense of humor." Wilcox took immense pride in both defeating the *U-550* and saving twelve of its crew. "Once those men were in the water," he told his children, "they were no longer my enemy. They would have died if we didn't get to them." He married three times and eventually relocated to Florida where he devoted his time to golf and charity work.

Wilcox regularly attended USS *Joyce* reunions although, according to Dick Wilcox, "he couldn't talk about the USS *Leopold* without crying." His grief was sharpened by a sense of guilt over twice aborting the *Leopold* rescue, an action he had taken only because John Bender's hydrophone picked up incoming torpedoes. Yet these had not sounded like German torpedoes and, after the war, the *U-255* commander assured Wilcox (in person) that he had fired no additional eels that night. Finally, in 2017, a theory originally proposed by Wilcox himself was confirmed through the efforts of one survivor's brother: the *Leopold*'s own torpedoes, primed to fire at the *U-255* in the moments before she was hit, had streaked toward the *Joyce* as the *Leopold* foundered. Wilcox had not been dodging phantoms after all.

Bob Wilcox died in 1995 at age 81 and was buried at Arlington National Cemetery with full military honors. In attendance was John Bender, the *Joyce*'s antisubmarine officer. "I don't need to remind you that we are alive today because of the leadership of Robert Wilcox," he wrote in a subsequent letter to his shipmates. Of "Taps" being played at the funeral, Bender wrote that "I have never heard it played so beautifully."[38]

Several weeks after Task Group 21.5 sank the *U-550*, Kapitänleutnant Klaus Hänert arrived at the Bowmanville POW camp in Canada. He was repatriated to West Germany in late 1947 and worked for a bakery and an oil company before joining the Bundesmarine. He penned letters to the families of his forty-four fallen crewmen, writing to one man's parents: "You can be assured that your son did his duty with bravery and dignity until the end … Your brave boy will never leave my thoughts." Axel Niestlé, who knew him personally, stated that Hänert "never stopped thinking about his men who lost their lives with the *U-550*."

Klaus Hänert later commanded the destroyer *Z-1*, and his attendance at a 1966 conference in the United States provided the opportunity to visit Bob Wilcox at his Baltimore home. Described as "very Prussian" by his son, Hänert retained the spiritual role of the *U-550* survivors' commander at annual reunions and fostered bonds between his crew and the veterans of Task Group 21.5. Neither his sense of duty nor frugality ever wavered, and he once justified his sparse wardrobe by stating that "a uniform is enough."

His son, Wolf, also became a Bundesmarine officer and shared with me his father's most important lessons. Klaus taught his son to "Always take care of your men" and "Never hide behind an order. Do what *you* feel is right." Wolf became a Bundesmarine naval doctor and attended the US Navy dive school. His father's wartime experience led him to specialize in treating cold water immersion casualties. When the elder Hänert developed Alzheimer's in his final years, only an "order" from his naval doctor son could deter Klaus' compulsion to again don his uniform and report for duty. Klaus Hänert died in 2003 at age 84, but the family naval tradition lives on. Wolf's two sons became naval officers and, at the time of this writing, Tom Hänert was the second watch officer aboard the *U-36*.[39]

In Hugo Renzmann's correspondence with Bob Wilcox, the *U-550*'s chief engineer spoke of postwar struggles and hopes for reconciliation: "Always I hope that our former enemies examine one day that the German people are the heart of Europe, and that Europe cannot live without this people." Renzmann eventually entered

Klaus Hänert and his son, Wolf, circa 1954. (Courtesy of Wolf Hänert)

the Bundesmarine and settled in Kiel, where he lived just a few houses away from Klaus Hänert. His journey with Otto von Bülow to take over the *Z-6* brought him to the United States in 1960. Before proceeding from Philadelphia to Charleston, however, Renzmann made a detour north.

"You've put on some weight, haven't you?" Wilcox joked upon meeting Renzmann at a Manhattan bus terminal. The onetime foes embraced and retreated to a bar, where Wilcox used pencils on a tabletop to demonstrate USS *Joyce's* maneuvers during their encounter sixteen years earlier. "We found you right away, but I was too dumb to know it," Wilcox stated regarding the poor sonar conditions. Renzmann shared the German perspective. "We waited and waited and could hear nothing, so we thought the escort vessels had gone east, but as soon as we started to move, *bang!*" The pair had dinner that evening at Wilcox's home on Staten Island, and Renzmann spoke fondly of that day for the rest of his life.[40]

Friedrich Torge, the *U-550*'s doctor, became a dermatologist and reserve naval physician in West Berlin. He forever referred to 16 April as his "second birthday" and irritated his family by leaving windows open during the winter, a lifelong habit instilled by the foul air inside the *U-550*. Dr Torge remained close with Klaus Hänert, and the name of his friend and former commanding officer was one of the few things he remembered when his cognitive faculties failed during his last days. Friedrich Torge died in 2009 and was buried with full military honors.

U-550 torpedoman Johann "Hans" Rauh relocated to Queens in New York City, earned an engineering degree, and worked for an aerospace components manufacturer. He eventually married fellow German immigrant Helga Christiansen after they met on a bus ride to Florida. They settled on Long Island and had two children, John and Gloria. "He loved being an American," John Rauh told me in 2021.

The few wartime memories Hans shared with his children were jarring. "Johnny, when those things would explode," he recounted about the depth charges, "you felt like you were gonna be ripped apart." John believes that his father's sincere appreciation for life "probably had a lot to do with what happened on April 16th, 1944." Hans found solace in former comrades, especially his longtime friend Albert Nitsche, and took his young son to *U-550* reunions in Bavaria. Hans Rauh died in 2005 at age 80.

Albert Nitsche picked cotton as a POW in Mississippi before returning home. He settled in Frankfurt, where he helped rebuild his war-ravaged country by working as a carpenter. Nitsche and his wife visited Hans Rauh in New York more than once, and both men attended regular *U-550* reunions. Nitsche also traveled to Washington, D.C. to meet USS *Peterson* radarman and New Jersey native Collingwood Harris.

The German and American veterans of 16 April found an enduring comradeship. Donald Macchia, a USS *Poole* veteran from Bloomfield, New Jersey, invited Klaus Hänert and his former crew to a Task Group 21.5 reunion in 1989. Collingwood Harris was particularly active in cultivating this relationship. He attended a *U-550* reunion in 1988, and Klaus Hänert wrote the following year that "he became a friend of all of us." Harris' recollections were documented by the Coast Guard Oral

History Program in 1984 and constitute the most vivid firsthand accounts of both the USS *Leopold* and *Pan Pennsylvania* incidents.[41]

The forward half of the tanker *Pan Pennsylvania* was located intact and upside-down at a depth of 240 feet in 1994, but the remainder continued to elude searchers. The bow section's discovery was made from the *Seeker*, the same New Jersey dive boat from which Richie Kohler and John Chatterton located the *U-869*. The conclusion of the *U-Who* mystery three years later, however, still left one U-boat unaccounted for off New Jersey. Where was the *U-550*?

Some of the Northeast's best wreck divers searched for Klaus Hänert's lost U-boat for years, but none were as determined as New Jersey attorney and technical diver Joe Mazraani. He first made his name in underwater salvage by recovering the helm of the freighter *Ayuruoca* off Asbury Park in 2010. That same year, he purchased a 45-foot lobster boat and outfitted it for diving under the name D/V *Tenacious*. The hunt for the *U-550* was on.

The search began in the summer of 2011. Aided by side-scan sonar expert Garry Kozak, Mazraani's team systematically "mowed the lawn" with a towed sonar array at hang numbers near the approximate coordinates of the 1944 battle. This proved fruitless, but the search resumed the following summer. A cigar-shaped image finally appeared on Kozak's monitor on 23 July 2012, and a lighted drop camera confirmed what lay on the seabed below. Sixty-eight years after Hugo Renzmann watched it sink, the *U-550* had been found.

Six divers descended 330 feet through a dark but clear sea. "When I landed on the deck, I had a reverential feeling," Mazraani recalled. Swarms of pollock and krill flitted through flashlight beams as the awestruck discoverers finned over the derelict war machine. They found the upright Type IXC/40 bedecked in hydroids and fishing nets, but remarkably well-preserved and still bearing visible damage from USS *Joyce*'s depth charges. Klaus Hänert's instinct for battle prior to surrendering is also evident. Tube two is open with a homing torpedo visible inside—bared fangs forever frozen in time.

The news shocked and thrilled Wolf Hänert, who was featured on a *Norddeutscher Rundfunk* television segment about the discovery. "When I saw for the first time that the boat was there, I read '*U-550*' and thought 'that can't be … that's my father's boat.'" John Rauh, son of Hans Rauh, accompanied the divers aboard D/V *Tenacious* and laid a wreath on the water over the wreck in honor of all those lost that day. "Human destinies also lay behind this," explained Friedrich Torge's granddaughter in the magazine *Cicero*. "It has come full circle for me and my family."[42]

Garry Kozak's sonar also identified something else on the seabed during Mazraani's search for the U-boat. When diving the site revealed an enormous and largely intact wreck rising nearly 70 feet off the seafloor, the team realized they had discovered the stern half of the *Pan Pennsylvania*. "It was a sight to see," Mazraani told one reporter. "We were in awe at the size of it. I had never seen a wreck so big."

The following year, the divers visited the New Jersey home of *Pan Pennsylvania* radio officer Mort Raphelson. "I wasn't expecting anything," stated Raphelson, age 92. "I just was interested in talking to them about their dive to the ship last year." They instead presented him with two ceramic bowls, one of which was mounted in a wood and glass frame. Tom Packer recovered them from the *Pan Pennsylvania* wreck. It was a fitting gift considering that the *U-550*'s attack interrupted Raphelson's breakfast. "Oh boy, a dish out of the ocean from my old ship!" Raphelson exclaimed. "Where's my soup?"

Mazraani and the others traveled to Germany in 2013 in the hope of learning from the three living *U-550* veterans what had transpired during the boat's chaotic and violent final minutes. Hugo Renzmann and Robert Ziemer both turned down requests to meet, but Albert Nitsche happily accepted. He greeted the divers at his home near Heidelberg with his trademark grin and surprising vigor, and conversed with them for hours. A letter from Robert Wilcox's granddaughter was read aloud, prompting Nitsche to remove his glasses and dab the tears welling in his eyes. After composing himself, Nitsche declared a simple and heartfelt "*Gut.*" *Good.*

Renzmann unexpectedly reconsidered and agreed to meet, and a television camera filmed his conversation with Joe Mazraani while Wolf Hänert interpreted. Renzmann excitedly remembered Bob Wilcox, and the exchange seemed to soothe an anxiety that had plagued the elderly chief engineer for seven decades. Finally, as Mazraani stated, "the man was at peace." Renzmann concluded their discussion with a hoarse expression of gratitude: "Thank you for finding the boat." Mazraani has also resolved to protect it, and the *U-550*'s exact location remains a closely guarded secret.[43]

***

Kenneth Pugh Gillmore, the Chilean naval officer who lost his brother Norman on the *Toltén*, corresponded with New Jersey firefighter and dive boat captain Duane Clause in the early 2000s. Kenneth Pugh was pleased to learn that Clause had recovered an anchor from the *Toltén* in 1996. The anchor would adorn Clause's backyard in Wall Township until 2019 when he donated it to the New Jersey Historical Divers Association. Pugh also found great satisfaction in the knowledge that his brother's grave is anything but abandoned.

Clause told him how the *Toltén*'s quiet repose instead teems with sea life and divers, serving as a living memorial to Norman and the thousands more whose wartime journeys ended in the Atlantic's cold embrace. If you visit Norman Pugh's final resting place off New Jersey, or any of the other silent tombs of those who perished in American waters during World War II, you will better understand Kenneth Pugh's sentiments. "You will feel how the shattered hull of the *Toltén* sends you this message," he wrote:

"Navigator, go and tell the homeland that here we lie, fulfilling our duty."[44]

Acknowledgements

If *Killing Shore* is ultimately a human story, then it is fitting that its creation hinged on the patience, generosity, and enthusiasm of dozens of individuals across three continents. Most were either naval/maritime subject matter experts or blood relatives of a character from this book, with a few occupying both categories. Without their gracious assistance, this would be a much different work.

Near the top of the list is Captain Jerry Mason, (USN, Ret), a former naval aviator who manages UboatArchive.net. His website provided the German archival documentation so critical to telling this story, and *Killing Shore*'s factual accuracy was further burnished through my extensive email correspondence with Jerry. Naval expertise was provided by Lieutenant Commander Joshua Mills (USN), while Captain Bob Desh (USCG, Ret.) and Commander Gary Thomas (USCG, Ret.) lent their knowledge of Coast Guard history. Their corollary across the Atlantic was Lucas Uhlemann, an active-duty German navy officer who became my go-to for all things related to the German language and German naval culture.

Captain Hugh Stephens (USMM, Ret.), a Merchant Marine combat veteran of World War II, brought realism to my portrayal of the merchant mariners by providing feedback on draft versions of the manuscript. He also answered a litany of questions and shared memories from seventy-eight years of service at sea and ashore. For a living legend and American hero like Captain Stephens to take such an interest in this project was enormously helpful and deeply humbling. Captain Jim McNamara (USMM, Ret.) and Armed-Guard.com webmaster Ron Carlson also contributed expertise on subjects ranging from lifeboats to steam engines.

Randall Peffer shared publishing advice, but his greatest contribution was his excellent 2014 book *Where Divers Dare: The Hunt for the Last U-boat*. This served as my guidepost for crafting a factual and stylistically distinct portrayal of the *Pan Pennsylvania* story in Chapter 15. I was also privileged to engage with Homer Hickam, famed NASA engineer and author of *Torpedo Junction*. Author Eric Wiberg referred me to illustrator Bob Pratt, whose talents produced two images featured in this book. Several old photographs were superbly restored and colorized by Peter Shafron (Heritage Studios). Joseph Bilby, an author specializing in New Jersey history, also provided three photographs from his personal collection.

My veritable platoon of subject matter experts included Northeast wreck divers Joe Mazraani, Jenn Sellitti, Gene Peterson, Dan Lieb, Steve Gatto, Harold Moyers, and Duane Clause. Captain Bill Manthorpe (USN, Ret.) made available his detailed knowledge of the Delaware Capes' wartime history, and further expertise was shared by Bjoern Pedersen (Norwegian Maritime Museum), Richard Van Treuren (Naval Airship Association), and Mike Laney (B-25 History Project). David Swope (New Jersey Maritime Museum) jumpstarted my research with a plethora of digital files, and John Arnold (NICOM, Inc) and his research team located several archived documents critical for reconstructing events in Chapters 7 and 10. Denise Wunder, a Thai boxing coach and native of Oberhausen, Germany also generously provided translation support for Chapter 8.

I am also indebted to the many friends and relatives who provided feedback on an interminable deluge of drafts. Notable mentions are extended to B. Chandler Brenneman, J.C. Wilt, Buddy Riggs, Mark Wood, James Jones, Giovanni Ferro, David Hamel, Bucky McCarthy, Eric Tannenbaum, and my parents. Their assistance constituted *Killing Shore*'s "user acceptance testing" by identifying everything from typos to shortfalls in clarity and continuity.

Finally, a wealth of documents, photographs, and memories were provided by characters' family members: Wolf Hänert, John Rauh, Mike Monichetti, James Tidwell, Eric Tidwell, Kenneth Pugh Olavarría, Sergio López Pugh, Aquiles Ramírez Astudillo, Wencke Hänert, Kimberly Wilcox Joshi, and Dick Wilcox. The insights they shared via video interviews, emails, and text messages were indispensable in bringing *Killing Shore*'s characters to life (if a stranger ever contacts you online regarding some long-dead relative, it's probably me). Earning their trust and gratitude was the most rewarding experience of this endeavor, and *Killing Shore* is as much their work as it is mine.

Endnotes

Chapter 1. Eins Zwei Drei

1 U-123 KTB (7th patrol), 14; Gannon, *Operation Drumbeat*, 230–231; Goralski & Freeburg, *Oil and War*, 105–106.

2 Kriegsmarine, "U-boat Commander's Handbook," 340; Dixon, *The U-boat Commanders*, 40–41; Gannon, *Operation Drumbeat*, 16–18, 62, 66–67, 77–79, 159; Letter from Reinhard Hardegen to George Betts (1986); Reinhard Hardegen interview by MourningTheAncient.com.

3 Gröner, *German Warships 1815–1945* Vol. II, 67–69; U-123 KTB (7th patrol), 1–2; Gannon, *Operation Drumbeat*, 1, 12, 127–128; UK MoD, *The U-boat War in the Atlantic*, Vol. I: 117.

4 Dönitz, *Memoirs*, 198–199; Gannon, *Operation Drumbeat*, 136–138; Padfield, *War Beneath the Sea*, 216.

5 U-123 KTB (7th patrol), 5, 8–9; Gannon, *Operation Drumbeat*, 191–192, 199; Philip Kaplan, *Grey Wolves: The U-boat War 1939–1945*, 24 (Skyhorse Publishing, 2014).

6 U-123 KTB (7th patrol), 10–11; Dönitz, *Memoirs*, 198–199; Uboat.net, "Cyclops."

7 Dimbleby, *The Battle of the Atlantic*, 245–246; Vaeth, *Blimps and U-boats*, 15; Padfield, *War Beneath the Sea*, 221–222; U-123 KTB (7th patrol), 12–13.

8 Reinhard Hardegen interview by Stephen Ames; Duffy, *Target: America*, 117, 119; Paterson, *U-boat Combat Missions*, 144; U-123 KTB (7th patrol), 13–14; Operation *Drumbeat*, 8, 229–232; Offley, *The Burning Shore*, 112.

9 Hadley, *Count Not the Dead*, 97; Reinhard Hardegen interview by MourningTheAncient.com; Gannon, *Operation Drumbeat*, 19–21.

10 U-123 KTB (7th patrol), 14–15; Gannon, *Operation Drumbeat*, 233–234; Padfield, *War Beneath the Sea*, 222; Offley, *The Burning Shore*, 113.

11 Mappen, *There's More to New Jersey Than the Sopranos*, 169–170; U-123 KTB (7th patrol), 9, 13, 15–18, 21–22; Dönitz, *Memoirs*, 203; Wiberg, *U-boats in New England*, 88; 4th ND War Diary: 15 Jan 1942; Gannon, *Operation Drumbeat*, 250.

Chapter 2. The Third Dimension of Warfare

1 Lender, *One State in Arms*, 75; Fernicola, *Twelve Days of Terror*, 1–5, 52; Capuzzo, *Close to Shore*, 7-8, 28, 59–61, 74, 88–98, 120–122, 212; Nagiewicz, *The Hidden History of Maritime New Jersey*, 15–16. Gentile, *The Lusitania Controversies* Book 1, 94.

2 Burke, *Torpedoes and Their Impact on Naval Warfare*, 1–3, 47–48, 55–56; Koerver, *The Kaiser's U-Boat Assault on America*, 7–9, 14; Padfield, *War Beneath the Sea*, 1–2; Shafter, *Destroyers in Action*, 42–43; German History in Documents and Images, "Bernhard von Bülow on Germany's 'Place in the Sun' (1897)" (GermanHistorySocs.ghi-dc.org).

3   Breemer, "Defeating the U-boat," 5–6; Hadley, *Count Not the Dead*, 16; Horton, *The Illustrated History of the Submarine*, 8–11, 66; Rudyard Kipling, "The Trade" (*Sea Warfare*, 1916).

4   Halpern, "Handelskrieg mit U-Booten," 136; Koerver, *The Kaiser's U-Boat Assault on America*, 13–17; Padfield, *Dönitz: The Last Führer*, 36; Rust, *Naval Officers Under Hitler*, 10–11.

5   Ballantyne, *The Deadly Deep*, 79–82, 96–99, 102–103, 145–146; Koerver, *The Kaiser's U-Boat Assault on America*, 11–12; Michael B. Miller, "Sea Transport and Supply" (Encyclopedia.1914-1918-Online.net, 24 Aug 2016).

6   Gray, *The U-boat War*, 56–58, 64–66; Koerver, *The Kaiser's U-Boat Assault on America*, 38, 92, 176; Ballantyne, *The Deadly Deep*, 103; Hodos, *The Kaiser's Lost Kreuzer*, 10–12, 18–22; Halpern, "Handelskrieg mit U-Booten," 140, 146–147.

7   Halpern, "Handelskrieg mit U-Booten," 145–146; Robinson & Robinson, *Der Kapitän*, 130; *Arizona Republican*, "Over Thousand Lost When Lusitania Sinks" (8 May 1915); *Los Angeles Times*, "American Papers Comment on Sinking of Lusitania" (8 May 1915).

8   Capuzzo, *Close to Shore*, 109, 119–122, 137, 143–146, 152, 164–165, 188–189, 209, 245; Fernicola, *Twelve Days of Terror*, 14–20.

9   Hadley, *Count Not the Dead*, 30; Ballantyne, *The Deadly Deep*, 156–162; Hodos, *The Kaiser's Lost Kreuzer*, 38–39; Capuzzo, *Close to Shore*, 17–27, 86, 102, 118; Fernicola, *Twelve Days of Terror*, 15, 31, 152–154; Dominic Etzold correspondence with author.

10   Capuzzo, *Close to Shore*, 206, 214–217, 226–246, 251–253, 259, 264, 269–272, 277, 280–282, 292–297; Fernicola, *Twelve Days of Terror*, 31, 37, 46–59, 139–140, 148–150.

11   Robinson & Robinson, *Der Kapitän*, 39–44, 264; Koerver, *The Kaiser's U-boat Assault on America*, 177–180; Ballantyne, *The Deadly Deep*, 156–159, 162; Hodos, *The Kaiser's Lost Kreuzer*, 39–40; Dominic Etzold correspondence with author.

12   Herwig, *Politics of Frustration*, 120–124; Hodos, *The Kaiser's Lost Kreuzer*, 11–12, 25–27; Ballantyne, *The Deadly Deep*, 148–152, 155–156, 165; Koerver, *The Kaiser's U-boat Assault on America*, 242–246, 255.

13   Maritime Archaeology Trust, "USS Jacob Jones," 5–6, 10–14; Woofenden, *Hunters of the Steel Sharks*, 10, 12–13; Edward N. Hurley, *The Bridge to France*, n.p. (J. B. Lippincott & Co., 1927); John W. Lawrence, "Hog Island" (PhiladelphiaEncyclopedia.org, 2014).

14   Ballantyne, *The Deadly Deep*, 172–176; Uboat.net, "Ships Hit During WWI"; Miller, "Sea Transport and Supply."

15   US Navy, "The Evolution of Naval Weapons," 46–47; Woofenden, *Hunters of the Steel Sharks*, 36, 174–175; Herwig, *Politics of Frustration*, 162–163; Breemer, "Defeating the U-boat," 1, 4–5; Ballantyne, *The Deadly Deep*, 178–181, 213; Padfield, *Dönitz: The Last Führer*, 114–115; Ballantyne, *The Deadly Deep*, 201, 220–221; Richard Woodman, *The Merchant Navy*, 31 (Shire Publications, 2013, Kindle).

16   Buchholz, *New Jersey Shipwrecks*, 144–147; Herwig, *Politics of Frustration*, 143–145; Gray, *The U-boat War*, 233–237; Office of Naval Records and Library, "German Submarine Activities on the Atlantic Coast …," 23–26, 139–141; Cox, "H-019-5: Black Sunday and the Battle of Orleans"; Bilby, et al., *Hidden History of New Jersey at War*, 79, 83; Manthorpe, "Submarines at the Cape"; Hodos, *The Kaiser's Lost Kreuzer*, 41–43, 89–91, 96–112, 151–154, 157–159; *New York Times*, "Press of Germany Gloats Over Raids" (9 Jun 1918) and "Tanker Escapes After Hot Pursuit" (4 Jun 1918); Sinkings and fatalities for 1918 tabulated by Dominic Etzold using a range of 400–500 nautical miles from North America.

17   Padfield, *Dönitz: The Last Führer*, 117–121, 125–127; Citino, *The Wehrmacht's Last Stand*, 10–11; Dönitz, *Memoirs*, 2–3; Herwig, *Politics of Frustration*, 146–149; Frank Blazich, "The End of the War as They Knew It" (Origins.OSU.edu, Sep 2012).

18   Dönitz, *Memoirs*, 4–5; Kershaw, *Hitler: A Biography*, 1–7, 20–21, 61–63; Hitler, *Mein Kampf*, 202–206; Padfield, *Dönitz: The Last Führer*, 18–19, 120–123, 128–129, 141.

Chapter 3. The Gray Wolves

1   Padfield, *Dönitz: The Last Führer*, 127–128, 139–143; Mulligan, *Neither Sharks Nor Wolves*, 220–225; Rust, *Naval Officers Under Hitler*, 13–14, 25–27, 31–32, 120; Title poem found by Eric Rust and republished by Jordan Vause.

2   Zabecki, *Dönitz: A Defense*, 99; Dönitz, *Memoirs*, 5–8, 12–13; Padfield, *Dönitz: The Last Führer*, 18–19, 29–32, 120–121, 167–168, 182–183, 651–652; Rose, *Power at Sea*, 124; Bercuson & Herwig, *Long Night of the Tankers*, xv; Werner, *Iron Coffins*, 16, 71.

3   Hinsley, *Hitler's Strategy*, 1–10; Speer, *Spandau: The Secret Diaries*, 116; Mallmann Showell, *Fuehrer Conferences on Naval Affairs*, 32–34 and *Hitler's Attack U-boats*, 16–25; Dönitz, *Memoirs*, 10–13; Blair, *The Hunters*, 36–39.

4   Kriegsmarine, "U-boat Commander's Handbook," 91, 197, 200, 235; Dönitz, *Memoirs*, 13–15, 20–23; Mallmann Showell, *Hitler's Navy*, 79–82; Padfield, *War Beneath the Sea*, 69.

5   Williamson, *U-boat Tactics in WWII*, 5–12, 29–36; UK MoD, *The U-boat War in the Atlantic*, Vol. I: 64–67; Rose, *Power at Sea*, 292–293.

6   Speer, *Spandau: The Secret Diaries*, 116; Horton, *The Illustrated History of the Submarine*, 111–112; Dönitz, *Memoirs*, 26–31, 42–43; Uboat.net, "U-boat Projects and Proposals"; Mulligan, *Neither Sharks Nor Wolves*, 41–42.

7   Rössler, *The Evolution and Technical History of German Submarines*, 94–114; Gröner, *German Warships 1815–1945* Vol. II, 43–46, 67–68; Mallmann Showell, *Hitler's Attack U-boats*, 52–56, 238–239; Mulligan, *Neither Sharks Nor Wolves*, 64–66.

8   Cremer, *U-boat Commander*, 21–22; UK Admiralty, "Interrogation of U-boat Survivors," 20; US Navy, "Report on the German Submarine of the U-570 Class …," 22, 51; Gröner, *German Warships 1815–1945* Vol. II, 43–46, 67–68.

9   UK Admiralty, "Report on U-570," 6, 45 and "Interrogation of U-boat Survivors," 20–21, 62; Gröner, *German Warships 1815–1945* Vol. II, 44, 68; Padfield, *War Beneath the Sea*, 5; Submarine History, Episode #13, "U-boat Batteries" (YouTube, 12 Jan 2022).

10 CAPT Jerry Mason correspondence with author; UK Admiralty, "Interrogation of U-boat Survivors," 32, 61; Brustat-Naval & Suhren, *Teddy Suhren, Ace of Aces*, 90; Ubootwaffe.pl, "Ship Tanks"; Gröner, *German Warships 1815–1945* Vol. II, 44, 68.

11 Kriegsmarine, "Preliminary U-boat Information for U-boat Type VIIC," 28–29, 35–40, 47; UK Admiralty, "Interrogation of U-boat Survivors," 24, 46, 51, 61–62; US Navy, "Design Study of Former German Submarine – Type IXC," S11, 2–4, S24, 1; Buchheim, *Das Boot*, 39–40, 100; Cremer, *U-boat Commander*, 21–22.

12 Kriegsmarine, "Preliminary U-boat Information for U-boat Type VIIC," 27–28, 38, 44–47, 71–78; Buchheim, *Das Boot*, 54–55; US Navy, "Report on the German Submarine of the U-570 Class …," 15, 18, 20–23, 27, 31, 61–62; Mulligan, *Neither Sharks Nor Wolves*, 11–12.

13 Goebeler & Vanzo, *Steel Boat, Iron Hearts*, 10; Mulligan, *Neither Sharks Nor Wolves*, 11–13; Paterson, *U-boat Combat Missions*, 48, 113–114; US Navy, "Report on the German Submarine of the U-570 Class …," 31.

14 US Navy, "Report on the German Submarine of the U-570 Class …," 16, 35–37, 69–75, and "Former German Submarine Type IXC-40," S1, 1–6; UK Admiralty, "Report on U-570," 4–5; Geroux, *The Mathews Men*, 44.

15 Dönitz, *Memoirs*, 205; US Navy, "Former German Submarine Type IXC-40," S33: 2; Gannon, *Operation Drumbeat*, 20; Buchheim, *U-boat War*, n.p.; World Documentary Films, "U-boats: The Most Feared Fighting Ships …"; Hirschfeld & Brooks, *The Secret Diary of a U-boat*, 135; Goebeler & Vanzo, *Steel Boat, Iron Hearts*, 19; Monsarrat, *The Cruel Sea*, 273; Williamson, *Grey Wolf*, 16–18, 24–25; Mulligan, *Neither Sharks Nor Wolves*, 22–23, 176.

16 Hadley, *Count Not The Dead*, 82; Dönitz, *Memoirs*, 13; Vause, *Wolf*, 28, 74; Hughes & Costello, *The Battle of the Atlantic*, 83.

17   Mulligan, *Neither Sharks Nor Wolves*, 185–186; Vause, *Wolf*, 80–81; Padfield, *Dönitz: The Last Führer*, 125–126; Rose, *Power at Sea*, 120.

18   Goebeler & Vanzo, *Steel Boat, Iron Hearts*, 93; Rust, *Naval Officers Under Hitler*, 120–121; Padfield, *Dönitz: The Last Führer*, 156, 296–298, 652–653; Mulligan, *Neither Sharks Nor Wolves*, 44–45, 183–184, 220–221; Vause, *Wolf*, 26.

19   Macintyre, *U-boat Killer*, 33–34; Mulligan, *Neither Sharks Nor Wolves*, 45, 132–136, 154–156, 180–181; Vause, *Wolf*, 19–20, 43, 50–53, 82–83, 95; Williamson, *Grey Wolf*, 42, 110; Goebeler & Vanzo, *Steel Boat, Iron Hearts*, 39, 62; Paterson, *U-boat Combat Missions*, 143, 147; UK Admiralty, "U 99 Interrogation of Survivors," 5 (C.B. 04051 20, Apr 1942) and "U-570 Interrogation of Crew," 31 (C.B. 4051 31, Oct 1941).

20   Davies & Smelser, *The Myth of the Eastern Front*, 39–47, 56–68, 90–119; Rust, *Naval Officers Under Hitler*, 20, 57, 120–123, 172; Padfield, *Dönitz: The Last Führer*, 20, 144, 208, 649–650; Vause, *Wolf*, 83, 96–100, 193–194; Mulligan, *Neither Sharks Nor Wolves*, 172, 215–216, 230–231; Kershaw, *Hitler: A Biography*, 816.

21   Macintyre, *U-boat Killer*, 43–44; Hadley, *Count Not the Dead*, 84–85; UK Admiralty, "Interrogation of U-boat Survivors," 6; Mulligan, *Neither Sharks Nor Wolves*, 215–218, 231–232; Vause, *Wolf*, 93, 96–100.

22   Mallmann Showell, *Hitler's Attack U-boats*, 182–185; Mulligan, *Neither Sharks Nor Wolves*, 2–7.

23   UK Admiralty, "Interrogation of U-boat Survivors," 24; Hadley, *Count Not the Dead*, 82, 131; Mulligan, *Neither Sharks Nor Wolves*, 7–10, 14; Uboat.net, "Torpedo Personnel"; Rottman, *SNAFU*, 220, 229; Paterson, *U-boat Combat Missions*, 79–80, 113; Mallmann Showell, *Hitler's Attack U-boats*, 179–181.

Chapter 4. A Tide of Steel

1   Hinsley, *Hitler's Strategy*, 1–2, 10; Kershaw, *Hitler: A Biography*, 550; Dönitz, *Memoirs*, 333, 403.

2   Padfield, *Dönitz: The Last Führer*, 171–172; Kershaw, *Hitler: A Biography*, 153–155, 628–631, 669; Hitler, *Zweites Buch*, 82–85; Monsarrat, *The Cruel Sea*, 441; Deutsche Forschungsgemeinschaft, "Wissenschaft, Planung, Vertreibung: Der Generalplan Ost der Nationalsozialisten" (dfg.de).

3   Lender, *One State in Arms*, 87; Rachlis, *They Came to Kill*, 21–22; Marc Mappen, *Jerseyana: The Underside of New Jersey History*, 205–209 (Rutgers University Press, 1992).

4   Dönitz, *Memoirs*, 46–47, 51, 110; Hinsley, *Hitler's Strategy*, 3, 48, 59–60; Blair, *The Hunters*, 53–55; Snow, *A Measureless Peril*, 103–104.

5   UK MoD, *The U-boat War in the Atlantic*, Vol. I: 40–46; Dönitz, *Memoirs*, 43–44, 54–59; Hinsley, *Hitler's Strategy*, 31–39, 55–59; Padfield, *War Beneath the Sea*, 59–60; Wright, "Wolves Without Teeth," 45–46, 50–51.

6   Lundvall, "En undersøkelse og analyse av bevæpningen av norske handelsskip ...," 24; McNab, *The Merchant Navy Seaman Pocket Manual*, 7–8; Tenold, *Norwegian Shipping in the 20th Century*, 21–24; Mawdsley, *War for the Seas*, 85–86, 166.

7   Roskill, *The Defensive*, 343–345; Offley, *Turning The Tide*, 13; Geroux, *The Mathews Men*, 46–47; Hughes & Costello, *The Battle of the Atlantic*, 63; Author's tabulation of shipping and U-boat losses.

8   Blair, *The Hunters*, 287–292; LT Joseph Leonard Jr., USCG & Carl Gibeault, "No Place for a Small Cutter" (*Naval History*, Vol. 7, No. 3, Oct 1993).

9   International Military Tribunal, *The Nuremberg Trials*, 2816; Morison, *The Battle of the Atlantic*, 7–8; Rose, *Power at Sea*, 49, 217, 282.

10   Williamson, "Lend-Lease to the USSR"; Freeburg & Goralski, *Oil and War*, 85–86; Yergin, *The Prize*, 335–336; Valery Romanenko, "The P-40 in Soviet Aviation" (Lend-Lease.net, 8 Jun

2019); Alexander Hill, "Did Russia Really Go it Alone? How Lend-Lease Helped the Soviets Defeat the Germans" (HistoryNet.com, 12 Jul 2008).

11   Ron Carlson correspondence with author; Brustat-Naval & Suhren, *Teddy Suhren, Ace of Aces*, 125; Mallmann Showell, *Fuehrer Conferences on Naval Affairs*, 281.

12   Author's tabulation of tonnage totals and losses; Mawdsley, *War for the Seas*, 85–86, 260; Roskill, *The Period of Balance*, 105; Dönitz, *Memoirs*, 124–126, 201.

13   Hughes & Costello, *The Battle of the Atlantic*, 104–106, 128–129; Offley, *Turning the Tide*, 141; Werner, *Iron Coffins*, 30–31; Uboat.net, "List of Wolfpacks" and "Famous Convoy Battles"; Leighton, "U.S. Merchant Shipping and the British Import Crisis," 201; Author's tabulation of 1941 tonnage losses.

14   Macintyre, *U-boat Killer*, 10–12, 42, 46, 50; Kriegsmarine, "U-boat Commander's Handbook," 57(a)(b), 58; Offley, *Turning the Tide*, 59–60, 72–74; Dönitz, *Memoirs*, 30–31, 495; Vause, *Wolf*, 90–92; Blair, *The Hunters*, 248–258, 279–285.

15   UK MoD, *The U-boat War in the Atlantic*, Vol. I: 87–92; Dönitz, *Memoirs*, 157–160; Blair, *The Hunters*, 129–135, 388–389; Rose, *Power at Sea*, 307; Alan Stripp, "How The Enigma Works" (PBS.org, Nov 2000); Kalika Prasad & Munesh Kumari, "A review on mathematical strength and analysis of Enigma," 4–11 (Central University of Jharkhand, 22 Apr 2020).

16   Hughes & Costello, *The Battle of the Atlantic*, 13–14; Gannon, *Operation Drumbeat*, 83–84; Morison, *The Battle of the Atlantic*, 33–38; American Historical Association, "How Much of What Goods Have We Sent to Which Allies?" (Historians.org); Mike Palumbo, "Inter-war Isolationism" (20thCenturySongbook.com); Fireside Chat No. 16, "On the Arsenal of Democracy" (29 Dec 1940); Winston Churchill, *The Second World War*, Vol. III: *The Grand Alliance*, 477 (The Reprint Society Ltd, 1952).

17   Monsarrat, *The Cruel Sea*, 159; O'Connor, "FDR's Undeclared War"; Morison, *The Battle of the Atlantic*, 74–98; Mallmann Showell, *Fuehrer Conferences on Naval Affairs*, 221–222; Hinsley, *Hitler's Strategy*, 169–175; Fireside Chat No. 17, "On An Unlimited National Emergency" (27 May 1941); Liberty Fleet Day address (27 Sep 1941); Navy Day Address (27 Oct 1941).

18   Hitler, *Mein Kampf*, 94–95 and *Zweites Buch*, 93, 124, 199; Duffy, *Target: America*, 13–15, 19; Weinberg, "Hitler's Image of the United States," 1008–1014; Padfield, *Dönitz: The Last Führer*, 172, 281–183; Trevor-Roper, *Hitler's Table Talk*, 178–179, 183, 300–301, 314–315; Herwig, *Politics of Frustration*, 207–214, 235, 253.

19   Kershaw, *Hitler: A Biography*, 656–660; Churchill, *The Grand Alliance*, 476–477.

20   Herwig, *Politics of Frustration*, 129; Capt Hugh Stephens interview by author; Waber, "Popular Perceptions of the American Merchant Marine During WWII," 5, 18–19, 36–37; Geroux, *The Mathews Men*, 98–99, 136; Dönitz, *Memoirs*, 228; Mawdsley, *War for the Seas*, 85–86; USMM. org, "African-Americans in the U.S. Merchant Marine and U.S. Maritime Service."

21   Mallmann Showell, *Fuehrer Conferences on Naval Affairs*, 281; Goralski & Freeburg, *Oil and War*, 107–108, 114, 349–350; Werner, *Iron Coffins*, xiii; Gropman, "Mobilizing U.S. Industry in World War II," 93–98; Bercuson & Herwig, *Long Night of the Tankers*, 7–15, 277; PBS. org, "War Production"; Palucka, "The Wizard of Octane"; Alexander J. Field, "The decline of US manufacturing productivity between 1941 and 1948" (*Economic History Review*, 16 Jan 2023).

22   Citino, *The Wehrmacht's Last Stand*, 10–11; Gannon, *Operation Drumbeat*, 77; Blair, *The Hunters*, 439; Williamson, "Lend-Lease to the USSR."

23   ESF War Diary, Jan 1942, Ch. 2: 5–6, Ch. 4: 3; BdU Ops Division KTB Vol. 29, Part A: 93; Clausewitz, *On War*, xxix–xxx, 147–148, 162–163; Dönitz, *Memoirs*, 154–155, 195–197; David Stahel, "The Wehrmacht and National Socialist Military Thinking," 339, 348–350, 358 (*War in History*, Vol. 24, No. 3, Jul 2017).

24 Author's tabulation of 1941 tonnage losses; BdU KTB: 11 Jan 1942; Kershaw, *Hitler: A Biography*, 12; Trevor-Roper, *Hitler's Table Talk*, 179; Roskill, *The Period of Balance*, 104–105; Dönitz, *Memoirs*, 195.

25 Gannon, *Operation Drumbeat*, 77; Herwig, *Politics of Frustration*, 240; Vause, *Wolf*, 127.

26 Blair, *The Hunters*, 438–441, 452–453; Dönitz, *Memoirs*, 196–199; UK MoD, *The U-boat War in the Atlantic*, Vol. II: 2–4; U-701 KTB (1st patrol), 3; Wiggins, *U-boat Adventures*, 218; Nicholas Monsarrat, *Monsarrat at Sea*, 53 (William Morrow and Co., 1976).

27 ESF War Diary, Dec 1941, Ch. 1: 1–3 and Jul 1942, Ch. 1: 1; Morison, *The Battle of the Atlantic*, 205–208; Offley, *The Burning Shore*, 97–98.

28 Morison, *The Battle of the Atlantic*, 114–116; Cox, "H-008–5: Admiral Ernest J. King …"; Buell, *Master of Sea Power*, 88–89, 573; Gannon, *Operation Drumbeat*, 168–170; Gerald Clarke, "Behind the Huck Finn Face" (*TIME*, 3 Aug 1981); Montgomery C. Meigs, *Slide Rules and Submarines*, 44–46 (National Defense University Press, 1990). | King was eventually asked whether the "sons-of-bitches" anecdote was true. He replied that it was not, "but if I had thought of it, then I would have said it."

29 ESF War Diary, Jan 1942, Ch. 2: 1–2; Blair, *The Hunters*, 453–455; Offley, *The Burning Shore*, 102–105.

30 USAAF Historical Division, "The Antisubmarine Command" (AAFRH-7, Apr 1945), 4–7; Geroux, *The Mathews Men*, 71; ESF War Diary, Dec 1941, Ch. 2: 2–4, Jan 1942, Ch. 2: 5–6, Ch. 3: 1–3, Feb 1942, Ch. 5: 1–4, Appx. I, Appx. II, and Mar 1942, Ch. 5: 4–6; Morison, *The Battle of the Atlantic*, 127, 254–255.

31 4th ND War Diary: 12 Jan 1942; U-123 KTB (7th patrol), 17, 19; Uboat.net, "Norvana"; ESF War Diary, Jan 1942, Ch. 2: 3, Appx. III; Vaeth, *Blimps & U-boats*, 15.

32 U-123 KTB (7th patrol), 9, 13, 18–22; U-66 KTB (4th patrol), 9; BdU KTB: 8 Feb 1942; Gannon, *Operation Drumbeat*, 258; Dimbleby, *The Battle of the Atlantic*, 243; Wiggins, *U-boat Adventures*, 218; Cremer, *U-boat Commander*, 51, 69.

33 Atlantic Fleet, "United States Atlantic Fleet Organization, First Quarter, Fiscal Year 1942"; Padfield, *War Beneath the Sea*, 210, 219, 228–229; Love, "The US Navy and Operation Roll of Drums, 1942," 120; Gannon, *Operation Drumbeat*, 238–240, 413–415; Offley, *The Burning Shore*, 100–105, 276–277; Reinhard Hardegen interview by Stephen Ames; ESF War Diary, Feb 1942, Ch. 3: 5–7 and Mar 1942, Ch. 2: 2–9; Blair, *The Hunters*, 444–447, 454–455, 465–466, 749–752.

34 Wiberg, *U-boats in New England*, 78; ESF War Diary, Mar 1942, Ch. 5: 1; Gannon, *Operation Drumbeat*, 339, 388–389.

35 4th ND War Diary: 25 Jan 1942; Love, "The U.S. Navy and Operation Roll of Drums, 1942," 107; ESF War Diary, Jan 1942, Ch. 2: 4, 6, Appx. III.

Chapter 5. *Varanger*

1 *Camden Courier-Post*, "Torpedoed Sailors Leave Gloucester Eager to Sail Again" (27 Jan 1942); Krigsseilerregisteret.no, "Carl Hjalmar Horne."

2 Tenold, *Norwegian Shipping in the 20th Century*, 133–136, 139, 143–146; WarSailors.com, "Nortraship" and "Odd Conrad: A Sailor at War"; WWIINorge.com, "Nortraship"; Bunker, *Heroes in Dungarees*, 16.

3 *Plainfield Courier-News*, "Torpedoing of Panama Tanker off Long Island Believed Start of Axis Sea Campaign" (Plainfield NJ, 15 Jan 1942); Offley, *The Burning Shore*, 113–115, 120–122; *TIME*, "U.S. at War: Attack by Sea" (1 Jun 1942); *New York Times*, "Navy Has No Word" (16 Jan 1942) and "New U-boat Victim Confirmed by Navy" (17 Jan 1942).

4   U-85 KTB (3rd patrol), 37; *TIME*, "U.S. at War: Attack by Sea"; Reinhard Hardegen interview by Stephen Ames; Cox, "H-008–5: Admiral Ernest J. King …"; Offley, *The Burning Shore*, 121; Taylor, *Fire on the Beaches*, 79; *New York Times*, "Sinkings Indicated" (24 Jan 1942), "Navy 'Doing Its Job', Says Knox" (29 Jan 1942), "'Sighted Sub, Sank Same' Radios a Modern Perry in Naval Plane" (30 Jan 1942), "Swedish Freighter is Sunk, But War on U-boats Gains" (8 Feb 1942), and "Knox Defends Policy of Withholding News" (18 Feb 1942).

5   Mike Monichetti interview by author; Croskey, "When the War Came to Sea Isle"; *New York Times*, "Ship is Sent Down" (26 Jan 1942); Dan Kelly, "Tradition Hangs Tough at the Jersey Shore" (*Reading Eagle*, 8 Apr 2013).

6   U-130 KTB (2nd patrol), 10–16; Wiberg, *U-boats in New England*, 129–130; Dönitz, *Memoirs*, 203–204; Mulligan, *Neither Sharks Nor Wolves*, 1–2.

7   Morgan & Taylor, *U-boat Attack Logs*, xxiv–xxvi; UK Admiralty, "Report on U-570," 19–21; US Navy, "Report on the German Submarine of the U-570 Class …," 58–60; Padfield, *War Beneath the Sea*, 6, 40–42; U-130 KTB (2nd patrol), 11.

8   U-130 KTB (2nd patrol), 12–16; Hirschfeld & Brooks, *The Secret Diary of a U-boat*, 182; Dixon, *The U-boat Commanders*, 156–157; Blair, *The Hunters*, 438; Kriegsmarine, "U-boat Commander's Handbook," 271–278 and "Diving Regulations for U-boats," 74–75; Werner, *Iron Coffins*, 16.

9   US Navy, "The Evolution of Naval Weapons," 46; AlternateWars.com, "Calculating Depth Charge Lethality"; Cremer, *U-boat Commander*, 73–74; Campbell, *Naval Weapons of WWII*, 163; Rottman, *SNAFU*, 232; COMINCH HQ, "Anti-Submarine and Escort of Convoy Instructions," 2345 (FTP 223A, 1 Jan 1945).

10   U-130 KTB (2nd patrol), 16–17; World Documentary Films, "U-boats: The Most Feared Fighting Ships …"; Cremer, *U-boat Commander*, 73; Padfield, *War Beneath the Sea*, 105.

11   *Lloyd's Register of Shipping 1940–41*; 4th ND, "Report of sinking of S.S. VARANGER" (25 Jan 1942); Ron Carlson, Capt Jim McNamara, and Bjoern Pedersen correspondence with author; U-130 KTB (2nd patrol), 21; Croskey, "When the War Came to Sea Isle"; Norwegian Maritime Museum, *Sjøforklaringer fra 2. verdenskrig* Vol. II, 351–352. | Gun model identified from the *Varanger* wreck by Gary Gentile.

12   Kriegsmarine, "U-boat Commander's Handbook," 197(a); Morgan & Taylor, *U-boat Attack Logs*, xii, xxi, xxiv; U-130 KTB (2nd patrol), 21; Office of Naval Intelligence, "Merchant Ship Shapes," 19, 34.

13   Kriegsmarine, "Torpedo Firing Regulations for U-boats," 9–11, 21–25; Wright, "Wolves Without Teeth," 27–28; UK Admiralty, "Report on U-570," 19–20; Rottman, *SNAFU*, 217; Campbell, *Naval Weapons of WWII*, 263; Schaeffer, *U-boat 977*, 52–53.

14   4th ND, "Report of sinking of S.S. VARANGER"; Norwegian Maritime Museum, *Sjøforklaringer fra 2. verdenskrig* Vol. II, 351; *Camden Courier-Post*, "Torpedoed Sailors Leave Gloucester Ready to Sail Again" (27 Jan 1942); Ron Carlson and Capt Jim McNamara correspondence with author; U-130 KTB (2nd patrol), 21; Bunker, *Heroes in Dungarees*, 161–162.

15   *Philadelphia Inquirer*, "Explosions Jar Shore, All 42 In Crew Saved" (26 Jan 1942); Norwegian Maritime Museum, *Sjøforklaringer fra 2. verdenskrig* Vol. II, 351; 4th ND, "Report of sinking of S.S. VARANGER"; U-130 KTB (2nd patrol), 21–22; Kriegsmarine, "U-boat Commander's Handbook," 175, 308; ESF War Diary, Jan 1942, Ch. 2: 3.

16   4th ND, "Report of sinking of S.S. VARANGER"; *Camden Courier-Post*, "Torpedoed Sailors Leave Gloucester Eager to Sail Again."

17   Croskey, "When the War Came to Sea Isle"; 4th ND War Diary: 25 Jan 1942; ESF War Diary, Jan 1942, Appx. III; 4th ND, "Report of sinking of S.S. VARANGER"; *New York Times*, "Ship is Sent Down." | "Poor devils" thought obtained from Dewey Monichetti's statements to reporters.

18   U-130 KTB (2nd patrol), 22–32; 43; Mulligan, *Neither Sharks Nor Wolves*, 45; Otto von Bülow interview by Clay Blair.

19   *Philadelphia Inquirer*, "Explosions Jar Shore, All 42 In Crew Saved"; Croskey, "When the War Came to Sea Isle"; *Camden Courier-Post*, "Torpedoed Sailors Leave Gloucester Eager to Sail Again."
20   Author's tabulation of coastal sinkings; ESF War Diary, Jan 1942, Ch. 2: 3–4, Mar 1942, Ch. 4: 1, and Apr 1942, Appx. I; Offley, *The Burning Shore*, 124–125.

Chapter 6. *India Arrow*

1   U-103 KTB (6th patrol), 14–15; Campbell, *Naval Weapons of WWII*, 255–256; Rottman, *SNAFU*, 198–199; UK Admiralty, "Interrogation of U-boat Survivors," 16, 18, "U 593 Interrogation of Survivors," 4–5, and "Report on U-570," 24–25; Richards & Banigan, *How to Abandon Ship*, 21–23; Title poem obtained from *Polaris* magazine via USMM.org.
2   *Asbury Park Press*, "Fearing Sub Trap, Vessels Sped from Arrow's Boats" (7 Feb 1942); Waber, "Popular Perceptions of the American Merchant Marine During WWII," 37.
3   Dönitz, *Memoirs*, 203–207, 223; Klingaman, *The Darkest Year*, 110; Author's tabulation of losses; ESF War Diary, Feb 1942, Ch. 2: 3; Goralski & Freeburg, *Oil and War*, 111. | Dönitz quote cited by Goralski & Freeburg, among others, though its historicity is unclear.
4   Hansen, *Execution for Duty*, 14–15; Dixon, *The U-boat Commanders*, 298–299; Padfield, *War Beneath the Sea*, 8; Neitzel & Welzer, *Soldiers*, 283.
5   U-103 KTB (6th patrol), 11; Hansen, *Execution for Duty*, 7–9, 15, 19, 106, 111–113; Wiggins, *U-boat Adventures*, 208; Rust, "The Case of Oskar Kusch …"
6   U-103 KTB (6th patrol), 11; Wright, "Wolves Without Teeth," 16, 64–65; Blair, *The Hunters*, 95; Cremer, *U-boat Commander*, 27; Michał Lipka, "Zapomniany sukces podwodnego drapieżnika" (Trojmiasto.pl, 9 Nov 2011).
7   Payne, *Principles of Naval Weapon Systems*, 359; Wright, "Wolves Without Teeth," 16, 32, 64–65; Cremer, *U-boat Commander*, 27; Mallmann Showell, *German Navy Handbook*, 183–185; Navy-Matters.blogspot.com, "Torpedo Lethality Myth" (4 July 2017).
8   U-103 KTB (6th patrol), 11–12; Hansen, *Execution for Duty*, 15; U-701 KTB (1st patrol), 3; Wiggins, *U-boat Adventures*, 218; Mulligan, *Neither Sharks Nor Wolves*, 8, 15–16; Goebeler & Vanzo, *Steel Boat, Iron Hearts*, 16.
9   U-103 KTB (6th patrol), 12–13; UK Admiralty, "Interrogation of U-boat Survivors," 24; Rössler, *The Evolution and Technical History of German Submarines*, 145; Payne, *Principles of Naval Weapon Systems*, 153–160.
10   *Lloyd's Register of Shipping, 1941–42*; Auke Visser's Renewed Historical Tankers Site, "Mobil Tankers" (AukeVisser.nl); Seerveld, "The Sinking of the SS India Arrow"; *Daily News*, "26 Missing in Sinking Of Tanker Off Jersey" (NYC, 7 Feb 1942); Capt Jim McNamara and Ron Carlson correspondence with author.
11   Seerveld, "The Sinking of the SS India Arrow"; Monsarrat, *The Cruel Sea*, 259; Sheila Boyer interview by author; Capt Hugh Stephens & Ron Carlson correspondence with author; War Shipping Administration, *Engineering Branch Training*, 55–58; Bunker, *Heroes in Dungarees*, 187–188; Geroux, *The Mathews Men*, 106; DVRBS.com, "Nicholas Hetz"; *Camden Courier-Post*, "12 Saved in Torpedoing Off New Jersey" (7 Feb 1942); *Suffolk County News*, "Suffolk Man Lost; Two Saved as Submarine Sinks Tanker" (13 Feb 1942).
12   U-103 KTB (6th patrol), 13; Mulligan, *Neither Sharks Nor Wolves*, 4; Taylor, *Fire on the Beaches*, 73; Brian McCue, "An Exploration of Zigzagging," 13–14, 29 (*Phalanx*, Vol. 37, No. 2, Jun 2004); Office of Naval Intelligence, "Remarks on Submarine Tactics Against Convoys," 11–13 (ONI Pub. No. 23, Dec 1917) and "Analysis of Advantage of Speed and Changes of Course in Avoiding Attack by Submarine," 14–17 (ONI Pub. No. 30, May 1918).

13   Kriegsmarine, "U-boat Commander's Handbook," 275(a)(1), 275(c)(3); Williamson, *U-boat Tactics in WWII*, 14–15; Campbell, *Naval Weapons of WWII*, 255–256; Goebeler & Vanzo, *Steel Boat, Iron Hearts*; 25; Buchheim, *U-boat War*, n.p.; U-103 KTB (6th patrol), 13; Paterson, *U-boat Combat Missions*, 104; Standard Oil of NJ, *Ships of the Esso Fleet in WWII*, 84; Uboat. net, "Culebra" and "Pan Norway."

14   U-103 KTB (6th patrol), 15; Office of Naval Intelligence, "Merchant Ship Shapes," 4–11, 19; US Coast Guard, "War Casualties Resulting from Enemy Action," 19 (21 Apr 1942); Padfield, *War Beneath the Sea*, 6–7; Seerveld, "The Sinking of the SS India Arrow"; Gannon, *Operation Drumbeat*, 185–186; Lender, *One State in Arms*, 89; Cremer, *U-boat Commander*, 69; *Evening News*, "Atlantic City Darkens Many Boardwalk Lights" (Harrisburg PA, 20 Mar 1942).

15   US Coast Guard, "Report on U.S. Merchant Tanker War Action Casualty" (18 Nov 1944); Moore, *A Careless Word ... A Needless Sinking*, 134; *Philadelphia Inquirer*, "26 Die Off N.J. as Sub Fires, Sinks Tanker" (7 Feb 1942); Seerveld, "The Sinking of the SS India Arrow"; *Camden Courier-Post*, "12 Saved in Torpedoing Off New Jersey"; *Suffolk County News*, "Suffolk Man Lost ..."; U-103 KTB (6th patrol), 15–16.

16   ESF War Diary, Feb 1942, Ch. 5: 1; *Philadelphia Inquirer*, "26 Die Off N.J. ..."; Seerveld, "The Sinking of the SS India Arrow"; *Camden Courier-Post*, "12 Saved in Torpedoing Off New Jersey."

17   Moore, *A Careless Word ... A Needless Sinking*, 134; Capt Jim McNamara and Ron Carlson correspondence with author; Richards & Banigan, *How to Abandon Ship*, 12, 41; *Camden Courier-Post*, "12 Saved in Torpedoing Off New Jersey"; *Suffolk County News*, "Suffolk Man Lost; Two Saved as Submarine Sinks Tanker" (13 Feb 1942); McNab, *The Merchant Navy Seaman Pocket Manual*, 144; War Shipping Administration, *Preliminary Training*, 5–9 (1943).

18   *Paterson Morning Call*, "17th Vessel Lost Off Atlantic Coast to Undersea Foe Raiders" (7 Feb 1942); *Philadelphia Inquirer*, "26 Die Off N.J. ..."; *Asbury Park Press*, "Fearing Sub Trap, Vessels Sped From Arrow's Boats."

19   U-103 KTB (6th patrol), 14, 16; *Scranton Tribune*, "Scranton Man is Missing In Torpedoing" (7 Feb 1942); *Paterson Morning Call*, "17th Vessel Lost Off Atlantic Coast ..."; *Asbury Park Press*, "Fearing Sub Trap, Vessels Sped from Arrow's Boats"; Goebeler & Vanzo, *Steel Boat, Iron Hearts*, 201.

20   *Camden Courier-Post*, "12 Saved in Torpedoing Off New Jersey"; *Suffolk County News*, "Suffolk Man Lost ..."; *Philadelphia Inquirer*, "26 Die Off N.J. ..."; *Scranton Tribune*, "Scranton Man is Missing In Torpedoing."

21   ESF War Diary, Feb 1942, Ch. 5: 1–4, Appx. IV; 4th ND War Diary: 4 Feb 1942.

22   *Paterson Morning Call*, "17th Vessel Lost Off Atlantic Coast ..."; *Philadelphia Inquirer*, "26 Die Off N.J. ..."; *Camden Courier-Post*, "12 Saved in Torpedoing Off New Jersey"; *Asbury Park Press*, "Fearing Sub Trap, Vessels Sped From Arrow's Boats"; *Fort Worth Star Telegram*, "Survivors of Vessel Tell of Struggle" (7 Feb 1942).

23   *Camden Courier-Post*, "Captain Asks 'Tow' But He and Men Get Ride from Rescuers" (7 Feb 1942), "Camden Sailor Among 26 Lost Aboard Tanker" (7 Feb 1942), and "12 Saved in Torpedoing Off New Jersey"; *Daily News*, "26 Missing in Sinking of Tanker Off Jersey"; *Paterson Morning Call*, "17th Vessel Lost Off Atlantic Coast ..." | Carl Johnson/Frank Marshall dialogue sourced from firsthand accounts published by newspapers.

24   4th ND War Diary: 6 Feb 1942; *Asbury Park Press*, "Fearing Sub Trap, Vessels Sped from Arrow's Boats"; *Philadelphia Inquirer*, "26 Die Off N.J. ..."; *Suffolk County News*, "Suffolk Man Lost ..."; *Scranton Tribune*, "Oiler's Family in Greenwood is Still Hoping" (7 Feb 1942); *Camden Courier-Post*, "26 Unreported in Sub Sinking Believed Dead" (7 Feb 1942); *Evening Star*, "26 Missing, 12 Safe After Torpedoing of Tanker Off Coast" (Washington D.C., 6 Feb 1942).

25 Standard Oil of NJ, *Ships of the Esso Fleet in WWII*, 83; Moore, *A Careless Word ... A Needless Sinking*, 51–52, 288; U-103 KTB (6th patrol), 17; 4th ND War Diary: 4 Feb 1942.

26 Wright, "Wolves Without Teeth," 32, 67, 121–122, 132, 148–149, 152–156; Rössler, *The Evolution and Technical History of German Submarines*, 143; Mulligan, *Neither Sharks Nor Wolves*, 79.

27 DVRBS.com, Written memories of Charles Seerveld; *Evening Star*, "26 Missing, 12 Safe ..."; *Camden Courier-Post*, "12 Saved in Torpedoing Off New Jersey"; *Philadelphia Inquirer*, "26 Die Off N.J. ..."; *Asbury Park Press*, "Fearing Sub Trap, Vessels Sped from Arrow's Boats."

Chapter 7. *R.P. Resor*

1 Kriegsmarine, "Diving Regulations for U-boats," 52–54, 79–80; U-578 KTB (3rd patrol), 11; Buchheim, *U-boat War*, n.p.; Title poem obtained via USMM.org.

2 Naturalization records of John J. Forsdal; *The Lookout*, "Vox Pop"; Standard Oil of NJ, *Ships of the Esso Fleet in WWII*, 108; Forsdal affidavit (28 Feb 1942), 1; *The Patchogue Advance*, "Three Town Men Lost in Action" (6 Mar 1942).

3 *Lloyd's Register of Shipping 1941–42*; *Marine Engineering and Shipping Review*, "Arcform Tanker R.P. Resor," 130–138; Standard Oil of NJ, *Ships of the Esso Fleet in WWII*, 106–108, 168–174; Forsdal affidavit (28 Feb 1942), 2–3.

4 ESF War Diary, Feb 1942, Ch. 4: 1–5, Appx. I and Mar 1942, Ch. 5: 1; Klingaman, *The Darkest Year*, 206; Roskill, *The Period of Balance*, 108–110; Hughes & Costello, *The Battle of the Atlantic*, 196; Goralski & Freeburg, *Oil and War*, 118; McCue, "An Exploration of Zigzagging," 29; Office of Naval Intelligence, "Analysis of the Advantage of Speed and Changes of Course in Avoiding Attack by Submarine," 32 (ONI Publication No. 30, May 1918).

5 ESF War Diary, Jan 1942, Ch. 2: 1, Feb 1942, Ch. 4: 4–5, and Mar 1942, Ch. 1: 3; Gannon, *Operation Drumbeat*, 355–356; Lawton, "Otto von Bülow"; Neprud, *Flying Minute Men*, 9–15; CentennialOfFlight.net, "Civil Air Patrol."

6 US Navy, "History of the Naval Armed Guard Afloat, World War II," 6, 15 and "Arming of Merchant Ships and Naval Armed Guard Service," 3–5; Bunker, *Heroes in Dungarees*, 22–23; *Seafarer's Log* (2 Feb 1942); Taylor, *Fire on the Beaches*, 93; USMM.org, "U.S. Naval Armed Guard Casualties During World War II"; *New York Times*, "21 Safe at Charleston" (22 Jan 1942).

7 Kriegsmarine, "U-boat Commander's Handbook," 197; ESF War Diary, May 1942, Appx. II.

8 Draft card for Daniel Hey; US Navy, "History of the Naval Armed Guard Afloat, World War II," iii and "Arming of Merchant Ships and Naval Armed Guard Service," 30; Morison, *The Battle of the Atlantic*, 299–300; Geroux, *The Mathews Men*, 31–32.

9 Forsdal affidavit (28 Feb 1942), 2–3; War Shipping Administration, *Deck Branch Training*, 48–50 (1943).

10 *Asbury Park Press*, "Men Are Saved in Flaming Sea" (28 Feb 1942); US Navy, "General Instructions for Commanding Officers of Naval Armed Guards on Merchant Ships," 4; Ron Carlson correspondence with author.

11 Forsdal affidavit (28 Feb 1942), 3–4; Standard Oil of NJ, *Ships of the Esso Fleet in WWII*, 108–109.

12 U-578 KTB (3rd patrol), 12; Ubootarchiv.de, "Ernst August Rehwinkel"; Author's tabulation of losses and patrols; Dönitz, *Memoirs*, 201, 204–205; BdU KTB: 1–31 Jan 1942.

13 Buchheim, *U-boat War*, n.p.; Geroux, *The Mathews Men*, 106–107; WarSailors.com, "M/S Breñas"; Ubootarchiv.de, "Raimund Tiesler"; U-578 KTB (3rd patrol), 12; Neitzel & Welzer, *Soldiers*, 54–55.

14 Golden & Tipton, *Essentials of Sea Survival*, 59–64; *The Lookout*, "Vox Pop"; Forsdal affidavit (28 Feb 1942), 4; US Coast Guard, "Report on U.S. Merchant Tanker War Action Casualty"

(21 Nov 1944). | "Daddy John" experience shared by Forsdal during interview published in *The Lookout*.

15   *Asbury Park Press*, "Men Are Saved in Flaming Sea"; Forsdal affidavit (9 Mar 1942); Geroux, *The Mathews Men*, 390.

16   Hänert & Hartmann, "Shipwreck and Hypothermia"; Golden & Tipton, *Essentials of Sea Survival*, 66–71; *U.S. Navy Diving Manual*, Ch. 2: 10–11, Ch. 3: 53–54; PADI, *Divemaster Manual*, 205 (2010); Forsdal affidavit (9 Mar 1942) and (28 Feb 1942), 4–5; War Shipping Administration, *Safety for Seamen*, 33; *Central New Jersey Home News*, "Two Tankers Sub Victims in Atlantic" (28 Feb 1942). | John Forsdal/Clarence Armstrong dialogue drawn partly from Forsdal's recollections.

17   *Asbury Park Press*, "When There's Danger Around, Look About and You'll See Daisey" (24 May 1942); USCG History Program, "Station Manasquan Beach, New Jersey"; US Coast Guard, *Assistance* Vol. II, 17, 148; *Coast Advertiser*, "Sub Sinks Tanker Off Belmar, 36 of Crew Perish" (Belmar NJ, 6 Mar 1942); Amagansett Life-Saving & Coast Guard Station Museum (AmagansettLSS.org); CAPT Bob Desh correspondence with author; Scheina, *US Coast Guard Cutters & Craft of WWII*, 256–257; Timothy R. Dring & William Wilkinson, *American Coastal Rescue Craft*, 48, 56 (University Press of Florida, 2009); Dennis R. Means, "A Heavy Sea Running: The Formation of the U.S. Life-Saving Service, 1846–1878" (*Prologue*, Winter 1987).

18   *U.S. Navy Diving Manual*, Ch. 3, 53–56; Golden & Tipton, *Essentials of Sea Survival*, 95–117, 119–130; *Central New Jersey Home News*, "Two Tankers Sub Victims in Atlantic"; Standard Oil of NJ, *Ships of the Esso Fleet in WWII*, 109; Forsdal affidavit (28 Feb 1942), 5.

19   Cressman, *The Official Chronology of the US Navy in WWII*, 161; *Asbury Park Press*, "When There's Danger Around, Look About and You'll See Daisey"; US Coast Guard, *Assistance* Vol. I, 6–7, 8–10 and Vol. II, 17, 147–148; Standard Oil of NJ, *Ships of the Esso Fleet in WWII*, 109.

20   Forsdal affidavit, 5 (28 Feb 1942) and (9 Mar 1942); *Asbury Park Press*, "Men Are Saved in Flaming Sea" and "When There's Danger Around, Look About and You'll See Daisey"; Standard Oil of NJ, *Ships of the Esso Fleet in WWII*, 109–110.

21   *The Lookout*, "Vox Pop"; *Asbury Park Press*, "Men are Saved in Flaming Sea"; US Coast Guard, *Assistance* Vol. I, 8 and Vol. II, 148; Forsdal affidavit (28 Feb 1942), 5.

22   E. Burke Maloney, "Crew of Camera Boat Unable to Haul in Oil-Covered Bodies of 4 Tanker Victims" and "The Day War Touched Home" (*Asbury Park Press*, 28 Feb 1942 and 26 Feb 1967); Erik Larsen, "The night World War II came to the Jersey Shore" (*The Coloradoan*, 28 Feb 2014); *Coast Advertiser*, "Our Day Will Come" and "Sub Sinks Tanker Off Belmar, 36 of Crew Perish" (Belmar NJ, 6 Mar 1942).

23   *New York Times*, "36 Survivors Here from the Norness" (17 Jan 1942) and "Sinkings Fail to Daunt Seamen" (24 Jan 1942); Standard Oil of NJ, *Ships of the Esso Fleet in WWII*, 79, 168–174; Moore, *A Careless Word … A Needless Sinking*, 230.

24   Kriegsmarine, "Preliminary Information for U-boat Type VIIC," 58, 74; US Navy, "Former German Submarine Type IX-C," S64: 8; ESF War Diary, Feb 1942, Appx. IV; U-578 KTB (3rd patrol), 11–12; 4th ND War Diary: 26–27 Feb 1942; Forsdal affidavit (28 Feb 1942), 4; Klingaman, *The Darkest Year*, 125.

Chapter 8. USS *Jacob Jones* (DD-130)

1   ESF War Diary, Feb 1942, Ch. 7: 2; Taylor, *Fire on the Beaches*, 97–98; Hickam, *Torpedo Junction*, 55–57.

2   Blair, *The Hunters*, 444–447; ESF War Diary, Feb 1942, Ch. 3: 1–6, Ch. 7: 2; Offley, *The Burning Shore*, 36–38; Klingaman, *The Darkest Year*, 100; *New York Times*, "Navy 'Doing Its Job' in East, Says Knox" (29 Jan 1942).

3   ESF War Diary, Dec 1941, Ch. 2: 10–15; Ernest King, "First Report to the Secretary of the Navy" (23 Apr 1944), 80; Cianflone, "The Eagle Boats of World War I"; Woofenden, *Hunters of the Steel Sharks*, 13; Blair, *The Hunters*, 450–451; Morison, *The Battle of the Atlantic*, 131.

4   ESF War Diary, Feb 1942, Ch. 3: 5–7, Mar 1942, Ch. 2: 8–9, and Apr 1942, Ch. 2: 1–3; Atlantic Fleet, "United States Atlantic Fleet Organization, First Quarter, Fiscal Year 1942"; Roskill, *The Period of Balance*, 106–108; Blair, *The Hunters*, 434–435; Offley, *The Burning Shore*, 99–102; Gannon, *Operation Drumbeat*, 266–267, 345–346.

5   Shafter, *Destroyers in Action*, 7–15, 17, 52, 86–92; ESF War Diary, Feb 1942, Ch. 2: 2; Macintyre, *U-boat Killer*, 21; Dimbleby, *The Battle of the Atlantic*, 121.

6   Office of Naval Records and History, "History of USS Jacob Jones (DD 130)"; Segars & Segars, "New Jersey's Jacob Jones"; Snow, *A Measureless Peril*, 12; Shafter, *Destroyers in Action*, 7–10; Bercuson & Herwig, *Deadly Seas*, 14–16; Norman Friedman, *U.S. Destroyers: An Illustrated Design History*, 43–47 (Naval Institute Press, 1982); Mark Lardas, *US Flush-Deck Destroyers 1916–45*, 5, 18, 48 (Osprey Publishing, 2018, Kindle).

7   *The Record*, "Oradell-born Black Earned Friends as Pupil, Athlete" (Hackensack NJ, 3 Mar 1942); Alexander Kendrick, "Destroyer Sunk Near Cape May" (*Philadelphia Inquirer*, 4 Mar 1942); USNA Virtual Memorial Hall, "Hugh D. Black, LCDR, USN"; Oberg, "The Jakie," 2–4; USS Jacob Jones, "Anti-Submarine Activity by Surface Ship, Report of" (23 Feb 1942).

8   Robinson & Robinson, *Der Kapitän*, 9–16; Maritime Archaeology Trust, "USS Jacob Jones," 10–23.

9   Eric Tidwell interview by author; *Central New Jersey Home News*, "Jacob Jones Survivors Stopped for Extra Clothes, Hot Coffee" (4 Mar 1942); USNA Virtual Memorial Hall, "Norman C. Smith, ENS, USN"; ESF War Diary, Feb 1942, Ch. 7: 3–4; *CIO News*, "Union Head Survives Sea Disaster" (7 Mar 1942).

10   ESF War Diary, Jan 1942, Ch. 2: 3 and Feb 1942, Ch. 7: 2; Dönitz, *Memoirs*, 202–203; Hickam, *Torpedo Junction*, 55–57.

11   U-578 KTB (3rd patrol), 12–13; Goebeler & Vanzo, *Steel Boat, Iron Hearts*, 21; Mulligan, *Neither Sharks Nor Wolves*; 16–17; Gannon, *Operation Drumbeat*, 196–197.

12   Oberg, "The Jakie," 5; ESF War Diary, Feb 1942, Ch. 7: 2–3; Salvini, *Historic Cape May, New Jersey*, 153–154; 4th ND War Diary: 27 Feb 1942; NAS Wildwood Aviation Museum, "NAS Wildwood History" (USNASW.org).

13   Office of Naval Intelligence, "Sinking of U.S.S. Jacob Jones," 2 (Form NNI-142); 4th ND, "Interviews with survivors of the USS JACOB JONES …," 2, 5, 7; ESF War Diary, Feb 1942, Ch. 7: 3.

14   U-578 KTB (3rd patrol), 13; Buchheim, *Das Boot*, 193; Kriegsmarine, "U-boat Commander's Handbook," 1, 11, 21; Clausewitz, *On War*, 26–27, 47–48, 163, 200; Neitzel & Welzer, *Soldiers*, 72.

15   Kriegsmarine, "U-boat Commander's Handbook, 105(f)(g), 204(b)(c); U-578 torpedo report and KTB (3rd patrol), 13–14; Buchheim, *Das Boot*, 193; Morgan & Taylor, *U-boat Attack Logs*, xxi, 209–210; Wright, "Wolves Without Teeth," 20–21, 27–28, 32–34, 153.

16   4th ND, "Interviews with survivors of the USS JACOB JONES …," 2–3, 6, 8; Eric Tidwell interview by author; ESF War Diary, Feb 1942, Ch. 7: 3–4; *Times Record*, "Jacob Jones' Bow was Carried Away by First Torpedo" (Troy NY, 4 Mar 1942).

17   U-578 KTB (3rd patrol), 14.

18   Hickam, *Torpedo Junction*, 60–61; 4th ND, "Interviews with survivors of the USS JACOB JONES …," 3–6, 8; ESF War Diary, Feb 1942, Ch. 7: 4–7; *Pittsburgh Press*, "Mercer Sailor Called Hero on Destroyer" (7 Mar 1942); Oberg, "The Jakie," 5; Monsarrat, *The Cruel Sea*, 281. | "What happened?" sourced from Homer Hickam's book.

19   *Philadelphia Inquirer*, "Seamen Drank Coffee, Donned Warm Clothes as Destroyer Sank" (4 Mar 1942); 4th ND, "Interviews with survivors of the USS JACOB JONES …," 2; *Intelligencer*

Journal, "Survivors Tell of Tarrying on Blasted Ship for Coffee" (Lancaster PA, 4 Mar 1942); *Times Record*, "Jacob Jones' Bow was Carried Away by First Torpedo."

20   Oberg, "The Jakie," 5–6; 4th ND, "Interviews with survivors of the USS JACOB JONES …," 2–8; Monsarrat, *The Cruel Sea*, 285; *Intelligencer Journal*, "Survivors Tell of Tarrying …"; *Pittsburgh Press*, "Mercer Sailor Called Hero on Destroyer"; *U.S. Navy Diving Manual*, Ch. 3: 33, 61.

21   Robinson & Robinson, *Der Kapitän*, 14–15; 4th ND, "Interviews with survivors of the USS JACOB JONES …," 2–3, 5–6; Taylor, *Fire on the Beaches*, 99; ESF War Diary, Feb 1942, Ch. 7: 6; *Intelligencer Journal*, "Survivors Tell of Tarrying …"; *Democrat and Chronicle*, "West Gaines Sailors Tells of Rescue in Torpedoing" (Rochester NY, 12 Mar 1942).

22   USS PE-56, Operational Remarks: 28 Feb 1942; ESF War Diary, Feb 1942, Ch. 7: 6–7; 4th ND War Diary: 28 Feb 1942.

23   U-578 KTB (3rd patrol), 14–16, 31–32; ESF War Diary, Mar 1942, Ch. 3: 1–3; Gannon, *Operation Drumbeat*, 61; Morgan & Taylor, *U-boat Attack Logs*, 210; Segars & Segars, "New Jersey's Jacob Jones."

24   *Cape May Star & Wave*, "Admiral Will House Naval Officers" (14 May 1942); NRHP Registration Form for Battery 223, Sec. 8: 12–13; Salvini, *Historic Cape May, New Jersey*, 165–167; John DeRosier, "A look back at Atlantic City's deep ties to World War II" (*Press of Atlantic City*, 29 May 2017); Bill Godfrey, "World War II's Lasting Mark" and "The Cape May Canal" (CapeMay. com, 1 Jun 2006 and 1 Aug 2006).

25   ESF War Diary, Feb 1942, Ch. 7: 7 and Mar 1942, Ch. 2: 1–9, Appx. III; Author's tabulation of sinkings and destroyer availability; Dimbleby, *The Battle of the Atlantic*, 251.

26   Kendrick, "Destroyer Sunk Near Cape May"; *Democrat and Chronicle*, "West Gaines Sailor Tells of Rescue in Torpedoing"; *Pittsburgh Press*, "Mercer Sailor Called Hero on Destroyer"; *Boston Globe*, "Lowell Youth Crew Member of Jacob Jones" (3 Mar 1942); *The Record*, "Memorial Service Held for H.D. Black" (16 Mar 1942); *Boston Globe*, "Cambridge Survivor of Jacob Jones Eager to Get Back" (6 Mar 1942) and "Only 11 Saved on Destroyer; Over 125 Die" (4 Mar 1942). | Howard Black's words as quoted by newspapers.

Chapter 9. *Gulftrade*

1   ESF War Diary, Mar 1942, Appx. VI; Naval History and Heritage Command, "Larch (YN-16)" (History.Navy.mil); Glenn Paulson, "World War II Net Tenders" (NavSource.org); *Austin American-Statesman*, "George B. Coale" (29 May 1994); Title poem obtained from *Seafarers Log* magazine (Seafarers International Union).

2   USCGC Antietam, "Cruise Report, 8 March to 14 March, 1942"; Scheina, *US Coast Guard Cutters & Craft of WWII*, 43–46; Galecki, *Rum Runners, U-boats, and Hurricanes*, 13–14, 22, 235.

3   ESF War Diary, Mar 1942, Ch. 1: 3, Appx. IV and Apr 1942, Ch. 1: 2, Ch. 2: 2–3; Roskill, *The Period of Balance*, 109; Larch deck log; 3rd ND INSPAT War Diary: 9 Mar 1942.

4   *Lloyd's Register of Shipping 1941–42*; Office of CNO, "Summary of Statements by Survivors, SS GULFTRADE …"

5   Capt Hugh Stephens, Ron Carlson, and Capt Jim McNamara correspondence with author; Bunker, *Heroes in Dungarees*, 29–30; USMM.org, "Poems About the Merchant Marine"; War Shipping Administration, *Engineering Branch Training*, 52; Herman Melton, *Liberty's War: An Engineer's Memoir of the Merchant Marine, 1942–1945*, n.p. (Naval Institute Press, 2017, Kindle).

6   US Coast Guard, "War Casualties Resulting From Enemy Action," 19 (21 Apr 1942); Office of CNO, "Summary of Statements by Survivors, SS GULFTRADE …"; *New York Times*, "U-boats Get 3 More Ships, One 3½ Miles Off Jersey" (11 Mar 1942).

7   War Shipping Administration, *Safety for Seamen*, 5; ESF War Diary, Mar 1942, Ch. 4: 1–2, Ch. 7: 4–7; Geroux, *The Mathews Men*, 98–99; ESF, "Coastwise routings between New York and Key West" (7 Mar 1942).

8   US Coast Guard, "War Casualties Resulting from Enemy Action," 19; *New York Times*, "U-boats Get 3 More Ships, One 3½ Miles Off Jersey"; *Corpus Christi Caller-Times*, "Bold U-boat Downs Tanker Off Jersey" (11 Mar 1942); 8th ND, "Routing Instructions" (28 Feb 1942). | Torger Olsen/George Parks dialogue sourced from Coast Guard report.

9   ESF War Diary, Jan 1942, Ch. 2: 3 and Apr 1942, Ch. 1: 1–2, Ch. 3: 1; U-124 KTB (2nd patrol), 10–19; Geroux, *The Mathews Men*, 118–122; *TIME*, "Battle of the Atlantic: Birth in a Boat" (13 Apr 1942).

10 Author's tabulation of tanker losses; ESF War Diary, Apr 1942, Ch. 1: 1, Ch. 7: 3–4; Klingaman, *The Darkest Year*, 132, 206; Goralski & Freeburg, *Oil and War*, 108, 113–114, 120; Yergin, *The Prize*, 375; *TIME*, "Oil: A Shortage, an If" (9 Mar 1942) and "World Battlefronts, Supply: Oil Can Lose the War" (16 Mar 1942).

11 U-588 KTB (2nd patrol), 10–16; Ubootarchiv.de, "Walter Wichmann"; Williamson, *Grey Wolf*, 50.

12 Olsen affidavit; Office of CNO, "Summary of Statements by Survivors, SS GULFTRADE …"; *New York Times*, "U-boats Get 3 More Ships, One 3½ Miles Off Jersey"; *The Evening Herald*, "Tanker Blown in Two, 19 Missing" (10 Mar 1942); US Coast Guard, "Report on U.S. Merchant Tanker War Action Casualty" (22 Nov 1944).

13 USCGC Antietam, "Cruise Report, 8 March to 14 March, 1942"; Office of CNO, "Torpedoing of SS GULFTRADE"; USCG Philadelphia District War Diary: 1–31 Mar 1942; 3rd ND INSPAT War Diary: 9–10 Mar 1942.

14 Chadwick affidavit; Office of CNO, "Summary of Statements by Survivors, SS GULFTRADE …"; *Corpus Christi Caller-Times*, "Bold U-boat Downs Tanker Off Jersey."

15 USCGC Antietam, "Cruise Report, 8 March to 14 March, 1942"; Galecki, *Rum Runners, U-boats, and Hurricanes*, 14, 81–82; US Coast Guard, *Assistance* Vol. I, 10; Olsen affidavit.

16 Chadwick affidavit; Larch deck log; *Corpus Christi Caller-Times*, "Bold U-boat Downs Tanker Off Jersey"; *Daily News*, "Tanker Lights Up off N.J., Sub Cuts it in Half" (NYC, 11 Mar 1942).

17 USCGC Antietam, "Cruise Report, 8 March to 14 March, 1942"; Larch deck log.

18 Larch deck log; Naval History and Heritage Command, "Larch (YN-16)"; Chadwick affidavit; US Coast Guard, *Assistance* Vol. I, 10; *Corpus Christi Caller-Times*, "Bold U-boat Downs Tanker Off Jersey"; *New York Times*, "U-boats Get 3 More Ships, One 3½ Miles Off Jersey." | "Stick with the ship" quote taken from Chadwick's statements to reporters.

19 ESF War Diary, Mar 1942, Appx. IV; USCG Philadelphia District War Diary: 1–31 Mar 1942; Snow, *A Measureless Peril*, 209; Gentile, *Shipwrecks of New Jersey*, 65.

20 U-588 torpedo report and KTB (2nd patrol), 16; Olsen affidavit; Neprud, *Flying Minute Men*, 12, 15; USCGC Antietam, "Cruise Report, 8 March to 14 March, 1942"; Office of CNO, "Torpedoing of SS GULFTRADE"; Larch deck log.

21 Author's tabulation of March 1942 losses; Bill Manthorpe correspondence with author; Wiberg, *U-boats in New England*, 98; Geroux, *The Mathews Men*, 122; Lender, *One State in Arms*, 88; ESF War Diary, Feb 1942, Ch. 4: 2, Appx. I and Mar 1942, Ch. 1: 2–3, Ch. 2: 1, Ch. 5: 1–3, Appx. I; *TIME*, "U.S. At War: Attack by Sea" (1 Jun 1942) and "Battle of the Atlantic: Not So Hot" (6 Apr 1942).

22 ESF War Diary, Mar 1942, Ch. 2: 1, Appx. IV and Oct 1942, Ch. 2: 9–34; U-123 KTB (8th patrol), 10–11; Offley, *The Burning Shore*, 154–156; Hickam, *Torpedo Junction*, 109–112.

Chapter 10. *Toltén*

1   3rd ND INSPAT War Diary: 13 Mar 1942.

2   *Lloyd's Register of Shipping 1941–42*; Pugh Gillmore, "El vapor Toltén, torpedeado en 1942 en su recalada a Nueva York," 4, 9, 18–19; Biographical essay by Aquiles Ramírez Astudillo; Sandoval Hernández, "¡Vapor 'Toltén' torpedeado!," 366; Sergio López Pugh and Kenneth Pugh Olavarría correspondence with author.

3   U-404 KTB (2nd patrol), 11.

4   Pugh Gillmore, "El vapor Toltén, torpedeado en 1942 …," 2, 4, 19, 36–37; Sergio López Pugh correspondence with author; Sandoval Hernández, "¡Vapor 'Toltén' torpedeado!," 366; Vásquez Méndez, "El Hundimiento del Toltén," 96–99.

5   Bercuson & Herwig, *Long Night of the Tankers*, xvi, 2, 7–11, 277–279; Goralski & Freeburg, *Oil and War*, 40, 107; Yergin, *The Prize*, 383; Dönitz, *Memoirs*, 221; Palucka, "The Wizard of Octane."

6   Vásquez Méndez, "El Hundimiento del Toltén," 97; Pugh Gillmore, "El vapor Toltén, torpedeado en 1942 …," 11, 16–17; Sandoval Hernández, "¡Vapor 'Toltén' torpedeado!," 365; *TIME*, "Chile: New President" (13 Apr 1942); International Military Tribunal, *The Nuremberg Trials*, 3321; Francis, "The United States and Chile During the Second World War," 95–96, 99–100. | "Gringo" remark taken from Kenneth Pugh Gillmore's essay, though its historicity is unclear.

7   Capt Hugh Stephens interview by author; Monsarrat, *The Cruel Sea*, 223; USMM.org, "The Most Dangerous Positions for Mariners during WWII"; Bunker, *Heroes in Dungarees*, 30.

8   Vásquez Méndez, "El Hundimiento del Toltén," 97–99; Buchheim, *Das Boot*, 289; Monsarrat, *The Cruel Sea*, 222–223; Pugh Gillmore, "El vapor Toltén, torpedeado en 1942 …," 36–39; Biographical essay by Aquiles Ramírez Astudillo; *Dayton Herald*, "Chilean Break With Axis Demanded After Sinking" (17 Mar 1942).

9   U-404 KTB (2nd patrol), 11–14; U-96 KTB (8th patrol), 24.

10 FamilieVonBuelow.de; VonBulow.se; Lawton, "Otto von Bülow"; Otto von Bülow interview by Clay Blair; Rust, *Naval Officers Under Hitler*, 9–10; Padfield, *Dönitz: The Last Führer*, 653; Dixon, *The U-boat Commanders*, 25; Mallmann Showell, *Hitler's Navy*, 95.

11 U-404 KTB (2nd patrol), 12–13; Busch & Röll, *German U-boat Commanders of WWII*, 230; Mallmann Showell, *Hitler's Navy*, 569–571.

12 Vásquez Méndez, "El Hundimiento del Toltén," 98–101; Sandoval Hernández, "¡Vapor 'Toltén' Torpedeado!," 366–367; Pugh Gillmore, "¿Quién hundió al Toltén?" and "El vapor Toltén, torpedeado en 1942 …," 8, 18–16, 20.

13 *La Hora*, "Torpedearon un vapor chileno" (Santiago, 17 Mar 1942); Vásquez Méndez, "El Hundimiento del Toltén," 101–102; Sandoval Hernández, "¡Vapor 'Toltén' torpedeado!," 366; Pugh Gillmore, "El vapor Toltén, torpedeado en 1942 …," 19; 3rd ND INSPAT War Diary: 12–13 Mar 1942; Biographical essay by Aquiles Ramírez Astudillo; Sergio López Pugh correspondence with author.

14 U-404 torpedo report and KTB (2nd patrol), 15–16; Kriegsmarine, "Torpedo Firing Regulations for Submarines," 9–11, 21–25; Torpedo Vorhaltrechner Project, "Torpedo calculator T. Vh. Re. S3" (TVRE.org); Otto von Bülow reply letter to Tom Roach (7 May 1975); Werner, *Iron Coffins*, 27.

15 Vásquez Méndez, "El Hundimiento del Toltén," 102; Sandoval Hernández, "¡Vapor 'Toltén' torpedeado!," 366; *La Hora*, "Torpedearon un vapor chileno"; U-404 KTB (2nd patrol), 16; *Dunkirk Evening Observer*, "Chile Aroused Over Sinking of Ship" (17 Mar 1942).

16 3rd ND INSPAT War Diary: 13 Mar 1942; ESF War Diary, Mar 1942, Appx. IV; Naval History and Heritage Command, "Larch (YN-16)."

17 Pugh Gillmore, "El vapor Toltén, torpedeado en 1942 …," 10–11, 14, 32; *Dayton Herald*, "Chilean Break With Axis Demanded After Sinking"; Pugh Gillmore, "¿Quién hundió al Toltén?";

New York Times, "Chilean Freighter Sunk Off Our Coast; 27 Lost, One Saved" (17 Mar 1942) and "Chileans Attack Axis Properties" (18 Mar 1942).

18   Otto von Bülow interview by Clay Blair; BdU Ops Division KTB Vol. 31, Part A: 266; Vásquez Méndez, "El Hundimiento del Toltén," 104; U-404 KTB (2nd patrol), 19; *New York Times*, "Chileans Stirred by Tolten Sinking" (17 Mar 1942) and "Nazis Offer to Pay for Chilean Ship" (26 Mar 1942).

19   Hernández, "¡Vapor 'Toltén' torpedeado!," 366–368; Vásquez Méndez, "El Hundimiento del Toltén," 100–101; Pugh Gillmore, "El vapor Toltén, torpedeado en 1942 ...," 5–7, 10–11, 19–21, 28 and "¿Quién hundió al Toltén?"; USCGC Antietam, "Cruise Report, 8 March to 14 March, 1942."

20   Pugh Gillmore, "El vapor Toltén, torpedeado en 1942 ...," 12–13, 31–32; Vásquez Méndez, "El Hundimiento del Toltén," 99–100, 103; *La Hora*, "Torpedearon un vapor chileano"; Sandoval Hernández, "¡Vapor 'Toltén' Torpedeado!," 366–367; Biographical essay by Aquiles Ramírez Astudillo.

21   Roskill, *The Period of Balance*, 108; ESF War Diary, Feb 1942, Ch. 4: 1–4 and Mar 1942, Ch. 5: 1–6; Morison, *The Battle of the Atlantic*, 255–256; Gannon, *Operation Drumbeat*, 391.

22   Bilby, et al., *Hidden History of New Jersey at War*, 111–114; Taylor, *Fire on the Beaches*, 78–79, 116; ESF War Diary, Mar 1942, Ch. 1: 2–3; Gannon, *Operation Drumbeat*, 344–345; Morison, *The Battle of the Atlantic*, 129–130; *TIME*, "U.S. at War: The Great White Way" (11 May 1942); *Philadelphia Inquirer*, "Survivor Signs Again, Hits Shore Lights" (18 Mar 1942); H.H. Kroh, "Fun at Jersey Beaches Knows No Dimout" (*New York Times*, 7 Jun 1942); New Jersey War Cabinet meeting minutes: 28 Apr, 4 May, 19 May 1942.

23   U-404 KTB (2nd patrol), 17–18; Gannon, *Operation Drumbeat*, 343–345; Office of the CNO, "Summary of Statements by Survivors, American Collier LEMUEL BURROWS, Mystic Steamship Line" (31 Mar 1942); *Boston Globe*, "Collier Sinking Brings Demand N.J. Black Out" (18 Mar 1942); WarSailors.com, "M/S Chr. Knudsen"; Jane Deedy, "Lawrence T. Sullivan, the Lemuel Burrows, and U-boat 404" (Deedy.com, 28 May 2007).

24   ESF War Diary, Apr 1942, Ch. 4: 1–3; USS Roper, "Destruction of German submarine – Report of," 1–2 (15 Apr 1942); Office of Naval Intelligence, "Report on the Sinking of the U-85," 7 (20 May 1942); 5th ND, "Sinking of German Submarine U-85, disposition of bodies and effects, report on," 4 (17 Apr 1942).

Chapter 11. *Persephone*

1   ZP-12 War Diary: 24 May 1942; Vaeth, *Blimps & U-boats*, 36–37.

2   Mallmann Showell, *Fuehrer Conferences on Naval Affairs*, 280–282; Kershaw, *Hitler: A Biography*, 498, 624, 787–789; International Military Tribunal, *The Nuremberg Trials*, 10918; Yergin, *The Prize*, 336; Dobbs, *Saboteurs*, 7–8. | Dönitz's dialogue at Wolf's Lair sourced from meeting transcript.

3   U-593 KTB (2nd patrol), 6–8; US Navy, "Report on the German Submarine of the U-570 Class ...," 36; UK Admiralty, "Report on U-570," 30–31; Busch & Röll, *German U-boat Commanders of WWII*, 123; UK Admiralty, "U 593 Interrogation of Survivors," 1.

4   ZP-12 War Diary: 25 May 1942; U-593 KTB (2nd patrol), 14; Shock, *US Navy Airships*, 9, 89, 163.

5   Goodyear, *US Navy K-Type Airship Pilot's Manual*, 1–3 (Sep 1943); Shock, *US Navy Airships*, 165; Vaeth, *Blimps & U-boats*, 40, 63, 74–82; ZP-12 War Diary: 25 May 1942; Mason Sutherland, "Aboard a Blimp Hunting U-boats," 79 (*National Geographic*, July 1943); *TIME*, "U.S. at War: Attack by Sea" (1 Jun 1942); Roy Grossnick, ed., *Kite Balloons to Airships ... the Navy's Lighter-than-Air Experience*, 33–39 (Government Printing Office, 1987).

6   Quistgaard affidavit; ESF War Diary, Apr 1942, Ch. 3: 1–7, Appx. I and May 1942, Ch. 4: 3–6; Neprud, *Flying Minute Men*, 12–13; BdU KTB: 21, 26–27 May 1942; Morison, *The Battle of the Atlantic*, 254–257.

7   *Lloyd's Register of Shipping 1941–42*; *Bristol Daily Courier*, "Capt Quistgaard Maps His Voyages" (2 Aug 1942); Quistgaard affidavit; Draft card for Helge Quistgaard; *New York Times*, "Tankers Replace Germans in Crews" (8 Sep 1939).

8   Capt Hugh Stephens interview by author; Monsarrat, *The Cruel Sea*, 286–290; Wiberg, *U-boats in New England*, 99; Author's tabulation of fatalities through 1 May 1942; Lawrenson, "Damn the Torpedoes"; ESF War Diary, Mar 1942, Ch. 2: 1, Ch. 7: 2–3 and Apr 1942, Ch. 7: 4–5.

9   H.H. Kroh, "Fun at Jersey Beaches Knows No Dimout" (*New York Times*, 7 Jun 1942); George Barrett, "Glow of Cities Aids U-boats" (*New York Times*, 24 May 1942); U-593 KTB (2nd patrol), 8–9; ESF War Diary, May 1942, Appx. V.

10   ZP-12 War Diary: 25 May 1942; Vaeth, *Blimps & U-boats*, 37–40, 63–64.

11   USAAF Historical Division, "The Antisubmarine Command," 4–6 (AAFRH-7, Apr 1945); ESF War Diary, Jan 1942, Appx. II and May 1942, Appx. IV; Cate & Craven, *US Army Air Forces in WWII* Vol. I, 528–531; Mallmann Showell, *Fuehrer Conferences on Naval Affairs*, 280–283; U-593 KTB (2nd patrol), 9; CentennialofFlight.net, "Civil Air Patrol"; Roger Thiel, "When the Antiques Went to War" (*Vintage Airplane*, Vol. 20, No. 7, Jul 1992).

12   393rd Bombardment Squadron, "Attack on Submarine" and "Mission Report 329"; Eastern Sea Frontier, "Analysis of Aircraft Attack"; Mike Laney correspondence with author; U-593 KTB (2nd patrol), 9.

13   U-593 KTB (2nd patrol), 9–14; Roskill, *The Defensive*, 357; Breemer, "Defeating the U-boat," 63; VAdm Peter Gretton, *Convoy Escort Commander: A Memoir of the Battle of the Atlantic*, 155–156 (Sapere Books, 2021, Kindle).

14   Kriegsmarine, "Torpedo Firing Regulations for U-boats," 9–11, 21–25; Cremer, *U-boat Commander*, 22; U-593 KTB (2nd patrol), 14; US Navy, "Report on the German Submarine of the U-570 Class …," 23.

15   ZP-12 War Diary: 25 May 1942; Vaeth, *Blimps & U-boats*, 20.

16   Larry Waddell, "Tanker's Luck Ran Out Off Barnegat Inlet" (*Asbury Park Press*, 8 Jul 2002); Office of CNO, "Summary of Statements by Survivors MS PERSEPHONE …"; U-593 KTB (2nd patrol), 14–15; Quistgaard affidavit.

17   US Coast Guard, *Assistance* Vol. I, 16 and Vol. II, 163; USCG Philadelphia District War Diary: 24–30 May 1942; Standard Oil of NJ, *Ships of the Esso Fleet in WWII*, 222; Quistgaard affidavit; Office of CNO, "Summary of Statements by Survivors MS PERSEPHONE …"; *Asbury Park Press*, "9 Lost in Daylight Attack 3 Miles Offshore" (29 May 1942).

18   Office of CNO, "Summary of Statements by Survivors MS PERSEPHONE …"; Quistgaard affidavit; USCG Philadelphia District War Diary: 24–30 May 1942; US Coast Guard, *Assistance* Vol. I, 16 and Vol. II, 163; ZP-12 War Diary: 24 May 1942.

19   *Harrisburg Telegraph*, "28 Are Saved in Sub Attack Seen on Shore" (29 May 1942); US Coast Guard, *Assistance* Vol. I, 16 and Vol. II, 163; Waddell, "Tanker's Luck Ran Out Off Barnegat Inlet."

20   ZP-12 War Diary: 25 May 1942; U-593 KTB (2nd patrol), 15; Vaeth, *Blimps & U-boats*, 23–24; Kriegsmarine, "Diving Regulations for U-boats," 50–51; UK Admiralty, "Interrogation of U-boat Survivors," 20–21.

21   US Coast Guard, *Assistance* Vol. I, 16 and Vol. II, 163–164; Quistgaard affidavit; Standard Oil of NJ, *Ships of the Esso Fleet in WWII*, 222.

22   Richard Van Treuren interview by author; ESF War Diary, May 1942, Appx. V; ZP-12 War Diary: 25 May 1942; Vaeth, *Blimps & U-boats*, 24–25; Payne, *Principles of Naval Weapons Systems*, 198–200, 205–206; U-593 KTB (2nd patrol), 15–16.

23 Buchholz, *New Jersey Shipwrecks*, 172–173; US Coast Guard, *Assistance* Vol. I, 16–18 and Vol. II, 163–164; USCG Philadelphia District War Diary: 24–30 May 1942; U-593 KTB (2nd patrol), 15–17.

24 Quistgaard affidavit; Standard Oil of NJ, *Ships of the Esso Fleet in WWII*, 221–223, 443–444; USCG Philadelphia District War Diary: 24–30 May 1942; *Harrisburg Telegraph*, "28 Are Saved in Sub Attack Seen on Shore" (29 May 1942); 4th ND, "Body washed ashore – Report of" (3 Jun 1942).

25 Lawrenson, "Damn the Torpedoes"; Wiberg, *U-boats in New England*, 99; Geroux, *The Mathews Men*, 92, 99; ESF War Diary, Apr 1942, Ch. 7: 1; S.E. Smith, *The United States Navy in World War II*, 122 (William & Morrow Co, Inc, 1966).

26 Rottman, *SNAFU*, 203; USCGC Icarus, "Report of Action of 9 May 1942 on Enemy Submarine," 1–3 (15 May 1942); Office of CNO, "Final Report of Interrogation of Survivors From U-352, Sunk by U.S.C.G. Icarus on May 9, 1942 in Approximate Position Latitude 34.12.05 N., Longitude 76.35 W.," 1–2, 6–12, 13, 20, 25–26 (31 Aug 1942); Atlantic Fleet, "Destruction of Enemy Submarine by U.S.C.G. ICARUS," 1 (15 May 1942), "Action Report, U.S.C.G. ICARUS, Analysis of" (25 May 1942), and "Summary of information of the engagement between ICARUS and German U/boat obtained by visit to Charleston, S.C.," 2 (18 May 1942).

Chapter 12. *Berganger*

1 U-578 KTB (4th patrol), 12–15, 18–19, 38; Topp, "A Visit With a U-Boat Ace: Erich Topp"; Buchheim, *U-boat War*, n.p.; WarSailors.com, "M/S Breñas"; Vause, *Wolf*, 42; Ubootarchiv.de, "Raimund Tiesler"; Title poem obtained from USMM.org.

2 International Military Tribunal, *The Nuremberg Files*, 10870–10871, 3336–3337, 3347; Padfield, *Dönitz: The Last Führer*, 273, 332–339; Cremer, *U-boat Commander*, 43; U-578 KTB (4th patrol), 18–19.

3 *Lloyd's Register of Shipping 1941–42*; U-213 KTB (2nd patrol), 32–35; Krigsseilerregisteret.no, "Alm Normann Nymann"; ESF War Diary, Apr 1942, Ch. 3: 2 and Jun 1942, Ch. 1: 1–2, 6; Norwegian Maritime Museum, *Sjøforklaringer fra 2. verdenskrig* Vol. I, 85–87; 3rd ND, "Summary of Statements by Survivors of SS BERGANGER and SS ANNA" (5 Jun 1942).

4 Royal House of Norway, "World War II" and "King Haakon VII (1872–1957)" (RoyalCourt.no); WWIINorge.com, "Nortraship"; *TIME*, "Norway: H7" (30 Sep 1957); Jess Isle, "Alt for Norge: The Motto That Unites Three Kings" (RoyalCentral.co.uk, 15 Jan 2021).

5 U-578 torpedo report and KTB (4th patrol), 19; Kriegsmarine, "Torpedo Firing Regulations for U-boats," 9–11, 21–25; Schaeffer, *U-boat 977*, 52–53.

6 US Navy, "Mine Disposal Handbook," Pt. IV, Ch. 3: 23–25; Wright, "Wolves Without Teeth," 67, 132, 136; U-578 KTB (4th patrol), 19; Krigsseilerregisteret.no, "M/S Berganger"; Eberhard Rössler, *Die Torpedos der deutschen U-Boote*, 79 (Mittler Verlag, 2005); Office of CNO, "Summary of Statements by Survivors of the MV 'BERGANGER', Norwegian cargo vessel ..."

7 3rd ND, "Enemy Attack on Merchant Ship," 3 (5 Jun 1942) and "Summary of Statements by Survivors of SS BERGANGER and SS ANNA"; Norwegian Maritime Museum, *Sjøforklaringer fra 2. verdenskrig* Vol. I, 85–87; Berganger deck log excerpt; War Shipping Administration, *Safety for Seamen*, 7.

8 U-578 KTB (4th patrol), 19; Office of CNO, "Summary of Statements by Survivors of the MV 'BERGANGER', Norwegian cargo vessel ..."; Krigsseilerregisteret.no, "Johan Kolbjørn Mathiassen Vidnes" and "Olaf Parelius Olbertsen Brevik"; Norwegian Maritime Museum, *Sjøforklaringer fra 2. verdenskrig* Vol. I, 85–87.

9 Admiralty Merchant Ship Defence Instructions No. 4; Campbell, *Naval Weapons of WWII*, 59; War Shipping Administration, *Deck Branch Training*, 47.

10   Capt Hugh Stephens interview by author; Office of CNO, "Summary of Statements by Survivors of the MV 'BERGANGER', Norwegian cargo vessel ..."; Norwegian Maritime Museum, *Sjøforklaringer fra 2. verdenskrig* Vol. I, 85–87.

11   U-578 KTB (4th patrol), 19; Wiggins, *U-boat Adventures*, 214.

12   Office of CNO, "Summary of Statements by Survivors of the MV 'BERGANGER', Norwegian cargo vessel ..."; Norwegian Maritime Museum, *Sjøforklaringer fra 2. verdenskrig* Vol. I, 85–87; WarSailors.com, "M/S Berganger"; 3rd ND, "Combat Intelligence Report on Torpedoing of M/V Berganger" and "Summary of Statements by Survivors of SS BERGANGER and SS ANNA"; U-578 KTB (4th patrol), 19.

13   U-578 torpedo reports and KTB (4th patrol), 19; Norwegian Maritime Museum, *Sjøforklaringer fra 2. verdenskrig* Vol. I, 85–87; Hirschfeld & Brooks, *The Secret Diary of a U-boat*, 52, 220; Neitzel & Welzer, *Soldiers*, 74.

14   3rd ND, "Combat Intelligence Report on Torpedoing of M/V Berganger"; Office of CNO, "Summary of Statements by Survivors of the MV 'BERGANGER', Norwegian cargo vessel ..."

15   3rd ND, "Enemy Attack on Merchant Ship," 6–7 and "Combat Intelligence Report on Torpedoing of M/V Berganger"; U-578 KTB (4th patrol), 20; Norwegian Maritime Museum, *Sjøforklaringer fra 2. verdenskrig* Vol. I, 85–87; Williamson, *U-boat Tactics in WWII*, 55.

16   Wiberg, *U-boats in New England*, 185–186; Norwegian Maritime Museum, *Sjøforklaringer fra 2. verdenskrig* Vol. I, 85–87; Krigsseilerregisteret.no, "M/S Berganger"; WarSailors.com, "M/S Reinholt."

17   BdU KTB: 17 May 1942; ESF War Diary, May 1942, Appx. IV and Jun 1942, Appx. V; U-578 KTB (4th patrol), 38; Mallmann Showell, *Fuehrer Conferences on Naval Affairs*, 280–283; Padfield, *Dönitz: The Last Führer*, 322–323; International Military Tribunal, *The Nuremberg Trials*, 3335–3336; Rössler, *The Evolution and Technical History of German Submarines*, 143.

Chapter 13. *Rio Tercero*

1   ESF War Diary, Jun 1942, Ch. 6: 2 and Apr 1942, Ch. 1: 2; US Coast Guard, *Beach Patrol*, 1, 7, 9; Cohen, "The Keystone Commandos"; Cullen, "Interview of John C. Cullen," 1–3, 10; Eastern Defense Command, "History of the New York-Philadelphia Sector," 20–24, 80–83, 104–106; Lender, *One State in Arms*, 88; Dobbs; *Saboteurs*, 124–125; Nazi Saboteur Military Commission, "Stenographic Transcript of Proceedings before the Military Commission to Try Persons Charged With Offenses Against the Law of War and the Articles of War," 101 (Session #1, 8 Jul 1942).

2   Nazi Saboteur Military Commission, "Stenographic Transcript of Proceedings ...," 101–107; ESF War Diary, Jun 1942, Ch. 6: 2–4; Cullen, "Interview of John C. Cullen," 8–12; Dasch, *Operation Pastorius*, 87; Dobbs, *Saboteurs*, 21, 28, 126–130; Rachlis, *They Came to Kill*, 30, 112–114; Thiesen, "Jack Cullen, Nazi Spies and the Founding of the USCG Beach Patrol"; Cohen, "The Keystone Commandos"; George Dasch statement to FBI, 14–15 (2 Jul 1942). | Dialogue drawn from Cullen's recollections in 1942 and 2006 and from Dasch's book.

3   Office of CNO, "Summary of Statements of Survivors SS Rio Tercero ..."; Francis, "The United States and Chile During the Second World War," 91; William Z. Slany, *U.S. and Allied Wartime and Postwar Relations and Negotiations With Argentina, Portugal, Spain, Sweden and Turkey on Looted Gold and German External Assets and U.S. Concerns*, xxxv (US Government Printing Office, 1998). | Scalese's attire as shown in photographs taken after rescue.

4   *Lloyd's Register of Ships 1941–42*; Paz, "El hundimiento del Rio III"; Slany, *U.S. and Allied Wartime and Postwar Relations and Negotiations With Argentina ...*, xxxv; Pablo Mendelevich, *El final: cómo dejan el gobierno los presidentes argentinos*, 138–139 (Ediciones B Argentina S.A., 2010); Norberto Galasso, *Perón: Formación, ascenso y caída, 1893–1955*, 118, 133, 135,

137–138 (Colihue, 2005); Raimundo Siepe & Monserrat Llairó, "Perón y la política marítima en la Argentina," 3–6 (Centro de Estudios Internacionales para el Desarrollo, 2001).

5   Office of CNO, "Sinking of Argentine Vessel, RIO TERCERO" and "Summary of Statements of Survivors SS Rio Tercero …"; Bunker, *Heroes in Dungarees*, 29. | Neutrality markings as seen in USCG photo dated 16 June 1942.

6   Dobbs, *Saboteurs*, 23, 46–47, 70, 80; Watson, *The Nazi Spy Pastor*, 84-85; BdU KTB: 26 May 1942; Cohen, "The Keystone Commandos"; Padfield, *Dönitz: The Last Führer*, 168; FBI.gov, "Black Tom 1916 Bombing"; Lender, *One State in Arms*, 76; Frenzel, "Hitler's Unfulfilled Dream of a New York in Flames"; UK MoD, *The U-boat War in the Atlantic*, Vol. II: 19; Christopher Maag, "Lyndhurst Marks 100th Anniversary of Kingsland Explosion" (NorthJersey.com, 10 Jan 2017).

7   U-202 KTB (6th patrol), 1-8, 11; Cohen, "The Keystone Commandos"; Dobbs, *Saboteurs*, 116; Rachlis, *They Came to Kill*, 6–8, 12, 92–93; Gannon, *Operation Drumbeat*, 223; Dasch, *Operation Pastorius*, 84–85.

8   Hickam, *Torpedo Junction*, 268–269; Office of CNO, "Summary of Statements of Survivors SS Rio Tercero …"; Raguso, "The Rio Tercero."

9   Cullen, "Interview of John C. Cullen," 13; ESF War Diary, Jun 1942, Ch. 6: 2, 4–5; Nazi Saboteur Military Commission, "Stenographic Transcript of Proceedings …," 107–108; Thiesen, "Jack Cullen, Nazi Spies and the Founding of the USCG Beach Patrol." | Coast Guard station dialogue sourced from William's Thiesen's article.

10   U-202 KTB (6th patrol), 8–9; UK Admiralty, "U 202 Interrogation of Survivors," 15; Frenzel, "Hitler's Unfulfilled Dream of a New York in Flames."

11   Office of CNO, "Summary of Statements of Survivors SS Rio Tercero …"; *Richmond Times-Dispatch*, "Sinking of Ship by Germans Shakes Argentina's War Policy" (24 Jun 1942); War Shipping Administration, *Safety for Seamen*, 28; Buchheim, *U-boat War*, n.p.

12   U-202 KTB (6th patrol), 9–10; UK Admiralty, "U 202 Interrogation of Survivors," 15.

13   Rachlis, *They Came to Kill*, 107; Dobbs, *Saboteurs*, 91; Office of CNO, "Summary of Statements of Survivors SS Rio Tercero …"; *Richmond Times-Dispatch*, "Sinking of Ship by Germans Shakes Argentina's War Policy."

14   Office of CNO, "Summary of Statements of Survivors SS Rio Tercero …"; 3rd ND, "Sinking of SS Rio Tercero (Argentinian) by German Submarine," 6 (23 Jun 1942); U-202 KTB (6th patrol), 16; COMINCH HQ incident report; ESF War Diary, Jun 1942, Appx. VI.

15   393rd Bombardment Squadron, "Attack on Enemy Submarine" and "Form Mike 526"; U-202 KTB (6th patrol), 16; Office of CNO, "Sinking of Argentine Vessel, RIO TERCERO"; *Camden Courier-Post*, "Argentina Aroused at 2nd Ship Sinking" (24 Jun 1942).

16   Paz, "El hundimiento del Rio Tercero"; ESF War Diary, Jun 1942, Appx. VI; Office of CNO, "Sinking of Argentine Vessel, RIO TERCERO"; Raguso, "The Rio Tercero"; *El Bien Público*, "Llego a Buenos Aires el Capitán del Rio Tercero" (4 Jul 1942).

17   BdU Ops Division KTB Vol. 34, Part A: 296, 299; *The Record*, "Hostile Crowds Stone Windows" (Hackensack NJ, 26 Jun 1942); Raguso, "The Rio Tercero"; Paz, "El hundimiento del Rio Tercero."

18   Dobbs, *Saboteurs*, 48, 135, 194–208, 242; Watson, *The Nazi Spy Pastor*, 86–87; Dasch, *Operation Pastorius*, 90, 106–107; Cohen, "The Keystone Commandos"; Puleo, *Due to Enemy Action*, 54; Frenzel, "Hitler's Unfulfilled Dream of a New York in Flames"

19   Lender, *One State in Arms*, 88; US Coast Guard, *Beach Patrol*, 5, 11, 21; Army Historical Foundation, "The Dogs of War: The U.S. Army's Use of Canines in WWII" (ArmyHistory.org).

20   Richards & Banigan, *How to Abandon Ship*, 42; Office of CNO, "Summary of Statements of Survivors SS Rio Tercero …"; U-202 KTB (6th patrol), 15–17; Uboat.net, "USS Cythera (PY 26)"; Tony

Bridgland, *Waves of Hate: Naval Atrocities of the Second World War*, 113–137 (Leo Cooper, 2002); Michael Sturma, "Atrocities, Conscience, and Unrestricted Warfare," 456–462 (*War in History*, Vol. 16, No. 4, Nov 2009).

21 John F. White, *The Milk Cows: The U-boat Tankers 1941–1945*, 28–34, 80–81 (Pen & Sword Military, 2009, Kindle); U-202 KTB (6th patrol), 17, 23–26, 31–32, 43.

22 ESF War Diary, Feb 1942, Ch. 2: 2–3, Apr 1942, Ch. 1: 2; UK MoD, *U-boat War in the Atlantic*, Vol. II: 12–13; Goralski & Freeburg, *Oil and War*, 115; U-103 KTB (7th patrol), 6–7, 14–15; *Salt Lake Tribune*, "Heroic Gunner Dies Trying to Bag U-boat" (28 May 1942); *The Miami News*, "Another Vessel Smashed in the Gulf" (28 May 1942).

Chapter 14. *John R. Williams*

1 ESF War Diary, Jun 1942, Appx. VI; Wiggins, *America's Anchor*, 200–201.

2 BdU KTB: 30 Apr, 17 May 1942; Dönitz, *Memoirs*, 215–216, 220; Mallmann Showell, *Fuehrer Conferences on Naval Affairs*, 281–282.

3 Offley, *The Burning Shore*, 183; ESF War Diary, Jan 1942, Ch. 2: 5 and Jun 1942, Ch. 2: 1–3.

4 Payne, *Principles of Naval Weapons Systems*, 294; ESF War Diary, Jun 1942, Ch. 2: 2–3; Office of Naval Records and Library, "German Submarine Activities on the Atlantic Coast …," 136–138; BdU KTB: 19 May 1942; Rottman, *SNAFU*, 219; *TIME*, "U.S. at War: Attack by Sea" (1 Jun 1942); Benson Lossing, *The Pictorial Field-Book of the War of 1812*, 240–243, 693 (1868).

5 US Navy, "German Underwater Ordnance: Mines," 80–81; Campbell, *Naval Weapons of WWII*, 269, 272–273; Holland, "The Tidewater confronts the storm," 80–81; U-373 KTB (5th patrol), 1; BdU KTB: 19 May 1942; Mallmann Showell, *Fuehrer Conferences on Naval Affairs*, 282.

6 ShipbuildingHistory.com, "Dravo Wilmington"; New York Shipbuilding Corporation, "The Story of New York Ship" (NewYorkShip.org); Wiggins, *America's Anchor*, 198, 203–204, 207–208; Yergin, *The Prize*, 383; Sun Ship Historical Society, "The Sun Ship 'History Panel' Page" (SunShip.org); T2Tanker.org, "A Brief History of the T2 Tanker"; Herbert Ershkowitz, "World War II" and Jean-Pierre Beugoms, "Arsenals" (PhiladelphiaEncyclopedia.org); Colin Ainsworth, "The Sun Also Rises" (*Delco Times*, 30 Oct 2017); ExplorePAHistory.com, "The Arsenal of America: Pennsylvania During the Second World War"; Mark Hostutler, "It Has Been 120 Years Since the First Crude Oil Shipment at Marcus Hook. A lot has changed since 1902" (*VISTA Today*, 20 Apr 2022).

7 Wiggins, *America's Anchor*, 28, 35–50, 199; Bill Manthorpe correspondence with author; Coastal Defense Study Group, "Harbor Defenses of the Delaware" (CDSG.org); Eastern Defense Command, "History of the New York-Philadelphia Sector," 21, 37–39, 88, 144–146, 150–155; National Register of Historic Places Registration Form for Battery 223, Sec. 7: 1, Sec. 8: 1–5, 8, 10–12 (Form 10–900, 19 Feb 2008); Grayson, *Delaware's Ghost Towers*, 41, 44–45.

8 Holland, "The Tidewater confronts the storm," 38–40, 80–81; Grayson, *Delaware's Ghost Towers*, 17; Duffy, *Target: America*, 1–5, 14; Eastern Defense Command, "History of the New York-Philadelphia Sector," 154–155; Walding, "Cape Henlopen (Fort Miles) – Delaware"; Tyler Dreiblatt, "History of Fort Miles at Cape Henlopen State Park" (DEStateParks.blog, 17 Sep 2020); Herwig, *Politics of Frustration*, 42–66; Richard Severo, "A Footnote: Kaiser's Plan to Invade the U.S." (*New York Times*, 24 Apr 1971).

9 ESF War Diary, Jun 1942, Ch. 2: 3–6, 12, Ch. 4: 1–3; Offley, *The Burning Shore*, 170, 184, 189–190.

10 U-373 KTB (5th patrol), 12–13; Kriegsmarine, "Diving Regulations for U-boats," 52–54, 79–80; Ubootarchiv.de, "Paul Karl Loeser"; Busch & Röll, *German U-boat Commanders of WWII*, 149.

11 Grayson, *Delaware's Ghost Towers*, 40; U-373 KTB, 15–19 (4th patrol), 12–13 (5th patrol), and minelaying orders.

12   US Navy, "German Underwater Ordnance: Mines," 3, 80–81 and "Mine Disposal Handbook," Pt. 4, Ch. 1: 2–4, 107; U-373 minelaying orders, minelaying report, and KTB (5th patrol), 13.

13   Walding, "How the Anti-submarine Harbor Defense System Worked" and "Cape Henlopen (Fort Miles) – Delaware"; Bill Manthorpe correspondence with author; ESF War Diary, Jun 1942, Appx. VI; Wiggins, *America's Anchor*, 200; 4th ND INSPAT War Diary: 17–18 Jun 1942.

14   *Lloyd's Register of Shipping 1941–42*; John Ward, "There's a Lot of Push and Pull in His Work" (*TowLine*, Sep 1959); *Shamokin News-Dispatch*, "Seagoing Tug is Sunk by Mine Off US Coast" (30 Jun 1942); George, *Shipwrecks of the Delaware Coast*, 103; Moore, *A Careless Word, A Needless Sinking*, 157; "US Navy, Mine Disposal Handbook," Pt. 4, Ch. 1: 2–4, 14–19; ESF War Diary, Jun 1942, Ch. 4: 5, Appx. VI.

15   Payne, *Principles of Naval Weapon Systems*, 358–359; US Navy, "German Underwater Ordnance: Mines," 127; Costanzo, "Underwater Explosion Phenomena and Shock Physics," 3; ESF War Diary, Jun 1942, Ch. 4, 5–6, Appx. VI; George, *Shipwrecks of the Delaware Coast*, 104–105; *Shamokin News-Dispatch*, "Seagoing Tug Is Sunk by Mine Off US Coast."

16   U-373 KTB (5th patrol), 16, 30; ESF War Diary, Jun 1942, Appx. VI; 4th ND INSPAT War Diary: 16 Jun 1942; U-87 minelaying orders and KTB (3rd patrol), 9, 11, 25; Wiberg, *U-boats in New England*, 345; *New York Times*, "Port Here Closed by Mines in 1942" (16 Jun 1945).

17   Office of CNO, "Report of Interrogation of Survivors of U-701, Sunk By U.S. Army Attack Bomber on July 7, 1942," 15–17, Annex B (17 Sep 1942); Offley, *The Burning Shore*, 202–204, 217–223, 232, 254; Holland, "The Tidewater confronts the storm," 85; ESF War Diary, Jun 1942, Ch. 1: 2 and Aug 1942, Ch. 3: 1–2; Uboat.net, "USS Dorado (SS 248)"; Maritime Education & Research Society, "USS Dorado (SS-248): On Eternal Patrol" (MERSFoundation.org).

18   ESF War Diary, Jun 1942, Ch. 3: 4 and Aug 1942, Ch. 3: 5–6, Ch. 4: 1–2; UK MoD, *The U-boat War in the Atlantic*, Vol. II: 12–13, 15, 18; Morison, *The Battle of the Atlantic*, 157, 260–263; Author's tabulation of Apr–Jul 1942 losses and patrols.

19   WarHistoryOnline.com, "Crossroads of War—A Reevaluation Of The Allied Victory At The Second Battle Of El Alamein" (5 Jan 2018); Dwight Jon Zimmerman, "Seatrain Texas to the Rescue" (Defense Media Network, 18 Jul 2016).

20   *TIME*, "U.S. at War: Attack by Sea" (1 Jun 1942); Author's tabulation of US coast sinkings and fatalities for Jan–Aug 1942; Freeburg & Goralski, *Oil and War*, 119; Leighton, "U.S. Merchant Shipping and the British Import Crisis," 201; Snow, *A Measureless Peril*, 208–209; Morison, *The Battle of the Atlantic*, 127; U-402 KTB (4th patrol), 11–14; Nathan Miller, *The War at Sea: A Naval History of World War II*, 316–317 (Oxford University Press, 1995).

21   Speer, *Spandau: The Secret Diaries*, 223–224; Padfield, *Dönitz: The Last Führer*, 327, 346; Author's tabulation of worldwide sinkings for Nov 1942; Roskill, *The Period of Balance*, 393–395; Offley, *Turning the Tide*, 100–104.

Chapter 15. *Pan Pennsylvania*

1   Harris, "Reflections of Collingwood Harris," 44; Andrews, *Tempest, Fire and Foe*, 27–30; Peffer & Nersasian, *Never to Return*, 121–127, 129–137.

2   Wolf Hänert correspondence with author; BdU KTB: 7 Feb–17 Mar, 11 May 1944; UK Admiralty, "U 448 and U 550 Interrogation of Survivors," 7–8, 15; Peffer, *Where Divers Dare*, 19–20, 260–261; Letter from Klaus Hänert to Eric-Jan Bakker (24 Jul 1989).

3   Padfield, *Dönitz: The Last Führer*, 390; Cremer, *U-Boat Commander*, 1–4; Sternhell & Thorndike, "Antisubmarine Warfare in World War II," 82; Mulligan, *Neither Sharks Nor Wolves*, 44; Rose, *Power at Sea*, 313–314; Uboat.net, "ONS-5." | Similar versions of Hitler's "can't go on" remark quoted by Cremer and Padfield.

4   Cremer, *U-boat Commander*, 81; Hinsley, *Hitler's Strategy*, 208; Bunker, *Heroes in Dungarees*, 13–14; Mulligan, *Neither Sharks Nor Wolves*, 56–57; PBS.org, "War Production"; Author's tabulation of shipping and U-boat losses; Sternhell & Thorndike, "Antisubmarine Warfare in World War II," 42–43; Mallmann Showell, *Hitler's Navy*, 93.

5   Letter from Klaus Hänert to Eric-Jan Bakker (24 Jul 1989); Wolf Hänert correspondence with author; Goebeler & Vanzo, *Steel Boat, Iron Hearts*, 218; Andrews, *Tempest, Fire and Foe*, 13–14; Richard Overy, *The Bombers and the Bombed*, 142–144, 306–307 (Penguin Books, 2015, Kindle).

6   Grier, "The Appointment of Admiral Karl Dönitz as Hitler's Successor," 186–187; Werner, *Iron Coffins*, 277, 236–237; Vause, *Wolf*, 98, 194–195; Speer, *Spandau: The Secret Diaries*, 334; Goebeler & Vanzo, *Steel Boat, Iron Hearts*, 2; Wolf Hänert interview by author.

7   UK Admiralty, "U 448 and U 550 Interrogation of Survivors," 7; RCAF No. 162 Squadron, U-boat Attack Assessment Form; BdU KTB: 8 Apr 1944; Peffer, *Where Divers Dare*, 14–17; Letters from Klaus Hänert to Michael Hadley (27 Apr 1982) and Eric-Jan Bakker (24 Jul 1989).

8   John Rauh interview by author; Peffer, *Where Divers Dare*, 22.

9   *Lloyd's Register of Shipping 1943–44*; ESF War Diary, Apr 1944, Ch. 2: 5; Delmar Leidy affidavit (23 May 1944); Armed Guard, "Voyage Report of SS PAN PENNSYLVANIA," 5; National Archives, "Camp Kilmer" (Archives.gov); Peffer, *Where Divers Dare*, 29–30, 39–40; NavSource. org, "YP-387, ex-AMc-200."

10 ESF War Diary, Apr 1944, Ch. 2: 1–6; Munro, "Eyewitnesses to World War II, U-550"; Offley, *Turning the Tide*, 74; 3rd ND, "Convoy CU-21" (14 Apr 1944).

11 UK Admiralty, "U 448 and U 550 Interrogation of Survivors," 2, 7–8; Letters from Klaus Hänert to Michael Hadley (27 Apr and 3 Sep 1982) and Eric-Jan Bakker (24 Jul 1989); John Rauh and Wolf Hänert interview by author; Hänert, "Versenkungsbericht des Kommandanten von U 550"; Peffer, *Where Divers Dare*, 25–28, 250–251; Rackow, "Hier wird U-550 vor New York versenkt"; Cicero, "Mein Großvater, vom Feind gerettet"; Mulligan, *Neither Sharks Nor Wolves*, 6; Wiberg, *U-boats in New England*, 421; ESF War Diary, Apr 1944, Ch. 2: 1–4.

12 USS Joyce, Gandy, and Peterson, Operational Remarks; Harris, "Reflections of Collingwood Harris," 45–47; ESF War Diary, Apr 1944, Ch. 2: 2; Peffer, *Where Divers Dare*, 34–41, 52; Peffer & Nersasian, *Never to Return*, 92–100, 166, 170, 189–190.

13 Rössler, *The Evolution and Technical History of German Submarines*, 143; Rottman, *SNAFU*, 233; Peffer & Nersasian, *Never to Return*, 39–40, 167–169, 198, 209; Peffer, *Where Divers Dare*, 36–37, 286; Harris, "Reflections of Collingwood Harris," 46–47.

14 Andrews, *Tempest, Fire and Foe*, 1–3, 415; Peffer & Nersasian, *Never to Return*, 37–41, 54–60, 63, 144; Harris, "Reflections of Collingwood Harris," 2–3, 52–53; Rottman, *SNAFU*, 23; Morison, *The Battle of the Atlantic*, 298.

15 Colimor, "Memories of Sub Attack"; Mazraani & Sellitti, "From Ordinary to Extraordinary"; Peffer, *Where Divers Dare*, 29, 32–33, 63–64; Uboat.net, "HX 228."

16 Hänert, "Versenkungsbericht des Kommandanten von U 550"; UK Admiralty, "U 448 and U 550 Interrogation of Survivors," 8; Peffer, *Where Divers Dare*, 56–62, 71–72.

17 Delmar Leidy affidavit; Armed Guard, "Voyage Report of SS PAN PENNSYLVANIA," 1, 4–5; USNOB Londonderry, "Torpedoing of S.S. PAN PENNSYLVANIA," 3; Mazraani & Sellitti, "From Ordinary to Extraordinary"; Peffer, *Where Divers Dare*, 63–64.

18 UK Admiralty, "U 448 and U 550 Interrogation of Survivors," 8; Hänert, "Versenkungsbericht des Kommandanten von U 550"; Peffer, *Where Divers Dare*, 71–75.

19 Delmar Leidy affidavit; Armed Guard, "Voyage Report of SS PAN PENNSYLVANIA," 4–5.

20 Kriegsmarine, "U-boat Commander's Handbook," 57(a), 254(b); Payne, *Principles of Naval Weapon Systems*, 164–168; UK Admiralty, "U 448 and U 550 Interrogation of Survivors," 8; Hänert, "Versenkungsbericht des Kommandanten von U 550."

21   USS Joyce, Form ASW-1 and "Contact and Action Reports"; Peffer, *Where Divers Dare*, 68–70. | "I want this guy" borrowed from Randall Peffer's depiction of events.

22   Colimor, "Memories of Sub Attack"; Armed Guard, "Voyage Report of SS PAN PENNSYLVANIA," 1–4; USNOB Londonderry, "Torpedoing of S.S. PAN PENNSYLVANIA," 3; Delmar Leidy affidavit; Mazraani & Sellitti, "From Ordinary to Extraordinary"; Comegno, "Divers Help Reunite 92-year-old man with WW2 Relics"; Office of the CNO, "Summary of Statements by Survivors SS PAN PENNSYLVANIA, U.S. Tanker, 11,017 G.T., owners National Bulk Carriers, chartered to W.S.A." (23 May 1944).

23   USS Peterson, "Narrative of Anti-Submarine Action 16 April 1944."

24   COMINCH HQ, "Analysis of Combined Anti-submarine Action Reports ...," 1; USS Joyce, War Diary: 16 Apr 1944, Form ASW-1, and "Contact and Action Reports"; Harris, "Reflections of Collingwood Harris," 54; ESF War Diary, Apr 1944, Ch. 2: 3; Armed Guard, "Voyage Report of SS PAN PENNSYLVANIA," 3; USS Peterson, "Narrative of Anti-Submarine Action 16 April 1944."

25   Hänert, "Versenkungsbericht des Kommandanten von U 550"; *Pasadena Independent*, "German Meets His Nemesis" (26 Feb 1960); UK Admiralty, "U 448 and U 550 Interrogation of Survivors," 2, 8; Peffer, *Where Divers Dare*, 79–81, 273–276, 282–283; Paterson, *U-boat Combat Missions*, 129; Goebeler & Vanzo, *Steel Boat, Iron Hearts*, 141–142.

26   US Navy, "Depth Charge, Mark 9 and Modifications," 8, 13, 16 (OP 866); USS Joyce, "Contact and Action Reports"; Peffer, *Where Divers Dare*, 76–77; COMINCH HQ, "Analysis of Combined Anti-submarine Action Reports ...," 2; USS Gandy, War Diary: 16 Apr 1944; Macintyre, *U-boat Killer*, 10–11, 50; USS Peterson, "Narrative of Anti-Submarine Action 16 April 1944"; Task Group 21.5 radio transcript for 16 Apr 1944; Colin F. Baxter, "Torpex and the Atlantic Victory" (*International Journal of Naval History*, Vol. 16, No. 1, May 2021). | All radio dialogue quoted verbatim from Task Group 21.5 radio transcript.

27   USS Joyce, Form ASW-1; US Navy, "Depth Charge, Mark 9 and Modifications," 28–30; UK Admiralty, "U 448 and U 550 Interrogation of Survivors," 8; Rackow, "Hier wird U-550 vor New York versenkt"; *Pasadena Independent*, "German Meets His Nemesis"; Padfield, *War Beneath the Sea*, 104–105, 132; Werner, *Iron Coffins*, 45; Neitzel & Welzer, *Soldiers*, 258; Peffer, *Where Divers Dare*, 76–80. | Some dialogue drawn from Hugo Renzmann's recollections as published in Rackow's article.

28   Dick Wilcox & Kimberly Wilcox Joshi interview by author; UK Admiralty, "U 448 and U 550 Interrogation of Survivors," 9; USS Joyce, "Contact and Action Reports" and Operational Remarks; USS Gandy, "Contact and Action Reports" and Operational Remarks. | Sessions' orders quoted verbatim from Contact and Action Reports.

29   USS Peterson, Form ASW-1; UK Admiralty, "U 448 and U 550 Interrogation of Survivors," 9; Armed Guard, "Voyage Report of SS PAN PENNSYLVANIA," 3; *Cicero*, "Mein Großvater, vom Feind gerettet"; Hänert, "Versenkungsbericht des Kommandanten von U 550"; Peffer, *Where Divers Dare*, 85–87, 243–244, 251, 256–257, 295; Harris, "Reflections of Collingwood Harris," 51.

30   Harris, "Reflections of Collingwood Harris," 51–53; Task Group 21.5 radio transcript for 16 Apr 1944; USS Peterson, "Narrative of Antisubmarine Action 16 April 1944"; Peffer, *Where Divers Dare*, 88–93, 284–286; Atlantic Fleet, "Summary of information of the engagement between ICARUS and German U/boat obtained by visit to Charleston, S.C.," 3 (18 May 1942).

31   Armed Guard, "Voyage Report of SS PAN PENNSYLVANIA," 3; Peffer, *Where Divers Dare*, 91, 243–244, 264–265; Monsarrat, *The Cruel Sea*, 234–235; Peffer & Nersasian, *Never to Return*, 211, 214–215, 218. | Conning tower scene as captured in USCG photograph.

32   Letter from Klaus Hänert to Eric-Jan Bakker (24 Jul 1989); UK Admiralty, "U 448 and U 550 Interrogation of Survivors," 9; Rackow, "Hier wird U-550 vor New York versenkt"; Peffer, *Where Divers Dare*, 89–90, 262, 264–265.

33   Munro, "Eyewitnesses to World War II, U-550"; Peffer, *Where Divers Dare*, 93, 103, 252, 262; John Rauh interview by author; Hänert & Hartmann, "Shipwreck and Hypothermia"; *US Navy Diving Manual*, Ch. 3: 53–54.

34   *Salisbury Post*, "Bill Stanback recalls his time aboard USS Gandy in WWII" (25 Mar 2014); Hänert, "Versenkungsbericht des Kommandanten von U 550"; USS Peterson, Operational Remarks and "Narrative of Antisubmarine Action 16 April 1944"; Peffer, *Where Divers Dare*, 244, 295; Wiberg, *U-boats in New England*, 426–428.

35   Armed Guard, "Voyage Report of SS PAN PENNSYLVANIA," 4; USS Joyce, Gandy, and Peterson, Operational Remarks; USNOB Londonderry, "Torpedoing of S.S. PAN PENNSYLVANIA," 4; Mazraani & Sellitti, "From Ordinary to Extraordinary"; Peffer, *Where Divers Dare*, 98, 103–104; Cressman, *The Official Chronology of the U.S. Navy in WWII*, 472; Peffer & Nersasian, *Never to Return*, 215.

36   USS Joyce, War Diary: 16 Apr 1944; Peffer, *Where Divers Dare*, 98–101; Werner, *Iron Coffins*, n.p.

37   Harris, "Reflections of Collingwood Harris," 55–56; Peffer, *Where Divers Dare*, 102–105; Armed Guard, "Voyage Report of SS PAN PENNSYLVANIA," 4. | Parting words between Wilcox & Hänert as portrayed by Randall Peffer.

Chapter 16. Wolfsdämmerung

1   Cianflone, "The Eagle Boats of WWI"; Puleo, *Due to Enemy Action*, 9, 76, 85, 91–92, 111–118, 144–147; Koster, "Tightrope Walker"; Author's tabulation of Eastern/Gulf Sea Frontier attacks, 1943–45.

2   Neitzel & Welzer, *Soldiers*, 257; Grier, "The Appointment of Admiral Karl Dönitz as Hitler's Successor," 186–189; Citino, *The Wehrmacht's Last Stand*, 10–11, 160; Mulligan, *Neither Sharks Nor Wolves*, 56–58, 178, 194, 220; Werner, *Iron Coffins*, xv–xvii, 280–281; Padfield, *Dönitz: The Last Führer*, 383–386, 424–425; Assmann, "Why U-boat Warfare Failed," 670.

3   Kershaw, *Hitler: A Biography*, 781–782, 798, 900; Padfield, *Dönitz: The Last Führer*, 322, 353–355, 386–387, 400–403, 480–483; Speer, *Spandau: The Secret Diaries*, 335; Grier, "The Appointment of Admiral Karl Dönitz as Hitler's Successor," 186–189; Mitchell Williamson, "Jürgen Oesten and the End of the U-boats" (WeaponsAndWarfare.com, 18 Jul 2021).

4   Hansen, *Execution for Duty*, 49–81, 97–102, 112–133; Rust, "The Case of Oskar Kusch …"; Vause, *Wolf*, 189–190; Padfield, *Dönitz: The Last Führer*, 474–476; Mulligan, *Neither Sharks Nor Wolves*, 232–233.

5   Mallmann Showell, *Hitler's Attack U-boats*, 42, 103–106 and *German Navy Handbook*, 155; Dönitz, *Memoirs*, 234–236, 352–357, 421–428; Sternhell & Thorndike, "Antisubmarine Warfare in World War II," 79; Rössler, *The Evolution and Technical History of German Submarines*, 208.

6   Smelser & Davies, *The Myth of the Eastern Front*, 1–2; Gropman, "Mobilizing U.S. Industry in World War II," 98; Rüdiger Overmans, "Deutsche militärische Verluste im Zweiten Weltkrieg," 228, 265 (*Beiträge zur Militärgeschichte*, Vol. 46, 2000).

7   Williamson, "Lend-Lease to the USSR"; Serhii Pyvovarov & Gleb Gusev, "79 years ago, the USSR was accepted into the Lend-Lease program" (Babel.ua, 11 Jun 2021); Robert Coalson, "We Would Have Lost: Did U.S. Lend-Lease Aid Tip The Balance In Soviet Fight Against Nazi Germany?" (Radio Free Europe, 7 May 2020); US Department of War, "Quantities of Lend-Lease Shipments," Sec. IIIB: 2–7, IIIC: 13–14, VII: 3–11 (31 Dec 1946).

8   Dönitz, *Memoirs*, 422; Mulligan, *Neither Sharks Nor Wolves*, 53–54; Author's tabulation of losses off Normandy; BdU KTB: 6 Jun 1944; US European Command, "D-Day: The Beaches" (DoD.defense.gov); Office of CNO, "History of the Naval Armed Guard Afloat," 176, 180–185; Bunker, *Heroes in Dungarees*, 282–283; Puleo, *Due to Enemy Action*, 65.

9   Duffy, *Target: America*, 16; Robert Goldich, "Manpower and the German Fixation" (WarOnTheRocks.com, 12 Jul 2013); Peter R. Mansoor, *The GI Offensive in Europe: The Triumph of American Infantry Divisions, 1941–1945*, 266–267 (University Press of Kansas, 1999).

10   Speer, *Spandau: The Secret Diaries*, 76; Padfield, *Dönitz: The Last Führer*, 384; Watson, *The Nazi Spy Pastor*, 11, 16, 21–23, 73, 108–109, 136, 151–159.

11   Duffy, *Target: America*, 105–108; Mallmann Showell, *German Navy Handbook*, 188; Blair, *The Hunted*, 682–683, 686–687; Philip K. Lundeberg, "Operation Teardrop Revisited," 210–226 (in *To Die Gallantly* by Runyan & Copes) and "The Treatment of Survivors and Prisoners of War, at Sea and Ashore" (*International Journal of Naval History*, Vol. 13, No. 1, 26 May 2016); Office of CNO, "Report on the Interrogation of German Agents, Gimpel and Colepaugh, Landed on the Coast of Maine from U-1230," 14 (13 Jan 1945).

12   Padfield, *Dönitz: The Last Führer*, 526, 537–543; Kershaw, *Hitler: A Biography*, 20–21, 946–955, 959; Dönitz, *Memoirs*, 439–444; Speer, *Spandau: The Secret Diaries*, 98; Friedrich Karl Engel, "Who played Bruckner's Adagio (from his Seventh Symphony)?" (*Funkgeschichte*, Vol. 41, Oct–Nov 2018).

13   Werner, *Iron Coffins*, 303–304; Puleo, *Due to Enemy Action*, 127, 131–133; Blair, *The Hunted*, 699–700.

14   Puleo, *Due to Enemy Action*, 131–133, 166–172; Lynch, "Kill and Be Killed?"; Ralph DiCarpio, "The Battle of Point Judith" (Destroyer Escort Sailors Association, 2003); David Arnold, "The Final Hours of U-853" (*Boston Globe*, 5 May 1985); Submarine Force Atlantic, "Divers' Examination of U-Boat" (9 May 1945); 1st ND, "For Release in Morning Newspapers Thursday, May 17" (16 May 1945); Task Group 60.7, "Narrative of Search, Attack and Sinking of German Submarine at 090T, 14500 yards from Sandy Point, conducted by vessels attached to Task Group SIXTY POINT SEVEN, 5–6 May 1945" (10 May 1945).

15   Derek Waller correspondence with author; Manthorpe, "Submarines at the Cape"; Padfield, *Dönitz: The Last Führer*, 542–559, 567–572; Dixon, *The U-boat Commanders*, 43–44; Busch & Röll, *German U-boat Commanders of WWII*, 43–44, 91, 149; Vause, *Wolf*, 207; Pathé Gazette No. 45/44, "Flensburg Fiasco" (31 May 1945). | "Words would be superfluous" quote obtained from Vause's book and corroborated by the memoirs of Walter Lüdde-Neurath, Dönitz's adjutant.

16   Author's tabulation of total Allied merchant fleet losses; Office of CNO, "History of the Naval Armed Guard Afloat," 12; UK MoD, *The U-boat War in the Atlantic*, Vol. III: 119–121; Tenold, *Norwegian Shipping in the 20th Century*, 133; Ballantyne, *The Deadly Deep*, 432–438; War Shipping Administration Press Release 2514 (Jan 1946); USMM.org, "U.S. Merchant Marine Casualties during World War II"; BBC.co.uk, "Fact File: Merchant Navy"; Malcolm Holley, "An Analysis of the devastation wrought by U-boats during World War Two" (Uboat.net).

17   Niestlé, *German U-boat Losses During WWII*, 1–4; Mulligan, *Neither Sharks Nor Wolves*, 251–256, 309; Hansen, *Execution for Duty*, xxi; Author's tabulation of sinkings and fatalities along US coast; Office of CNO, "History of the Naval Armed Guard Afloat," 14–15; USMM. org, "U.S. Naval Armed Guard Casualties During World War II"; *All Hands*, "Sea Lane Vigilantes" (Nov 1945).

18   Rose, *Power at Sea*, 284.

Chapter 17. Bones in the Ocean

1   Eric Tidwell interview by author; Title poem obtained from American Seamen's Friend Society via USMM.org.

2   Waber, "Popular Perceptions of the American Merchant Marine During WWII," 6–7; Bunker, *Heroes in Dungarees*, 38; War Shipping Administration Press Release #2514 (Jan 1946); Geroux, *The Mathews Men*, 98–100, 136, 294–295; Anton Otto Fisher, "Delaware Valley Ships Lost to War" (MaritimeDelRiv.com); Pete Bannan, "Remembering 141 sailors of Sun Oil who died in World War II" (*Delco Times*, 20 Feb 2022).

3   Armed-Guard.com, "Dedication of Merchant Marine Memorial; Camden, New Jersey; June 11, 2005"; AtlasObscura.com, "The American Merchant Mariner's Memorial"; Tenold, *Norwegian Shipping in the 20th Century*, 133–135; WarSailors.com, "Memorials" and "Nortraship."

4   Vause, *Wolf*, 223–224; Niestlé, *German U-boat Losses During WWII*, 4; Werner, *Iron Coffins*, xvii, 273–274; Kurson, *Shadow Divers*, 142–143; Mappen, *There's More to New Jersey Than the Sopranos*, 171; Gannon, *Operation Drumbeat*, n.p.; Padfield, *Dönitz: The Last Führer*, 661; Dimbleby, *The Battle of the Atlantic*, 451; Legacy.com, "Herbert Werner Obituary" (7 Jun 2013).

5   TIME, "U.S. At War: Attack by Sea" (1 Jun 1942); Buell, *Master of Sea Power*, 348–349; Gannon, *Operation Drumbeat*, 298, 240, 413–414; Blair, *The Hunters*, 449–451, 455–460; Mawdsley, *War for the Seas*, 258; Cox, "H-008–5: Admiral Ernest J. King …"; Dimbleby, *The Battle of the Atlantic*, 264; Doug Stanton, *In Harm's Way: The Sinking of the USS Indianapolis and the Extraordinary Story of Its Survivors*, 262–267, 274–275, 280–285 (Henry Holt and Company, 2022; 2001).

6   International Military Tribunal, *The Nuremberg Trials*, 52, 72–73, 337–338, 484–491, 492–495, 660, 2775, 2816, 3347, 6365–6366, 148178–148183; Yergin, *The Prize*, 357–358; Gannon, *Operation Drumbeat*, 416; Padfield, *Dönitz: The Last Führer*, 283, 660; Zabecki, *Dönitz: A Defense*, 14; Joint Army-Navy Assessment Committee, "Japanese Naval and Merchant Shipping Losses During World War II by All Causes," vii (NAVEXOS P-468, Feb 1947).

7   Morio, "Oskar Kusch – Briefe und Texte"; Zabecki, *Dönitz: A Defense*, 95; International Military Tribunal, *The Nuremberg Trials*, 489, 491, 10918; Padfield, *Dönitz: The Last Führer*, 403–404, 466–467, 651, 661; Rems, "Götterdämmerung: German Admirals on Trial."

8   Speer, *Spandau: The Secret Diaries*, 42, 77–78, 116, 213–214, 223, 295–296; Vause, *Wolf*, 184, 222; Rems, "Götterdämmerung"; Padfield, *Dönitz: The Last Führer*, 425–429, 496, 643, 649–651, 661; Grier, "The Appointment of Admiral Karl Dönitz as Hitler's Successor," 187–188.

9   Dixon, *The U-boat Commanders*, 43–44; Reinhard Hardegen interview by Stephen Ames; Uboat.net, "Most Successful U-boat Commanders"; Gannon, *Operation Drumbeat*, 418; Ken Ringle, "The Submerged Story of the U-boat War" (21 Aug 1990); Harrison Smith, "Reinhard Hardegen, U-boat commander who menaced American shores, dies at 105" (*Washington Post*, 18 Jun 1942).

10   National Register of Historic Places Registration Form for Battery 223, Sec. 8: 2 (Form 10–900, 19 Feb 2008); AtlasObscura.com, "Bunker At Cape May Point"; CapeMayMAC.org, "World War II Lookout Tower"; Civil Air Patrol, "About CAP" and "About New Jersey Wing" (NJWG. CAP.gov); Margaret Montet, "Pleasure Cruise: Touring the historic Cape May Canal" (NJ.com, 27 Apr 2011); Navy Lakehurst Historical Society (NLHS.com).

11   Author's tabulation of NJ sinkings; Grote, "What lies beneath"; Atkinson, "Impacts of Bottom Trawling on Underwater Cultural Heritage," 25; Nagiewicz, *Hidden History of Maritime New Jersey*, 19–20; NJ Dept of Environmental Protection, "Artificial Reef Management Plan for New Jersey 2005" (Dec 2005), 12–14.

12   Joe Mazraani correspondence and Dan Lieb interview by author; Kurson, *Shadow Divers*, 194–197; Grote, "What lies beneath"; Gentile, *The Lusitania Controversies* Book 1, 70, 221–222 and *Shadow Divers Exposed*, 22–41, 56–59, 127–129, 138–139, 160–161; McCarthy, "How Shipwreck Divers Scour Jersey's Ocean Floor"; *Philadelphia Inquirer*, "John Dudas, 38, deep-sea diver" (16 Jul 1982); Women Divers Hall of Fame, "Evelyn Dudas" (wdhof.org); Chuck Bennett, "Wreck Valley, New York-New Jersey" (ScubaDiving.com, 7 Sep 2008).

13 McCarthy, "How Shipwreck Divers Scour New Jersey's Ocean Floor"; Duane Clause correspondence with author; Atkinson, "Impacts of Bottom Trawling on Underwater Cultural Heritage," 38–39, 102; National Register of Historic Places Multiple Property Registration Form for "World War II Shipwrecks along the East Coast and Gulf of Mexico," Sec. F: 51–53 (Form 10–900-b, 26 Apr 2013).

14 Kurson, *Shadow Divers*, 90–91; Segars & Segars, "New Jersey's Jacob Jones."

15 US Coast Guard, "Sunken Tanker Project Report," 1–3, 8–11 (1967); NOAA, "Risk Assessment for Potentially Polluting Wrecks in US Waters," A-3, A-5, A-7, ES-1 (Mar 2013) and "More than 450,00 Gallons of Oil Recovered from WWII Shipwreck" (19 Jul 2019); *New York Times*, "Wrecks Checked for Oil Pollution" (16 Aug 1967); Tom Schlichter, "The Coimbra's Oil Issue" (SouthernBoating.com, 2 Jul 2019); Frank Roylance, "WWII shipwrecks could threaten U.S. coast" (*Baltimore Sun*, 8 Jul 2011).

16 *Asbury Park Press*, "Trawler Tragedy Is Linked to Wartime 'Torpedo Alley'" (25 Jul 1965) and "Live Torpedo Warhead Among Fishing Catch" (23 Sep 1978); Tom Gogola, "Caught in the Net Off Block Island: A Live WWII Bomb" (*East Hampton Star*, 3 Nov 2022); Steve Giegerich, "U-boat torpedo shuts down part of Shore resort" (*Asbury Park Press*, 14 May 1985).

17 Niestlé, *German U-boat Losses During WWII*, 8, 229–230; Author's tabulation of U-boat losses and crew fatalities along US coast; Kurson, *Shadow Divers*, 148–149; National Park Service, "Sunken Military Craft Act of 2004" (NPS.gov).

18 Kurson, *Shadow Divers*, 12–13, 19–21, 42–56, 63–66, 100–104, 106–111, 117–119, 134–140, 167–175, 194, 216–223, 253–264, 311–323; Nagiewicz, *Hidden History of Maritime New Jersey*, 110; Chatterton, *et al.*, "The Fate of U-869 Reexamined," Pt. 2 and 3; PBS, "Hitler's Lost Sub"; Gentile, *The Lusitania Controversies* Book 1, 221–222.

19 Harold Moyers correspondence with author; US Navy, "Mine Disposal Handbook," 2, 9; Chatterton, *et al.*, "The Fate of U-869 Reexamined," Pt. 2 and 3; Williamson, *U-boat Tactics in WWII*, 45; Kurson, *Shadow Divers*, 281–282; Gentile, *Shadow Divers Exposed*, 210–218, 226–232.

20 Mike Monichetti interview by author; Croskey, "When the War Came to Sea Isle"; Donald Wittkowski, "The Day Sea Isle Made International News" (*Sea Isle News*, 25 Jan 2021).

21 Busch & Röll, *German U-boat Commanders*, 121; Dixon, *The U-boat Commanders*, 156–158; Uboat.net, "Most Successful U-boat Commanders" and "U-130"; Rust, "The Case of Oskar Kusch …"

22 Duane Clause correspondence with author; Gentile, *Shipwrecks of New Jersey*, 146; NJScuba.net, "Varanger"; WarSailors.com, "M/T Varanger"; John Raguso, "The Varanger (28 Mile Wreck)" (*The Fisherman*, 2 May 1985).

23 Dixon, *The U-boat Commanders*, 298–299; Uboat.net, "Werner Winter" and "U-103."

24 Morio, "Oskar Kusch – Briefe und Texte"; Hansen, *Execution for Duty*, 135, 188–193, 197–210; Rust, "The Case of Oskar Kusch …"; Lucas Uhlmann correspondence with author; Vause, *Wolf*, 188–191.

25 Harold Moyers correspondence with author; Brandon McWilliams, "India Arrow" (DownTooLong.com, 2007).

26 Nagiewicz, *Hidden History of Maritime New Jersey*, 114; NJWreckDivers.com, "Cape May and other Shipwreck Information"; Tom Baker, "After the Inferno: A Visit to the Resor" (*Sub Aqua Journal*, Vol. 2, No. 11, Nov 1992).

27 Chamberlain, "Jacob Jones survivor's grandson dives wreck"; Uboat.net, "USS Bronstein" (DE 189); Eric Tidwell and Jim Tidwell interview by author; *All Hands*, 35 (No. 600, Jan 1967); *The Naval Reservist*, 7–8 (May 1966); Andrew Wulfeck, "Divers find wreckage of first US Navy destroyer sunk by enemy fire" (*New York Post*, 14 Aug 2022).

28 Boyd, "Sad Saga of the Jacob Jones"; Segars & Segars, "New Jersey's Jacob Jones"; Morgan & Taylor, *U-boat Attack Logs*, 211; Seibold & Adams, *Shipwrecks and Legends 'Round Cape May*, 77; Puleo,

Due to Enemy Action, 5, 10–12, 311–318; Eric Tidwell interview by author; Riordan, "A Deep-Sea Dive Stirs a Navy Commander's Family Pride"; NJScuba.net, "USS Jacob Jones DD-130 (1/2)"; Gary Gentile, *Shipwrecks of Delaware and Maryland*, 98 (Gary Gentile Productions, 1990); David Sharp, "Navy vessel sunk by German sub in WWII finally found" (*Navy Times*, 18 Jul 2019).

29   Niestlé, *German U-boat Losses During WWII*, 196–197, 229–230; Morgan & Taylor, *U-boat Attack Logs*, 211; WarSailors.com, "M/S Breñas"; Ubootarchiv.de, "Raimund Tiesler"; Louie Smith, "WW2 hero who sunk German U-boat has struck up friendship with survivor" (*The Mirror*, 29 May 2019).

30   Author's dives on Gulftrade wreck; US Coast Guard, *Assistance* Vol. II, 69–71; Wiberg, *U-Boats in New England*, 77; Gentile, *Shipwrecks of New Jersey*, 65; Atlantic Divers, "Cape May and other Shipwreck Information"; NJScuba.net, "Gulf Trade"; Ubootarchiv.de, "U 588."

31   Pugh Gilmore, "El vapor Toltén, torpedeado en 1942 en su recalada a Nueva York," 3–4, 13–14, 29 and "¿Quién hundió al Toltén?" 1; Vásquez Méndez, "El hundimiento del Toltén," 104; Author's correspondence with Kenneth Pugh Olavarría, Sergio López Pugh, and Aquiles Ramírez Astudillo; John Raguso, "The Tolten" (*The Fisherman*, 13 Jun 1985).

32   U-404 KTB, 15–16; NJScuba.net, "Tolten"; Author's dives on Toltén wreck; Atlantic Divers, "Cape May and other Shipwreck Information"; Lawton, "Otto von Bülow"; Dixon, *The U-boat Commanders*, 25–26; Busch & Röll, *German U-boat Commanders of WWII*, 43; Uboat.net, "U-404"; Otto von Bülow reply letter to Tom Roach (7 May 1975).

33   *Bristol Daily Courier*, "Captain Quistgaard Maps his Voyages" (2 Aug 1952); Index to Petitions for Naturalization in New York City (1792–1989); Social Security Death Index.

34   UK Admiralty, "U 593 Interrogation of Survivors," 3–4; Uboat.net, "U-593"; Dixon, *The U-boat Commanders*, 158–160; Craig Francis, "Kursk crew face cold, dark, scary wait" (CNN, 15 Aug 2000); Der Spiegel, "Furchtbare psychische Situation" (15 Aug 2000); Christian Mayer, "Gefangen in einem von Bomben getroffenen U-Boot" (*Süddeutsche Zeitung*, 18 Aug 2000); John Raguso, "The Persephone" (*The Fisherman*, 19 Jun 1986).

35   Joe Mazraani correspondence with author; Watson, *The Nazi Spy Pastor*, 159–164, 171; Raguso, "The Rio Tercero"; UK Admiralty, "U 202 Interrogation of Survivors," 8–9; Ubootarchiv.de, "Hans-Heinz Linder"; Thiesen, "Jack Cullen, Nazi Spies and the Founding of the USCG Beach Patrol"; Richard Goldstein, "John Cullen, Coast Guardsman Who Detected Spies, Dies at 90" (*New York Times*, 2 Sep 2011); Amagansett Life-Saving & Coast Guard Station Museum (AmagansettLSS.org); Michael Mueller, *Canaris: The Life and Death of Hitler's Spymaster*, 335–336 (Frontline Books, 2017, Kindle).

36   Tommy Rowan, "Merchant ship sunk by Nazi U-boat off Cape May reveals secret that is changing an episode in WWII history books" (*Philadelphia Inquirer*, 16 Jul 2018); Gene Peterson, "Tragedy of the S.S. Miraflores – Able Bodied Seaman Robert Bing" (NJWreckDivers.com, 18 Apr 2013).

37   Peffer, *Where Divers Dare*, 106; Givnish Funeral Homes, "Morton Raphelson" (26 Mar 2016).

38   Letter from John L. Bender to USS Joyce veterans (12 Jun 1995); Peffer & Nersasian, *Never to Return*, 257–263; Kimberly Wilcox Joshi and Dick Wilcox interview by author; Peffer, *Where Divers Dare*, 93, 106–107; Abbey Glaser, "Robert Wilcox, 81, WWII Veteran" (*South Florida Sun Sentinel*, 1 Jun 1995).

39   Wiberg, *U-boats in New England*, 427; Wolf Hänert interview and correspondence with author; Klaus Hänert letters to Eric-Jan Bakker (24 Jul 1989) and Michael Hadley (3 Sep 1982); Peffer, *Where Divers Dare*, 107–108, 231–232, 295–296.

40   Rackow, "Hier wird U-550 vor New York versenkt"; *Pasadena Independent*, "German Meets His Nemesis" (26 Feb 1960); Wolf Hänert interview by author; Peffer, *Where Divers Dare*, 226–229; Klaus Hänert letters to U-550 veterans (29 May 1989) and Donald Macchia (30 May 1989); *York Dispatch*, "German, US Navy Officers Recall 1944 Battle" (York PA, 22 Feb 1960).

41 *Cicero*, "Mein Großvater, vom Feind gerettet"; Harris, "Reflections of Collingwood Harris," 43–56; John Rauh interview by author; Peffer, *Where Divers Dare*, 107–108, 230, 254–255.

42 Peffer, *Where Divers Dare*, 161–163, 216, 274–275, 286–289; Joe Mazraani correspondence with author; Colimor, "Memories of Sub Attack"; *Cicero*, "Mein Großvater, vom Feind gerettet"; Mazraani & Sellitti, "From Ordinary to Extraordinary"; Gentile, *Shadow Divers Exposed*, 167–168; Norddeutscher Rundfunk, "Die Todesfahrt von U 550" (15 Dec 2013).

43 Norddeutscher Rundfunk, "Die Todesfahrt von U 550"; Colimor, "Memories of Sub Attack"; Comegno, "Divers help reunite 92-year-old man with World War II relics"; Peffer, *Where Divers Dare*, 243–253, 263–265.

44 Duane Clause correspondence with author; Pugh Gillmore, "El vapor Toltén, Torpedeado en 1942 en su recalada a Nueva York," 34 and "¿Quién hundió al Toltén?," 6–7.

Selected Bibliography

Academic Papers

Atkinson, Christopher Michael. "Impacts of Bottom Trawling on Underwater Cultural Heritage." Master's thesis, Texas A&M University (May 2012).

Holland, Brett Leo. "The Tidewater confronts the storm: antisubmarine warfare off the capes of Virginia during the first six months of 1942." Master's thesis, University of Richmond (May 1994).

Lundvall, Erlend. "En undersøkelse og analyse av bevæpningen av norske handelsskip i Nortraship i krigsårene 1940–1945." Master's thesis, University of Oslo (Spring 2019).

Waber, Andrew J. "Popular Perceptions of the American Merchant Marine During World War II." Master's thesis, University of Florida (Spring 2008).

Wright, David Habersham. "Wolves Without Teeth: The German Torpedo Crisis in World War Two." Master's thesis, Georgia Southern University (Summer 2010).

Journal Articles

"Arcform Tanker R.P. Resor." *Marine Engineering and Shipping Review*, Vol. 33 (Mar 1936).

Assmann, Kurt, VAdm (Bundesmarine). "Why U-Boat Warfare Failed." *Foreign Affairs*, Vol. 28, No. 4 (Jun 1950).

Breemer, Jan S. "Defeating the U-boat: Inventing Antisubmarine Warfare." Newport Papers 36, US Naval War College (Aug 2010).

Cianflone, Frank A. "The Eagle Boats of World War I." *Proceedings*, Vol. 99/6/844 (Jun 1973).

Francis, Michael J. "The United States and Chile During the Second World War: The Diplomacy of Misunderstanding." *Journal of Latin American Studies*, Vol. 9, No. 1 (1977).

Gropman, Alan L. "Mobilizing U.S. Industry in World War II: Myth and Reality." McNair Paper 50. Institute for National Strategic Studies (Aug 1996).

Halpern, Paul G. "Handelskrieg mit U-Booten: The German Submarine Offensive in World War I." In *Commerce Raiding: Historical Case Studies, 1755–2009* (Newport Papers 40), edited by Bruce Elleman and S.C.M. Paine. Newport: US Naval War College, 2013.

Hänert, W. & V. Hartmann. "Shipwreck and Hypothermia: Experience Gained by the German Navy, 1939–1945." *Medical Aspects of Harsh Environments*, Vol. 1 (2001).

Lynch, Adam. "Kill and Be Killed? The U-853 Mystery." *Naval History*, Vol. 22, No. 3 (Jun 2008).

McCue, Brian. "An Exploration of Zigzagging." *Phalanx*, Vol. 37, No. 2 (Jun 2004).

O'Connor, Jerome M. "FDR's Undeclared War." *Naval History*, Vol. 18, No. 1 (Feb 2004).

Palucka, Tim. "The Wizard of Octane." *Invention & Technology*, Vol. 20, No. 3 (Winter 2005).

Pugh Gillmore, Kenneth. "El vapor Toltén, torpedeado en 1942 en su recalada a Nueva York." *Boletín*, No. 5, Chilean Academy of Maritime History (Dec 2001).

Pugh Gillmore, Kenneth. "¿Quién hundió al Toltén?" *Revista de Marina*, Vol. 121, No. 878 (1 Feb 2004).

Rems, Alan P. "Götterdämmerung: German Admirals on Trial." *Naval History*, Vol. 29, No. 6 (Dec 2015).

Rust, Eric C. "The Case of Oskar Kusch and the Limits of U-boat Camaraderie in World War II: Reflections on a German Tragedy." *International Journal of Naval History*, Vol. 1, No. 1 (Apr 2002).

Sandoval Hernández, Ariel. "Vapor 'Toltén' Torpedeado!" *Revista de Marina*, Vol. 94, No. 706 (Jun 1975).

Vásquez Méndez, Claudio. "El Hundimiento del Toltén." *Revista Mar*, No. 205 (2019).

Weinberg, Gerhard L. "Hitler's Image of the United States." *The American Historical Review,* Vol. 69, No. 4 (Jul 1964).

Books

Andrews, Lewis M, Jr. *Tempest, Fire and Foe: Destroyer Escorts in World War II and the Men Who Manned Them*. Magnolia: Narwhal Press, 1999.

Ballantyne, Iain. *The Deadly Deep: The Definitive History of Submarine Warfare*. New York: Pegasus Books Ltd, 2018.

Bercuson, David J. & Holger H. Herwig. *Deadly Seas: The Duel Between the St Croix and the U305 in the Battle of the Atlantic*. Vintage Canada, 1998; Toronto: Random House of Canada, 1997.

Bercuson, David J. & Holger H. Herwig. *Long Night of the Tankers: Hitler's War Against Caribbean Oil*. Calgary: University of Calgary Press, 2014.

Bilby, Joseph G., James M. Madden, & Harry Ziegler. *Hidden History of New Jersey at War*. Charleston: The History Press, 2014. Kindle.

Blair, Clay. *Hitler's U-boat War: The Hunters, 1939–1942*. Modern Library, 2000; Random House, Inc, 1996.

Blair, Clay. *Hitler's U-boat War: The Hunted, 1942–1945*. New York: Random House Inc, 1998.

Brustat-Naval, Fritz & Teddy Suhren. *Teddy Suhren, Ace of Aces: Memoirs of a U-boat Rebel*. Translated by Frank James. Yorkshire: Frontline Books, 2011; Köhlers Verlagsgellschaft (as *Nasses Eichlenlaub*), 1983. Kindle.

Buchheim, Lothar-Günther. *Das Boot*. London: Cassell, 1999; Piper Verlag GmbH, 1973.

Buchheim, Lothar-Günther. *U-boat War*. Translated by Gudie Lawaetz. Bantam Books, 1979; R. Piper & Co. Verlag GmbH (as *U-Boot-Krieg*), 1976.

Buchholz, Margaret Thomas. *New Jersey Shipwrecks: 350 Years in the Graveyard of the Atlantic*. Harvey Cedars: Down the Shore Publishing, 2004.

Buell, Thomas B. *Master of Sea Power: A Biography of Fleet Admiral Ernest J. King*. Annapolis: Naval Institute Press, 2012; Boston: Little, Brown & Company, 1980.

Bunker, John. *Heroes in Dungarees: The Story of the American Merchant Marine in World War II*. Annapolis: Naval Institute Press, 2006; 1995. Kindle.

Burke, Arthur E. *Torpedoes and Their Impact on Naval Warfare*. Naval Undersea Warfare Center Division Newport, 2017.

Busch, Rainer & Hans-Joachim Röll. *German U-boat Commanders of World War II*. London: Greenhill Books & Annapolis: Naval Institute Press, 1999; Herford: Verlag E.S. Mittler & Sohn GmbH (as *Die Deutschen U-Boot-Kommandanten*), 1996.

Campbell, John. *Naval Weapons of World War II*. London: Conway Maritime Press, 2002; 1985.

Capuzzo, Michael. *Close to Shore: The Terrifying Shark Attacks of 1916*. Broadway Books, 2001. Kindle.

Cate, James & Wesley Craven. *The Army Air Forces in World War II*. Vol. 1, *Plans and Early Operations, January 1939 to August 1942*. University of Chicago Press, 1948.

Citino, Robert. *The Wehrmacht's Last Stand: The German Campaigns of 1944–1945*. University Press of Kansas, 2017. Kindle.

Clausewitz, Carl von. *On War*. Translated by Michael Howard & Peter Paret. New York: Oxford University Press, Inc, 2007.

The Coast Guard at War: XIV, Assistance. 2 vols. US Coast Guard. Public Information Division, 1944.

The Coast Guard at War: XVII, Beach Patrol. US Coast Guard. Public Information Division, 1945.

Cremer, Peter. *U-boat Commander: A Periscope View of the Battle of the Atlantic*. Translated by Lawrence Wilson. Annapolis: Naval Institute Press, 1984; The Bodley Head Ltd, 1984 (as *U-333*); Berlin: Verlag Ullstein GmbH, 1982 (as *Ali Cremer: U-333*).

Cressman, Robert J. *The Official Chronology of the U.S. Navy in World War II*. Naval Historical Center Contemporary History Branch, 1999.

Dasch, George J. *Operation Pastorius: Eight Nazi Spies Against America*. Eumenes Publishing, 2019; Macbride, 1959 (as *Eight Spies Against America*). Kindle.

Davies, Edward J, II & Ronald Smelser. *The Myth of the Eastern Front: The Nazi-Soviet War in American Popular Culture*. New York: Cambridge University Press, 2008.

Dimbleby, Jonathan. *The Battle of the Atlantic: How the Allies Won the War*. New York: Oxford University Press, 2016; Viking Press, 2015. Kindle.

Dixon, Jeremy. *The U-boat Commanders: Knight's Cross Holders 1939–1945*. Yorkshire: Pen & Sword Military, 2019. Kindle.

Dobbs, Michael. *Saboteurs: The Nazi Raid on America*. New York: Vintage Books, 2005. Kindle.

Dönitz, Karl. *Memoirs: Ten Years and Twenty Days*. Yorkshire: Frontline Books, 2012; George Weidenfeld and Nicolson Ltd, 1959. Kindle.

Duffy, James P. *Target: America: Hitler's Plan to Attack the United States*. Lanham: Lyons Press, 2004.

Fernicola, Richard G, M.D. *Twelve Days of Terror: Inside the Shocking 1916 New Jersey Shark Attacks*. Lyons Press, 2016.

Galecki, Bryan. *Rum Runners, U-boats, and Hurricanes: The Complete History of the Coast Guard Cutters Bedloe and Jackson*. 2nd ed. Pine Belt Publishing, 2005.

Gannon, Michael. *Operation Drumbeat: The Dramatic True Story of Germany's First U-boat Attacks Along the American Coast in World War II*. HarperCollins Publishers, 2020; Harper & Row, 1990. Kindle.

Gentile, Gary. *The Lusitania Controversies*. Book 1, *Atrocity of War and a Wreck-Diving History*. 1st ed. Philadelphia: Gary Gentile Productions, 1998.

Gentile, Gary. *Shipwrecks of New Jersey*. Norwalk: Sea Sports Publications, 1988.

George, Pam. *Shipwrecks of the Delaware Coast: Tales of Pirates, Squalls, and Treasure*. Charleston: The History Press, 2011; 2010. Kindle.

Geroux, William. *The Mathews Men: Seven Brothers and the War Against Hitler's U-boats*. Penguin Books, 2017; Viking, 2016. Kindle.

Goebeler, Hans & John Vanzo. *Steel Boat, Iron Hearts: A U-boat Crewman's Life Aboard U-505*. Savas Beatie LLC, 2008; Wagnerian Publications, 1999. Kindle.

Golden, Frank, & Michael Tipton. *Essentials of Sea Survival*. Human Kinetics, 2002.

Goralski, Robert & Russel W. Freeburg. *Oil and War: How the Deadly Struggle for Fuel in World War II Meant Victory or Defeat*. Quantico: Marine Corps University Press, 2021.

Gray, Edwyn A. *The U-boat War: 1914–1918*. London: Leo Cooper, 1994; Seeley, Service and Co. Ltd, 1972 (as *The Killing Time*).

Grayson, William C. *Delaware's Ghost Towers: The Coast Artillery's Forgotten Last Stand During the Darkest Days of World War II*. Bloomington: AuthorHouse, 2005.

Grier, David. "The Appointment of Admiral Karl Dönitz as Hitler's Successor." In *The Impact of Nazism: New Perspectives on the Third Reich and Its Legacy*, edited by Daniel Rogers & Alan Steinweis. Lincoln & London: University of Nebraska Press, 2003.

Gröner, Erich. *German Warships 1815–1945*. Vol. 2, *U-boats and Mine Warfare Vessels*. London: Conway Maritime Press, 1991; Bernard & Graefe Verlag, 1983 (as *Die deutschen Kriegsschiffe 1815–1945*).

Hadley, Michael L. *Count Not the Dead: The Popular Image of the German Submarine*. Montreal: McGill-Queen's University Press, 1995.

Hansen, Peter C. *Execution for Duty: The Life, Trial, and Murder of a U-boat Captain*. Yorkshire: Pen & Sword Maritime, 2005.

Herwig, Holger H. *Politics of Frustration: The United States in German Naval Planning, 1889–1941*. Little, Brown & Company, 1976.

Hickam, Homer. *Torpedo Junction: The U-boat War Off America's East Coast, 1942*. Annapolis: US Naval Institute Press, 1996; 1989.

Hinsley, F. H. *Hitler's Strategy*. New York & Tokyo: Ishi Press, 2011; Cambridge: Cambridge University Press, 1951.

Hirschfeld, Wolfgang & Geoffrey Brooks. *Hirschfeld: The Secret Diary of a U-boat*. Yorkshire: Frontline Books, 2011; Leo Cooper, 1996. Kindle.

Hitler, Adolf. *Mein Kampf*. Translated by Ralph Manheim. Boston: Houghton Mifflin, 1943.

Hitler, Adolf. *Zweites Buch: Hitler's Secret Book*. Translated by Salvatore Attanasio. New York: Grove Press, 1961.

Hodos, Paul N. *The Kaiser's Lost Kreuzer: A History of U-156 and Germany's Long-Range Submarine Campaign Against North America, 1918*. Jefferson: McFarland & Company Inc, 2018. Kindle.

Horton, Edward. *The Illustrated History of the Submarine*. New York: Doubleday & Company, 1974.

Hughes, Terry & John Costello. *The Battle of the Atlantic*. New York: The Dial Press & Collins Sons & Co. Ltd, 1977.

Kershaw, Ian. *Hitler: A Biography*. W.W. Norton & Company, 2008; 1998. Kindle.

Klingaman, William K. *The Darkest Year: The American Homefront, 1941–1942*. New York: St. Martin's Press, 2019. Kindle.

Koerver, Hans Joachim. *The Kaiser's U-Boat Assault on America: Germany's Great War Gamble in the First World War*. Yorkshire & Philadelphia: Pen & Sword Military, 2020. Kindle.

Kurson, Robert. *Shadow Divers: The True Adventure of Two Americans Who Risked Everything to Solve One of the Last Mystery of World War II*. New York: Random House Trade Paperbacks, 2005; Random House, 2004.

Leighton, Richard M. "U.S. Merchant Shipping and the British Import Crisis." In *Command Decisions* (CMH Pub. 70-7-8), edited by Kent Roberts Greenfield. Washington, D.C.: US Army Center for Military History, 1960.

Lender, Mark Edward. *One State in Arms: A Short Military History of New Jersey*. Trenton: New Jersey Historical Commission, 1991.

Love, Robert W., Jr. "The U.S. Navy and Operation Roll of Drums, 1942." In *To Die Gallantly: The Battle of the Atlantic*, edited by Timothy Runyan & Jan Copes. Kindle.

Macintyre, Donald, Capt (RN). *U-boat Killer: Fighting the U-boats in the Battle of the Atlantic*. Eumenes Publishing, 2019; Avon Books, 1956. Kindle.

Mallmann Showell, Jak P, ed. *Fuehrer Conferences on Naval Affairs 1939–1945*. Stroud: The History Press, 2015; Greenhill Books/Lionel Leventhal Ltd, 1990.

Mallmann Showell, Jak P. *German Navy Handbook: 1939–1945*. Sutton Publishing Limited, 2002; 1999.

Mallmann Showell, Jak P. *Hitler's Attack U-boats: The Kriegsmarine's WWII Submarine Strike Force*. Yorkshire & Philadelphia: Frontline Books, 2020.

Mallmann Showell, Jak P. *Hitler's Navy: A Reference Guide to the Kriegsmarine 1935–1945*. Barnsley: Seaforth Publishing, 2009; Arms and Armour Press, 1979 (as *The German Navy in World War Two*). Kindle.

Mappen, Marc. *There's More to New Jersey Than the Sopranos*. New Brunswick: Rivergate Books, 2009.

Mawdsley, Evan. *The War for the Seas: A Maritime History of World War II*. New Haven & London: Yale University Press, 2019.

McNab, Chris, ed. *The Merchant Navy Seaman Pocket Manual 1939–1945*. Oxford & Havertown: Casemate Publishers, 2018. Kindle.

Monsarrat, Nicholas. *The Cruel Sea*. Cornwall: House of Stratus, 2011; London: Cassell & Co., 1951.

Moore, Arthur. *A Careless Word … A Needless Sinking: A History of the Staggering Losses Suffered By the U.S. Merchant Marine, Both in Ships and Personnel, During World War II*. American Merchant Marine Museum, 1983.

Morgan, Daniel & Bruce Taylor. *U-boat Attack Logs: A Complete Record of Warship Sinkings from Original Sources 1939–1945*. Yorkshire: Seaforth Publishing, 2011.

Morison, Samuel Eliot. *History of United States Naval Operations in World War II*. Vol. 1, *The Battle of the Atlantic, September 1939–May 1943*. Annapolis: Naval Institute Press, 2010; Boston: Little, Brown & Company, 1947.

Mulligan, Timothy P. *Neither Sharks Nor Wolves: The Men of Nazi Germany's U-boat Arm, 1939–1945*. Annapolis: Naval Institute Press, 2011; 1999. Kindle.

Nagiewicz, Stephen D. *Hidden History of Maritime New Jersey*. Charleston: The History Press, 2016. Kindle.

Neitzel, Sönke & Harald Welzer. *Soldiers: German POWs on Fighting, Killing, and Dying*. Translated by Jefferson Chase. Vintage Books, 2013; Frankfurt am Main: S. Fischer Verlag GmbH, 2011 (as *Soldaten: Protokolle vom Kämpfen, Töten und Sterben*). Kindle.

Neprud, Robert E. *Flying Minute Men: The Story of the Civil Air Patrol*. New York: Duell, Sloan, and Pearce, 1948.

Niestlé, Axel. *German U-boat Losses During World War II: Details of Destruction*. London: Frontline Books, 2022, 2014; Annapolis: Naval Institute Press, 1998.

Norwegian Maritime Museum. *Sjøforklaringer fra 2. verdenskrig*. 2 vols. 2003.

The Nuremberg Trials (Vol. 1–22): Complete Transcript of the Trials: From the Beginning until the Sentencing. International Military Tribunal. 2nd ed. E-artnow, 2022. Kindle.

Offley, Ed. *The Burning Shore: How Hitler's U-boats Brought World War II to America*. New York: Basic Books, 2014. Kindle.

Offley, Ed. *Turning the Tide: How a Small Band of Allied Sailors Defeated the U-boats and Won the Battle of the Atlantic*. New York: Basic Books, 2011. Kindle.

Padfield, Peter. *Dönitz: The Last Führer*. London: Lume Books, 2021; Victor Gollancz Ltd, 1984. Kindle.

Padfield, Peter. *War Beneath the Sea: Submarine Conflict 1939–1945*. London: Lume Books, 2020; John Murray Ltd, 1995. Kindle.

Paterson, Lawrence. *U-boat Combat Missions: The Pursuers & the Pursued: First-Hand Accounts of U-boat Life and Operations*. London: Chatham Publishing, 2007.

Payne, Craig, LCDR (USN). *Principles of Naval Weapons Systems*. Annapolis: Naval Institute Press, 2006.

Peffer, Randall. *Where Divers Dare: The Hunt For the Last U-boat*. New York: Berkley Caliber, 2016. Kindle.

Peffer, Randall & Col. Robert Nersasian. *Never to Return: Surviving the Worst Combat Loss in the History of the US Coast Guard*. Guilford: Lyons Press, 2017. Kindle.

Puleo, Stephen. *Due to Enemy Action: The True World War II Story of the USS Eagle 56*. Ginny Glass and Untreed Reads Publishing, 2012. Kindle.

Rachlis, Eugene. *They Came to Kill: The Story of Eight Nazi Saboteurs in America*. Eumenes Publishing, 2019; Random House, 1961. Kindle.

Richards, Phil & John J. Banigan. *How to Abandon Ship: The World War II Classic That Can Save Your Life*. New York: Skyhorse Publishing, 2016; Cornell Maritime Press, 1942. Kindle.

Robinson, Gertrude J. & Markus F. Robinson. *Der Kapitän: U-boat Ace Hans Rose*. Gloucestershire: Amberley, 2018.

Rose, Lisle A. *Power at Sea: The Breaking Storm, 1919–1945*. Columbia & London: University of Missouri Press, 2007.

Roskill, S.W. *The War at Sea 1939–1945*. Vol. 1, *The Defensive*. Edited by J.R.M. Butler. Hertfordshire: Wordsworth Editions Ltd, 1998; London: Collins Ltd, 1960.

Roskill, S.W. *The War at Sea 1939–1945*. Vol. 2, *The Period of Balance*. Edited by J.R.M. Butler. London: Her Majesty's Stationary Office, 1956. Kindle.

Rössler, Eberhard. *The U-boat: The Evolution and Technical History of German Submarines*. London: Cassell & Co., 2001; J.G. Lehmanns Verlag, 1975 (as *Geschichte des deutschen Ubootbaus*).

Rottman, Gordon L. *SNAFU: Sailor, Airman, and Soldier Slang of World War II*. Oxford: Osprey Publishing, 2013. Kindle.

Runyan, Timothy J. & Jan M. Copes, eds. *To Die Gallantly: The Battle of the Atlantic*. New York & Abingdon: Routledge, 2019; Westview Press, 1994. Kindle.

Rust, Eric C. *Naval Officers Under Hitler: The Men of Crew 34*. Annapolis: Naval Institute Press, 2017; Praeger Publishers, 1991.

Safety for Seamen. Medical Division, War Shipping Administration. New York: Carey Press Corporation, 1943.

Salvini, Emil R. *Historic Cape May, New Jersey: The Summer City by the Sea*. Charleston: The History Press, 2012. Kindle.

Schaeffer, Heinz. *U-boat 977: The U-boat That Escaped to Argentina*. Bristol: Cerberus Publishing Ltd, 2005; William Kimber, 1952.

Scheina, Robert L. *U.S. Coast Guard Cutters & Craft of World War II*. Annapolis: Naval Institute Press, 1982.

Seibold, David J. & Charles J. Adams III. *Shipwrecks and Legends 'Round Cape May*. Reading: Exeter House Books, 1987.

Shafter, Richard A. *Destroyers in Action*. Eumenes Publishing, 2019; Cornell Maritime Press, 1945. Kindle.

Shock, James R. *U.S. Navy Airships 1915–1962*. Edgewater: Atlantis Productions, 2001.

Snow, Richard. *A Measureless Peril: America in the Fight for the Atlantic, the Longest Battle of World War II*. New York: Scribner, 2010.

Speer, Albert. *Spandau: The Secret Diaries*. Translated by Richard & Clara Winston. New York & Tokyo: Ishi Press, 2010; Verlag-Ullstein GmbH, 1975 (as *Spandauer Tagebücher*).

Standard Oil Company of New Jersey. *Ships of the Esso Fleet in World War II*. New York: Conway Publishing, 1946.

Taylor, Theodore. *Fire on the Beaches*. New York: W.W. Norton & Company, 1958.

Tenold, Stig. *Norwegian Shipping in the 20th Century: Norway's Successful Navigation of the World's Most Global Industry*. Bergen: Palgrave Macmillan, 2018.

Trevor-Roper, Hugh. *Hitler's Table Talk, 1941–1944: His Private Conversations*. Translated by Norman Cameron & R.H. Stevens. New York: Enigma Books, 2000; London: Weidenfeld & Nicolson Ltd, 1953.

The U-boat War in the Atlantic 1939–1945. 3 vols. Ministry of Defence. London: Her Majesty's Stationary Office, 1992; 1989.

Vaeth, J. Gordon. *Blimps and U-Boats: U.S. Navy Airships in the Battle of the Atlantic*. Annapolis: Naval Institute Press, 1992.

Vause, Jordan. *Wolf: The U-boat Commanders in World War II*. Annapolis: Naval Institute Press, 1997.

Watson, J. Francis. *The Nazi Spy Pastor: Carl Krepper and the War in America*. Praeger: 2014.

Werner, Herbert. *Iron Coffins: A Personal Account of the German U-boat Battles of World War II*. Da Capo Press, 2002; 1998; New York: Holt, Rinehart, and Winston, 1969.

Wiberg, Eric. *U-boats in New England: Submarine Patrols, Survivors and Saboteurs, 1942–45*. Fonthill Media Ltd, 2019. Kindle.

Wiggins, Kennard R. Jr. *America's Anchor: A Naval History of the Delaware River and Bay, Cradle of the United States Navy*. Jefferson: McFarland & Company, Inc: 2019.

Wiggins, Melanie. *U-boat Adventures: Firsthand Accounts from World War II*. Annapolis: Naval Institute Press, 2010.
Williamson, Gordon. *Grey Wolf: U-boat Crewmen of World War II*. Oxford: Osprey Publishing, 2001.
Williamson, Gordon. *U-boat Tactics in World War II*. Long Island City: Osprey Publishing, 2010.
Woofenden, Todd A. *Hunters of the Steel Sharks: The Submarine Chasers of WWI*. Bowdoinham: Signal Light Books, 2006.
Yergin, Daniel. *The Prize: The Epic Quest for Oil, Money, and Power*. New York: Simon & Schuster, 1991.
Zabecki, David T. *Dönitz: A Defense*. 6th ed. Bennington: Merriam Press, 2008; 1988.

Interviews & Correspondence

Cullen, John C. "Interview of John C. Cullen." Interviewed by Dr William Thiesen, USCG Atlantic Area Historian. US Coast Guard Oral History Program. Chesapeake, VA. 30 March 2006.
Hardegen, Reinhard. Interview by Stephen Ames. Deutsches Schiffahrtsmuseum, Bremerhaven. 1992. Uboat.net.
Harris, Collingwood. "Reflections of Collingwood Harris." Interviewed by LT Arthur Johnson, USCGR. US Coast Guard Oral History Program. Washington, D.C. 18 October 1984.
Topp, Erich. Interview by Craig McLean. "A Visit with a U-Boat Ace: Erich Topp." Süssen. July 2004, published 17 February 2007. Uboat.net.
Von Bülow, Otto. Interview by Clay Blair. Clay Blair Collection, American Heritage Center, University of Wyoming. 1987.
Author interviews and correspondence with:
  Sheila Boyer—Grandniece of Ira Buhrman
  Ron Carlson—Webmaster of Armed-Guard.com
  Duane Clause—New Jersey wreck diver and dive boat captain
  Bob Desh—Captain, USCG (Ret.) and Foundation for Coast Guard History
  Dominic Etzold—New Jersey-based historian of the Kaiserliche Marine
  Wencke Hänert—Granddaughter of Klaus Hänert
  Wolf Hänert—Physician and son of Klaus Hänert
  Mike Laney—B-25 History Project
  Dan Lieb—President of New Jersey Historical Divers Association
  Sergio López Pugh—Grandson of Norman Pugh Cook
  Jerry Mason—Commander, USN (Ret.) and UboatArchive.net founder and webmaster
  Joe Mazraani—Technical diver and U-550 wreck discoverer
  Jim McNamara—Captain, US Merchant Marine (Ret.)
  Mike Monichetti—Grandson of Dewey Monichetti and owner of Mike's Seafood
  Bjoern Pedersen—Norwegian Maritime Museum
  Kenneth Pugh Olavarría—Nephew of Norman Pugh Cook, Chilean senator, retired admiral
  Aquiles Ramírez Astudillo—Grandson of Aquiles Ramírez Bárcena
  John Rauh—Son of Johann "Hans" Rauh
  Hugh Stephens—Captain, US Merchant Marine (Ret.) and World War II combat veteran
  Gary Thomas—Commander, USCG (Ret.) and Foundation for Coast Guard History
  Eric Tidwell—Commander, USN (Ret.) and grandson of Joseph "Paul" Tidwell
  Jim Tidwell—Son of Paul Tidwell
  Richard Van Treuren—Naval Airship Association
  Derek Waller—Air Commodore, Royal Air Force (Ret.) and U-Boat historian
  Kim Joshi Wilcox & Dick Wilcox—Son and granddaughter of Robert Wilcox
  Lucas Uhlemann—German naval officer

Miscellaneous

Costanzo, Frederick A. "Underwater Explosion Phenomena and Shock Physics". Naval Surface Warfare Center Carderock Division (February 2010).

Oberg, Albert E. "The Jakie." Written memories obtained by E. Andrew Wilde Jr. in 2006.

Ramírez Astudillo, Aquiles. Biographical essay about Captain Aquiles Ramírez Bárcena. 2012.

"USS Jacob Jones: The first US destroyer sunk by enemy action." Report from the 2014–2018 project "Forgotten Wrecks Of the First World War." Maritime Archaeology Trust. May 2020.

Official Records—German

"Diving Regulations for U-boats" (M.Dv.Nr. 381). Oberkommando der Kriegsmarine, August 1943.

Hänert, Klaus. "Versenkungsbericht des Kommandanten von U 550." Debriefing by West German government in 1948.

Kriegstagebücher (KTBs) translated and published by Jerry Mason (UboatArchive.net).

"Preliminary U-boat Information for U-boat Type VIIC" (M.Dv.Nr. 371,181). Naval Construction Office, Oberkommando der Kriegsmarine. 23 December 1936.

"Torpedo Firing Regulations for U-boats" (M.Dv.Nr. 416/3). Oberkommando der Kriegsmarine. 1943.

"U-boat Commander's Handbook" (M.Dv.Nr. 906). Oberkommando der Kriegsmarine. 1943.

Official Records—US & UK

Affidavit by Guy F. Chadwick. Sworn in New York, NY before notary John C. Coles. 11 March 1942.

Affidavit by Helge Quistgaard. "Statement by Captain Helge Quistgaard, Master, MS 'Persephone', Torpedoed—May 25, 1942." Sworn in Queens County, NY before notary Eugene X. Ottenant. 5 June 1942.

Affidavit by John J. Forsdal. "SS 'R.P. RESOR' — February 27, 1942." Sworn in Hudson County, NJ before notary John C. Coles. 28 February 1942.

Affidavit by John J. Forsdal. Sworn in Hudson County, NJ before notary John J. Garrity. 9 March 1942.

Affidavit by Torger Olsen. Sworn in New York, NY before notary John C. Coles. 12 March 1942.

"Analysis of Aircraft Attack." Memo to First Air Force and Eastern Defense Command regarding CPT Fitzgerald's attack on 14 May 1942. Eastern Sea Frontier. 18 September 1942.

"Analysis of Combined Anti-Submarine Action Reports: USS JOYCE (DE317), USS GANDY (DE764) and USS PETERSON (DE152)." Incident No. 5992. Headquarters of US Fleet Commander-in-Chief, US Navy. Undated.

"Arming of Merchant Ships and Naval Armed Guard Service" (OPNAV-P421-514). United States Naval Administration in World War II No. 172. Office of the Chief of Naval Operations, US Navy. 1946.

"Attack on Enemy Submarine." Report by 2LT Hugh Maxwell to squadron commander. 393rd Bombardment Squadron, First Bomber Command, US Army Air Forces. 22 June 1942.

"Attack on Submarine." Memo from CPT Maurice Fitzgerald to First Bomber Command HQ. 393rd Bombardment Squadron, US Army Air Forces. 15 May 1942.

"Combat Intelligence and Information of Possible Value as Combat Intelligence Gathered From Interviews with Surviving Members of the USS JACOB JONES, sunk by Enemy Action at 0500, February 28, 1942, position 74° 29'W, 38° 42'N." District Intelligence Office, Fourth Naval District, US Navy. 2 March 1942.

"Combat Intelligence Report on Torpedoing of 'M/V Berganger.'" Office of the Chief of Naval Operations, US Navy. 24 June 1942.

"Cruise Report, 8 March to 14 March, 1942." USCGC Antietam (WSC-128) commanding officer. US Coast Guard. 16 March 1942.

Deck Log Book (N. Nav. 330). Larch (YN-16). Covers 8–15 March 1942.

"Depth Charge, Mark 9 and Modifications" (OP 866). Bureau of Ordnance, US Navy. 12 February 1944.

"Design Study of Former German Submarine—Type IXC" (Report 2G-9C). Portsmouth Naval Shipyard, US Navy. July 1946.

"Enemy Attack on Merchant Ship" (Form NNI-142) for attack on *Berganger*. District Intelligence Office, Third Naval District, Eastern Sea Frontier. 5 June 1942.

"The Evolution of Naval Weapons" (NAVPERS 91066-A). Bureau of Naval Personnel, US Navy. March 1949.

"Form Mike 526." B-25B attack by 2LT Hugh Maxwell. 393rd Bombardment Squadron, First Bomber Command, US Army Air Forces. 22 June 1942.

"General Instructions for Commanding Officers of Naval Armed Guards on Merchant Ships" (OPNAV 23L-2). 4th ed. US Department of the Navy. March 1944.

"German Submarine Activities on the Atlantic Coast of the United States and Canada" (Publication No. 1). Historical Section, Office of Naval Records and Library, US Navy. 1920.

"German Underwater Ordnance: Mines" (OP-1673A). Bureau of Ordnance, US Navy. 14 June 1946.

"History of Convoy and Routing." United States Naval Administration in World War II No. 11. Headquarters of US Fleet Commander-in-Chief & 10th Fleet Commander, US Navy. 1945.

"History of the Naval Armed Guard Afloat, World War II" (OP-414). United States Naval Administration in World War II No. 173. Office of the Chief of Naval Operations, US Navy. 1946.

"History of the New York–Philadelphia Sector." Eastern Defense Command, US Army. 18 July 1944.

"History of USS Jacob Jones (DD 130)." Ships' Histories Section, Office of Naval Records and History, US Navy. Undated.

"Interrogation of U-boat Survivors: Cumulative Edition" (C.B. 04051 103). Naval Intelligence Division, UK Admiralty. June 1944.

"Interviews with survivors of the USS JACOB JONES, sunk by enemy action at 0500, 28 February, 1942." District Intelligence Office, Fourth Naval District, Eastern Sea Frontier. 1 March 1942.

"Merchant Ship Shapes" (ONI 223-M). Office of Naval Intelligence, US Navy. January 1944.

"Mine Disposal Handbook" (OP-1330). Bureau of Ordnance, US Navy. 1 March 1945.

"Mission Report 329." B-25A attack on U-593 by CPT Maurice Fitzgerald. 393rd Bombardment Squadron, First Bomber Command, US Army Air Forces. 14 May 1942.

"Remarks on Submarine Tactics Against Convoys" (ONI Publication No. 23). Office of Naval Intelligence, US Navy. December 1917.

"Report on the German Submarine of the U-570 Class Captured by the British in August 1941." Office of Naval Intelligence, US Navy. 28 September 1941.

"Report on 'U-570' (H.M.S. Graph)" (C.B. 4318). Naval Intelligence Division, UK Admiralty. January 1943.

"Sinking of Argentine Vessel, RIO TERCERO." Memorandum to COMINCH. Office of the Chief of Naval Operations, US Navy. 23 June 1942.

Sternhell, Charles M. & Alan M. Thorndike. "Antisubmarine Warfare in World War II" (OEG Report No. 51). Operations Evaluation Group, Office of the Chief of Naval Operations, US Navy. April 1946.

"Summary of Statements by Survivors MS PERSEPHONE, Panamanian Tanker 8426 G.T., Panama Transport Company (Standard Oil of New York)." Memorandum for file. Office of the Chief of Naval Operations, US Navy. 10 June 1942.

"Summary of Statements by Survivors of the MV 'BERGANGER', Norwegian cargo vessel, 6826 G.T., Nortraship (Westfall Larsen) owners, chartered to Norwegian Shipping and Trade Mission." Memorandum for file. Office of the Chief of Naval Operations, US Navy. 24 June 1942.

"Summary of Statements by Survivors, SS GULFTRADE, American Tanker, Gulf Oil Corporation." Memorandum for file. Office of Chief of Naval Operations, US Navy. 23 April 1942.

"Summary of Statements of Survivors SS Rio Tercero, Argentinian Cargo-Passenger Ship, 3342 G.T., Owned by Argentine Government, Chartered by Boyd, Wier, and Sewell, Inc." Office of the Chief of Naval Operations, US Navy. 24 June 1942.

"Summary of Statements by Survivors, SS RP RESOR, Standard Oil Company Tanker." Memorandum for file. Office of the Chief of Naval Operations, US Navy. 6 March 1942.

"Torpedoing of SS GULFTRADE." Memorandum for file. Summary of *Jonancy* captain's report. Office of the Chief of Naval Operations, US Navy. 19 March 1942.

"Torpedoing of S.S. PAN PENNSYLVANIA." Intelligence Report: Enemy Attack on Merchant Ships (NNI-142). US Naval Operating Base Londonderry. 26 April 1944.

U-boat Attack Assessment Form. No. 162 Squadron, Royal Canadian Air Force. 22 February 1944.

"United States Atlantic Fleet Organization, First Quarter, Fiscal Year 1942" (Confidential Memorandum 12CM-42). Atlantic Fleet, US Navy. 29 January 1942.

US Maritime Service Training Manual: Deck Branch Training. US Coast Guard. War Shipping Administration, 1943.

US Maritime Service Training Manual: Engineering Branch Training. US Coast Guard. War Shipping Administration, 1944.

US Maritime Service Training Manual: Preliminary Training. US Coast Guard. War Shipping Administration, 1943.

U.S. Navy Diving Manual. Rev. 7. Naval Sea Systems Command, US Navy. 1 December 2016.

USS Joyce. Form ASW-1 (Antisubmarine Action by Surface Ship). Escort Division 22. 16 April 1944.

USS Peterson. "Narrative of Anti-Submarine Action 16 April 1944." Escort Division 22. 16 April 1944.

"U 202 Interrogation of Survivors" (C.B. 04051 72). Naval Intelligence Division, UK Admiralty. July 1943.

"U 448 and U 550 Interrogation of Survivors." Naval Intelligence Division, UK Admiralty. August 1944.

"U 593 Interrogation of Survivors" (C.B. 04051 94). Naval Intelligence Division, UK Admiralty. February 1944.

"Voyage Report of SS PAN PENNSYLVANIA." ENS John J. Melican report to Chief of Naval Operations. 27 May 1944.

Magazine Articles

Chatterton, John, Richie Kohler, and John Yurga. "The Fate of U-869 Reexamined." Parts 1–3. *Wreck Diving*, Nos. 17, 18, and 19, 2009.

Cohen, Gary. "The Keystone Commandos." *The Atlantic*, Vol. 289, No. 2, February 2002.

Frenzel, Eike. "Hitler's Unfulfilled Dream of a New York in Flames." *Der Spiegel*, 16 September 2010.

Lawrenson, Helen. "Damn the Torpedoes!" *Harper's Magazine*, July 1942.

Raguso, John. "The Rio Tercero." *The Fisherman*, 1 August 1985.

Segars, Herbert & Veronica Segars. "New Jersey's Jacob Jones." *Skin Diver*, May 1991.

"Vox Pop." *The Lookout*, Vol. 33, No. 5, May 1942. Seamen's Church Institute of New York.

News Articles

Chamberlain, Cain. "Jacob Jones Survivor's Grandson Dives Wreck." *Cape May Star and Wave*, 27 July 2011.

Colimor, Edward. "Memories of Sub Attack." *Philadelphia Inquirer*, 1 May 2014.

Comegno, Carol. "Divers help reunite 92-year-old man with World War II relics." *Courier-Post* (Cherry Hill, NJ), 3 May 2013.

Croskey, David. "When the War Came to Sea Isle." *Sea Isle Times*, August 2012.

Grote, Dan. "What lies beneath: N.J.'s coast lined with shipwrecks." *Press of Atlantic City*, 26 January 2015.

McCarthy, Breanne. "How Shipwreck Divers Scour Jersey's Ocean Floor." *New Jersey Monthly*, 21 July 2020.

Miller, Michael. "Sunken WWII Destroyer off Cape May Holds Family's Fascination and its Fate." *Press of Atlantic City*, 22 July 2011.

Riordan, Kevin. "A Deep-Sea Dive Stirs a Navy Commander's Family Pride." *Philadelphia Inquirer*, 26 July 2011.

Web

Auke Visser's Renewed Historical Tankers Site. Webmaster Auke Visser. aukevisser.nl/mobil/id31.htm

Armed-Guard.com. Webmaster Ron Carlson, founded by Thomas R. Bowerman. armed-guard.com

Boyd, Ellsworth. "Sad Saga of the Jacob Jones." National Underwater and Marine Agency. 3 June 2015. numa.net/2015/06/sad-saga-of-the-jacob-jones

"Calculating Depth Charge Lethality." Alternate Wars. 15 Sep 2017. alternatewars.com/BBOW/Subsurface/Depth_Charge_Lethality.htm

Cox, Samuel J. "H-008-5: Admiral Ernest J. King—Chief of Naval Operations, 1942." Naval History and Heritage Center. 6 May 2019. history.navy.mil/about-us/leadership/director/directors-corner/h-grams/h-gram-008/h-008-5.html

Cox, Samuel J. "H-019-5: Black Sunday and the Battle of Orleans." Naval History and Heritage Center. 8 May 2019. history.navy.mil/about-us/leadership/director/directors-corner/h-grams/h-gram-019/h-019-5.html

Hardegen, Reinhard. "Reinhard Hardegen." MourningTheAncient.com. October 1994. mourningtheancient.com/ww2-x10.htm

Koster, John. "Tightrope Walker." HistoryNet. 1 July 2016. historynet.com/tightrope-walker/

Krigsseilerregisteret. "A digital monument documenting the wartime seafarers." krigsseilerregisteret.no

"Larch (YN-16)." Naval History and Heritage Command. 21 August 2019. history.navy.mil/research/histories/ship-histories/danfs/l/larch.html

Lawton, John. "Otto von Bülow." Mac's Web Log. 16 Jun 2006. ahoy.tk-jk.net/macslog/ConvoyRB1.html

Manthorpe, William. "Submarines at the Cape: Friend and Foe." NavyAtCapeHenlopen.info. navyatcapehenlopen.info/submarinesatthecapefriendandfoe.html

Manthorpe, William. "World War II: Harbor Entrance Control Post (HECP) and Captain of the Port (COTP)." NavyAtCapeHenlopen.info navyatcapehenlopen.info/harborentrancecontrolpost.html

"Mein Großvater, vom Feind gerettet." *Cicero* cicero.de/kultur/mein-grossvater-vom-feind-gerettet/51469

Miller, Michael B. "Sea Transport and Supply." International Encyclopedia of the First World War. 24 August 2016. encyclopedia.1914-1918-online.net/article/sea_transport_and_supply

Morio, Bert. "Oskar Kusch—Briefe und Texte." Apt-Holtenau.de. 3 April 2018. apt-holtenau.de/holtenau-info/history/kusch-oskar-briefe.htm

Naval Grid Calculator. navalgrid.com

Paz, Roberto Marcelo. "El hundimiento del Rio III." El Snorkel. 6 November 2002. elsnorkel.com/2002/11/el-hundimiento-del-rio-iii.html

Rackow, Alexander. "Hier wird U-550 vor New York versenkt." *Bild*. 5 August 2012. bild.de/news/ausland/u-boot/hier-wird-u-550-vor-new-york-versenkt-25495950.bild.html

Seerveld, Charles. "The Sinking of the SS India Arrow." DVRBS.com. dvrbs.com/ccwd-ww2/ww2-mm-clseerveld.htm

Seerveld, Charles. Written memories of Merchant Marine service (untitled). DVRBS.com. dvrbs.com/ccwd-ww2/ww2-mm-clseerveld.htm

Thiesen, William H. "Jack Cullen, Nazi Spies and the Founding of the USCG Beach Patrol." The Maritime Executive. 16 September 2019. maritime-executive.com/features/jack-cullen-nazi-spies-and-founding-of-the-uscg-beach-patrol-8

Torpedo Vorhaltrechner Project. Founder Maciek Florek. TVRE.org

UboatArchive.net. Webmaster Jerry Mason. uboatarchive.net

Uboat.net. uboat.net

U-Boot-Archiv Wiki. ubootarchiv.de

Ubootwaffe.pl. ubootwaffe.pl

USMM.org. usmm.org

US Naval Academy Virtual Memorial Hall. usnamemorialhall.org

Walding, Richard. "Cape Henlopen (Fort Miles)—Delaware." IndicatorLoops.com. indicatorloops.com/usn_miles.htm

Walding, Richard. "How the Anti-Submarine Harbour Defence System Worked." IndicatorLoops.com. indicatorloops.com/loopworks.htm

WarSailors.com. Webmaster Siri Lawson. warsailors.com

Williamson, Mitchell. "Jürgen Oesten and the End of the U-boats." WeaponsAndWarfare.com. 18 July 2021. weaponsandwarfare.com/2021/07/18/jurgen-oesten-and-the-end-of-the-u-boats

Williamson, Mitchell. "Lend-Lease to the USSR." WeaponsAndWarfare.com. weaponsandwarfare.com/2020/06/08/lend-lease-to-the-ussr

Wrecksite.eu. wrecksite.eu

Film, Television, and Online Video

Kils, Bjoern, Maureen Langevin, and Steve Langevin, producers. *Pioneers of Northeast Wreck Diving.* 2008; Dive Voyage Expeditions. Short documentary film.

Mazraani, Joe & Jennifer Sellitti. "From Ordinary to Extraordinary: The Merchant Marine Experience in WWII." Presentation for New Jersey Historical Divers Association 17th Annual Shipwreck Symposium. YouTube video, 49:27. 1 May 2021. youtu.be/LEKofZREPbw

Munro, Mark. "Eye Witnesses of World War II, U-550." Vimeo video, 00:12. 23 February 2012. vimeo.com/37325432

World Documentary Films. "U-boats: The Most Feared Fighting Ships of the Battle of the Atlantic." YouTube video, 45:13. 19 June 2015. youtube.com/watch?v=YvyfcmkhFiY&ab_channel=WorldDocumentaryFilmsHD

Index